WORLD TRADE ORGANIZATION

Dispute Settlement Reports

2017
Volume VIII

Pages 3767-4372

THE WTO DISPUTE SETTLEMENT REPORTS

The *Dispute Settlement Reports* of the World Trade Organization (the "WTO") include panel and Appellate Body reports, as well as arbitration awards, in disputes concerning the rights and obligations of WTO Members under the provisions of the *Marrakesh Agreement Establishing the World Trade Organization*. The *Dispute Settlement Reports* are available in English. Volumes comprising one or more complete cases contain a cumulative list of published disputes. The cumulative list for cases that cover more than one volume is to be found in the first volume for that case.

This volume may be cited as DSR 2017:VIII

CAMBRIDGE
UNIVERSITY PRESS

University Printing House, Cambridge CB2 8BS, United Kingdom

One Liberty Plaza, 20th Floor, New York, NY 10006, USA

477 Williamstown Road, Port Melbourne, VIC 3207, Australia

314–321, 3rd Floor, Plot 3, Splendor Forum, Jasola District Centre, New Delhi – 110025, India

79 Anson Road, #06–04/06, Singapore 079906

Cambridge University Press is part of the University of Cambridge.

It furthers the University's mission by disseminating knowledge in the pursuit of
education, learning, and research at the highest international levels of excellence.

www.cambridge.org
Information on this title: www.cambridge.org/9781108482875
DOI: 10.1017/9781108609906

© World Trade Organization 2018

First published 2018

Printed and bound in Great Britain by Clays Ltd, Elcograf S.p.A.

A catalogue record for this publication is available from the British Library.

ISBN 978-1-108-48287-5 Hardback

TABLE OF CONTENTS

TABLE OF CONTENTS

INDONESIA - MEASURES CONCERNING THE IMPORTATION OF CHICKEN MEAT AND CHICKEN PRODUCTS

Report of the Panel
WT/DS484/R and Add.1

*Adopted by the Dispute Settlement Body
on 22 November 2017*

TABLE OF CONTENTS

LIST OF ANNEXES

ANNEX A

WORKING PROCEDURES FOR THE PANEL

ANNEX B

ARGUMENTS OF THE PARTIES

ANNEX C

ARGUMENTS OF THE THIRD PARTIES

Contents		Page
Annex C-8	Integrated executive summary of the arguments of Paraguay	4117
Annex C-9	Integrated executive summary of the arguments of Qatar	4119
Annex C-10	Integrated executive summary of the arguments of the United States	4122

CASES CITED IN THIS REPORT

Short title	Full case title
Argentina – Financial Services	Appellate Body Report, *Argentina – Measures Relating to Trade in Goods and Services*, WT/DS453/AB/R and Add.1, adopted 9 May 2016
Argentina – Hides and Leather	Panel Report, *Argentina – Measures Affecting the Export of Bovine Hides and Import of Finished Leather*, WT/DS155/R and Corr.1, adopted 16 February 2001, DSR 2001:V, p. 1779
Argentina – Import Measures	Appellate Body Reports, *Argentina – Measures Affecting the Importation of Goods*, WT/DS438/AB/R / WT/DS444/AB/R / WT/DS445/AB/R, adopted 26 January 2015
Argentina – Import Measures	Panel Reports, *Argentina – Measures Affecting the Importation of Goods*, WT/DS438/R and Add.1 / WT/DS444/R and Add.1 / WT/DS445/R and Add.1, adopted 26 January 2015, as modified (WT/DS438/R) and upheld (WT/DS444/R / WT/DS445/R) by Appellate Body Reports WT/DS438/AB/R / WT/DS444/AB/R / WT/DS445/AB/R
Australia – Apples	Appellate Body Report, *Australia – Measures Affecting the Importation of Apples from New Zealand*, WT/DS367/AB/R, adopted 17 December 2010, DSR 2010:V, p. 2175
Australia – Automotive Leather II	Panel Report, *Australia – Subsidies Provided to Producers and Exporters of Automotive Leather*, WT/DS126/R, adopted 16 June 1999, DSR 1999:III, p. 951
Australia – Salmon	Appellate Body Report, *Australia – Measures Affecting Importation of Salmon*, WT/DS18/AB/R, adopted 6 November 1998, DSR 1998:VIII, p. 3327
Australia – Salmon (Article 21.5 – Canada)	Panel Report, *Australia – Measures Affecting Importation of Salmon – Recourse to Article 21.5 of the DSU by Canada*, WT/DS18/RW, adopted 20 March 2000, DSR 2000:IV, p. 2031
Brazil – Desiccated Coconut	Appellate Body Report, *Brazil – Measures Affecting Desiccated Coconut*, WT/DS22/AB/R, adopted 20 March 1997, DSR 1997:I, p. 167
Brazil – Retreaded Tyres	Appellate Body Report, *Brazil – Measures Affecting Imports of Retreaded Tyres*, WT/DS332/AB/R, adopted 17 December 2007, DSR 2007:IV, p. 1527

Short title	Full case title
Brazil – Retreaded Tyres	Panel Report, *Brazil – Measures Affecting Imports of Retreaded Tyres*, WT/DS332/R, adopted 17 December 2007, as modified by Appellate Body Report WT/DS332/AB/R, DSR 2007:V, p. 1649
Canada – Renewable Energy / Canada – Feed-in Tariff Program	Panel Reports, *Canada – Certain Measures Affecting the Renewable Energy Generation Sector / Canada – Measures Relating to the Feed-in Tariff Program*, WT/DS412/R and Add.1 / WT/DS426/R and Add.1, adopted 24 May 2013, as modified by Appellate Body Reports WT/DS412/AB/R / WT/DS426/AB/R, DSR 2013:I, p. 237
Canada – Wheat Exports and Grain Imports	Appellate Body Report, *Canada – Measures Relating to Exports of Wheat and Treatment of Imported Grain*, WT/DS276/AB/R, adopted 27 September 2004, DSR 2004:VI, p. 2739
Chile – Price Band System	Panel Report, *Chile – Price Band System and Safeguard Measures Relating to Certain Agricultural Products*, WT/DS207/R, adopted 23 October 2002, as modified by Appellate Body Report WT/DS207AB/R, DSR 2002:VIII, p. 3127
China – Electronic Payment Services	Panel Report, *China – Certain Measures Affecting Electronic Payment Services*, WT/DS413/R and Add.1, adopted 31 August 2012, DSR 2012:X, p. 5305
China – HP-SSST (Japan) / China – HP-SSST (EU)	Appellate Body Reports, *China – Measures Imposing Anti-Dumping Duties on High-Performance Stainless Steel Seamless Tubes ("HP-SSST") from Japan / China – Measures Imposing Anti-Dumping Duties on High-Performance Stainless Steel Seamless Tubes ("HP-SSST") from the European Union*, WT/DS454/AB/R and Add.1 / WT/DS460/AB/R and Add.1, adopted 28 October 2015
China – Intellectual Property Rights	Panel Report, *China – Measures Affecting the Protection and Enforcement of Intellectual Property Rights*, WT/DS362/R, adopted 20 March 2009, DSR 2009:V, p. 2097
China – Publications and Audiovisual Products	Appellate Body Report, *China – Measures Affecting Trading Rights and Distribution Services for Certain Publications and Audiovisual Entertainment Products*, WT/DS363/AB/R, adopted 19 January 2010, DSR 2010:I, p. 3
China – Rare Earths	Panel Reports, *China – Measures Related to the Exportation of Rare Earths, Tungsten, and Molybdenum*, WT/DS431/R and Add.1 / WT/DS432/R and Add.1 / WT/DS433/R and Add.1, adopted 29 August 2014, upheld by Appellate Body Reports WT/DS431/AB/R / WT/DS432/AB/R / WT/DS433/AB/R, DSR 2014:IV, p. 1127
China – Raw Materials	Appellate Body Reports, *China – Measures Related to the Exportation of Various Raw Materials*, WT/DS394/AB/R / WT/DS395/AB/R / WT/DS398/AB/R, adopted 22 February 2012, DSR 2012:VII, p. 3295
China – Raw Materials	Panel Reports, *China – Measures Related to the Exportation of Various Raw Materials*, WT/DS394/R, Add.1 and Corr.1 / WT/DS395/R, Add.1 and Corr.1 / WT/DS398/R, Add.1 and Corr.1, adopted 22 February 2012, as modified by Appellate Body Reports WT/DS394/AB/R / WT/DS395/AB/R / WT/DS398/AB/R, DSR 2012:VII, p. 3501
Colombia – Ports of Entry	Panel Report, *Colombia – Indicative Prices and Restrictions on Ports of Entry*, WT/DS366/R and Corr.1, adopted 20 May 2009, DSR 2009:VI, p. 2535

Short title	Full case title
Colombia – Textiles	Appellate Body Report, *Colombia – Measures Relating to the Importation of Textiles, Apparel and Footwear*, WT/DS461/AB/R and Add.1, adopted 22 June 2016
Dominican Republic – Import and Sale of Cigarettes	Appellate Body Report, *Dominican Republic – Measures Affecting the Importation and Internal Sale of Cigarettes*, WT/DS302/AB/R, adopted 19 May 2005, DSR 2005:XV, p. 7367
Dominican Republic – Import and Sale of Cigarettes	Panel Report, *Dominican Republic – Measures Affecting the Importation and Internal Sale of Cigarettes*, WT/DS302/R, adopted 19 May 2005, as modified by Appellate Body Report WT/DS302/AB/R, DSR 2005:XV, p. 7425
EC – Approval and Marketing of Biotech Products	Panel Reports, *European Communities – Measures Affecting the Approval and Marketing of Biotech Products*, WT/DS291/R, Add.1 to Add.9 and Corr.1 / WT/DS292/R, Add.1 to Add.9 and Corr.1 / WT/DS293/R, Add.1 to Add.9 and Corr.1, adopted 21 November 2006, DSR 2006:III, p. 847
EC – Asbestos	Appellate Body Report, *European Communities – Measures Affecting Asbestos and Asbestos-Containing Products*, WT/DS135/AB/R, adopted 5 April 2001, DSR 2001:VII, p. 3243
EC – Asbestos	Panel Report, *European Communities – Measures Affecting Asbestos and Asbestos-Containing Products*, WT/DS135/R and Add.1, adopted 5 April 2001, as modified by Appellate Body Report WT/DS135/AB/R, DSR 2001:VIII, p. 3305
EC and certain member States – Large Civil Aircraft	Appellate Body Report, *European Communities and Certain Member States – Measures Affecting Trade in Large Civil Aircraft*, WT/DS316/AB/R, adopted 1 June 2011, DSR 2011:I, p. 7
EC – Bananas III	Appellate Body Report, *European Communities – Regime for the Importation, Sale and Distribution of Bananas*, WT/DS27/AB/R, adopted 25 September 1997, DSR 1997:II, p. 591
EC – Bananas III	Panel Reports, *European Communities – Regime for the Importation, Sale and Distribution of Bananas*, WT/DS27/R/ECU *(Ecuador)* / WT/DS27/R/GTM, WT/DS27/R/HND *(Guatemala and Honduras)* / WT/DS27/R/MEX *(Mexico)* / WT/DS27/R/USA *(US)*, adopted 25 September 1997, as modified by Appellate Body Report WT/DS27/AB/R, DSR 1997:II, p. 695 to DSR 1997:III, p. 1085
EC – Chicken Cuts	Appellate Body Report, *European Communities – Customs Classification of Frozen Boneless Chicken Cuts*, WT/DS269/AB/R, WT/DS286/AB/R, adopted 27 September 2005, and Corr.1, DSR 2005:XIX, p. 9157
EC – Commercial Vessels	Panel Report, *European Communities – Measures Affecting Trade in Commercial Vessels*, WT/DS301/R, adopted 20 June 2005, DSR 2005:XV, p. 7713
EC – Computer Equipment	Appellate Body Report, *European Communities – Customs Classification of Certain Computer Equipment*, WT/DS62/AB/R, WT/DS67/AB/R, WT/DS68/AB/R, adopted 22 June 1998, DSR 1998:V, p. 1851
EC – Export Subsidies on Sugar	Appellate Body Report, *European Communities – Export Subsidies on Sugar*, WT/DS265/AB/R, WT/DS266/AB/R, WT/DS283/AB/R, adopted 19 May 2005, DSR 2005:XIII, p. 6365

Short title	Full case title
EC – Export Subsidies on Sugar (Australia)	Panel Report, *European Communities – Export Subsidies on Sugar, Complaint by Australia*, WT/DS265/R, adopted 19 May 2005, as modified by Appellate Body Report WT/DS265/AB/R, WT/DS266/AB/R, WT/DS283/AB/R, DSR 2005:XIII, p. 6499
EC – Export Subsidies on Sugar (Brazil)	Panel Report, *European Communities – Export Subsidies on Sugar, Complaint by Brazil*, WT/DS266/R, adopted 19 May 2005, as modified by Appellate Body Report WT/DS265/AB/R, WT/DS266/AB/R, WT/DS283/AB/R, DSR 2005:XIV, p. 6793
EC – Export Subsidies on Sugar (Thailand)	Panel Report, *European Communities – Export Subsidies on Sugar, Complaint by Thailand*, WT/DS283/R, adopted 19 May 2005, as modified by Appellate Body Report WT/DS265/AB/R, WT/DS266/AB/R, WT/DS283/AB/R, DSR 2005:XIV, p. 7071
EC – Fasteners (China)	Appellate Body Report, *European Communities – Definitive Anti-Dumping Measures on Certain Iron or Steel Fasteners from China*, WT/DS397/AB/R, adopted 28 July 2011, DSR 2011:VII, p. 3995
EC – Hormones	Appellate Body Report, *EC Measures Concerning Meat and Meat Products (Hormones)*, WT/DS26/AB/R, WT/DS48/AB/R, adopted 13 February 1998, DSR 1998:I, p. 135
EC – IT Products	Panel Reports, *European Communities and its member States – Tariff Treatment of Certain Information Technology Products*, WT/DS375/R / WT/DS376/R / WT/DS377/R, adopted 21 September 2010, DSR 2010:III, p. 933
EC – Sardines	Panel Report, *European Communities – Trade Description of Sardines*, WT/DS231/R and Corr.1, adopted 23 October 2002, as modified by Appellate Body Report WT/DS231/AB/R, DSR 2002:VIII, p. 3451
EC – Seal Products	Appellate Body Reports, *European Communities – Measures Prohibiting the Importation and Marketing of Seal Products*, WT/DS400/AB/R / WT/DS401/AB/R, adopted 18 June 2014, DSR 2014:I, p. 7
EC – Selected Customs Matters	Appellate Body Report, *European Communities – Selected Customs Matters*, WT/DS315/AB/R, adopted 11 December 2006, DSR 2006:IX, p. 3791
EC – Tariff Preferences	Appellate Body Report, *European Communities – Conditions for the Granting of Tariff Preferences to Developing Countries*, WT/DS246/AB/R, adopted 20 April 2004, DSR 2004:III, p. 925
EU – Biodiesel (Argentina)	Appellate Body Report, *European Union – Anti-Dumping Measures on Biodiesel from Argentina*, WT/DS473/AB/R and Add.1, adopted 26 October 2016
Guatemala – Cement I	Appellate Body Report, *Guatemala – Anti-Dumping Investigation Regarding Portland Cement from Mexico*, WT/DS60/AB/R, adopted 25 November 1998, DSR 1998:IX, p. 3767
India – Autos	Panel Report, *India – Measures Affecting the Automotive Sector*, WT/DS146/R, WT/DS175/R, and Corr.1, adopted 5 April 2002, DSR 2002:V, p. 1827
India – Solar Cells	Appellate Body Report, *India – Certain Measures Relating to Solar Cells and Solar Modules*, WT/DS456/AB/R and Add.1, adopted 14 October 2016

Short title	Full case title
Indonesia – Autos	Panel Report, *Indonesia – Certain Measures Affecting the Automobile Industry*, WT/DS54/R, WT/DS55/R, WT/DS59/R, WT/DS64/R, Corr.1 and Corr.2, adopted 23 July 1998, and Corr.3 and Corr.4, DSR 1998:VI, p. 2201
Indonesia – Import Licensing Regimes	Panel Report, *Indonesia – Importation of Horticultural Products, Animals and Animal Products*, WT/DS477/R, WT/DS478/R, Add.1 and Corr.1, circulated to WTO Members 22 December 2016 [appealed; adoption pending]
Japan – Alcoholic Beverages II	Appellate Body Report, *Japan – Taxes on Alcoholic Beverages*, WT/DS8/AB/R, WT/DS10/AB/R, WT/DS11/AB/R, adopted 1 November 1996, DSR 1996:I, p. 97
Korea – Alcoholic Beverages	Panel Report, *Korea – Taxes on Alcoholic Beverages*, WT/DS75/R, WT/DS84/R, adopted 17 February 1999, as modified by Appellate Body Report WT/DS75/AB/R, WT/DS84/AB/R, DSR 1999:I, p. 44
Japan – Apples	Appellate Body Report, *Japan – Measures Affecting the Importation of Apples*, WT/DS245/AB/R, adopted 10 December 2003, DSR 2003:IX, p. 4391
Korea – Dairy	Appellate Body Report, *Korea – Definitive Safeguard Measure on Imports of Certain Dairy Products*, WT/DS98/AB/R, adopted 12 January 2000, DSR 2000:I, p. 3
Korea – Various Measures on Beef	Appellate Body Report, *Korea – Measures Affecting Imports of Fresh, Chilled and Frozen Beef*, WT/DS161/AB/R, WT/DS169/AB/R, adopted 10 January 2001, DSR 2001:I, p. 5
Mexico – Corn Syrup (Article 21.5 – US)	Appellate Body Report, *Mexico – Anti-Dumping Investigation of High Fructose Corn Syrup (HFCS) from the United States – Recourse to Article 21.5 of the DSU by the United States*, WT/DS132/AB/RW, adopted 21 November 2001, DSR 2001:XIII, p. 6675
Mexico – Taxes on Soft Drinks	Panel Report, *Mexico – Tax Measures on Soft Drinks and Other Beverages*, WT/DS308/R, adopted 24 March 2006, as modified by Appellate Body Report WT/DS308/AB/R, DSR 2006:I, p. 43
Peru – Agricultural Products	Panel Report, *Peru – Additional Duty on Imports of Certain Agricultural Products*, WT/DS457/R and Add.1, adopted 31 July 2015, as modified by Appellate Body Report WT/DS457/AB/R
Philippines – Distilled Spirits	Appellate Body Reports, *Philippines – Taxes on Distilled Spirits*, WT/DS396/AB/R / WT/DS403/AB/R, adopted 20 January 2012, DSR 2012:VIII, p. 4163
Russia – Pigs (EU)	Panel Report, *Russian Federation – Measures on the Importation of Live Pigs, Pork and Other Pig Products from the European Union*, WT/DS475/R and Add.1, adopted 21 March 2017, as modified by Appellate Body Report WT/DS475/AB/R
Russia – Tariff Treatment	Panel Report, *Russia – Tariff Treatment of Certain Agricultural and Manufacturing Products*, WT/DS485/R, Corr.1, Corr.2, and Add.1, adopted 26 September 2016
Thailand – H-Beams	Appellate Body Report, *Thailand – Anti-Dumping Duties on Angles, Shapes and Sections of Iron or Non-Alloy Steel and H-Beams from Poland*, WT/DS122/AB/R, adopted 5 April 2001, DSR 2001:VII, p. 2701
Turkey – Rice	Panel Report, *Turkey – Measures Affecting the Importation of Rice*, WT/DS334/R, adopted 22 October 2007, DSR 2007:VI, p. 2151

Short title	Full case title
US – Animals	Panel Report, *United States – Measures Affecting the Importation of Animals, Meat and Other Animal Products from Argentina*, WT/DS447/R and Add.1, adopted 31 August 2015
US – Anti-Dumping and Countervailing Duties (China)	Appellate Body Report, *United States – Definitive Anti-Dumping and Countervailing Duties on Certain Products from China*, WT/DS379/AB/R, adopted 25 March 2011, DSR 2011:V, p. 2869
US – Carbon Steel	Appellate Body Report, *United States – Countervailing Duties on Certain Corrosion-Resistant Carbon Steel Flat Products from Germany*, WT/DS213/AB/R and Corr.1, adopted 19 December 2002, DSR 2002:IX, p. 3779
US – Clove Cigarettes	Appellate Body Report, *United States – Measures Affecting the Production and Sale of Clove Cigarettes*, WT/DS406/AB/R, adopted 24 April 2012, DSR 2012: XI, p. 5751
US – Clove Cigarettes	Panel Report, *United States – Measures Affecting the Production and Sale of Clove Cigarettes*, WT/DS406/R, adopted 24 April 2012, as modified by Appellate Body Report WT/DS406/AB/R, DSR 2012:XI, p. 5865
US – Continued Zeroing	Appellate Body Report, *United States – Continued Existence and Application of Zeroing Methodology*, WT/DS350/AB/R, adopted 19 February 2009, DSR 2009:III, p. 1291
US – COOL	Panel Reports, *United States – Certain Country of Origin Labelling (COOL) Requirements*, WT/DS384/R / WT/DS386/R, adopted 23 July 2012, as modified by Appellate Body Reports WT/DS384/AB/R / WT/DS386/AB/R, DSR 2012:VI, p. 2745
US – Countervailing and Anti-Dumping Measures (China)	Appellate Body Report, *United States – Countervailing and Anti-Dumping Measures on Certain Products from China*, WT/DS449/AB/R and Corr.1, adopted 22 July 2014, DSR 2014:VIII, p. 3027
US – FSC	Panel Report, *United States – Tax Treatment for "Foreign Sales Corporations"*, WT/DS108/R, adopted 20 March 2000, as modified by Appellate Body Report WT/DS108/AB/R, DSR 2000:IV, p. 1675
US – Gasoline	Appellate Body Report, *United States – Standards for Reformulated and Conventional Gasoline*, WT/DS2/AB/R, adopted 20 May 1996, DSR 1996:I, p. 3
US – Gambling	Appellate Body Report, *United States – Measures Affecting the Cross-Border Supply of Gambling and Betting Services*, WT/DS285/AB/R, adopted 20 April 2005, DSR 2005:XII, p. 5663 (and Corr.1, DSR 2006:XII, p. 5475)
US – Oil Country Tubular Goods Sunset Reviews	Appellate Body Report, *United States – Sunset Reviews of Anti-Dumping Measures on Oil Country Tubular Goods from Argentina*, WT/DS268/AB/R, adopted 17 December 2004, DSR 2004:VII, p. 3257
US – Poultry (China)	Panel Report, *United States – Certain Measures Affecting Imports of Poultry from China*, WT/DS392/R, adopted 25 October 2010, DSR 2010:V, p. 1909
US – Upland Cotton	Appellate Body Report, *United States – Subsidies on Upland Cotton*, WT/DS267/AB/R, adopted 21 March 2005, DSR 2005:I, p. 3
US – Section 301 Trade Act	Panel Report, *United States – Sections 301-310 of the Trade Act of 1974*, WT/DS152/R, adopted 27 January 2000, DSR 2000:II, p. 815

Short title	Full case title
US – Shrimp (Thailand)	Panel Report, *United States – Measures Relating to Shrimp from Thailand*, WT/DS343/R, adopted 1 August 2008, as modified by Appellate Body Report WT/DS343/AB/R / WT/DS345/AB/R, DSR 2008:VII, p. 2539
US – Tuna II (Mexico) (Article 21.5 – Mexico)	Appellate Body Report, *United States – Measures Concerning the Importation, Marketing and Sale of Tuna and Tuna Products – Recourse to Article 21.5 of the DSU by Mexico*, WT/DS381/AB/RW and Add.1, adopted 3 December 2015
US – Tuna II (Mexico)	Appellate Body Report, *United States – Measures Concerning the Importation, Marketing and Sale of Tuna and Tuna Products*, WT/DS381/AB/R, adopted 13 June 2012, DSR 2012:IV, p. 1837
US – Wool Shirts and Blouses	Appellate Body Report, *United States – Measure Affecting Imports of Woven Wool Shirts and Blouses from India*, WT/DS33/AB/R, adopted 23 May 1997, and Corr.1, DSR 1997:I, p. 323
US – Wool Shirts and Blouses	Panel Report, *United States – Measure Affecting Imports of Woven Wool Shirts and Blouses from India*, WT/DS33/R, adopted 23 May 1997, upheld by Appellate Body Report WT/DS33/AB/R, DSR 1997:I, p. 343
US – Corrosion-Resistant Steel Sunset Review	Appellate Body Report, *United States – Sunset Review of Anti-Dumping Duties on Corrosion-Resistant Carbon Steel Flat Products from Japan*, WT/DS244/AB/R, adopted 9 January 2004, DSR 2004:I, p. 3
US – Zeroing (EC)	Appellate Body Report, *United States – Laws, Regulations and Methodology for Calculating Dumping Margins ("Zeroing")*, WT/DS294/AB/R, adopted 9 May 2006, and Corr.1, DSR 2006:II, p. 417
US – Zeroing (Japan) (Article 21.5 – Japan)	Appellate Body Report, *United States – Measures Relating to Zeroing and Sunset Reviews – Recourse to Article 21.5 of the DSU by Japan*, WT/DS322/AB/RW, adopted 31 August 2009, DSR 2009:VIII, p. 3441
Thailand – Cigarettes (Philippines)	Appellate Body Report, *Thailand – Customs and Fiscal Measures on Cigarettes from the Philippines*, WT/DS371/AB/R, adopted 15 July 2011, DSR 2011:IV, p. 2203
Thailand – Cigarettes (Philippines)	Panel Report, *Thailand – Customs and Fiscal Measures on Cigarettes from the Philippines*, WT/DS371/R, adopted 15 July 2011, as modified by Appellate Body Report WT/DS371/AB/R, DSR 2011:IV, p. 2299

TABLE OF FREQUENTLY CITED EXHIBITS

Exhibit	Title	Short Title (if applicable)
BRA-01/IDN-24	Ministry of Agriculture Regulation 58/Permentan/ PK.210/11/2015	MoA 58/2015
BRA-03/IDN-39	Ministry of Trade Regulation No. 5/2016 Regarding Provisions on Export and Import of Animal and Animal Products.	MoT 05/2016
BRA-04	OECD Review of Agricultural Policies: Indonesia 2012	
BRA-08/IDN-100	Ministry of Agriculture Regulation 20/Permentan/ OT.140/4/2009	MoA 20/2009
BRA-14	Minutes of the Fourth Meeting of Consultative Committee on agriculture (CCA) between the Ministry of Agriculture of the Republic of Indonesia and the Ministry of Agriculture, Livestock and Food Supply of Federative Republic of Brazil	Minutes of the CCA meeting of 15 and 16 September 2010
BRA-29/IDN-1	Law of the Republic of Indonesia Number 18/2009 on Husbandry and Animal Health	Law 18/2009
BRA-34	Ministry of Agriculture Regulation 139/Permentan PD/410/12/2014	MoA 139/2014
BRA-42/IDN-127	Ministry of Trade Regulation 46 /M-DAG/PER/8/2013	MoT 46/2013
BRA-43	Brazilian Veterinary Certificates for poultry (2009) and turkey and duck (2010) proposed by Brazil to Indonesia	
BRA-46/IDN-05	Law of Republic of Indonesia N. 33/2014 concerning Halal Product Assurance	Law 33/2014
BRA-48/IDN-93	Ministry of Agriculture Regulation 34/Permentan/ PK210/7/2016	MoA 34/2016
BRA-56	Online article entitled: Indonesia aims for poultry and beef self-sufficiency	
IDN-31	Government Regulation No. 95/2012 Concerning Veterinary Public Health and Animal Welfare.	GR 95/2012
IDN-56	Online article entitled: Indonesia aims for poultry and beef self-sufficiency	
IDN-74	Government Regulation No. 69/1999 on Food Labelling and Advertisement.	GR 69/1999
IDN-84	Regulation EC No. 852/2004 of the European Parliament and of the Council on the Hygiene of Foodstuffs of 29 April 2004	EC Reg 852/2004

Exhibit	Title	Short Title (if applicable)
IDN-88	Import Recommendation by the Minister of Agriculture for beef from New Zealand in December 2015	
IDN-109	MoT Regulation No. 59/2016 concerning Export and Import Prohibitions on Animal and Animal Products	MoT 59/2016

ABBREVIATIONS USED IN THIS REPORT

Abbreviation	Description
Animal Law	Law 18/2009
API	Importer Identification Number
BPJPH	Halal Product Organizing Agency
CCA	Consultative Committee on agriculture
Consumer Law	Law 8/1999
DSB	Dispute Settlement Body
DSU	Understanding on Rules and Procedures Governing the Settlement of Disputes
Food Law	Law 18/2012 of Indonesia
GATT 1994	General Agreement on Tariffs and Trade 1994
Halal Law	Law 33/2014
LPH	Halal examination agencies
Import Licensing Agreement	Agreement on Import Licensing Procedures
MoA	Minister of Agriculture or Ministry of Agriculture
MoA Regulation	Regulation of the Minister of Agriculture or Regulation of the Ministry of Agriculture
MoT	Minister of Trade or Ministry of Trade
MoT Regulation	Regulation of the Minister of Trade or Regulation of the Ministry of Trade
MUI	Indonesian Ulama Council
OECD	Organisation for Economic Co-operation and Development
OIE	World Organisation for Animal Health
SPS Agreement	Agreement on the Application of Sanitary and Phytosanitary Measures
TBT Agreement	Agreement on Technical Barriers to Trade
WTO	World Trade Organization

1.   INTRODUCTION

1.1   Complaint by Brazil

1.   On 16 October 2014, Brazil requested consultations with Indonesia pursuant to Articles 1 and 4 of the Understanding on Rules and Procedures Governing the Settlement of Disputes (DSU), Article XXII of the General Agreement on Tariffs and Trade 1994 (GATT 1994), Article 11 of the Agreement on the Application of Sanitary and Phytosanitary Measures (SPS Agreement), Article 6 of the Agreement on Import Licensing Procedures (Import Licensing Agreement), Article 14 of the Agreement on Technical Barriers to Trade (TBT Agreement), Article 19 of the Agreement on Agriculture, and Article 8 of the Agreement on Preshipment Inspection with respect to the measures and claims set out below.[1]

2.   Consultations were held on 15 and 16 December 2014. These consultations failed to resolve the dispute.

1.2   Panel Establishment and Composition

3.   On 15 October 2015, Brazil requested the establishment of a panel pursuant to Article 6 of the DSU with standard terms of reference.[2] At its meeting on 3 December 2015, the Dispute Settlement Body (DSB) established a panel pursuant to the request by Brazil in documents WT/DS484/8 and WT/DS484/8/Corr.1, in accordance with Article 6 of the DSU.[3]

4.   The Panel's terms of reference are the following:

> To examine, in the light of the relevant provisions of the covered agreements cited by the parties to the dispute, the matter referred to the DSB by Brazil in documents WT/DS484/8 and WT/DS484/8/Corr.1, and to make such findings as will assist the DSB in making the recommendations or in giving the rulings provided for in those agreements.[4]

5.   Argentina, Australia, Canada, Chile, China, the European Union, India, Japan, the Republic of Korea, New Zealand, Norway, Paraguay, the Russian Federation, the Separate Customs Territory of Taiwan, Penghu, Kinmen and Matsu (Chinese Taipei), Thailand, the United States, and Viet Nam notified their interest in participating in the Panel proceedings as third parties.

---

[1]   See WT/DS484/1.
[2]   WT/DS484/8 and WT/DS484/8/Corr.1.
[3]   See WT/DSB/M/371.
[4]   WT/DS484/9.

6.   On 22 February 2016, Brazil requested the Director-General to determine the composition of the panel, pursuant to Article 8.7 of the DSU. On 3 March 2016, the Director-General accordingly composed the Panel as follows:

Chairperson: Mr Mohammad Saeed

Members: Mr Sufyan Al-Irhayim

                        Ms Claudia Orozco

7.   On 28 April 2016 and 23 May 2016, Oman and Qatar respectively requested to join as third parties. On 25 May 2016, the Panel consulted with the parties. Brazil took the view that neither request should be accepted. Indonesia had no objections to the requests. On 3 June 2016, the Panel informed Oman, Qatar, and the parties of its decision to accept the requests. On 6 June 2016, the Panel informed the other third parties of its decision to accept the requests. The Panel's ruling on the requests is set out in section 7.1.1 below.

1.3   Panel Proceedings

1.3.1   General

8.   On 16 March 2016, after consulting with the parties, the Panel adopted its Working Procedures[5] and timetable.

9.   On 22 April 2016 and 10 June 2016, Brazil and Indonesia respectively submitted their first written submissions.

10.   On 13 and 15 July 2016, the Panel held its first substantive meeting with the parties. A session with the third parties took place on 14 July 2016. Following the meeting, on 19 July 2016, the Panel sent written questions to the parties and third parties. On the same date, the parties sent written questions to each other. The Panel received the responses to questions on 2 August 2016.

11.   On 2 September 2016, Brazil and Indonesia submitted their second written submissions.

12.   On 11 and 12 October 2016, the Panel held a second substantive meeting with the parties. Following the meeting, on 21 October 2016, the Panel sent written questions to the parties. The Panel received the responses to those questions on 4 November 2016. The Panel gave the parties an opportunity to comment on each other's responses. The Panel received the comments on 18 November 2016.

13.   On 15 December 2016, the Panel issued the descriptive part of its Report to the parties. The Panel issued its Interim Report to the parties on 15 March 2017. The Panel issued its Final Report to the parties on 10 May 2017.

---

[5]   See the Panel's Working Procedures in Annex A-1.

1.3.2   Preliminary ruling

14.   On 10 June 2016, together with its first written submission, Indonesia presented a request for a preliminary ruling concerning certain alleged defects in the panel request and certain inconsistencies between the scope of the panel request and Brazil's first written submission.

15.   On 13 June 2016, the Panel invited Brazil to comment on Indonesia's preliminary ruling request. On the same date, the Panel also invited the third parties to comment on Indonesia's preliminary ruling request and to file those comments together with their third-party submissions.

16.   On 17 June 2016, the United States, as a third party, provided its views. No other third party provided comments. On 27 June 2016, the Panel received comments from Brazil.

17.   On 13 and 15 July 2016, in the course of the first meeting with the parties, the Panel posed questions to both parties in connection with Indonesia's request for a preliminary ruling.

18.   On 19 July 2016, the Panel informed the parties of its conclusions with respect to Indonesia's preliminary ruling request. On 27 July 2016, the Panel informed the third parties of its conclusions. The Panel's conclusions as well as the reasoning supporting those conclusions are set out in section 7.1.2 below.

2.   **FACTUAL ASPECTS**

2.1   The Measures at Issue

19.   This dispute concerns measures imposed by Indonesia on imports of certain chicken meat and chicken products from Brazil.[6]

20.   Brazil makes claims against two categories of measures: (i) an alleged general prohibition on the importation of chicken meat and chicken products; and (ii) specific restrictions and prohibitions on the importation of chicken meat and chicken products.

2.1.1   Alleged general prohibition

21.   In its panel request, Brazil describes the alleged general prohibition as follows:

> Indonesia imposes several prohibitions or restrictions on the importation of chicken meat and chicken products which,

---

[6]   Brazil describes the products at issue in this dispute as meat and products from fowls of the species *Gallus domesticus*, corresponding to the following HS codes: (i) 0207.11 (whole chicken, not cut into parts, fresh or chilled); (ii) 0207.12 (whole chicken, not cut into parts, frozen); (iii) 0207.13 (chicken cuts and offal, fresh or chilled); (iv) 0207.14 (chicken cuts and offal, frozen); and (v) 1602.32 (chicken meat, other leftover meat and blood that has been processed or preserved). See Brazil's panel request, p. 1.

combined, have the effect of a general prohibition on the importation of these products, as follows:

a. Indonesia does not allow the importation of animal and animal products not listed in the appendices of the relevant regulations[7]. With regard to chicken, the list only contemplates HS codes referred to as whole chicken, fresh or chilled and frozen[8]. The HS codes for chicken meat cut into pieces[9] are not described in any of the "positive lists" which contain the products that can be imported into Indonesia's territory;[10]

b. Domestic food production (including "staple food"[11], which encompasses chicken meat and chicken products) and national food reserve are prioritized over food import, which is only authorized as an exception, when domestic food supply in Indonesia is not considered "sufficient" by the government;[12]

c. Imports of essential and strategic goods may be prohibited and/or restricted and prices may be controlled by the Indonesian government.[13] Thus, import and export operations may be postponed by the Minister of Trade during a force majeure event. As chicken meat and chicken products fit into the categories of essential and strategic goods[14], even if they were allowed to enter into Indonesia, their effective importation would be subject to the discretion of the Minister of Trade;

d. The Indonesian government limits the importation of chicken meat and chicken products to certain intended uses. The importation of chicken meat and chicken products shall only be allowed to meet the needs of "hotel, restaurant, catering, manufacturing, other special needs, and modern market";[15]

---

[7] (footnote original) The products allowed to be imported by Indonesia are currently listed in the Appendix I and II of MoA Regulation 139/2014 and the Appendix II of MoT Regulation 46/2013.

[8] (footnote original) HS Codes 020711 and 020712.

[9] (footnote original) HS Codes 020713 and 020714.

[10] (footnote original) Furthermore, the HS code for processed chicken products is not described in the "positive list" of MoA Regulation 139/2014.

[11] (footnote original) According to Article 1.15 of Law 18/2012 ("Food Law"), the term "staple food" means "[…] food that is intended as the main daily food according to local potential resources and wisdom".

[12] (footnote original) The determination of self-sufficiency is under the discretion of the Government authorities. The Government is empowered to establish a tax and/or tariff policy in favor of national interests or to regulate the import of staple food (Articles 14, 15, 36, 55 and 56 of Law 18/2012).

[13] (footnote original) Law 7/2014 ("Trade Law") imposes a number of measures that institutionalize the government's central role in trade management as well as provides further instruments towards government intervention and protectionist actions.

[14] (footnote original) According to the Trade Law, strategic goods are defined as goods that have "a strategic role in the smooth running of national development".

[15] (footnote original) See Article 32(2) of MoA Regulation 139/2014.

e.   Indonesia has unduly refused to examine and approve the Health Certificates for poultry products (including chicken meat and chicken products) proposed by Brazil since 2009;

f.   Indonesia imposes prohibitions and/or restrictions to importation through its Import Licensing Regime.[16] In order to import chicken meat and chicken products, importers must obtain import licenses after several approval and overlapping authorization stages, covered by different regulations and authorities; and

g.   Indonesia establishes an import prohibition through different regulations regarding halal slaughtering and labelling requirements for imported chicken meat and chicken products.[17, 18]

22.   In its subsequent submissions, Brazil did not make reference to the last element, identified above, in its description of the alleged general prohibition. Reference to this last element was made, however, when discussing specific restrictions and prohibitions applied by Indonesia to its imports of chicken meat and chicken products. This is discussed in section 7.8 below.

2.1.2   Specific restrictions and prohibitions

23.   In addition to the alleged general prohibition on the importation of chicken meat and chicken products, Brazil also challenges a number of individual measures. Four of those individual measures, albeit described in slightly different terms in their own section of the panel request, correspond to items (a), (d), (e), and (f) of the previous section. They pertain respectively to (i) the non-inclusion of certain chicken products in the list of products that may be imported; (ii) the limitation of imports of chicken meat and chicken products to certain intended uses; (iii) Indonesia's alleged undue delay in the approval of health certificates for chicken products; and (iv) Indonesia's import licensing regime.

24.   In addition, Brazil challenges two more individual measures:

a.   Surveillance and implementation of halal slaughtering and labelling requirements for imported chicken meat and chicken products established by different Indonesian regulations, which are much stricter than the surveillance and the implementation of

---

[16]   (footnote original) Imports of animals and animal products, including chicken cuts, which are not listed in the HS codes described in the positive lists of MoA Regulation 139/2014 and of MoT Regulation 46/2013, are prohibited. Furthermore, through the Trade Law and MoA Regulation 139/2014, the Indonesian government controls the type, quantity, price and use of chicken meat and chicken products allowed to be imported into Indonesia.

[17]   (footnote original) See MoA Regulation 139/2014 and Law 33/2014.

[18]   Brazil's panel request, pp. 1-2. For ease of reference, bullet points in the original were replaced with letters.

        halal requirements applied to the domestic production in Indonesia[19]; and

b.   Restrictions on the transportation of imported products by requiring direct transportation from the country of origin to the entry points in Indonesia.[20]

25.   Brazil's panel request identifies a further two individual measures. However, Brazil has not developed claims in its subsequent submissions in respect of these measures.[21]

2.2   *Other Factual Aspects*

26.   During the proceedings, certain legal instruments underlying a number of the measures at issue were either revoked or revoked and replaced. Table 1 below indicates the two legal instruments that are central to this dispute, as identified by Brazil in its panel request, and the corresponding legal instruments that revoked and replaced them, as indicated by the parties in their respective submissions.[22]

---

[19]   Brazil's panel request, part II, item No. iv, fourth bullet. See also Brazil's first written submission, paras. 136-139.

[20]   Brazil's panel request, part II, item Nos. i, third bullet and ii, third bullet. See also Brazil's first written submission, paras. 132-135.

[21]   First, when challenging restrictions on the transportation of imported products, Brazil's panel request also indicates that such restrictions are in place by virtue of "limiting the ports of entry for chicken meat and chicken products". Second, Brazil's panel request refers to Indonesia's failure to notify the relevant laws and regulations constituting an inconsistency with Indonesia's WTO's "transparency requirements".

[22]   Other legal instruments have also been modified in the course of the proceedings. The changes to those other instruments will be identified, as relevant, in the examination of the different claims.

Table 1. Amendments and revisions in the relevant legal instruments

Panel request[23] ("first set of legal instruments")	First written submission[24] ("second set of legal instruments")	Second[25] written submission ("third set of legal instruments")
• MoA 139/2014 of 23 December 2014[26] • MoT 46/2013 of 30 August 2013[27]	• MoA 58/2015 of 25 November 2015[28] • MoT 05/2016 of 28 January 2016[29]	• MoA 34/2016 of 15 July 2016[30] • MoT 59/2016 of 15 August 2016[31]

27.   The Panel discusses its approach with regard to the changes in the different sets of legal instruments in section 7.2.4 below.

3.   PARTIES' REQUESTS FOR FINDINGS AND RECOMMENDATIONS

28.   Brazil requests the Panel to find that:

a.   Indonesia's general prohibition on the importation of chicken meat and chicken products is inconsistent with Article XI:1 of the GATT 1994 and Article 4.2 of the Agreement on Agriculture;

b.   Indonesia's prohibition on the importation of chicken cuts and other prepared or preserved chicken meat is inconsistent with Article XI:1 of the GATT 1994 and Article 4.2 of the Agreement on Agriculture;

c.   Indonesia's restrictions on the use of imported chicken meat and chicken products is inconsistent with Article XI:1 of the GATT 1994 and Article 4.2 of the Agreement on Agriculture;

---

[23]   The panel request was filed by Brazil on 15 October 2015. The Panel was established on 3 December 2015.

[24]   Brazil's first written submission was received by the Panel on 22 April 2016. Indonesia's first written submission was received by the Panel on 10 June 2016.

[25]   The parties' second written submissions were received on 2 September 2016.

[26]   See Brazil's first written submission, para. 58. See also Indonesia's second written submission, para. 6.

[27]   *Ibid.*

[28]   *Ibid.*

[29]   *Ibid.*

[30]   See Indonesia's second written submission, para. 32. See also Indonesia's second written submission, para. 6.

[31]   MoT 37/2016, which was enacted on 23 May 2016 amended MoT 05/2016. On 15 August 2016, MoT 5/2016, as amended by MoT 37/2016, was replaced by MoT 59/2016. See Indonesia's second written submission, para. 6.

    d.   Indonesia's restrictive import licensing procedures is inconsistent with Article XI:1 of the GATT 1994, Article 4.2 of the Agreement on Agriculture, and Article 3.2 of the Agreement on Import Licensing Procedures;

    e.   Indonesia's restrictive transportation requirements for imported chicken meat and chicken products is inconsistent with Article XI:1 of the GATT 1994 and Article 4.2 of the Agreement on Agriculture;

    f.   Indonesia's restrictions on the use of imported chicken meat and chicken products is inconsistent with Article III:4 of the GATT 1994;

    g.   Indonesia's surveillance and implementation of halal labelling requirements is inconsistent with Article III:4 of the GATT 1994; and

    h.   Indonesia's undue delay with regard to the approval of sanitary requirements is inconsistent with Article 8 and Annex C of the SPS Agreement.[32]

29.   Indonesia requests that the Panel reject Brazil's' claims in this dispute in their entirety.[33]

4.   ARGUMENTS OF THE PARTIES

30.   The arguments of the parties are reflected in their executive summaries, provided to the Panel in accordance with paragraph 21 of the Working Procedures adopted by the Panel (see Annexes B-1 and B-2).

5.   ARGUMENTS OF THE THIRD PARTIES

31.   The arguments of Argentina, Australia, Canada, the European Union, Japan, New Zealand, Norway, Paraguay, Qatar, and the United States are reflected in their executive summaries, provided in accordance with paragraph 22 of the Working Procedures adopted by the Panel (see Annexes C-1, C-2, C-3, C-4, C-5. C-6, C-7, C-8, C-9, and C-10). Chile, China, India, the Republic of Korea, Oman, the Russian Federation, Chinese Taipei, Thailand, and Viet Nam did not submit written or oral arguments to the Panel.

---

[32] Brazil's first written submission, para. 316. See also Brazil's second written submission, para. 225.

[33] Indonesia's first written submission, para. 373. See also Indonesia's second written submission, para. 178.

6.   INTERIM REVIEW

6.1   Introduction

32.   On 15 March 2017, the Panel issued its Interim Report to the parties. On 29 March 2017, Brazil and Indonesia submitted written requests for the Panel to review aspects of the Interim Report. On 12 April 2017, the parties submitted comments on each other's request for review. Neither party requested an interim review meeting.

33.   In accordance with Article 15.3 of the DSU, this section of the Report sets out our response to the parties' requests for review of precise aspects of the Report made at the interim review stage. We discuss the parties' requests for substantive modifications below, in sequential order. In addition to the substantive requests discussed below, we have made editorial and drafting improvements to the Report, including, where relevant, those suggested by the parties.

34.   The numbering of some of the paragraphs and the footnotes in the Report has changed from that in the Interim Report. The discussion below refers to the numbering in the Interim Report, and where it differs, the corresponding numbering in the Report is included.

6.2   Preliminary Ruling: Whether the Alleged General Prohibition is Within the Panel's Terms of Reference

35.   Regarding **paragraph 7.33**, Indonesia notes that Brazil's panel request does not mention the word "unwritten" and thus requests the Panel to reconcile its description of the measure at issue with that provided in Brazil's panel request. Brazil disagrees with Indonesia and considers that the wording of paragraph 7.33 is adequate. Brazil suggests an alternative wording should the Panel decide to amend this paragraph.

36.   We see no need to amend this paragraph as suggested by Indonesia. We are cognizant of the fact that Brazil's panel request does not include the term "unwritten" in its description of the alleged general prohibition. However, we read that description to be referring to an unwritten measure and find confirmation for this in Brazil's submissions. This paragraph of the Interim Report reflects our conclusion, which is based on our understanding of Brazil's panel request.

6.3   Order of Analysis: Whether Article XI of the GATT 1994 and Article 4.2 of the Agreement on Agriculture Are Mutually Exclusive

37.   Regarding **paragraph 7.73**, Indonesia requests the Panel to delete its reference to "the exceptions set out" when referring to Article XI:2 of the GATT 1994, because Indonesia considers that this reference could lead to confusion

about the nature of that provision. Brazil does not comment on Indonesia's request.

38. We accept Indonesia's suggestion, because we agree with Indonesia that the expression "the exceptions set out" may lead to confusion.

6.4 Individual Measure 1: Positive List Requirement

39. Brazil requests the Panel to complement the first sentence of **paragraph 7.149** to reflect more accurately Brazil's suggestion of an alternative less-trade restrictive measure. Indonesia does not comment on Brazil's request.

40. We see no need to amend this paragraph as suggested by Brazil. The language that Brazil requests us to add is not included in the relevant sections of Brazil's submissions referred to in the relevant footnote to this paragraph of the Interim Report. Moreover, in our view, the context provided by the preceding paragraphs makes this addition unnecessary.

41. Regarding **paragraph 7.152**, Brazil requests the Panel to complement this paragraph to clarify that certification does not apply to products whose importation is prohibited by virtue of the positive list requirement. Indonesia does not comment on Brazil's request.

42. We see no need to amend this paragraph as suggested by Brazil. Brazil is requesting us to complement this sentence with an argument developed in the subsequent paragraph of the Interim Report.[34] In our view, this addition would disrupt the manner in which we present the question before us.

6.5 Individual Measure 2: Intended Use Requirement

43. Regarding **paragraph 7.207**, Brazil considers that the Interim Report mischaracterizes its argument and requests the Panel to quote directly Brazil's submissions stating that "from a public health perspective, frozen chicken is much safer than fresh chicken because freezing is considered to be a preservation method that inhibits microbial growth and delays metabolic activities". Indonesia requests the Panel not to accept Brazil's proposed change. Indonesia considers that Brazil's argument does not address Indonesia's primary concern, and that it is therefore irrelevant.

44. We made changes to paragraph 7.207 to better summarize Brazil's argument. However, we did not include the requested quote as we consider that Brazil's argument is described in more detail in paragraph 7.211 which also reflects the above statement made by Brazil.[35] Furthermore, we slightly

---

[34] See para. 7.153 below, where we explain that "[a]s noted above, chicken cuts that cannot be imported into Indonesia, neither require certification nor need to be traced. A product cannot be certified and banned at the same time. Thus, in respect of the banned products subject to the measure at issue, certification is a new measure, not one that already exists as part of a comprehensive policy."

[35] See para. 7.211 below, where we state that "[i]t points to the food safety benefits of freezing meat and submits that □the freezing process the imported chicken undergoes […] is capable of

shortened the description of Indonesia's argument because we consider that that argument is already described in more detail in paragraph 7.210.[36]

45.   Brazil requests the Panel to rephrase Indonesia's argument in **paragraph 7.210,** submitting that the wording does not adequately reflect the evidence presented by Indonesia, which concerns re-freezing alone. Indonesia considers that Brazil's suggestions are without merit and should not be accepted. Indonesia argues that the evidence is on point with respect to both the thawing and the re-freezing argument it made. Indonesia also refers to additional evidence that it considers to be on point a reference to which it suggests should be included in paragraph 7.210.

46.   We made changes to paragraph 7.210 to better reflect Indonesia's argument and the evidence it has submitted. However, we disagree with Brazil's specific suggestion for the following reasons. First, we disagree with Brazil's contention that Indonesia's argument is only about re-freezing. While Indonesia's first written submission may have put more emphasis on the issue of re-freezing, its subsequent submissions clearly focus on the issue of improper thawing (prior to re-freezing).[37] Brazil's specific suggestion would therefore be an inaccurate account of Indonesia's arguments. Second, there is a difference between an argument a party makes and the evidence it submits. Even in a case where a party's argument is not substantiated by evidence, it would be erroneous for a panel to indicate that such argument was not made by the party.[38] Paragraph 7.210 of the Interim Report first describes Indonesia's argument and then lists the evidence submitted by Indonesia. (As requested by Indonesia, we have reflected in that paragraph in a more comprehensive manner the relevant evidence submitted by Indonesia.) Paragraph 7.213 is the Panel's assessment of the relevant evidence including those that Brazil itself has submitted. We discuss the parties' comments regarding that assessment below.

47.   Regarding **paragraphs 7.213, 7.214 and 7.215** Brazil essentially disagrees with the Panel's assessment of Brazil's evidence and requests the Panel to revisit that assessment. Brazil takes the view that a higher degree of reliability should have been given to the Ingham et al. research note submitted by Brazil compared to Indonesia's evidence consisting of governmental guidelines and instructions. In support of its argument Brazil refers to the Appellate Body's jurisprudence in *EC – Hormones* regarding divergent opinions. Indonesia considers that Brazil's request is without merit. Indonesia (here and in its comments on paragraph 7.210) offers its own views on how to assess the

---

ensuring that the meat will remain fresh for a longer period, as compared to meat that has never been frozen☐" (footnotes omitted).

[36]   We also made changes to para. 7.210 below.

[37]   See e.g. Indonesia's opening statement at first meeting of the Panel, para. 66. See also para. 7.213 below, where we address the relationship between these two issues.

[38]   A panel, in that case, would have to indicate in its report that the argument was made but was not substantiated.

evidence. Furthermore, Indonesia considers Brazil's reference to *EC – Hormones* to be misplaced.

48.   We made some changes to paragraphs 7.213 and 7.214 to clarify our reasoning in light of the parties' comments. However, we reject Brazil's request for the following reasons. First, our finding that Indonesia's argument on the existence of a health risk is supported by evidence, is based on a review of all the evidence taken together, including, importantly, the evidence submitted by Brazil itself.[39] Brazil is correct in pointing out that exhibit IDN-56 is not directly on point, as we state in paragraph 7.213. We added a similar comment in paragraph 7.213 regarding exhibit IDN-64. However, while it is true that Indonesia has not submitted scientific papers that directly demonstrate the risk it refers to, it has nevertheless submitted evidence that refers to the existence of such a risk, including expert advice from a governmental source. That evidence is corroborated by Brazil's own scientific evidence. We consider that for purposes of proving the alleged risk under Article XX(b) of the GATT 1994, this evidence, taken together, is sufficient to support Indonesia's defence.[40] Furthermore, we are of the view, similar to Indonesia, that Brazil's reading of *EC – Hormones* is misplaced. We read this jurisprudence to suggest that a Member may base its measure on scientifically sound evidence, regardless of whether that evidence represents a mainstream scientific view or a divergent/minority view. Contrary to what Brazil implies, that jurisprudence *in casu* favours Indonesia, not Brazil, as it is Indonesia's measure that is at issue, not Brazil's. Thus, the Ingham et al. research note, even if scientifically sound, cannot "nullify" (to use Brazil's words) the mainstream view that Indonesia relies on.

49.   Brazil requests us to move the content of **footnote 343** into the main text, in a new paragraph, right after **paragraph 7.226**. Indonesia does not comment on Brazil's request.

50.   We reject Brazil's request as we consider that the issue discussed in footnote 343 was not sufficiently developed to properly fit in the necessity analysis. Inserting the text in the place indicated by Brazil would, in our view, disrupt the flow of the analysis, thereby potentially confusing the reader. We note that Brazil's right to take issue with what we state is not impacted by the placement of that statement either in a footnote or in the main text.

51.   Brazil takes issue with, and, therefore proposes to delete, language in **paragraph 7.230** suggesting that Brazil did not elaborate on the less trade restrictive alternative measures that it proposed. Indonesia considers that Brazil's request is without merit, because Brazil has failed to develop its proposed less trade restrictive alternative measures. Therefore, Indonesia requests the Panel

---

[39]   See Appellate Body Report, *Korea – Dairy Safeguards*, para. 137.
[40]   Whether it would have been sufficient for purposes of rebutting, for example, an Article 5.1. claim under the SPS Agreement, can be left open, as Brazil chose not to pursue its SPS claims, see also fn 318 below.

not to accept Brazil's suggestion and to retain the original wording in paragraph 7.230.

52.   We made the changes proposed by Brazil, but also deleted additional language from paragraph 7.230. We note that the paragraph in question contains a description of Brazil's arguments, whereas subsequent paragraphs contain our analysis of these arguments. Our view that Brazil has not sufficiently described the alternative measures it proposed is set out in those paragraphs. To delete the corresponding language from paragraph 7.230, therefore, does not change or affect the assessment we made. We noted, however, that the description in paragraph 7.230 was inaccurate in that it referred to an argument that Brazil specifically made in the context of Article XX(d) rather than under Article XX(b). We have, therefore, deleted that argument.

53.   Brazil requests specific changes to **paragraph 7.235** which reflect its disagreement with the Panel's understanding that Indonesia's primary concern is the thawing of frozen chicken in tropical temperatures. Indonesia requests the Panel not to accept Brazil's suggestion, because in its view, Indonesia's arguments and evidence address more than the re-freezing of thawed meat alone.

54.   We reject Brazil's request as we see no reason to change our understanding, as discussed above, that Indonesia's primary concern is the thawing of frozen chicken at tropical temperatures.[41]

55.   Brazil's request in respect of **paragraphs 7.236 and 7.237** is twofold. First, Brazil, referring to its previous comments regarding its arguments on less trade restrictive alternative measures, requests that the first sentence of paragraph 7.236 be deleted. Second Brazil requests that the Panel "revisit" this section of the report in respect of the cold storage requirement to better reflect Brazil's argument. Brazil submits that "contrary to what the Panel suggested, [it] never argued that [the cold storage] requirement would not be a less trade restrictive alternative to the intended use requirement". Furthermore Brazil states that "it was clear from the discussions and the evidence on the record that having or not a cold storage facility was not an issue behind the intended use restriction". Finally, Brazil submits that "the reference to cold storage in relation to the intended use requirement was only introduced after the first meeting with the Panel, when Brazil had already submitted its arguments...." Indonesia requests the Panel not to accept Brazil's suggestion, because in its view it is without merit. In particular, Indonesia considers that Brazil's assertion that the cold storage requirement was not related to the intended use requirement is incorrect. Indonesia further considers that it referred to the cold storage as part of the intended use requirement in its first written submission. Indonesia further refers to its comments to paragraph 7.230-7.239, regarding the less trade restrictive alternative measures proposed by Brazil.

---

[41]   See also para. 6.15 above.

56.   We reject Brazil's request for the following reasons. First, we see no reason to change the first sentence in paragraph 7.236, which contains the conclusion of our analysis of the less trade restrictive measures proposed by Brazil; which, as seen above, we found unnecessary to modify. Second, as regards the cold storage requirement, we cannot find in Brazil's submissions that Brazil considered the cold storage requirement a less trade restrictive alternative. Brazil may, as it claims, never have argued that the cold storage requirement *would not be* a less trade restrictive alternative to the intended use requirement; however, it also never argued that it *would be*. At the same time, contrary to what Brazil contends, the need for cold storage was referred to by Indonesia as early as in its first written submission.[42] Brazil, thus, could have picked up on Indonesia's argument and pointed to cold storage as a less trade-restrictive alternative, but chose not to do so. To better reflect our understanding of Brazil's arguments, we have slightly modified paragraph 7.236.

57.   Indonesia requests the Panel to delete the last two sentences of **paragraph 7.238.** Indonesia takes the view that there is a contradiction between rejecting Brazil's proposed measure of "rules regulating the thawing of frozen chicken" and referring back to these same rules as possibly encompassing a cold storage requirement. Brazil disagrees with this request and submits that it never argued that the cold storage requirement would not be a less trade restrictive alternative to the intended use requirement. Moreover, Brazil reiterates that it did not understand the concern with proper storage to be related to the intended use requirement.

58.   We accept Indonesia's request and have, therefore, deleted the last two sentences of paragraph 7.238. We acknowledge that the prohibition to let frozen chicken meat thaw, which is implied in a cold storage requirement, may be considered the exact opposite of a rule on thawing, in which case, it would be contradictory to consider that rules on proper thawing could encompass a cold storage requirement.

59.   Brazil requests the Panel to modify **paragraph 7.256** to better reflect Brazil's argument regarding consumer information as a less trade-restrictive alternative and to better explain why the Panel considered that it is not a less trade restrictive alternative. Indonesia requests the Panel not to accept Brazil's suggestion, which it considers to be without merit. Indonesia further considers that Brazil's "alternative" does not address Indonesia's objective of protecting consumers from deceptive practices.

60.   We accept Brazil's request and have made the relevant changes.

61.   Brazil requests changes to **paragraph 7.313.** The suggested changes reflect its disagreement with the Panel's understanding that Indonesia's primary concern is the thawing of frozen chicken in tropical temperatures rather than re-

---

[42]   See Indonesia's first written submission, para. 191; opening statement at the first meeting of the Panel, paras. 64 and 66; and second written submission, paras. 138-139.

freezing. Indonesia requests the Panel not to accept Brazil's suggestion, stressing that Indonesia's arguments and evidence address both re-freezing and thawing of meat.

62.   We reject Brazil's request, because, as already indicated in paragraphs 6.15 and 6.23, we see no reason to change our understanding that Indonesia's primary concern is the thawing of frozen chicken at tropical temperatures.

63.   Brazil proposes specific changes to **paragraph 7.317** and also requests the Panel to make further changes as appropriate. More specifically, Brazil considers that it provided enough evidence to support that thawed chicken is safer than fresh chicken left on display outside. Brazil thus suggests specific changes to reflect this view. Furthermore, Brazil requests the Panel to explain why it considered that the evidence before it leads to find that there are differences in health risks arising from previously frozen thawing chicken and fresh chicken that could justify differences in treatment. Indonesia requests the Panel not to accept Brazil's request which in its view, is without merit. In particular, Indonesia considers that it has not disputed that freezing is used as a hazard-based control measure; however, in Indonesia's view, this does not address the risks with which Indonesia is concerned.

64.   We reject Brazil's request as we see no reason to change our assessment. Brazil's reference to Codex's guideline for the control of *Campylobacter* in chicken meat (Codex CAC/GL 78-2011) in its response to Panel question No. 90, does not address the health risks arising from or relative to leaving fresh chicken displayed at outside temperatures. We therefore decline to amend this paragraph as suggested by Brazil.

65.   Brazil requests the Panel to modify **paragraphs 7.318 and 7.320** to better reflect Brazil's arguments on likeness of thawed and fresh chicken. In this context, Brazil also refers to the Panel's analysis on consumer tastes in respect of the food safety issue and points out that Indonesia did not make any argument to this effect. Indonesia considers Brazil's request to be without merit and requests the Panel to reject it.

66.   We made changes to paragraph 7.318 to accommodate Brazil's request.

6.6   *Individual Measure 5: Halal Labelling Requirements*

67.   Regarding **paragraph 7.532**, Indonesia requests the Panel to make changes to better reflect Indonesia's arguments on why it conducts a holistic assessment of the exporters' compliance with sanitary requirements and halal requirements. Brazil opposes Indonesia's request and notes that regardless of Indonesia's right to adopt its own halal requirements, it is settled that the verification of sanitary requirements comprises exclusively SPS-related matters.

68.   We accept Indonesia's request and have changed paragraph 7.532 (paragraph 7.533 in the Report) accordingly. Contrary to what Brazil seems to imply, we consider that Indonesia's request does not affect the outcome of the

Panel's analysis; it rather clarifies the arguments raised by Indonesia addressed by the Panel.

6.7 Individual Measure 6: Transportation Requirement

69.   Regarding **paragraph 7.598**, Brazil requests the Panel to include or make a specific reference in item (g) of section 8 (conclusions and recommendations) of the Interim Report to the Panel's understanding that the direct transportation requirement, as enshrined in Article 19(a) of MoA 34/2016 includes transhipment. Indonesia is of the view that it is not necessary for the Panel to refer to transhipment in its findings in item (g), because this finding refers specifically to the direct transportation requirement as challenged in Brazil's panel request.

70.   We see no need to reflect this finding in section eight (conclusions and recommendations) of the Report. As Brazil notes, the Panel's factual finding that the transportation requirement, as enshrined in Article 19(a) of MoA 34/2016, allows for transit (including transhipment) is contained in paragraph 7.598 of the Interim Report (paragraph 7.599 of the Report). We observe that this finding is one of two intermediate findings that lead to the overall finding and conclusion contained in section 8. We are of the view that there is no need for section 8 to contain all the detailed and intermediate findings that we have made in the course of our examination, in particular those that have no bearing on implementation under Article 21.5 of the DSU. Furthermore, in our view, the legal value of a finding made by the Panel is not defined by whether it is contained in section seven (findings) or section eight (conclusions and recommendations) of the Report.

6.8 Claims Relating to the Alleged General Prohibition

71.   Indonesia requests the Panel to add a sentence at the end of **paragraph 7.620**, to reflect Brazil's characterization of the alleged general prohibition as "on-going conduct" of "general and systematic application", made during the first meeting. Indonesia refers to the Appellate Body's finding in *Argentina – Import Measures* that the constituent elements that must be substantiated with evidence and arguments in order to prove the existence of a measure challenged will be informed by how such measure is described or characterized by the complainant. Brazil opposes Indonesia's request because it considers it to be misleading. Brazil notes that its reference to "on-going conduct" or "general and prospective application" at the first meeting of the Panel served only to highlight possible analytical tools available to the Panel in WTO case law so as to ascertain the existence of an unwritten measure.

72.   We see no need to amend this paragraph as suggested by Indonesia. However, in light of the parties' comments, we have changed paragraph 7.620 (paragraph 7.621 in the Report) to better reflect Brazil's arguments. Brazil has described the content and scope of the alleged general prohibition in several sections of its submissions. Notably, in paragraph 172 of its first written

submission, Brazil provided a description of the nature of the alleged general prohibition. In that description, Brazil did not refer to the measure being an "on-going conduct" of "general and systematic application". Indonesia refers to a statement made by Brazil in response to questions posed by the Panel during the first substantive meeting. After the first meeting, the Panel sent written questions to both parties, which included questions similar to those formulated during the meeting. One such question is Panel question No. 5(c). As noted by Indonesia, in its response to this question, Brazil replied that characterizing the measure in a particular way does not change the nature of the measure itself or the evidentiary threshold necessary to demonstrate its existence. This point is now also reflected in the summary of Brazil's arguments. We are cognizant of the Appellate Body's finding referred to by Indonesia, and specifically discuss its implications in section 7.10.4.3 of the Report.

73.   Indonesia requests the Panel to add a footnote to **paragraph 7.656** to better reflect Indonesia's position that the delay in the approval of the veterinary health certificate is caused by the actions of Brazil's exporters. Brazil considers that request should be disregarded by the Panel, because this paragraph does not deal with the question of attribution of any delays in the approval of veterinary health certificates, but rather with the question of attribution of the unwritten measure.

74.   We accept Indonesia's request and have added footnote 848 to paragraph 7.656 (paragraph 7.657 in the Report). We acknowledge that Indonesia did raise an objection with respect to the attribution of the delay in the approval of the veterinary certificate to Indonesia's authorities. To the extent that Brazil included the undue delay as constituent measure of the alleged general prohibition, we consider Indonesia's argument to be pertinent in this section.

75.   Regarding **paragraphs 7.658 and 7.659:** Brazil requests the Panel to modify those paragraphs to better reflect Brazil's arguments. Brazil considers that the Panel failed to reflect Brazil's arguments on the trade effects of Indonesia's overarching measure. Brazil further notes that it has provided sufficient evidence of the causal link between the absence of chicken imports and the Indonesian legislation applicable to the imports of chicken meat and chicken products since 2009 (referring to Exhibits BRA-09, BRA-08, and BRA-10). Indonesia requests the Panel not to accept Brazil's request. Indonesia considers that Brazil's request is based on its erroneous assumptions and apparent misunderstanding of the Panel's reasoning. Moreover, Indonesia considers Brazil's request to modify these paragraphs to be imprecise.

76.   We see no need to amend these paragraphs as suggested by Brazil. In section 7.10.3 of the Report, the Panel summarized Brazil's arguments, and referred to the relevant evidence submitted by Brazil in support of its claims against the alleged general prohibition. The paragraphs that Brazil refers to are part of section 7.10.4 (Panel's assessment) of the Report, where the Panel engages with each of the arguments that Brazil raised in support of the existence of the alleged general prohibition. Those two paragraphs address, specifically, whether the trade data submitted by Brazil proves the existence of the measure.

To that extent, we consider that these paragraphs are not dealing with Brazil's arguments. They are rather setting out the Panel's assessment of the arguments that the Panel summarised in an earlier section of the Report. Therefore, we see no need to modify the paragraphs mentioned by Brazil. Moreover, we consider that the additional arguments raised by Brazil in respect of the demonstration of the casual link between the absence of chicken imports and the Indonesian legislation applicable to the imports of chicken meat and chicken products since 2009 are addressed in the remainder of section 10.4.

77.   Regarding **paragraphs 7.670 and 7.686**: Brazil requests the Panel to modify those paragraphs to better reflect Brazil's arguments. Brazil notes that it never suggested that as long as chicken meat and chicken products could not be imported into Indonesia the unwritten measure would be in place. Brazil emphasizes that it was rather concerned with the connection of the set of individual measures that operates together to ban imports of chicken from Brazil. Indonesia requests the Panel not to accept Brazil's request. As a preliminary matter, Indonesia considers that Brazil's request for review of these paragraphs is very unclear. Indonesia further considers that in light of Brazil's submissions throughout the proceedings the Panel did not mischaracterize Brazil's arguments.

78.   We see no need to amend those paragraphs as suggested by Brazil. In section 7.10.3.3, the Panel set out Brazil's arguments in respect of the distinction between the individual measures constituting the alleged general prohibition and the alleged general prohibition itself. On the basis of its understanding of those arguments, the Panel developed its assessment in section 7.10.4. In the Panel's view, the manner in which the Panel formulated its understanding of Brazil's arguments for the purposes of its assessment, both in paragraphs 7.670 and 7.686, corresponds with the arguments that Brazil raised throughout its submissions in these proceedings.

6.9   Conclusions and Recommendations

79.   Indonesia requests the Panel to include in its list of conclusions and recommendations its findings that the Panel has no jurisdiction to rule on Brazil's claims with respect to certain measures. Brazil does not comment on Indonesia's request.

80.   We see no need to accept Indonesia's request. Similarly to what we stated in paragraph 6.39 above we consider that it is not necessary to include every jurisdictional finding in the section on conclusions and recommendations of the Report.

7.   FINDINGS

81.   Before turning to our review of Brazil's claims, as a preliminary matter, we first set out two rulings of interest which we made early on in the proceedings.

7.1 Preliminary Matters

7.1.1 Requests to join the Panel proceedings as third parties after the ten-day period

82.   As described in section 1.2 above, Oman and Qatar requested to join these proceedings as third parties over three months after the Panel was established (see paragraph 1.7 above). Neither Member provided an explanation for the timing of its request.

83.   After consulting with the parties, the Panel decided to accept the requests. The Panel's decision, as communicated to Oman and Qatar, as well as to the parties and the other third parties, is set out below:

> Oman and Qatar respectively addressed the DSB Chair on 28 April 2016 and 23 May 2016, requesting to participate as third parties in DS 484. The requests were made over 3 months after the Panel was established. Neither Member provided an explanation for the timing of its request. On 25 May 2016, the Panel consulted the parties. Brazil took the view that neither request should be accepted. Indonesia had no objections to the requests.

> The Panel notes that Article 10 of the DSU is silent on when Members are to notify their interest in participating in a dispute as third party and recalls the Appellate Body's statement in *EC - Hormones* that "the DSU leaves panels a margin of discretion to deal, always in accordance with due process, with specific situations that may arise in a particular case and that are not explicitly regulated".[43]

> In exercising its discretion, the Panel has taken into account the following. First, the Panel recalls that, once a panel is established, the DSB Chair invites delegations wishing to reserve their third-party rights to raise their flags, after which the Chair reads out the names of those Members who have indicated such interest. The Chair then states as follows:

> > Those Members who have reserved their third-party rights by raising their flags do not need to send any confirmation in writing to the Secretariat. Other delegations who may wish to reserve their third-party rights should do so through a written communication within the next 10 days after this meeting.

---

[43]   (footnote original) Appellate Body Report, *EC – Hormones*, fn 138 to para. 152.

This approach, which was developed in the GATT, has been followed for the more than 230 panels established by the DSB since 1995.[44]

Second, in 10 cases, so far, panels have accepted requests that were made beyond the 10 day period.[45] In doing so, these panels considered whether accepting the request would interfere with the panel's composition, and whether the proceedings would be hampered or due process rights affected. In those cases, requests for third party participation were either filed before or shortly after panel composition.[46]

Third, the Panel notes that both Oman and Qatar are developing countries with very little experience in dispute settlement cases.

The Panel notes that accepting Qatar's and Oman's requests would have no consequences for panel composition, as neither Member has a national on the Panel. Furthermore, the requests, while quite late in the proceedings still allow Qatar and Oman to participate in accordance with the timetable adopted by the Panel, particularly the deadline for third parties submissions (17 June 2016) and the session of the Panel with the third parties (14 July 2016). Thus, accepting the requests does not affect the development of the proceedings.

Finally, the Panel notes that Brazil indicated *inter alia* that the requests should be denied because it had "already submitted its First Written Submission" and "considers that it would seem inadequate to permit new Third Parties at this stage". The Panel notes that Brazil did not allege or explain that participation by Qatar and Oman would affect its due process rights. Furthermore, Brazil neither asked for confidential treatment of the information it presented in its first written submission, nor did it indicate in any other way a need to limit third parties' access to such information.

---

[44] (footnote original) See GATT Council Minutes 21 June 1994, C/M/273 and WT/DSB/M/101. The Panel also notes that in the ongoing DSU negotiations a proposal is under consideration to insert the 10-day notice rule into the text of Article 10(2) of the DSU. See WTO Doc. TN/DS/25, page A-7; and TN/DS/27, para. 3.16.

[45] (footnote original) In some of those disputes, the third-party notifications were made after panel establishment but before panel composition. See Panel Reports, *EC – Export Subsidies on Sugar*, paras. 2.1-2.4 and *Peru – Agricultural Products,* fn 6 to para. 1.6. See also Secretariat Notes WT/DS431/7 in *China – Rare Earths* and WT/DS267/15 in *US –Upland Cotton*. In other disputes, the third-party notifications were made after panel composition. See Panel Reports *Turkey – Rice*, paras. 6.1-6-2; *US – Shrimp (Thailand)*, fn 4 to para. 1.9; *EC – IT Products*, paras. 1.9 and 7.73-7.75; *China – Electronic Payment Services*, fn 7 to para. 1.4; and *EC –Seal Products*, fn 13 to para. 1.10. See also *China – HP-SSST(EU)*, note by the Secretariat on the constitution of the Panel, WT/DS460/5/Rev.1, para. 4.

[46] (footnote original) The latest filing after composition hitherto was 15 days. See Panel Report, *Turkey – Rice*, paras. 6.1-6.2.

Accordingly, Brazil's first written submission was sent to the third parties without any restrictions. The Panel further notes that Brazil will have an opportunity to comment on the views that may be submitted by Oman and Qatar as third parties. The Panel therefore does not consider that accepting the requests by Oman and Qatar would affect the due process rights of the parties or third parties in these proceedings.

On the basis of the above considerations, the Panel accepts Oman's and Qatar's requests for third-party participation. This acceptance is subject to maintaining the timetable adopted by the Panel for the participation of third parties. The Panel is cognizant that, as Brazil points out, no request for third-party participation has ever been made as late as in these proceedings. Accepting these requests recognizes the limited experience of the requesting Members but should not be taken as encouragement to other Members to disregard the long-standing norm of indicating third-party interest at the DSB meeting where the panel is established or within 10 days thereafter.

7.1.2 Preliminary ruling request by Indonesia

84.   As described in section 1.3.2 above, Indonesia presented along with its first written submission, a request for a preliminary ruling concerning certain alleged defects in the panel request as well as alleged inconsistencies between the scope of the panel request and Brazil's first written submission. The Panel, on 19 July 2016, communicated its conclusions. This section describes Indonesia's request as well as the Panel's ruling.

7.1.2.1 Indonesia's request

85.   Indonesia requested the Panel to find that:

a.   The alleged general prohibition/overarching measure is not properly within the terms of reference of the Panel;

b.   Brazil's challenge to the import licensing regime "as a whole" is not properly within the terms of reference of the Panel;

c.   Brazil's claims with regard to other prepared or preserved chicken meat were not identified in the panel request and therefore are not within the terms of reference of the Panel; and

d.   Brazil is precluded from raising claims under Article 1 of the Agreement on Import Licensing Procedures.[47]

86.   In its comments, Brazil requested the Panel to disregard the requests presented by Indonesia.[48]

---

[47]   Indonesia's request for a preliminary ruling, para. 6.1.

7.1.2.2   The Panel's conclusions and reasoning

87.   In its communication of 19 July 2016, the Panel informed the parties of its conclusions with respect to Indonesia's request for a preliminary ruling, namely that it:

> 1. Finds that the alleged general prohibition/overarching measure is properly within the terms of reference of the Panel, and in particular, that (a) Brazil's panel request provides a brief summary of the complaint sufficient to present the problem clearly, (b) the measure described in Brazil's first written submission is not altered to the point of falling outside the terms of reference of the Panel, and (c) the alleged general prohibition is properly identified in Brazil's panel request.

> 2. Finds that the panel request does not contain a challenge to the import licensing regime "as a whole", and such measure is therefore not within the terms of reference of the Panel.

> 3. Finds that Brazil's claims with regard to other prepared or preserved chicken meat are identified in Brazil's panel request and are therefore within the terms of reference of the Panel.

> 4. Takes note of Brazil's statement that it is not making any claims under Article 1 of the Agreement on Import Licensing Procedures and therefore sees no need to rule that Brazil is precluded from making such claims.[49]

88.   The Panel indicated in its communication that its reasoning in reaching these conclusions would be elaborated in this report. Accordingly, we now turn to set out those reasons. We will first refer to the legal standard governing a panel's terms of reference and then provide the reasoning for each of the conclusions.

7.1.2.2.1   Legal standard applicable to a panel's terms of reference

89.   As noted by the Appellate Body, pursuant to Article 7.1 of the DSU, a panel's terms of reference are governed by the panel request, unless the parties agree otherwise.[50] The panel request, thus, delimits the scope of a panel's jurisdiction.[51]

90.   Article 6.2 of the DSU, which governs the panel request, states:

---

[48]   Brazil's response to Indonesia's request for a preliminary ruling, para. 52.

[49]   (footnote original) Brazil's response to Indonesia's request for a preliminary ruling, para. 51, confirmed also at the first substantive meeting of the parties.

[50]   See e.g. Appellate Body Reports, *US – Carbon Steel*, para. 124; and *Argentina – Import Measures*, para. 5.11.

[51]   See e.g. Appellate Body Reports, *China – HP-SSST (Japan) / China – HP-SSST (EU)*, para. 5.12.

> The request for the establishment of a panel shall be made in writing. It shall indicate whether consultations were held, identify the specific measures at issue and provide a brief summary of the legal basis of the complaint sufficient to present the problem clearly.

91.   Article 6.2 contains two distinct requirements, namely (1) the identification of the specific measures at issue; and (2) the provision of a brief summary of the legal basis of the complaint (or the claims) sufficient to present the problem clearly. Together these two elements comprise the "matter referred to the DSB", and form the basis of the panel's terms of reference under Article 7.1 of the DSU.[52] Therefore, a measure that has not been properly identified in the panel request is outside a panel's terms of reference. Similarly, a panel has no jurisdiction over claims that have not been briefly summarized in a manner sufficient to present the problem clearly.

92.   As the Appellate Body found, by establishing and defining the jurisdiction of the panel, the panel request fulfils the due process objective of providing the respondent and third parties notice regarding the nature of the complainant's case so as to enable them to respond accordingly.[53]

93.   Furthermore, the Appellate Body summarized the manner in which a panel must determine whether a panel request fulfils the requirements of Article 6.2:

> A panel request's compliance with the requirements of Article 6.2 of the DSU must be demonstrated on its face as it existed at the time of its filing. Consequently, any defects in the panel request cannot be "cured" by the subsequent submissions of the parties.[54] Nevertheless, subsequent submissions, such as the complaining party's first written submission, may be consulted to the extent that they may confirm or clarify the meaning of the words used in the panel request.[55,56]

94.   The parties generally agree on this legal standard. However, Brazil adds a further element. Based on the Appellate Body report in *Korea – Dairy*, Brazil

---

[52]   See e.g. Appellate Body Reports, *Guatemala – Cement I*, paras. 72 and 73; *US – Carbon Steel*, para. 125; *US – Continued Zeroing*, para. 160; *US – Zeroing (Japan) (Article 21.5 – Japan)*, para. 107; and *Australia – Apples*, para. 416.

[53]   See e.g. Appellate Body Report, *US – Countervailing and Anti-Dumping Measures (China)*, para. 4.7 (citing Appellate Body Reports, *Brazil – Desiccated Coconut*, p. 22, DSR 1997:I, p. 186; *Chile – Price Band System*, para. 164; and *US – Continued Zeroing*, para. 161).

[54]   (footnote original) Appellate Body Report, *US – Countervailing and Anti-Dumping Measures (China)*, para. 4.9.

[55]   (footnote original) Appellate Body Reports, *US – Carbon Steel*, para. 127; *US – Countervailing and Anti-Dumping Measures (China)*, para. 4.9.

[56]   Appellate Body Reports, *Argentina – Import Measures*, para. 5.42. See also Appellate Body Reports, *China - HP-SSST (Japan)/ China - HP-SSST(EU)*, para. 5.13; and *China – Raw Materials*, para. 233.

argues that a party that alleges an impairment of its right of defence must provide evidence to support such impairment.[57] Brazil submits in this regard, that Indonesia has failed to present any evidence relating to the prejudice that it alleges to have suffered.[58]

95.   We note that Appellate Body statements in recent cases contradict Brazil's argument. In *EC and certain member States – Large Civil Aircraft*, the Appellate Body emphasized that "this due process objective is not constitutive of, but rather follows from, the proper establishment of a panel's jurisdiction".[59] In *US – Countervailing and Anti-Dumping Measures (China)*, the Appellate Body, referring back to this statement, explicitly ruled out the need for any demonstration that a respondent's ability to defend itself was effectively impaired:

> [A] determination of whether due process has been respected does not necessitate a separate examination of whether the parties suffered prejudice, considering that "[t]his due process objective is not constitutive of, but rather follows from, the proper establishment of a panel's jurisdiction."[60],[61] (emphasis added)

96.   On the basis of the foregoing, we do not agree with Brazil that in our assessment of whether Brazil's panel request satisfies the requirements of Article 6.2, we should examine whether Indonesia suffered prejudice in its ability to defend itself.

7.1.2.2.2   Whether the alleged general prohibition is within the Panel's terms of reference

97.   We turn to examine the first issue identified by Indonesia in its request for a preliminary ruling. Indonesia develops three lines of arguments to submit that the alleged general prohibition is not within the Panel's terms of reference. The first argument refers to Brazil's panel request not providing a brief summary of the legal basis sufficient to present the problem clearly. The second argument pertains to a discrepancy between the measure described in Brazil's panel request and in Brazil's first written submission. The third argument pertains to the panel request not referring to the objective linking together the seven measures that constitute the general prohibition, thus affecting its proper identification. We turn to discuss each of these arguments.

---

[57]   Brazil's response to Indonesia's request for a preliminary ruling, para. 10 (quoting Appellate Body Report, *Korea – Dairy*, para. 131).
[58]   Brazil's response to Indonesia's request for a preliminary ruling, para. 11.
[59]   Appellate Body Report, *EC and certain member States – Large Civil Aircraft*, para. 640.
[60]   (footnote original) Appellate Body Report, *EC and certain member States – Large Civil Aircraft*, para. 640.
[61]   Appellate Body Report, *US – Countervailing and Anti-Dumping Measures (China)*, para. 4.7. See also Appellate Body Reports, *China – Raw Materials*, para. 233.

7.1.2.2.2.1   Whether the panel request contains a brief summary of the legal basis of the complaint sufficient to present the problem clearly

98.   Indonesia's first argument, concerns the description of the claims in respect of the alleged general prohibition, as set out in Brazil's panel request. Indonesia takes issue with the fact that Brazil refers to seven separate measures, contained in at least six legal instruments, allegedly breaching 15 WTO legal provisions. Indonesia considers that in doing so, Brazil does no more than repeat the text of these legal provisions without connecting them to the specific measures and the specific legal instruments at issue.[62] Brazil considers that the general prohibition is described as independent from its components[63], and that the panel request lists the WTO provisions with which the general prohibition is considered to be inconsistent.[64]

99.   We note that the summary of the legal basis of the complaint aims to explain succinctly how or why the challenged measure is considered to be violating the WTO obligations in question.[65] The Appellate Body found that:

> [I]n order to "present the problem clearly", a panel request must "plainly connect" the challenged measure(s) with the provision(s) claimed to have been infringed such that a respondent can "know what case it has to answer, and ... begin preparing its defence".[66,67]

100.   We will examine Brazil's panel request following the Appellate Body's guidance, to determine whether it provides a brief summary of the legal basis of the complaint sufficient to present the problem clearly.

101.   Brazil's panel request starts with an introduction indicating the procedural history of the dispute and summarizing the measures at issue.[68] Under heading I, it then describes the general prohibition, including its seven constitutive elements, and lists the underlying legal instruments, and the articles of the covered agreements that the general prohibition is allegedly inconsistent with.[69] Under heading II, there are different sections, which describe the specific restrictions and prohibitions on the importation of chicken meat and chicken products, and list their underlying legal instruments as well as the articles of the covered agreements that each measure is allegedly inconsistent with.[70]

102.   We understand Indonesia's main concern to be the lack of sufficient clarity on which aspects of the general prohibition are inconsistent with which

---

[62]   Indonesia's request for a preliminary ruling, paras. 1.14-1.16.
[63]   Brazil's response to Indonesia's request for a preliminary ruling, para. 16.
[64]   Brazil's response to Indonesia's request for a preliminary ruling, para. 22.
[65]   Appellate Body Report, *US – Countervailing Measures (China)*, para. 4.9.
[66]   (footnote original) Appellate Body Report, *US – Oil Country Tubular Goods Sunset Reviews*, para. 162 (quoting Appellate Body Report, *Thailand – H-Beams*, para. 88).
[67]   Appellate Body Report, *US – Countervailing and Anti-Dumping Measures (China)*, para. 4.8.
[68]   Brazil's panel request, p. 1.
[69]   Brazil's panel request, pp. 1-3.
[70]   Brazil's panel request, pp. 3-9.

articles of the covered agreements listed by Brazil, including a brief indication of how and why.[71] We agree with Indonesia that Brazil's panel request could have been structured in a clearer manner. However, in our view it does not fall short of the requirement to provide a brief summary of the legal basis of the complaint sufficient to present the problem clearly for the following reasons.

103. First, in the introductory paragraph of the section addressing the alleged general prohibition, Brazil's panel request describes this measure as follows: "Indonesia imposes several prohibitions or restrictions on the importation of chicken meat and chicken products which, combined, have the effect of a general prohibition on the importations of these products". We consider this language to clearly indicate that the challenge is against one measure, not seven separate ones.

104. Second, we note that the last part of the section of Brazil's panel request concerning the alleged general prohibition begins with the following introductory clause: "Brazil considers that the *general import prohibition described above* is inconsistent with Indonesia's obligations under the following provisions" (emphasis added).[72] Brazil then lists several articles of the covered agreements and briefly explains why "these measures", generally referring to the alleged general prohibition, are inconsistent with each of the respective articles. In our view, the degree of detail provided in this section meets the minimum required under Article 6.2, because it includes a list of the articles of the covered agreements that the measure is considered to be inconsistent with, and briefly indicates why the challenged measure is inconsistent with them.[73]

105. Third, in our view, the second part of Brazil's panel request, describing the specific restrictions and prohibitions also challenged by Brazil, serves as context in understanding what the problem is. Four of the constitutive elements of the general prohibition are also challenged as individual restrictions.[74] In the sections that relate to each of those elements, the panel request provides an explanation of why each measure is inconsistent with certain provisions of the covered agreements. Thus, this further clarifies how certain elements of the general prohibition relate to each of the 15 WTO provisions allegedly breached by this measure.[75]

106. Fourth, Indonesia argues that the situation that we are confronted with is similar to that examined by the Appellate Body in *China – Raw Materials*.[76] In that case, the Appellate Body found that the complainants' panel requests did not present the problem clearly. This is, because the relevant section of the complainants' panel requests (section III) referred generically to "Additional

---

[71] Indonesia's request for a preliminary ruling, para. 1.28.
[72] Brazil's panel request, p. 3.
[73] Brazil's panel request, p. 3. See Appellate Body Report, *US – Countervailing and Anti-Dumping Measures (China)*, para. 4.8.
[74] See para. 2.5 above.
[75] In this respect, see also Indonesia's request for a preliminary ruling, para. 1.26.
[76] Indonesia's request for a preliminary ruling, paras. 1.18-1.19.

Restraints Imposed on Exportation" and raised multiple problems relative to different obligations arising under several provisions of the GATT 1994, China's Accession Protocol, and China's Working Party Report. The Appellate Body observed that neither "the titles of the measures nor the narrative paragraphs reveal the different groups of measures that are alleged to act collectively to cause each of the various violations, or whether certain of the measures is considered to act alone in causing a violation of one or more of the obligations".[77] In our view, the fact pattern in the present case differs from that addressed by the Appellate Body in *China – Raw Materials*. Brazil's panel request does not refer to several measures independently and then list a number of WTO provisions without briefly explaining why it considers that the challenged measure is inconsistent with them. Rather, Brazil's panel request describes only one measure and briefly indicates why this measure is inconsistent with each of the relevant WTO provisions.

107.   Fifth, in our view, the amount of detail that Indonesia considers necessary would require Brazil to develop arguments in addition to setting out the claims. Indeed, Indonesia seems to expect Brazil's panel request to describe the precise and specific manner in which each of the constitutive elements of the general prohibition, not the measure itself, are inconsistent with the relevant articles of the covered agreements. The Appellate Body has been clear in acknowledging that Article 6.2 requires that the *claims* – not the *arguments* – be set out in a panel request in a way that is sufficient to present the problem clearly.[78] In our view, accepting Indonesia's arguments would require us to blur this distinction.

108.   On the basis of the foregoing, we consider that Brazil's panel request satisfies the minimum standard set out in Article 6.2. This is, the panel request lists the specific articles of the covered agreements that it claims are breached by the general prohibition, and it plainly connects, albeit in a general manner, the aspects of the general prohibition that it considers to be inconsistent with the relevant article of the covered agreements.

7.1.2.2.2.2   Whether the measure has been properly identified

109.   As indicated above, Indonesia makes the following two arguments in connection with the proper identification of the general prohibition. First, Indonesia takes issue with the fact that the panel request lists *seven* elements of the alleged general prohibition, whereas the first written submission lists only *six*.[79] Second, Indonesia argues that to properly identify the alleged general prohibition, Brazil should have included in its panel request a description of the policy objective pursued by such measure.[80] Brazil considers that Article 6.2

---

[77] Appellate Body Reports, *China – Raw Materials*, para. 230.
[78] Appellate Body Report, *EC – Selected Customs Matters*, para. 153.
[79] Indonesia's request for a preliminary ruling, paras. 1.29-1.30.
[80] Indonesia's request for a preliminary ruling, paras. 1.37-1.38; and opening statement at the first meeting of the Panel, paras. 15-18.

does not require a panel request to describe the policy objective of an unwritten measure.[81] Brazil also argues that not referring in its first written submission to one of the components of the general prohibition mentioned in the panel request does not alter the nature of this measure, and that it is its prerogative to better formulate and develop its claims, respecting the panel's terms of reference.[82]

110.   We note that both of these arguments relate to the proper identification of the measure, albeit in differing ways. An assessment of whether a panel request has sufficiently identified a specific measure has to be done on a case-by-case basis.[83] The Appellate Body has observed that a panel should undertake this assessment: (a) on an objective basis, and (b) considering the particular context in which the measures exist and operate.[84] The Appellate Body has also noted that "the measures at issue must be identified with sufficient precision so that what is referred to adjudication by a panel may be discerned from the panel request".[85]

111.   In the specific context of identifying an unwritten measure, the Appellate Body has made a clear distinction between the standard required for the proper *identification* of an unwritten measure and the demonstration of its *existence*.[86] While the former is a matter of Article 6.2 of the DSU – at issue here – the latter is a substantive question to be addressed with the merits of the case. The Appellate Body stated in particular, that, "the identification of a measure within the meaning of Article 6.2 need be framed *only with sufficient particularity so as to indicate the nature of the measure and the gist of what is at issue*".[87] Consequently, we understand that there is no requirement for perfect identity between what is described in the panel request and what is described in the submission, as long as the "nature and gist of the measure" remains the same.

112.   Turning to the first argument, Indonesia essentially argues that the measure described in the first written submission is not the one identified in the Panel request and is, therefore outside the Panel's terms of reference.[88]

113.   As we understand it, the "nature and gist of the measure" as described in the panel request is that it is an unwritten measure that consists of a number of individual measures, which allegedly operate together in such a way as to result in a general prohibition. Thus, the unwritten measure constitutes the framework for a number of different measures.

114.   At this general level of identifying the "nature and gist" of the measure, we consider that the alleged general prohibition is not significantly altered just because there is one less constitutive element in its description. It is still a

---

[81]   Brazil's response to Indonesia's request for a preliminary ruling, paras. 42-44.
[82]   Brazil's response to Indonesia's request for a preliminary ruling, paras. 36 and 39.
[83]   Appellate Body Report, *US – Countervailing and Anti-Dumping Measures (China)*, para. 4.9.
[84]   *Ibid.*
[85]   Appellate Body Report, *US – Continued Zeroing*, para. 168.
[86]   Appellate Body Report, *US – Continued Zeroing*, para. 169.
[87]   Appellate Body Report, *US – Continued Zeroing*, para. 169 (emphasis added).
[88]   Indonesia's request for a preliminary ruling, paras. 1.29-1.30.

measure that allegedly constitutes the framework for a number of different measures. Whether the six elements make up the unwritten measure or whether other allegedly equally trade-restrictive measures – possibly including the seventh measure described in the panel request – are or are not part of that unwritten measure, is a question of demonstrating the existence of the alleged general prohibition, but not of its proper identification. For the purposes of the latter, the Panel considers that the measure as described in Brazil's first written submission is within the Panel's terms of reference.

115. Turning to the second argument, we understand Indonesia to allege a deficiency in Brazil's panel request, insofar as it does not describe the objective of the alleged unwritten measure. As seen above, in our view, Brazil's panel request is clear in providing the elements necessary to discern the measure.[89]

116. In our assessment, whether there is an objective that links the different elements of the general prohibition together is a question of demonstrating the existence of the measure.[90] Thus, contrary to what Indonesia argues[91], we do not consider that to properly identify the alleged general prohibition, Brazil necessarily had to include a description of the objective of the measure in the panel request. We will address this issue when we assess, on the merits, whether Brazil has established a *prima facie* case that the general prohibition is a measure attributable to Indonesia, and that it is contrary to a number of WTO provisions. We therefore conclude that Brazil was under no obligation to describe the objective of the alleged general prohibition in its panel request to satisfy the requirements of Article 6.2 of the DSU.[92]

117. On the basis of the foregoing, the Panel finds that the alleged general prohibition/overarching measure is properly within the terms of reference of the Panel, and in particular, that (a) Brazil's panel request provides a brief summary of the complaint sufficient to present the problem clearly, (b) the measure described in Brazil's first written submission is not altered to the point of falling outside the terms of reference of the Panel, and (c) the alleged general prohibition is properly identified in Brazil's panel request.

---

[89] We note that Indonesia referred to the explicit inclusion of the policy objective in the European Union's panel request in *Argentina – Import Measures*, as indication of the deficiencies in Brazil's panel request (Indonesia's opening statement at the first meeting of the Panel, paras. 17-18). The fact that the European Union included such description in its panel request does not mean that Article 6.2 requires the policy objective of an unwritten measure to be included in a panel request.

[90] See the European Union's third-party submission, para. 58. See also section 7.10.4.2.4 below.

[91] Indonesia's request for a preliminary ruling, paras. 1.37-1.40.

[92] In this respect, see also United States' third-party submission, paras. 97-98.

7.1.2.2.3 Whether Brazil's panel request properly identified Indonesia's import licensing regime "as a whole"

118.   Indonesia argues that Brazil's challenge to Indonesia's import licensing regime as a whole is not within the Panel's terms of reference.[93] In particular, Indonesia submits that Brazil's panel request, when addressing Indonesia's import licensing regime refers to a limited number of aspects of Indonesia's import licensing regime[94], and that it is only in its first written submission that Brazil challenges Indonesia's import licensing regime as a whole.[95] Brazil rejects Indonesia's arguments, and submits that it has properly identified in its panel request the challenged measure as Indonesia's import licensing regime, as a whole. Brazil submits that when read as a whole, and on the basis of the language used, it is clear that Brazil's panel request was not referring to specific provisions of Indonesia's licensing procedures, but to the import licensing regime as a whole.[96]

119.   As indicated above, a measure at issue must be identified with sufficient precision so that what is referred to adjudication by a panel may be discerned from the panel request.[97] Previous panels confronted with claims against a regime as a whole, found that such a measure was at issue because the relevant panel request clearly indicated that to be the case.[98] We thus consider that for a panel request to properly challenge a regime as a whole, it should clearly indicate that the whole regime is a measure at issue.

120.   We do not find such a clear indication in Brazil's panel request. In section II.v of its panel request, Brazil addresses "Restrictions on the importation of chicken meat and chicken products through Indonesia's Licensing Regime". In that section, Brazil, in describing Indonesia's licensing regime, neither uses the expression "as a whole" nor describes issues in a way that suggests that the regime as a whole is the cause of nullification and impairment. Instead, Brazil refers to specific aspects of Indonesia's licensing regime and describes those as trade-restrictive.[99] In addition, Brazil challenges a number of import licensing conditions as individual measures elsewhere in the panel request. A plain reading of the panel request, therefore, suggests that Indonesia's import licensing

---

[93]   Indonesia's request for a preliminary ruling, para. 5.6.
[94]   Indonesia's opening statement at the first meeting of the Panel, para. 21.
[95]   Indonesia's request for a preliminary ruling, para. 5.2.
[96]   Brazil's response to Indonesia's request for a preliminary ruling, paras. 47-48.
[97]   Appellate Body Report, *US – Continued Zeroing*, para. 168.
[98]   See Appellate Body Report, *EC – Selected Customs Matters*, paras. 165-172 (finding that the United States' panel request presented with sufficient clarity, as required by Article 6.2 of the DSU, that the claim made under Article X:3(a) concerned the European Communities' system of customs administration as a whole or overall); and Panel Report, *Indonesia – Import Licensing Regimes*, paras. 2.49 (regarding Indonesia's import licensing regime for horticultural products) and 2.64 (regarding Indonesia's import licensing regime for animals and animal products).
[99]   Brazil's panel request, pp. 7-8.

regime as a whole is not a measure that Brazil challenges, but rather, that it challenges specific aspects of the import licensing regime.

121.   We see the above reading confirmed in Brazil's own submissions. In its submissions, Brazil listed a limited number of specific aspects of Indonesia's import licensing regime that it is challenging.[100]

122.   On this basis, we find that Brazil's panel request does not contain a challenge to the import licensing regime "as a whole", and that this measure is therefore not within the Panel's terms of reference.

> 7.1.2.2.4   Whether Brazil's claims with regard to the import prohibition on other prepared or preserved chicken meat are within the Panel's terms of reference

123.   The panel request describes a specific import prohibition on certain chicken products in a number of places. Indonesia argues that the Panel should decline to rule on that import prohibition to the extent it covers other prepared or preserved chicken meat.[101] Indonesia submits that in its panel request, Brazil only challenged the prohibition on the importation of fresh, chilled or frozen poultry cuts and offal (HS subheadings 020713 and 020714), but did not challenge the prohibition on the importation of prepared or preserved chicken meat (HS heading 1602).[102] According to Indonesia, Brazil's identification of the challenged measure as the prohibition on the importation of chicken cuts prevents Brazil from including additional products under the scope of that measure.[103] Brazil argues that it has identified in its panel request the products at issue, including prepared or preserved chicken meat (HS subheading 1602.32). Brazil considers this category of products is therefore within the Panel's terms of reference.[104]

124.   In our view, Indonesia's arguments go to the manner in which Brazil's panel request identified the measure at issue, and how such identification affects the product coverage of the measure at issue. Article 6.2 of the DSU does not refer to the identification of the products at issue; rather, it refers to the identification of the measures at issue. A number of cases have addressed the question of whether it is necessary to identify the products at issue in the panel request. Previous panels and the Appellate Body have concluded that with respect to certain WTO obligations (e.g. related to tariff classification), the identification of the products to which the specific measures at issue apply may

---

[100]   Brazil's first written submission, paras. 200 and 228; Brazil's response to Panel question No. 15; and Brazil's second written submission, para. 104.
[101]   Indonesia's request for a preliminary ruling, para. 1.48.
[102]   Indonesia's request for a preliminary ruling, para. 1.43.
[103]   Indonesia's request for a preliminary ruling, paras. 1.46-1.47.
[104]   Brazil's response to Indonesia's request for a preliminary ruling, paras. 49-50.

be necessary to identify the products subject to the measure in dispute.[105] Moreover, the Appellate Body has noted that in certain circumstances, the scope of the products identified in a panel request may limit the scope of a panel's terms of reference.[106]

125.   In the introductory paragraph of the panel request, Brazil refers to the products at issue as "meat from fowls of the species *Gallus domesticus* and products from fowls of the species *Gallus domesticus* hereinafter referred to as chicken meat and chicken products".[107] A footnote to the above quoted sentence in the panel request, provides that the products concerned in the present dispute are referred to by the following HS codes "(i) 0207.11 (whole chicken, not cut into parts, fresh or chilled); (ii) 0207.12 (whole chicken, not cut into parts, frozen); (iii) 0207.13 (chicken cuts and offal, fresh or chilled); (iv) 0207.14 (chicken cuts and offal, frozen) and; (v) 1602.32 (chicken meat, other leftover meat and blood that has been processed or preserved)".[108] Thus, as Brazil rightly points out, its panel request includes a general reference to the products at issue, which includes an explicit reference to prepared or preserved chicken meat.

126.   Brazil's panel request then provides three different descriptions of the specific prohibition on the importation of certain products. First, when referring to the elements of the alleged general prohibition:

> Indonesia does not allow the importation of animal and animal products not listed in the appendices of the relevant regulations[109]. With regard to chicken, the list only contemplates HS codes referred to as whole chicken, fresh or chilled and frozen[110]. The HS codes for chicken meat cut into pieces[111] are not described in any of the "positive lists" which contain the products that can be imported into Indonesia's territory;[112,113]

---

[105]   Appellate Body Report, *EC – Computer Equipment*, para. 67. See also Appellate Body Report, *EC – Chicken Cuts*, para. 167. The following panels have addressed the issue of whether it is necessary to identify the products at issue in the panel request: Panel Reports: *Korea – Alcoholic Beverages*, paras. 10.14-10.16; *US – FSC*, paras. 7.23 and 7.29; *EC – IT Products*, paras. 7.194-7.197; and *US – Clove Cigarettes*, paras. 7.137-7.142. See also para. 2.17 of Annex A to the Panel Report, *Russia – Tariff Treatment*.

[106]   Appellate Body Report, *Australia – Salmon*, paras. 102-103 (where the Appellate Body concluded that the products at issue in that dispute were limited to "fresh, chilled or frozen salmon").

[107]   Brazil's panel request, p. 1.

[108]   Brazil's panel request, p. 1. We note that Brazil refers to heading HS 1602 in its panel request. In the World Customs Organization Harmonized System, this particular heading refers to "Other prepared or preserved meat, meat offal or blood". We thus understand Brazil, where it refers to "processed or preserved" meat, to mean "prepared or preserved" meat. We thus use the words "processed" and "prepared" interchangeably in this report.

[109]   (footnote original) The products allowed to be imported by Indonesia are currently listed in the Appendix I and II of MoA Regulation 139/2014 and the Appendix II of MoT Regulation 46/2013.

[110]   (footnote original) HS Codes 020711 and 020712.

[111]   (footnote original) HS Codes 020713 and 020714.

[112]   (footnote original) Furthermore, the HS code for processed chicken products is not described in the "positive list" of MoA Regulation 139/2014.

127. The second description of the measure features in sections II.i (measures that do not conform to nor are based on international standards) and II.ii (measures that are more trade restrictive than required to achieve its appropriate level of protection). In both these sections the specific import prohibition on certain chicken products is described as:

> Prohibition on the importation of chicken cuts, as the relevant regulations only allow the whole chicken, fresh or chilled and frozen.[114] The HS codes for chicken meat cut into pieces[115] are not described in any of the "positive lists" which contain the products that can be imported into Indonesia's territory;[116]

128. The third description of the measure features in Section II.iv (measures that discriminate against imported chicken meat and chicken products):

> Indonesia prohibits the importation of chicken meat cut into pieces[117] while domestically produced chicken cuts are largely traded in its domestic market;[118]

129. We recall that a panel must examine a panel request as a whole and on the basis of the context in which the measure at issue exists and operates. A panel may seek confirmation or clarification of the meaning of the panel request in subsequent submissions.[119]

130. The first description above is focused on the existence of a "positive list", while the second and third descriptions are focused on the absence of chicken cuts from that list. Furthermore, the first description contains a reference to prepared or preserved chicken in a footnote, while the second and third do not. Notwithstanding these apparent differences, by reading Brazil's panel request as a whole, it is clear to us that all of the above-enumerated descriptions focus on the same measure. That measure is the requirement for certain products to be listed in the relevant appendices of Indonesia's regulations governing the importation of animal products, for their importation to be permitted. We consider that our conclusion is further reinforced by the manner in which Brazil formulated its arguments in respect of its claims against this measure as well by Brazil's answers during the first substantive meeting to the Panel's question on

---

[113] Brazil's panel request, p. 2.
[114] (footnote original) HS Codes 020711 and 020712.
[115] (footnote original) HS Codes 020713 and 020714.
[116] Brazil's panel request, pp. 4-5.
[117] (footnote original) According to the "positive lists" established by the Appendices of MoA Regulation 139/2014 and MoT Regulation 46/2013.
[118] Brazil's panel request, p. 6.
[119] Appellate Body Reports, *China - HP-SSST (Japan)/ China - HP-SSST(EU)*, para. 5.13; and *Argentina – Import Measures*, paras. 5.40. and 5.42.

what is the measure at issue.[120] Finally, we do not see Indonesia contest that there is only one measure despite the various, differing descriptions.[121]

131.   Thus, the product coverage within the Panel's terms of reference must be construed on the basis of that one challenged measure, in reading the panel request as a whole. As seen above, while not in every description, Brazil's panel request does contain one description that refers to chicken cuts and prepared or preserved chicken meat as being excluded from the list. The panel request indicates this to be the case in at least one relevant regulation. In addition, the panel request generally defines the product scope as including that product. Read as a whole, therefore, we consider that Brazil's claims with respect to the positive list requirement do not exclude prepared or preserved chicken meat from the Panel's terms of reference.

132.   Furthermore, the Appellate Body in *EC – Selected Customs Matters* found that the arguments included in a panel request "should not be interpreted to narrow the scope of the measures or the claims".[122] In our view, this logic also applies to situations where the description of the measure varies slightly throughout different sections of a panel request. Accordingly, we consider that the references to chicken cuts in the second part of Brazil's panel request should not be read in such a manner as to narrow down the scope of the positive list.

133.   Based on the foregoing, we find that Brazil's claims with regard to other prepared or preserved chicken meat are identified in Brazil's panel request and are therefore within the terms of reference of the Panel.

> 7.1.2.2.5   Whether claims raised by Brazil under Article 1 of the Import Licensing Agreement are within the Panel's terms of reference

134.   Indonesia submits that if Brazil were raising a separate claim under Article 1 of the Import Licensing Agreement, it would be outside the Panel's terms of reference.[123] Brazil observes that "it did not make any claim under Article 1" of the Import Licensing Agreement. Brazil clarifies that its references to Article 1 in its first written submission are for the purposes of contextualization.[124]

---

[120]   Brazil's first written submission, paras. 77-79. In this panel report, in line with what the parties have done we refer to this measure as the "positive list requirement"; see also section 7.4 below.

[121]   See Indonesia's request for a preliminary ruling, paras. 1.43-1.44 and 1.48; and opening statement at the first meeting of the Panel, paras. 19-20.

[122]   Appellate Body Report, *EC – Selected Customs Matters*, para. 153.

[123]   Indonesia's request for a preliminary ruling, paras. 1.49-1.52.

[124]   Brazil's response to Indonesia's request for a preliminary ruling, para. 51, confirmed also at the first meeting of the Panel.

135.   The Panel takes note of Brazil's statement that it is not making any claims under Article 1 of the Import Licensing Agreement and therefore does not see a need to rule on this issue.

136.   This concludes our section on preliminary matters. We now turn to our review of Brazil's claims.

7.2   Panel's Order of Analysis

7.2.1   General

137.   We recall that as a general principle panels are free to structure their order of analysis in the way they consider most appropriate as long as the structure of the analysis adopted accords with their mandate and functions under the DSU.[125] In deciding on how to proceed to examine the matter referred to us, we need to decide on the sequence of our analysis as it relates to three elements of the case: (a) the order of analysis between claims brought against a general prohibition and claims against individual measures some of which are part of the general prohibition; (b) the order of analysis for a plurality of claims when they all refer to the same aspect of a measure; and (c) the sequence for the analysis of measures in force at the time of establishment of the panel and as subsequently amended to the extent that they are covered by the Panel's terms of reference.

7.2.2   Order of analysis in respect of claims against the general prohibition and against individual measures

138.   Concerning the sequence of analysis in respect of the claims against the alleged general prohibition as a single unwritten measure and claims against individual measures, we note that Brazil as a complainant presented its submissions addressing first the alleged general prohibition.[126] Brazil has not indicated any particular reason for the manner in which it has structured its claims. Considering however that Brazil has characterized the general prohibition as a "single unwritten measure" composed of a number of individual measures, we will proceed first with a review of the claims against each of the individual measures before addressing the general prohibition. This sequence allows us to have an understanding of the content and operation of each of the measures individually, which is useful when assessing how the individual measures may interact to form a single unwritten measure as claimed by Brazil.

---

[125]   See e.g. Appellate Body Report, *Colombia – Textiles*, para. 5.20.
[126]   Brazil's first written submission, paras. 73-76.

7.2.3   Order of analysis of claims

7.2.3.1   Introduction

139.   Brazil has raised claims under Article XI:1 of the GATT 1994 and Article 4.2 of the Agreement on Agriculture, Article III:4 of the GATT 1994, and Article 3.2 of the Import Licensing Agreement. Indonesia submits that for all the measures for which Brazil made claims of a breach of Article 4.2 of the Agreement on Agriculture and Article XI of the GATT 1994, Article 4.2 of the Agreement on Agriculture applies to the exclusion of Article XI:1 of the GATT 1994.[127] In addition, Indonesia submits that Articles III:4 and XI:1 of the GATT 1994 are mutually exclusive and cannot be applied to the same aspect of a measure.[128] Finally, Indonesia considers that some of the measures challenged are not import licencing procedures and thus the Import Licencing Agreement is not applicable.[129] In this section, we address the first of these challenges, i.e. the relation between Article 4.2 of the Agreement on Agriculture and Article XI:1 of the GATT 1994. We limit our analysis in this section to that challenge because it touches upon five of the seven measures. As the remaining two challenges concern only one measure each, we address them in the relevant sections concerning these measures.

7.2.3.2   Whether Article XI of the GATT 1994 and Article 4.2 of the Agreement on Agriculture are mutually exclusive

140.   Indonesia argues that there is a conflict between Article 4.2 of the Agreement on Agriculture and Article XI of the GATT 1994 which pursuant to Article 21.1 of the Agreement on Agriculture, must lead to the exclusion of Article XI of the GATT 1994.[130] The conflict, according to Indonesia, arises from the difference in the allocation of the burden of proof in respect of a defence under Article XX of the GATT 1994 for, on the one hand, a violation of a GATT provision (e.g. of Article XI), and, on the other hand, a measure subject to Article 4.2 of the Agreement on Agriculture. Indonesia submits that under Article 4.2, a complaining party has the burden of demonstrating that the challenged measures are not maintained under Article XX of the GATT 1994. Indonesia contrasts this with the general rule applicable in respect of a defence under Article XX in the context of a claim under Article XI of the GATT 1994, namely that the burden of proof is on the responding party.[131] In Indonesia's view, Article 21.1 of the Agreement on Agriculture, thus, would apply as a conflict rule with the effect that Article 4.2 of the Agreement on Agriculture

---

[127]   Indonesia's first written submission, paras. 65-74.
[128]   Indonesia's first written submission, para. 81.
[129]   Indonesia's first written submission, para. 76.
[130]   Indonesia's first written submission, paras. 65-74.
[131]   Indonesia's first written submission, paras. 67-74; and second written submission, paras. 80-86.

would prevail over, and, therefore, exclude the application of Article XI of the GATT 1994.

141.   In Brazil's view[132], which is shared by the third parties that have commented on this issue[133], there is no conflict between the two provisions.

142.   In deciding whether Article 4.2 of the Agreement on Agriculture applies to the exclusion of Article XI of the GATT 1994 by virtue of Article 21.1 of the Agreement on Agriculture we will be guided by an analysis of the text of each provision and the principle of harmonious treaty interpretation.[134]

143.   Article 21.1 of the Agriculture Agreement states:

> The provisions of GATT 1994 and of other Multilateral Trade Agreements in Annex 1A to the WTO Agreement shall apply subject to the provisions of this Agreement.

144.   We agree with Indonesia that Article 21.1 of the Agreement on Agriculture is a conflict rule similar to that set out in the General Interpretative Note to Annex 1A.[135] Therefore, if there were a conflict between Article 4.2 of the Agreement on Agriculture and Article XI of the GATT 1994, Article 4.2 would indeed prevail and Article XI would not apply.

145.   We note that Indonesia's argument that there is a conflict is premised on what it considers as a difference in the allocation of the burden of proof in Article 4.2 of the Agreement on Agriculture and in Article XX as a defence to a claim under Article XI of the GATT 1994.

146.   We therefore, turn to the question whether the burden of proof in respect of Article XX of the GATT 1994 is reversed in Article 4.2 of the Agreement on Agriculture.

147.   The question of whether the burden of proof in respect of a possible justification under Article XX of the GATT 1994 is reversed under Article 4.2 of the Agreement on Agriculture, goes to the meaning of the footnote to the latter provision, which states:

---

[132]   Brazil's opening statement at the first meeting of the Panel, paras. 32-37; and second written submission, paras. 15-21.

[133]   Argentina's third-party statement, paras. 15-19; Australia's third-party statement, para. 11; Australia's third-party response to Panel question No. 6; European Union's third-party written submission, paras. 22-29; European Union's third-party statement, paras. 10-11; European Union's third-party response to Panel question No. 6; Japan's third-party statement, paras. 3-6; Japan's third-party response to Panel question No. 6; New Zealand's third party submission, paras. 63-71; New Zealand's third-party statement, paras. 8-9; New Zealand's third-party response to Panel question No. 6; Norway's third-party statement, paras. 2-3; Norway's third-party response to Panel question No. 6; United States' third party submission, paras. 11-15; and United States' third-party response to Panel question No. 6.

[134]   See Appellate Body Report, *US – Anti-Dumping and Countervailing Duties (China)*, para. 570 (citing Appellate Body Report, *US – Upland Cotton*, paras. 549-550).

[135]   See Appellate Body Report, *EC – Export Subsidies on Sugar*, para. 221. See also Indonesia's first written submission, para. 67.

These measures include quantitative import restrictions, variable import levies, minimum import prices, discretionary import licensing, non-tariff measures maintained through state-trading enterprises, voluntary export restraints, and similar border measures other than ordinary customs duties, whether or not the measures are maintained under country-specific derogations from the provisions of GATT 1947, *but not* measures maintained under balance-of-payments provisions or under other general, non-agriculture-specific provisions of GATT 1994 or of the other Multilateral Trade Agreements in Annex 1A to the WTO Agreement. (emphasis added)

148.   As is uncontested by the parties, the second part of the footnote ("but…") limits the scope of Article 4.2 of the Agreement on Agriculture.[136] Thus, Article 4.2 does not apply if a measure is listed in the first part of the footnote, and also fulfils the conditions of the second part of the footnote.[137] It is furthermore, uncontested by the parties that Article XX of the GATT 1994 is one of the "other general non-agriculture specific provisions of GATT 1994" referred to in the second part of the footnote.[138] Thus, if a measure is justified by Article XX of the GATT 1994, Article 4.2 of the Agreement on Agriculture will not apply. This view is in accordance with relevant case law as well as supported by the negotiating history of Article 4.2 of the Agreement on Agriculture.[139]

149.   Indonesia's argument that the burden of proof in respect of Article XX is different to that in footnote 1 to Article 4.2 of the Agreement on Agriculture is essentially based on the logic that a complaining party must prove all the elements of its claim under Article 4.2 of the Agreement on Agriculture. Since the question of a justification under Article XX of the GATT 1994 is part of determining the scope of Article 4.2 of the Agreement on Agriculture (through the reference in the second part of the footnote), in Indonesia's view, the complainant accordingly must prove that the measure at issue is not justified under any of the general, non-agriculture-specific provisions of the GATT 1994, including Article XX. According to Indonesia, it is the manner in which footnote

---

[136]   See Indonesia's first written submission, para. 70; and Brazil's opening statement at the first meeting of the Panel, para. 37; and second written submission, para. 21.

[137]   See e.g. Panel Report, *Indonesia - Import Licensing Regimes*, para. 7.33.

[138]   See Indonesia's first written submission, para. 70; and Brazil's second written submission, para. 21.

[139]   Panel Report, *Chile – Price Band System*, para. 7.68. Regarding the negotiating history, starting at the end of 1991, certain delegations proposed that this provision should not apply to measures justified under Articles XII, XVIII, XIX, XX and XXI of GATT 1947. This proposal became the basis for the current language. It indicates that the language was intended to exclude certain measures from the obligation of converting them into ordinary customs duties, rather than modifying the burden of proof with respect to such exceptional measures. See e.g. MTN.TNC/W/89/Add.1, MTN.GNG/AG/W/6, MTN.GNG/AG/W/7, MTN.GNG/AG/W/8, MTN.GNG/AG/W/9, MTN.GNG/MA/W/24, MTN.TNC/W/122. See also Press Release (NUR/080).

1 to Article 4.2 is structured, that alters the allocation of the burden of proving that a measure is justified through a general non-agriculture exception.[140]

150.   In assessing whether the burden of proof is reversed in Article 4.2 of the Agreement on Agriculture, we consider the following.

151.   First, in WTO dispute settlement, the burden of proof in respect of a defence under Article XX of the GATT 1994 is on the responding party.[141]

152.   Second, in the context of the footnote to Article 4.2, Article XX is part of the applicability and scope of Article 4.2, as opposed to providing for exceptions to a potential violation of that provision.[142] In the same context, however, Article XX of the GATT 1994, still provides for exceptions, albeit not to violations of Article 4.2 of the Agreement on Agriculture itself, but of GATT provisions, in respect of which, measures are "maintained under".

153.   Third, there are certain provisions in the covered agreements that carve out specific measures from their scope.[143] An example is Article XI:2 of the GATT 1994, which provides that the prohibition on quantitative restrictions in Article XI:1 does not extend to certain measures listed in Article XI:2; which means that Article XI:2 limits the scope of the obligation contained in Article XI:1.[144] A party invoking Article XI:2 bears the burden of proving that the conditions set out in the provision are met.[145] A further example is the Enabling Clause, which allows developed country Members to grant developing Members special and differential treatment without violating the most-favoured nation (MFN) principle. The Enabling Clause constitutes an exception, which rather than justifying a violation of the MFN principle, leads to its non-application.[146] Consequently, based on the general rule of the allocation of the

---

[140]   Indonesia's first written submission, paras. 69-73.

[141]   See e.g. Appellate Body Reports, *US – Gasoline,* pp. 22-23, DSR 1996:I, 3 at 21; *US – Wool, Shirts and Blouses,* pp. 15-16, DSR 1997:I, 323 at 337; *Korea – Various Measures on Beef,* para. 157; *EC – Tariff Preferences,* para. 104; and *Thailand - Cigarettes (Philippines),* para. 176.

[142]   In fact, contrary to the examples that Indonesia provides from the TRIMs Agreement or the Trade Facilitation Agreement (Indonesia's opening statement at the first meeting of the Panel, para. 32.), Footnote 1 to Article 4.2 does not create a "general rule-exception relationship" for the Agreement on Agriculture.

[143]   In *Canada – Renewable Energy/ Canada – Feed-in-Tariff Program,* when assessing Article III:8(a) of the GATT 1994 (which derogates from the national treatment principle contained in Article III by exempting certain measures from its scope), the Appellate Body surmised "the characterization of the provision as a derogation does not pre-determine the question as to which party bears the burden of proof with regard to the requirements stipulated in the provision." Appellate Body Reports, *Canada – Renewable Energy/ Canada – Feed-in-Tariff Program,* para. 5.56. See also Appellate Body Report, *India – Solar Cells,* para. 5.18 (where the Appellate Body confirms that Article III:8(a) sets out a derogation from the national treatment obligation contained in Article III of the GATT 1994).

[144]   See Appellate Body Reports, *China – Raw Materials,* para. 334.

[145]   See Panel Report, *China – Raw Materials,* paras. 7.209-7.213 (where the panel rejected an argument raised by China indicating that the complainants had the burden to demonstrate that the conditions in Article XI:2(a) did not apply). This view was implicitly endorsed by the Appellate Body. See Appellate Body Reports, *China – Raw Materials,* para. 344.

[146]   Appellate Body Report, *EC – Tariff Preferences,* para. 102.

burden of proof[147], a respondent raising a justification under this provision has the burden of proving it.[148] These examples demonstrate that even where provisions operate explicitly as a "carve out" to another provision rather than as justification of a violation of that provision, the burden of proof may still fall on the responding party as the one benefitting from such "carve out".

154.   Fourth, Indonesia submits that there "are many examples of provisions in the covered agreements that convert exceptions under Article XX of the GATT 1994 into positive obligations, thereby shifting the burden of proof to the complainant".[149] In our view this argument is misplaced. The second part of footnote 1 to Article 4.2 of the Agreement on Agriculture, contrary to the examples provided by Indonesia, does not create "positive obligations" that require a complaining party to prove a violation.

155.   Based on the foregoing, we consider that the underlying premise of Indonesia's argument, that there is a reversal of burden of proof in respect of Article XX in Article 4.2, is incorrect. We therefore, leave open the question of whether the alleged difference in the allocation of burden of proof would have amounted to a conflict within the meaning of Article 21.1. Since Article 21.1 does not apply, Article 4.2 of the Agreement on Agriculture does not exclude the application of Article XI of the GATT 1994.

156.   Having established that the two provisions are not mutually exclusive, we need to decide on the sequence of analysis of the two claims. We note Indonesia's argument that Article 4.2 of the Agreement on Agriculture is *lex specialis* because the goods at issue in this dispute are agricultural goods.[150] We are not convinced that the scope of goods covered by a claim, in and of itself, decides over whether an agreement is more specific than another. As some third parties have pointed out, in terms of nature of substantive obligation violated (i.e. quantitative restriction), Article XI could be considered more specific than Article 4.2.[151] In addition, we note the prominent role that Article XX plays in Indonesia's defence. Consequently, we consider appropriate to first assess Brazil's claims under Article XI:1, and then review Indonesia's defences under

---

[147]   This rule provides that "the burden of proof rests upon the party, whether complaining or defending, who asserts the affirmative of a particular claim or defence." Appellate Body Report, *US – Wool Shirts, and Blouses*, pp. 14, DSR 1997:I, 323 at 335.

[148]   Note that the Appellate Body, because of the special role of the Enabling Clause, took the view that the complaining party had to *identify* the provisions of the Enabling Clause with which the measure is allegedly inconsistent, whereas the respondent has to *establish* the facts necessary to support the consistency of the challenged measure with the relevant provisions of the Enabling Clause. Appellate Body Report, *EC – Tariff Preferences*, paras. 105-115.

[149]   Indonesia's opening statement at the first meeting of the Panel, para. 34 (referring to Article 2.2 of the TBT Agreement, Article 5.6 of the SPS Agreement, and Article 11.6(b) of the Agreement on Trade Facilitation).

[150]   Indonesia's first written submission, para. 66. See also Indonesia's first written submission, para. 178.

[151]   United States' third-party submission, para. 13; New Zealand's third-party submission, para. 66.

Article XX, before turning to Brazil's claims under Article 4.2 of the Agreement on Agriculture.

7.2.4   Order of analysis of amended measures

7.2.4.1   Introduction

157.   In section 2.2 above, we noted that the legal instruments underlying some of the measures at issue were either revoked or revoked and replaced after the establishment of the Panel. The two main legal instruments underlying these measures changed twice over the course of the proceedings.[152] The second set was adopted shortly after the establishment of the Panel and before the first submission was due.[153] The third set was adopted after the end of the period foreseen for answers to questions by the Panel following the first meeting of the Panel with the parties.[154]

158.   Based on the changes enacted through the third set of legal instruments, Indonesia takes the view that three of the challenged measures that existed under the first set of legal instruments have expired.[155] Brazil contests the expiry claimed by Indonesia and presents arguments in support of its claims in respect of relevant provisions in the third set of legal instruments.[156]

159.   In response to a question from the Panel, Brazil explained that it requests the Panel "to make findings on the measures originally identified by Brazil at the time of establishment of the Panel" as well as "to make specific and additional findings on the measures identified in its panel request, in light of the amendments brought to the Indonesian regulatory framework, to the extent that they affect the original measures."[157]

160.   Indonesia, for its part, submits that while the Panel may make findings on expired measures, it cannot make any recommendation in their respect. Furthermore, as regards the review of measures as enacted through the new legal instruments, Indonesia submits that the Panel does not have jurisdiction to review them if they are not in essence the same as the measure set out in the

---

[152]   See Table 1 above in section 2.2. As noted in fn 31, with respect to the MoT Regulations, MoT 46/2013 was replaced by MoT 05/2016, which was subsequently amended by MoT 37/2016. The amended version of MoT 05/2016 was replaced by MoT 59/2016. For ease of reference, the Panel treats the sequence of changes to MoT 05/2016 through MoT 37/2016 and MoT 59/2016 as *one* change.

[153]   MoA 58/2015 of 25 November 2015 entered into force on 7 December 2015; MoT 05/2016 of 28 January 2016 entered into force as of the promulgation date.

[154]   MoA 34/2016 of 15 July 2016 entered into force on 19 July 2016; MoT 59/2016 of 15 August 2016 entered into force on 16 August 2016. As noted in fn 31, MoT 59/2016 consolidated MoT 05/2016 and MoT 37/2016. See also fn 144 above.

[155]   The three measures are as follows: (1) positive list requirement; (2) intended use requirement; (3) the application and validity periods (licensing requirements).

[156]   See e.g. Brazil's response to Panel question No. 66(a).

[157]   Brazil's response to Panel question No.66(a).

panel request.[158] According to Indonesia, where measures have expired, the essence has necessarily changed, with the consequence that relevant provisions in the new legal instruments are outside the Panel's terms of reference.[159] While contesting the Panel's authority to review their WTO consistency, Indonesia does not contest that the Panel may take subsequent legislative changes into account as evidence.[160]

7.2.4.2 Jurisdiction with respect to the measures as enacted through the legal instruments adopted after the panel establishment

161.   We first address the issue of jurisdiction, cognizant that we can only rule on Brazil's claims of WTO inconsistency in respect of measures that are covered by our terms of reference. In addressing this issue, we are mindful of the difference between the measures at issue and the legal instruments embodying those measures.[161]

162.   In deciding whether the measures as incorporated in the second and third set of legal instruments are covered by our terms of reference, we recall that pursuant to Article 7.1 of the DSU, a panel's terms of reference are governed by the panel request, unless the parties agree otherwise.[162] The panel request, thus, delimits the scope of a panel's jurisdiction.[163] In accordance with Article 6.2, the matter referred to a panel by the DSU comprises the specific measure identified in the panel request and the legal basis of the complaint.

163.   We note that, Brazil as complaining party considers that the measures as incorporated in the third set of legal instruments continue to affect its rights under the same covered agreements as the measures included in the panel request. The claims developed in the second submission and during the second meeting with the Panel elaborate on the claims made in the first written submission.[164]

164.   To decide on whether we have jurisdiction on the measures as incorporated in the second and third sets of legal instruments, we will first examine Brazil's panel request, to determine whether its terms are broad enough to cover these legal changes. We then assess the relationship between the legal instruments identified in Brazil's panel request and the subsequent legal instruments. Lastly, we analyse the text contained in the relevant provisions of the subsequent legal instruments and determine how they affect the measures in

---

[158]   Indonesia's response to Panel question Nos. 66a and No. 149.
[159]   Indonesia's response to Panel question No. 149.
[160]   Indonesia's response to Panel question No. 66(a).
[161]   Panel Report, *Argentina – Footwear*, paras. 8.40 and 8.41; see also Appellate Body Report, *US – Upland Cotton*, paras.262 and 270.
[162]   See e.g., Appellate Body Reports, *Argentina – Import Measures*, para. 5.11.
[163]   Appellate Body Reports, *China – HP-SSST (Japan) / China – HP-SSST (EU)*, para. 5.12.
[164]   See e.g. Brazil's second written submission, para. 82; opening statement at the second meeting of the Panel, paras. 15 and 18; and response to Panel question No. 103.

light of Brazil's panel request. In this regard, in line with the Appellate Body's ruling in *Chile – Price Band System*, we consider that we only have jurisdiction over such subsequent changes, if and to the extent that, the measures at issue, as enacted through the relevant legal instruments, remain in essence the same as those identified in the panel request.[165]

165.   Regarding the panel request, we note that Brazil's panel request contains a description of the challenged measures followed by an identification of the legal instruments through which each measure was enacted and an indication that the measure includes also "any amendments, replacements, related measures, or implementing measures". Thus, Brazil's panel request is broad enough to cover such changes.

166.   Regarding the relationship between the different sets of legal instruments, we note that the second set revokes and replaces the first set; the second set is in turn, revoked and replaced by the third.[166] They have identical scope and subject matter and follow the same structure. The three MoA regulations concern "the Importation of Carcass, meat and/or processed product thereof into the territory of the Republic of Indonesia".[167] Likewise, the three MoT regulations concern "export and import provisions on animal and animal products".[168] Thus, the subsequent legal instruments are replacements of the preceding legal instruments.

167.   Regarding the *essence* test, as noted above, it requires an analysis of the text contained in the relevant provisions in each subsequent legal instrument with a view to determining how they affect the measures in light of Brazil's panel request. We will carry out this analysis and make a final determination on jurisdiction on a case-by-case basis, as we proceed with the review of the concerned measures in the relevant sections of this report.

7.2.4.3   Scope and sequence of the Panel's analysis

168.   Having set out our views on the relevant test for jurisdiction, we now turn to the question as to which sets of legal instruments to evaluate and in what sequence. In deciding this question we are mindful of the objectives of achieving prompt settlement of disputes and securing a positive solution to disputes encapsulated in Articles 3.3 and 3.4 of the DSU, as well as the importance of due process. Regarding the latter, we note that both parties have generally

---

[165] Appellate Body Report, *Chile – Price Band System*, paras.135-139. See also Appellate Body Reports, *EC – Chicken Cuts*, paras. 156-161; *EC – Selected Customs Matters*, para. 4.4; *US – Zeroing, Art. 21.5 (EC)*, paras. 190-191 and 383; and *China – Raw Materials*, fn 524 to para. 262.

[166] Each legal instrument contains a provision that upon entry into force, that regulation revokes and declares null and void the previous regulation. See Article 40 of MoA 58/2015; Article 40 of MoA34/2016; Article 37 of MoT 05/2016; and Article 36 of MoT 59/2016.

[167] See title page of MoA 139/2914 (Exhibit BRA-34); MoA 58/2015 (Exhibit BRA-01/IDN-24); and MoA 34/2016 (Exhibit BRA-48/IDN-93).

[168] See title page of MoT 46/2013 (Exhibit BRA-42); MoT 05/2016 (Exhibit BRA-03); and MoT 59/2016 (Exhibit IDN-109).

assured us that they have had enough opportunities to set out their arguments and submit the necessary supporting evidence to present their claims and defences.[169]

169. As noted above, Brazil requests us "to make findings on the measures originally identified by Brazil at the time of establishment of the Panel" as well as "to make specific and additional findings on the measures identified in its panel request, in light of the amendments brought to the Indonesian regulatory framework, to the extent that they affect the original measures".[170] Brazil has made arguments with respect to the measures as enacted through the second and third set of legal instruments, but did not make arguments in respect of the first set of legal instruments. This suggests that Brazil considers it possible and reasonable, in order to secure a positive solution to this dispute, to commence with the second set of legal instruments.

170. Taking into account the above, we have decided as follows: Subject to the Panel having jurisdiction, we will start with a review of the measures as enacted by the second set of legal instruments. We will make findings on these measures before addressing the issue, where relevant, of whether they have expired as argued by Indonesia. We agree with Indonesia's reading of the relevant case law that the expiry of a measure would not prevent us from making findings on that measure.[171] In light of Brazil's request in this respect, we consider that such findings are necessary to secure a positive solution to the dispute and for this reason, we review all measures and make findings irrespective of whether they have expired.

171. Where Indonesia has so argued, we will examine the issue of expiry. We observe that the concept of "expiry" of a measure has had limited development in the case law so far.[172] We infer from the relevant jurisprudence that a measure has expired if it has ceased to exist.[173] We note, however, that in the cases decided so far, the measures at issue were terminated *without* the underlying legal instrument being replaced by a new one.[174] In contrast, we are confronted with a situation where the legal instruments underlying the challenged measures have been replaced by new legal instruments. Mindful of the difference between measures and the legal instruments enacting them, we do not exclude that a

---

[169] Parties' response to Panel question No. 66(b). We note Indonesia's reservations in respect of certain aspects of one measure, namely the intended use requirement, and discuss them in the relevant section concerning this measure.

[170] Brazil's response to Panel question No. 66(a).

[171] See Appellate Body Reports, *China – Raw Materials*, para. 263 referring to Panel Reports, *US – Wool Shirts and Blouses*, para. 6.2; *Indonesia – Autos*, para. 14.9; *Chile – Price Band System*, para. 7.126; *Dominican Republic – Import and Sale of Cigarettes*, para. 7.344; and *EC – Approval and Marketing of Biotech Products*, paras. 7.1303-7.1312. See also Appellate Body Report, *US – Upland Cotton*, para. 272, fn 214.

[172] See Appellate Body Reports, *US – Certain EC Products*, para. 81; *US – Upland* Cotton, paras. 272-273; *China – Raw Materials*, paras. 264-265; and Panel Report, *US – Poultry*, para. 7.51.

[173] See, in particular, Appellate Body Report, *US – Upland Cotton*, para. 272.

[174] See fn 162 above.

measure may cease to exist even where a new legal instrument has replaced a preceding one. We will, therefore, review, on a case by case basis, as we examine the relevant measures, whether they have indeed ceased to exist. In this examination, we take into account as evidence relevant changes to the measures, as enacted through the third set of legal instruments.[175]

172.   We agree with Indonesia that the expiry of a measure, while not preventing a panel from making findings, may have a bearing on whether a panel can make a recommendation.[176] In *US – Certain EC Products* the Appellate Body found that the panel erred in making a recommendation in respect of a measure that was no longer in existence.[177] In subsequent cases, the Appellate Body provided guidance on specific situations where a panel may make a recommendation despite the expiry of a measure.[178] Such specific situations concern subsidies or measures that are annually adopted within a framework of measures. We are of the view that none of the measures at issue fall within these specific situations. Accordingly, if we find that a measure has expired, we will not make a recommendation.

173.   In addition to reviewing the measures as enacted through the second set of legal instruments, we will, jurisdiction permitting, review Brazil's claims with respect to the measures as enacted through the third set of legal instruments, where Brazil has made arguments to this effect and where we have found that the measure has not expired.

174.   As a final remark, we observe, that the rapid succession of legislative changes has created a few challenges in these proceedings.[179] As noted above, the parties have generally assured us that they have had enough opportunities to set out their arguments and submit the necessary supporting evidence to present their claims and defences.[180] Nevertheless, we have been mindful of the particular importance of safeguarding due process under these unusual circumstances. At the same time, the same unusual circumstances have

---

[175]   See Panel Reports, *China – Raw Materials*, para. 7.25 citing *China – Publications and Audiovisual Products*, para. 177; *China - Auto Parts*, para. 225; *US - Section 211 Appropriations Act*, para. 105; India - Patents (US), paras. 65. See also Appellate Body Report, *EC – Selected Customs Matters*, para. 188.

[176]   See Appellate Body Reports, *US – Upland Cotton*, paras. 272-273; and *China – Raw Materials*, paras. 264-265. We note that in a number of other cases the expiry of the measure was contested. In those cases, the panels refrained from making a finding on whether the measure had expired and instead adopted a recommendation that was qualified such that it would not apply if and to the extent the measure had expired. See Panel Reports, *EC – Biotech*, para. 8.16; and *Thailand – Cigarettes (Philippines)*, para. 8.8. See also Panel Report, *EC – Commercial Vessels*, para. 8.4; and Appellate Body Report, *Dominican Republic – Import and Sale of Cigarettes*, para. 129.

[177]   Appellate Body Report, *US – Certain EC Products*, para. 81.

[178]   Appellate Body Reports, *US – Upland* Cotton, paras. 272-273 and *China – Raw Materials*, paras. 264-265.

[179]   We note Brazil's reference to a "moving target", Brazil's opening statement at the second meeting of the Panel, para. 3.

[180]   See fn 160 above.

compelled us to exercise some flexibility in examining the parties' arguments, given their constant evolution in the course of the proceedings.

7.3 Background on the Measures at Issue

175.   Having provided explanations regarding the order of our analysis, we now turn to providing some explanations regarding the factual context of this dispute. Our description in this section is brief. More detailed descriptions of the relevant legal instruments as well as of specific factual aspects follow in the relevant sections on each measure.

176.   As noted above, this dispute concerns a number of measures affecting the importation of chicken meat and chicken products into Indonesia. To import such products into Indonesia, an importer has to apply for and obtain an import recommendation from the Minister of Agriculture (MoA Import Recommendation) and an import approval from the Minister of Trade (MoT Import Approval). The former is a necessary step in obtaining the latter. The relevant MoA and MoT regulations set out the procedural and substantive requirements for obtaining an MoA Import Recommendation and an MoT Import Approval. It is these two regulations that have been revoked and replaced twice over the course of the proceedings as discussed in section 7.2.4 above.

177.   Importers can only apply for an MoA Import Recommendation if the exporting country has been approved in advance as a "country of origin". Similarly, the relevant business unit in the exporting country is required to be pre-approved before an application for an MoA Import Recommendation can be made. The country of origin approval serves to verify animal health conditions for the relevant product in the exporting country. The business unit approval serves to verify the animal health, food safety and halal slaughtering conditions at the relevant business units in the country of origin.[181]

178.   In addition to having country of origin approval and business unit approval, importers must produce a number of other documents when applying for an MoA Import Recommendation.

179.   The chart below provides an overview of the basic features of Indonesia's import licensing regime. We provide further details along with additional charts in the relevant sections of this report.

---

[181]   We note that in the relevant laws and regulations, this step is referred to as "country of origin and business unit stipulation". For ease of reference, we refer to this as "approval", which we understand to have the same legal meaning as "stipulation".

Figure 1 Overview of Indonesia's import licensing regime

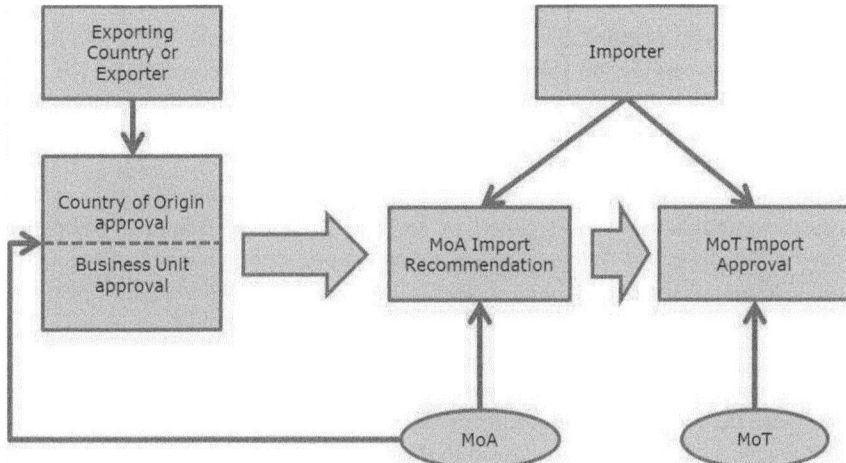

180.   As is uncontested by Indonesia, there have been virtually no imports of chicken cuts (since 2006) and whole chicken (since 2009) into Indonesia, including from Brazil.[182]

181.   Furthermore, as is undisputed between the parties, a feature of Indonesia's chicken market is that most of the chicken meat consumed in Indonesia is sold in the traditional markets (also called "wet markets").[183] Moreover, most of the chicken meat sold in these markets is from freshly slaughtered chickens. All chicken meat, whether imported into or produced in Indonesia, must be halal.

182.   We now turn to assess Brazil's claims in respect of the six individual measures Brazil has described in its first written submission.

---

[182]   See Brazil's first written submission, paras. 23, referring to Table 2; 204; and 234; and Brazil's second written submission, paras. 126 and 147. See also Indonesia's response to Panel question No. 9, which refers to TradeMap import statistics from 2004-2015 for HS Codes 0207.11, 0207.12, 0207.13, 0207.14 as well as 1602.32 (Exhibit IDN-89). The data provided by Brazil in Table 2 of its first written submission is corroborated by Exhibit IDN-89. Indonesia explains further that imports of chicken from 1988 to 2008 as reflected on the tables were on account of a partial exemption that was made for imports destined for the Batam Industrial Area Indonesia, pursuant to MoA Decree 229/1988. See Indonesia's response to Panel question No. 9.

[183]   See Brazil's first written submission, paras. 224 and 289, where Brazil asserts that around 70% of Indonesian chicken meat and chicken products in Indonesia are sold in traditional or wet markets. See also Indonesia's first written submission, paras. 135, 159 and 326, where Indonesia submits that 80 to 85% of chicken meat is sold in traditional or wet markets.

7.4   Individual Measure 1: Positive List Requirement

7.4.1   Introduction

183.   The first measure concerns provisions in the relevant MoA and MoT regulations governing the importation of meat, which prescribe the type of carcass for which an importer may obtain an MoA Import Recommendation and an MoT Import Approval. Chicken cuts and other chicken products cannot be the subject either of an MoA Import Recommendation or an MoT Import Approval, because they are not listed in the relevant appendices[184] of the respective regulations.[185] As noted in section 2.1 above, Brazil, in its panel request, has described this measure as an import prohibition on certain products; in the course of the proceedings, Brazil referred to this measure as the "positive list requirement", the term also used by Indonesia.[186] We do likewise.

184.   As we explained above[187], the legal instruments enacting the positive list requirement have been revoked and replaced twice since panel establishment. The table below sets out relevant provisions in the three different sets of legal instruments as they will be discussed in this section.

Table 2.   Relevant provisions regarding the positive list requirement

First set of legal instruments	Second set of legal instruments	Third set of legal instruments
MoA 139/2914 (Exhibit BRA-34)	**MoA 58/2015 (Exhibit BRA-01/IDN-24)**	**MoA 34/2016 (Exhibit BRA-48/IDN-93)**
Art. 8	*Art. 7*	*Art. 7*
Requirements for meat … and carcass and/or meat from other than bovine, as well as its processed as Listed in Appendix 2 which are integral parts of this Ministerial Regulation.	In addition to the requirements referred in Article 4, Article 5, and Article 6, the importation of carcass, meat and/or the processed product thereof must comply with the requirements of:	… (2) …type of carcass, meat, and/or offal other than cattle including its processed products … are listed in Annex II which is an integral part of this Ministerial Regulation.
	a. Type of carcass, meat and the processed product thereof;	(3) The type of carcass … other than cattle which is not listed in … Annex II … may still be granted recommendation, as long as it meets the requirements of safe, healthy,
	Art. 8	
	…	
	(2) Types of non-cattle carcass	

---

[184]   We use the term "appendix" to refer to the section of the relevant legal instrument that contains the list of products that are allowed to be imported into Indonesia. For the purposes of this report, "appendix" is synonymous with "annex" and "attachment", which are terms that are also used in the various translations of the relevant regulations to refer to the same section of the legal instrument.

[185]   See also Brazil's first written submission, para. 77 and 191; and Indonesia's first written submission, para. 223.

[186]   Indonesia's first written submission, para. 218.

[187]   See sections 2.2 and 7.2.4 above.

First set of legal instruments	Second set of legal instruments	Third set of legal instruments
	and the processed product thereof as referred to in Article 7 letter a, are included in Attachment II which is an inseparable part of this Ministerial Regulation.	wholesome and halal ….
MoT 46/2013 **(Exhibit BRA-42)** *Art. 2* … (2) The Type of Animal and Animal Product that can be imported as included in Appendix I and Appendix II is an integral part of this Ministerial Regulation. *Article 11* (2) To obtain Import Approval … company that will import Animal and/or Animal Product must submit application by attaching: (a) recommendation from the Minister of Agriculture or official appointed by the Minister of Agriculture, for importing Animal and fresh Animal Product as stated in Appendix II of this Ministerial Regulation;	MoT 05/2016 (Exhibit BRA-03) *Art. 7* … (2) The type of Animal and Animal Product that can be imported shall be as per Appendices II, III, and IV forming integral part hereof. *Article 10* (2) To obtain Approval to Import … the company shall submit the application … by attaching: … (e) Recommendation of the Minister of Agriculture or official so appointed by the Minister of Agriculture, for Import of Animal and Animal Product as per Appendices III and IV hereto;	MoT 59/2016 (Exhibit IDN-109) *Art. 7* … (2) The types of Animals and Animal Products which are limited for importation are as included in Annex II and III, which is an integral part of this Minister Regulation. *Art 11* (1) To obtain the Import Approval … for the importation of Animals and Animal Products … the API holder company... shall submit an application … by attaching: … (e) Recommendation from the Minister of Agriculture or an official appointed by the Minister of Agriculture, for the Import of Animals and Animal Products as listed in Annex II and Annex III in which an integral part of this Minister Regulation; *Article 29* Animal and animal products that are not contained in the attachment of this Minister Regulation may be imported after obtaining Import Approval from Import Director by attaching Recommendation as referred to in Article 11 paragraph (1) letter e or f.

185.   As explained in section 7.2.4.3 above, we will first analyse the measure as enacted through the second set of legal instruments (i.e. regulations MoA 58/2015 and MoT 05/2016), the version Brazil refers to in its first written submission. We then move on to examine the relevant provisions of the third set of legal instruments.

7.4.2 Panel's analysis of the positive list requirement as enacted through MoA 58/2015 and MoT 05/2016

186. We note that the relevant provisions of regulations MoA 58/2015 and MoT 05/2016 are virtually identical to those of MoA 139/2014 and MoT 46/2013, which were in force at the time of the panel establishment (i.e. first set of legal instruments). Thus, given that the measure remains in essence the same, we consider that we have jurisdiction to review its WTO consistency.[188]

187. Brazil contends that the positive list requirement constitutes a violation of Article XI of the GATT 1994 and Article 4.2 of the Agreement on Agriculture.[189] Indonesia does not dispute that MoA 58/2015 and MoT 05/2016 establish a prohibition on the importation of chicken cuts.[190] Indonesia however submits that the measure is justified under Article XX(d) of the GATT 1994.[191]

7.4.2.1 Preliminary issue of fact – whether prepared or preserved chicken meat can be imported into Indonesia

188. Before we address the parties' arguments regarding the merits of Brazil's claims we first need to address a factual issue. The issue is whether prepared or preserved chicken meat can be imported into Indonesia. While Brazil claims it cannot, Indonesia submits that it can.

189. We recall that, in our preliminary ruling set out in section 7.1.2.4 above, we addressed a jurisdictional issue regarding prepared or preserved chicken meat. More specifically, we found that our terms of reference covered Brazil's claims on the positive list requirement in respect of prepared or preserved chicken meat.

190. Following our ruling, Indonesia, in its second written submission, asserted that prepared or preserved chicken meat could be imported into Indonesia. Indonesia's assertion was notably based not on the above set of legal instruments, but on a different regulation. Indonesia argued that pursuant to MoT 87/2015, prepared or preserved chicken meat could be imported into Indonesia.[192]

191. We clarified the issue through a number of questions to the parties.[193] Based on their responses and comments, our understanding is as follows: MoT 87/2015[194] is a regulation that imposes a number of conditions on certain

---

[188] See paras. 7.84 and 7.93 above.
[189] See Brazil's first written submission, paras. 191-194. See also Brazil's first written submission paras. 99-101.
[190] See Indonesia's first written submission, para. 223.
[191] See Indonesia's first written submission, paras. 223 and 229-234.
[192] Indonesia's second written submission, paras. 25-27.
[193] See parties' responses to Panel question Nos. 72 (a), (b), and (c).
[194] We note that MoT 87/2015 was not in force at the time of panel establishment. As explained by Indonesia, MoT 87/2015 was originally scheduled to enter into force on 1 November 2015 until 31 December 2018 (Article 26). However, MoT 94/2015 (Exhibit IDN-113) amended Article 26 and

products upon importation; for example, the regulation limits the choice of ports of destination in Indonesia for the concerned products.[195] The regulation applies to some 800 tariff lines, including certain processed animal products such as prepared or preserved chicken meat. However, the fact that a good is subject to the import conditions set out in MoT 87/2015 does not mean that it cannot at the same time be subject to other import regulations, including that its importation may be prohibited altogether by virtue of provisions set out elsewhere.[196] This is the case with respect to the product at issue in this dispute. Prepared or preserved chicken meat is not listed in the relevant appendix of MoA 58/2015 or in that of MoT 05/2016. Thus, its importation is not allowed by virtue of those regulations.[197]

192.   We therefore find that notwithstanding the fact that prepared or preserved chicken meat is covered by MoT 87/2015, it cannot be imported pursuant to MoA 58/2015 and MoT 05/2016.

7.4.2.2   Whether the positive list requirement is inconsistent with Article XI of the GATT 1994

193.   Brazil submits that the positive list requirement prohibits the importation of chicken cuts and other prepared or preserved chicken meat and is, therefore, contrary to Article XI of the GATT 1994.[198] As noted above, Indonesia does not dispute that the positive list requirement establishes a prohibition on the importation of chicken cuts and offers no arguments under Article XI.[199]

---

provided that MoT 87/2015 shall come into effect on 1 January 2016 until 31 December 2016 (See Indonesia's response to Panel question No. 72 (b)). The predecessor regulation that was in force at the time of panel establishment was MoT 83/2012. It provides for a similar set of import conditions and also applies to prepared or preserved chicken meat, (Exhibit IDN-128).

[195]   See Articles 2 and 4 of MoT 87/2015 (Exhibit IDN-33).

[196]   See Indonesia's response to Panel question No. 72 (a) and (c).

[197]   We note that the predecessor of MoT 05/2016, namely MoT 46/2013, did list prepared or preserved chicken meat in its relevant appendix. Thus, the importation of prepared or preserved chicken meat was allowed by virtue of that regulation. However, as seen in section 7.3 above, the granting of an MoT Import Approval under the MoT regulation is dependent on an MoA Import Recommendation under the MoA regulation. Therefore, because the product was not listed in the relevant appendix of the MoA regulation applicable at the time (MoA 139/2014), no MoA Import Recommendation could be granted, and consequently, no MoT Import Approval could be granted under MoT 46/2013. See also Indonesia's response to Panel question No. 72(c).

[198]   Brazil's first written submission, paras. 191-194. See also Brazil's first written submission, paras 99-101.

[199]   Indonesia's first written submission, para. 228. As noted in section 7.2.3.2 above, Indonesia takes the view that Article XI of the GATT 1994 does not apply and, therefore, made its main arguments under Article 4.2 of the Agreement on Agriculture. We note that also under Article 4.2 of the Agreement on Agriculture, Indonesia does not contest that there is a quantitative restriction on imports within the meaning of footnote of Article 4.2. See Indonesia's first written submission, para. 223.

194.   Article XI:1 of the GATT 1994 reads as follows:

> No prohibitions or restrictions other than duties, taxes or other charges, whether made effective through quotas, import or export licences or other measures, shall be instituted or maintained by any contracting party [Member] on the importation of any product of the territory of any other contracting party [Member] or on the exportation or sale for export of any product destined for the territory of any other contracting party [Member].

195.   Accordingly, we need to assess the following two questions with regard to the positive list requirement: (1) whether it is a prohibition or restriction on the importation of chicken meat and chicken products, and (2) whether it is made effective through quotas, import or export licences or other measures.

196.   As regards the first question, the Appellate Body has identified the meaning of the term "prohibition" as a "legal ban on the trade or importation of a specified commodity".[200] In our view, the positive list requirement qualifies as a "legal ban" because the direct legal consequence of not being listed as a product is that importation of that product is not allowed. The positive list requirement, therefore, is a prohibition within the meaning of Article XI.

197.   As regards the second question, the Appellate Body in *Argentina – Import Measures* analysed the meaning of measures "made effective" and concluded that it covers "measures through which a prohibition or restriction is produced or becomes operative".[201] We recall that the positive list requirement means that no import recommendation and/or no import approval are granted if and when a product is not contained in the relevant appendices.[202] The import approval operates as a licence in that it constitutes the permission required to import chicken meat and chicken products into Indonesia.[203] Thus, the positive list requirement is made effective through a licence.

198.   We therefore conclude that the positive list requirement is inconsistent with Article XI of the GATT 1994.

---

[200] Appellate Body Reports, *China – Raw Materials*, para. 319; and *Argentina – Import Measures*, para. 5.217.

[201] Appellate Body Reports, *Argentina – Import Measures*, para. 5.218.

[202] See description in paragraph 7.103 above.

[203] The Panel notes that Article XI of the GATT 1994 does not define the concept of "import licence". The Shorter Oxford English Dictionary defines "licence" as "liberty to do something, leave, permission". (*Shorter Oxford English Dictionary*, 6th edn, W.R. Trumble (ed.) (Oxford University Press, 2007), Vol. 2, p. 2363). The panel in *Turkey – Rice,* while noting that the concept of "import licence" is not defined under Article XI, referred to the definition of "import licensing" contained in Article 1.1 of the Import Licensing Agreement, i.e. "administrative procedures used for the operation of import licensing regimes requiring the submission of an application or other documentation (other than that required for customs purposes) to the relevant administrative body as a prior condition for importation into the customs territory of the importing Member". See Panel Report, *Turkey – Rice*, para. 7.126.

7.4.2.3   Whether the positive list requirement is
          justified under Article XX(d) of the GATT
          1994

199.   Indonesia raises a defence under Article XX(d) of the GATT 1994, submitting that the positive list requirement is necessary to secure compliance with Indonesia's laws and regulations dealing with halal requirements, as well as deceptive practices and customs enforcement relating to halal.[204] Indonesia's concern is that chicken parts would be sourced from non–halal slaughtering houses and passed off as halal. Indonesia does not put forward arguments to justify the prohibition on prepared or preserved chicken meat.[205]

200.   Brazil considers that the positive list requirement is not justified[206] and asserts, *inter alia,* that halal certification would be a less trade-restrictive alternative measure.[207]

201.   Article XX states in its relevant part:

> Subject to the requirement that such measures are not applied in a manner which would constitute a means of arbitrary or unjustifiable discrimination between countries where the same conditions prevail, or a disguised restriction on international trade, nothing in this Agreement shall be construed to prevent the adoption or enforcement by any contracting party [Member] of measures:
>
> …
>
> (d) necessary to secure compliance with laws or regulations which are not inconsistent with the provisions of this Agreement, including those relating to customs enforcement, the enforcement of monopolies operated under paragraph 4 of Article II and Article XVII, the protection of patents, trade marks and copyrights, and the prevention of deceptive practices;

202.   In order to assess Indonesia's defence, we need to proceed in two steps.[208] First, we need to assess whether the measure is provisionally justified under subparagraph (d) of Article XX, as set out above. If that is the case, we go on to examine whether the measure satisfies the requirements of the chapeau of Article

---

[204]   See Indonesia's first written submission, para. 230. For a brief description of what "halal" means in respect of chicken meat, see para. 7.536 below.

[205]   See Indonesia's first written submission, para. 232; and Indonesia's opening statement at the first meeting of the Panel, para. 89.

[206]   Brazil's opening statement at the first meeting of the Panel, paras. 56-59, and 63 and second written submission, paras. 85-103.

[207]   Brazil's second written submission, para. 93.

[208]   Appellate Body Reports, *US – Gasoline,* p. 22 (DSR 1996:I, 3, at 20); and *EC – Seal Products,* para. 5.169.

XX. Furthermore, we note that Indonesia, as the party asserting the defence, generally has the burden of proof.[209]

203.   We turn to assess whether the positive list requirement is provisionally justified under subparagraph (d) of Article XX. In line with relevant guidance provided by the Appellate Body[210], we consider that this assessment requires us to address the following two questions: (1) whether the positive list requirement is designed to secure compliance with laws or regulations that are not themselves inconsistent with some provision of the GATT 1994; and (2) whether the positive list requirement is necessary to secure compliance with those laws and regulations.

7.4.2.3.1   Whether the positive list requirement is designed to secure compliance with laws or regulations that are not themselves inconsistent with the GATT 1994

204.   Turning to the first of these questions, we note that Indonesia refers to three different laws, namely Law 18/2009 (Animal Law), Law 33/2014 (Halal Law), and Law 8/1999 (Consumer Law).[211] Brazil has not called into question the consistency of these laws with the GATT 1994, and we agree with Indonesia that it must, therefore, be presumed.[212]

205.   In terms of specific provisions, Indonesia refers to a provision of Law 18/2009 that addresses the Indonesian authorities' duty to "supervise, inspect, examine, standardize, certify and register animal products" in order "to secure safe, healthy, intact and rightful animal products".[213] In the same law, indeed the same article, Indonesia points to the requirement for imported products to have a "rightful certificate".[214] Indonesia also refers to the obligation "to provide honest information about the condition and quality of products", which Law 8/1999

---

[209] Appellate Body Report, *US – Wool Shirts and Blouses*, pp. 14, DSR 1997:I, 323 at 335. However, the Appellate Body also noted that in respect of the less trade-restrictive alternative measure, the complaining party has the burden of proof. See Appellate Body Report, *US – Gambling* para. 309. See also para. 7.136 below.

[210] Appellate Body Report, *Korea – Various Measures on Beef*, para. 157. See also Appellate Body Report, *Argentina – Financial Services*, para. 6.202.

[211] See Indonesia's first written submission, para. 230. See also Law of the Republic of Indonesia Number 18/2009 on Husbandry and Animal Health (Exhibit BRA-29/IDN-1); Law of Republic of Indonesia No. 33/2014 concerning Halal Product Assurance (Exhibit BRA-46/IDN-5); and Law of the Republic of Indonesia No. 8/1999 concerning Consumer Protection (Exhibit IDN-70).

[212] Indonesia's first written submission, para. 231 and opening statement at the first meeting of the Panel, para. 84. See in this regard, Appellate Body Report, *US – Carbon Steel*, para. 157. We note that Indonesia does not refer to any law or regulation concerning specifically customs enforcement; but see para. 7.119 above.

[213] Indonesia's first written submission, para. 230 referring to Article 58(1) of Law 18/2009 (Exhibit IDN-1/BRA-29).

[214] Indonesia's first written submission, para. 230, referring to Article 58(4) of Law 18/2009 (Exhibit IDN-1/BRA-29).

imposes on entrepreneurs.[215] In terms of specific halal requirements in Indonesian law, Indonesia limits itself to a general reference to "the process of certification" in Law 33/2014.[216]

206.   Indonesia explains that the positive list requirement "served to ensure the traceability of imported chicken meat and chicken products to specific foreign establishments that obtained halal certificates".[217] Elsewhere, Indonesia, in referring to the preamble of MoA 58/2015 asserts that that regulation "was created 'in view of' certain Indonesian laws, including [the three laws referred to above]" and that its stated purpose is to provide the legal basis to ensure the compliance with safety, healthy, wholesome and halal requirements.[218]

207.   The Appellate Body has described the relevant test that we need to apply as "an initial examination of the relationship between the inconsistent measure and the relevant laws or regulations" which requires a panel to "scrutinize the design of the measures sought to be justified".[219] The Appellate Body has further clarified that the standard for ascertaining whether such a relationship exists is whether the assessment of the design of the measure reveals that the measure is *not incapable* of securing compliance with the relevant laws and regulations in Indonesia.[220] Finally, we note that the Appellate Body has described this test as "not... particularly demanding", in contrast to the requirements of the next step of the analysis, namely the necessity test.[221]

208.   With this in mind we turn to analyse Indonesia's arguments. In our view, the provisions that Indonesia refers to, as well as its explanation on traceability, at least when taken at face value, do not directly explain how the positive list requirement was designed to ensure compliance with Indonesia's stated concern that non-halal chicken cuts would be passed off as halal. We consider that the provisions referred to in the relevant laws are geared towards *allowing* the importation of animal products into the country rather than *banning* them as is effectively the case for chicken cuts, prepared or preserved chicken meat (and other products).[222] Certification and traceability are tools whose use is premised on importation being possible in the first place, as is the case for whole chicken. Chicken cuts that cannot be imported into Indonesia, neither require certification

---

[215]   Indonesia's first written submission, para. 230 and fn 335, referring to Articles 4, 7, 9(1) and (3) of Law 8/1999 (Exhibit IDN-70).
[216]   Indonesia's first written submission, para. 230.
[217]   Indonesia's first written submission, para. 232.
[218]   Indonesia's opening statement at the first meeting of the Panel, para. 85.
[219]   Appellate Body Report, *Argentina – Financial Services*, para. 6.203. See also Appellate Body Report, *Colombia – Textiles,* para. 5.124 referring to this standard (developed under Article XIV of the GATS) as relevant in the context of Article XX(a) of the GATT 1994..
[220]   Appellate Body Report, *Colombia – Textiles*, paras. 5.68 (referring to the test applicable in the context of Article XX(a)) and 5.125-5.128 (indicating that the test is also applicable to Article XX(d)).
[221]   Appellate Body Report, *Colombia – Textiles*, para. 5.70.
[222]   As Indonesia explains in response to Panel question No.81, turkey cuts and duck cuts have not been included in the positive list for the same reason as chicken cuts.

nor need to be traced. In other words, the provisions referred to above as well as Indonesia's explanation regarding traceability, when taken at face value, do not seem to account for the ban that the positive list requirement puts in place.

209. However, Indonesia has also described a factual background of certain incidents allegedly involving importation into Indonesia of non-halal chicken cuts. Against this background we understand Indonesia to suggest that the ban on chicken cuts was adopted because certification and traceability could *not* ensure what Indonesia seeks to ensure, namely that all imported chicken products are halal.[223] It may be possible therefore, to understand Indonesia's arguments above as focusing on demonstrating how the regulatory system in Indonesia is generally geared towards ensuring the halalness of meat products, including imported meat products. The specific measure of the positive list requirement could then be explained as working towards the same objective, namely to ensure halalness in the specific factual circumstances that Indonesia referred to.

210. As regards these specific factual circumstances, we note the following. Indonesia suggests that there were a number of incidents of imported non-halal meat being passed off as halal.[224] As evidence of this Indonesia submits a letter from the Indonesian Minister of Agriculture to his US counterpart dated 2002.[225] In this letter reference is made to three incidents. One is described as involving imports of chicken quarter legs "illegally" entering the Indonesian market. The chicken legs were produced by a US company that was known to have only one halal certified food processing plant. Indonesia, elsewhere, describes the shipment in question as "part halal, part non-halal" and explains that it was this incident that led to the adoption of the positive list requirement and, therefore, to the ban on chicken cuts in 2006.[226] The second incident involved a shipment of chicken cuts that were destined for Russia, but ended up in the Indonesian market, which, as Indonesia explains elsewhere, "caused unrest amongst Muslim consumers as they considered those products were not halal".[227] The third reference in the Indonesian Minister's letter to his US counterpart is to a US meat producer that has "firmly stated" that its products imported into Indonesia, which were accompanied by a halal certificate, have never been produced under halal procedures. The letter neither identifies the company in question nor offers any other factual information in this regard.

---

[223] Indonesia's response to Panel question No. 80.

[224] See Indonesia's response to Panel question No. 78, referring to Indonesia Ministry of Agriculture's response dated 5 April 2002 to the Letter from United States Secretary of Agriculture (Exhibit IDN-82). See also Indonesia's response to Panel question No. 80.

[225] See Letter by Indonesia's Minister of Agriculture (Exhibit IDN-82).

[226] Indonesia's response to Panel question No.78(a). Note that chicken cuts have never been included in the positive list since its first adoption in 2006. See Indonesia's response to Panel question No. 78(b). See also section 7.3 above.

[227] Indonesia's response to Panel question No.78(a).

211. We have some doubts with regard to these explanations. First of all, if the risk of non-halal chicken cuts being passed off as halal exists, as Indonesia argues, why would the same risk not exist with regard to whole chicken, which is not prohibited? Indonesia explains that there were no incidents involving whole chicken and that it addresses problems as they arise on a case-by-case basis.[228] We are not persuaded by this argument, as we do not see why non-halal whole chicken could not as easily be passed off as halal as in the case of chicken cuts.[229] Second, we are not sure about the extent to which the incidents mentioned above involved shipments being passed off as halal, rather than simply shipments, which were never meant to be imported into Indonesia and, for that reason, should have been stopped upon importation.[230] Third we note that in Indonesia's own description, it is an incident that dates back to 1999, which led to the adoption of a regulation in 2006.[231] This means that, Indonesia decided to put in place a measure after as long a period as seven years to address a risk, which moreover does not seem to have materialized again in the intervening years.

212. The above factors cast some doubt on the link claimed by Indonesia between the incidents and the putting in place of the positive list requirement. However, we are mindful that our task is not to evaluate historic facts, but to assess whether a measure, independent of the reasons cited for its adoption, can objectively be considered to have a relationship with the laws and regulations in question. As noted above, this is the case if the measure is *not incapable* of securing compliance with them. We found above that the positive list requirement has the effect akin to a ban as it effectively prohibits import of chicken cuts and other chicken products into Indonesia. We consider that a ban is not incapable of securing halalness insofar as it excludes any risk of non-halal products being imported into the country. That it also excludes products that are halal, is a different issue to be addressed in the level of necessity. We recall that the Appellate Body has highlighted a panel's duty to structure its analysis in such a way that it does not "truncate [that analysis] prematurely and thereby foreclose consideration of crucial aspects of the respondent's defence relating to the 'necessity' analysis".[232]

---

[228] Indonesia's response to Panel question No.79.

[229] We also have some doubts regarding Indonesia's explanations as to why lamb cuts and goat cuts are not prohibited. Indonesia explains that, due to their size, those animals cannot be slaughtered with a rotary blade (Indonesia's response to Brazil's question No. 1(a)). However, in our view they could still be slaughtered in a non-halal manner and be passed off as halal irrespective of whether they can be slaughtered with a rotary blade.

[230] The Russia shipment, for example, since it was not destined for the Indonesian market, should not have passed import control. Similarly, in respect of the first incident referred to above, it is not clear whether the shipment was certified halal or not.

[231] Indonesia's response to Panel question No.78(a).

[232] Appellate Body Report, *Colombia - Textiles*, para. 5.77 (citing Appellate Body Report, *Argentina – Financial Services*, para. 6.203).

213.   For these reasons we find that the positive list requirement is designed to secure compliance with the halal requirements laid down in Indonesian law.

7.4.2.3.2   Whether the positive list requirement is necessary to secure compliance with the relevant laws and regulations in Indonesia

214.   The second question we need to address to establish whether the positive list requirement is provisionally justified under Article XX(d) of the GATT 1994, is whether that measure is necessary to secure compliance with Indonesia's halal requirements.

215.   In line with the Appellate Body's guidance in *Colombia – Textiles,* the assessment of the "necessity" of a measure "entails an in-depth, holistic analysis" of the relationship between the measure and the objective it pursues, which in the current dispute, is to secure compliance with Indonesia's halal requirements.[233]

216.   The test involves a process of "weighing and balancing" a series of factors, including (1) the importance of the objective, (2) the contribution of the measure to that objective, and (3) the trade-restrictiveness of the measure.[234] In most cases, a comparison between the challenged measure and (4) possible alternatives should then be undertaken. The burden to identify any alternative measures that would be less trade-restrictive is on the complaining party.[235] The Appellate Body has described the process of weighing and balancing these factors as:

> a holistic operation that involves putting all the variables of the equation together and evaluating them in relation to each other after having examined them individually, in order to reach an overall judgement.[236]

217.   Thus, we examine each of the four factors individually before reaching an overall conclusion on whether the measure is necessary.

218.   Turning to the first factor – the societal value at stake – a panel needs to assess the relative importance of the interests or values furthered by the challenged measure.[237] The more vital or important the interests or values that

---

[233] Appellate Body Report, *Colombia - Textiles,* para. 5.70. See also Appellate Body Report, *Argentina – Financial Services,* para. 6.204.
[234] Appellate Body Reports, *Colombia – Textiles,* para. 5.70; and *EC - Seal Products,* para. 5.169.
[235] Appellate Body Reports, *US – Gambling,* paras. 309 and 311; and *Brazil – Retreaded Tyres,* para. 156.
[236] Appellate Body Report, *Brazil – Retreaded Tyres,* para. 182.
[237] Appellate Body Report, *US – Gambling,* para. 306 (citing *Korea – Various Measures on Beef,* para. 162).

are reflected in the objective of the measure are, the greater their weight is in the overall weighing and balancing exercise.[238]

219.   Indonesia emphasizes the importance of halalness for its population which is predominantly Muslim.[239] Brazil acknowledges that importance and emphasizes in turn that it does not take issue with Indonesia's halal requirements.[240] We see no disagreement between the parties on this issue. To us, there is no doubt that halalness is of great importance to the Indonesian population and, thus, represents a societal value of considerable weight.

220.   Turning to the second factor – contribution – a panel must assess "in a qualitative or quantitative manner, the extent of the measure's contribution to the end pursued".[241] As the Appellate Body observed, "[t]he greater the contribution, the more easily a measure might be considered to be 'necessary'".[242] However, the Appellate Body also pointed out that since a measure's contribution is only one component of the necessity calculus under Article XX, the assessment of whether a measure is "necessary" cannot be determined by the degree of contribution alone, but will depend on the manner in which the other factors of the "necessity" standard inform the analysis.[243]

221.   Based on this guidance, we apply a qualitative assessment of the contribution that the ban on chicken cuts makes in ensuring halalness of chicken meat in Indonesia. On the one hand, a ban on chicken cuts contributes to ensure respect for halal requirements insofar as it effectively reduces the risk of non-halal imported chicken cuts being passed off as halal to something close to zero: where no imported chicken cuts can enter the country, non-halal chicken cuts cannot be passed off as halal. We note in this context that Indonesia refers to its level of protection in respect of halalness as "zero tolerance" or "zero risk".[244] We point out, however, that there is some doubt as to the extent of the risk of non-halal chicken cuts being passed off as halal, in the first place. As seen above, Indonesia points to only three incidents, not all of which necessarily demonstrate the risk in question and which, furthermore, date back to 1999. Moreover, Indonesia has not been able to explain why no such risk would exist for whole chicken.

222.   On the other hand, a ban prevents *all* imported chicken cuts from entering the country, including those that are in full compliance with the Indonesian halal requirements. As noted above, Indonesia's regulatory system is geared towards allowing halal products to enter the country. Viewed from this perspective, the

---

[238]   See Appellate Body Report, *Korea – Various Measures on Beef*, para. 162.
[239]   See e.g. Indonesia's first written submission, para. 26; and opening statement at the first meeting of the Panel, paras. 3-4.
[240]   Brazil's opening statement at the first meeting of the Panel, para. 59; closing statement at the first meeting of the Panel, para. 10; and second written submission, para. 94.
[241]   Appellate Body Report, *Argentina – Financial Services*, para. 6.234.
[242]   Appellate Body Report, *Korea – Various Measures on Beef*, para. 163.
[243]   Appellate Body Reports, *EC – Seal Products*, para. 5.215.
[244]   Indonesia's response to Panel question Nos. 78(a) and 84.

ban makes no contribution and is in fact counterproductive to allowing Indonesian consumers to buy imported halal chicken cuts.

223.   These considerations bring us to the third factor to be considered in the context of a "necessity" assessment, namely the trade-restrictiveness of the measure. We note that, similar to the above analysis on contribution, a panel must assess the degree of trade-restrictiveness and may do so in a qualitative or quantitative manner.[245] Furthermore, following the same logic as above, the less trade-restrictive a measure is the better its chances are of being considered necessary, bearing in mind, however, that trade-restrictiveness is only one component in the overall analysis.[246]

224.   Indonesia submits that "the fact that the measure imposed a prohibition on the importation of certain specific categories of chicken products, which undermined Indonesia's objective, does not mean that the measure was a ban". Indonesia adds that "nothing prevented Brazilian exporters from exporting to Indonesia whole carcasses of chicken, provided that Indonesia's halal requirements were fulfilled". In Indonesia's view, therefore, the measure is not highly trade-restrictive.[247] We are somewhat puzzled by this argument given that it is Indonesia's own legislation that applies two different measures, by allowing one product and banning the other.

225.   A ban, as the panel in *Brazil – Retreaded Tyres* put it, is "as trade-restrictive as can be".[248] It thus weighs heavily against considering a measure necessary.[249] The Appellate Body noted as much in *Brazil – Retreaded Tyres* by pointing out that

> [W]hen a measure produces restrictive effects on international trade as severe as those resulting from an import ban, it appears to us that it would be difficult for a panel to find that measure necessary unless it is satisfied that the measure is apt to make a material contribution to the achievement of its objective.[250]

226.   We note that the Appellate Body in this context rejected an argument made by Brazil that the high level of protection sought through the ban meant that even a marginal or insignificant contribution should be considered necessary.[251]

---

[245]   Appellate Body Report, *Korea – Various Measures on Beef,* para. 163.

[246]   Appellate Body Reports, *EC – Seal Products,* para. 5.125.

[247]   See Indonesia' opening statement at the first meeting of the Panel, para. 88.

[248]   Panel Report, *Brazil – Retreaded Tyres,* para. 7.211.

[249]   The Appellate Body has emphasized that there is no predetermined threshold of contribution in analysing the necessity of a measure under Article XX. See Appellate Body Reports, *EC – Seal Products,* para. 5.213.

[250]   Appellate Body Report, *Brazil – Retreaded Tyres,* para. 150. See also Appellate Body Report, *EC – Seal Products,* para. 5.213, where the Appellate Body stressed that in *Brazil – Retreaded Tyres,* "the Appellate Body was careful not to suggest that its approach in that dispute was requiring the use of a generally applicable threshold for a contribution analysis".

[251]   Appellate Body Report, *Brazil – Retreaded Tyres,* para. 150.

227.   Applying this guidance to the present case, we note that our earlier assessment of the contribution of the measure has been a "mixed bag": the ban prevents the importation of non-halal chicken meat, but also the importation of halal chicken meat – thus, it makes a contribution regarding non-halal meat, but no contribution regarding halal meat. The actual risk of non-halal meat being passed off as halal, to the extent it has been proven to have materialized, dates back to 1999. Indonesia pursues a zero risk policy, but according to the Appellate Body's pronouncement cited in paragraph 7.146 above, that does not mean that any kind of contribution must be considered necessary.

228.   Without reaching any preliminary conclusion on necessity[252], we turn to the fourth factor to be considered in the overall assessment of necessity, namely the question of a less trade-restrictive alternative measure.

229.   Brazil submits that a less trade-restrictive alternative measure would be certification in slaughterhouses in the exporting countries.[253] Indonesia submits that Brazil, in referring to this less trade-restrictive measure in just two sentences, has not met its burden of proof. Furthermore, Indonesia seems to suggest that Brazil cannot propose, as a less trade-restrictive alternative, a measure that already exists.[254]

230.   We note that a panel must compare the challenged measure and possible alternative measures that achieve the same level of protection while being less trade restrictive.[255] The Appellate Body has explained that an alternative measure must be "reasonably available" and, thus, may not impose "an undue burden on that Member, such as prohibitive costs or substantial technical difficulties".[256] Indonesia is correct in pointing out that the burden of proving the existence of an alternative measure that satisfies the aforementioned elements falls on Brazil as the complainant.[257] We will, therefore examine whether this burden has been met.

231.   Brazil refers to halal certification as the less trade-restrictive alternative. We note that halal certification already exists in Indonesian law (both for domestic and imported products). At the time that is relevant to assessing this measure, halal certification of imported meat products was a requirement set out in the relevant legislation.[258] Furthermore, Law 33/2014, which, among other

---

[252]   Appellate Body Reports, *EC– Seal Products*, para. 5.215. See also fn 1299 to the same paragraph.
[253]   Brazil's second written submission para. 93; opening statement at first meeting of the Panel, para. 58.
[254]   Indonesia's response to Panel question No. 83.
[255]   Appellate Body Report, *US – Gambling*, para. 307.
[256]   Appellate Body Report, *US – Gambling*, para. 308.
[257]   See para. 7.136 above.
[258]   See Government Regulation No. 95/2012 Concerning Veterinary Public Health and Animal Welfare (Exhibit IDN-31). Articles 26 and 54, and Article 31 provides that domestic and imported animal meat products respectively, must have a halal certificate. See also Law 33/2014 which provides in its Article 4 that "[p]roducts that enter, circulate, and traded in the territory of Indonesia must be certified halal". Furthermore, regarding specifically imported products, Article 14(1)(e) of

---

things, refers to halal certification, had already been put in place.[259] We do not understand Brazil to be proposing certification procedures other than those that are already in place.

232.   Thus, in our view, the issue is not whether Brazil has met its burden of proof. It clearly has since the content of the proposed alternative measure is clear and there is no doubt that it is reasonably available. The issue rather is whether Brazil can propose as a less trade-restrictive alternative, a measure that Indonesia already has in place. We understand Indonesia to suggest that it cannot.[260] The relevant jurisprudence that Indonesia refers to in this context is *Brazil – Retreaded Tyres*. In that dispute the panel and the Appellate Body rejected some of the alternative measures proposed by the complainant on the grounds that they were already in place as part of a comprehensive strategy. The Appellate Body reasoned:

> Substituting one element of this comprehensive policy for another would weaken the policy by reducing the synergies between its components, as well as its total effect.[261]

233.   In our view, the situation in the present case differs from the facts at issue in *Brazil – Retreaded Tyres*. At issue in *Brazil – Retreaded Tyres* was a measure that already applied to the product in question. Here, while certification already exists in Indonesian law, it is not a measure that already applies to the banned products. As noted above, chicken cuts that cannot be imported into Indonesia, neither require certification nor need to be traced. A product cannot be certified and banned at the same time. Thus, in respect of the banned products subject to the measure at issue, certification is a new measure, not one that already exists as part of a comprehensive policy. We therefore, see no reason why Brazil should be prevented from proposing certification as an alternative measure. Whether that measure achieves Indonesia's objective of ensuring halalness, bearing in mind Indonesia's strict level of protection, is a different question.

234.   On that question, we consider relevant the submissions Indonesia made in the context of explaining the latest developments on the positive list requirement as they have occurred through the adoption of MoA 34/2016 and MoT

MoA 58/2015 requires a business unit (in order to receive approval as exporting business unit. See section 7.3 above) to "have halal-certified butchers for animal slaughterhouse other than swine slaughterhouse and supervised by halal certification institution acknowledged by Indonesian halal authority". Furthermore, Article 36(4) refers to a "halal certificate" as one of the documents that is checked by a Veterinary Public Health Supervisor once the meat products have been imported into the country.

[259] As Indonesia explains, the main purpose of Law 33/2014 was to unify existing halal assurance requirements and to create new government bodies to guarantee halal product assurance, in coordination with the Indonesian MUI. See Indonesia's response to Panel question Nos. 43 and 82.

[260] Indonesia argues that "Brazil did not however, explain the following essential elements of the 'less trade-restrictive alternative measure': … (ii) how this measure is different from the certification requirements that already exist in Indonesia; … (iv) why this measure is an alternative rather than a complement". See Indonesia's response to Panel question No. 83.

[261] Appellate Body Report, *Brazil – Retreaded Tyres*, para. 172.

59/2016.[262] As we discuss in more detail below, Indonesia submits that through these latest legal instruments the positive list requirement has been terminated.[263] What matters to the question discussed here is the reason that Indonesia puts forward to explain the alleged termination of the positive list requirement. According to Indonesia, it is the "more comprehensive certification requirements over a staggered period of time", which Law 33/2014 put in place, that led the relevant Indonesian authorities to consider that "the halalness of imported products, in particular, chicken cuts and processed products [could be protected] even without the positive list".[264] In other words, Indonesia considers that its current certification procedures are such that the positive list requirement is no longer necessary.

235.   We note that the certification procedures that Indonesia refers to in making this argument, were already in place when the positive list requirement was enacted through MoA 58/2015 and MoT 05/2016. As regards specifically imported chicken products, certification through a national body accredited by the MUI has been required since 2001. It is our understanding that it is not envisaged that accreditation will change with the establishment of a new certification agency as provided for in Law 33/2014.[265] Given this, we agree with Brazil, and we do not see why these certification procedures that Indonesia itself considers sufficient to meet its strict level of protection in respect of ensuring halalness, would not constitute a less trade-restrictive alternative measure for the purposes of the present "necessity" assessment.[266]

236.   Having examined the four factors of the "necessity" test individually, we now turn to the overall assessment of all these factors considered together. In weighing and balancing all factors together in a holistic assessment, we acknowledge the great importance that Indonesia attributes to halalness and we recall the trade-restrictiveness of the measure and the ambivalent nature of the contribution. Mindful of these factors and given that an alternative less-trade-restrictive measure exists that equally meets Indonesia's objective, we conclude that the measure does not comply with the requirements of the necessity test.

237.   We therefore find that the positive list requirement is not necessary pursuant to Article XX(d). As this means that the measure does not meet the requirements of a provisional justification under Article XX(d), there is no need for us to further examine whether it meets the requirements of the chapeau.

---

[262]   As regards taking into account subsequent developments in the context of Article XX of the GATT 1994. See Panel Reports, *China – Raw Materials*, para. 7.25 (citing Appellate Body Reports *China – Publications and Audiovisual Products,* para. 177; *China – Auto Parts*, para. 225; *US – Section 211 Appropriations Act*, para. 105; *India – Patents (US)*, para. 65). See also Appellate Body Report, *EC – Selected Customs Matters*, para. 188.

[263]   Indonesia's second written submission, paras. 28-29 and 32-34.

[264]   Indonesia's response to Panel question No. 82.

[265]   See MORA Decree 518/2001, (Exhibit IDN-107). For more details on the new agency, see para. 7.557 below.

[266]   Brazil's comment on Indonesia's response to Panel question No. 83, para.18.

238.   We therefore conclude that the positive list requirement is inconsistent with Article XI and not justified under Article XX(d) of the GATT 1994.

7.4.2.4   Whether the positive list requirement is inconsistent with Article 4.2 of the Agreement on Agriculture

239.   We recall that the aim of the dispute settlement mechanism is to "secure a positive solution to a dispute" (Article 3.7 of the DSU) and that our duty, according to Article 11 of the DSU is to "make such other findings as will assist the DSB in making the recommendations or in giving the rulings provided for in the covered agreements". As the Appellate Body has observed, it is on the basis of these provisions, that panels may exercise judicial economy.[267] The Appellate Body has also explained that the principle of judicial economy "allows a panel to refrain from making multiple findings that the same measure is *inconsistent* with various provisions when a single, or a certain number of findings of inconsistency, would suffice to resolve the dispute".[268] Thus, panels need address only those claims "which must be addressed in order to resolve the matter in issue in the dispute"[269], and panels "may refrain from ruling on every claim as long as it does not lead to a 'partial resolution of the matter'".[270]

240.   On the basis of the above, having found a violation of Article XI of the GATT 1994, we consider that it is not necessary to address Brazil's claim under Article 4.2 of the Agreement on Agriculture in order to secure a positive solution to this dispute.

7.4.3   Panel's analysis of the relevant provisions of MoA 34/2016 and MoT 59/2016

241.   Our findings above apply to the positive list requirement as enacted through MoA 58/2015 and MoT 05/2016. As noted at the beginning of this section, in the course of the proceedings, these two legal instruments were revoked and replaced by MoA 34/2016 and MoT 59/2016.

---

[267] See Appellate Body Report, *Argentina – Import Measures*, para. 5.189 (citing Appellate Body Report, *EC – Export Subsidies on Sugar*, para. 331).

[268] Appellate Body Report, *Canada – Wheat Exports and Grain Imports*, para. 133. (emphasis original)

[269] Appellate Body Reports, *US – Wool Shirts and Blouses*, p. 19, DSR 1997:I, p. 340; *US – Tuna II (Mexico)*, para. 403.

[270] Appellate Body Report; *US – Tuna II (Mexico)*, para. 404 (citing Appellate Body Report, *US – Upland Cotton*, para. 732).

242.   With this change, the parties' arguments have evolved. Indonesia submits that the positive list requirement has expired.[271] Brazil disagrees.[272] We will, therefore, examine, whether the positive list requirement has expired.

7.4.3.1   Whether the positive list requirement has expired by virtue of MoA 34/2016 and MoT 59/2016

243.   As discussed in section 7.2.4.3 above, we agree with Indonesia that the expiry of the measure at issue may have a bearing on whether we can make a recommendation. As we stated there, we consider that a measure has expired if it has ceased to exist. We thus need to examine whether the positive list requirement has ceased to exist by virtue of relevant provisions adopted in MoA 34/2016 and MoT 59/2016.[273] We note that Indonesia as the party that asserts expiry bears the burden of proving this.[274]

244.   We refer to the relevant provisions as set out in Table 2 above. Indonesia argues that by virtue of Article 7(3) of MoA 34/2016 and Article 29 of MoT 59/2016 chicken products may be imported into Indonesia even though they are not on the list, provided they meet the requirement of being safe, healthy, wholesome, and halal.[275] Brazil submits that the sole fact that the lists/appendices still exist is sufficient proof that Indonesia has not revoked the positive list, pointing also to language that suggests that entitlement to be imported is derived from the lists.[276] Brazil furthermore reads Article 7(3) as providing Indonesian authorities with full discretion on whether chicken products can be imported, concluding that that clause "does not indicate that the positive list is no longer in force but rather that these requirements are additional to that imposed by the positive list".[277]

245.   We recall that the measure that is at issue in this dispute and that we have examined is the requirement for chicken meat and chicken products to be listed in the relevant appendices of Indonesia's regulations governing the importation of animal products, in order for their importation to be permitted. In examining whether this measure has ceased to exist, we note, first of all, that the positive

---

[271]   See Indonesia's first written submission, para. 224; response to Panel question No. 13; second written submission, para. 135; and opening statement at the second meeting of the Panel, paras. 37-38.

[272]   Brazil's second written submission, para. 82.

[273]   We consider these provisions as evidence of subsequent legal developments. See Panel Report, *China – Raw Materials*, para. 7.25 (citing Appellate Body reports, *China – Publications and Audiovisual Products*, para. 177; *China - Auto Parts*, para. 225; *US - Section 211 Appropriations Act*, para. 105; and *India - Patents (US)*, para. 65). See also Appellate Body Report, *EC – Selected Customs Matters*, para. 188.

[274]   See Appellate Body Report, *US – Wool Shirts and Blouses*, p. 14, DSR 1997:I, 323 at 335.

[275]   Indonesia's response to Panel question No. 13; and second written submission, para. 34.

[276]   Brazil points to headings of the appendices. See Brazil's comments on Indonesia's response to Panel question No. 77, para. 13.

[277]   Brazil's comments on Indonesia's response to Panel question No. 77, para. 14.

list as such still exists. It is still in both regulations and still refers to whole chicken only.[278] We are mindful that the measure at issue is not the list as such, but rather the requirement to be on that list in order to be allowed to be imported. However, the continued existence of the positive list raises doubts as to what its role is in determining which products may be allowed into Indonesia. As Brazil points out, the wording of the headings describing the appendices has not changed from previous versions. They still describe those appendices as clearly establishing that only the products listed in those appendices are entitled to be imported into Indonesia.[279] Similarly, there are other provisions that have not been changed and, therefore, still refer to the list as the authority for whether products may be imported. Article 7 of MoT 59/2016, for example, prominently states the principle of imports being limited to certain products without mentioning or referring to what is now stated in Article 29.[280] Most importantly, however, Article 29 stipulates the need to obtain a recommendation "as referred to in Article 11 paragraph (1) letter e", which, in turn, refers to recommendations for products "as listed". Thus, this provision, on its face, refers to an MoA Import Recommendation obtained for products listed in Appendix III, (i.e. the positive list) but *not* to a recommendation obtained for products not listed in that appendix. Indonesia essentially suggests not to read Article 11 paragraph (1) subparagraph (e) too literally but to focus on the "operative part" of Article 29 which is about the need to have an MoA Import Recommendation.[281]

246.   In light of the plain meaning of Article 11 paragraph (1), subparagraph (e), therefore, we conclude that the positive list requirement continues to apply in the same manner. We further consider that because the positive list requirement continues to apply in the same manner, Article 7(3) does not have any application.

247.   We therefore find that the positive list requirement has not ceased to exist, and consequently that this measure has not expired.

---

[278] We note that the relevant appendix in MoA 34/2016 continues to be appendix II, whereas the relevant appendix in MoT 59/2016 is now appendix III (instead of appendix IV as it was in MoT 05/2016).
[279] See Brazil's comments on Indonesia's response to Panel question No. 77, para. 13.
[280] See Articles 7 and 29 of MoT 59/2016 (Exhibit IDN-109).
[281] See Indonesia's response to Panel question No.75.

7.4.3.2   Whether the positive list requirement as enacted through the relevant provisions of MoA 34/2016 and MoT 59/2016 is inconsistent with Article XI of the GATT 1994 and Article 4.2. of the Agreement on Agriculture

248.   As we indicate in section 7.2.4.3 above, Brazil requests the Panel to review its claims with regard to the positive list requirement as enacted through MoA 34/2016 and MoT 59/2016.

249.   We found above, that by virtue, in particular of Articles 11(1)(e) and 29 of MoT 59/2016 the positive list requirement continues to apply in the same manner as it applied by virtue of the relevant provision in MoA 58/2015 and MoT 05/2016. Given the unchanged, continued application of the positive list requirement, we consider that the measure remains in essence the same and that, therefore, we have jurisdiction to review its WTO consistency.

250.   Furthermore, the unchanged, continued application of the positive list requirement leads us to the conclusion that our findings above continue to apply in the same manner. Thus, the positive list requirement as enacted through MoA 34/2016 and MoT 59/2016 is inconsistent with Articles XI:1 and is not justified under Article XX(d) of the GATT 1994.

251.   As regards Article 7(3) of MoA 34/2016, we found above, that given the continued application of the positive list requirement, this clause does not find any application. Therefore, we will not address the consistency of Article 7(3) with Article XI of the GATT 1994.

252.   As with our findings above regarding the measure as enacted through MoA 58/2015 and MoT 05/2016, we apply judicial economy to Brazil's claim under Article 4.2. of the Agreement on Agriculture.

7.4.4   Conclusion

253.   To summarize, we find that the positive list requirement as enacted through MoA 58/2015 and MoT 05/2016 is inconsistent with Article XI of the GATT 1994 and not justified under Article XX(d) of the GATT 1994. Having found that the positive list requirement, as enacted through MoA 58/2015 and MoT 05/2016, is inconsistent with Article XI of the GATT 1994, we consider that it is not necessary to address Brazil's claim under Article 4.2 of the Agreement on Agriculture in order to secure a positive solution to this dispute.

254.   We further find that the positive list requirement has not ceased to exist by virtue of the relevant provisions in MoA 34/2016 and MoT 59/2016.

255.   Furthermore, given that the positive list requirement, as enacted through the relevant provisions of MoA 34/2016 and MoT 59/2016, continues to apply in the same manner as enacted through MoA 58/2015 and MoT 05/2016, our findings on Article XI and XX(d) of the GATT 1994, in respect of the positive

list requirement as enacted through MoA 58/2015 and MoT 05/2016, therefore, also apply to this measure as enacted through MoA 34/2016 and MoT 59/2016.

7.5   Individual Measure 2: Intended Use Requirement

7.5.1   Introduction

256.   We now turn to the second of the individual measures that Brazil challenges. This measure, which is contained in the relevant MoA regulation,[282] consists in limiting the uses of imported chicken meat products in the Indonesian market to specific "intended uses" as identified in the relevant MoA regulation.[283] The allowed use is spelled out in the MoA Import Recommendation; sanctions are provided in case of non-observance. The parties have referred to this measure as the "intended use requirement", a term which we hereby adopt.[284]

257.   As noted above, the MoA regulation enacting the intended use requirement has been revoked and replaced twice since panel establishment.[285] The table below sets out relevant provisions in the three successive versions of the MoA regulation, as they will be discussed in this section.

Table 3.   Relevant provisions in the three successive versions of the MoA regulation

First set of legal instruments	Second set of legal instruments	Third set of legal instruments
MoA 139/2014 (Exhibit BRA-34)	**MoA 58/2015 (Exhibit BRA-01/IDN-24)**	**MoA 34/2016 (Exhibit BRA-48/IDN-93)**
Art. 30	*Art. 29*	*Art. 4*
Recommendation ... shall at least consist of:	Recommendation ... shall at least contain:	...
...	...	(6) Business Actors, State Owned Enterprises, Regional Owned Enterprises, Social Institutions or International Institution Representatives as referred to in paragraph (1) are obliged to conduct importation in accordance with Recommendation as referred to in paragraph (3).
(j) Purpose of usage.	(j) the intended use.	
Art. 32	*Art. 31*	
...	(1) Intended use, as referred to in Article 29 letter j, of carcass and meat, as referred to in Article 8, is	
(2) Purpose of usage as referred to in		

---

[282]   We note that the relevant MoT regulation does not contain such a requirement in respect of chicken meat products, but only in respect of beef products. See the parties' responses to Panel question No. 86.

[283]   See also Brazil's first written submission, paras. 87 and 102 and Indonesia's first written submission, para. 129.

[284]   See Indonesia's first written submission, para. 129; and Brazil's second written submission, para. 24.

[285]   See sections 2.2 and 7.2.4 above.

First set of legal instruments	Second set of legal instruments	Third set of legal instruments
Article 30 letter j, for carcass, and/or meat other than beef and its processed as referred to in Article 8 includes: hotel, restaurant, catering, manufacturing, other special needs, and modern market.	for hotels, restaurants, caterings, industries, and other particular purposes. (2) Intended use, as referred to in Article 29 letter j, of the processed product is for hotels, restaurants, caterings, industries, and other particular purposes, as well as for modern market.	*Art. 22* (1) Application of a Recommendation … shall be enclosed with the following required documents: … (l) distribution plan … in accordance for format-2 *Art. 28* Recommendation … shall at least consist of: … (j) Purpose of usage.
Art. 39 Business Actors, State-Owned Entities, Regional Entities, Social Institutions, or Foreign Country/International Institution Representatives, or that violate the provisions in: … (d) Article 32; … shall be sanction[ed] by withdrawing of the recommendation, not given next recommendation , and shall be proposed to the Minister of Trade for a withdrawal of their Import Permit (PI) and company status as an Animal Product Registered Importer (IT).	*Art. 38* Business Player, State Owned Enterprise (SOE) and Regional Government Owned Enterprise (ROE), Social Institution, and Foreign Country Representative/International Institution that breaches the provision of: … (e) Art. 31 shall be sanctioned by revocation of their recommendation, denial of their next recommendation application, and propose to the Minister administrating governmental trade affairs to revoke the Import Approval (PI).	*Art. 31* (1) Purpose of usage as referred to in Article 28 letter j for carcass, meat, offal and/or its processed products which required a cold chain facility as referred to in Article 8 for hotels, restaurants, caterings, industries, markets with cold chain facilities, and other special needs. *Art. 32* (1) Business Actors, State-Owned Enterprises, Regional-Owned Enterprises, Social Institutions and Foreign Country/International Institution Representatives who imports carcass, meat, offal and/or their processed products is forbidden to: … (b) conduct importation of type/category of carcass, meat and/or their processed products other than what is stated in the Recommendation. (3) Business Actors, State-Owned Enterprises and Regional-Owned Enterprises which import carcass, meat and offal and/or their processed products as listed in Annex I and Annex II is required to submit a distribution report of the carcass and meat to the Director General online in accordance to format-4 on every Thursday. *Art. 38* (1) Business Actors, State Owned Enterprises, Regional Owned Enterprises, Social Institutions or Foreign Country/Institution Representatives which violate Article 4 paragraph (2) and paragraph (6) will be subject to temporary suspension of import recommendation for 1 year period, and proposed by the Minister to the ministry of trade to be imposed sanction

First set of legal instruments	Second set of legal instruments	Third set of legal instruments
		according to the prevailing laws and regulations. ... (3) Business Actors, State-Owned Enterprises, Regional-Owned Enterprises, Social Institutions or Foreign Country/Institution Representatives which violate the following articles: ... (b) Article 22 paragraph (1) letter l, will be subject to written warning and if it is ignored, will be subject to temporary suspension of import recommendation for 1 year period.
		(4) Business Actors, State-Owned Enterprises, Regional-Owned Enterprises, Social Institutions or Foreign Country/Institution Representatives which violate Article 32 will be subject to written warning and if it is ignored, will be subject to temporary suspension of import recommendation for 1 year period.

258.   As explained in section 7.2.4.3 above, we will first analyse the measure as enacted in MoA 58/2015, that is, the version Brazil refers to in its first written submission. We then move to examine the relevant provisions in MoA 34/2016 (the most recent legal instrument).

7.5.2   Analysis of the intended use requirement as enacted through MoA 58/2015

259.   In this section we consider the intended use requirement as enacted through MoA 58/2015. Brazil contends that this measure is inconsistent with Article XI of the GATT 1994, Article III:4 of the GATT 1994, and Article 4.2 of the Agreement on Agriculture.[286] Indonesia, as a threshold matter, submits that only Article III:4 of the GATT 1994 is applicable.[287] In respect of that provision Indonesia contends that there are no like products and, therefore, that there is no less favourable treatment.[288] Alternatively, Indonesia argues that the measure is justified under Article XX(b) and (d) of the GATT 1994.[289]

---

[286]   Brazil's first written submission, paras. 195-199, 224-227, and 268-293.
[287]   Indonesia's first written submission, paras. 81-89; see also para. 7.59 above.
[288]   Indonesia's first written submission, paras. 144-172.
[289]   Indonesia's first written submission, paras. 179-217.

7.5.2.1 Measure at issue and jurisdiction

260. We refer to Table 3 above, which sets out Article 31 of MoA 58/2015. According to this provision, imported frozen chicken may only be sold to hotels, restaurants, caterings and industries. In addition, processed products may also be sold to modern markets. Pursuant to Article 29(j) of MoA 58/2015 (see Table 3 above), these intended uses are explicitly indicated in the MoA Import Recommendation.[290] Article 38(e) provides for sanctions if an importer breaches Article 31. The sanctions consist in a revocation of the recommendation, denial of the next recommendation application and proposal to the MoT to revoke the import approval.

261. We note that these provisions differ slightly from the intended use requirement as laid down in the previous legal instrument, namely MoA 139/2014. In particular, the sale in modern markets was also allowed for (non-processed) chicken meat in the previous version. In our view, this does not affect our jurisdiction. As discussed above, in line with the Appellate Body's jurisprudence in *Chile – Price Band System*, we consider that our terms of reference cover subsequent amendments to the measure at issue so long as that measure in essence remains the same.[291] The intended use requirement consists in limiting allowed uses in the market; this essence has remained the same. As a matter of fact, the most important use that the measure does not include, as enacted through either set of legal instruments, is the use in traditional markets. Both parties agree that this is where most Indonesians buy their chicken.[292] We therefore consider that the intended use requirement, as laid down in MoA 58/2015, is within our terms of reference.

7.5.2.2 Whether Article III:4 of the GATT 1994 is applicable

262. As noted above, Brazil raises claims under both Article XI of the GATT 1994 and Article 4.2 of the Agreement on Agriculture, as well as under Article III:4 of the GATT 1994. Thus, Brazil challenges the intended use requirement both as a border and as an internal measure.

263. Indonesia argues that the intended use requirement can only be challenged under Article III:4 of the GATT 1994.[293] Indonesia submits that a measure is either an internal measure or a border measure but cannot be both at the same time.[294] Indonesia thus considers that these provisions are mutually exclusive. According to Indonesia, because it is applying, to like domestic

---

[290] See example of Import Recommendation by the Minister of Agriculture for beef from New Zealand in December 2015 (Exhibit IDN-88) and Import Recommendation by the Minister of Agriculture for beef from Australia (Exhibit IDN-92(b)).
[291] See section 7.2.4.2 above.
[292] See section 7.3 above, in particular, para. 7.101
[293] Indonesia's first written submission, para. 81.
[294] Indonesia's first written submission, paras. 84. See also Indonesia's response to Panel question No. 51.

products, a measure equivalent to the intended use requirement, the intended use requirement is an internal measure.[295]

264.   According to Brazil, the intended use requirement has effects both at the border and subsequently (i.e. after importation), when the good is offered for sale in the Indonesian market. In Brazil's view, therefore, to the extent the measure affects goods at the border, the measure must be assessed under Article XI, and to the extent the measure affects goods after passing through the border, the measure must be examined under Article III:4.[296] Brazil also argues that there is no equivalent measure that applies to domestic chicken.[297]

265.   We observe, first of all, that while the intended use requirement may have different effects, what Brazil identifies as the problematic aspect of the measure, i.e. the source or cause of the different effects, is one and the same, whether presented under Article III:4 or under Article XI and Article 4.2. This is thus different from other disputes, where different aspects of a measure were separately challenged under different provisions, as causing distinct effects relevant to the provisions cited.[298]

266.   Next, we note that both parties, albeit for different reasons, take the view that Article III:4 is applicable and have presented arguments under this provision. We observe that the question whether Article III:4 applies to the exclusion of Article XI of the GATT 1994 and Article 4.2 of the Agreement on Agriculture, only becomes relevant if and when Article III:4 is applicable to the measure at issue. We therefore examine whether the intended use requirement as laid down in MoA 58/2015, falls within the scope of Article III:4.

267.   Article III: 4 states as follows:

> The products of the territory of any contracting party [Member] imported into the territory of any other contracting party [Member] shall be accorded treatment no less favourable than that accorded to like products of national origin *in respect of all laws, regulations and requirements affecting their internal sale, offering for sale, purchase, transportation, distribution or use.* The provisions of this paragraph shall not prevent the application of differential internal transportation charges which are based

---

[295]   See Indonesia's opening statement at the first meeting of the Panel, para. 45. See also Indonesia's first written submission, para. 169, and second written submission, paras. 37-38.

[296]   Brazil's opening statement at the first meeting of the Panel, paras. 43, and 45-46. See also Brazil's response to Panel question No. 51.

[297]   Brazil's second written submission, para. 41.

[298]   See e.g. Panel Reports, *Argentina – Import Measures*, paras. 6.132-6.135. In this dispute, different aspects of the TRRs measure were challenged separately under Article XI:1 and Article III:4 of the GATT 1994. See also Panel Report, *India – Autos*, para. 7.297. In this dispute, the complainants challenged distinct aspects of the trade balancing condition. In contrast to the above two disputes, in the current dispute, although different effects of the measure are alleged, only one aspect of the measure is alleged to be problematic.

exclusively on the economic operation of the means of transport and not on the nationality of the product. (emphasis added)

268.   Thus, Article III:4 applies to "laws, regulations and requirements affecting their internal sale, offering for sale, purchase, transportation, distribution or use".[299] However, this scope defining element of Article III:4 is qualified through the interpretative note *Ad Article III* which states:

> Any internal tax or other *internal charge, or any law, regulation or requirement of the kind referred to in paragraph 1* which applies to an imported product and to the like domestic product and is collected or enforced in the case of the imported product at the time or point of importation, is *nevertheless* to be regarded as an internal tax or other internal charge, or a law, regulation or requirement of the kind referred to in paragraph 1, and is accordingly subject to the provisions of Article III. (emphasis added)

269.   We read this qualification[300] to mean that a measure that affects the internal sale, offering for sale, etc., when enforced at the time or point of importation, only comes under Article III:4 if it applies to an imported product *and* the like domestic product. In other words, measures which only apply to imported products affecting their internal sale, etc., but do not apply to like domestic products, do not fall under Article III:4.

270.   There are thus three questions that we need to address. The first question is whether the intended use requirement is a law, regulation or requirement affecting the internal sale, offering for sale, purchase, transportation, distribution or use of imported chicken meat. We consider that this is the case and do not understand either party to dispute the point.

271.   The second question is whether the intended use requirement is a measure that is enforced at the time or point of importation. We understand the relevant literal meaning of "enforce" in this context to be "to give legal force".[301] The question, therefore, is whether the intended use requirement is given legal force at the time or point of importation. As noted above, the allowed uses are spelt out in the MoA Import Recommendation. The imposition of sanctions in case of non-observance of the requirement directly affects the possibility to import. In

---

[299]   We discuss further elements of Article III:4 in section 7.5.3.3.3.2 below.

[300]   We note that the Appellate Body, in the context of Article III:2, described the relationship between the *AD Note* and that provision as follows: "Article III:2 second sentence, and the accompanying *Ad* Article have equivalent legal status in that both are treaty language which was negotiated and agreed at the same time. The *Ad* Article does not replace or modify the language contained in Article III:2 second sentence, but, in fact, clarifies its meaning. Accordingly, the language of the second sentence and the *Ad* Article must be read together in order to give them their proper meaning." See Appellate Body Report, *Japan – Alcoholic Beverages II*, p. 24, DSR 1996:I, 97 at 116.

[301]   The Online Oxford English Dictionary defines the word "enforce" as "to give legal force". <http://www.oed.com/view/Entry/62160#eid5398975> (last accessed on 16 January 2017).

our view, the intended use requirement is akin to a condition, on which importation depends. We therefore consider this to be a case of enforcement "at the point of importation".

272.   The third question is whether the measure applies to imported products *and* to like domestic products. The panel in *EC – Asbestos* took the view that this does not mean that the "identical" measure must apply to like domestic products; rather, that there is an *equivalent* measure for like domestic products.[302] We agree with this view. The very fact that one is enforced at the border and the other in the market may imply that measures are not identical. However, what matters is whether they are designed to achieve the same result.[303]

273.   Indonesia submits that there is an equivalent measure that applies to domestic chicken meat, pointing to certain provisions in MoA Decree 306/1994.[304] As stated in its title, the Decree governs the slaughtering and handling of poultry meat and its by-products.[305] It provides in Article 22(c) that a place for selling poultry meat in the market must "be provided with a table having a porcelain covered or other non-corrosive and smooth material for selling fresh poultry meat and be equipped with cooler facilities (refrigerator and or freezer) for selling chilled-fresh and or frozen poultry meat". Thus, frozen poultry meat cannot be sold in markets, including traditional wet markets, unless there is a cold storage facility. Similarly, Article 23 of the Decree provides that frozen meat and chilled-fresh poultry meat which is offered for sale in meat shops and supermarkets must be stored in cold storage. Generally, therefore, domestic frozen and chilled products are subject to a cold storage requirement when sold in the domestic market.

274.   In comparing these provisions to the intended use requirement, we note that the latter does not prescribe any cold storage requirement. Instead the intended use requirement effectively prohibits the sale in traditional markets whether or not they have cold storage facilities. Thus, the aim and content of the intended use requirement are substantially different from those of MoA Decree 306/1994.[306] We, therefore, find that there is no measure applying to domestic products that is equivalent to the intended use requirement as enacted through MoA 58/2015.

---

[302]   Panel Report, *EC – Asbestos*, paras. 8.91-8.95.
[303]   See Panel Report, *EC – Asbestos*, para. 8.92. (noting that "the regulations applicable to domestic and foreign products lead to the same result".)
[304]   MoA Decree 306/1994 of the Minister of Agriculture concerning Slaughtering of Poultry and Handling of Poultry Meat and its By-products (MoA Decree 306/1994) (Exhibit IDN-83).
[305]   We note that the Decree applies to chicken meat, not differentiating whether domestic or imported.
[306]   We also note that they have differing scopes insofar as the intended use requirement, *de jure*, applies to any kind of imported chicken, including fresh chicken, whereas the cold storage requirement under MoA Decree 306/1994 only applies to chilled and frozen chicken.

275.   Given the absence of an equivalent measure that applies to domestic like products, we conclude that the intended use requirement cannot be considered an internal measure for the purposes of Article III:4 of the GATT 1994. Article III:4, therefore, does not apply. As noted above, the question whether Article III:4 applies to the exclusion of Article XI of the GATT 1994 and Article 4.2 of the Agreement on Agriculture, therefore, is not relevant.

7.5.2.3   Whether the intended use requirement is inconsistent with Article XI of the GATT 1994

276.   We next turn to Brazil's claim under Article XI of the GATT 1994. We note that Indonesia's argument that Article XI does not apply was based on the premise that Article III:4 would apply. As seen above, this is not the case. In the alternative, Indonesia argues that Article 4.2 of the Agreement on Agriculture is *lex specialis* and on this ground maintains that Article XI does not apply.[307] As seen in section 7.2.3.2 above, we disagree with this view and have decided to examine Article XI before Article 4.2 throughout this report.

277.   We have discussed Article XI in section 7.4.2.2 above with regard to the positive list requirement. As we did with the positive list requirement, we structure our analysis of the intended use requirement around the following two questions: (1) Whether the intended use requirement is a prohibition or restriction on the importation of chicken meat and chicken products, and (2) whether it is made effective through quotas, import or export licences or other measures.

278.   As regards the first question, Brazil submits that the intended use requirement is a "restriction". Brazil points to the "restricted access of imported chicken meat and chicken products to the most important consumer markets in Indonesia, adversely affecting the competitive opportunities of the exported products".[308]

279.   The Appellate Body identified the meaning of the term "restriction" as "[a] thing which restricts someone or something, a limitation on action, a limiting condition or regulation" and concluded from it, that it is "generally, ... something that has a limiting effect".[309] Furthermore, in a contextual reading of the title of Article XI[310], the Appellate Body concluded that the limiting effect must be "on the quantity or amount of a product being imported".[311]

280.   As we noted above, the intended use requirement operates as a condition on the importation of chicken meat and chicken products. The importer must

---

[307]   Indonesia's first written submission, para. 178.
[308]   Brazil's first written submission, para. 195.
[309]   Appellate Body Reports, *China – Raw Materials*, para. 319 (quoting from the *Shorter Oxford English Dictionary*, 6th edn, W.R. Trumble, A. Stevenson (eds) (Oxford University Press, 2007), Vol. 2, p. 2553). See also Appellate Body Reports, *Argentina - Import Measures*, para. 5.217.
[310]   Article XI is entitled "General Elimination of Quantitative Restrictions".
[311]   Appellate Body Reports, *China – Raw Materials*, para. 320.

commit to not selling in modern (chicken meat) and in traditional markets (chicken meat and processed chicken) in order to obtain an MoA Import Recommendation and ultimately an MoT Import Approval. Breach of this condition results in the imposition of strict sanctions, including not permitting the importer to import any chicken meat whatsoever. Thus, while quantities of imported products are not directly regulated, the way the condition operates directly impacts on the volume imported: With more than 70 % of the market *de jure* inaccessible, "importers are not free to import as much as they desire or need".[312] Thus, the possibilities for export to Indonesia are reduced from the outset.[313] We, therefore, find that the intended use requirement is a "restriction" on imports within the meaning of Article XI of the GATT 1994.

281.   We turn to the second question, namely whether the restriction is made effective through quotas, import or export licences or other measures. We recall that the intended use requirement operates as a condition upon importation. Thus, the issuance of an MoA Import Recommendation, which in turn, is necessary to obtain an MoT Import Approval, is directly dependent on the importer committing to the allowed uses. As noted previously, the MoT Import Approval operates as a licence in that it constitutes the permission required to import chicken meat and chicken products into Indonesia.[314] Thus, we consider that the restriction is made effective through a licence.

282.   Since both questions are answered in the positive, we, therefore, find that the intended use requirement as enacted through MoA 58/2015 is inconsistent with Article XI of the GATT 1994.

7.5.2.4   Whether the intended use requirement is justified under Article XX(b) or (d) of the GATT 1994

283.   Indonesia raises a defence under Article XX(b) and (d) of the GATT 1994, essentially arguing that the intended use requirement serves to ensure that frozen chicken is not sold in markets without proper refrigeration facilities.[315] Brazil rejects the defence submitting that Indonesia has not met its evidentiary burden.[316]

284.   We have discussed Article XX in section 7.4.2.3 above with regard to the positive list requirement. As we noted in that section, an analysis under Article XX requires us to proceed in two steps. We first need to assess whether the measure is provisionally justified under the specific sub-paragraphs identified by the respondent – here subparagraphs (b) and (d). If that is the case, we go on to

---

[312]   Panel Reports, *Argentina – Import Measures*, para. 6.256.
[313]   See similar situation in Panel Reports, *Argentina – Import Measures*, para. 6.256.
[314]   See para. 7.117 above.
[315]   Indonesia's first written submission, paras 188-216. See in particular, para. 206.
[316]   Brazil's second written submission, paras. 58-77.

examine whether the measure satisfies the requirements of the chapeau of Article XX.

285.   Furthermore, we recall that the burden of proof in respect of an exception generally is on the responding party.[317]

7.5.2.4.1   Article XX(b)[318]

286.   Turning to the first step in our analysis under Article XX, we examine whether the intended use requirement is provisionally justified under subparagraph (b) of Article XX. Subparagraph (b) covers measures that are "necessary to protect human, animal or plant life or health".

287.   Indonesia argues that the intended use requirement serves to prevent a risk to human health in terms of food safety which, it argues, arises from improper thawing and re-freezing of previously frozen chicken.[319] Brazil considers that there is no meaningful connection between the measure and its purported objective and that the measure is not necessary.[320]

288.   There are two elements that we need to examine, namely whether the intended use requirement (1) pursues a human health objective, and (2) is necessary to achieve that objective.

7.5.2.4.1.1   Whether the intended use requirement pursues a human health objective

289.   As regards the first element, we follow previous panels in proceeding in two steps in the examination of this element.[321] Thus, we first establish whether Indonesia has demonstrated that there is a health risk. If such a risk is found, we proceed to examine whether the objective of the intended use requirement is to reduce that risk.

---

[317]   See para. 7.122 above.

[318]   We note that Indonesia's defence under Article XX(b) raises a food safety issue. We observe that the SPS Agreement, according to its Preamble, "elaborates rules for the application of the provisions of the GATT 1994 which relate to the use of sanitary or phytosanitary measures, in particular the provisions of Article XX(b)". Brazil, in its panel request, made a number of claims under the SPS Agreement, which it, however, did not develop in its submissions. In its response to a question from the Panel, Brazil took the view that it would have been for Indonesia to "claim" that the challenged measures are SPS (or TBT) measures (see Brazil's response to Panel's question No.1). We do not share the view that it would be for the responding party to make a "claim" that a measure is in the nature of an SPS measure. It is for a complaining party to raise claims under the specific covered agreements, not for the responding party to "invoke" such agreements. In our view, therefore, in the absence of evidence and arguments submitted by Brazil, we cannot address any SPS claims, even if we were to consider that they are applicable. See Appellate Body Report, *US – Gambling*, para. 281 (citing Appellate Body Report *Chile - Price Band System*, para. 173).

[319]   See Indonesia's second written submission, paras. 138-139.

[320]   See Brazil's opening statement at the first meeting of the Panel, para. 61; and Brazil's second written submission, para. 62.

[321]   Panel Reports, *Brazil – Retreaded Tyres*, paras. 7.42 and 7.43; and *EC – Asbestos*, para. 8.170.

Whether Indonesia has demonstrated that there is a health risk

290.   Indonesia's argument generally is that freezing and thawing increases microbial growth and facilitates product deterioration.[322] While Indonesia's argument initially emphasized the issue of re-freezing thawed chicken,[323] its subsequent submissions focus on the issue of improper thawing, and in particular thawing in tropical temperatures as these are the temperatures found in Indonesia's outdoor traditional markets.[324] In support of its argument, Indonesia submits the following evidence:

> a. A scientific publication on the "Differentiation of Deboned Fresh Chicken Thigh Meat from the Frozen-Thawed One Processed with Different Deboning Conditions".[325] (Sik Bae et al. study)
>
> b. A scientific publication regarding the "Effects of Freeze-Thaw Cycles on Lipid Oxidation and Myowater in Broiler Chicken".[326] (Ali et al. study)
>
> c. Advice that can be found on the website of the US Department of Agriculture.[327] The advice directly refers to the risk of foodborne illnesses by leaving chicken meat out to thaw for more than two hours at room temperature.
>
> d. A reference to an EU Regulation on the hygiene of foodstuffs, which requires food businesses to undertake thawing "of foodstuffs ..... in such a way as to minimize the risk of growth of pathogenic microorganisms or the formation of toxins in the foods" and stipulates that "[d]uring thawing, foods are to be subjected to temperatures that would not

---

[322]   Indonesia's first written submission, para. 191.

[323]   See Indonesia's first written submission, para. 134.

[324]   See Indonesia's opening statement at the first meeting of the Panel, para. 66; second written submission, para. 139; opening statement at the second meeting of the Panel, para. 42; comment on Brazil's response to Panel question No. 85, paras. 41-44; comment on Brazil's response to Panel question No. 90, paras. 56-60; and comment on Brazil's response to Panel question No. 90, para. 68.

[325]   Y. S. Bae, J. C. Lee, S. Jung, H. Kim, S.Y. Jeon, D.H. Park, S. L and C. Jo, Differentiation of Debone Fresh Chicken Thigh Meat from the Frozen-Thawed one Processed with Different Deboning Conditions, Korean Journal for Food Science of Animal Resources, Feb. 2014, at 1 (*Sik Bae et al. study*)(Exhibit IDN-64/IDN-69).

[326]   S. Ali, N. Rajput, C. Li, W. Zhang and G. Zhou, Effect of Freeze-Thaw Cycles on Lipid Oxidation and Myowater in Broiler Chickens, 18(1) Brazilian Journal of Poultry Science 35 (2016) (Ali et al. study) (Exhibit IDN-56).

[327]   United States Department of Agriculture, "The Big Thaw – Safe Defrosting Methods for Consumers" (Exhibit IDN-85).

result in a risk to health.[328] The regulation does not specify what temperature that is.[329,330]

291. Brazil contests the existence of a risk arising from thawing frozen chicken at outside temperatures. It points to the food safety benefits of freezing meat[331] and submits that "the freezing process the imported chicken undergoes [...] is capable of ensuring that the meat will remain fresh for a longer period, as compared to meat that has never been frozen".[332] As for multiple freezing, Brazil considers that the issue of re-freezing bears no relation to the measure at issue or can be addressed through other measures.[333] In support of its position Brazil submits two scientific publications:

a. A 2015 publication in the Brazilian Journal of Poultry Science discussing the "Meat Quality of Chicken Breast Subjected to Different Thawing Methods" ("Oliveira *et al.* paper").[334]

b. A 2005 Research Note in the (US) Journal of Food Protection on the "Growth of Salmonella Serovars, Escherichia coli O157:H7 and Staphylococcus aureus during Thawing of Whole Chicken and Retail Ground Beef Portions at 22 and 30°C" ("Ingham *et al.* research note").[335]

292. We note that it is uncontested between the parties that the traditional markets currently do not (or only marginally) have cold storage facilities available.[336] In the absence of such facilities, frozen meat would have to be sold

---

[328] Regulation EC No. 852/2004 of the European Parliament and of the Council on the Hygiene of Foodstuffs of 29 April 2004 (Exhibit IDN-84). See in particular, Chapter IX, para. 7.

[329] We note however that Article 1(c) of the regulation states:

Article 1

Scope

1. This Regulation lays down general rules for food business operators on the hygiene of foodstuffs, taking particular account of the following principles:

...

(c) it is important, for food that cannot be stored safely at ambient temperatures, particularly frozen food, to maintain the cold chain;

[330] Indonesia also submitted two exhibits (Exhibit IDN-150 and IDN-151) referring to relevant Brazilian legislation. However, Indonesia did not submit an English translation of these exhibits.

[331] See Brazil's second written submission, para. 62; and opening statement at the second meeting of the Panel, para. 57. See also Brazil's response to Panel question No. 90.

[332] See Brazil's second written submission, para. 62.

[333] See Brazil's second written submission, paras. 62-65.

[334] OLIVEIRA *et al* (2015), Meat Quality of Chicken Breast Subjected to Different Thawing Methods. Brazilian Journal of Poultry Science. v.17, n.2, p. 165-172 (Oliveira *et al.* paper). (Exhibit BRA-57).

[335] INGHAM *et al* (2005), Growth of Salmonella Serovars, Escherichia coli O157:H7, and Staphylococcus aureus during Thawing of Whole Chicken and Retail Ground Beef Portions at 22 and 30°C. Journal of Food Protection, v. 68, n. 7, pp. 1457–1461 (Ingham *et al.* research note). (Exhibit BRA-58).

[336] Brazil's opening statement at the second meeting of the Panel, para. 16; Indonesia's first written submission, para. 130. However, see discussion on the possibilities to put cold storage facilities on those markets, para. 7.267 below.

thawing at tropical temperatures. It is in this factual context that the parties discuss the above risks. What they do not discuss is the situation prevailing in what the relevant legislation refers to as "modern markets". Our understanding is that modern markets usually do have cold storage facilities and thus, the above discussion is not pertinent to that situation. A first observation to be made, therefore, is that Indonesia does not put forward arguments to justify the intended use requirement to the extent it applies to modern markets.[337]

293.   Turning to the risks discussed in the context of traditional markets, we note that the issue of re-freezing, only arises if and when meat has been allowed to thaw in the first place. Our focus at this point of the analysis, therefore, is to establish whether Indonesia has demonstrated that a risk to human health arises from leaving chicken meat to thaw outside at tropical temperatures. If it has, we do not need to discuss whether re-freezing constitutes an (additional) risk. We observe that the above-mentioned scientific publications submitted by Indonesia do not directly discuss food safety risks arising from thawing frozen meat at tropical temperatures. Both studies focus on other topics and all the thawing methods applied during these studies were carried out in controlled temperatures below 10° C rather than in room or tropical temperatures.[338] We note, however, that the Ali et al. study refers to thawing in the refrigerator as the "most common and widely preferred method of thawing frozen food".[339] The USDA advice, in contrast, is directly pertinent to the risk discussed. As noted above, it refers to the risk of foodborne illnesses by leaving chicken meat out to thaw for more than two hours at room temperature. We are mindful that the website publication is not a scientific publication itself. However, as official expert advice from a governmental source, we consider that it has some evidentiary weight. Moreover, the advice is corroborated not only by the above-mentioned reference in the scientific publication[340], but more importantly and more explicitly by the two scientific publications that Brazil itself has submitted. The Oliveira et al. paper, in several places, refers to this view citing other scientific publications, as well as a relevant legal standard in Brazilian law.[341] Furthermore, as we understand it, the very purpose of the second paper, namely the Ingham et al. research note, is to challenge that mainstream view which it describes as "longstanding advice from experts".[342] *Thus, in setting out to contest it, the*

---

[337]   As noted in para. 7.200 above, only preserved and prepared chicken meat can be sold in modern markets, carcass cannot.

[338]   The Sik Bae et al. study focuses on the quality of three categories of deboned chicken thigh meat: (a) slaughtered and deboned in the same plant; (b) slaughtered, deboned, frozen and thawed in the same plant; and (c) slaughtered in a plant, deboned in a different plant, but then transferred to the original plant, see *Sik Bae et al. study* (Exhibit IDN-64/IDN-69). The Ali et al. study focuses on the influence of freezing-thawing cycles on lipid oxidation and myowater contents and distribution in chicken breast meat, see Ali et al. study (Exhibit IDN-56).

[339]   See Ali et al. study (Exhibit IDN-56), p. 36

[340]   See fn 327.

[341]   See Oliveira *et al*, paper (Exhibit BRA-57), pp. 167-168.

[342]   See Brazil's response to Panel question No. 90, citing Ingham *et al.* research note (Exhibit BRA-58).

Ingham et al. research note, proves that the currently prevailing view in science is that there is a risk in thawing frozen meat at room temperatures and, therefore, a fortiori at tropical temperatures.

294.   Under these circumstances, we consider that Indonesia has demonstrated the existence of a risk arising from thawing frozen chicken at tropical temperatures. We further consider that while Brazil has submitted a scientific publication demonstrating that there is no such risk, that publication, at best, represents a divergent view.[343] The existence *of a divergent view would not prevent Indonesia from relying on the above view which, as the evidence shows, happens to be the currently prevailing view in science.*[344] Brazil's reference to the Ingham et al. research note, therefore, does not suffice to rebut Indonesia's assertion that there is a risk to human health.

295.   We, therefore, find that Indonesia has established that there is a risk to human health arising from thawing meat at tropical temperatures.

Whether the objective of the intended use requirement is to reduce that risk

296.   We next address the question whether the objective of the intended use requirement is to reduce that risk.

297.   Indonesia states that "the intended use requirement was designed to ensure that only *safe* imported chicken is sold in markets facilities".[345] For Indonesia this means "that frozen chicken cannot be sold in markets without proper cold storage".[346]

298.   Brazil argues "that there is no meaningful connection between limiting the sale of frozen chicken to places with cold chain facilities and the objective of ☐eliminating the risk of [frequent] freezing and thawing products for sale to consumers.☐"[347]

299.   We note that the task of ascertaining the objective pursued by a measure under Article XX(b) is similar to the task in Article XX(a) or (d). We, therefore, consider the case law referred to above in our analysis on Article XX(d) to be relevant also here.[348]

---

[343]   We do not take a view on the scientific value of this research note.

[344]   *We refer to the Appellate Body's jurisprudence in EC – Hormones which we read to suggest that a Member may base its measure on scientifically sound evidence, no matter whether that evidence represents a mainstream scientific view or a divergent/minority view. In other words, if there are mutually contradictory but equally respectable scientific opinions on a given question, a Member is free to base its measure on either opinion, see* Appellate Body Reports, *EC – Hormones*, para. 194; and *US – Continued Suspension / Canada – Continued Suspension*, para. 591.

[345]   Indonesia's first written submission, paras. 189 and 207 (emphasis original).

[346]   Indonesia's first written submission, para. 189.

[347]   Brazil's second written submission, para. 62.

[348]   In *Colombia – Textiles*, the Appellate Body held that while the terms "to protect" under paragraph (a) and "to secure compliance" under paragraph (d) of Article XX differ both terms involve establishing the existence of a relationship between the measure and those objectives. See Appellate Body Report, *Colombia – Textiles*, paras. 5.126-5.127.

300.   As noted above, the Appellate Body has described the relevant test under Article XX(d) as "an initial examination of the relationship between the inconsistent measure and the relevant laws or regulations" which requires a panel to "scrutinize the design of the measures sought to be justified".[349] The Appellate Body further clarified that the standard for ascertaining whether such a relationship exists is whether the assessment of the design of the measure reveals that the measure is *not incapable* of securing compliance with the relevant laws and regulations in Indonesia.[350] Finally, the Appellate Body has described this test as "not... particularly demanding", in contrast to the requirements of the next step of the analysis, namely the necessity test.[351]

301.   Applied *mutatis mutandis* to Article XX(b), we consider that our task is to ascertain whether the measure is *not incapable* of reducing the identified risk to human health.

302.   Applying this standard to the intended use requirement, we observe that it completely prevents the sale of imported frozen chicken in traditional markets. To the extent that no frozen chicken can be sold in such markets, no risks from thawing such chicken can possibly arise. Viewed this way, applying the above standard, the measure must be considered "not incapable" of achieving the objective of protecting human health. That it also prevents the sale of frozen chicken that is perfectly safe, is a question that matters to our necessity analysis. On this basis, we find that there is a relationship between the intended use requirement and the objective of protecting human health.

7.5.2.4.1.2   Whether the intended use requirement is necessary to protect human health

303.   Having established that the intended use requirement pursues the objective of protecting human health, we now address the second element of the test under Article XX(b), namely whether the measure is necessary to achieve that objective.

304.   As seen above, the "necessity" test involves a process of "weighing and balancing" a series of factors, including (1) the importance of the objective, (2) the contribution of the measure to that objective, and (3) the trade-restrictiveness of the measure.[352] In most cases, (4) a comparison between the challenged measure and possible less trade-restrictive alternatives should then be undertaken. The Appellate Body has also emphasized that "a complaining party must identify any alternative measures that, in its view, the responding party should have taken".[353]

---

[349] Appellate Body Report, *Argentina – Financial Services*, para. 6.203.
[350] Appellate Body Report, *Colombia – Textiles*, para. 5.68.
[351] Appellate Body Report, *Colombia – Textiles*, para. 5.70.
[352] Appellate Body Reports, *EC – Seal Products*, para. 5.169.
[353] Appellate Body Reports, *EC – Seal Products*, para. 5.169 (citing Appellate Body Report, *US – Gambling*, paras. 309-311).

305.   We first observe that the objective pursued through the intended use requirement, as noted above, is the protection of human health, an interest which Indonesia considers of the highest importance. [354] We agree and do not understand Brazil to disagree.

306.   Next we consider the contribution that the intended use requirement makes to protecting that interest. As noted above, the intended use requirement effectively reduces the risks arising from thawing chicken meat at tropical temperatures in the traditional market to a significant degree, since it does not allow any frozen chicken to reach that market. Viewed this way, the intended use requirement makes an important contribution to protecting human health. We observe, however, that the specific risk to human health associated with thawing meat at tropical temperatures, does not arise, for example if frozen chicken remains frozen by being kept, where available, in cold storage. For such perfectly safe chicken, the intended use requirement does not make any contribution to ensuring that (only) safe chicken is sold in the market.[355]

307.   With these considerations in mind, we turn to the third factor, which is the trade-restrictiveness of the measure. As seen above, the intended use requirement operates generally as a trade restriction directly impacting the volume of chicken that may be imported into Indonesia.[356] This restriction most notably affects access to modern markets and traditional markets, which are altogether excluded from the allowed uses. In terms, specifically, of access to traditional markets to which Indonesia's defence under Article XX(b) exclusively relates, the measure operates as a trade restriction to the highest degree.[357] As the Appellate Body made clear in *Brazil – Retreaded Tyres*, such trade-restrictiveness weighs heavily against considering a measure necessary.

---

[354]   Indonesia's first written submission, para. 191.

[355]   We also note, in this context, an argument that Brazil raises and which we understand to relate to the issue of necessity. Brazil refers to an incident that the United States mentioned in its oral statement, para. 7. As stated by the United States and later confirmed by Indonesia in its response to a question from Brazil, some 9000 tons of frozen meat were authorized to be sold in Indonesia's traditional markets in June 2016. Brazil considers that "this is evidence enough that the measure at issue is not necessary to fulfil Indonesia's policy objective, as the government itself does envisage some flexibility in the enforcement of the legislation". (Brazil's second written submission, para. 67.) We note that whether the chicken was sold frozen or in a thawing state is disputed between the parties. We note, furthermore, that Indonesia refers to exceptional circumstances in which the decision was made to authorize the sale (see Indonesia's response to Brazil's question No. 2). In our view, a one-time authorization, per se, cannot prove whether a measure is "necessary" in the context of Article XX. We do not exclude that it could be a relevant factor in a necessity analysis. However, in order to take this element into account, a careful consideration of the specific circumstances would be required. We consider that we do not have enough facts on hand to carry out such an examination. However, this issue can be left open, if we find that there is no necessity, based on other reasons.

[356]   See section 7.5.2.3 above.

[357]   See also Panel Report, *Brazil – Retreaded Tyres*, para. 7.211.

Depending on the circumstances, however, a material contribution made by the measure may still outweigh that trade-restrictiveness.[358]

308.   As seen above, we have some doubts whether the intended use requirement can be seen as making an important contribution. We acknowledge that it significantly reduces the risks arising from thawing chicken at tropical temperatures and, thus, materially contributes to preventing that risk. In doing so, however, the intended use requirement prevents the sale of frozen chicken in traditional markets, including of chicken that would *not* present the above risk, and in particular, chicken that is being kept frozen in cold storage, where available. In respect of such *safe* chicken the measure makes no contribution to achieving any objective. Put differently, the measure "overshoots" its intended objective, which, as Indonesia states, is to "ensure that only *safe* imported chicken is sold in markets facilities".[359]

309.   However, we are mindful that the Appellate Body cautioned panels not to consider as a pre-determined legal standard that a measure would have to make a "material contribution" in order for it to be necessary, despite being trade-restrictive in the extreme. The Appellate Body emphasized in this respect that all "dimensions" of necessity will have to be explored, including that of less trade-restrictive alternatives.[360] We, therefore, turn to consider Brazil's arguments regarding less trade-restrictive alternatives.

310.   In terms of less trade-restrictive alternatives, Brazil first pointed to labelling requirements, rules regulating the thawing of frozen chicken to be offered for sale[361], and restricting the possibility of refreezing previously thawed chicken for sale in traditional markets.[362] In its response to a question from the Panel, Brazil furthermore presented the following list:

> (a) a requirement limiting the number of times a product may undergo a freezing-thawing cycle;

> (b) requirement limiting the shelf-life of products that underwent more than one freezing-thawing cycle;

> (c) a requirement introducing guidelines for methods of thawing, especially for room-temperature thawing;

> (d) a requirement introducing a mandatory good hygienic practice (GHP) plan for establishment selling chicken meat;

> (e) provision of information to consumers that the product was previously frozen and should not be refrozen.[363]

---

[358]   Appellate Body Report, *Brazil – Retreaded Tyres*, para. 172. See also Appellate Body Reports *EC- Seal Products*, para. 5.215.
[359]   See Indonesia's first written submission, para. 189.
[360]   Appellate Body Reports, *EC – Seal Products*, para. 5.214.
[361]   Brazil's opening statement at first meeting of the Panel, para.62.
[362]   Brazil's second written submission, para. 64.
[363]   Brazil's response to Panel question No. 99.

311.   To us, the above proposed alternative measures can be divided in two categories. First, those that (potentially) address Indonesia's concern regarding the thawing of chicken meat at tropical temperatures in the market, namely (c) and (d) above. Second, those that address potential concerns regarding the refreezing of previously frozen chicken, namely (a), (b) and (e) above.

312.   Turning to the first category, in assessing Brazil's reference to "labelling requirements", we consider that such broad reference, without any explanation of what the label should state, is not sufficient. Given that Brazil takes the view that thawing chicken at tropical temperatures may be safe, it is not even possible to second-guess what the content of such labels should be. If Brazil is suggesting that the label should simply inform the consumer that chicken meat was previously frozen, we consider that such label would not address Indonesia's health concern.

313.   Similarly, as regards rules or guidelines regulating the thawing of chicken, we note that Brazil neither explains what the rules should be nor how they should apply in a traditional market. At the same time, we must assume that the alternative measures identified by Brazil are based on its view that thawing chicken in tropical temperatures is safe. Therefore, the alternative measures do not address Indonesia's own perception of the risks involved. As Indonesia points out, thawing should take place in a cold storage facility.[364]

314.   Finally, while Brazil proposes mandatory good hygienic practices as an alternative measure, which, as Indonesia argues, is already being applied, Brazil does not explain how this would address Indonesia's concern about thawing frozen chicken at tropical temperatures.

315.   Turning to the second category, namely measures relating to refreezing of previously frozen chicken, as stated previously, we note that Indonesia's concern primarily relates to thawing chicken at tropical temperatures. The alternative measures that Brazil proposes in respect of the re-freezing issue, however, do not address that concern. To the contrary, the proposed alternative measures address a concern that would only arise, if it were possible to sell thawed chicken. We, therefore, do not need to consider this category further.[365]

316.   We are, thus, in a situation where the less trade-restrictive alternative measures proposed by the complaining party cannot be meaningfully integrated in our necessity analysis. However, there is a concrete less trade-restrictive alternative which is plainly before us insofar as Indonesia, in the meantime, has enacted it in its legislation. We recall that the intended use requirement in the version that we are examining prohibits access to traditional markets altogether, irrespective of whether or not they may have cold storage facilities. As we will further discuss below, a subsequent amendment to this measure, enacted through MoA 34/2016, provides that imported frozen chicken meat may be sold in

---

[364] Indonesia's comments on Brazil's response to Panel question No. 99.
[365] See para. 7.213 above. See also Indonesia's comments on Brazil's response to Panel question No. 99, para. 68.

markets with cold storage facilities. As is clear from Brazil's comments on this later version, Brazil considers this new version to also be WTO-inconsistent despite the cold storage requirement, which may be the reason why it has not proposed the latter as a less trade-restrictive alternative.[366]

317.   We are mindful that the Appellate Body has cautioned panels not to take it upon themselves "to rebut the claim (or defence) where the responding party (or complaining party) itself has not done so".[367] However, the Appellate Body has also held that where a defence or rebuttal of a defence has been made, a panel may rule on the defence "relying on arguments advanced by the parties or developing its own reasoning".[368]

318.   We believe that, for the purposes of our analysis here, we can consider the cold storage requirement as a less-trade restrictive alternative, for the following reasons: First, given the subsequent legislative developments, we have before us evidence that this is an alternative measure that is reasonably available and meets Indonesia's objective.[369] Second, Indonesia's defence of the intended use requirement, in fact, reads like a reference to, and anticipation of, this subsequent legislation. In other words, we do not see Indonesia defending a complete ban from traditional markets, as enacted through MoA 58/2015, but rather the cold storage requirement as enacted through MoA 34/2016. Indonesia, for example, in discussing necessity, states the following: "Thus, by *requiring importers* to import frozen and chilled chicken meat and products to be sold *only in markets that have a proper cold-chain systems*...is capable of making and does make some contribution...".[370] The intended use requirement as enacted through MoA 58/2015, which Indonesia defends pertinently with this statement, notably does not require cold storage, but prohibits access to traditional markets altogether. Third, while Brazil does not suggest cold storage, it does, as seen above, suggest *inter alia* "rules regulating the thawing of frozen chicken to be offered for sale" as a less trade-restrictive alternative measure.[371] In our view a cold storage requirement could be considered to fall under "rules regulating the thawing of frozen chicken".

319.   For the above reasons we consider the cold storage requirement as a relevant factor in our necessity analysis. In weighing and balancing all factors

---

[366]   Brazil's second written submission, para. 62; and opening statement at the second meeting of the Panel, para. 16.
[367]   Appellate Body Report, *US – Gambling*, para. 282. See also Appellate Body Report, *Japan – Agricultural Products II*, para. 130.
[368]   Appellate Body Report, *US – Gambling*, para. 282. See also Appellate Body Reports, *EC – Hormones*, para. 156; and *US – Certain EC Products*, para. 123.
[369]   See Panel Reports, *China – Raw Materials*, para. 7.25 (citing Appellate Body Reports, *China – Publications and Audiovisual Products*, para. 177; *China - Auto Parts*, para. 225; *US - Section 211 Appropriations Act*, para. 105; and *India - Patents (US)*, para. 65). See also Appellate Body Report, *EC – Selected Customs Matters*, para. 188.
[370]   Indonesia's first written submission, para. 191. (emphasis added)
[371]   See Brazil's opening statement at the first meeting of the Panel, para. 62; and second written submission, para. 64.

together in a holistic assessment, we recall the trade-restrictiveness of the measure and the ambivalent nature of the contribution. Mindful of these factors and given that an alternative less-trade-restrictive measure exists that equally meets Indonesia's objective, we conclude that the measure does not comply with the requirements of the necessity test.

320.   We therefore find that the intended use requirement is not provisionally justified under Article XX(b).

7.5.2.4.2   Article XX(d)

321.   We now turn to the second defence that Indonesia has raised under Article XX, namely Article XX(d).

322.   Indonesia submits that the intended use requirement secures compliance with relevant provisions in Indonesian law which require that imported food must be safe. In addition, Indonesia refers to consumer protection pointing to the risk of consumers mistaking thawed chicken for fresh chicken when buying chicken in the traditional market.[372]

323.   Brazil submits that Indonesia failed to provide any evidence that the intended use requirement contributes to the enforcement of any particular law or regulation. Brazil also argues that "Indonesia has not indicated whether there would not be any less trade-restrictive alternative measures to secure compliance with its laws and regulations".[373]

324.   As set out in section 7.4.2.3 above, Article XX(d) covers measures "necessary to secure compliance with laws or regulations which are not inconsistent with the provisions of this Agreement [...]".

325.   We have already examined the food safety aspects in our analysis under Article XX(b). Under its Article XX(d) defence, Indonesia refers to the need to enforce relevant provisions in Indonesian Law that pursue the objective of protecting human health, including food safety, as discussed in sub-paragraph (b). In our view, therefore, the outcome of our analysis in sub-paragraph (d) here would not differ from our analysis in sub-paragraph (b) above. Our analysis below, therefore, will focus on consumer deception, an aspect of Indonesia's defence under Article XX that has not been covered so far.

326.   As we have noted in section paragraph 7.4.2.3 above, our assessment under Article XX(d) requires us to address the following two questions: (1) whether the intended use requirement is designed to secure compliance with laws or regulations that are not themselves inconsistent with the GATT 1994; and (2) whether the intended use requirement is necessary to secure compliance with such laws and regulations. We address these questions in turn.

---

[372] Indonesia's first written submission, paras. 203-206. Indonesia also refers to "customs enforcement", but does not develop any arguments subsequently.
[373] Brazil's second written submission, paras. 69 and 71.

7.5.2.4.2.1 Whether the intended use requirement is designed to secure compliance with laws and regulations that are not themselves inconsistent with the GATT 1994

327. Indonesia refers to Law 8/1999 (Consumer Protection), which, as it submits, "requires entrepreneurs to provide honest information about the condition and quality of products".[374] Indonesia argues that the intended use requirement is designed to ensure that imported frozen chicken meat and products are not sold in markets without proper refrigeration facilities. The sanctions, according to Indonesia, are designed to prevent importers from engaging in deceptive practices.[375] The deceptive practices Indonesia describes refer to "consumers being misled into buying thawed products believing they were fresh products".[376]

328. As noted previously, the legal standard as clarified by the Appellate Body requires a panel to apply "an initial examination of the relationship between the inconsistent measure and the relevant laws or regulations". A panel, thus, must "scrutinize the design of the measures sought to be justified".[377] The Appellate Body further clarified that the standard for ascertaining whether such a relationship exists is whether the assessment of the design of the measure reveals that the measure is *not incapable* of securing compliance with the relevant laws and regulations in Indonesia.[378] Finally, we note that the Appellate Body has described this test as "not... particularly demanding", in contrast to the requirements of the next step of the analysis, namely the necessity test.[379]

329. It is our understanding that Indonesian law does not specifically describe the passing off of thawed chicken as fresh chicken as a deceptive practice. However, we agree with Indonesia that it would be deceptive for a consumer to buy thawed chicken in the belief that it is freshly slaughtered chicken. We do not understand Brazil to disagree with that point. Thus, a measure designed to prevent consumer deception, could be considered to be a measure designed to secure compliance with Indonesian consumer protection laws. Furthermore, Brazil has not called into question the consistency of these laws with the GATT 1994, and we agree with Indonesia that it must, therefore, be presumed.[380]

330. In examining the design, structure and architecture of the measure we refer to our observation above, that the intended use requirement completely prevents the sale of imported frozen chicken in traditional markets. If no frozen chicken can be sold in such markets, sellers cannot readily engage in the deceptive practice of misleading consumers into buying thawed chicken. Viewed

---

[374] Indonesia's first written submission, para. 203.
[375] Indonesia's first written submission, para. 206.
[376] Indonesia's comments on Brazil's response to Panel question No. 99.
[377] Appellate Body Report, *Argentina – Financial Services*, para. 6.203.
[378] Appellate Body Report, *Colombia – Textiles*, paras. 5.68.
[379] Appellate Body Report, *Colombia – Textiles*, para. 5.70.
[380] Indonesia's first written submission, para. 205.

this way, and in applying the above standard, on the basis of its design, structure and operation, the measure must be considered to be "not incapable" of achieving the objective of securing compliance with Indonesia's consumer protection law. That it prevents the sale of chicken altogether is a different issue that is relevant to our necessity analysis. On this basis we find, that there is a relationship between the intended use requirement and the objective to secure compliance with the relevant laws and regulations.

Whether the intended use requirement is necessary to secure compliance with such laws and regulations

331. Turning to the necessity test, we examine the different factors as outlined in paragraph 7.136 above.

332. In terms of the importance of the objective pursued, we acknowledge the importance of the protection of consumers from deceptive practices, to which Indonesia refers.[381]

333. Regarding the contribution that the measure makes in achieving this objective, we note Indonesia's argument that "sanctions in case of lack of compliance contribute to preventing local sellers from sourcing frozen chicken meat, thawing it, and selling it as fresh chicken meat in markets without proper refrigeration facilities".[382] Indonesia submits that this "decreases [the] incidence of deceptive practices".[383] We are not persuaded by this argument. First of all, sanctions for breach of the intended use requirement apply to the importer, not to the local seller, who would be the one engaging in deceptive practices. Second, the prohibition on the sale of imported frozen chicken also applies to sellers who would not engage in deceptive practices, but would be selling either frozen or thawed chicken with the information that it was previously frozen. Based on these considerations, we are not convinced that the contribution is, as Indonesia argues, "substantial".[384]

334. As seen above, whether the contribution is substantial/material or not, in turn matters given the trade-restrictiveness of the intended use requirement which weighs heavily against considering the measure necessary.[385]

335. Turning to the issue of a less trade-restrictive alternative, we do not agree with Brazil's suggestion that the burden of putting forward less trade-restrictive alternatives is on Indonesia, a point that has been settled unambiguously in the case law.[386]

---

[381] Indonesia's first written submission, para. 208.
[382] Indonesia's first written submission, para. 207.
[383] *Ibid.*
[384] Indonesia's first written submission, para. 208.
[385] Appellate Body Report, *Brazil – Retreaded Tyres*, para. 150.
[386] Appellate Body Reports, *EC – Seal Products*, para. 5.169, citing Appellate Body Report, *US – Gambling*, paras. 309-311. See also para. 7.122 above.

336.   Furthermore, as regards the less trade-restrictive measures that Brazil itself refers to, we note that Brazil suggests, in particular, that there should be "regulation requiring sellers to inform that the imported product for sale is either frozen or has been 'previously frozen'".[387] These are, as we understand it, two different suggestions with different underlying scenarios. In the first scenario, the chicken is sold frozen. We note that chicken would only remain frozen if it were kept in cold storage. In that scenario, which we discuss above as a possible less trade-restrictive alternative under Article XX(b), the proposed labelling would be unnecessary, because the consumer would see that the chicken is frozen and, thus, could not be deceived into believing that it is fresh. In the second scenario, the chicken sold is "previously frozen", that is, thawing or thawed. This scenario, thus, presumes that the frozen chicken could be sold thawed. In our view, in considering this scenario, we cannot ignore that Indonesia, with the intended use requirement, is also pursuing a health protection objective. We have accepted Indonesia's argument that there is a risk in thawing chicken at tropical temperatures. We have also accepted that labelling, in the manner Brazil proposes, would not address Indonesia's health concern and thus would not achieve Indonesia's objective of protecting human health.[388] Therefore, even if labelling were a less trade-restrictive alternative in respect of the consumer protection objective alone, viewed cumulatively with the other objective pursued by the measure, it is not. We, therefore, do not consider this option as one that we need to discuss further.[389]

337.   This leaves us with the same situation as above under Article XX(b), namely that the less trade-restrictive alternative measures proposed by the complaining party are not such that we can meaningfully integrate them in our holistic analysis of necessity. For similar reasons as set out above, however, we take the view that we can consider as a less trade restrictive alternative the requirement to sell only in markets with cold storage facilities. We recall that Indonesia has enacted a measure through MoA 34/2016 which allows access to traditional markets provided they have cold storage facilities. In Indonesia's own assessment, therefore, this is an alternative measure which achieves Indonesia's objective, *inter alia*, of protecting its consumers against the deceptive practice of passing off thawed chicken as fresh. Indeed, Indonesia's defence under Article XX(d), similar to its defence under Article XX(b), reads as if Indonesia were already referring to its later measure enacted under MoA 34/2016. For example, Indonesia states "that the intended use requirement *prohibits* that imported frozen chicken meat and products are sold in markets *without proper cold-chain systems*" thereby contributing "to ensuring to a great extent that only safe imported chicken is sold to consumers".[390] The intended use requirement that

---

[387]   Brazil's opening statement at second meeting of the Panel, para. 59.
[388]   See para. 7.232. above.
[389]   We, therefore, can leave open the question of whether Brazil has provided enough detail in respect of this alternative.
[390]   Indonesia's first written submission, para. 207.

Indonesia seeks to defend with this statement, however, is no such prohibition; it is a prohibition of access to traditional markets altogether, whether or not they have cold storage facilities. For these reasons we consider the cold storage requirement as a factor relevant to our necessity analysis.

338.   In weighing and balancing all factors together we recall the trade-restrictiveness of the measure and the ambivalent nature of the contribution. Mindful of these factors and given that an alternative less-trade-restrictive measure exists that equally meets Indonesia's objective, we conclude that the measure does not comply with the requirements of the necessity test.

339.   We therefore find that the intended use requirement is not provisionally justified under Article XX(d).

340.   Given the absence of a (provisional) justification under either subparagraph (b) or (d), we see no need to proceed to an analysis under the chapeau of Article XX.

341.   In conclusion, we find that the intended use requirement is inconsistent with Article XI of the GATT 1994 and is not justified under Article XX of the GATT 1994.

7.5.2.5   Whether the intended use requirement is inconsistent with Article 4.2 of the Agreement on Agriculture

342.   As noted in section 7.4.2.4 above, the principle of judicial economy "allows a panel to refrain from making multiple findings that the same measure is *inconsistent* with various provisions when a single, or a certain number of findings of inconsistency, would suffice to resolve the dispute".[391] Thus, panels need address only those claims "which must be addressed in order to resolve the matter in issue in the dispute"[392], and panels "may refrain from ruling on every claim as long as it does not lead to a 'partial resolution of the matter'".[393]

343.   Having found a violation of Article XI of the GATT 1994, we consider that it is not necessary to address Brazil's claim under Article 4.2 of the Agreement on Agriculture in order to secure a positive solution to this dispute.

7.5.3   Analysis of the relevant provisions of MoA 34/2016

344.   Our findings above apply to the intended use requirement as enacted through MoA 58/2015. As noted in the beginning of this section, in the course of the proceedings, MoA 58/2015 was revoked and replaced by MoA 34/2016.

---

[391] Appellate Body Report, *Canada – Wheat Exports and Grain Imports*, para. 133. (emphasis original)

[392] Appellate Body Reports, *US – Wool Shirts and Blouses*, p. 19, DSR 1997:I, p. 340; *US – Tuna II (Mexico)*, para. 403.

[393] Appellate Body Reports, *US – Upland Cotton*, para. 732; and *US – Tuna II (Mexico)*, para. 404.

345.   With this change the parties' arguments have evolved. Indonesia submits that the intended use requirement has expired.[394] Brazil contests this assertion. Brazil also contends that MoA 34/2016 introduced additional features which reinforce the restriction caused by the intended use requirement.[395]

346.   We first describe the relevant provisions at issue before turning to the question of whether their adoption has led to the expiry of the intended use requirement. We, then, consider the question whether the Panel has jurisdiction to review the relevant provisions under MoA 34/2016 against Brazil's claims. If so, we consider whether the modified features of the intended use requirement change the analysis that we provided above in respect of the intended use requirement.

7.5.3.1   Provisions at issue

7.5.3.1.1   Limitation on the intended use to markets with cold chain facilities

347.   We refer to Table 3 above which sets out Article 31(1) of MoA 34/2106. According to this provision imported frozen chicken may be sold in modern and traditional markets provided they have cold chain facilities. It is not disputed between the parties that currently most traditional markets do not have any cold storage facilities.[396] Indonesia explains that almost all traditional markets have access to electricity, that no authorization is required to install cold chain facilities and that the cost for doing so would have to be borne by the entity installing them.[397] Indonesia also refers to recent government plans to revitalize 5,000 traditional markets and open the cold storage industry to foreign investment.[398]

348.   In terms of sanctions applying to breach of the above requirement, Indonesia refers to Article 32(1)(b) which requires importers to abide by the intended uses listed in the MoA Import Recommendation.[399] Pursuant to Article 38(4), a breach of Article 32 may result in a temporary suspension of import recommendation for one year.[400] In addition, we note that Article 38(1) also

---

[394]   See Indonesia's response to Panel question No. 2, where Indonesia describes the intended use requirement as an "expired" measure stating that it has been "removed". See also Indonesia's second written submission, para. 6, where Indonesia states that the intended use requirement has been "eliminated"; and Indonesia's responses to Panel question No. 66(a) and 85.

[395]   Brazil's opening statement at second meeting of the Panel, paras. 15 and 18.

[396]   See Brazil's opening statement at second meeting of the Panel, para.16. See also Indonesia's first written submission, para. 130.

[397]   Indonesia's response to Panel question No. 98.

[398]   Indonesia's response to Panel question No. 98(b).

[399]   See Table 3 above.

[400]   *Ibid.*

provides for sanctions for a breach of Article 4(6) which requires importers to conduct importation in accordance with the MoA Import Recommendation.[401]

7.5.3.1.2   Enforcement of the intended use through distribution plan and weekly distribution report

349.   In addition, MoA 34/2016 has introduced two new provisions, which, Indonesia describes as "part of the enforcement framework to ensure that chilled and frozen chicken meat and chicken products are sold in markets with cold chain facilities".[402]

350.   The first is Article 22(1)(l) of MoA 34/2016 which provides that the application for an MoA Import Recommendation which is to be submitted by the importer shall contain a "distribution plan of carcass, meat, offal and its processed products in accordance to format-2". Format 2[403] requires the importer not only to list country of origin, type of meat and quantity, but also to list the name and address of the buyer, as well as the price.[404]

351.   The second new provision that MoA 34/2016 has introduced is Article 32(3), which provides that the importer "is required to submit a distribution report of the carcass and meat to the Director General online in accordance to format-4 on every Thursday". Format 4[405] requires the importer to submit information on the following five items: (1) Arrival schedule, (2) Import realization, (3) distribution to industry/hotel, restaurant, catering/market with cold chain facility, (4) final stock on the importer, and (5) number of delivery orders. We note that the information required in the distribution plan as described above, in particular, the quantity sold as well as name and address of buyer and the price, must also be submitted through Format 4 (namely in items 2 and 3).

352.   In terms of sanctions, starting with the distribution report, Indonesia refers to Article 38(4) of MoA 34/2016. This provision provides for sanctions for non-submission of the weekly report with a written warning followed by a temporary suspension of the MoA Import Recommendation for one year.[406] As for the distribution plan, Article 38(3)(b) provides that violation of Article

---

[401]   See Table 3 above. We note that subparagraph (6) has been added through MoA 34/2016. No such subparagraph existed in MoA 58/2015.

[402]   Indonesia's response to Panel question No. 88(b).

[403]   We note that Format 2 has the heading "Distribution Plan of Carcass and Meat from Cattle". However, as Indonesia explains, the original Indonesian version translates as "Distribution Plan for carcass, meat, offal and processed products". See Indonesia's response to Panel question No.88(c)(i).

[404]   MoA 34/2016 (Exhibit BRA-48).

[405]   We note that Format 4 has the following heading: "Distribution Plan of Carcass and Meat from Cattle". However, as Indonesia explains, the original Indonesian version translates as "Distribution Plan for carcass, meat, offal and processed products". See Indonesia's response to Panel question No.88(a).

[406]   See Table 3 above. See also Indonesia's response to Panel question No. 88(a).

22(1)(l) may be subject to a temporary suspension of the MoA Import Recommendation for one year.[407]

7.5.3.2 Whether the intended use requirement has expired

353.   Indonesia submits that with the adoption of MoA 34/2016 the intended use requirement has expired. According to Indonesia, this is, because Article 31(1) of MoA 34/2016 "removed the limitation on the specific intended uses referred to by Brazil in its Panel Request".[408] Brazil argues that "the intended use requirement is still in place, now in a new restrictive guise". Brazil explains that "[b]ecause traditional markets have no (or only marginal) cold chain facilities available, Brazilian frozen or chilled chicken will not have access to this segment due to the restriction imposed by Indonesia".[409]

354.   As noted in section 7.2.4.3 above, we agree with Indonesia that the expiry of the measure at issue may have a bearing on whether we can make a recommendation. We consider that a measure has expired if it has ceased to exist.

355.   Indonesia's argument is that the importer now has access to all segments of the markets including traditional markets (provided they have cold chain facilities). Indonesia, therefore, contends that the intended use requirement as a "limitation on the specific intended uses" has been removed with the consequence that the measure no longer exists.[410]

356.   We described in paragraph 7.181 above the intended use requirement as a measure consisting in limiting allowed uses in the market. It is true, as Indonesia points out, that amongst the "allowed uses" there is now also sale in modern and traditional markets, whereas these were not included in the intended use requirement as enacted through MoA 58/2015. However, these allowed uses remain subject to a condition - the cold storage requirement – condition which must be fulfilled in order for the use to be allowed. The condition, thus, directly determines whether or not the use is allowed. Therefore, allowed uses are still limited. That limitation results in the same effect, namely preventing access to traditional markets, since the latter currently do not have (or only marginally have) cold storage facilities.[411] No access to traditional markets in turn means no access to the largest portion of the chicken market in Indonesia.[412]

---

[407] See Table 3 above.

[408] Indonesia's response to Panel question No.85. See also Indonesia's response to Panel question No. 66(a). See also Indonesia's response to Panel question No. 2 and second written submission, para. 6.

[409] Brazil's opening statement at second meeting of the Panel, paras. 15-16.

[410] Indonesia's response to Panel question No. 85.

[411] We recall our conclusion that the cold storage requirement could be a less trade restrictive alternative to not allowing the use of imported chicken products in modern and traditional markets. See para. 7.257 above. We point out that there is a difference between the question of the (continued)

357.   In light of the foregoing, we find that the measure has not ceased to exist and, therefore, that there is no expiry.

7.5.3.3   Whether the intended use requirement, as enacted through the relevant provisions of MoA 34/2016, is WTO-inconsistent as claimed by Brazil

358.   We next turn to the claims which Brazil has raised in respect of the above provisions. Brazil's position essentially is that the intended use requirement continues to be a WTO-inconsistent measure and that the new enforcement provisions (i.e. distribution plan and weekly distribution report) have only reinforced the restrictions.[413] We first establish whether we have jurisdiction before turning to a due process issue which Indonesia has raised.

7.5.3.3.1   Jurisdiction

359.   As regards the cold storage requirement, we note that Article 31(1) of MoA 34/2016, in substance, has amended Article 31(1) and Article 31(2) of MoA 58/2015. Indonesia submits that because the measure, in its view, has expired, its essence is no longer the same.[414] We agree with the underlying logic that our discussion on expiry immediately above, is directly relevant. As we have found, the essence of the intended use requirement is to limit allowed uses in the market, and because this has not changed with the adoption of Article 31(1) of MoA 34/2016, the measure has not expired. That finding implies that the measure, in essence has remained the same. As noted above, in line with the Appellate Body's guidance in *Chile – Price Band System*, we consider that because the measure has in essence remained the same and because the terms of Brazil's Panel request are broad enough, we have jurisdiction to review the intended use requirement as enacted through Article 31(1) of MoA 34/2016.

360.   As regards both the distribution plan and the weekly distribution report, we recall that these are new requirements introduced through MoA 34/2016. In Indonesia's view, they are not covered by the Panel's terms of reference. In that regard, Indonesia reiterates that the intended use requirement has expired. Indonesia also submits that the distribution plan does not relate to or implement the intended use requirement as set out in Brazil's panel request.[415]

361.   As noted above, Indonesia describes these requirements as "part of the enforcement framework to ensure that chilled and frozen chicken meat and

---

existence of a measure and its WTO-consistency. In respect of the WTO-consistency of the amended intended use requirement we assess the latter in section 7.5.3.3 below.

[412]   See para. 7.101 above.

[413]   Brazil's opening statement at second meeting of the Panel, in particular paras. 18 and 21.

[414]   Indonesia's response to Panel question No. 85.

[415]   Indonesia's response to Panel question No.88(e).

chicken products are sold in markets with cold chain facilities".[416] We understand this to mean that these requirements are enforcement provisions for the intended use requirement as laid down in Article 31(1) of MoA 34/2016. Indeed if there were no intended use requirement, i.e. no limitation whatsoever on the use of imported chicken meat, the distribution plan and the weekly report would make little sense. In other words, the *raison d'être* of both the distribution plan and the distribution report is directly contingent on the existence of the intended use requirement. Moreover, we note Brazil's argument that these two requirements reinforce the restrictions caused by the intended use requirement.[417] Given these factors, we consider that the two requirements are closely related to the intended use requirement such that they form part of that measure. That measure, in turn, is, as we have found above, in essence still the same measure that Brazil challenged in its panel request. Moreover we take the view that Indonesia could reasonably anticipate or foresee that any new enforcement provision that it adopts in respect of a measure that is at issue in the dispute, could be relevant to the dispute.[418] We, thus, find that the distribution plan and the distribution report are closely related to the intended use requirement such that they form part of that measure.

362. We thus consider that the intended use requirement as enacted through MoA 34/2016, which includes the limitation on cold storage as well as the distribution plan and the distribution report, is within our terms of reference.

7.5.3.3.2 Admissibility of claims in terms of due process

363. Brazil's position, as seen above, is that the intended use requirement continues to be a WTO-inconsistent measure and that the new enforcement provisions (i.e. distribution plan and weekly distribution report) have only reinforced the restrictions.[419] Indonesia, however, submits, in respect of the distribution plan and distribution report, that Brazil "did not make a proper claim". Indonesia argues that it is not clear which aspects of which WTO provisions these requirements are inconsistent with" and refers to Brazil's challenge as "vague and unprecise". As a consequence Indonesia considers that its ability to defend itself is undermined.[420] We understand Indonesia to raise a due process concern, which requires us to examine whether the claims that Brazil makes in respect of the distribution plan and weekly report, are admissible.

364. Brazil essentially argues that the changes that the new measures have brought about have not changed the nature of the violations. To us it is clear,

---

[416] See para. 7.269 above.
[417] Brazil's opening statement at second meeting of the Panel, paras. 18-21.
[418] Whether there are other due process concerns relating to the manner in which Brazil has presented its claims, is a different issue which we discuss below.
[419] Brazil's opening statement at the second meeting of the Panel, in particular paras. 18-21.
[420] Indonesia's response to Panel question No. 66(b).

therefore, that the claims that we have to examine are those set out above in paragraph 7.182 above, namely Article XI of the GATT 1994, Article 4.2 of the Agreement on Agriculture and Article III:4 of the GATT 1994. Brazil made arguments specifically on the new enforcement provisions at the second meeting.[421] While those arguments clearly point to the trade-restrictive and discriminatory nature alleged by Brazil, they remain somewhat limited and were only further developed in Brazil's responses to questions.[422] It seems to us that this is mainly because Indonesia first had to provide some factual explanations regarding these new requirements – a fact which in our view should not be counted against Brazil. We also note that Indonesia was given ample opportunity to explain the measures in its responses to questions and was able to – and did – react to Brazil's arguments in its comments to Brazil's responses.[423] Under these circumstances we do not consider that Indonesia has identified a valid due process concern that would prevent us from proceeding with the examination of Brazil's claims regarding the new enforcement provisions.

365.   As we have stated above, our analysis of Brazil's claims will focus on whether the modified and additional features of the intended use requirement change the analysis that we provided above in respect of the intended use requirement.

7.5.3.3.3   Claims under Article III:4 of the GATT 1994

366.   As noted above, Brazil raises claims both under Article XI of the GATT 1994 and Article 4.2 of the Agreement on Agriculture, as well as under Article III:4 of the GATT 1994. Thus, Brazil challenges the intended use requirement both as border and as internal measure. As seen above, the parties disagree on whether it is possible to challenge (the same aspect of) a measure both under Article XI of the GATT 1994 (or Article 4.2. of the Agreement on Agriculture) and under Article III of the GATT 1994.

367.   We started our analysis above, regarding the intended use requirement as enacted under the previous regulation MoA 58/2015, under Article III:4 of the GATT 1994. As we explained above, both parties, albeit for different reasons, take the view that Article III:4 is applicable and have presented arguments under this provision. We observed that the question whether Article III:4 applies to the exclusion of Article XI of the GATT 1994 and Article 4.2 of the Agreement on Agriculture, only becomes relevant if and when Article III:4 is applicable to the measure at issue. We, therefore examined whether the intended use requirement as laid down in MoA 58/2015 was covered by Article III:4. We now examine

---

[421] Brazil's opening statement at the second meeting of the Panel, paras. 18-21.
[422] Brazil's response to Panel question No. 87; and comments on Indonesia's response to Panel question No. 88.
[423] See Indonesia's responses to Panel question Nos. 88 and 89. See also Indonesia's comments on Brazil's response to Panel question No. 87.

whether this analysis still stands in light of the changes made to the intended use requirement through MoA 34/2016.

7.5.3.3.3.1   Whether Article III:4 is applicable

368.   We set out Article III:4 in paragraph 7.187 above. As we explained there, the scope of Article III:4 is qualified through the interpretative note *Ad Article III*, the text of which we set out in paragraph 7.188 above. We read the qualification made through the *Ad Note* to mean that a measure that affects the internal sale, offering for sale, etc., when enforced at the time or point of importation, only comes under Article III:4 if it applies to an imported product *and* the like domestic product. We, therefore need to examine the following three elements: (1) whether the measure is a law, regulation or requirement affecting the internal sale, offering for sale, purchase, transportation, distribution or use of imported chicken meat; (2) whether the measure that is enforced at the time or point of importation, and (3) whether it applies to imported products *and* to like domestic products.

369.   In paragraphs 7.190-7.194 above, we examined these three elements with regard to the intended use requirement in its previous version and arrived at the conclusion that it was *not* covered by the *Ad Note*, and that therefore, Article III:4 was not applicable. The changes to the intended use requirement that the above provisions under MoA 34/2016 have brought about raise the question whether that result remains the same. There are two issues that we need to consider, both of which concern the third element above. We recall that this element requires us to consider whether there is an "equivalent" domestic measure.

Cold storage requirement

370.   The first issue we need to address, concerns the cold storage requirement introduced through Article 31(1) of MoA 34/2016. We recall that Indonesia submits that there is an "equivalent" measure to the intended use requirement, namely a cold storage requirement applicable to the sale of frozen and chilled meat in markets in domestic law, as laid down in MoA Decree 306/1994.

371.   In our analysis of the intended use requirement as previously enacted through MoA 58/2015, we found that there was no "equivalence" because that version of the intended use requirement did not contain any reference to cold storage. Access to traditional markets was prohibited, whether or not they had cold storage facilities. We, therefore, concluded, that the aim and content of the respective provisions was substantially different, such that there was no equivalence. With the adoption of MoA 34/2016, however, there is now a cold storage requirement which, in terms of scope, exactly matches the cold storage requirement under MoA Decree 306/1994. We further note that both Article 31(1) of MoA 34/2016 and the relevant provisions in MoA Decree 306/1994

apply to the same products, namely frozen and chilled chicken meat.[424] This indicates to us that there is now equivalence.

Enforcement provisions

372.   This preliminary conclusion leads us to the second issue, namely whether the "equivalence" assessment of two measures is affected by the way these measures are enforced. If it were, differences in enforcement could lead to "non-equivalence" taking the measure outside the scope of Article III. We note that both parties as well as the European Union as third party, consider that enforcement is part of the equivalence analysis.[425] In our view it is not.

373.   A first point to be made is that the very situation that the *Ad Note* contemplates is already one that builds on a difference in enforcement – one measure is enforced at the border, the other is not. The *Ad Note* makes clear that this difference does not take the measure outside the scope of Article III.

374.   Second, enforcement of a measure is a question of how a measure is applied. Differences in how a measure is applied are relevant in the assessment of whether there is less favourable treatment. In our view, the "equivalence" assessment in the *Ad Note* is not to be conflated with the question of whether there is less favourable treatment and, therefore, a violation of Article III. An equivalence assessment is limited to ascertaining *whether* a measure is applied both to domestic and imported products, not *how* it is applied. If it were otherwise, the equivalence assessment itself would amount to a less favourable treatment analysis and an assessment under Article III would be redundant.

375.   Applying our view to the case at hand, we do not see a need, for purposes of the equivalence analysis, to address the enforcement provisions in the intended use requirement and compare them to the way the domestic cold storage requirement is enforced. Instead, we consider that these are questions that are relevant to our analysis under Article III:4.

376.   We, therefore, confirm our preliminary analysis above, that there is an equivalent domestic measure. Thus we conclude that pursuant to the *Ad Note,* Article III:4 is applicable to the intended use requirement as enacted through MoA 34/2016.

7.5.3.3.3.2   Whether there is inconsistency with Article III:4

377.   Brazil's argument essentially is that the intended use requirement imposes restrictions on imported chicken whereas no such restrictions are imposed on domestic chicken.[426] Indonesia's defence consists mainly in arguing that there is

---

[424]   We note that our assessment of substantive compliance with Article III:4 of the GATT 1994, owing to the nature of Brazil's arguments, requires a "likeness" analysis going beyond the "likeness" established for the purpose of equivalence. See in particular, section 7.5.3.3.3.2 below.

[425]   See Brazil and Indonesia's response to Panel question No. 91(a). See also European Union's third-party response to Panel question No. 11.

[426]   Brazil's first written submission, paras. 269 and 270; second written submission, paras. 54-56.

no difference in treatment between imported frozen and domestic frozen chicken; as for any difference in treatment between imported frozen and domestic fresh chicken, Indonesia submits that they are not like products.[427]

378. We have set out the text of Article III:4 in paragraph 7.187 above. To assess whether there is a violation of Article III:4 we need to examine the following three questions: (1) whether the imported and domestic products at issue are "like products"; (2) whether the measure at issue is a "law, regulation, or requirement affecting their internal sale, offering for sale, purchase, transportation, distribution or use"; and (3) whether the imported products are accorded "less favourable" treatment than that accorded to like domestic products.[428]

379. We do not see an issue with the second of these elements. As we have already established in paragraph 7.190 above, we consider that the intended use requirement is a regulation or requirement that affects the internal sale and offering for sale. Neither party contests this point.

380. As for the other two elements, our assessment differs depending on the specific aspect of the intended use requirement addressed by Brazil's arguments. We see two different aspects, namely the cold storage requirement, on the one hand, and the enforcement provisions on the other.

Whether the intended use requirement is inconsistent with Article III:4 with respect to its cold storage requirement

381. Regarding the cold storage requirement, Brazil does not contest that a cold storage requirement also applies to domestic frozen and chilled chicken. What Brazil considers to be discriminatory is that no such requirement applies to fresh chicken — a fact, which in turn is uncontested by Indonesia.[429] Brazil's argument that such difference in treatment results in a discrimination of imported products vis-à-vis domestic products, is based on the uncontested fact that imported chicken, due to the nature of its transportation from the exporting

---

[427] Indonesia's first written submission, para. 147-172.

[428] Appellate Body Report, *Korea – Various Measures on Beef*, para. 133.

[429] Brazil's response to Panel question No. 96; Detailed Study on the Indonesian Chicken Market (Exhibit BRA-02); Indonesia's first written submission paras. 130 and 135, referring to Carrick Devine, M. Dikeman, Encyclopedia of Meat Sciences, (2nd ed. Elsevier, 2014)(Exhibit IDN-48); Daryanto, Arief, Diederik De Boer, Dikky Indrawan, Ferry Leenstra, Huub Mudde, Idqan Fahmi, and Peter Van Horne, Socio-economic Analysis of the Slaughtering Systems in the Poultry Meat Sector in Greater Jakarta Area (2014) (Exhibit IDN-57), para. 14; and USAID, Indonesia's Poultry Value Chain: Costs, Margins, Prices, and Other Issues (2013), at 4, Aug. 2013 (Exhibit IDN-58). We observe that whether fresh chicken is exempted from a refrigeration requirement is not entirely clear in MoA Decree 306/1994. While Article 22 seems to make a distinction between "fresh poultry meat" and "fresh-chilled poultry meat", other provisions in the Decree (such as Article 14(1)) seem to suggest that also fresh chicken meat needs to be cooled at all times. Irrespective of what is legally required, however, we note that the parties agree on what the factual situation is in the traditional markets, namely that freshly slaughtered chicken is offered for sale without being refrigerated.

country, is always frozen and can never be fresh.[430] It is also uncontested that while there is some domestic frozen chicken, most chicken sold in Indonesia is sold fresh in traditional markets.[431] Finally, as noted previously both parties agree that currently most traditional markets do not have cold storage facilities.[432]

382.   With respect to this alleged discrimination, we consider that the relevant products for the likeness assessment as submitted by Brazil are frozen and fresh chicken. We therefore turn to assessing whether fresh and frozen chicken are like.

Likeness

383.   A first argument that Brazil makes is that "likeness" must be assumed, because the origin of the product is the only factor that distinguishes the imported and domestic products.[433] While we agree on the principle, which the Appellate Body has confirmed in *Argentina – Financial Services*, we do not think it applies to the dispute at hand.[434] In our view, this would be the case if the cold storage requirement *de jure* only applied to imported products.[435] It is true, as Brazil points out, that Article 31(1) only applies to imported products.[436] However, as established in our equivalence assessment under the Note *Ad Article III* above, an equivalent cold storage requirement applies also to domestic products. *De jure*, therefore, even if contained in different legal instruments (Article 31(1) of MoA 34/2016, on the one hand, and Article 22 of MoA Decree 306/1994 on the other), no distinction is made between imported and domestic products, insofar as frozen and chilled products are concerned. Furthermore, *de jure*, fresh chicken is not covered by that requirement, whether domestic or imported.[437] That the latter (imported fresh chicken), in practice, does not exist, because all chicken is imported frozen, is not an issue of law but of fact. We, therefore, find that origin of the product, *de jure*, is not the factor that distinguishes frozen imported and fresh domestic chicken. Likeness, thus, needs

---

[430]   Brazil's opening statement at the second meeting of the Panel, para. 17; Indonesia's first written submission, paras. 149 and 318.
[431]   See para. 7.101 above.
[432]   Brazil's second written submission, para. 66; Brazil's opening statement at the second meeting of the Panel, para. 16; Indonesia's first written submission, para. 130.
[433]   Brazil's second written submission, para. 48. See also Brazil's response to Panel question No. 96.
[434]   Appellate Body Report, *Argentina – Financial Services*, para. 6.36.
[435]   The Appellate Body stated: "…we note that measures allowing the application of a presumption of "likeness" will typically be measures involving a *de jure* distinction between products of different origin." See Appellate Body Report, *Argentina – Financial Services*, para. 6.36.
[436]   Brazil opening statement at the first meeting of the Panel, para. 66.
[437]   But see comment in fn 417.

to be established and the burden of doing so is on Brazil as the complaining party.[438]

384. Brazil, as does Indonesia, argues on the basis of the four likeness criteria developed in previous disputes, namely (1) products characteristics/physical properties, (2) end uses, (3) consumer tastes and preferences, and (4) tariff classification.[439]

385. Regarding the first criterion the parties mainly debate differences in physical properties arising from the freezing process. Brazil considers that the freezing process does not change the relevant properties of the product and points out that "freezing is a process capable of retaining the characteristics of chicken meat and chicken products, guaranteeing their quality and sanity".[440] Indonesia, for its part, points, *inter alia*, to the possible presence of additional substances (brine) and to the risks concerning the quality and safety of the meat arising from undue variations in temperature in the handling of frozen chicken.[441]

386. Regarding the second criterion, Indonesia concedes that frozen and fresh chicken have similar end uses, which Brazil also describes as "food consumption".[442]

387. Regarding the third criterion, Brazil considers that the Indonesian consumers' tastes and habits related to chicken meat and chicken products would be adequately met by the Brazilian products.[443] Indonesia refers to the fact that currently most consumers source their chicken from traditional markets and contends that Indonesians prefer fresh over frozen chicken.[444]

388. Finally, regarding the fourth criterion, Brazil points out that "both imported and domestic products are subject to the same HS codes of the *Gallus domesticus* species chicken meat"[445], whereas Indonesia focuses on the differences in HS codes at the six-digit level as regards fresh and frozen chicken.[446]

---

[438] See Appellate Body Report, *Argentina – Financial Services*, paras. 6.30 and 6.42. In this dispute, the Appellate Body considered the "likeness" test under Article III:4 of the GATT in its examination of claims under Article II:1 and Article XVII:1 of the GATS, and ruled that:

Regarding the burden of proof in establishing "likeness" relying on the presumption approach, we note that, in keeping with the general rule that the burden of proof rests upon the party that asserts the affirmative of a particular claim, the complainant bears the burden of making a *prima facie* case that a measure draws a distinction between services and service suppliers based exclusively on origin. In this regard, a panel is required to assess objectively the evidence and arguments forming the basis of such a contention. (footnotes omitted)

[439] Appellate Body Report, *EC – Asbestos*, para. 101.
[440] Brazil's opening statement at the first meeting of the Panel, para. 72.
[441] Indonesia's first written submission, paras. 152-157, in particular, paras. 155 and 156.
[442] Brazil's first written submission, para. 273; Indonesia's first written submission, para. 159.
[443] Brazil's first written submission, para. 273.
[444] Indonesia's first written submission, para.159.
[445] Brazil's first written submission, para. 273.
[446] Indonesia's first written submission, para. 163.

389.   We recall the Appellate Body's guidance that the assessment of likeness of products is fundamentally about their competitive relationship in the marketplace.[447] A panel may carry out this assessment by relying on the above four likeness criteria, which the Appellate Body described as "tools" to assist a panel in sorting and examining the relevant evidence.[448] The Appellate Body also noted that "the kind of evidence to be examined in assessing the ☐likeness☐ of products will, necessarily, depend upon the particular products and the legal provision at issue".[449]

390.   Both parties refer to the need for the panel to look at the specific marketplace when assessing the competitive relationship in light of the above criteria.[450] We agree. We consider the specific marketplace to be the one which is affected by the measure at issue. In other words, the concrete circumstances envisaged by the measure at issue define the specific marketplace in respect of which the competitive relationship is to be assessed. That assessment is about how the products compete with each other *but for the measure*.[451]

391.   We observe that the cold storage requirement concerns the offering for sale in markets and that the discrimination that Brazil alleges, specifically concerns the offering for sale in traditional markets. As we noted above, in those traditional markets, which currently do not have (or only marginally have) cold storage facilities, chicken is mostly sold freshly slaughtered.[452] As Indonesia explains the chicken is mostly slaughtered in nearby slaughter points during the night or in the early morning hours and then brought to the market in plastic crates.[453] It is then displayed in the traditional market without being in cold storage.

392.   *But for the measure*, frozen chicken would not have to be kept in cold storage, but would be offered – thawing - alongside fresh chicken.[454] In our

---

[447]   Appellate Body Report, *EC – Asbestos*, para. 103.
[448]   Appellate Body Report, *EC – Asbestos*, para. 102.
[449]   Appellate Body Report, *EC – Asbestos*, para. 103.
[450]   Indonesia's first written submission, para. 160; and Brazil's second written submission, para. 45.
[451]   We are mindful of the Appellate Body's caveat, stated in the context of Article III:2 that a "but for" test could be "overly restrictive" if it assumes that the measure at issue is the only factor influencing competition. (See Appellate Body Report, *Philippines – Distilled Spirits*, para. 227). However, we consider the "but for" test a useful starting point for a likeness analysis and do not exclude consideration of other factors.
[452]   See para. 7.101 above.
[453]   Indonesia's first written submission, para. 135; Indonesia's response to Panel question No. 100; Daryanto, Arief, Diederik De Boer, Dikky Indrawan, Ferry Leenstra, Huub Mudde, Idqan Fahmi, and Peter Van Horne, Socio-economic Analysis of the Slaughtering Systems in the Poultry Meat Sector in Greater Jakarta Area (2014) (Exhibit IDN-57). See also Brazil's response to Panel question No. 100 referring to a market study according to which some of the chicken is slaughtered directly in the market (Exhibit BRA-02). According to Indonesia the latter is not permitted under the law. See Indonesia's comments on Brazil's response to Panel question No. 100. In our view, the question of whether chickens are slaughtered directly in the market regardless of whether it is permitted by law, does not affect our analysis, as they are in any event, freshly slaughtered.
[454]   Brazil seems to acknowledge that this is the situation envisaged. See Brazil's opening statement at the first meeting of the Panel, para. 69.

view, it is this specific situation that we need to consider when assessing the competitive relationship between the products.

393.   We observe that with regard to this specific situation — frozen chicken thawing outside at tropical temperatures — Indonesia has pointed to food safety concerns. As seen above, Indonesia's argument is that thawing frozen chicken outside at tropical temperatures increases microbial growth which can lead to food borne illnesses.[455] In the context of our analysis under Article XX(b), we have found that Indonesia has demonstrated the existence of this risk, which Brazil has failed to rebut.

394.   As noted above, in the context of the likeness analysis, Indonesia has referred to this issue in its discussion of physical properties.[456]

395.   We recall that in *EC – Asbestos*, the Appellate Body considered the health risks associated with the product at issue to be relevant to the assessment of physical properties.[457] The health risk that the Appellate Body considered in that case was the carcinogenicity and toxicity of fibres containing asbestos as opposed to fibres not containing asbestos (which were found not to present the same risk).[458] The Appellate Body found that physical difference to be "highly significant" indicating that the products were not like.[459] The Appellate Body held that in order to overcome such indication, a higher burden was placed on the complaining Member to establish likeness on the basis of other criteria.[460] In addition to being relevant to physical properties, the Appellate Body also considered it "very likely" that the consumers' tastes and habits would be shaped by the health risk associated with the product.[461] Because it had failed to present, *inter alia*, evidence on consumer tastes and habits (which would have had to show that the health risk did not affect consumer choice), the Appellate Body found that the complaining party had not met its burden of proof in establishing likeness.[462]

396.   We are mindful that our case presents certain differences. In particular, the health risk discussed here (food-borne illnesses) is not associated with the product as such (frozen chicken) but rather with the process of thawing it at tropical temperatures. In our view, however, this difference does not make the above ruling by the Appellate Body less pertinent. The reason is that it is this specific process that the cold storage requirement, alleged to be discriminatory, seeks to prevent, not the sale of the product (frozen chicken) as such.

---

[455]   See section 7.5.2.4.1.1 above.
[456]   See para. 7.305 above; Indonesia's first written submission, para. 156.
[457]   Appellate Body Report, *EC – Asbestos*, para. 116. See also Appellate Body Report, *US – Clove Cigarettes*, para.118.
[458]   Appellate Body Report, *EC – Asbestos*, para. 114.
[459]   *Ibid.*
[460]   Appellate Body Report, *EC – Asbestos*, para. 118.
[461]   Appellate Body Report, *EC – Asbestos*, para. 122. See also Appellate Body Report, *US – Clove Cigarettes*, para. 118.
[462]   Appellate Body Report, *EC – Asbestos*, paras. 139 and 141.

397.   Therefore, in relying on the Appellate Body's jurisprudence in the above case, we consider the health risk associated with thawing frozen chicken at tropical temperatures to be relevant to our assessment of physical properties of the product at issue. As noted above, we have found that Indonesia has established that there is such a risk. Brazil has suggested that there is a similar if not greater risk with leaving fresh chicken on display outside.[463] However, Brazil has not submitted any evidence to this effect. On the basis of the evidence before us, we therefore find that the difference in health risk arising from previously frozen/thawing chicken and fresh chicken presents a difference in physical properties that indicates non-likeness.[464]

398.   Turning to the other criteria, in light of the health risk identified, we consider the assessment of consumer tastes and habits to be particularly relevant. In line with the above case law, we take the view that the health risk associated with improperly thawed chicken may well be an aspect that would affect a consumer's choice between buying such a thawed chicken and buying a fresh one. We are cognizant of the fact that neither party has specifically discussed this aspect in its submissions nor presented any evidence in this regard. However, as noted above, the physical difference in health risks between fresh and thawing chicken indicates that there is no likeness.[465] As the Appellate Body noted, in the absence of evidence on consumer tastes, "there is no basis for overcoming the inference, drawn from the different physical properties of the products that the products are not □like□".[466] The absence of evidence, therefore, is one that Brazil is accountable for as the party bearing the burden of proof.[467]

399.   Finally, we address the remaining two elements. Regarding end use we note the parties' agreement on the end use (food consumption), a point, which, therefore, does not add weight to either side of the analysis. As regards the tariff line, we note that the parties debate the difference between frozen and fresh, while our analysis is focused on thawing versus fresh. Therefore, we consider that the difference at six-digit level, between frozen and fresh is to be considered with some caution, even if it supports the above conclusion that non-likeness is indicated. As seen above, Brazil has not been able to rebut that indication.

400.   We, therefore, find that frozen and fresh chicken are not like in the specific circumstances envisaged by the cold storage requirement. Consequently we find that the intended use requirement does not breach Article III:4 with respect to its cold storage requirement.

---

[463]   Brazil's second written submission, para. 62; and response to Panel question No. 90.
[464]   We refrain from taking a position on the duration for which fresh chicken can be displayed at outside temperatures for it to become unfit for human consumption.
[465]   See para. 7.315 above.
[466]   Appellate Body Report, *EC-Asbestos*, para. 121.
[467]   Appellate Body Report, *EC-Asbestos*, para. 139.

Whether the intended use requirement is inconsistent with Article III:4 with respect to its enforcement provisions

401.   The second alleged discriminatory aspect raised by Brazil concerns the enforcement provisions of the intended use requirement. Brazil's argument essentially is that the cold storage requirement is enforced in a much stricter and more burdensome way for imported products than for domestic products.[468] Indonesia factually contests certain aspects raised by Brazil and generally takes the view that enforcement provisions are only "slightly different".[469]

Likeness

402.   We observe that the enforcement provisions concern those products which are covered by the cold storage requirement, be it under Article 31(1) of MoA 34/2016 or under MoA Decree 306/1994. These are frozen and chilled chicken meat, both on the imported and on the domestic side. Thus, contrary to the alleged discrimination discussed above, likeness can be presumed insofar as origin is the only factor that distinguishes the enforcement provisions as they apply to imported frozen/chilled chicken and those applying to domestic frozen/chilled chicken.

Less favourable treatment

403.   We, therefore, turn to the question whether there is less favourable treatment. We recall that the Appellate Body pointed out that a "formal difference in treatment between imported and like domestic products is [...] neither necessary, nor sufficient, to show a violation of Article III:4".[470] Instead, as the Appellate Body explained, to establish whether there is less favourable treatment, a panel needs to examine whether "a measure modifies the *conditions of competition* in the relevant market to the detriment of imported products".[471]

404.   To assess this question, we first need to establish the factual situation. Starting with the domestic side of the enforcement provisions, Indonesia explains that MoA Decree 306/1994 itself does not contain enforcement provisions, but that those are contained in "higher laws", to which the Decree refers and which are currently Law 18/2009 and Government Regulation 95/2012.[472] Indonesia describes these enforcement provisions as essentially consisting in surveillance carried out by a public health supervisor, who has the authority to inspect "animal product business units" and, *inter alia*, to postpone or stop the production process.[473] Indonesia further submits that local regulation contributes to supervision. Indonesia provides the example of Jakarta, which

---

[468] Brazil's opening statement at the second meeting of the Panel, paras. 19-21.
[469] Indonesia's response to Panel question Nos. 88 and 91.
[470] Appellate Body Report, *Korea – Various Measures on Beef*, para. 137.
[471] *Ibid.*
[472] Indonesia's response to Panel question No.89.
[473] *Ibid.*

requires meat distributors to obtain a meat distributor licence, requiring them to provide information, *inter alia*, about place of sale including storage facilities.[474] To obtain the licence, meat distributors also need to submit a sales report for the last three months.[475]

405.   Turning to the imported products side of the enforcement provisions, we recall our above description of the requirement to submit a distribution plan and a weekly distribution report, as well as our description of the various sanction provisions set out in Article 38 of MoA 34/2016.

406.   In addressing the differences between these enforcement provisions, Brazil highlights three issues. The first is the strict sanctions that apply to importers deviating from the limitation on the allowed uses, which could result in a total exclusion of the importer from the Indonesian market for one year.[476] Indonesia confirms that the sanction provided for under Article 38(4) (written warning and, if ignored, temporary suspension for one year) applies "when an importer fails to comply with Article 32(1)(b) by selling chicken meat and chicken product at a market without cold chain facilities".[477] In comparison, domestic sellers who would sell frozen or chilled chicken without respecting the cold storage requirement, do not face a comparable sanction – if any sanction at all. While Indonesia has referred to supervision by the public health supervisor over animal products business units, we are not convinced that there is a legal requirement for such supervision to apply to sellers in the traditional market.[478] However, even if there were, the strictest "sanction" which the public health supervisor seems to be able to apply is to stop or postpone the production process. Furthermore, we note that Indonesia has not referred to any sanction that could apply to the domestic distributor who sold the frozen chicken to the seller in the traditional market. For these reasons, we find that the stricter sanctions applying to imported frozen and chilled chicken, result in a competitive disadvantage for imported products

407.   The second issue that Brazil refers to is that the commitment to certain intended uses (to obtain an MoA Import Recommendation) restricts the importer to not selling elsewhere, whereas no such restriction exists for domestic sellers.[479] We note that the MoA Import Recommendation itself refers to the intended uses on a general basis as "hotel, restaurant, market with cold chain

---

[474]   Indonesia's response to Panel question No. 88(d). See also Requirements to Obtain a Meat Distributor License, retrieved from: http://pelayanan.jakarta.go.id/site/detailperizinan/472 (Exhibit IDN-131).

[475]   *Ibid.*

[476]   Brazil's first written submission, paras.104 and 105.

[477]   Indonesia's response to Panel question No. 88(a).

[478]   We note that Article 37(2) of Regulation 95/2012 defines "animal product business units" as including "a milking place, egg production place, other Animal origin food production place, non food Animal products production place, and collecting and sales place".

[479]   Brazil's response to Panel question No. 87.

facilities".[480] Thus, the import recommendation itself does not prevent an importer from switching within those allowed uses.[481] However, with the requirement to provide a distribution plan and a weekly distribution report, the situation has changed. We recall that the importer, in the distribution plan, has to identify, *inter alia*, the name and address of the buyer as well as the price.[482] Like Brazil, we take the view that the importer is effectively bound by this list, which is checked through the weekly distribution reports. As a consequence the importer is prevented "from actually distributing the imported chicken meat and chicken product after the import operation occurs to the best business offers it may be able to get".[483]

408. Indonesia argues that the distribution plan has no binding effect.[484] Central to its argument is the sanction provision contained in Article 38(3)(b).[485] Indonesia submits that this sanction relates to an importer not submitting *any* distribution plan.[486] We note however that Article 23(2) provides that the application for an MoA Import Recommendation would be "rejected" if it is "incomplete and/or incorrect".[487] To us, the scenario suggested by Indonesia, that an importer would not submit any distribution plan, is covered by this provision. An application that does not have a distribution plan attached would never proceed, but would be rejected due to it being incomplete. Indonesia's reading of Article 38(3)(b), therefore, in our view, is in direct conflict with Article 23(2), which already provides for a sanction for not submitting a distribution plan. A reasonable reading of Article 38(3)(b) would reflect that this provision addresses the particular situation where the importer, while having submitted such a plan, does not do what is stated in it. In our reading, therefore, Article 38(3)(b) does provide for a sanction if and when the importer does not carry out the sales as contained in the distribution plan. We therefore find that the distribution plan has the effect of binding the importer to specific sales identified at the moment of the

---

[480] See example provided in Import Recommendation by the Minister of Agriculture for beef from Australia (Exhibit IDN-92(b)).

[481] See also Indonesia's second written submission, para. 141.

[482] See Format-2, Ministry of Agriculture Regulation 34/Permentan/PK210/7/2016 (Exhibit BRA-48).

[483] Brazil's response to Panel question No. 87.

[484] Indonesia's response to Panel question No. 88 (a); and Indonesia's comments on Brazil's response to Panel question No. 87.

[485] Indonesia's comments on Brazil's response to Panel question No. 87, in particular, para. 51. See also Indonesia's response to Panel question No. 88(a).

[486] *Ibid.*

[487] Article 23 states in relevant part:

(1) The head of PPVTPP after receiving the application online as referred to in Article 20 is to verify the completeness of administration requirements as referred to in Article 22, within a maximum period of one (1) working day shall provide answer either to reject or approve.

(2) The application is *rejected* as referred to in paragraph (1) if the administrative requirements as referred to in Article 22 is *incomplete and/or incorrect*.

(3)...

(emphasis added)

application for an MoA Import Recommendation. This results in a competitive disadvantage for imported products given that no such restriction exists for domestic sellers of frozen and chilled chicken meat.

409.   The third issue that Brazil refers to is the burden and cost arising from having to submit a distribution plan and a weekly distribution report.[488] We agree that a one-time requirement for domestic meat distributors to submit a sales report for the last three months, (at least in the area of Jakarta) does not compare with the burden and cost incurred by the importer, which arises on a continuous basis.[489] We, therefore, find that the increased administrative burden and cost result in a competitive disadvantage for imports of frozen and chilled chicken.

410.   On the basis of these three issues, collectively and individually, we find that there is less favourable treatment of imported frozen and chilled chicken meat and chicken products in respect of the enforcement provisions of the intended use requirement.

411.   Consequently we find that the intended use requirement is inconsistent with Article III:4 of the GATT 1994 with respect to its enforcement provisions.

7.5.3.3.3.3   Whether the enforcement provisions are justified under Article XX of the GATT 1994

412.   Indonesia submits that its defence under Article XX(b) and (d) of the GATT 1994 applies *mutatis mutandis* to measures under the new regime, i.e. MoA 34/2016.[490]

413.   In line with the relevant jurisprudence, we note that what Indonesia would need to justify is the difference in treatment the enforcement provisions make for domestic and imported products.[491] Indonesia's arguments under Article XX(b) and (d) pertain to the health risk from improperly thawed chicken meat and to the risk of consumers being deceived into buying thawed chicken instead of fresh chicken.[492] We observe that these arguments do not explain the difference in treatment of domestic and imported products in respect of the enforcement provisions.

414.   We, thus, find that Indonesia has not put forward a *prima facie* case justifying the specific breach of Article III:4 which we identified above.

415.   We, therefore, conclude that the intended use requirement, where its enforcement provisions are concerned, is inconsistent with Article III:4 and is not justified under Article XX(b) or (d) of the GATT 1994.

---

[488]   Brazil's comments on Indonesia's response to Panel question No. 88(d).
[489]   We recall that the distribution plan has to be submitted with every application for an MoA Import recommendation; furthermore, the distribution report has to be submitted on a weekly basis.
[490]   Indonesia's response to Panel question No. 66(b).
[491]   Appellate Body Report, *Thailand – Cigarettes*, para. 177.
[492]   See section 7.5.2.4 above.

7.5.3.3.3.4   Claims under Article XI of the GATT 1994 and Article 4.2 of the Agreement on Agriculture

416.   Brazil also makes claims under Article XI of the GATT 1994 and Article 4.2 of the Agreement on Agriculture. We recall that the aim of the dispute settlement mechanism is to "secure a positive solution to a dispute" (Article 3.7 of the DSU) and that our duty, according to Article 11 of the DSU is to "make such other findings as will assist the DSB in making the recommendations or in giving the rulings provided for in the covered agreements". We consider that the findings that we have made above are sufficient to secure a positive solution to the dispute. We are mindful that we have not considered the intended use requirement in its latest enactment under MoA 34/2016, under Article XI of the GATT 1994 or Article 4.2 of the Agreement on Agriculture. However, we consider that certain findings that we made above make clear that the outcome of a consideration under Article XI would be the same as under Article III:4. We refer, in particular to our finding in respect of the previous version of the intended use requirement (as enacted through MoA 58/2015) which already identified the cold storage requirement as a less trade-restrictive alternative that would have justified the intended use requirement under Article XX(b). We also find relevant, in this context, our findings above, in the context of our Article III:4 analysis of the most recent version of the intended use requirement, that the cold storage requirement also applies to domestic frozen and chilled products and does not constitute a breach of Article III:4. On this basis, we apply judicial economy to Article XI (and Article 4.2 of the Agreement on Agriculture). Under the circumstances, we consider that we do not need to address and answer the question raised by Indonesia, whether the application of Article XI is excluded because of the applicability Article III:4.

7.5.4   Conclusion

417.   In sum, we find that the intended use requirement as enacted through MoA 58/2015 is inconsistent with Article XI of the GATT 1994 and not justified under Article XX(b) or Article XX(d) of the GATT 1994. Having found that the intended use requirement as enacted through MoA 58/2015 is inconsistent with Article XI of the GATT 1994, we consider that it is not necessary to address Brazil's claim under Article 4.2 of the Agreement on Agriculture in order to secure a positive solution to this dispute.

418.   We further find that the intended use requirement has not ceased to exist by virtue of the relevant provisions in MoA 34/2016. Furthermore, we find that we have jurisdiction over these provisions. In respect of the cold storage requirement, we find that the intended use requirement as enacted through the relevant provisions in MoA 34/2016, is not inconsistent with Article III:4 of the GATT 1994. With respect to the enforcement provisions, we find that the intended use requirement is inconsistent with Article III:4 of the GATT 1994 and is not justified under Article XX(b) or (d) of the GATT 1994. We apply judicial economy with regard to Brazil's claims under Article XI of the GATT

1994 and Article 4.2 of the Agreement on Agriculture and, therefore, leave open the question as to whether Articles III:4 and XI are mutually exclusive.

7.6   Individual Measure 3: Certain Aspects of Indonesia's Import Licensing Regime

7.6.1   Introduction

419.   We now turn to the third of the individual measures that Brazil challenges. Brazil claims that certain aspects of Indonesia's import licensing regime are inconsistent with a number of Indonesia's obligations under the covered agreements. We recall that in section 7.3 above we provide a brief overview of the main features of Indonesia's import licensing regime, some of which are germane to this section.

420.   As indicated in section 7.1.2.3 above, we found that Brazil has not challenged Indonesia's import licensing regime as a whole. Instead, Brazil has raised a number of claims in respect of certain aspects of the licensing regime. The main elements of Indonesia's import licensing regime challenged by Brazil, and the respective claims raised by Brazil throughout these proceedings, are summarized in the following table[493]:

Table 4.   Overview of claims made by Brazil

Measure		Provisions allegedly breached
Positive list requirement		Articles: XI:1 of the GATT 1994. 4.2 of the Agreement on Agriculture, and 3.2 of the Import Licensing Agreement
Intended use requirement		
Application windows and validity periods		
Fixed licence terms		
Discretionary import licensing	Letter of recommendation from provincial livestock services office	Articles: 4.2 of the Agreement on Agriculture and 3.2 of the Import Licensing Agreement
	Supervision on the compliance of veterinary public health requirements	
	MoT's discretion to determine the amount of imported goods in the MoA Import Recommendation	

421.   We note that Brazil additionally argues that certain other elements of Indonesia's import licensing regime are WTO-inconsistent. In particular, Brazil claims that the following elements are inconsistent with Indonesia's obligations

---

[493]   Brazil's first written submission, paras. 200, 228 and 244; response to Panel question No. 15(a); second written submission, paras. 104-105; and response to Panel question No. 108(a).

under the covered agreements: (i) the denial of import licences to secure price stabilization[494]; and (ii) additional restrictions on "certain products" and "processed products".[495]

422.   In the subsequent sections, we will separately address each of the elements listed in the table above. We will discuss, in a final section, the two elements indicated in the previous paragraph. Before moving on to the examination of each element, we will provide a brief overview of Indonesia's import licensing regime as well as present the order of analysis that we will follow in addressing the parties' claims and defences.

7.6.2   Overview of Indonesia's import licensing regime

423.   As noted in section 7.3 above, an importer wishing to import chicken products into Indonesia must first obtain an MoA Import Recommendation and an MoT Import Approval. The figure below provides an overview of the steps and timeframes relative to obtaining these licensing documents, on the basis of the relevant provisions of MoA 58/2015 and MoT 05/2016.[496]

Figure 2   Overview of the application and approval of the MoA Import Recommendation and the MoT Import Approval

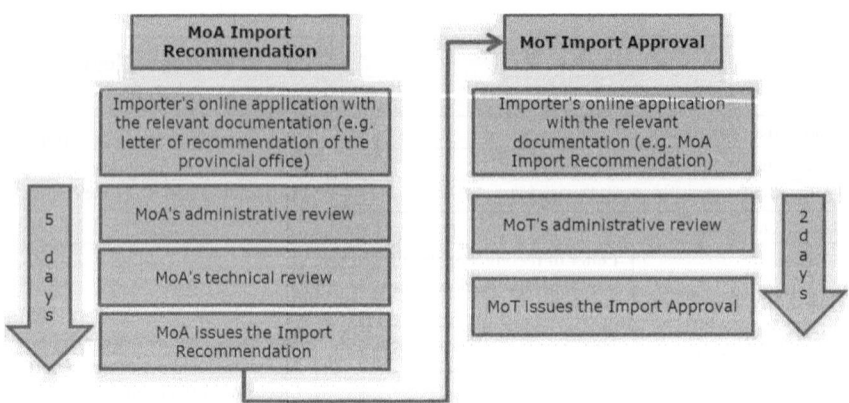

424.   As explained in detail below, Brazil takes issue with certain aspects relative to these two licensing documents, as well as with some of the documents

---

[494]   Brazil's response to Panel question No. 129.
[495]   Brazil's response to Panel question No. 15(b).
[496]   The time-frames for the issuance of the MoA Import Recommendation and the MoT Import Approval indicated in the figure above are based on Articles 24(1) and 25(1) of MoA 58/2015 (Exhibit BRA-01/IDN-24) and Article 10(3) of MoT 05/2016 (Exhibit BRA-03/IDN-39), for the MoA Import Recommendation and the MoT Import Approval, respectively.

required to obtain the MoA Import Recommendation and the MoT Import Approval.[497]

7.6.3 Order of analysis

425. Brazil has raised claims under Article XI:1 of the GATT 1994 and Article 4.2 of the Agreement on Agriculture, on the one hand, and Article 3.2 of the Import Licensing Agreement, on the other hand, for most elements of Indonesia's import licensing regime.

426. Indonesia argues that Brazil wrongly raised these claims, on the basis of the same arguments, under Article XI:1 of the GATT 1994 and Article 4.2 of the Agreement on Agriculture, and Article 3.2 of the Import Licensing Agreement, because it failed to distinguish between the scope of application of the provisions in these three agreements.[498] Brazil does not disagree with Indonesia that import licensing rules are not subject to the Import Licensing Agreement, but considers that all the elements of Indonesia's import licensing regime

---

[497] According to Article 23(1) of MoA 58/2015 (Exhibit BRA-01/IDN-24), an importer must submit the following documents with an application for an MoA Import Recommendation: (a) Identification Card (KTP) and/or company management identification; (b) Taxpayer Identification Number (NPWP); (c) Business and Trade License (SIUP); (d) Livestock and Animal Health Registration Certificate or Business Licence; (e) Company's deed of incorporation and the last amendment thereof; (f) Veterinary Control Number (NKV); (g) Importer Identity Number (API); (h) Statement Letter with stamp duty affixed accompanied with supporting document which declare ownership of cold storage and refrigerated vehicle, with the exception of ready-to-eat processed food that do not need cold storage facility as informed on the product label; (i) Letter of recommendation from provincial livestock services office; (j) Employing veterinarian with competency in the field of veterinary public health, proven by an assignment letter or work contract from company management; (k) Report of import realization from the previous period; (l) Provide the evidence of local cattle procurement verified by provincial and/or district/municipality livestock services offices of the origin of the cattle; and (m) Statement letter with stamp duty affixed declaring the document submitted is correct and valid.

According to Article 10(2) of MoT 5/2016 (Exhibit BRA-03/IDN-39), an importer must submit the following documents with an application for an MoT Import Approval: (a) Company's Deed of Establishment together with amendment thereto, for Import of Animal and Animal Product as per Appendix III hereto; (b) API; (c) evidence of ownership of maintenance place and evidence of ownership of Animal Slaughterhouse or work contract with Animal Slaughterhouse already fulfilling the standard based on the provisions in the legislation, for Import of Juvenile as per Appendix III hereto; (d) evidence of ownership of cold storage and evidence of ownership of cold transportation means, for Import of Animal Product as per Appendix III hereto; and (e) Recommendation of the Minister of Agriculture or official so appointed by the Minister of Agriculture, for Import of Animal and Animal Product as per Appendices III and IV hereto; or (f) Recommendation of the Head of Drug And Food Administration Agency or official so appointed by the Head of Drug And Food Administration Agency for Import of Processed Animal Product and Recommendation of the Minister of Agriculture or official so appointed by the Minister of Agriculture for Import of Processed Animal Product still having risk of zoonosis spread as per Appendix IV hereto.

[498] Indonesia's first written submission, paras. 76-79.

---

constitute import licensing procedures.[499] Moreover, both parties agree that an import licensing procedure can simultaneously breach these three provisions.[500]

427.   We consider that the disagreement between the parties does not relate to the scope of application of the Import Licensing Agreement. Rather, the parties have differing views on whether some of the challenged measures constitute import licensing procedures and thus fall within the scope of the Import Licensing Agreement.

428.   The Appellate Body has made it clear that the Import Licensing Agreement applies to import licensing *procedures* and not to import licensing *rules*.[501] If we find that any of the challenged measures is an import licensing rule, we will not need to examine Brazil's claims under Article 3.2 of the Import Licensing Agreement, given that it would not be applicable to that measure. However, the question of the proper order of analysis arises when we are confronted with a measure that we have found to constitute an import licensing procedure.

429.   As we have already noted (see paragraph 7.57 above), a panel is free to structure its order of analysis. In doing so, a panel should follow a proper logical sequence.[502] Nonetheless, previous panels and the Appellate Body have determined the proper logical sequence in examining claims raised under different agreements of Annex 1A of the WTO Agreement by first identifying the most relevant provision in a dispute.[503]

430.   The question that we are confronted with is whether we should begin our examination of the challenged measures with Article 3.2 of the Import Licensing Agreement, on the one hand, or with Article XI:1 of the GATT and Article 4.2 of Agreement on Agriculture, on the other hand.[504]

431.   Brazil considers that Article XI:1 of the GATT 1994, Article 4.2 of the Agreement on Agriculture, and Article 3.2 of the Import Licensing Agreement can and should apply simultaneously.[505] Indonesia considers that Article 4.2 is

---

[499]   Brazil's first written submission, paras. 135, 137, 139, and 143.
[500]   Brazil's response to Panel question No. 49; and Indonesia's response to Panel question No. 49.
[501]   Appellate Body Report, *EC – Bananas III*, para. 197.
[502]   See para. 7.58 above.
[503]   See Appellate Body Reports, *EC – Bananas III*, para. 204 (concluding that the panel should have applied the Agreement on Import Licensing Procedures (Article 1.3) before the GATT 1994 (Article X:3(a)). See also Panel Reports, *Indonesia - Import Licensing Regimes (New Zealand/US)*, para. 7.33 (examining first Article XI:1 of the GATT 1994 before Article 4.2 of the Agreement on Agriculture because it deals more specifically with import restrictions); *US – Animals*, paras. 7.7-7.12 (first examining claims under the SPS Agreement as it is more specific than the GATT 1994; such approach was followed by other panels referred to in para. 7.10); and *EC – Sardines*, paras. 7.15-7.19 (first examining claims under the TBT Agreement as it is a more specific agreement than the GATT 1994).
[504]   We recall that in section 7.2.3.2 above, we concluded and explained why we begin our analysis under Article XI:1 of the GATT 1994 and only turn to Article 4.2 of the Agreement on Agriculture if there is no finding of inconsistency under Article XI:1.
[505]   See Brazil's response to Panel question No. 49.

lex specialis in respect of both the GATT 1994 and the Import Licensing Agreement. Indonesia considers that this is less clear for the relationship between Article XI:1 of the GATT 1994 and Article 3.2 of the Import Licensing Agreement, because the scope of application of these provisions is different. Indonesia further notes that the general approach of other panels has been to exercise judicial economy with respect to claims under the Import Licensing Agreement when they had already found the substantive aspects of the import licensing regime to be inconsistent with Article XI:1.[506]

432.   We consider that the most appropriate manner to structure our analysis is by first assessing Brazil's claims under Article XI:1 or Article 4.2, as relevant. We will then examine Brazil's claims under Article 3.2 of the Import Licensing Agreement. In our view, this approach provides a logical sequence for the following reasons.[507]

433.   First, we note that Article XI:1 of the GATT 1994 imposes a substantive obligation on Members to refrain from imposing prohibitions or restrictions on the importation or the exportation of goods. In contrast, Article 3.2 of the Import Licensing Agreement deals with the administration of import licensing procedures.[508] Regarding which of these provisions is *lex specialis*, previous panels have considered that provisions of the covered agreement that deal with the substantive content of a measure, such as Article XI:1 of the GATT 1994, are more specific than those that deal with the application and administration of a measure, such as Article 3.2 of the Import Licensing Agreement.[509] These panels reached this conclusion when confronted with claims under these two provisions.[510]

434.   Second, we note that the Appellate Body in *EC – Bananas III* referred to the decision of the panel in that dispute to begin its analysis of the claims raised by the complainants under Article X:3(a) of the GATT 1994 before assessing those raised under the Import Licensing Agreement. The Appellate Body observed that "the Panel, in our view, should have applied the *Licensing Agreement* first, since this agreement deals specifically, and in detail, with the administration of import licensing procedures".[511] We consider the situation in that dispute to be different from the one before us. In *EC – Bananas III*, the Appellate Body was confronted with a situation where the complainants raised claims under provisions that govern the administration and application of measures, rather than their substantive content. In particular, the Appellate Body

---

[506]   See Indonesia's response to Panel question No. 49.
[507]   We note that at least three previous panels followed the same order of analysis. See Panel Reports, *Indonesia – Import Licensing Regimes*, para. 7.35; *Argentina – Import Measures*, paras. 6.359-6.361; and *Turkey – Rice*, paras. 7.38-7.42.
[508]   Appellate Body Report, *EC – Bananas III*, para. 197.
[509]   See Panel Reports, *Turkey – Rice*, paras. 7.38-7.42; and *Argentina – Import Measures*, paras. 6.359-6.361.
[510]   *Ibid.*
[511]   Appellate Body Report, *EC – Bananas III*, para. 204.

dealt with claims under Articles X:3(a) of the GATT 1994 and 1.3 of the Import Licensing Agreement. We are examining a different situation. Brazil has raised claims under provisions that set out substantive obligations, such as Articles XI:1 of the GATT 1994 and 4.2 of the Agreement on Agriculture, as well as under provisions pertaining to the administration and application of measures, such as Article 3.2 of the Import Licensing Agreement.

435.   We will thus begin our analysis by examining the challenged elements with regard to Article XI:1 of the GATT 1994 or Article 4.2 of the Agreement on Agriculture, as relevant.

7.6.4   Analysis of the positive list requirement and the intended use requirement as specific aspects of Indonesia's licensing regime

436.   We recall that Brazil challenged the positive list requirement and the intended use requirement individually and as elements of Indonesia's import licensing regime. Both Brazil[512] and Indonesia[513] have indicated that their claims and defences concerning these measures as elements of Indonesia's import licensing regime, are the same as those discussed with respect to these measures considered individually. We have already assessed Brazil's claims under Article XI:1 of the GATT 1994 in respect of these measures (see section 7.4 above with respect to the positive list requirement and section 7.5 with respect to the intended use requirement).[514] We therefore see no need for us to further discuss the claims and defences under Article XI:1 in respect of these measures, when considered as elements of Indonesia's import licensing regime.

437.   Brazil has further claimed that the positive list requirement and the intended use requirement are inconsistent with Article 3.2 of the Import Licensing Agreement.[515] Indonesia argues that these measures are not procedural in nature and therefore fall outside the scope of the Import Licensing

---

[512]   Brazil's first written submission, paras. 201 and 228-231; and second written submission, para. 148. See also Brazil's opening statement at the first meeting of the Panel, para. 79.

[513]   Indonesia's first written submission, paras. 247 and 295.

[514]   As indicated above, we have found that the positive list requirement, as enacted through the relevant provisions of MoA 58/2015 and MoT 05/2016 is inconsistent with Article XI:1, is not justified under Article XX(d) of the GATT 1994 (see para. 7.173 above), and has not ceased to exist (see para. 7.174 above). We also found that this measure, as enacted through the relevant provisions of MoA 34/2016 and MoT 59/2016, is inconsistent with Article XI:1 and not justified under Article XX(d), because it continues to apply in the same manner as enacted through MoA 58/2015 and MoT 05/2016 (see para. 7.175 above). With respect to the intended use requirement, we have found that this measure, as enacted through MoA 58/2015 is inconsistent with Article XI of the GATT 1994 and not justified under Article XX(b) or (d). We also found that this measure as enacted through MoA 34/2016, where its enforcement provisions are concerned, is inconsistent with Article III:4, and is not justified under Article XX(b) or (d) of the GATT 1994 (see paras. 7.337-7.338 above).

[515]   Brazil's first written submission, paras. 253-257; and second written submission, paras. 123-124 and 133-143. See also Brazil's response to Panel question Nos. 15, 16, 48; and opening statement at the second meeting of the Panel, paras. 33-34.

Agreement.[516] We, therefore, turn to address the applicability of the Import Licensing Agreement to these measures.

438.   Article 1.1 of the Import Licensing Agreement defines import licensing:

> as administrative procedures[1] used for the operation of import licensing regimes requiring the submission of an application or other documentation (other than that required for customs purposes) to the relevant administrative body as a prior condition for importation into the customs territory of the importing Member.

---

[1] (footnote original) Those procedures referred to as "licensing" as well as other similar administrative procedures.

439.   Brazil argues that there might be certain grey areas when determining whether a measure is exclusively substantive in nature or whether it can also have a procedural dimension. Brazil considers this to be the case with the positive list requirement and the intended use requirement. Brazil considers that the positive list requirement is a procedural licensing requirement to the extent that it must be declared in the application to obtain the import licence and appears in the import licence itself. Moreover, Brazil indicates that the importer who intends to renew a licence has to adduce evidence that it has fully complied with such requirement.[517] On the basis of similar arguments, Brazil considers that the intended use requirement constitutes an import licensing procedure.[518] Indonesia considers these elements to constitute substantive requirements for importation and that Brazil has failed to demonstrate that they fall under the scope of the Import Licensing Agreement.[519]

440.   In our view, the positive list requirement and the intended use requirement are in the nature of an import licensing rule. The positive list refers to the products that can be imported. To that extent, it does not impose a requirement to submit a particular document or constitute a requirement for importation. Instead, it is a requirement that simply prohibits trade in respect of specific products not included therein. The intended use requirement is a substantive requirement that importers commit to respect when applying both for an MoA Import Recommendation and for an MoT Import Approval. Clearly such representation by the importers is made through the submission of a

---

[516] Indonesia's response to Panel question No. 48. See also Indonesia's first written submission, para. 287.
[517] Brazil's response to Panel question No. 16; and second written submission, paras. 133-143. See also Brazil's response to Panel question Nos. 15 and 48; and opening statement at the second meeting of the Panel, paras. 33-34.
[518] Brazil's response to Panel question No. 16; and second written submission, paras. 133-143. See also Brazil's response to Panel question Nos. 15 and 48.
[519] Indonesia's first written submission, para. 287; response to Panel question No. 48; and second written submission, para. 124.

particular document, which in this case is the online application. Contrary to what Brazil argues, however, we do not consider that this makes the intended use requirement an administrative procedure used for the operation of an import licensing regime. We thus conclude that the positive list requirement and the intended use requirement do not fall under the purview of the Import Licensing Agreement.

7.6.5 Analysis of the application windows, validity periods and fixed licence terms

7.6.5.1 Introduction

441. Brazil is challenging the WTO-consistency of the application windows, the validity periods and the fixed licence terms. The application windows refer to the time in the year during which an importer may apply for an MoA Import Recommendation or an MoT Import Approval. The validity periods concern the period of time during which an importer can use such recommendation and approval. We understand Brazil to challenge the combined operation of the application windows and the validity periods resulting in specific trade restrictions, i.e. the impossibility to import the products at issue during certain periods of time.[520] Lastly, the fixed licence terms relate to the limitation imposed by the relevant regulations of MoA and MoT on the possibility of an importer to modify certain aspects of an MoA Import Recommendation and an MoT Import Approval.

442. As noted in section 7.2.4 above, the legal instruments enacting the application windows, the validity periods and the fixed licence terms have been revoked and replaced twice since panel establishment. The following tables reproduce the provisions relevant to our subsequent analysis in each of the three sets of legal instruments.

Table 5. Relevant provisions regarding the application and validity periods

First set of legal instruments	Second set of legal instruments	Third set of legal instruments
MoA 139/2014	MoA 58/2015	MoA 34/2016
Art. 23	*Art. 22*	*Art. 21*
(1) Application for a Recommendation made by Business Actors, State Owned	(1) Business Player, State Owned Enterprise (SOE) and Regional Government Owned	Application for a Recommendation for Business Actors, State-Owned

---

[520] Brazil's first written submission, paras. 200, 202-209. See also Brazil's opening statement at the first meeting of the Panel, para. 91; second written submission, para. 155; and response to Panel question No. 111.

First set of legal instruments	Second set of legal instruments	Third set of legal instruments
Entities, and Regional Entities s shall be submitted on the period of 1 – 31 December on the previous year, 1 – 31 March, 1 – 30 June, 1 – 30 September of the current year.	Enterprise (ROE) must submit Recommendation Application on 1st -31st of December of the preceding year, on 1st - 30th of April, and on 1st - 31st of August of the current year.	Enterprises, Regional-Owned Enterprises, Social Institutions or International Institution Representatives may be submitted at any time during working days.
Art. 31	*Art. 30*	*Art 27*
(1) Recommendation as referred to in Article 30 letter i is valid since the date of issuance until to December 31st of the current year at the latest.	(1) Validity period of the Recommendation as referred to in Article 29 letter i shall be performed in three periods within one year as follows: a. First period shall enter into force as of 1st of January up to 30th of April; b. Second period shall enter into force as of 1st of May up to 30th of August; c. Third period shall enter into force as of 1st of September up to 31st of December.	(1) Applicant upon receiving the recommendation as referred to in Article 26 paragraph (2) must within maximum 3 months since the issuance date, to submit an import approval to the ministry which is carrying out the governmental affairs in the trade issues. (2) The recommendation as referred to in Article 26 paragraph (2) is only valid for one submission of an import license. (3) If within the period referred to in paragraph (1) the applicant did not apply for an import approval, the recommendation will be declared invalid. *Art. 30* (1) The validity period of the Recommendation as referred to in Article 28 letter(i) is for 6 (six) months commencing from the issuance date.
MoT 46/2013	**MoT 05/2016**	**MoT 59/2016**
Art. 12	*Art.11*	*Art. 12*
(1) Application for Import Approval of Animal and Animal Product as stated in Appendix I for: a. The first quarter, period of January to March, can only be submitted in the month of December. b. The second quarter, period of April to June, can only be submitted in the month of March. c. The third quarter, period of July to September, can only be submitted in the month of June. d. The fourth quarter, period of	(3) The application for Approval to Import for Animal and Animal Product as per Appendix IV hereto may be submitted at any time. *Art. 12* (1) The validity term of Approval to Import for Animal and Animal Product as per Appendices II and IV hereto shall be in accordance with the validity term of the Recommendation as of the issue date. *Art. 19* (1) The Certificate of Health in	The application for Import Approval as referred to in Article 11 may be submitted at any time. *Art. 13* The validity period of an Import Approval as referred to in Article 11 is in line with the validity period of the Recommendation, from the date of issuance. *Art. 18* (1) Certificate of Health in the country of origin of imported animal and/or animal product is issued after the issuance of

First set of legal instruments	Second set of legal instruments	Third set of legal instruments
October to December, can only be submitted in the month of September. (2) Import Approval is issued at the start of each quarter. (3) Import Approval as intended in Article 11 paragraph (3) item a is valid for 3 (three) months commencing from the date of issuance of the Import Approval. *Art. 15.* (1) Certificate of Health of the imported Animal and/or Animal Product in the country of origin is issued after RI-Animal and Animal Product have obtained Import Approval. (2) Import Approval Number is attached on the Certificate of Health as intended in paragraph (1).	the country of origin of Animal and/or Animal Product to import shall be issued after the issue of Approval to Import. (2) The Number of Approval to Import shall be affixed on the Certificate of Health as referred to in paragraph (1).	Import Approval. (2) Import Approval Number shall be included in the Certificate of Health as referred to in paragraph (1).

Table 6.   Relevant provisions regarding the fixed licence terms

First set of legal instruments	Second set of legal instruments	Third set of legal instruments
MoA 139/2014	**MoA 58/2015**	**MoA 34/2016**
Art. 33	*Art. 32*	*Art. 32*
Business Actors, State-Owned Entities, Regional Entities, Social Institutions, and Foreign Country/International Institution Representatives, that import carcass, meat, and/or its processed: a. are prohibited to request the change of country of origin, point of entry, type/category of carcass, meat, and/or its processed for the issued recommendation; … *Art. 39* Business Actors, State-Owned Entities, Regional Entities, Social Institutions, or Foreign	Business Player, State Owned Enterprise (SOE) and Regional Government Owned Enterprise (ROE), Social Institution, and Foreign Country Representative/International Institution, conducting importation: a. are not allowed to make any alteration to the Country of Origin, Business Unit of Origin, port of discharge, type/category of carcass, meat, and/or the processed product thereof to a Recommendation that has been issued; … *Art. 38*	(1) Business Actors, State-Owned Enterprises, Regional-Owned Enterprises, Social Institutions and Foreign Country/International Institution Representatives who imports carcass, meat, offal and/or their processed products is forbidden to: a. propose changes to the Country of Origin, Business Unit of origin, port of entry, type/category of the carcass, meat, offal and/ or their processed products to the recommendation that has been published; …

First set of legal instruments	Second set of legal instruments	Third set of legal instruments
Country/International Institution Representatives, or that violate the provisions in: ... e. Article 33 shall be sanction by withdrawing of the recommendation, not given next recommendation , and shall be proposed to the Minister of Trade for a withdrawal of their Import Permit (PI) and company status as an Animal Product Registered Importer (IT).	Business Player, State Owned Enterprise (SOE) and Regional Government Owned Enterprise (ROE), Social Institution, and Foreign Country Representative/ International Institution that breaches the provision of: (f) Article 32, shall be sanctioned by revocation of their recommendation, denial of their next recommendation application, and propose to the Minister administrating governmental trade affairs to revoke the Import Approval (PI).	*Art. 38* (4) Business Actors, State-Owned Enterprises, Regional-Owned Enterprises, Social Institutions or Foreign Country/Institution Representatives which violate Article 32 will be subject to written warning and if it is ignored, will be subject to temporary suspension of import recommendation for 1 year period.
MoT 46/2013 *Art. 30* (2) Imported Animal and/or Animal Product with quantity, type, business unit, and/or country of origin that is not in accordance with the Import Approval and/or not in accordance with the provision in this Ministerial Regulation shall be re-exported.	**MoT 05/2016** *Art. 27* (2) The Animal and/or Animal Product imported of which the quantity, type, business unit, and/or country of origin are not in accordance with the Approval to Import and/or not in accordance with the provisions herein shall be re-exported.	**MoT 59/2016** *Art. 26* (2) Imported Animal and/or animal products of which the amount, type, business unit, and/or country of origin not in conformity with import approval and/or the requirements of this Minister Regulation must be re-exported.

443.   As explained in section 7.2.4.3 above, we first analyse the measures as enacted in MoA 58/2015 and MoT 05/2016, that is, the version Brazil has used to develop its claims in its first written submission. We undertake this analysis only after confirming that we have jurisdiction in respect of the challenged measures as enacted through this (second) set of legal instruments.

444.   With the adoption of the third and most recent set of legal instruments (i.e. MoA 34/2016 and MoT 59/2016) the parties' arguments have evolved. Indonesia submits that the application windows no longer exist and that, therefore, that measure has expired.[521] Brazil, however contests expiry.[522] We address these arguments in section 7.6.5.2.2 below.

---

[521]   Indonesia's response to Panel question No. 24; second written submission, paras. 19-22 and 129; response to Panel question No. 113; and comments on Brazil's response to Panel question No. 103, para. 80.
[522]   Brazil's response to Panel question No. 103.

7.6.5.2   Panel's analysis of the application windows, validity periods and the fixed licence terms as enacted through MoA 58/2015 and MoT 05/2016

445.   Brazil has challenged the joint operation of the application windows and the validity periods, and separately, the fixed licence terms. We will thus first examine the application windows and the validity periods, as a single measure, before turning to our assessment of the fixed licence terms. This part of our assessment will focus on our jurisdiction and the consistency of these measures with Article XI:1 of the GATT 1994. We note that Indonesia raised a joint defence for all three measures[523], we therefore pursue a joint examination of Indonesia's defence of these measures under Article XX(d). Lastly, we address Brazil's claims in respect of these measures under Article 4.2 of the Agreement on Agriculture and Article 3.2 of the Import Licensing Agreement.

7.6.5.2.1   Application windows and validity periods

7.6.5.2.1.1   Measure at issue and Panel's jurisdiction

446.   On the basis of Table 5 above, we consider the following to be the main features of the provisions at issue:

a.   Limit an importer's opportunity to apply for an MoA Import Recommendation to three application periods each year[524];

b.   Allow for the re-submission of an application for an MoA Import Recommendation to be made before the end of the validity period of the relevant recommendation[525];

c.   Limit the issuance of an MoA Import Recommendation to three times a year[526];

d.   Condition the issuance of an MoT Import Approval to the issuance of an MoA Import Recommendation[527];

e.   Allow for an importer to apply for an MoT Import Approval at any time[528];

f.   Limit the validity of an MoA Import Recommendation to three periods a year, of four months each[529];

---

[523]   Indonesia's response to Panel question No. 113.
[524]   See Article 22(1) of MoA 58/2015 (Exhibit BRA-1/IDN-24).
[525]   See Article 30(3) of MoA 58/2015 (Exhibit BRA-1/IDN-24).
[526]   See Article 28 of MoA 58/2015 (Exhibit BRA-1/IDN-24).
[527]   See Article 10(2)(e) of MoT 05/2016 (Exhibit BRA-3/IDN-39).
[528]   See Article 11(3) of MoT 05/2016 (Exhibit BRA-3/IDN-39).
[529]   See Article 30(1) of MoA 58/2015 (Exhibit BRA-1/IDN-24).

g. Set the validity of an MoT Import Approval to that of the MoA Import Recommendation upon which it is based.[530]

h. Require the inclusion of the number of the MoT Import Approval on the veterinary health certificate,[531] thus limiting the possibility of exporters to ship products before importers obtain an MoT Import Approval.

447. As shown in Table 5 above, the relevant provisions in MoA 58/2015 and MoT 05/2016, through which the application windows and the validity periods are enacted, differ from those in MoA 139/2014 and MoT 46/2013. As discussed above, in line with the Appellate Body's jurisprudence in *Chile – Price Band System*, we consider that our terms of reference cover subsequent amendments to the measure at issue so long as that measure remains in essence the same.[532]

448. The application windows for an MoA Import Recommendation, albeit changing from four times to three times a year, remain in place in MoA 58/2015. Moreover, although an importer could apply for an MoT Import Recommendation at any time, according to MoT 05/2016 an importer can only apply for MoT Import Approval if it has already received an MoA Import Recommendation. In our view, this has the practical effect of limiting the application windows for an MoT Import Approval to those time periods during which an importer has an existing MoA Import Recommendation. This means that if an importer does not hold an MoA Import Recommendation, it will have to wait until the next application period for such a recommendation before being able to apply for an MoT Import Approval. On this basis, we consider that the application windows for MoA Import Recommendations and MoT Import Approvals, as enacted through MoA 58/2015 and MoT 05/2016, remain in essence the same as those identified in Brazil's panel request.

449. The validity period for an MoA Import Recommendation, changed from the time remaining between its issuance and the 31st of December of that year (as enacted in Article 31(1) of MoA 139/2014), to three four-month periods. Thus, despite that difference the validity period remains in place. In addition, the validity period of the MoT Import Approval corresponds to that of the MoA Import Recommendation. In our view, the fact that MoT Import Approvals are valid for an additional month, under MoT 05/2016, does not affect the fact that their term of validity is still limited. On this basis, we consider that the validity periods for MoA Import Recommendations and MoT Import Approvals, as enacted through MoA 58/2015 and MoT 05/2016, remain in essence the same as those identified in Brazil's panel request.

450. On the basis of the foregoing we find that the application windows and the validity periods, as enacted through MoA 58/2015 and MoT 05/2016, fall

---

[530] See Article 12(1) of MoT 05/2016 (Exhibit BRA-3/IDN-39).
[531] Article 19 of MoT 05/2016 (Exhibit BRA-3/IDN-39).
[532] See section 7.2.4 above.

within our terms of reference, and we thus have jurisdiction to rule on their WTO consistency.

7.6.5.2.1.2 Whether the application windows and the validity periods are inconsistent with Article XI:1 of the GATT 1994

451. Brazil argues that the application windows and the validity periods limit trade because, through their combined operation, they prevent exports from entering Indonesia's market during the beginning of each validity period.[533] According to Indonesia, the application windows and validity periods set out in MoA 58/2015 and MoT 05/2016 do not have any trade-limiting effects.[534] Indonesia considers that under this regime, importers would be able to import their products throughout the year.[535]

452. As indicated above, we will examine the application windows and the validity periods as a single measure. We set out Article XI:1 of the GATT 1994 above.[536] As we have done for the positive list requirement and the intended use requirement, we structure our analysis under Article XI:1 around the following two questions: (1) whether the measures at issue constitute a prohibition or restriction on the importation of chicken meat and chicken products; and (2) whether they are made effective through quotas, import or export licences or other measures.

453. Regarding the second question, we note that the parties have not explicitly debated the specific nature of the application windows and the validity periods. To the extent that these are elements of Indonesia's import licensing regime, we consider them to constitute an import licence for the purposes of Article XI:1 of the GATT 1994.

454. As regards the first question, we recall that the Appellate Body identified the meaning of the term "restriction" as "[a] thing which restricts someone or something, a limitation on action, a limiting condition or regulation" and concluded from it, that it is "generally ... something that has a limiting effect".[537] Furthermore, in a contextual reading of the title of Article XI[538] the Appellate

---

[533] Brazil's first written submission, paras. 206 and 208-209; opening statement at the first meeting of the Panel, para. 91; second written submission, para. 155; and response to Panel question No. 111.
[534] Indonesia's second written submission, paras. 14 and 127. As noted above, Indonesia considers that Article XI:1 does not apply in this dispute. As we discussed in section 7.2.3.2 above, we do not agree with Indonesia that Article 4.2 of the Agreement on Agriculture applies to the exclusion of Article XI:1 of the GATT 1994.
[535] Indonesia's second written submission, paras. 17-18.
[536] See section 7.4.2.2 above.
[537] Appellate Body Reports, *China – Raw Materials*, para. 319; and *Argentina – Import Measures*, para. 5.217.
[538] The title of Article XI is "General Elimination of Quantitative Restrictions".

Body concluded that the limiting effect must be "on the quantity or amount of a product being imported".[539]

455.   Brazil submits that the exportation process of the products at issue takes its exporters, on average, up to 100 days.[540] Because the validity periods are limited to 120 days, Brazil considers that the export transactions could only effectively happen during 20 days of each validity period.[541] Indonesia submits that because they are able to re-apply for a new MoA Import Recommendation a month before the expiry of the validity period, importers can import their products into Indonesia throughout the year without interruption.[542]

456.   According to the evidence submitted by Brazil, the whole export process would take an exporter on average 100 days. This is the result of adding the time required to take the following three steps to export. The first is the sales of the products (e.g. finding a buyer, etc.), which, according to Brazil, lasts 30 days on average. The second is production, which, Brazil asserts, lasts from 20 to 30 days. The final step is the loading, documentation, shipping and transit, which, as Brazil submits, lasts from 35 to 45 days.[543] We note that Indonesia has not rebutted the accuracy of this time-frame, although indicating that Brazil has not provided evidence for the existence of any type of "dead zone".[544]

457.   We do not consider the first two steps described by Brazil (e.g. sales of products and production), to be relevant for our analysis. The sales and production steps, correspond to time that is under the control of the exporter. We do not see how such time could depend on the specific time-frames set out by the application windows or the validity periods. We thus consider that the only relevant time-frame, for the purposes of our analysis, is the maximum 45 days that correspond to the last step, namely, documentation and shipment.

458.   To understand better the design, architecture, and revealing structure of this measure and its expected operation, we examine a hypothetical scenario. We assume that an importer has obtained an MoA Import Recommendation and an MoT Import Approval for the validity period of January to April 2016 and that it takes, on average, six weeks (45 days) for the importer to load, prepare the relevant documentation, and ship the products from Brazil to Indonesia. This means that at the latest, the importer must make its last shipment by mid-March for the products to arrive in time to be admitted to Indonesia, before the validity

---

[539] Appellate Body Reports, *China – Raw Materials*, para. 320. See also Appellate Body Reports, *Argentina – Import Measures*, para. 5.217.

[540]   See Letter of ABPA informing the average deadlines necessary to conclude an export process of chicken meat and chicken products from Brazil to Indonesia (ABPA letter) (Exhibit BRA-44).

[541]   Brazil's first written submission, para. 206. See also Brazil's first written submission, paras. 208-209; opening statement at the first meeting of the Panel, para. 91; second written submission, para. 155; and response to Panel question No. 111.

[542]   Indonesia's second written submission, paras. 17-18.

[543]   See ABPA Letter (Exhibit BRA-44). See also MSC Routefinder and Maersk Line Schedules informing that there is no direct vessel's line from Brazil to Indonesia (Exhibit BRA-45).

[544]   Indonesia's second written submission, para. 13.

of the MoA Import Recommendation and the MoT Import Approval expire. We also assume that the importer applied in April, at the earliest opportunity, for an MoA Import Recommendation and an MoT Import Approval for the next validity period of May to August 2016. We assume that the MoA Import Approval would be issued in April, one week after the importer made the on-line application.[545] Therefore, the earliest the importer would be able to ship animals and animal products under the validity period of May to August, would be the second week of April after reapplying and obtaining the new MoA Import Recommendation and the MoT Import Approval. If the importer is able to ship the products immediately after obtaining the MoT Import Approval, the products would arrive at the end of May. Therefore, in this scenario, there would be no imports between the end of April and the end of May. Hence, the importer would have to stop shipments in mid-March and could only resume after obtaining a new MoT Import Approval in mid-April. These shipments would only arrive in Indonesia at the end of May, following the time for loading, documentation, and shipment indicated above.

459.   The hypothetical scenario, which was modelled to closely follow how the different elements or requirements encompassed in these measures operate, shows that under Indonesia's import licensing regime, between the time of application and the end of the licensing period there is always a period of time during which no chicken is actually imported into Indonesia. It is worth noting that this period of no imports can be attributed to three separate causes: (i) the timing of the application windows, which is very close to the expiration of the previous import documents, (ii) the requirements that preclude importers from shipping products before having obtained the new MoT Import Approval, that would otherwise allow importers to save time by shipping their products in advance while waiting for the new MoT Import Approval, and (iii) the shipping time from the country of origin, which creates a gap between the time where the new MoT Import Approval is received and the time when the goods subject to such MoT Import Approval arrive in Indonesia. Of these three causes, the first two are attributable to Indonesia's regulations while the third one is due to geographical factors when shipping products from Brazil to Indonesia. However, the manner in which the application windows and the validity periods are designed could have taken this fact into account to avoid trade-restrictiveness. The breadth of the trade restrictiveness of these measures is represented in the following figure:

---

[545] We acknowledge Indonesia's indication that according to the relevant provisions of MoA 58/2015, the issuance of an MoA Import Recommendation can take up to five working days. Similarly, according to the relevant provisions of MoT 05/2016, the issuance of an MoT Import Approval can take up to two working days. See Indonesia's second written submission, para. 14.

Figure 3   "Dead zone" scenario on the importation of chicken

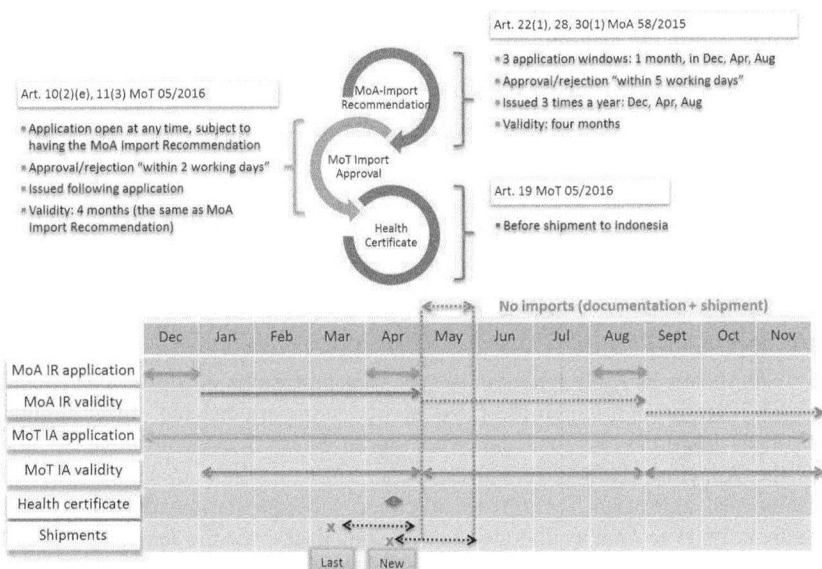

Sources: Based on MoA 58/2015 (Exhibit BRA-01/IDN-24), MOT 5/2016 (Exhibit BRA-03/IDN-39), and Exhibits BRA-44 and BRA-45.

460.   We recall that one of the features of the measures at issue is that the number of the MoT Import Approval must be indicated on the veterinary health certificate.[546] Indonesia argues that any delay caused by the fact that the veterinary certificate has to include the number of the MoT Import Approval would be a consequence of the administrative process for the issuance of the certificate by the authorities in the country of origin.[547]

461.   In our view, this argument is misplaced. The moment when exporters may request the relevant veterinary health certificate is limited because of Indonesia's import licensing regime. In particular, due to the requirement set forth in Article 19 of MoT 05/2016 that the veterinary health certificate is issued after the issuance of the MoT Import Approval. Thus, absent this requirement, exporters could have saved time by requesting the issuance of the veterinary health certificate in parallel to the renewal of the MoT Import Approval. On this basis, we consider that Indonesia's argument does not alter our conclusion resulting from the preceding analysis.

462.   Brazil has demonstrated that the application windows and validity periods, considered as a single measure, by virtue of its design, constitutes a restriction having a limiting effect on the competitive opportunities of importers.

---

[546]   Article 19 of MoT 05/2016 (Exhibit BRA-3/IDN-39).
[547]   Indonesia's second written submission, paras. 15-16.

In practice, importers will not be able to import products during at least four weeks of each import period, thus restricting the market access of the products at issue into Indonesia. We thus consider that these measures constitute an import restriction within the meaning of Article XI:1 of the GATT 1994.

463.   We therefore find that the single measure consisting of the application windows and the validity periods, as enacted through MoA 58/2015 and MoT 05/2016, is inconsistent with Article XI:1 of the GATT 1994.

7.6.5.2.2   Fixed licence terms

7.6.5.2.2.1   Measure at issue and Panel's jurisdiction

464.   In this section we consider the fixed licence terms as enacted through MoA 58/2015 and MoT 05/2016.

465.   As shown in Table 6 above, the relevant provisions in MoA 58/2015 and MoT 05/2016 through which the fixed licence terms are enacted, differ slightly from those in MoA 139/2014 and MoT 46/2013. As discussed above, in line with the Appellate Body's jurisprudence in *Chile – Price Band System*, we consider that our terms of reference cover subsequent amendments to the measure at issue so long as that measure remains in essence the same.[548]

466.   There are only marginal differences in the manner in which the fixed licence terms are set out in the first two sets of legal instruments. The only change in the MoA Import Recommendation is that the sanction no longer includes proposing to the Minister to withdraw the company status as animal product registered importer. In our view, this does not change, in any way the essence of the terms of this licensing requirement as being fixed.[549] The same holds true for the MoT Import Approval, where the wording used in the relevant provisions of both MoT 46/2013 and MoT 05/2016 is almost identical.[550]

467.   On the basis of the foregoing we find that the fixed licence terms, as enacted through the second set of legal instruments, fall within our terms of reference, and that we thus have jurisdiction to rule on their WTO consistency.

---

[548] See section 7.2.4 above.

[549] Article 33(a) of MoA 139/2014 establishes that importers "are prohibited to request the change of country of origin, point of entry, type/category of carcass, meat, and/or its processed for the issued recommendation". Moreover, Article 39 provides that a violation to the provisions of Article 33 shall be sanctioned by "withdrawing of the recommendation, not given next recommendation, and shall be proposed to the Minister of Trade for a withdrawal of their Import Permit (PI) and company status as an Animal Product Registered Importer (IT)".

[550] Article 30(2) of MoT 46/2013 provides that animals and animal products imported with "quantity, type, business unit, and/or country of origin that is not in accordance with the Import Approval" shall be re-exported.

7.6.5.2.2.2   Whether the fixed licence terms are inconsistent with Article XI:1 of the GATT 1994

468.   Brazil argues that the fixed licence terms limit trade because by prohibiting adjustments to the relevant licensing documents, they impede importers from having the necessary flexibility to respond to changes in market conditions.[551] Indonesia rejects Brazil's arguments and considers that Brazil has failed to demonstrate that this measure has any limiting effect on imports.[552]

469.   We set out Article XI:1 of the GATT 1994 above.[553] As we have done for the previous measures we have examined under this provision, we structure our Article XI:1 analysis around the following two questions: (1) whether the measures at issue constitute a prohibition or restriction on the importation of chicken meat and chicken products, and (2) whether it is made effective through quotas, import or export licences or other measures.

470.   Regarding the second question, we note that the parties have not explicitly debated the specific nature of the fixed licence terms. In our view, the fixed licence terms are elements of Indonesia's import licensing regime, as they condition the manner in which the import licensing documents will be enforced. On this basis, we consider that the fixed licence terms constitute an import licence for the purposes of Article XI:1 of the GATT 1994.

471.   As regards the first question, we recall that the Appellate Body identified the meaning of the term "restriction" as "[a] thing which restricts someone or something, a limitation on action, a limiting condition or regulation" and concluded from it, that it is "generally ... something that has a limiting effect".[554]

472.   Indonesia raises what we consider a preliminary defence. According to Indonesia, the terms of the import licensing requirements are at the complete discretion of the importers, and thus, are not measures maintained by Indonesia.[555] Brazil considers this defence to be misplaced as the fixed licence terms are a measure instituted and maintained by Indonesia.[556] We agree with Indonesia that it is the importer who initially defines the terms of the licensing documents, when submitting the relevant applications. However, this is in no way dispositive of the consequences arising from a subsequent amendment to those terms after the relevant licensing document has been issued. It is Articles 32(a) of MoA 58/2015 and 27(2) of MoT 05/2016 that prohibit such amendments. Moreover, the sanctions imposed in case of any change to the fixed licence terms results from the text of Articles 38 and 27(2) of MoA 58/2015 and MoT 05/2016, respectively. All these are part of legal instruments adopted by

---

[551]   Brazil's first written submission, paras. 210-211; and second written submission, para. 160.
[552]   Indonesia's first written submission, para. 294.
[553]   See section 7.4.2.2 above.
[554]   Appellate Body Reports, *China – Raw Materials*, para. 319; and *Argentina – Import Measures*, para. 5.217.
[555]   Indonesia's first written submission, para. 262.
[556]   Brazil's second written submission, paras. 159-160.

the government of Indonesia, which we thus consider to be attributable to Indonesia.[557]

473.   Brazil argues that foreclosing the possibility to amend the terms of the MoA Import Recommendation and the MoT Import Approval forces importers to have all the details of transactions in advance of importation. Brazil considers this to run counter to market practices.[558] Brazil further submits that by not being entitled to request adjustments in the licensing terms, importers are unable to respond to new business opportunities during the validity period.[559] Brazil thus considers that the fixed licence terms: (a) unduly restrict market access for Brazilian products; (b) create uncertainty as to an applicant's ability to import; and (c) impose a significant burden on importers unrelated to their normal importing activity.[560] Brazil further notes that it does not question a Member's right to require that the country of origin and the product be identified in an import licence whenever the measure is justified in light of the legitimate trade restrictions the licensing regime is supposed to administer.[561]

474.   In our view, the design and structure of the fixed licence terms is such that if an importer modifies the relevant terms of the import licensing documents it will be subject to severe sanctions (e.g. revocation of the MoA Import Recommendation or re-exportation of the relevant consignment).

475.   We understand Brazil's arguments to imply that only those requirements that stem from illegitimate trade restrictions have the trade-restrictive effect that Brazil is complaining about. We note that there is certain information that appears in the import licensing documents, which is objectively verified in the process of the issuance of an MoA Import Recommendation. In particular, the relevant MoA regulations provide for an approval process of a country of origin and of business units (see paragraph 7.97 above). Moreover, such verification, which entails the assessment of the animal disease status of a country, may impact the products that can be authorized to enter. If an importer desires to modify any of these terms, it would need to apply for a new MoA Import Recommendation, to the extent that Indonesian authorities would need to verify such information in respect of the new country of origin or the new business units. Against this back-drop, we fail to see how limiting the possibility to amend this information could create any trade-restrictiveness.

476.   We do not consider this to be the case with respect to the port of entry and the quantity of the products. We agree with Brazil that limiting these requirements impedes importers from making adjustments to the licensing

---

[557]   See Appellate Body Report, *US – Corrosion-Resistant Steel Sunset Review*, para. 81; *Australia – Apples*, para. 171; *US – Shrimp*, para. 173; and Panel Reports, *Canada – Renewable Energy / Feed-In Tariff Program*, fn 37; and *Australia – Salmon (Article 21.5 – Canada)*, para. 7.12 and fn 146.
[558]   Brazil's first written submission, para. 210.
[559]   Brazil's first written submission, para. 211.
[560]   Brazil's first written submission, para. 212. See also Brazil's opening statement at the first meeting of the Panel, para. 93; and response to Panel question No. 23.
[561]   Brazil's response to Panel question No. 23.

documents that arise in the normal course of business. Brazil refers to Norway's third-party statement, indicating that "the fact that importers are prevented from responding to changes in market conditions has a limiting effect on trade".[562] We agree with Brazil's assumption that there may be circumstances arising in the normal course of business that may require an importer to modify the ports of entry or the quantity it initially indicated in the application for the licensing documents. The trade-restrictive effect of this measure arises from its design and structure. Importers are simply not allowed to amend in any way the information on the ports of entry. Furthermore, importers are also not allowed to increase the quantity of the products for a given validity period.[563] Moreover, importers who infringe this prohibition are subject to sanctions that entail grave consequences for business opportunities, such as the revocation of the relevant licensing documents or the re-exportation of the products. In our view, these sanctions result in a limitation on imports of products that can either not be imported through the port of entry initially designated or exceed the quantity indicated in the application form.[564] We thus consider both these aspects of the fixed licence terms, as enforced through the applicable sanctions, to constitute conditions limiting the importation of the products at issue.

477.   We note Indonesia's argument, that importers are free to alter the terms of importation from one licence application to the next.[565] In our view, this argument does not alter our preceding analysis. Although an importer could modify the conditions of importation from one period to the next, it is still nonetheless limited by the licence terms for each period. As described above, such limitation results in importers not being able to amend the ports of entry or the quantity of imported products. As we have noted, doing so entails grave sanctions.

478.   In addition, Indonesia argues that some of the terms of importation are not as stringent as Brazil portrays them. For instance, an importer can indicate several ports of entry and not be sanctioned if it only imports through one of them.[566] Despite Indonesia's explanation, we consider that the requirement to list upfront the ports of entry through which imported products could enter has a trade-restrictive effect. According to Indonesia, the only situation in which an importer would not be sanctioned if changing the port of entry is, if it listed several or all possible ports in its application. It seems unreasonable to impose such burden on the applicant. Moreover, if all importers were to do this, this requirement would not serve Indonesia to gather the information on the specific ports through which particular consignments would enter the country.

---

[562] Brazil's second written submission, para. 159.
[563] Indonesia's response to Panel question No. 113.
[564] See United States' third-party submission, para. 46 (referring to the limitation on the quantity of products that may be imported in a given validity period).
[565] Indonesia's first written submission, para. 263.
[566] *Ibid.*

479.   Similarly, Indonesia argues that an importer may indicate that it will import a certain quantity and change the desired amount from one period to the next.[567] Although this might be true, it does not change the fact that imports beyond the stipulated quantity will entail severe sanctions. In addition, if all importers were to indicate extremely high numbers of desired imports, this requirement would not serve Indonesia to gather precise information of quantity of imports that would occur in a specific day.

480.   On the basis of the foregoing, we find that the fixed licence terms, in respect of the limitation on the ports of entry and the quantity of imported products, are inconsistent with Article XI:1 of the GATT 1994.

7.6.5.2.3   Whether the application windows, the validity periods, and the fixed licence terms are justified under Article XX(d) of the GATT 1994

7.6.5.2.3.1   Introduction

481.   We have found that the application windows, the validity periods and the fixed licence terms, as enacted through MoA 58/2015 and MoT 05/2016, are inconsistent with Article XI:1 of the GATT 1994.[568]

482.   We recall that Indonesia set out its defence under Article XX of the GATT 1994 for the three measures referred to above. On this basis, and in order to provide the clearest and most expedient analysis, we will examine Indonesia's defence under Article XX for the application windows, the validity periods and the fixed licence terms jointly.

483.   Indonesia raises its defence under Article XX(d) of the GATT 1994, essentially arguing that these measures allow the allocation of human resources to ensure compliance with Indonesia's laws and regulations addressing halal, public health, consumer protection, and customs enforcement relating to halal and safety.[569] Brazil rejects the defence on procedural and substantive grounds. Procedurally, Brazil argues that Indonesia developed, too late in the proceedings, its arguments on how the challenged measures secure compliance with the

---

[567] Indonesia's second written submission, para. 18; and response to Panel question No. 113.

[568] See paras. 7.383 (regarding the application windows and the validity periods) and 7.400 (regarding the fixed licence terms) above.

[569] Indonesia's first written submission, para. 297; opening statement at the first meeting of the Panel, para. 97; and responses to Panel question Nos. 24 and 113.

relevant laws and regulations.[570] On substance, Brazil submits that Indonesia has not met its evidentiary burden.[571]

484.   Before pursuing our substantive examination of Indonesia's defence under Article XX, we will address Brazil's procedural objections.

7.6.5.2.3.2   Admissibility of certain aspects of Indonesia's defence under Article XX(d)

485.   In commenting on Indonesia's responses to the Panel's questions after the second meeting, Brazil challenged the Panel's ability to assess Indonesia's arguments on how the application windows and the validity periods and the fixed licence terms could be justified under Article XX(d).[572] In Brazil's view, Indonesia developed certain arguments too late in the proceedings.[573]

486.   Brazil is particularly concerned with certain evidence submitted by Indonesia at this late stage in support of its defence under Article XX(d), namely, that certain importers present a monthly arrival plan.[574] Brazil argues that according to paragraph 8 of the Panel's Working Procedures, Indonesia was expected to submit all relevant evidence during the first meeting. Moreover, these arguments were not developed as part of a rebuttal to new arguments brought by Brazil and the Panel granted no authorization to submit them. Brazil signals that Indonesia did not provide any good cause that would justify this late submission.[575] On this basis Brazil claims that Indonesia's arguments on the relationship between the challenged measures and Article XX(d) of the GATT, as well as the arrival plan, are not properly before the Panel.[576]

487.   We disagree with Brazil that Indonesia "waited until the very last opportunity to develop" its defence under Article XX(d).[577] It is true that Indonesia refined its arguments, however it raised its defence under Article XX(d) from the first written submission itself.[578] Moreover, Indonesia argues that these measures contribute to the claimed objective by allowing "Indonesia to manage better its resources by providing an estimate on the volume of imports

---

[570]   Brazil's comments on Indonesia's response to Panel question No. 113, paras. 37-41. We note that in paras. 36-41 of its comments to Indonesia's responses to question of the Panel, Brazil referred to question No. 133, however we understand Brazil's comments to be referring to Indonesia's response to Panel question No. 113. On this basis, we refer to Brazil's comments on Indonesia's response to Panel question No. 113.

[571]   Brazil's second written submission, paras. 157 and 161-163; opening statement at the second meeting of the Panel, paras. 36-38; and comments on Indonesia's response to Panel question No. 113, para. 52.

[572]   Brazil's comments on Indonesia's response to Panel question No. 113, paras. 37-41.

[573]   Brazil's comments on Indonesia's response to Panel question No. 113, para. 37.

[574]   Brazil's comments on Indonesia's response to Panel question No. 113, para. 38.

[575]   Brazil's comments on Indonesia's response to Panel question No. 113, paras. 39-40.

[576]   Brazil's comments on Indonesia's response to Panel question No. 113, para. 41.

[577]   Brazil's comments on Indonesia's response to Panel question No. 113, para. 37.

[578]   Indonesia's first written submission, paras. 296-301.

that would enter Indonesia through a particular port at a given time".[579] We consider that it would be preferable if the parties raise their arguments and defences at the earliest opportunity. However, we are cognizant that argumentation unfolds in the course of the proceedings, including through responses to questions from the Panel. The latter, in fact, is the case here.[580] We note that Indonesia developed these arguments and submitted a new exhibit in response to a question from the Panel, which, in turn, was triggered by arguments developed by both parties in the course of the second meeting on Indonesia's defence under Article XX(d). Lastly, we observe that Brazil has had an opportunity to respond to Indonesia's arguments.[581]

488. On the basis of the foregoing, we consider that Indonesia's defence under the general exceptions provided in Article XX(d) and references to the monthly arrival plan are properly before us. We therefore turn to the substantive assessment of Indonesia's defence under Article XX(d).

7.6.5.2.3.3   Whether the application windows, the validity periods and the fixed licence terms are justified under Article XX(d)

489. We have set out Article XX in section 7.4.2.3 above. As we noted there, the analysis under Article XX requires us to proceed in two steps. We first need to assess whether the measure is provisionally justified under the specific sub-paragraphs identified by the respondent – here subparagraph (d). If that is the case, we go on to examine whether the measure satisfies the requirements of the chapeau of Article XX. Furthermore, we recall that the burden of proof in respect of an exception is on the responding party.[582]

Article XX(d)

490. As already seen in section 7.4.2.3 above, Article XX(d) covers measures "necessary to secure compliance with laws or regulations which are not inconsistent with the provisions of this Agreement […]".

---

[579] Indonesia's response to Panel question Nos. 24 and 113.
[580] We recall that it is the Panel's prerogative to ask questions and scrutinize the parties' argumentation. See Appellate Body Reports, *US – Zeroing (EC)*, para. 260; and *EC – Fasteners (China)*, para. 566.
[581] In *US – Gambling*, the Appellate Body addressed a similar question to the one raised by Brazil. In that dispute Antigua argued that the panel had erred in considering the United States' defence under Article XIV of the GATS because it was raised too late in the proceedings (i.e. in the second written submission to the Panel). The Appellate Body considered that in the circumstances of that dispute, where Antigua had an opportunity to comment on the United States' defence, the panel had not deprived Antigua's full and fair opportunity to respond to the defence. (Appellate Body Report, *US – Gambling*, para. 276) Similarly, we consider that if a complaining party has had the opportunity to comment on the arguments developed by the respondent, a panel should consider those arguments in its assessment of the respondent's defence.
[582] See para. 7.122 above.

491.   In paragraph 7.123 above, we noted that, in line with relevant guidance provided by the Appellate Body[583], our assessment under Article XX(d) requires us to address the following two questions: (1) whether the application windows, the validity periods and the fixed licence terms are designed to secure compliance with laws or regulations that are not themselves inconsistent with a provision of the GATT 1994, and (2) whether these are measures necessary to secure compliance with such laws and regulations. We address these questions in turn.

Designed to secure compliance with laws or regulations

492.   Indonesia's defence has evolved throughout these proceedings. At the outset, Indonesia argued that these measures, as part of Indonesia's import licensing regime, are designed to secure compliance with Indonesia's laws and regulations addressing halal, public health, as well as deceptive practices (consumer protection) and customs enforcement relating to halal and safety. Indonesia refers to the following provisions: Articles 58(1), 58(4), and 59(1) of Law No. 18/2009 (Animal Law); halal certification as set out in Law 33/2014; and Articles 4,7, 9(1) and 9(3) of Law 8/1999 (Consumer Protection Law).[584] Indonesia indicates that none of these laws and regulations are inconsistent with the provisions of the GATT 1994, and that Brazil has not provided proof otherwise.[585]

493.   Indonesia further explained that the immediate manner in which these measures secure compliance with those laws and regulations is by facilitating the supervision by customs and quarantine officials over the importer's compliance with the relevant halal, safety, and consumer protection requirements at the time of importation.[586] Indonesia considers that these measures, especially the fixed licence terms, give the government a general indication of where, when, and what, will be imported.[587]

494.   Brazil considers that Indonesia has failed to demonstrate that these measures are necessary to secure the immediate objective that Indonesia argues these measures pursue.[588] Brazil further argues that Indonesia's rationale and regulatory behaviour is contradictory, to the extent that it says that it requires detailed information of the volume of imports to determine the manner in which it will allocate its human resources. However, Brazil also claims that the

---

[583] Appellate Body Report, *Korea – Various Measures on Beef*, para. 157. See also Appellate Body Reports, *Argentina – Financial Services*, para. 6.202; and *Colombia– Textiles*, paras. 5.123 and 5.124.

[584] Indonesia's first written submission, para. 297; opening statement at the first meeting of the Panel, para. 97; and response to Panel question Nos. 24 and 113.

[585] Indonesia's first written submission, para. 298.

[586] Indonesia's response to Panel question No. 113.

[587] Indonesia's response to Panel question No. 115.

[588] Brazil's second written submission, paras. 157 and 161-163; opening statement at the second meeting of the Panel, paras. 36-38; and comments on Indonesia's response to Panel question No. 113, para. 52.

regulations are flexible, which would defeat such a purpose.[589] Brazil further submits that there are less trade-restrictive alternatives that could achieve Indonesia's claimed objective.[590]

495.   As noted previously, the Appellate Body has described our task as "an initial examination of the relationship between the inconsistent measure and the relevant laws or regulations" which requires a panel to "scrutinize the design of the measures sought to be justified".[591] The Appellate Body further clarified that the standard for ascertaining whether such a relationship exists is whether the assessment of the design of the measure reveals that the measure is *not incapable* of securing compliance with the relevant laws and regulations in Indonesia.[592] Finally, we note that the Appellate Body has described this test as "not… particularly demanding", in contrast to the requirements of the next step of the analysis, namely the necessity test.[593]

496.   It is our understanding that Indonesian law does not specifically require the planned allocation of human resources in customs or quarantine control posts.[594] To that extent, we understand that Indonesia is not claiming that the challenged measures directly secure compliance with the relevant laws and regulations. However, we agree with Indonesia that an appropriate management of human resources at the time of importation is necessary for the proper enforcement of customs laws and regulations, particularly the provisions on halal, public health, consumer protection and food safety referred to by Indonesia. To that extent, we accept the argument that the challenged measures may indirectly secure compliance with the laws and regulations identified by Indonesia.

497.   In further exploring this matter, we have some doubts about these measures being designed to secure the objective identified by Indonesia. As we point out above[595], we consider there to be a degree of contradiction in Indonesia's arguments. In particular, we do not see how a measure that is flexible, in terms of providing only indicative information that can vary greatly (e.g. allowing importers to indicate all the ports of entry and only use one or to

---

[589]   Brazil's comments on Indonesia's response to Panel question No. 113, paras. 42-45.

[590]   Brazil's comments on Indonesia's response to Panel question No. 113, paras. 46-52.

[591]   Appellate Body Report, *Argentina – Financial Services*, para. 6.203. See also para. 6.113 where the Appellate Body states that "[t]he GATS sets out general exceptions and security exceptions from obligations under that Agreement in the same manner as does the GATT 1994" and that "[s]ome of these objectives are the same under both provisions, such as protection of public morals, protection of human, animal or plant life or health, and securing compliance with WTO-consistent laws and regulations".

[592]   Appellate Body Report, *Colombia – Textiles*, paras. 5.68 (referring to the test applicable in the context of Article XX(a)) and 5.125-5.128 (indicating the test applicable to Article XX(d)).

[593]   Appellate Body Report, *Colombia – Textiles*, para. 5.70.

[594]   In its responses to the Panel's questions, Indonesia has confirmed that understanding. See Indonesia's response to Panel question No. 115.

[595]   See paras. 7.402 and 7.403. In this regard, see also Brazil's comments on Indonesia's response to Panel question No. 113, paras. 42-45.

indicate the maximum amount to be imported for a three-month period), will make any meaningful contribution to knowing precisely where, when and how many imports will take place. Moreover, we do not consider that as explained by Indonesia, the existence of a monthly arrival plan confirms the contribution of the challenged measures.[596] Instead, as we discuss further below, we consider it to undermine the need for the fixed licence terms. These considerations call into question whether this measure is designed to facilitate the supervision by customs and quarantine officials over the importer's compliance with the relevant halal, safety, and consumer protection requirements at the time of importation, and thus to secure compliance with the relevant laws and regulations.

498.   At the same time, we see that Indonesia's arguments support the view that the challenged measures, by virtue of their design, structure and expected operation, may provide Indonesian authorities with an estimate of (1) how many imports will occur during each validity period, and (2) through which ports in Indonesia those imports will enter. In our view, however, such an estimate will be too general to provide useful information to facilitate the allocation of customs and quarantine officials.

499.   Despite our doubts, in applying the above standard, we acknowledge that the measures at issue are "not incapable" of achieving the objective of facilitating the allocation of customs and quarantine officers to secure compliance with Indonesia's laws and regulations pertaining to halal, public health, consumer protection and food safety. As Indonesia argues, the information it collects through the measures is useful in facilitating the allocation of the relevant officers. On this basis we find, that there is a relationship between the application windows, the validity periods and the fixed licence terms, and the objective of securing compliance with the relevant laws and regulations through the allocation of human resources in charge of supervising compliance with such laws and regulations at the time of importation.

Necessary to secure compliance with laws and regulations

500.   As seen above, the "necessity" test involves a process of weighing and balancing a series of factors, including (1) the importance of the objective, (2) the contribution of the measure to that objective, and (3) the trade-restrictiveness of the measure.[597] In most cases, (4) a comparison between the challenged measure and possible less trade-restrictive alternatives should then be undertaken. We turn to examine these factors.

501.   In terms of the importance of the objective pursued, we acknowledge the importance of complying with Indonesia's laws and regulations pertaining to

---

[596]   Indonesia's response to Panel question Nos. 113 and 115.
[597]   Appellate Body Reports, *EC - Seal Products*, para. 5.169.

halal, public health, consumer protection and food safety.[598] Moreover, we recognize the importance of facilitating the allocation of human resources for government officials to be able to supervise an importer's compliance with Indonesia's halal, safety, and consumer protection requirements at the time of importation.[599]

502.   We have noted above that we have some doubts on whether these measures are designed to achieve the objective claimed by Indonesia. Those same doubts are relevant for our assessment of the degree of contribution of these measures to the objective of facilitating the allocation of human resources for government officials to be able to supervise importer's compliance with Indonesia's halal, safety, and consumer protection requirements at the time of importation. In particular, we do not consider that the information collected by Indonesian authorities is that meaningful, so as to facilitate an appropriate allocation of the customs and quarantine officers in charge of supervision. Thus, we do not consider the degree of contribution of the challenged measures significant. We rather consider it to be limited.

503.   As seen above, whether the contribution is substantial/material or not, in turn matters in light of the degree of trade-restrictiveness of the challenged measures. We have found that the application windows and the validity periods foreclose the possibility of imports occurring during at least four weeks of each validity period. Moreover, the fixed licence terms limit an importers' ability to amend the port of entry or quantity in the import licensing documents, thus limiting trade in respect of situations where such changes are required due to changes in market conditions. Thus, these measures constitute limitations on trade. Such limitations are not of the magnitude of an import ban, however they do distort the normal trade flows that would occur in their absence. Consideration of these measures as trade-restrictive, notwithstanding their extent, weighs against considering them necessary.

504.   Turning to the issue of a less trade-restrictive alternative, Brazil has submitted two alternative measures.[600] The first is allocating human resources on the basis of the normal influx of imported cargo. Brazil considers that the evidence provided by Indonesia with respect to the reduction in the dwelling time at certain ports demonstrates that most of the imports enter Indonesia through one port. This information could be used by Indonesia to decide on the best manner of allocating its human resources.[601] Brazil submits as the second alternative that if the Panel were to accept the evidence submitted by Indonesia in respect of the monthly arrival plan, then, such a monthly arrival plan alone

---

[598]   Indonesia's first written submission, para. 297; opening statement at the first meeting of the Panel, para. 97; and responses to Panel question Nos. 24 and 113.

[599]   Indonesia's response to Panel question No. 113.

[600]   Brazil's second written submission, para. 158; and comments to Indonesia's response to Panel question No. 113.

[601]   Brazil's comments on Indonesia's response to Panel question No. 113, paras. 47-51.

could provide the accurate information that Indonesia is seeking in a much less-trade restrictive manner than the challenged measures.[602]

505.   We agree with Brazil that the first option provides useful information to Indonesia in forecasting the quantity of imports and the ports through which they will enter. However, we do not consider this information to be entirely accurate. We thus do not consider that this measure, in itself, can achieve the objective indicated by Indonesia. This however, does not prevent Indonesia from using this methodology in combination with other measures.

506.   We agree with Brazil that the monthly arrival plan is a less-trade restrictive alternative that achieves Indonesia's desired objective. It is a measure that could be required from importers, which would provide Indonesia with the precise information necessary to allocate customs and veterinary officials to supervise compliance with the relevant laws and regulations at importation. This alternative would more accurately reflect the details of importation, while allowing importers to amend, as necessary, the quantity and the ports of entry initially indicated in the application for the relevant licensing requirements. To that extent, this measure is an available alternative that has a much less-trade restrictive effect.

507.   As indicated above, the forecast of the amount of imports and ports of entry could be combined with the monthly import plan to provide Indonesian authorities the necessary information to facilitate the allocation of human resources for government officials to be able to supervise an importer's compliance with Indonesia's halal, safety, and consumer protection requirements at the time of importation. These two alternative measures could work in a way that the forecast provides Indonesia with estimates that are later confirmed through the monthly import plans, providing Indonesian authorities with the information they require in a much less-trade restrictive manner than the challenged measures.

508.   In weighing and balancing all factors together we consider that Indonesia has failed to demonstrate that the measures make a significant contribution to the immediate objective that it is pursuing. Moreover, Brazil has successfully submitted an alternative measure available to Indonesia that would meet Indonesia's objective and have a less-trade restrictive effect. On this basis, we reach the conclusion that the application windows, the validity periods and the fixed licence terms are not necessary to facilitate the allocation of human resources for government officials to be able to supervise importer's compliance with Indonesia's halal, safety, and consumer protection requirements at the time of importation. We therefore find that the application windows, the validity periods and the fixed licence terms, as enacted through MoA 58/2015 and MoT 05/2016, are not provisionally justified under Article XX(d).

---

[602]   Brazil's comments on Indonesia's response to Panel question No. 113, para. 46.

509.   Given the absence of a (provisional) justification under subparagraph (d), we see no need to proceed to an analysis under the chapeau of Article XX.

510.   In conclusion, we find that the limited application windows, the validity periods, and the fixed licence terms are inconsistent with Article XI of the GATT 1994 and are not justified under Article XX(d) of the GATT 1994.

7.6.5.2.4   Whether the application windows, the validity periods, and the fixed licence terms are inconsistent with Article 4.2 of the Agreement on Agriculture and Article 3.2 of the Import Licensing Agreement

511.   We note that the parties agree that the application windows, the validity periods, and the fixed licence terms are all import licensing procedures within the meaning of Article 1.1 of the Import Licensing Agreement.[603] We agree with the parties' view, because all these elements of Indonesia's import licensing regime fall under the definition of Article 1.1, as they are part of Indonesia's administrative procedures used for the operation of Indonesia's import licensing regime.

512.   In paragraph 7.159 above we have discussed the legal test applicable to the exercise of judicial economy.

513.   In this regard, having found a violation of Article XI of the GATT 1994 in respect of these elements of Indonesia's import licensing regime, we consider that it is not necessary to address Brazil's claim under Article 4.2 of the Agreement on Agriculture or Article 3.2 of the Import Licensing Agreement to secure a positive solution to this dispute.

7.6.5.3   Analysis of the relevant provisions of MoA 34/2016 and MoT 59/2016

7.6.5.3.1   Introduction

514.   Our findings above apply to the application windows, the validity periods, and the fixed licence terms as enacted through MoA 58/2015 and MoT 05/2016. As noted in the beginning of this section, in the course of the proceedings, these regulations were revoked and replaced by MoA 34/2016 and MoT 59/2016.

515.   With this change, the parties' arguments have evolved in respect of the application windows and the validity periods. Indonesia submits that the

---

[603]   Brazil's first written submission, paras. 245-247; response to Panel question No. 12(a); second written submission, para. 151; and Indonesia's first written submission, paras. 79 and 287. We note that in Indonesia's view, Brazil did not raise claims against the fixed licence terms under Article 3.2 of the Import Licensing Agreement.

application windows no longer exist and therefore that the measure has expired.[604] Brazil contests expiry.[605]

> 7.6.5.3.2   Whether the application windows and the validity periods, as a single measure, has expired

516.   As discussed in section 7.2.4 above, we agree with Indonesia that, having made findings on the application windows and the validity periods, the expiry of the measure at issue may have a bearing on whether we can make a recommendation. We consider that a measure has expired if it has ceased to exist. We thus need to examine whether the application and validity periods, as a single measure, have ceased to exist. We note that Indonesia as the party that asserts expiry, bears the burden of proving this.

517.   It is uncontested between the parties that the application windows as enacted through MoA 58/2016 have been revoked and eliminated through Article 21 of MoA 34/2016 (see Table 5 above). We understand Brazil to contest expiry. Brazil argues that the single measure persists through the new condition that importers who have received an MoA Import Recommendation must apply for the respective MoT Import Approval within the following three months (Article 27(1) of MoA 34/2016 – see Table 5 above). Brazil argues that this means that an application for an MoT Import Approval cannot be submitted at any time.[606]

518.   Moreover, Brazil argues that extending the validity period of the MoA Import Recommendation from four to six months does not eliminate the trade-restrictiveness of the measure.[607] Indonesia contests Brazil's view. Indonesia considers that by eliminating the application windows, the six-month validity periods allow importers to undertake imports throughout the year without interruption.[608] Indonesia further submits that Brazil has failed to demonstrate that there are any "dead zones" arising from the new validity periods.[609]

519.   As we have explained above, the trade restrictiveness that we found in respect of the application windows and the validity periods as enacted through MoA 58/2015 and MoT 05/2016 resulted from the combined operation of these measures, which, as we found above, creates certain periods in a year during which no imports can occur. As uncontested by the parties, Article 21 of MoA

---

[604]   Indonesia's response to Panel question No. 24; second written submission, paras. 19-22 and 129; response to Panel question No. 113; and comments on Brazil's response to Panel question No. 103, para. 80.

[605]   Brazil's response to Panel question No. 103.

[606]   *Ibid.*

[607]   *Ibid.*

[608]   Indonesia's response to Panel question No. 24 (last paragraph); second written submission, paras. 19-22 and 129; and response to Panel question No. 113.

[609]   Indonesia's comments to Brazil's response to Panel question No. 103, paras. 81-85.

34/2016 eliminates any limitation on the application windows. In our view, the removal of the application period substantially alters the combined operation of the application windows and validity periods, as examined above. This alteration goes to the source of the trade-restrictiveness arising from that combined operation of the application windows and the validity periods. There no longer is a limitation on when an importer can apply for an MoA Import Recommendation. In our view, this means that an importer would now be able to apply for an MoA Import Recommendation at any time during the year, and if it so wishes, it can request as many MoA Import Recommendations as would be necessary to conclude the relevant business transactions throughout the year. We further note that Brazil has not challenged this.[610]

520.   Brazil's view is that the measure has not expired because of the new deadline to apply for an MoT Import Approval. We agree on that Article 27(1) introduces a deadline on when an importer who has received an MoA Import Recommendation must apply for an MoT Import Approval. However, as we noted above, importers are free to apply for the import licensing documents at any time of the year. This contrasts with the limited application windows as enacted through MoA 58/2015 which only allowed importers to apply for an MoA Import Recommendation during three months of the year. We, thus, agree with Indonesia, that there are no longer any "dead zones" arising from the new validity periods. On this basis, we consider that the application windows and the validity periods, as a single measure, have ceased to exist, and has, therefore, expired .

<blockquote>
7.6.5.3.3   Whether the limited validity period, as enacted through MoA 34/2016, is inconsistent with Article XI:1 of the GATT 1994, Article 4.2 of the Agreement on Agriculture and Article 3.2 of the Import Licensing Agreement
</blockquote>

521.   We understand Brazil to maintain its claim that the new validity period enacted through Article 30(1) of MoA 34/2016 is inconsistent with Article XI:1 of the GATT 1994, Article 4.2 of the Agreement on Agriculture and Article 3.2 of the Import Licensing Agreement.[611] On this basis, we first turn to the question of whether the new validity period, as enacted through MoA 34/2016, is within our terms of reference.

522.   Before turning to this question, we note that we have analysed the application windows and the validity periods as a single measure. We followed this analytical approach in response to the manner in which Brazil presented its case. However, we do not consider that this analytical approach prevents us from

---

[610]   Brazil's response to Panel question No. 103.
[611]   *Ibid.*

considering subsequent developments as relevant to only one of those two aspects of the single measure we examined.

523.   As discussed above, in line with the Appellate Body's jurisprudence in *Chile – Price Band System*, we consider that our terms of reference cover subsequent amendments to the measure at issue so long as that measure remains in essence the same.[612] In our view, Article 30(1) of MoA 34/2016 is an amendment to a measure identified in Brazil's panel request, namely, the limited validity period.[613] Through this amendment, the validity period of the MoA Import Recommendation has changed from four to six months. We consider this change not to be such that the measure is no longer in essence the same.

524.   We further note that both Indonesia[614] and Brazil[615] agree that the validity period, as enacted in Article 30 of MoA 34/2016, is within the Panel's terms of reference. On this basis, we consider that the new validity period is within our terms of reference, and we thus have jurisdiction to review its WTO consistency.

525.   Brazil has not adduced any further evidence or arguments explaining why the new validity period, absent the application windows, is inconsistent with Article XI:1 of the GATT 1994, Article 4.2 of the Agreement on Agriculture or Article 3.2 of the Import Licensing Agreement.

526.   We recall that the Appellate Body indicated that:

> A *prima facie* case must be based on "evidence *and* legal argument" put forward by the complaining party in relation to *each* of the elements of the claim.[616] A complaining party may not simply submit evidence and expect the panel to divine from it a claim of WTO-inconsistency.[617] Nor may a complaining party simply allege facts without relating them to its legal arguments.[618]

527.   On the basis of the foregoing, and applying this standard, we consider that Brazil has failed to make a *prima facie* case that the validity period, as enacted through MoA 34/2016 and MoT 59/2016, is inconsistent with Article

---

[612]   See section 7.2.4 above.

[613]   Brazil's panel request, p. 7.

[614]   Indonesia's response to Panel question No. 102.

[615]   Brazil's comments on Indonesia's response to Panel question No. 102, para. 29.

[616]   (footnote original) Appellate Body Report, *US – Wool Shirts and Blouses*, p. 16, DSR 1997:I, 323, at 336. (emphasis added) As not every claim of WTO-inconsistency will consist of the same elements, "the nature and scope of evidence required to establish a *prima facie* case 'will necessarily vary from measure to measure, provision to provision, and case to case'". (Appellate Body Report, *Japan – Apples*, para. 159 (quoting Appellate Body Report, *US – Wool Shirts and Blouses*, p. 14, DSR 1997:I, 323, at 335))

[617]   (footnote original) In *Canada – Wheat Exports and Grain Imports*, para. 191, the Appellate Body made a similar observation in the context of an appeal under Article 11 of the DSU:

… it is incumbent upon a party to identify in its submissions the relevance of the provisions of legislation—the evidence—on which it relies to support its arguments. It is not sufficient merely to file an entire piece of legislation and expect a panel to discover, on its own, what relevance the various provisions may or may not have for a party's legal position.

[618]   Appellate Body Report, *US – Gambling*, para. 140.

XI:1 of the GATT 1994, Article 4.2 of the Agreement on Agriculture and Article 3.2 of the Import Licensing Agreement.

> 7.6.5.3.4 Whether the fixed licence terms, as enacted through MoA 34/2016 and MoT 59/2016, are inconsistent with Article XI:1 of the GATT 1994, Article 4.2 of the Agreement on Agriculture and Article 3.2 of the Import Licensing Agreement

528.   As noted above, the parties do not develop new arguments in respect of the fixed licence terms as enacted through MoA 34/2016 and MoT 59/2016. As can be seen from Table 6 above, the provisions in MoA 34/2016 and MoT 59/2016 through which the fixed licence terms are enacted are virtually identical to the relevant provisions in the previous legal instruments, namely MoA 58/2015 and MoT 05/2016. For this reason, we consider that the fixed licence terms, as enacted through MoA 34/2016 and MoT 59/2016 are within our terms of reference and we have jurisdiction to rule on them.

529.   Furthermore, because the relevant provisions of MoA 34/2016 and MoT 59/2016 are almost identical to those in the previous legal instruments, we find that the fixed licence terms continue to apply in the same manner. Our findings on Article XI and XX(d) of the GATT 1994, in respect of the measure as enacted through MoA 58/2015 and MoT 05/2016, therefore, also apply to the measure as enacted through MoA 34/2016 and MoT 59/2016. In addition, for the reasons explained above, we do not consider it necessary to make findings under Article 4.2 of the Agreement on Agriculture or under Article 3.2 of the Import Licensing Agreement.

7.6.5.4   Conclusion

530.   On the basis of the foregoing, we find that the application windows, the validity periods and the fixed licence terms, as enacted through MoA 58/2015 and MoT 05/2016, are inconsistent with Article XI:1 of the GATT 1994 and are not justified under Article XX(d) of the GATT 1994.

531.   We also find that the combined operation of the application windows and the validity periods expired with the adoption of MoA 34/2016. Consequently, we will not make a recommendation in respect of the measure as enacted through MoA 58/2015 and MoT 05/2016.

532.   Finally, we find that the new validity period, as enacted through MoA 34/2016, is a measure that falls within our terms of reference. However, we find that Brazil failed to make a *prima facie* case that the new validity period, as enacted through MoA 34/2016, is inconsistent with Article XI:1 of the GATT 1994, Article 4.2 of the Agreement on Agriculture and Article 3.2 of the Import Licensing Agreement. We also find that the fixed licence terms as enacted through MoA 34/2016 and MoT 59/2016 are within our terms of reference and

that the above findings on Article XI:1 and on Article XX(d) of the GATT 1994 apply.

7.6.6 Discretionary import licensing

7.6.6.1 Introduction

533. Brazil argues that there are certain elements of Indonesia's import licensing regime, which, by virtue of their design and structure, constitute discretionary import licensing in terms of Article 4.2 of the Agreement on Agriculture. These include (i) letter of recommendation from provincial livestock services office, (ii) supervision on the compliance of veterinary public health requirements, and (iii) MoT's power to determine the amount of imports.[619] Indonesia considers that none of these measures constitute discretionary import licensing.[620] In the alternative, Brazil submits that these requirements constitute similar border measures to discretionary import licensing within the meaning of Article 4.2 of the Agreement on Agriculture.[621] Indonesia considers that because Brazil made an unsubstantiated assertion that these measures constitute similar border measures to discretionary import licensing, Brazil has failed to make its *prima facie* case.[622]

534. In response to a question from the Panel the parties expressed their views on whether these measures are within the Panel's terms of reference. Indonesia considers that these measures are not within the Panel's terms of reference.[623]

7.6.6.2 Panel's jurisdiction

535. We first examine whether the elements of Indonesia's import licensing regime which Brazil challenges as discretionary import licensing are within the Panel's terms of reference.

536. Brazil considers these elements to be part of what Brazil described in its panel request as "several approvals, authorizations and recommendations granted under the discretion of Indonesian authorities".[624] Brazil further argues that to the extent that the discretionary elements of the MoA Recommendation and

---

[619] Brazil's first written submission, paras. 234 and 237; second written submission, paras. 165 and 169; and response to Panel question No. 108(a).

[620] Indonesia's first written submission, paras. 268-271. See also response to Panel question No. 57. See Indonesia's comments on Brazil's response to Panel question No. 108 (referring to Indonesia's first written submission, paras. 272-274; second written submission, para. 13; and responses to Panel question Nos. 12, 17, 18, 104(e), 105, 113 and 117).

[621] Brazil's first written submission, para. 237.

[622] Indonesia's first written submission, para. 276.

[623] Indonesia's response to Panel question No. 105.

[624] Brazil's response to Panel question No. 105 (citing section II(v) of Brazil's panel request, p. 7). See also response to Panel question No. 108(c).

MoT Approval are within the Panel's terms of reference, the process to obtain the documents required for each are also within the panel's terms of reference.[625]

537.   Indonesia contests this view and argues that the discretionary elements challenged by Brazil are not closely related to any of the measure identified in Brazil's panel request. Indonesia considers that Brazil's overly broad reference to "authorizations and recommendations" comprising Indonesia's import recommendations and approvals, does not amount to having provided Indonesia with adequate notice of the specific measures challenged as discretionary import licensing.[626]

538.   As explained in section 7.1.2.2.1 above, Article 6.2 of the DSU contains two distinct requirements, namely (1) the identification of the specific measures at issue and (2) the provision of a brief summary of the legal basis of the complaint (or the claims) sufficient to present the problem clearly. Together these two elements comprise the "matter referred to the DSB", and form the basis of the panel's terms of reference under Article 7.1 of the DSU.[627] In our view, Indonesia's challenge to these measures being within the Panel's terms of reference relates to the identification of the measures at issue.

539.   The Appellate Body has noted that "the measures at issue must be identified with sufficient precision so that what is referred to adjudication by a panel may be discerned from the panel request".[628]

540.   In our preliminary ruling, as set out in section 7.1.2.3 above, we found that Brazil's claims only pertained to specific aspects of Indonesia's import licensing regime. Section II.v of Brazil's panel request refers to "Restrictions on the importation of chicken meat and chicken products through Indonesia's Import Licensing regime". This section contains an introductory paragraph followed by a bullet point list describing different aspects of the licencing regime.[629]

541.   The bullet point list contains, *inter alia*, the following item: "the MoA Regulations – and a MoT Recommendation – limit the type and quantity of animal products allowed to be imported by determining the types and quantities of products specified in a Recommendation or Import Approval[630]".[631] In our

[625]   Brazil's comments on Indonesia's response to Panel question No. 105, paras. 31-34.

[626]   Indonesia's response to Panel question No. 105.

[627]   Appellate Body Report, *US – Countervailing and Anti-Dumping Measures (China)*, para. 4.6 (citing Appellate Body Report, *EC and certain member States – Large Civil Aircraft*, para. 639 (referring to Appellate Body Reports, *Guatemala – Cement I*, paras. 72 and 73; *US – Carbon Steel*, para. 125; *US – Continued Zeroing*, para. 160; *US – Zeroing (Japan) (Article 21.5 – Japan)*, para. 107; and *Australia – Apples*, para. 416).

[628]   Appellate Body Report, *US – Continued Zeroing*, para. 168.

[629]   The introductory paragraph ends as follows: "Moreover, Indonesia's trade-restrictive import licensing regime for chicken meat and chicken products includes, but is not limited to, the following measures:"

[630]   (footnote original) See, e.g., Article 28 of MoA Regulation 139/2014 (stating that the quantity of animal product specified in a Recommendation is set by the Ministry of Trade).

[631]   Brazil's panel request, p. 7

view, this item properly identifies MoT's power to determine the amount of imported goods, as a specific aspect of Indonesia' licensing regime at issue in this dispute. On this basis, we consider this measure to be properly within our terms of reference.

542.   In contrast, the bullet point list does not contain any item or reference to the letter of recommendation of the provincial livestock services office nor the supervision on the compliance of veterinary public health requirements let alone any discretion relating to these. We therefore turn to examine the introductory paragraph to section II.v of Brazil's panel request.

543.   This paragraph of Brazil's panel request refers to importers obtaining import licensing after "several approvals, authorizations and recommendations granted *under the discretion* of Indonesian authorities, which comprises (i) an Importer Designation from the Ministry of Trade for animals and animal products; (ii) an animal and animal products Import Recommendation from the Ministry of Agriculture; and (iii) an Import Approval from the Ministry of Trade."[632] Thus, the introductory paragraph generally refers to "discretion" in the context of referring, *inter alia*, to the Import Recommendation. We note that the letter of recommendation is part of what an importer has to submit when applying for an MoA Import Recommendation.[633] The letter is issued by an entity different from the one in charge of issuing the MoA Import Recommendation. It is, thus, one step removed from the process of issuance of the MoA Import Recommendation and possible issues arising in respect of discretion are not the same as those that may arise with respect to the issuance of the MoA Import Recommendation itself. In our view, therefore, the general reference to "discretion" contained in the introductory paragraph, is not specific enough to encompass possible discretionary aspects of the letter of recommendation.

544.   As regards the supervision on the compliance of veterinary public health requirements, we observe that this is a process of verification of certain health requirements, which is carried out *upon* importation of a product.[634] This supervision, thus, is not part of the (*ex ante*) licencing process that involves the issuance of an MoA Import Recommendation and MoT Import Approval. In our view, therefore, the general reference to "discretion" contained in the introductory paragraph, is not pertinent to the supervision on the compliance of veterinary health requirements.

545.   We find support for this reading of the introductory paragraph of this section of Brazil's panel request in the fact that Brazil, as seen above, has

---

[632]   *Ibid.*
[633]   See Article 24(1)(i) of MoA 139/2014 (Exhibit BRA-34/IDN-126), Article 23(1)(i) of MoA 58/2015 (Exhibit BRA-01/IDN-24), and Article 22(1)(i) of MoA 34/2016 (Exhibit BRA-48/IDN-93).
[634]   See Articles 34 and 38(2) of MoA 139/2014 (Exhibit BRA-34/IDN-126), Articles 33 and 37(2) of MoA 58/2015 (Exhibit BRA-01/IDN-24), and Articles 33 and (37(2) of MoA 34/2016 (Exhibit BRA-48/IDN-93).

specifically identified other alleged discretionary aspects of Indonesia's licensing system in the bullet points following that paragraph.

546.   On the basis of the foregoing, we consider that the wording of Brazil's panel request does not allow us to discern that Brazil was challenging the letter of recommendation from provincial livestock services office nor the supervision on the compliance of veterinary public health requirements. In our view, the reference in the introductory paragraph to section II.v of Brazil's panel request is insufficient to satisfy the requirement of Article 6.2 of the DSU to identify these two challenged measures.[635] We further note that in response to a question from the Panel, Brazil did not refer to discretionary import licensing as part of the specific aspects of Indonesia's import licensing regime that it challenged.[636]

547.   We will therefore only examine MoT's power to determine the amount of imported products, which according to Brazil constitutes discretionary import licensing under Article 4.2 of the Agreement on Agriculture and is inconsistent with Article 3.2 of the Import Licensing Agreement.

548.   In section 7.6.3 above the Panel set out its preferred order of analysis. As explained above, we first examine Brazil's claim under Article 4.2 of the Agreement on Agriculture. Then we turn to our assessment of this element under Article 3.2 of the Import Licensing Agreement.

7.6.6.3   WTO consistency of MoT's power to determine the amount of imported goods

7.6.6.3.1   Whether MoT's power to determine the amount of imported goods is inconsistent with Article 4.2 of the Agreement on Agriculture

549.   Article 4.2 of the Agreement on Agriculture provides:

Members shall not maintain, resort to, or revert to any measures of the kind which have been required to be converted into ordinary customs duties[1], except as otherwise provided for in Article 5 and Annex 5.

---

[635] We note that in its first and second written submissions, Indonesia provides substantive arguments in respect of these measures not constituting discretionary import licensing (Indonesia's first written submission, paras. 268-271. See also response to Panel question No. 57. See Indonesia's comments on Brazil's response to Panel question No. 108 (referring to Indonesia's first written submission, paras. 272-274; second written submission, para. 13; and responses to Panel question Nos. 12, 17, 18, 104(e), 105, 113 and 117)). In addition, Indonesia did not raise any objections with respect to these measures in its request for a preliminary ruling. Indonesia only objected to these measures being within our terms of reference as a result of a question posed by the Panel.

[636] Brazil's response to Panel question No. 15.

¹ (footnote original) These measures include quantitative import restrictions, variable import levies, minimum import prices, discretionary import licensing, non-tariff measures maintained through state-trading enterprises, voluntary export restraints, and similar border measures other than ordinary customs duties, whether or not the measures are maintained under country-specific derogations from the provisions of GATT 1947, but not measures maintained under balance-of-payments provisions or under other general, non-agriculture-specific provisions of GATT 1994 or of the other Multilateral Trade Agreements in Annex 1A to the WTO Agreement.

550.   An assessment of whether MoT's power to determine the amount of imported goods is consistent with Article 4.2 requires us to answer two questions: (1) whether the challenged measure is of the type required to be converted into ordinary customs duties (e.g. it constitutes discretionary import licensing or a similar border measure); and (2) whether such a measure is maintained under balance-of-payments provisions or other general, non-agriculture-specific provisions. As discussed in section 7.2.3.2 above, this second question will only be relevant to the extent that the respondent has claimed this to be the case.[637]

551.   Indonesia has not argued that this measure is maintained under balance-of-payments provisions or other general, non-agriculture-specific provisions. We will thus focus our analysis on the first question, that is, whether this measure constitutes discretionary import licensing.

552.   As noted in section 7.2.4 above, the legal instruments enacting MoT's power to determine the amount of imported goods have been revoked and replaced twice since panel establishment. The following table reproduces the provisions relevant for our subsequent analysis in each of the three sets of legal instruments.

Table 7.   Minister's power to determine the amount of imported goods

First set of legal instruments	Second set of legal instruments	Third set of legal instruments
MoA 139/2014	**MoA 58/2015**	**MoA 34/2016**
Art. 28	*Art. 27*	No equivalent provision
The quantity allocation in the recommendation per Business Actors, State-owned Entities, Regional Entities, Social Institutions, and Foreign Country/International Institution	Determination of the amount in Recommendation per Business Player, Social Institution, and Foreign Country Representative/ International Institution, shall be stipulated by the minister administrating governmental	

---

[637]   See Panel Report, *Turkey – Rice*, para. 7.137.

First set of legal instruments	Second set of legal instruments	Third set of legal instruments
Representatives is defined by the Minister of Trade.	trade affairs.	

553.   Article 27 of MoA 58/2015 provides that determination of the amount of imported goods in the MoA Import Recommendation shall be stipulated by the Minister of Trade. This provision reproduces, almost word for word, Article 28 of MoA 139/2014, which was identified in Brazil's panel request.[638] On this basis we consider that the measure is in essence the same as the one identified in Brazil's panel request and therefore we have jurisdiction to review its WTO consistency.

554.   We note that Brazil developed its claim that MoT's power to determine the amount of imported goods in the MoA Import Recommendation constitutes discretionary import licensing in two paragraphs of its second written submission.[639]

555.   We recall that the Appellate Body reasoned that "a *prima facie* case must be based on 'evidence *and* legal argument' put forward by the complaining party in relation to *each* of the elements of the claim.[640],[641] The Panel considers that Brazil's arguments and evidence are insufficient to support a *prima facie* case that Article 27 of MoA 58/2015 is inconsistent with Article 4.2 of the Agreement on Agriculture. In our view, Brazil has merely asserted that the text of this provision can be read to mean that the Minister of Trade has discretion to establish the amount of the imported goods. However, Brazil has failed to explain the manner in which this measure relates to the issuance of an MoA Import Recommendation or how this measure constitutes "import licensing" for the purposes of our analysis under Article 4.2 of the Agreement on Agriculture. In addition, Brazil has not rebutted the explanation provided by Indonesia that

[638]   Brazil's panel request, p. 8.
[639]   Brazil's second written submission, para. 170. We note that in *EC – Fasteners (China)* the respondent challenged the procedural stage at which the complainant developed certain arguments in support of a measure identified in its panel request. In addressing this issue, the Appellate Body concluded that the "late assertion of a claim ..., and the absence of proper argumentation and of the provision of relevant evidence in support of this assertion, demonstrates that the European Union was not called upon to respond to China's claim under Article 6.5". (Appellate Body Report, *EC – Fasteners (China)*, para. 574.). Indonesia has not objected to Brazil developing its arguments in its second written submission.
[640]   (footnote original) Appellate Body Report, *US – Wool Shirts and Blouses*, p. 16, DSR 1997:I, 323, at 336. (emphasis added) As not every claim of WTO-inconsistency will consist of the same elements, "the nature and scope of evidence required to establish a *prima facie* case 'will necessarily vary from measure to measure, provision to provision, and case to case'". (Appellate Body Report, *Japan – Apples*, para. 159 (quoting Appellate Body Report, *US – Wool Shirts and Blouses*, p. 14, DSR 1997:I, 323, at 335)).
[641]   Appellate Body Report, *US – Gambling*, para. 140.

the amount in the MoA Import Recommendation is determined by the importer applying for it and endorsed by the MoT and the MoA.[642]

556.   Moreover, we note that MoA 34/2016 no longer includes any reference to the wording of Article 27 of MoA 58/2015.

557.   On the basis of the foregoing, we find that Brazil failed to make a *prima facie* case that Article 27 of MoA 58/2015 is inconsistent with Article 4.2 of the Agreement on Agriculture.

7.6.6.3.2   Whether MoT's discretion to determine the amount of imported goods is inconsistent with Article 3.2 of the Import Licensing Agreement

558.   In this section we address the consistency of MoT's power to determine the amount of imported goods with Article 3.2 of the Import Licensing Agreement.

559.   Article 3.2 of the Import Licensing Agreement provides:

> Non-automatic licensing shall not have trade-restrictive or — distortive effects on imports additional to those caused by the imposition of the restriction. Non-automatic licensing procedures shall correspond in scope and duration to the measure they are used to implement, and shall be no more administratively burdensome than absolutely necessary to administer the measure.

560.   An assessment of this matter requires us to determine first whether we are in the presence of a non-automatic import licensing system. If that is the case, we then need to examine, in respect of the first sentence, whether the import licensing procedure at issue has a trade-restrictive or -distortive effect additional to that caused by the underlying restriction. In addition, under the second sentence, we would need to examine whether the measure at issue corresponds "in scope and duration to the measure they are used to implement" and whether it is "more administratively burdensome than absolutely necessary to administer the measure".

561.   We note that Brazil developed its claim that MoT's power to determine the amount of imported goods is inconsistent with Article 3.2 of the Import Licensing Agreement in one paragraph of its second written submission.[643]

---

[642]   Indonesia's response to Panel question No. 12.

[643]   Brazil's second written submission, para. 171. We note that in *EC – Fasteners (China)* the respondent challenged the procedural stage at which the complainant developed certain arguments in support of a measure identified in its panel request. In addressing this issue, the Appellate Body concluded that the "late assertion of a claim ..., and the absence of proper argumentation and of the provision of relevant evidence in support of this assertion, demonstrates that the European Union was not called upon to respond to China's claim under Article 6.5". (Appellate Body Report, *EC –*

Report of the Panel

562.   We recall that the Appellate Body reasoned that "a *prima facie* case must be based on 'evidence *and* legal argument' put forward by the complaining party in relation to *each* of the elements of the claim.[644],[645] We consider that Brazil's arguments and evidence are insufficient to support a *prima facie* case that Article 27 of MoA 58/2015 is inconsistent with Article 3.2 of the Import Licensing Agreement. In our view, Brazil has merely asserted that:

> [I]t is easy to see that they [the three elements challenged as discretionary import licensing] fail under Article 3.2 of the ILA, as they impose a heavy burden on the exporter, who needs to comply with a series of overlapping import controls that are not "absolutely" necessary to achieve Indonesia's policy objectives.[646]

563.   By limiting its arguments to this statement, Brazil has failed to explain each of the elements of this claim and to adduce arguments and evidence in support of its contention. We therefore find that Brazil failed to make a *prima facie* case that Article 27 of MoA 58/2015 is inconsistent with Article 3.2 of the Import Licensing Agreement.

7.6.6.4   Conclusion

564.   On the basis of the foregoing, we conclude that the letter of recommendation from the provincial livestock services office and the supervision on the compliance with veterinary public health requirements are outside our terms of reference.

565.   We further find that Brazil has failed to make a *prima facie* case that MoT's power to determine the amount of imported goods is inconsistent with Article 4.2 of the Agreement on Agriculture or Article 3.2 of the Import Licensing Agreement.

Fasteners (China), para. 574.). Indonesia has not objected to Brazil developing its arguments in its second written submission.

[644] (footnote original) Appellate Body Report, *US – Wool Shirts and Blouses*, p. 16, DSR 1997:I, 323, at 336. (emphasis added) As not every claim of WTO-inconsistency will consist of the same elements, "the nature and scope of evidence required to establish a *prima facie* case 'will necessarily vary from measure to measure, provision to provision, and case to case'". (Appellate Body Report, *Japan – Apples*, para. 159 (quoting Appellate Body Report, *US – Wool Shirts and Blouses*, p. 14, DSR 1997:I, 323, at 335)).

[645] Appellate Body Report, *US – Gambling*, para. 140.

[646] Brazil's second written submission, para. 171. We note that in *EC – Fasteners (China)* the respondent challenged the procedural stage at which the complainant developed certain arguments in support of a measure identified in its panel request. In addressing this issue, the Appellate Body concluded that the "late assertion of a claim …, and the absence of proper argumentation and of the provision of relevant evidence in support of this assertion, demonstrates that the European Union was not called upon to respond to China's claim under Article 6.5". (Appellate Body Report, *EC – Fasteners (China)*, para. 574.). Indonesia has not objected to Brazil developing its arguments in its second written submission.

3936   DSR 2017:VIII

7.6.7   Other aspects of Indonesia's import licensing regime

566.   We note that in addition to the claims that we have examined on Indonesia's import licensing regime, Brazil raised two additional claims. The first pertains to the denial of import licences to secure price stabilization. The second concerns what Brazil identified as additional restrictions on "certain products" and "processed products". We will address each of these by first examining whether they fall within our terms of reference and then assessing Brazil's claims.

7.6.7.1   Denial of import licences to secure price stabilization

567.   The bullet point list contained in section II.v of Brazil's panel request includes the following item: "[t]o secure price stabilization, import licenses may not be granted by the Indonesian authorities to attend its objectives of price policy and import management".[647] This reference clearly places this element of Indonesia's import licensing regime within our terms of reference, and we thus have jurisdiction to review its WTO consistency.

568.   Brazil has not developed specific arguments against this element of Indonesia's import licensing regime. However, following a question from the Panel, Brazil indicates that it maintains its claim regarding the denial of import licences to secure price stabilization.[648] Indonesia considers that Brazil did not develop this claim and thus failed to make a *prima facie* case for this measure.[649]

569.   We agree with Indonesia that Brazil has not developed any significant arguments in respect of this measure. The references made by Brazil in response to a question from the Panel regarding the basis of its claim are limited to a section on the factual description of Indonesia's import licensing regime in its first written submission. In our view, this is far from sufficient for a complainant to raise a *prima facie* case. On this basis we find that Brazil has not made a *prima facie* case that the denial of import licences to secure price stabilization is inconsistent with any of the covered agreements.

7.6.7.2   Additional restrictions on "certain products" and "processed products"

570.   In its first written submission Brazil referred to a number of additional restrictions on "certain products" and "processed products".[650] In response to a question from the Panel on whether Brazil considered these additional

---

[647]   Brazil's panel request, p. 8.
[648]   Brazil's response to Panel question No. 129 (referring to Brazil's first written submission, paras. 84-86).
[649]   Indonesia's comments on Brazil's response to Panel question No. 129.
[650]   Brazil's first written submission, fn 138 to para. 124.

restrictions to be part of its claims against certain aspects of Indonesia's import licensing regime, Brazil replied in the affirmative.[651]

571.   In perusing Brazil's panel request, we cannot find any reference to a challenge being raised in respect of measures referring to "certain products" or "processed products" as part of Brazil's claims against Indonesia's import licensing regime or elsewhere in the panel request. We therefore consider that the challenge against these measures is not within our terms of reference.

7.6.8   Overall conclusion

572.   In sum, we find that the positive list requirement and the intended use requirement are in the nature of an import licensing rule. We thus conclude that these measures do not fall under the purview of the Import Licensing Agreement.

573.   We find that the application windows, the validity periods and the fixed licence terms, as enacted through MoA 58/2015 and MoT 05/2016, are inconsistent with Article XI:1 of the GATT 1994 and are not justified under Article XX(d) of the GATT 1994. Having found that the application windows, the validity periods and the fixed licence terms, as enacted through MoA 58/2015 and MoT 05/2016 are inconsistent with Article XI of the GATT 1994, we consider that it is not necessary to address Brazil's claims under Article 4.2 of the Agreement on Agriculture and Article 3.2 of the Import Licensing Agreement in order to secure a positive solution to this dispute.

574.   We further find that the application windows and the validity periods, as a single measure, has expired because of the amendments introduced through the relevant provisions in MoA 34/2016 and MoT 59/2016. We thus refrain from making a recommendation in respect of the application windows and the validity period, as a single measure. Moreover, with respect to the new validity period, as enacted through MoA 34/2016, we find that Brazil has failed to demonstrate that this measure is inconsistent with Article XI:1 of the GATT 1994, Article 4.2 of the Agreement on Agriculture or Article 3.2 of the Import Licensing Agreement. We have also found that because of the almost identical language in the relevant provisions governing the fixed licence terms, our findings on Article XI and XX(d) of the GATT 1994, in respect of this measure as enacted through MoA 58/2015 and MoT 05/2016, also apply to this measure as enacted through MoA 34/2016 and MoT 59/2016.

575.   We have also found that the letter of recommendation from the provincial livestock, the supervision on the compliance of veterinary health requirements, and additional restrictions on "certain products" and "processed products" are not within our terms of reference.

---

[651]   Brazil's response to Panel question No. 15(b).

576.   Moreover, we conclude that Brazil failed to make a *prima facie* case that the following aspects of Indonesia's import licensing regime are WTO-inconsistent: (1) MoT's power to determine the amount of imported goods in the MoA Import Recommendation, as enacted through MoA 58/2015; and (2) the denial of import licences to secure price stabilization.

7.7   Individual Measure 4: Undue Delay in the Approval of the Veterinary Health Certificate

7.7.1   Introduction

577.   Brazil claims that Indonesia has caused an undue delay with respect to the approval of a veterinary certificate for the importation of poultry from Brazil into Indonesia. Brazil posits that this constitutes a violation of Indonesia's obligations under Article 8 and Annex C(1)(a) of the SPS Agreement.[652] Indonesia rejects Brazil's claim on two main grounds. First, Indonesia submits that it has not caused a delay in undertaking the relevant approval proceedings.[653] Second, Indonesia argues that even if there were a delay, it cannot be deemed undue.[654]

7.7.2   Relevant facts

578.   Before referring to the relevant legal provisions and assessing the merits of the parties' arguments, the Panel will present its understanding of certain factual aspects relative to Brazil's claim.

7.7.2.1   Background to the relevant SPS approval procedure

579.   It is our understanding that as part of sanitary and health surveillance, governments will normally require that, at the time of importation, certain animal products are accompanied by a veterinary health certificate. A veterinary health certificate is a document issued by an officially recognized veterinarian in the country of origin, attesting certain health characteristics of the traded product and of its place of origin. These health characteristics pertain to aspects, such as the pest or disease status of the product or the animal from which it is derived and of its place of origin; the type of veterinary inspection to which the animal was subject; the conditions of the establishment in which the products were

---

[652]   Brazil's first written submission, paras. 35-36 and 128-131; opening statement at the first meeting of the Panel, paras. 96-105; and second written submission, paras. 195-215.
[653]   Indonesia's response to Panel question No. 65; and second written submission, paras. 161 and 166.
[654]   Indonesia's first written submission, paras. 363-367; response to Panel question No. 65; and second written submission, paras. 161-163 and 166.

obtained; the type of monitoring to which the establishments are subject; and the product's wholesomeness and suitability for human consumption.[655]

580.   The health characteristics contained in a veterinary health certificate are usually the result of a bilateral process between the two trading partners. As part of this process, a Member normally evaluates the veterinary service of the trading partner interested in exporting animal products and verifies certain sanitary requirements in the country of origin.[656] Sometimes this process also entails an examination of the business units interested in exporting. After the evaluation process is concluded, the relevant trading partners would normally agree to the text of a model veterinary health certificate.

581.   As seen in 7.6.6 above, under Indonesian law, imported animal products must be accompanied by a veterinary health certificate.[657] As set out in Indonesia's laws and regulations, the process of obtaining an agreed model veterinary health certificate (as described in the previous paragraph), is part of the country of origin approval procedure. That approval procedure along with the business unit approval, both of which we have outlined in 7.3 above have been in place since 2006.

582.   In 2009, the year relevant to the facts at issue, the country of origin and business unit approvals were regulated through MoA 20/2009.[658] That regulation set out, *inter alia,* the sanitary conditions that imported chicken products must satisfy to enter Indonesia[659], as well as the criteria that Indonesia uses to evaluate its trading partners' veterinary services.[660] The country's disease status, which refers to the sanitary conditions of the place of origin of the relevant products, had to be based on an evaluation of and a report on the relevant country, which may be recognized by the OIE.[661] The evaluation also had to include a review of the documents submitted to Indonesian authorities and through on-site verification, in the country of origin, of such information. This regulation furthermore included requirements relating to animal health and food safety, as well as to halal slaughtering, that specific business units interested in exporting

---

[655] The veterinary health certificate proposed by Brazil to Indonesia for chicken products covers most of these aspects. See Brazilian veterinary certificate proposals for poultry meat (2009) and for turkey and duck (2010), p. 4 (Brazil's proposed model veterinary health certificates) (Exhibit BRA-43).

[656] Chapter 3.2 of Volume I of the World Organization for Animal Health (OIE) Terrestrial Animal Health Code, on "evaluation of veterinary services" refers to the criteria that may be used in the process of evaluating the veterinary service of a country. See OIE, Terrestrial Animal Health Code (25th edition, 2016), Vol. I, Chapter 3.2. Available at: http://www.oie.int/index.php?id=169&L=0&htmfile=chapitre_eval_vet_serv.htm (last accessed on 2 February 2017).

[657] This has been required since 1992. See Indonesia's response to Panel question No. 28.

[658] MoA 20/2009 (Exhibits BRA-08/IDN-100). See Indonesia's responses to Panel question Nos. 28(a) and 130.

[659] Article 13 of MoA 20/2009 (Exhibits BRA-08/IDN-100).

[660] Article 9(3) of MoA 20/2009 (Exhibits BRA-08/IDN-100).

[661] Article 14 of MoA 20/2009 (Exhibits BRA-08/IDN-100). The OIE's disease status recognition can be found in the OIE's website: http://www.oie.int/animal-health-in-the-world/official-disease-status/ (last visited on 23 January 2017).

should satisfy.[662] Relevant teams in charge of verifying the information had to evaluate these requirements, both through a document review and an on-site inspection.[663] After concluding the desk review and the on-site inspection, the relevant authorities in Jakarta had to undertake a risk analysis. Following the risk analysis, the authorities would issue a country of origin and a business unit approval.[664] That stipulation could be followed by the conclusion of a bilateral health protocol[665], which would include, *inter alia*, the model veterinary health certificate to be used.[666]

Figure 4   Steps to obtain country of origin and business unit approvals

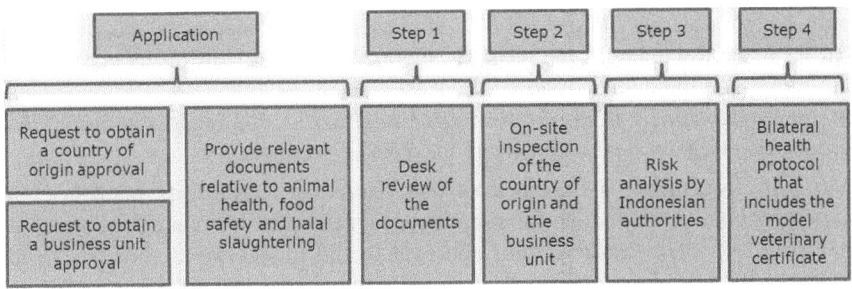

583.   The regulations currently in force (GR 95/2012[667] and MoA 34/2016[668]) follow this same structure[669], and include more detailed provisions on these procedures.[670]

> 7.7.2.2   Brazil's request for the approval of a veterinary health certificate

584.   It is uncontested by the parties that in June or July 2009, Brazil sent a communication to Indonesia requesting the approval of a veterinary health certificate for the importation of chicken products from Brazil.[671] Brazil

---

[662] Article 15 of MoA 20/2009 (Exhibits BRA-08/IDN-100).

[663] Article 16 of MoA 20/2009 (Exhibits BRA-08/IDN-100).

[664] Article 18 of MoA 20/2009 (Exhibits BRA-08/IDN-100).

[665] Article 17 of MoA 20/2009 (Exhibit BRA-08/IDN-100).

[666] Article 1.28 of MoA 20/2009 (Exhibit BRA-08/IDN-100), defines an animal health and veterinary health protocol as the document containing requirements for animal health and veterinary health already approved by the Director General of Animal Husbandry.

[667] See Articles 29 and 30 of Government Regulation No. 95/2012 Concerning Veterinary Public Health and Animal Welfare (GR 95/2012) (Exhibit IDN-31).

[668] See Articles 9 through 16 of MoA 34/2016 (Exhibit BRA-48/IDN-93).

[669] See Indonesia's response to Panel question No. 30(a).

[670] See Indonesia's response to Panel question No. 28(b).

[671] Brazil's first written submission, para. 35; Indonesia's response to Panel question No. 30(b); and Brazil's response to Panel question No. 35(a). See Brazil's proposed model veterinary health

---

formulated this request as part of efforts to find trade opportunities for its poultry meat industry.[672] These efforts also included bilateral meetings between government officials in the agriculture sector from Brazil and Indonesia. These were meetings of the Consultative Committee on Agriculture (CCA), which is part of the formal bilateral cooperation that had been set up.[673] Brazil reiterated its interest to export chicken products to Indonesia during several CCA meetings that took place between 2009 and 2011.[674]

585.   The minutes of the meeting of 15 and 16 September 2010 indicate that Indonesia accepted the proposed model health veterinary certificate. The meeting addressed the necessity of an audit mission to inspect the producing establishments and the halal procedures. Brazil invited the audit mission to come to Brazil during November 2010 and Indonesia mentioned the mission would only be possible in March 2011.[675] However, it is uncontested between the parties that subsequent to the meeting, Indonesia did not confirm its acceptance in writing and the audit mission did not take place. As Indonesia acknowledged in these proceedings, it has not responded to Brazil's 2009 request to accept the proposed veterinary health certificate for chicken products.[676]

586.   In December 2012, at least one Brazilian enterprise, interested in exporting chicken to Indonesia, submitted the relevant SPS related information necessary to obtain business unit approval to the Indonesian authorities.[677] In January 2013, Indonesia informed the Brazilian embassy in Jakarta that in

---

certificates (Exhibit BRA-43). Brazil also refers to having submitted, on August 2009, the answers to the "questionnaire to assess the Export of Meat and Meat Products to Indonesia", which Brazil submitted as Exhibit BRA-59. See Brazil's response to Panel question No. 133; and comments to Indonesia's response to Panel question No. 133. We further note that, as discussed in section 7.10.3.4 below, Brazil submitted to the Panel the letter dated 17 July 2009 from the Director General of Livestock at the Department of Agriculture to the Brazilian Ambassador in Jakarta (Exhibit BRA-52). Brazil submitted this exhibit as evidence of the alleged general prohibition and neither party referred to it in the context of Brazil's claim on undue delay. In this letter, Indonesian authorities rejected Brazil's proposal to export poultry because domestic poultry industries in Indonesia have been well developed towards their self-sufficiency. We note that this letter predates the subsequent indication of Indonesia's acceptance of Brazil's proposed veterinary certificate at the CCA meeting that took place in December 2010.

[672] Brazil's first written submission, paras. 24-35.

[673] Brazil's first written submission, para. 34.

[674] See Minutes of the Third Meeting of Consultative Committee on agriculture (CCA) between the Ministry of Agriculture of the Republic of Indonesia and the Ministry of Agriculture, Livestock and Food Supply of Federative Republic of Brazil (Minutes of the CCA meeting of 4 and 5 May 2009) (Exhibit BRA-13); Minutes of the Fourth CCA Meeting between the Ministry of Agriculture of the Republic of Indonesia and the Ministry of Agriculture, Livestock and Food Supply of the Federative Republic of Brazil (Minutes of the CCA meeting of 15 and 16 September 2010) (Exhibit BRA-14); and Minutes of the Fifth CCA Meeting between the Ministry of Agriculture of the Republic of Indonesia and the Ministry of Agriculture, Livestock and Food Supply of Federative Republic of Brazil (Minutes of the CCA meeting of 24 and 25 May 2011) (Exhibit BRA-16).

[675] Minutes of the CCA meeting of 15 and 16 September 2010, p. 5 (Exhibit BRA-14).

[676] Indonesia's response to Panel question No. 36.

[677] Questionnaire on food safety submitted by Cooperativa Central Aurora Alimentos on 27 December 2012 (Exhibit IDN-125).

addition to the information on the food safety assurance system, the Brazilian enterprise should submit information regarding its halal assurance system.[678] The letter indicated that the review would only be performed once the completed questionnaire of "Information On Halal Practices In Exporting Poultry Slaughterhouse" had been received.[679]

587.   On 17 July 2014, Brazil sent a communication to Indonesia, pursuant to Article 5.8 of the SPS Agreement, requesting an explanation of the sanitary basis of certain import restrictions applicable to the importation of chicken products. In particular, Brazil asked Indonesia to provide the reasons for the delay in the approval procedures of the veterinary health certificate for Brazilian poultry.[680] In September 2014, Indonesia replied to Brazil, indicating, among other things, that the delay was due to the applicant's failure to comply with existing procedures. As Indonesia explained in its response, this failure related to the fact that the relevant information on the halal assurance system in Brazil had not been submitted.[681]

588.   Throughout these proceedings Indonesia has confirmed that the reason for not proceeding with the review of both country of origin and business unit approval is that the relevant information on halal requirements was still outstanding.[682] Brazil, for its part, at the second meeting with the Panel, confirmed that to date, it has not submitted any halal information to Indonesia.[683]

7.7.3   Whether Indonesia has acted in a manner inconsistent with Article 8 and Annex C(1)(a) of the SPS Agreement

589.   Article 8 of the SPS Agreement reads:

> Members shall observe the provisions of Annex C in the operation of control, inspection and approval procedures, including national systems for approving the use of additives or for establishing tolerances for contaminants in foods, beverages or feedstuffs, and

---

[678]   Letter from the Ministry of Agriculture to the Embassy of Brazil in Jakarta, 22 January 2013 (Letter from Indonesia to Brazil of 22 January 2013) (Exhibit IDN-40). In October 2012, Indonesia informed the Brazilian embassy in Jarkata of the need to submit food safety and halal assurance information to obtain country and establishment approval for the importation of turkey and duck from Brazil to Indonesia. Letter from Director General of Livestock and Animal Health Services to Ambassador of Brazil in Jakarta, dated 15 October 2012 (Exhibit IDN-124).

[679]   See Letter from the Ministry of Agriculture to the Embassy of Brazil in Jakarta, 22 January 2013 (Exhibit IDN-40).

[680]   Brazil - Letter from Ambassador Marcos Galvão to Ambassador H.E. Triyono Wibowo (Brazil's Article 5.8 SPS request of July 2014) (Exhibit BRA-19).

[681]   See Indonesia - Answers related to the Article 5.8 SPS request (Exhibit BRA-20), in particular, response to question No. 4.

[682]   See Indonesia's response to Panel question No. 37(d); and second written submission, para. 172.

[683]   Brazil explains that exporters would not reasonably make investments to meet Indonesia's halal slaughtering requirements if Indonesia's market is not open to accept importation of chicken products. See Brazil's opening statement at the second meeting of the Panel, para. 72.

> otherwise ensure that their procedures are not inconsistent with the provisions of this Agreement.

590.   Annex C(1)(a) of the SPS Agreement reads:

> 1. Members shall ensure, with respect to any procedure to check and ensure the fulfilment of sanitary or phytosanitary measures, that:
>
> > (a) such procedures are undertaken and completed without undue delay and in no less favourable manner for imported products than for like domestic products;

591.   Article 8 mandates that Members observe the provisions of Annex C in the operation of control, inspection and approval procedures. Thus, a violation of the obligations contained in Annex C entails a violation of Article 8.[684]

592.   A Panel assessing the consistency of a measure with the first clause of Annex C(1)(a) needs to determine (1) that the challenged measure is an SPS control, inspection, or approval procedure subject to Annex C; (2) that there has been a delay in a Member undertaking or completing such SPS procedure; and (3) that such delay is undue.[685]

593.   Before turning to our examination of each of the elements necessary to determine whether the challenged measure is inconsistent with Annex C(1)(a), we will refer to an argument raised by Indonesia. Indonesia argues that Brazil did not properly raise its undue delay claim because Brazil had failed to identify the relevant legislation requiring the submission of a veterinary certificate at the time of importation of chicken products into Indonesia.[686] Brazil submits that regardless of the specific legal basis it referred to, the key issue is that such requirement is clearly established in Indonesia's legislation.[687]

594.   We observe that Brazil's claim concerns a failure by Indonesia to undertake and complete the relevant SPS approval procedure without undue delay. The measure at issue, thus, is not the relevant legislation applicable at the time, but Indonesia's alleged failure to comply with Brazil's request.[688] That claim is premised on the fact that Indonesia's legal framework requires imported chicken products to be accompanied by a veterinary health certificate. In our view, despite Brazil not referring to the correct legal instrument governing that requirement, the fact that it exists is uncontested by Indonesia.[689] Thus, we are not persuaded by Indonesia's argument.

---

[684]   Appellate Body Report, *Australia – Apples*, para. 434.
[685]   See Panel Reports, *Russia – Pigs (EU)*, paras. 7.505 and 7.1051; and *US – Animals*, para. 7.53.
[686]   Indonesia's first written submission, paras. 360-362; and Indonesia's response to Panel question No. 34.
[687]   Brazil's response to Panel question No. 33.
[688]   See also Argentina's third-party statement, paras. 3-4.
[689]   See Brazil's first written submission, Annex 1 (referring to Indonesian sanitary requirements for importation, specifically MoA 139/2014 (Exhibit BRA-34) that requires a protocol for importation,

595.   We turn to examine (1) whether Indonesia's refusal to examine and approve the veterinary health certificate for poultry products proposed by Brazil is subject to Annex C(1) of the SPS Agreement; (2) whether it amounts to a delay; and (3) whether such delay is undue.

7.7.3.1 Whether the approval of Brazil's proposed veterinary health certificate for chicken is subject to Annex C of the SPS Agreement

596.   Annex C applies to different "control, inspection and approval procedures"[690], which the footnote to this title describes as, "*inter alia*, procedures for sampling, testing and certification". Paragraph 1 of Annex C, in turn, refers to the relevant procedures as "any procedure to check and ensure the fulfilment of sanitary or phytosanitary measures".

597.   It is uncontested among the parties that the approval of a veterinary health certificate is an SPS approval procedure within the above meaning and, therefore, subject to Annex C of the SPS Agreement.[691] We agree with the parties. As established in footnote 7 to Annex C, referred to above, Annex C applies to procedures for certification. We understand that the approval of a veterinary health certificate falls within this category. In addition, the approval of a veterinary health certificate is part of a procedure to check the fulfilment of specific sanitary measures, that is, sanitary requirements.

598.   As noted above, pursuant to Indonesia's laws and regulations, the approval of the veterinary health certificate is part of the country of origin approval procedure which, in turn is bundled with a business unit approval procedure. To the extent that these approval procedures check and ensure the fulfilment of sanitary requirements (in addition to what is required for the approval of the veterinary health certificate), they also qualify as SPS approval procedures within the above meaning and, are, therefore, subject to Annex C.

7.7.3.2 Whether there has been a delay in Indonesia's consideration of Brazil's proposed veterinary health certificate for chicken

599.   As noted by the Appellate Body, the ordinary meaning of the word "delay" is "(a period of) time lost by inaction or inability to proceed".[692] With this in mind, we turn to examine the facts in this dispute.

---

which includes a veterinary certificate). See also Indonesia's first written submission, paras. 361-362 (referring to Articles 27, 29 and 31 of GR 95/2012 (Exhibit IDN-31)).

[690]   The title of Annex C is "Control, Inspection and Approval Procedures".

[691]   Brazil's first written submission, para. 302; and second written submission, para. 199. See also Indonesia's response to Panel question No. 65; and second written submission, para. 161.

[692]   Appellate Body Report, *Australia – Apples*, para. 437 (citing *Shorter Oxford English Dictionary*, 6th edn, A. Stevenson (ed.) (Oxford University Press, 2007), Vol. 1, p. 635).

600.   In mid-2009, Brazil submitted to Indonesia a request for the approval of a veterinary health certificate for chicken products.[693] As noted above, Indonesia has confirmed to the Panel that it has not responded to this request.[694] The request for the approval of a veterinary health certificate is step four in a country of origin approval procedure; however, in the present case, the request for approval has not yet progressed to step two, namely an on-site inspection. The reason for this "hold up" is, as Indonesia explains, that an application for business unit approval is not yet complete, because the relevant halal assurance documentation has not been submitted.[695] Indonesia has also indicated that until Brazil provides such information, it will not move on to the on-site field inspection either of the country of origin approval or the business unit approval.[696] These facts suggest to us, that there is a declared intention by Indonesia not to proceed.

601.   On the basis of the above, however, Indonesia makes two arguments, namely (1) that due to the incompleteness of the application the SPS approval procedure has not yet commenced with the consequence that no delay can have occurred, and (2) given the outstanding information to be received from the applicant, even if there were a delay, it would not be attributable to Indonesia but to the applicant itself.[697]

602.   We are not persuaded by Indonesia's argument on the incompleteness of Brazil's request for the following reasons. First, we do not consider that an SPS approval procedure starts only when *all* the relevant information is submitted. Rather, the procedure is triggered with submission of an application for approval, whether or not it satisfies all the relevant requirements.[698] We find support for this view in the relevant context of Annex C(1)(a). In particular, we recall that Annex C(1)(b) requires Members to promptly examine "the completeness of the documentation" and inform "the applicant in a precise and complete manner of all deficiencies; ... even when the application has deficiencies, the competent body proceeds as far as practicable with the procedure if the applicant so requests".[699] Therefore, the competent body is required to take an action or proceed, despite the irregularities in the application,

---

[693]   Brazil's proposed model veterinary health certificates (Exhibit BRA-43).

[694]   Indonesia's response to Panel question No. 36.

[695]   See answer to question No. 4 of Indonesia's answers to Article 5.8 SPS request (Exhibit BRA-20); Indonesia's response to Panel Question No. 37(d); second written submission, para. 172; and response to Panel question No. 133(b).

[696]   Indonesia's second written submission, para. 172; and response to Panel question No. 133(b).

[697]   Indonesia's second written submission, paras. 161 and 163.

[698]   See Panel Report, *EC – Approval and Marketing of Biotech Products*, paras. 7.1494, 7.1501 and 7.1502 (finding that the phrase "undertake and complete" covers all stages of relevant procedures and should be taken as meaning that, once an application has been received, approval procedures must be started and then carried out from beginning to end).

[699]   See Annex C(1)(b) of the SPS Agreement, which states that "when receiving an application, the competent body promptly examines the completeness of the documentation and informs the applicant in a precise and complete manner of all deficiencies".

to the extent practical as opposed to waiting for the submission of *all* relevant information.

603.   Second, we do not consider that in establishing whether there is a delay, we are required to consider the question of whether the delay is attributable to one side or the other. That question, in our view, pertains to the examination of whether the delay is undue, discussed in detail in section 7.7.3.3 below.[700]

604.   Third, the SPS approval procedure at issue here is the approval of the veterinary health certificate, which is in turn the fourth step in the country of origin approval process. In respect of this approval procedure Indonesia has not argued that there is any outstanding information which is due, and only pointed towards halal information being due, which is non-SPS related and is dealt with in greater detail in the subsequent section below.

605.   On the basis of the foregoing, we consider that Indonesia's declared inaction has led to a loss of time in the relevant SPS approval procedure, constituting a delay.

7.7.3.3   Whether the delay in Indonesia's consideration
of Brazil's proposed veterinary health
certificate for chicken is undue

606.   Annex C(1)(a) requires Members to ensure that relevant procedures are undertaken and completed without undue delay. The Appellate Body has interpreted this to mean that such procedures should be undertaken with appropriate dispatch, or in other words, should not involve periods of time that are unwarranted, or otherwise excessive, disproportionate or unjustifiable.[701]

607.   As mentioned above, Indonesia indicates that the procedure has not moved forward because of Brazil's failure to submit the relevant halal assurance questionnaire. In addition, both parties agree that halal slaughtering requirements are not SPS related.[702] The legal question we are confronted with is whether a Member may delay the completion of an SPS approval procedure because of outstanding non-SPS related information that it requires the applicant to submit. If the answer is in the affirmative, then Indonesia would be correct in arguing that the delay is attributable to Brazil and is therefore justified. If the answer is in the negative, Brazil would be correct in arguing that Indonesia is unjustifiably holding back the relevant SPS approval procedure.

608.   Our assessment is set forth below. As noted above, Annex C(1) of the SPS Agreement identifies the types of procedures to which the obligations

---

[700] See Panel Reports, *EC – Approval and Marketing of Biotech Products*, paras. 7.1494 and 7.1497; *US- Poultry (China)*, para. 7.354; and *Russia – Pigs*, paras. 7.532 and 7.534.
[701] Appellate Body Report, *Australia – Apples*, para. 437. See also Panel Report, *EC – Approval and Marketing of Biotech Products*, para. 7.1495 (finding that Annex C(1)(a) dictates that approval procedures should be undertaken and completed with no unjustifiable loss of time).
[702] See Indonesia's first written submission, para. 371; and Brazil's second written submission, para. 212.

contained in subparagraphs (a) through (i) apply, namely, "any procedure to check and ensure the fulfilment of sanitary or phytosanitary measures". This means that the purpose of the relevant procedure is to check and ensure the fulfilment of sanitary requirements.[703] Thus, in our view, the scope of Annex C already delimits what delays may be warranted or justified, namely, those needed for a Member to be able to check and ensure the fulfilment of the relevant SPS requirements.[704] This reading is confirmed by Annex C(1)(c) which requires Members to ensure that "information requirements are *limited to what is necessary for appropriate control, inspection and approval procedures*". Therefore, requesting information that is not necessary to check and ensure fulfilment of sanitary requirements would run counter to this obligation.

609.   We find support for our view in the submissions of certain third parties to this dispute. Argentina and the European Union both argue that inaction caused by the applicant's failure to submit information would only be relevant if it relates to evidence required in order to conduct a risk assessment or other controls designed to protect human, animal or plant life or health.[705]

610.   Furthermore, we note that previous panels have taken the view that whenever a Member delays the relevant procedure because it has required information which has been found not to be necessary under Annex C(1)(c), such delay would be undue under Annex C(1)(a).[706]

611.   Returning to the above legal question, on the basis of these considerations, we conclude that a Member may *not* delay the completion of an SPS approval procedure because non-SPS related information, which the Member requires the applicant to submit, is outstanding from an application.

612.   Applying this conclusion to the facts at issue, we recall that the only information which is outstanding relates to halal assurances, which both parties agree is not SPS related.[707] We agree. Accordingly we find that the delay is not justified and, is therefore undue. We note that given the scope of Brazil's claim, this finding applies to the approval procedure relevant to obtain the veterinary health certificate, which, as seen above, is part of the country of origin approval procedure. As noted above, this procedure is bundled with the business unit

---

[703] Appellate Body Report, *Australia – Apples*, para. 435; and Panel Report, *EC – Approval and Marketing of Biotech Products*, para. 7.1498.

[704] See Panel Reports, *EC – Approval and Marketing of Biotech Products*, paras. 7.1498 and 7.1500; and *US – Animals*, para. 7.143 (referring to a situation where a Member needs time to assess new or additional information). We further note that the delays attributable to action or inaction of an applicant cannot be held against the Member carrying out the procedure. See Panel Reports, *EC – Approval and Marketing of Biotech Products*, para. 7.1497; *US- Poultry (China)*, para. 7.354; and *Russia – Pigs*, paras. 7.532 and 7.534.

[705] See Argentina's third-party submission, paras. 19-23; Argentina's third-party statement, paras. 10 and 13; European Union's third-party submission, paras. 92-93; and European Union's third-party statement, para. 13.

[706] See Panel Report, *Russia – Pigs (EU)*, paras. 7.534, 7.583 and 7.1097.

[707] Indonesia's first written submission, para. 371; and Brazil's opening statement at the first meeting of the Panel, para. 99.

approval procedure, which, has an SPS component as well as the halal component at issue.

613.   We note Indonesia's argument that there are practical reasons to merge the procedures to verify both SPS and non-SPS related matters, which is what Indonesia has done with respect to animal health, food safety and halal assurances. In particular, Indonesia states that "it would be inefficient to start the Document Desk Review process of the food safety assurance system of the business unit in Brazil and proceed to the field on-site inspection for food safety, if it is not known whether the business unit has a halal assurance system. To make separate trips to assess food safety and halal requirements separately would entail unnecessary costs for Indonesia, which is a developing country."[708] While we have some sympathy for this argument, we do not believe that it can overrule what we consider to be a clear requirement laid down in the SPS Agreement, namely that the verification of sanitary requirements is undertaken and completed without undue delay.[709]

614.   We emphasize that our finding does not concern or affect Indonesia's right to impose halal requirements as a pre-marketing condition for the importation of chicken. We also note that Brazil has not contested this right. We recognize that a Member has the right to impose halal requirements in a manner consistent with its WTO obligations.

7.7.4   Conclusion

615.   On the basis of the foregoing, we find that Indonesia has caused an undue delay in the approval of the veterinary health certificate inconsistent with Article 8 and Annex C (1)(a) of the SPS Agreement.

7.8   *Individual Measure 5: Halal Labelling Requirements*

7.8.1   Introduction

616.   Brazil submits that Indonesia discriminates against imported chicken products through the manner in which it enforces its halal labelling requirements. On this basis, Brazil claims that Indonesia breaches Article III:4 of the GATT 1994.[710] Indonesia rejects Brazil's claim by arguing that the halal labelling requirements apply equally to the relevant like products.[711]

---

[708]   Indonesia's second written submission, para. 164.

[709]   We note that in some instances it is the Member interested in exporting who pays for the costs of the mission that will undertake the on-site evaluation. See, e.g. G/SPS/GEN/204/Rev.9/Add.1, paras. 121-126.

[710]   Brazil's first written submission, paras. 137-138 and 285-293; and second written submission, paras. 179-180.

[711]   See Indonesia's first written submission, paras. 329-330

Alternatively, Indonesia submits that the challenged measure is justified under Article XX(a) and (d) of the GATT 1994.[712]

7.8.2 Factual background

617. As seen in section 7.3 above, all chicken meat sold in Indonesia, whether domestic or imported, must be halal. Halalness is a requirement in Islam. For meat it generally means that the animal: (1) must be permitted for Muslims to eat, (2) must have been slaughtered upon the pronouncing of specific words, and (3) must have been slaughtered in a manner that allows the animal to bleed to death.[713] The specific standards on the exact details of the slaughtering procedure may vary from country to country. In Indonesia, Fatwa 12/2009 sets out the applicable standards.[714]

618. Indonesia has enacted several laws and regulations providing for the certification of halalness (that is, certification that an animal has been slaughtered in accordance with the halal requirements) and for the labelling of halal products as "halal".[715] Before 2014, the laws and regulations relating to halal products in Indonesia were not contained in a single law. There were rules applicable to halal labelling of certain products[716], verification of halalness of certain products[717], and the entity in charge of such verification.[718] It is our understanding that imported animal products have been required to bear a halal label since 1999[719], and to be halal certified since 2001.[720] These requirements are also contained, in the same manner, in all three sets of legal instruments at issue in this dispute.[721]

---

[712] See Indonesia's first written submission, paras. 342-355; and opening statement at the first meeting of the Panel, paras. 117-132.

[713] Food that conforms to Islamic law is described as halal, which is Arabic for permissible. Non-halal food is called *haram*. *Haram* food is not permitted to be consumed by Muslims. The halal requirements prohibit not only the consumption of pork but also, among others, the consumption of meat not slaughtered according to the prescribed methods. See Indonesia's first written submission, paras. 15-18; and Fatwa 12/2009 on Halal Certification Standards (Exhibit IDN-104).

[714] See Indonesia's first written submission, paras. 36-37, referring to Fatwa 12/2009 on Halal Certification Standards (Exhibit IDN-104).

[715] Indonesia's first written submission, paras. 27-37; and response to Panel question No. 43.

[716] Government Regulation No. 69/1999 on Food Labelling and Advertisement (GR 69/1999) (Exhibit IDN-74/IDN-88).

[717] Ministry of Religious Affairs Decree No. 518/2001 (MoRA 518/2001) (Exhibit IDN-107).

[718] Ministry of Religious Affairs Decree No. 519/2001 On Halal Food Inspection Implementing Agencies (MoRA 519/2001) (Exhibit IDN-28/IDN-108).

[719] Articles 2(1) and 10(1) of GR 69/1999 (Exhibit IDN-74/IDN-88).

[720] Article 3(1)(b) of MoRA 518/2001 (Exhibit IDN-107).

[721] See Articles 7, 14(2), and 19 of MoA 139/2014; Articles 7(d), 18, and 19(e) of MoA 58/2015; and Articles 6(d), 17, and 18 of MoA 34/2016. See also Brazil's first written submission, fn 151 to para. 137; fn 267 to para. 286; and fn 268 to para. 287.

619. On 17 October 2014, the Congress of Indonesia issued Law 33/2014 concerning halal product assurance.[722]

620. Article 4 of Law 33/2014 provides that products that enter, circulate, and are traded in Indonesia must be certified halal.[723]

621. Article 38 of Law 33/2014 provides that those business operators who have received a halal certification must include a halal label on: (a) the product's packaging; (b) a specific part of the product; and/or (c) a specific place of the product.[724]

622. Brazil does not take issue with the fulfilment of the halal certification and labelling, as required by Indonesia and explicitly recognizes the importance of both these requirements.[725]

623. What Brazil takes issue with is the alleged discrimination in enforcing the halal requirements. Brazil refers to the fact that imported products must be labelled halal, which is controlled at the border. Brazil contrasts this with the uncontested fact that fresh chicken, which constitutes a majority of the chicken sold in traditional markets, is not required to bear a halal label.[726]

7.8.3   Whether Indonesia's enforcement of halal labelling requirements is inconsistent with Article III:4 of the GATT 1994

624. Brazil's bases its claim on two grounds. The first pertains to a transition period provided for in Law 33/2014, which according to Brazil, exempts domestic chicken from halal certification for a period of five years. The second ground, which Brazil raises, pertains to an exception from the labelling requirement for meat sold in small quantities.[727] We address these in turn.

---

[722] Law of Republic of Indonesia N. 33/2014 concerning Halal Product Assurance (Law 33/2014) (Exhibit BRA-46/IDN-5).
[723] Article 4 of Law 33/2014 (Exhibit BRA-46/IDN-5).
[724] Article 38 of Law 33/2014 (Exhibit BRA-46/IDN-5).
[725] Brazil's first written submission, para. 139; opening statement at the first meeting of the Panel, para. 53; response to Panel question No. 45; and second written submission, paras. 173 and 185;
[726] See Brazil's first written submission, para. 137.
[727] See Brazil's first written submission, para. 287. See also Brazil's response to Panel question No. 46.

7.8.3.1 Whether the enforcement of the grace period for the application of certain aspects of Law 33/2014 is inconsistent with Article III:4

7.8.3.1.1 Introduction

625. Brazil submits that Article 67 of Law 33/2014 provides for a five-year grace period regarding the halal certification obligation. According to Brazil, in practice, only domestic products can benefit from the grace period.[728]

626. In response, Indonesia argues that the grace period pertains to the entity in charge of issuing the halal certification, rather than to certification itself. According to Indonesia, therefore, both domestic and imported products are subject to the same substantive requirements regarding halal certification, including the obligation to obtain a halal certificate from the competent authorities.[729]

627. In addition, during the second substantive meeting, Indonesia argued that "the halal certification requirement and the related five-year grace period fall outside of the Panel's terms of reference". According to Indonesia, Brazil's challenge is limited to another regulation regarding halal slaughtering and labelling, including the difference in treatment in the surveillance and implementation of halal labelling. Indonesia posits that, accordingly, Brazil's claim does not include challenges on halal certification.[730]

7.8.3.1.2 Whether Brazil's claim regarding the grace period provided in Article 67 of Law 33/2014 falls within the Panel's terms of reference

628. In light of the foregoing , we will first address whether Brazil's claim that the grace period provided in Article 67 of Law 33/2014 is inconsistent with Indonesia's obligations under Article III:4 of the GATT 1994 is within our terms of reference.

629. In section 7.1.2.2.1 above, we discuss the legal standard that the Panel should follow to determine whether a measure and a claim are within its terms of reference. We are guided by that standard when developing the following considerations. In addition, we recall that the Appellate Body has drawn a distinction between claims and arguments:

> By "*claim*" we mean a claim that the respondent party has violated, or nullified or impaired the benefits arising from, an

---

[728] Brazil's first written submission, para. 287; and response to Panel question No. 44.

[729] Indonesia's opening statement at the first meeting of the Panel, paras. 113-115; response to Panel question No. 43; and second written submission, para. 156. See also Indonesia's response to Panel question No. 47.

[730] Indonesia's opening statement at the second meeting of the Panel, para. 47.

identified provision of a particular agreement. Such a *claim of violation* must, as we have already noted, be distinguished from the *arguments* adduced by a complaining party to demonstrate that the responding party's measure does indeed infringe upon the identified treaty provision.[731]

630.   Section II.iv of Brazil's panel request indicates that Indonesia discriminates against chicken meat and chicken products imported from third countries *vis-à-vis* its domestic like products through different measures. One of the measures identified therein is "the surveillance and implementation of halal slaughtering and labelling requirements".[732] Brazil considers this measure to be inconsistent with Article III:4 of the GATT 1994 as it accords to imported products less favourable treatment than that accorded to like domestic products.[733]

631.   The measure at issue, thus, is the surveillance and implementation of halal slaughtering and labelling requirements and the claim is the inconsistency of this measure with Article III:4 of the GATT 1994.

632.   As discussed in detail below, the parties disagree on the scope and meaning of the grace period for the application of Law 33/2014. Brazil submits that Article 67 exempts domestic chicken meat from the halal certification requirement with the consequence that it does not need to be labelled "halal" when offered for sale. We understand Brazil, thus, to rely on its reading of Article 67 as the reason why domestic chicken sold in markets is not labelled halal. In our view, Brazil's references to the grace period fall within the category of *arguments* made in order to develop the *claim* under Article III:4 of GATT 1994 in respect of the measure identified, namely "...implementation of halal...labelling requirements". On this basis, we reject Indonesia's view that the halal certification requirement and the related five-year grace period fall outside the Panel's terms of reference, and find that this reference is an argument developed by Brazil in support of a claim falling within our terms of reference.

7.8.3.1.3   Whether Article 67 of Law 33/2014 exempts domestic chicken from halal certification in a manner inconsistent with Article III:4

633.   We recall that for a claim of violation of Article III:4 of the GATT 1994 to succeed the complainant must demonstrate that imported like products are treated less favourably compared to like domestic products. Brazil essentially argues that Article 67 of Law 33/2014 exempts domestic chicken from halal certification, whereas it does not exempt imported chicken.

---

[731]   Appellate Body Report, *Korea – Dairy*, para. 139. (emphasis original; footnote omitted)
[732]   Brazil's panel request, p. 6.
[733]   Brazil's panel request, p. 7.

634.   We therefore turn to examine whether Brazil's reading of Indonesia's relevant laws and regulations, in particular Article 67 of Law 33/2014, is correct. In assessing this matter, we need to determine the meaning of a number of provisions of Law 33/2014. As noted above, the Appellate Body has found that in determining the meaning of a domestic regulation, a Panel should undertake a holistic assessment of all relevant elements, starting with the text of the relevant provision.[734] We will therefore begin our examination with the text of the relevant provision.

635.   The grace period referred to by both parties is contained in Article 67 of Law 33/2014. This provision establishes:

> (1) Obligation of halal certification for Product that circulate and traded in the territory of Indonesia as intended in Article 4 come into effect 5 (five) years from the legislation of this Law.

> (2) Prior to the obligation of halal certification as intended in paragraph (1) is in effect, the type of Product which require halal certification is regulated in stages.[735]

636.   The first paragraph of Article 67 refers back to Article 4 of Law 33/2014. As seen above, this provision establishes that products that enter, circulate, and are traded in Indonesia must be certified halal.[736]

637.   We observe that, read outside its context, on its face, Article 67 could indeed be understood to provide, as Brazil suggests, that certification is not required during the five-year transitional period.

638.   However, as Indonesia submits, a number of other provisions in Law 33/2014, suggests a different reading. Law 33/2014, among other things, sets up an institutional framework for halal product assurance. Such institutional framework includes the creation of the Halal Product Organizing Agency (BPJPH) and the recognition, by the BPJPH, of halal examination agencies (LPH).[737]

639.   According to Article 64 of Law 33/2014, the formation of BPJPH is intended to occur within the three years following the legislation of Law 33/2014.[738] This provision suggests the need for a transitional period before the new institutional framework is fully operative.

640.   Moreover, Articles 59 and 60 of Law 33/2014 refer to the renewal and request of halal certificates before the formation of BPJPH. Article 60 is particularly relevant, because it establishes that "MUI still conducts its task in

---

[734] Appellate Body Reports, *EU – Biodiesel (Argentina)*, para. 6.156; and *US – Countervailing and Anti-Dumping Measures* (China), para. 4.101.
[735] Article 67 of Law 33/2014 (Exhibit BRA-46/IDN-5).
[736] Article 4 of Law 33/2014 (Exhibit BRA-46/IDN-5).
[737] Articles 1, 5 and 6 of Law 33/2014 (Exhibit BRA-46/IDN-5).
[738] Article 64 of Law 33/2014 (Exhibit BRA-46/IDN-5).

Halal Certification until BPJPH is formed".[739] There are other provisions that regulate the transition before BPJPH is formed, referring to LPHs already recognized (Article 61), halal auditors already recognized (Article 62), and halal supervisors of company already recognized (Article 63). In addition, Article 66 establishes that at "the time this Law is enacted, all Regulating Legislation that regulates regarding JPH is considered valid as long as it does not contradict with the provision in this Law".[740]

641.   The foregoing, in our view, unequivocally confirms that, during the grace period, the obligation to be halal certified is still in place. We understand that such an obligation should be carried out according to the rules and regulations in force at the time of the approval of Law 33/2014, namely, MoRA 518/2001 and 519/2001.

642.   Hence, we consider Brazil's description of the meaning and scope of application of Indonesia's domestic regulation to be inaccurate. In our view, contrary to Brazil's submission, the grace period provided in Article 67 of Law 33/2014 does not suspend the obligation for producers of chicken products sold in Indonesia to obtain halal certification. Article 67, therefore, is not the reason for, and does not explain the absence of, halal labels on chicken sold in traditional markets.

643.   Given our factual finding regarding the meaning of the five-year grace period set out in Article 67 of Law 33/2014, we consider that Brazil has failed to demonstrate the manner in which the five-year grace period set out in Article 67 of Law 33/2014 constitutes a violation of Article III:4 of the GATT 1994.

> 7.8.3.2   Whether the exemption from the halal labelling requirement for food directly sold and packed before the buyer in small number is inconsistent with Article III:4

644.   We next turn to examine Brazil's second ground in support of its claim, namely that Indonesia discriminates against imported chicken products in respect of an exemption from the halal labelling requirement that applies to chicken directly sold to the consumer in small quantities.[741]

645.   Brazil developed this argument in the course of the proceedings in response to the following argument put forward by Indonesia. Referring to the absence of halal labels on chicken sold in traditional markets, Indonesia

---

[739]   Article 60 of Law 33/2014 (Exhibit BRA-46/IDN-5).
[740]   Article 66 of Law 33/2014 (Exhibit BRA-46/IDN-5).
[741]   We note that this exemption applies only to halal *labelling*. As Indonesia stresses, chicken sold in this manner, would still have to be halal. In this regard, see also Qatar's general comment in Qatar's third-party statement, para. 11.

explained that by virtue of Article 63(b) of GR 69/1999, labels do not need to be applied on food products sold before buyers.[742]

646.   In reaction to this explanation from Indonesia, Brazil submits that exempting certain types of food from the halal labelling requirement epitomizes the discrimination that concerns Brazil.[743] In Brazil's view, imported previously frozen (thawed) chicken meat must also be allowed to be sold unpackaged and unlabelled before consumers.[744] The difference in treatment between fresh chicken and imported frozen chicken, according to Brazil, amounts to discrimination.

647.   We turn to examine the scope of the exemption from the obligation to bear a halal label foreseen in Indonesia's regulation applicable to certain food products and whether Brazil has made its case in this respect.

7.8.3.2.1   Factual description of the
exemption of certain food products
from bearing the halal label

648.   As seen above, the requirement for halal products to bear a halal label is set out in Article 38 of Law 33/2014.

649.   Outside Law 33/2014, a number of relevant laws and regulations generally address labelling requirements, including halal labelling. Article 2(1) of GR 69/1999 establishes that anybody producing or importing packaged food into Indonesia for trading shall put labels on, in and or as part of food packages.[745] Article 10(1) establishes that anybody producing or importing packed food into Indonesia for trading and declaring that food is permissible for Muslims, "shall be responsible for the truth of the statement and put the information or word 'halal' on labels".[746]

650.   It is with reference to GR 69/1999 that Indonesia submits that certain categories of food products are exempted from labelling requirements, including halal labelling. In particular, Indonesia refers to Article 63(b) of GR 69/1999.[747]

651.   Article 63 of GR 69/1999 provides:

The provisions on labels and advertisements as meant in this government regulation shall not be effective for:

---

[742] Indonesia's closing statement at the first meeting of the Panel, para. 15; and second written submission, para. 155.
[743] Brazil's responses to Panel question Nos. 143-144.
[744] Brazil's response to Panel question No. 144.
[745] Article 2(1) of GR 69/1999 (Exhibit IDN-74/IDN-88).
[746] Article 10(1) of GR 69/1999 (Exhibit IDN-74/IDN-88).
[747] Indonesia's closing statement at the first meeting of the Panel, para. 15; and second written submission, para. 155.

    a. food whose package is too small, so that it is impossible to contain all kinds of information as meant in this government regulation;

    b. food directly sold and packed before buyers in a small number;

    c. food sold in a large amounts (bulk)[748]

652.   Indonesia submits that this exemption is more specific than Article 38 of Law 33/2014 and applies to fresh chicken sold in traditional markets. In its most recent submissions, Brazil indicates that it agrees with Indonesia that Article 63(b) is more specific, and thus provides for an exemption to a specific category of products from the obligation to bear a halal label. Brazil's grievance is that in its view, the exemption does not apply to imported frozen chicken.

7.8.3.2.2   Panel's analysis under Article III:4

653.   We therefore turn to consider whether the exemption to the labelling requirement set out in Article 63/1999 results in less favourable treatment inconsistent with Article III:4.

654.   As seen above, Brazil considers that imported previously frozen chicken meat that underwent thawing must also be allowed to be sold unpackaged and unlabelled before consumers.[749] We understand this argument to refer to a *de facto* discrimination between fresh domestic chicken and frozen imported chicken.[750] Brazil argues that "the restriction on imported products to be sold only packaged affects the conditions of competition" by: (i) limiting the manner by which imported products can be displayed to consumers; and (ii) preventing consumers from examining the product they intend to purchase.[751] Moreover, Brazil argues that the fact that imported products have to bear a halal label imposes additional costs on Brazilian exporters.[752]

655.   As discussed above[753], an assessment pursuant to Article III:4 of the GATT 1994 requires the Panel to determine: (1) whether the imported and domestic products at issue are like products; (2) whether the measure at issue is a "law, regulation, or requirement affecting their internal sale, offering for sale, purchase, transportation, distribution or use"; and (3) whether the imported products are accorded "less favourable" treatment than that accorded to like domestic products.[754]

---

[748] Article 63 of GR 69/1999 (Exhibit IDN-74/IDN-88).

[749] Brazil's response to Panel question No. 144.

[750] See Appellate Body Report, *US – Tuna II (Article 21.5 – Mexico)*, paras. 7.28-7.29 (regarding the manner in which a panel should assess a complainant's claim of *de facto* detrimental impact).

[751] Brazil's response to Panel question No. 144.

[752] Brazil's response to Panel question No. 145.

[753] See section 7.5.3.3.3.2 above.

[754] Appellate Body Report, *Korea – Various Measures on Beef*, para. 133.

656.   Furthermore, the Appellate Body has indicated that "there must be in every case a genuine relationship between the measure at issue and its adverse impact on competitive opportunities for imported *versus* like domestic products".[755] According to the Appellate Body:

> [I]n determining whether the detrimental impact on competitive opportunities for like imported products is *attributable to*, or has a *genuine relationship with*, the measure at issue, the relevant question is "whether it is the governmental measure at issue that 'affects the conditions under which like goods, domestic and imported, compete in the market within a Member's territory'".[756] (emphasis added)

657.   In our assessment, given the facts as well as the nature of Brazil's arguments, it is this question of whether there is a genuine relationship between the challenged measure and the adverse impact claimed by Brazil, that is at the forefront of our Article III:4 analysis, and must therefore be addressed first. As we see it, Article 63 of GR 69/1999 is not the cause of Brazil's problem; rather, the detriment described above by Brazil, stems from and, therefore, is attributable to requirements regulated elsewhere. Imported chicken products are packaged and labelled before they reach the (traditional) market; the requirement to do so is laid down in other provisions of Indonesia's laws and regulations.[757] The cost of labelling is already incurred at that point. Furthermore, imported chicken meat, because it is frozen, must be in cold storage when sold in traditional markets. That requirement, which we have examined under Article III:4 in section 7.5.3.1.1 above, is set out elsewhere, not in Article 63 of GR 69/1999. It is because of this requirement, not because of Article 63 of GR 69/1999, that imported chicken meat cannot be put on display in the same manner as fresh chicken meat (to which the cold storage requirement does not apply). Finally, in our view, Article 63 of GR 69/1999 would apply if and when frozen chicken products, for example chicken cuts, are sold and individually packed in front of the buyer.[758]

658.   Based on these considerations, we take the view that there is no *genuine relationship* between that measure and what Brazil perceives as detrimental impact on the competitive opportunities for imported chicken, namely, the difference in display and the cost of labelling. Put differently, that impact on the conditions of competition is not attributable to the measure at issue. Since we

---

[755]   Appellate Body Report, *Thailand – Cigarettes (Philippines)*, para. 134. See also Appellate Body Report, *EC – Seal Products*, para. 5.101.

[756]   Appellate Body Report, *EC – Seal Products*, para. 5.105 (referring to Appellate Body Reports, *US – COOL*, para. 270 (in turn referring to Appellate Body Report, *Korea – Various Measures on Beef*, para. 149)).

[757]   See e.g. Articles 7(d), 18, and 19 of MoA 58/2015; and Articles 6(d), 17, and 18 of MoA 34/2016.

[758]   This could be the case, for example, if frozen chicken cuts were imported in "bulk" and then sold individually at the market.

have found that there is no genuine relationship between the challenged measure and the alleged detrimental impact, we do not consider it necessary to return to the other elements of the test set out above.

659.   We, therefore, consider that Brazil has not demonstrated that Article 63 of GR 69/1999 provides *de facto* less favourable treatment between fresh domestic chicken and frozen imported chicken, within the meaning of Article III:4 of the GATT 1994.

7.8.4   Conclusion

660.   On the basis of the foregoing, we consider that Brazil has failed to demonstrate that Indonesia's implementation of its halal labelling requirements is inconsistent with Indonesia's obligations under Article III:4 of the GATT 1994.

7.9   *Individual Measure 6: Transportation Requirement*

7.9.1   Introduction

661.   We turn to the last of the individual measures challenged by Brazil, which Brazil has described as a direct transportation requirement.[759] The measure consists in a requirement, laid down in the relevant MoA regulation, that transportation shall be conducted "directly" from the country of origin to the port of discharge in Indonesia.

662.   Brazil claims that the direct transportation requirement mandates that shipments cannot stop in transit at any port between the port of dispatch in Brazil and the port of destination in Indonesia.[760] Brazil argues that this requirement is a quantitative restriction, in violation of Article XI:1 of the GATT 1994 and Article 4.2 of the Agreement on Agriculture.[761]

663.   Indonesia submits that Brazil wrongly interprets the concerned provision in the relevant MoA regulation. According to Indonesia, its legal framework allows for imported goods to transit through ports located in countries other than those in the country of origin and the country of destination.[762]

664.   In reaction to Indonesia's explanation of the direct transportation requirement, Brazil argues that the "legal uncertainties generated by the murky language" of the relevant provision "amount to a quantitative restriction".[763]

665.   As noted above, the relevant MoA regulation enacting, *inter alia*, the direct transportation requirement has been revoked and replaced twice since

---

[759] Brazil's panel request, pp. 4-5.
[760] Brazil's first written submission, paras. 60, 132 and 214.
[761] Brazil's first written submission, paras. 134-135 and 216-217; second written submission, paras. 218-222; and response to Panel question No. 139.
[762] Indonesia's first written submission, paras. 304-310; and second written submission, paras. 148 and 151.
[763] Brazil's second written submission, para. 222. See also response to Panel question No. 139.

panel establishment. The following table sets out the relevant provisions of the different sets of legal instruments underlying the direct transportation requirement as discussed in this report.

Table 8. Relevant provisions regarding the direct transportation requirement

First set of legal instruments	Second set of legal instruments	Third set of legal instruments
MoA 139/2014	**MoA 58/2015**	**MoA 34/2016**
Art. 20	*Art. 20*	*Art. 19*
(1) Transportation/shipment of carcass, meat, and/or its processed as referred to in Article 17 is conducted directly from the country of origin to the point entry within the territory of the Republic of Indonesia. ... (3) Importation of carcass, meat, and/or its processed by way of transit is conducted in accordance with the Law and Regulation regarding animal quarantine.	Transportation requirements of carcass, meat and/or the processed product thereof as referred to in Article 7 letter d shall be as follows: a. Conducted directly from the Country of Origin to the port of discharge within the territory of the Republic of Indonesia. ... c. Transit during importation shall be carried out pursuant to the animal quarantine laws and regulations.	The requirements of transportation/shipment of carcass, meat, offal and/or their processed products as referred to in Article 6 letter d are as follows: a. conducted directly from the Country of Origin to the port of entry within the territory of the Republic of Indonesia ... c. importation by way of transit is conducted in accordance with the laws and regulations regarding animal quarantine;

666.   As reflected in Table 8 above, the provisions enacting the direct transportation requirement are virtually identical from one legal instrument to the next. On this basis, we consider that the direct transportation requirement, as enacted through Article 19(a) of MoA 34/2016 falls within the Panel's terms of reference and we thus have jurisdiction to review its WTO consistency. Our findings below, therefore, are relevant to any of the three enactments of the measure, including the most recent one. Brazil, in its most recent submissions, refers to the relevant provision in MoA 34/2016, namely Article 19(a). We, therefore, do so as well.

667.   We first examine whether the direct transportation requirement means what Brazil alleges it to mean, namely that it requires non-stop shipment. If we find that this is the case, we examine, whether it is inconsistent with Article XI of the GATT 1994 or Article 4.2 of the Agreement on Agriculture. If we find that the direct transportation requirement does not mean what Brazil alleges it to mean, but allows for transit, as argued by Indonesia, we go on to consider the second issue raised by Brazil, namely that the direct transportation requirement is inconsistent with Article XI of the GATT 1994 and Article 4.2 of the Agreement on Agriculture, due to its "murky language".

7.9.2   Whether the direct transportation requirement is
        inconsistent with Article XI of the GATT 1994 and
        Article 4.2 of the Agreement on Agriculture

668.   As noted above, Brazil initially developed its claim by arguing that the
direct transportation requirement, enshrined in Article 19(a) of MoA 34/2016,
prohibits the possibility of goods shipped from Brazil to Indonesia from being
imported into Indonesia, if they have stopped in transit in a third country.[764]

7.9.2.1   Whether the direct transportation requirement
          mandates non-stop shipment without transit or
          transhipment

669.   The first step of our analysis is therefore to ascertain the meaning of the
direct transportation requirement in Article 19(a) of MoA 34/2016.

670.   The Appellate Body has found that in determining the meaning of a
domestic regulation, a panel should undertake a holistic assessment of all
relevant elements, starting with the text of the relevant provision.[765] We will
therefore begin our examination with the text of the relevant provision.

671.   Brazil understands that the term "conducted directly" in Article 19(a),
means that if the transportation is not direct, or, if by any reason, a stop in a third
country or port during the transportation is necessary before the arrival at the
port of destination, then the products could not be imported into Indonesia.[766]

672.   Indonesia explains that sub-paragraph (a) of Article 19 should be read
together with the other paragraphs of this article. In particular, Indonesia refers
to sub-paragraph (c) in the same provision, according to which "importation by
way of transit" must be conducted "in accordance with the laws and regulations
regarding animal quarantine".[767] Indonesia also refers to specific provisions of
the relevant laws and regulations (Law 16/1992 and GR 82/2000) in support of
its reading that Article 19(a) does not prohibit transit.[768] Indonesia furthermore
explains that a violation of the direct transportation requirement is limited to a
specific situation, namely when goods originating in one country are imported
into a third country and then re-exported to Indonesia.[769]

---

[764]   Brazil's first written submission, paras. 132 and 214.
[765]   Appellate Body Reports, *EU – Biodiesel (Argentina)*, para. 6.156; and *US – Countervailing and Anti-Dumping Measures (China)*, para. 4.101.
[766]   Brazil's first written submission, paras. 132 and 214.
[767]   Indonesia's first written submission, para. 305; response to Panel question No. 39; and second written submission, para. 151. We recall that Indonesia explains that the term "direct" may be used in the same manner as it is used in the airline industry, where there is a distinction between "direct" and "non-stop" flights. See Indonesia's second written submission, para. 151.
[768]   See Indonesia's first written submission, paras. 306-308; and second written submission, para. 148. See also Indonesia's responses to Panel question Nos. 41 and 42, where Indonesia explains the relationship between these legal instruments and Indonesia's import licensing regime.
[769]   Indonesia's response to Panel question No. 39. See also Indonesia's response to Panel question No. 137.

673.   We note that the text of Article 19(a), read in isolation from other provisions of MoA 34/2016, could indeed be understood, as argued by Brazil, to indicate that transportation must be non-stop from the port of origin in Brazil to the port of destination in Indonesia. However, the text of paragraph (c) is explicit in referring to "importation by way of transit". This provision clearly indicates that the importation of goods is allowed even if it occurs after such goods stopped in transit on their journey from the port of origin in Brazil to the port of destination in Indonesia. The text of paragraph (c) requires that when this happens, transit should be conducted in accordance with animal quarantine laws and regulations. Indonesia has pointed to Law 16/1992 concerning Animal, Fish and Plant Quarantine and to GR 82/2000 on Animal Quarantine. Both instruments address, *inter alia*, the quarantine treatment of shipments of animal products (as potential carriers of animal pests and diseases) arriving in Indonesia, which have stopped in third country ports on the way.[770] GR 82/2000 specifically defines "transit" as a "temporary stop of transportation means in a harbour during their journey that brings in animal, material derived from animal, animal product material and other thing[s], before arriving in the designated harbour".[771] To us, these provisions unequivocally acknowledge that animal products shipped from Brazil to Indonesia can be imported even if they transit through ports in third countries.

674.   We further note that the MoA Import Recommendation template contains a field on transit.[772] In our view, the inclusion of this field in the MoA Import Recommendation template suggests that an importer may indicate the port or ports of transit of the imported products, and that transit is therefore contemplated and allowed.

675.   Indonesia's reading is further corroborated by evidence on record. Indonesia submitted to the Panel a Bill of Lading dated 25 April 2016 and an Import Notification dated 24 May 2016, both of which demonstrate that a shipment of frozen boneless beef from Australia transited through Singapore before arriving at Tanjung Priok in Indonesia.[773] Indonesia also submitted to the Panel an MoA Import Recommendation for beef from New Zealand, which has the field for transit filled out, indicating "Singapore Container Terminal".[774] This evidence supports Indonesia's assertion that its authorities allow the import of

---

[770]   Indonesia's first written submission, paras. 306-308; and second written submission, para. 148.

[771]   Article 1(8) of GR 82/2000 (Exhibit IDN-78). We note that this definition resembles that of "transit" as set out in Article V(1) of the GATT 1994.

[772]   Indonesia's second written submission, para. 151 (referring to Format I in MoA 58/2015 (Exhibit BRA-01/IDN-24), p. 27.

[773]   Indonesia's opening statement at the first meeting of the Panel, para. 133 (referring to Bill of Lading dated 25 April 2016 and Import Notification dated 24 May 2016 (Bill of Lading and Import Notification of 2016) (Exhibit IDN-79).

[774]   Indonesia's response to Panel question No. 40 (referring to Import Recommendation by the Minister of Agriculture for beef from New Zealand in December 2015 (MoA Recommendation for beef) (Exhibit IDN-88)).

animal products that transit through third-countries, in a manner consistent with quarantine laws and regulations, before getting to Indonesia.

676.   Brazil furthermore posits that Indonesia's description of how the direct transportation requirement operates, implies that transhipment is excluded from Indonesia's definition of transit.[775] Brazil has not put forward any evidence in support of this view. It is our understanding that transhipment is the process through which the cargo is moved from one ship onto another.[776] Transhipment is, therefore, a process, which may or may not happen during transit as defined in the above government regulation. Since transit is allowed, as we established, transhipment is necessarily also allowed subject to quarantine laws and regulations.

677.   On the basis of the foregoing, we disagree with Brazil's view that a plain reading of Article 19(a) of MoA 34/2016 does not support the conclusion that transit is allowed by Indonesian authorities.[777] We have read this provision together with other provisions in Indonesia's laws and regulations, and come to the conclusion that transit (including transhipment) is allowed.

678.   We consider that Indonesia's representations support our own reading of Article 19(a), and we attach importance to Indonesia's official explanation of this provision.[778]

679.   We, therefore, conclude that the direct transportation requirement, as enshrined in Article 19(a) of MoA 34/2016, allows importation into Indonesia of goods transiting through third-country ports, including those that involve transhipment.

680.   Thus, contrary to what Brazil argues, the direct transportation requirement does not prohibit imported products from entering Indonesia after transiting through ports in third countries. To that extent, we consider that Brazil has failed to demonstrate how this measure constitutes a violation of Article XI of the GATT 1994 and Article 4.2 of the Agreement on Agriculture.

---

[775]   Brazil's second written submission, para. 219; and response to panel question No. 139.

[776]   Transhipment is defined in Chapter 2 of Annex E of the International Convention on the Simplification and Harmonization of Customs Procedures (Revised Kyoto Convention) as a "Customs procedure under which goods are transferred under Customs control from the importing means of transport to the exporting means of transport within the area of one Customs office which is the office of both importation and exportation". (Available at: http://www.wcoomd.org/en/topics/facilitation/instrument-and-tools/conventions/pf_revised_kyoto_conv/kyoto_new/spane.aspx, last visited on 26 January 2017).

[777]   Brazil's second written submission, para. 218.

[778]   See Panel Report, *US – Section 301 Trade Act*, paras. 7.118-7.126.

7.9.2.2   Whether the meaning of the direct transportation requirement is so unclear as to constitute an import restriction inconsistent with Article XI of the GATT 1994 and Article 4.2 of the Agreement on Agriculture

681.   Having established that the direct transportation requirement does not mean what Brazil alleges and therefore does not violate Article XI of the GATT 1994 and Article 4.2 of the Agreement on Agriculture, we turn to Brazil's second point. We recall that Brazil, in reaction to Indonesia's explanation of the direct transportation requirement, argues that even if transit was allowed, the "murky" language in Article 19(a) of MoA 34/2016 creates legal uncertainties that amount to a quantitative restriction.[779]

7.9.2.2.1   Whether Brazil's claim that the legal uncertainties arising from the "murky" language in Article 19(a) of MoA 34/2016 amount to a quantitative import restriction falls within the Panel's terms of reference

682.   Noting that it is our responsibility, even if not raised by the parties, to examine issues that go to the root of our jurisdiction[780], we asked both parties at the second substantive meeting for their views on whether this particular claim was within the Panel's terms of reference.[781]

683.   In its response, Brazil argues that the characterization of the direct transportation requirement as a quantitative restriction falls within the panel request.[782] Indonesia submits that the direct transportation requirement is the measure at issue, and therefore, the claim pertaining to the legal uncertainties arising from the murky language of Article 19(a) goes beyond the Panel's terms of reference.[783]

684.   Pursuant to Article 7.1 of the DSU, a panel's terms of reference are governed by the panel request.[784] Article 6.2 requires that a panel request: (1) identifies the specific measures at issue, and (2) provides a brief summary of the legal basis of the complaint (or the claims) sufficient to present the problem clearly.[785]

---

[779] Brazil's second written submission, para. 222.
[780] Appellate Body Report, *Mexico – Corn Syrup (Article 21.5 – US)*, paras. 36 and 53.
[781] See Panel question No. 139.
[782] Brazil's response to Panel question No. 139.
[783] Indonesia's response to Panel question No. 139.
[784] Appellate Body Report, *US – Carbon Steel*, para. 124. See also, Appellate Body Reports, *Argentina – Import Measures*, para. 5.11.
[785] Appellate Body Reports, *China – HP-SSST (Japan)* / *China – HP-SSST (EU)*, para. 5.12.

685.   On its face, Brazil's panel request identifies the measure at issue as the direct transportation requirement, which consists of "restrictions on the transportation of imported products ... by requiring direct transportation from the country of origin to the entry points in Indonesia".[786] The panel request further explains that this measure is maintained through Article 20(1) of MoA 139/2014[787] (currently reproduced in Article 19(a) of MoA 34/2016).

686.   Brazil's panel request has identified the direct transportation requirement as the requirement contained in the concerned provision of the relevant MoA regulation. It is this provision that Brazil interprets to mean "non-stop" transport resulting in a violation of Article XI:1 of the GATT 1994 and Article 4.2 of the Agreement on Agriculture. It is also this provision that Brazil now alleges to create uncertainty in a manner inconsistent with Article XI:1 and Article 4.2 of the Agreement on Agriculture. In our view, therefore, the description of the measure as "direct transportation requirement" in the panel request is broad enough to allow for different arguments on why there is inconsistency with Article XI and Article 4.2. We consider "non-stop" to be one such argument and "murky language" to be another. We recall that the Appellate Body has distinguished between claims and arguments, pointing out that parties do not need to develop their arguments in the panel request, but may do so in their submissions.[788] On that basis, we have the authority to consider Brazil's argument.

> 7.9.2.2.2   Whether the language in Article 19(a) of MoA 34/2016 amounts to an inconsistency with Article XI:1 of the GATT 1994 and Article 4.2 of the Agreement on Agriculture

687.   We turn to Brazil's argument that the murky language in Article 19(a) of MoA 34/2016 constitutes a trade-restriction.

688.   In support of this claim, Brazil refers to the findings of the panels in *Colombia – Ports of Entry* and *Argentina – Import Measures*. In particular, Brazil recalls that these panels have acknowledged that a measure constitutes a quantitative restriction when it creates uncertainties and affects investment plans,

---

[786]   Brazil's panel request, pp. 4-5.

[787]   Ministry of Agriculture Regulation 139/Permentan/PD/410/12/2014 (MoA 139/2014) (Exhibit BRA-34).

[788]   We recall that the Appellate Body has distinguished claims from arguments, in the following terms:

> Claims, which are typically allegations of violation of the substantive provisions of the *WTO Agreement*, must be set out clearly in the request for the establishment of a panel. Arguments, by contrast, are the means whereby a party progressively develops and supports its claims. These do not need to be set out in detail in a panel request; rather, they may be developed in the submissions made to the panel.

Appellate Body Report, *Dominican Republic – Import and Sale of Cigarettes*, para. 121.

restricts market access for import, makes importation prohibitively costly, creates uncertainty as to an importer's ability to import, and more generally has an implication on the competitive situation of an importer.[789]

689.   We note that neither of these cases addressed the issue of legal uncertainty potentially created through "murky language". In *Colombia – Ports of Entry* the measure at issue was a limitation on the ports of entry for imports. In setting out and summarizing the case law supporting a broad reading of the concept of "quantitative restrictions" in Article XI, that panel also referred to measures creating uncertainties or affecting investment plans as falling in that category.[790] In *Argentina – Import Measures*, the measure at issue was an import procedure which, in the panel's view created "uncertainty by conditioning an applicant's ability … upon compliance with an unidentified number of requirements".[791] In both these cases the trade-restrictive effects found to constitute a violation of Article XI were a result of the measure *as such*. Thus, in our view, these two cases reaffirm that a panel may establish what the content of a measure is and determine whether such content causes uncertainty that amounts to an import restriction under Article XI.

690.   In this dispute, the content of the measure *as such*, as understood by the Panel (see above) has not been shown to have any trade-restrictive effect. The uncertainty that Brazil refers to, is notably *not* one that we experienced while carefully reading the relevant provision in its context. Neither has Brazil submitted any evidence that would demonstrate that such uncertainty exists or is experienced by its exporters.[792] Thus, while it is conceivable that a Member could adduce evidence that demonstrates that the measure's drafting causes legal uncertainty (e.g. through other laws and regulations or evidence of its application)[793], no such evidence has been presented here. We, therefore, leave open the question, whether, had such uncertainty been demonstrated, this could amount to a "quantitative restriction" within the meaning of Article XI.

7.9.3   Conclusion

691.   On the basis of the foregoing, we conclude that Brazil has failed to demonstrate that the direct transportation requirement, as enacted through Article 19(a) of MoA 34/2016, is inconsistent with Article XI:1 of the GATT 1994 and Article 4.2 of the Agreement on Agriculture.

---

[789] Brazil's second written submission, para. 222.
[790] Panel Report, *Colombia – Ports of Entry*, para. 7.240.
[791] Panel Reports, *Argentina – Import Measures*, para. 6.468.
[792] One could, for example, think of contradictory advice received from Indonesian authorities.
[793] See Appellate Body Report, *EU – Biodiesel*, para. 6.156 (referring to the evidentiary elements that a complainant may submit to support its understanding of the meaning of municipal law).

7.10 Claims Relating to the Alleged General Prohibition

7.10.1 Introduction

692.   Having examined the individual measures that Brazil challenges, we now turn to examine the alleged general prohibition. We recall that Brazil describes this measure as an unwritten measure.[794] Brazil raises claims of violations of Article XI of the GATT 1994 and Article 4.2 of the Agreement on Agriculture.

693.   As seen above, Indonesia requested the Panel to find that the alleged measure is not within its terms of reference. Our preliminary ruling, which rejects this request, is set out in section 7.1.2.2.2 above. Indonesia further submits that Brazil has not demonstrated the existence of this measure.[795] In the alternative, Indonesia contends that Brazil has failed to prove that the measure violates Article 4.2 of the Agreement on Agriculture or Article XI of the GATT 1994.[796]

694.   As is well established, any act or omission attributable to a WTO Member can be challenged as a measure under the WTO dispute settlement system.[797] Such measure does not necessarily have to be expressed in written form or laid down in a legal instrument, but may be unwritten instead.[798]

695.   The parties disagree on whether Brazil has established that the unwritten measure it describes exists. Our task, therefore, requires that we first assess whether Brazil has demonstrated the existence of the alleged unwritten measure. We address the claims of violation made by Brazil only if we find that the alleged unwritten measure exists.

696.   In undertaking our task we recall the legal standard applicable to ascertaining the existence of an unwritten measure. As the Appellate Body explained, a complaining party will need to demonstrate, cumulatively, (1) that a measure is attributable to the responding Member, (2) its precise content, and (3) other elements depending on whether it is of general and prospective application or of a different nature.[799] We note, furthermore, that Brazil asserts the existence of an unwritten single measure that results from the combined operation of six individual measures. Consequently, we consider applicable the observation by the Appellate Body in *Argentina – Import Measures* that "[a] complainant challenging a single measure composed of several different instruments will normally need to provide evidence of how the different components operate

---

[794]   See e.g. Brazil's comments on Indonesia's request for preliminary ruling, paras. 17, 19, and 28; opening statement at the first meeting of the Panel, para. 11; and second written submission, para. 2.
[795]   Indonesia's first written submission, paras. 101 and 109.
[796]   Indonesia's first written submission, paras. 118, 124, 125, 127, and 128.
[797]   Appellate Body Report, *US – Corrosion-Resistant Steel Sunset Review*, para. 81.
[798]   Appellate Body Report, *US – Zeroing (EC)*, para. 192.
[799]   Appellate Body Reports, *Argentina – Import Measures*, para 5.108. On the basis of the Appellate Body's findings in *Argentina – Import Measures*, we disagree with Brazil's view that the Panel should not examine this element.

together as part of a single measure and how a single measure exists as distinct from its components".[800]

697.   We will first summarize how Brazil has described the measure. We then summarize the evidence that Brazil has submitted to demonstrate the existence of this measure before turning to our own assessment.

7.10.2   Brazil's description of the measure

698.   Brazil argues that the measure at issue in this dispute is an unwritten overarching measure that results from the combined interaction of several individual measures "conceived to implement an official trade policy based on the overriding objective of restricting imports to protect domestic production".[801] Brazil asks the Panel to consider this measure as a single, self-standing measure.[802]

699.   According to Brazil, Indonesia has put in place a set of measures "founded on the premise that the importation of animal products should be made only if domestic animal production were insufficient to fulfil the needs for the people's consumption". Brazil considers this to result in a *de jure* and a *de facto* prohibition on the importation of chicken meat and chicken products from Brazil.[803]

700.   Brazil asserts that the precise content of the unwritten measure is a general ban on the importation of chicken meat and chicken products from Brazil, which results from, and is implemented through, the combined operation of written regulations and procedures (and one omission[804]) conceived to protect Indonesia's domestic poultry industry.[805] According to Brazil, the unwritten measure has existed at least since 2009[806], applies to imports from any country, and covers all chicken meat and chicken products.[807]

701.   Brazil considers that the general ban is independent and different from its constitutive elements and therefore will not cease to exist even if one or more of its elements is altered, replaced or eliminated. According to Brazil, the unwritten

---

[800]   Appellate Body Reports, *Argentina – Import Measures*, para 5.108. On the basis of the Appellate Body's findings in *Argentina – Import Measures*, we disagree with Brazil's view that the Panel should not examine other elements relative to specific nature of the measure.
[801]   Brazil's first written submission, paras. 75-76. See also opening statement at the first meeting of the Panel, para. 11; and second written submission, paras. 11 and 13.
[802]   Brazil's first written submission, para. 75; opening statement at the first meeting of the Panel, para. 9; response to Panel question No. 5(a)(iii); and second written submission, para. 2.
[803]   Brazil's first written submission, para. 76.
[804]   Brazil refers to the undue delay in examining and approving Brazil's proposal for a veterinary health certificate for poultry. See section 7.7 above.
[805]   Brazil's response to Panel question No. 5(a)(i). See also Brazil's first written submission, para. 75; and opening statement at the first meeting of the Panel, para. 11.
[806]   *Ibid.*
[807]   Brazil refers to chicken meat and chicken products from the species *Gallus domesticus*, commonly classified on HS Codes 0207.11, 0207.12, 0207.13, 0207.14 and 1602.32. See Brazil's response to Panel question No. 5(a)(ii).

measure responds to an overriding objective that goes beyond the specific impact of each constitutive element and results from the combined operation of the measures.[808] Brazil describes this measure in different ways in its submissions.[809] Brazil submits that whether the general ban is qualified as a rule or norm of general and prospective application, an ongoing conduct, or a concerted action or practice, does not change the nature of the measure itself or the evidentiary threshold necessary to demonstrate its existence.[810]

702.   Brazil emphasizes that even if an element of the alleged general prohibition is found not to be WTO-inconsistent, it does not mean that the general prohibition itself is not WTO-inconsistent.[811]

703.   Based on the description of the measure by Brazil, the unwritten measure has three relevant features: (a) it consists of several individual measures; (b) it derives from and is implemented through the combined operation of several individual measures, resulting in a general ban on chicken meat and chicken products, and (c) it was conceived for the fulfilment of a single overriding objective.[812] We set out in more detail below Brazil's description of these features.

7.10.2.1   Individual measures as constitutive elements

704.   Brazil describes six individual measures as constitutive elements of the alleged general prohibition.[813] Brazil emphasizes that it is not excluding the possibility that other measures exist or may be adopted in the future that could also form part of the constitutive elements of the alleged general prohibition.[814]

705.   The six individual measures are as follows:

a.   positive list requirement;

b.   domestic food production (including "staple food"[815], which encompasses chicken meat and chicken products) and national food reserve are prioritized over food import, which is only authorized as an exception, when domestic food supply is not considered "sufficient" by the government;

---

[808]   Brazil's response to Panel question No. 5(a)(iii).
[809]   See Brazil's first written submission, para. 172; opening statement at the first meeting of the Panel, para. 9; response to Panel question No. 5(c); and second written submission, para. 10.
[810]   Brazil's response to Panel question No. 5(c).
[811]   Brazil's response to Panel question No. 6.
[812]   Brazil's response to Panel question No. 5(a)(i).
[813]   Brazil's panel request, p. 2 and first written submission, para. 76. See also the discussion in our preliminary ruling in section 7.1.2.2.2 above, concerning whether the alleged general prohibition, as described in Brazil's first written submission, is within the Panel's terms of reference.
[814]   Brazil's response to Panel question No. 69.
[815]   According to Article 1.15 of Law 18/2012 ("Food Law"), the term "staple food" means "[...] food that is intended as the main daily food according to local potential resources and wisdom". See Exhibit BRA-31/IDN-3.

c.   imports of essential and strategic goods, which include chicken and chicken products may be prohibited or restricted and prices may be controlled by the Indonesian government. Thus, import and export operations may be postponed by the Minister of Trade during a force majeure event and if allowed to enter into Indonesia, their effective importation would be subject to the discretion of the Minister of Trade;

d.   intended use requirement;

e.   undue delay in examining and approving the health certificates for chicken meat and chicken products proposed by Brazil since 2009; and

f.   restrictions on importation through Indonesia's import licensing regime.

706.   As noted previously, Brazil has challenged four of these six measures separately, namely the positive list requirement, the intended use requirement, undue delay, and import licensing requirements (letters, a, d, e, and f above). We have examined these four measures in sections 7.4 (positive list requirement), 7.5 (intended use requirement), 7.6 (import licensing requirements), and 7.7 (undue delay) above. The two measures not challenged separately are a so-called "self-sufficiency requirement"(letter b above) and "a restriction on imports of essential goods"(letter c above). Brazil's descriptions of these measures as well as Indonesia's comments on these descriptions are as follows.

7.10.2.2   Self-sufficiency requirement

707.   Concerning the self-sufficiency requirement, Brazil submits that it allows for, or requires, imports of animal and animal products to be restricted when the Indonesian authorities deem that domestic production is sufficient.[816] In describing this requirement, Brazil refers to relevant provisions of three different laws.

708.   First, Brazil refers to Article 36(4) of Law 18/2009. That provision is currently contained in Article 36B of Law 41/2014[817], and reads:

Import of Livestock and Animal based products from overseas to the territory of Republic of Indonesia shall be made if the production and supply of Livestock and Animal based products in

---

[816]   Brazil's first written submission, paras. 80- 83; and response to Panel question No. 5(b).

[817]   Article 36(4) is worded in a slightly different manner to Article 36B. Article 36(4) states:

Article 36

...

(4) The import of animals, livestock and animal products from abroad may be allowed if domestic production and supply of animals or livestock is not sufficient for the local community.

Article 36(4) of Law of the Republic of Indonesia Number 18/2009 on Husbandry and Animal Health (Law 18/2009) (Exhibit BRA-29/IDN-1).

the home country is not yet sufficient to meet the domestic consumption.[818]

709.   Second, Brazil refers to Article 36 Law 18/2012, and asserts that in the context of paragraph 2 chicken meat and chicken products are considered as "staple food".[819] The provision reads as follows:

(1) Food Import can only be implemented if domestic Food Production is not sufficient and/or cannot be produced domestically.

(2) Staple Food Import can only be implemented if domestic Food Production and National Food Reserve are not sufficient.

(3) Sufficiency of domestic Staple Food Production and Government Food Reserve is determined by minister or government institution with the task of executing governmental orders in the Food sector.[820]

710.   Third, Brazil refers to Article 30(1) of Law 19/2013 which states:

Every Person is prohibited from importing Agricultural Commodities when the availability of domestic Agricultural Commodities is sufficient for consumption and/or Government food reserves.[821]

711.   Indonesia contests Brazil's factual description of this self-sufficiency requirement. Indonesia submits that "self-sufficiency is a general principle described in some provisions of some of Indonesia's laws, and is commonly understood to relate to food security".[822] Indonesia contends that "this principle has not had any practical effect on the importation of chicken into Indonesia".[823]

712.   As discussed further below, Brazil also refers to the self-sufficiency requirement as the overriding objective of the alleged general prohibition.

7.10.2.3   Restrictions on imports of essential goods

713.   Concerning the "restrictions on the importation of essential goods", Brazil submits that certain provisions of Law 7/2014 allow Indonesian authorities to impose additional restrictions on the importation of "essential goods", conferring a large margin of discretion on them.[824] Brazil stresses that the term "essential

---

[818]   Law 41/2014 (amending 18/2009) (Exhibit BRA-30/IDN-2).
[819]   Brazil's first written submission, fn 97 to para. 82. Indonesia's first written submission, para. 38.
[820]   Law 18/2012 (Exhibit BRA-31/IDN-3).
[821]   Law 19/2013 (Exhibit BRA-33). We note that neither Brazil's panel request nor the section on legal arguments in Brazil's first written submission refers to Law 19/2013.
[822]   Indonesia's first written submission, para. 12. See also Indonesia's response to Panel question No. 10.
[823]   Indonesia's first written submission, para. 92. See also Indonesia's responses to Panel question Nos. 10 and 11.
[824]   Brazil's first written submission, paras. 84-86.

goods" as defined in Law 7/2014, includes "chicken meat and chicken products".[825] Indonesia confirms this point.[826]

714.   Brazil identifies the following provisions of Law 7/2014 as relevant to its claims[827]:

    a. Article 25(1), which states:

The Government and Local Government to control the availability of basic needs goods and / or important items in the entire territory of the Republic of Indonesia in sufficient quantity, good quality, and affordable prices.

    b. Article 26(3), which states:

In order to guarantee the supply and stabilize prices of basic needs goods and essential items, the Minister set a price policy, stock management and logistics, as well as the management of Export and Import.

    c. Article 38, in particular, paragraphs (1) and (4), which read in relevant part:

(1) The Government shall regulate the activities of foreign trade through policies and control in the field of Export and Import.

…

(4) Foreign Trade Control include:

licensing;

Standards; and

prohibition and restriction.

715.   According to Indonesia, the qualification of products as "essential goods" does not affect the ability of importers from other countries to import these products into Indonesia.[828] In support of this argument Indonesia cites beef as an example (also identified as an "essential good") and argues that beef is allowed to be imported into Indonesia.[829] As regards Articles 26(3) and 38, Indonesia essentially does not deny that these provisions provide a legal basis to regulate imports, but submits that "no MoA Import Recommendation or MoT Import Approval has ever been denied on the basis of [the above] provisions".[830]

---

[825] Brazil's first written submission, fn 99 to para. 84, referring to Law of the Republic of Indonesia Number 7/2014 concerning trade, Explanatory notes to Article 25 (Law 7/2014). (Exhibit BRA-32).
[826] Indonesia's response to Panel question No. 4.
[827] Law 07/2014 (Exhibit BRA-32). See Brazil's first written submission, para. 55.
[828] Indonesia's response to Panel question No. 4.
[829] Ibid.
[830] Ibid.

7.10.2.4   Combined operation

716.   The second feature of the alleged unwritten measure is that it "derives from and is implemented through the combined operation" of the individual measures.[831] Brazil asserts that the ban on imports of chicken products is not just an effect, but the intended result of "an unwritten measure adopted by Indonesia".[832] According to Brazil, it is the "expected joint operation" of these measures, that constitutes the self-standing, independent measure.[833]

717.   In terms of how the individual measures operate together, Brazil explains that "each of these different components creates an additional layer of protection of Indonesia's market, reinforcing a maze of restrictions that, combined, prevent imports of chicken meat and chicken products and serves to implement Indonesia's self-sufficiency policy".[834] Furthermore, Brazil refers to the different elements as operating either to decrease the attractiveness of Indonesia's market or to increase costs and risks for exporters.[835] Brazil argues that "put together, these different layers [of trade-restrictiveness] form a thick, virtually impenetrable barrier to imports of any amount of chicken meat and chicken products".[836]

718.   Brazil explains that "[a]s currently formulated, the single operation of any of the different components identified by Brazil is capable of seriously limiting the importation of Brazilian chicken into the Indonesian market. Together they work as a general ban, which results in graver consequences to international trade. It follows that, even if some of these individual elements could be altered, replaced or removed, the 'overarching' import ban would still be in place".[837]

7.10.2.5   Overriding objective

719.   The third feature of the alleged unwritten measure according to Brazil, is that the individual measures that operate together to create the unwritten measure are all "conceived to implement an official trade policy based on the overriding objective of restricting imports to protect domestic production".[838] Brazil also refers to this objective as an official policy of self-sufficiency.[839]

720.   The overriding objective of restricting imports to protect domestic production is, according to Brazil, the "glue" that binds together all the

---

[831]   Brazil's response to Panel question No. 5(a)(i).
[832]   Brazil's response to Panel question No. 5(a)(iv).
[833]   *Ibid.*
[834]   Brazil's response to Panel question No. 5(a)(vi).
[835]   Brazil's second written submission, para. 13.
[836]   *Ibid.*
[837]   Brazil's response to Panel question No. 5(a)(vi).
[838]   Brazil's first written submission, paras. 75-76.
[839]   Brazil's first written submission, para. 76. See also Brazil's response to Panel question Nos. 5(b) and 71.

individual components of the general ban and informs its implementation.[840] Brazil explains that "as long as the underlying official trade policy of restricting imports to protect domestic production remains in place" the general prohibition would still be in force.[841]

7.10.3 Evidence and argument submitted by Brazil

721. We turn next to the evidence and arguments that Brazil has submitted to demonstrate the existence of the alleged unwritten measure. These pertain mostly to the measure's precise content, and its operation as a single measure. We examine the following points made by Brazil.

7.10.3.1 Trade data

722. Brazil presents trade data that shows that since 2009 there have been virtually no imports of chicken meat and chicken products into Indonesia from any country, including from Brazil.[842] As seen above, Indonesia does not contest the data.[843]

723. Brazil argues that 2009 was the year when a series of different pieces of legislation, conceived for the fulfilment of the single overriding objective of protecting the domestic industry, were enacted.[844] Brazil points in particular to the following legal instruments: Law 18/2009 ("Law on Husbandry and Animal Health"), whose Article 36(4) provides that imports of animal or animal products should only be authorized if domestic animal products and supply or livestock are insufficient to fulfil the needs for the people's consumption and MoA 20/2009, which established several requirements for the importation of carcass, meat and/or offal.[845]

724. Brazil contends that the fact, that virtually no imports have occurred, "by itself is evidence enough of the existence of the policy" and thus of the general prohibition.[846] Brazil also points out that Indonesia fails to explain why no imports have been authorized.[847]

725. Brazil argues that while the measure is not to be confounded with its effect, in this particular case, the effects of the measure are particularly relevant from an evidentiary point of view to confirm the measure's existence.[848]

---

[840] Brazil's response to Panel question No. 5(b). See also Brazil's second written submission, para. 167.
[841] Brazil's response to Panel question No. 5(a)(iv).
[842] Brazil's first written submission, paras. 22-23. Indonesia's response to Panel question No. 9.
[843] See section 7.3 above.
[844] Brazil's response to Panel question No. 5(a)(i).
[845] Brazil's first written submission, fn 19 to para. 23.
[846] Brazil's closing statement at the first meeting of the Panel, paras. 3 and 4.
[847] Brazil's opening statement at the first meeting of the Panel, para. 13.
[848] Brazil's response to Panel question No. 5(a)(iv).

7.10.3.2   Written nature of the constitutive elements

726.   Brazil points out that because the individual measures are written acts or derived from written acts (undue delay) "the precise content of the import ban and its attribution to Indonesia is clear and self-evident". Brazil contends that thus, "these [written] legal acts, in conjunction with the undue delay, provide enough evidence of the existence of the measure".[849]

7.10.3.3   Elements of distinction between individual measures and single measure

727.   In support of its contention that the alleged general prohibition is a measure that is "distinct" from its constitutive elements, Brazil highlights the following.

728.   First, Brazil submits that the alleged general prohibition will not cease to exist, if one or more of its elements are altered, replaced or no longer implemented. Brazil gives as an example the fact that an individual measure such as the "undue delay" could be addressed and would potentially solve specific trade concerns, but it would not dismantle the general prohibition because other elements of the unwritten measure would continue to act jointly to prevent imports.[850] For Brazil, "to address the measures only individually would not solve the problem".[851]

729.   Second, in the same vein, Brazil considers that even if some products at issue are exceptionally allowed to be imported, for instance, in the case of a short-term collapse on domestic production, the general prohibition would still be in force. In Brazil's view, this would be the case as long as the underlying official trade policy of restricting imports to protect domestic production remains in place and "permeates Indonesia's trade measures".[852]

730.   Third, Brazil argues that the "legal nature" of the alleged general prohibition is different insofar as it is a quantitative restriction (an import ban), whereas the legal nature of its constitutive parts varies from more limited quantitative restrictions (such as the prohibition on the importation of certain chicken products not included in the "positive list" of permitted products) to discrimination between domestic and imported products and licensing procedures that are more burdensome than necessary.[853]

731.   Fourth, Brazil considers that differences in product coverage between the different individual measures only prove the existence of the general prohibition. Brazil refers to the positive list requirement, which does not affect individually all HS Codes, but only those which are not included in the list of products

---

[849]   Brazil's opening statement at the second meeting of the Panel, para. 48. See also Brazil's second written submission, para. 12.
[850]   Brazil's response to Panel question Nos. 5(a)(ii) and 5(a)(iii).
[851]   Brazil's response to Panel question No. 5(a)(iii).
[852]   Brazil's response to Panel question No. 5(a)(iv).
[853]   Brazil's response to Panel question No. 5(a)(iii).

allowed to be imported into Indonesia. Brazil points out that "when this element is combined with the other components, they result in an import ban to the products previously mentioned [chicken meat and chicken products from the species *Gallus domesticus,* commonly classified on HS Codes 0207.11, 0207.12, 0207.13, 0207.14 and 1602.32]".[854]

7.10.3.4 Evidence that all individual elements pursue the same single objective

732.   Brazil points to the provisions on self-sufficiency in Indonesian law and asserts that "in its current formulation, self-sufficiency is also an important component of the general prohibition, because it consists of a mandatory requirement that has to be applied by Indonesian authorities before imports are authorized".[855] However, Brazil also distinguishes this component from the overriding objective, arguing that "even if the explicit references to such operational requirement were written out of Indonesia's legal framework, the general prohibition could subsist as an independent, single, unwritten measure whose objective is to implement the self-sufficiency policy".[856]

733.   To prove that self-sufficiency has been adopted as an overriding policy objective, Brazil submitted a number of documents as evidence. First, Brazil submitted two OECD reports, namely (1) a Review of Indonesia's Agricultural Policies dated 2012; and (2) the OECD FAO Agricultural Outlook 2014-2023.[857]

734.   Second, in its responses to questions from the Panel, Brazil referred to "several declarations of Indonesian authorities"[858], and subsequently submitted five documents, which consist of four press articles and one letter from the Indonesian Director General of Livestock at the Ministry of Agriculture to the Brazilian Ambassador to Indonesia.[859] Indonesia submits that these last five documents are inadmissible as evidence because they have been submitted too late.[860]

7.10.4 Panel's assessment

735.   Having set out Brazil's arguments and evidence describing the alleged unwritten measure and its features, we now turn to assess whether Brazil has demonstrated the existence of the measure.

736.   We recall that the legal standard applicable to ascertaining the existence of an unwritten measure requires (1) evidence to demonstrate that the measure is

---

[854]   Brazil's response to Panel question No. 5(a)(ii).
[855]   Brazil's response to Panel question No. 5(b).
[856]   *Ibid.*
[857]   See OECD Review of Agricultural Policies: Indonesia 2012 (Exhibit BRA-04) and OECD-FAO. Agricultural Outlook 2014-2023 (Exhibit BRA-05).
[858]   Brazil's response to Panel question No. 5(c).
[859]   Brazil's response to Panel question No. 70 (referring to Exhibits BRA-52 through BRA-56).
[860]   Indonesia's comment on Brazil's response to Panel question No. 70.

attributable to the respondent; (2) evidence to demonstrate the precise content of the challenged measure[861], including evidence of how the different components operate together as part of a single measure and how such single measure exists as distinct from its components[862]; and (3) evidence on the specific nature of the measure, i.e. whether it is of general and prospective application or of a different nature.[863] Furthermore, the Appellate Body has pointed out that the evidentiary threshold for proving the existence of an unwritten measure is high.[864] We address these elements in turn.

7.10.4.1 Attribution

737. Given that the constitutive elements of the alleged unwritten measure are provisions laid down in legal instruments enacted by Indonesia, there can be no doubt that the unwritten measure, if proven to exist, would be attributable to Indonesia.[865]

7.10.4.2 Precise content

7.10.4.2.1 Whether the trade data proves the existence of the measure

738. We first consider Brazil's argument regarding the absence of any imports of chicken meat and chicken products into Indonesia since 2009. We note that Indonesia does not contest this fact. Indonesia however points to the requirement to obtain an import approval[866], and argues that the absence of imports can be attributed to other factors, such as lack of interest to export to Indonesia or non-compliance with requirements to import.[867]

739. We refer to the well-established case law according to which trade effects are neither necessary nor sufficient to prove a violation.[868] That case law is based on the logic that what a complainant has to prove is not the effect itself but the causal link between the challenged measure and the observed (or potential) effect.[869] We consider that this logic applies, all the more so, where the very existence of the challenged measure itself is at issue.

---

[861] Appellate Body Reports, *Argentina – Import Measures*, para 5.104.
[862] Appellate Body Reports, *Argentina – Import Measures*, para. 5.108.
[863] *Ibid.*
[864] Appellate Body Report, *US – Zeroing (EC)*, para. 198.
[865] The Panel notes that in Indonesia's view, the delay in the approval of the veterinary health certificate is caused by actions of Brazil's exporters and is thus not attributable to Indonesia. Indonesia's first written submission, para. 108.
[866] Indonesia's response to Panel question No. 9.
[867] See Indonesia's second written submission, para. 102.
[868] See e.g. Panel Report, *Colombia – Ports of Entry*, paras. 7.252–7.253. See also Appellate Body Report, *EC – Bananas III*, paras. 252-253 (citing GATT Panel Report, *US – Superfund (1987)*, para. 5.1.9).
[869] Panel Report, *Argentina – Hides and Leather*, paras. 11.20-11.21.

740.   Consequently, Brazil's argument that there have been virtually no imports of chicken meat and chicken products since 2009, describes an effect but does not serve to establish the source of the effect. We, therefore, agree with Indonesia that absence of trade, by itself, does not prove the existence of an unwritten measure.[870] The absence of trade could confirm the existence of an unwritten measure, if it has already been proven through other means.[871]

7.10.4.2.2   Whether the written nature of the constitutive elements proves the existence of the measure

741.   Next, we address Brazil's arguments that the written nature of (most of) the individual measures that it has identified as constitutive elements, is enough evidence to prove the existence of the measure.[872]

742.   Brazil contrasts this evidentiary situation with that in *Argentina – Import Measures* where the constitutive elements of the unwritten measure were not laid down in any legal act.[873] We agree with Brazil that the situation we are dealing with is quite different from that in *Argentina – Import Measures*. In that case, the constitutive elements of the unwritten measure – a set of different conditions imposed upon importation or investment – were not contained in any legal act. To show that these conditions existed, the complainants were required to submit evidence of their application, i.e. show instances where they had been imposed. We note that in addition to showing the application of the different conditions, the complainants demonstrated that such application was intended to implement a specific policy decision – a point we come back to below.

743.   In this dispute, the constitutive elements of the alleged unwritten measure are laid down in written legal instruments. Thus, unlike in *Argentina – Import Measures*, in this dispute, it is not necessary to show instances of the application of the individual constitutive elements to prove *their* existence. However, Brazil's burden is not to prove the existence of those individual measures but rather to prove the existence of an (unwritten) measure that it argues is *distinct* from these individual measures.

7.10.4.2.3   Whether the single measure can be discerned from the design, structure and architecture of the constitutive elements

744.   We understand Brazil to contend that the existence of the alleged unwritten measure can be inferred from the written individual measures insofar as their combined operation and the resulting effect of a total ban on imports

---

[870]   Indonesia's second written submission, para. 102.
[871]   We understand Brazil to concede this point. See e.g. Brazil's second written submission, para. 10.
[872]   Brazil's second written submission, para. 12.
[873]   Brazil's second written submission, para. 11.

would be proof of that existence. In other words, the existence of the alleged unwritten measure could be demonstrated through the design, structure and architecture of the individual constitutive measures.

745.   The design, structure and architecture of the individual measures could prove the existence of the unwritten measure if it can be demonstrated that their operation involves a certain interdependence and that such combined operation results in a single measure that is distinct from its components.[874] In this regard we note that the panel in *US – COOL* identified factors that have been considered by panels and the Appellate Body in past analogous disputes. We note in particular the legal status of the requirements, their relationship and whether they have autonomous status.[875]

746.   Brazil has described the combined operation by pointing to the multi-layered restrictiveness of the different individual measures, which "forms a thick, virtually impenetrable barrier to imports".[876] Indonesia contests that the different measures operate together as part of a single measure.[877]

747.   We note that the four individual measures also challenged separately are all part of the legal instruments that generally govern the conditions for importation of animal products including chicken meat and chicken products into Indonesia. The fact that they are part of the same import regime means that, at some level, they operate together and relate to each other. The two additional individual measures, namely the self-sufficiency clause and the essential goods clause, are contained in other legal instruments. More specifically, they are contained in laws which to our understanding, are at a higher normative level than the two ministerial regulations that govern the conditions for importation of animal products. We note that, at least the latest version of the two ministerial regulations, refer to these laws in their preamble. Thus, it could be said that there is some relationship between the different legal instruments.

748.   However, a relationship based merely on the co-existence in the same legal instrument or a connection between different legal instruments, is not enough to assume that different measures operate as a single measure. This is particularly the case where measures operate in their own right.[878] To consider the several individual measures as a single distinct measure they must be inter-dependent in respect of the overall impact assessed.[879] Here, we see a number of

---

[874]   Appellate Body Reports, *Argentina – Import Measures*, para. 5.108.
[875]   The factors identified by the panel are as follows: (i) the manner in which the complainant presented its claim(s) in respect of the concerned instruments; (ii) the respondent's position; and (iii) the legal status of the requirements or instrument(s), including the operation of, and the relationship between, the requirements or instruments, namely whether a certain requirement or instrument has autonomous status. Panel Report, *US – COOL*, para. 7.50. See also Appellate Body Reports, *Argentina – Import Measures*, fn 451 to para. 5.108.
[876]   Brazil's second written submission, para. 13.
[877]   See Indonesia's second written submission, paras. 100-101. See also Indonesia's response to Panel question No. 68.
[878]   Panel Report, *US – Export Restraints*, para. 8.85.
[879]   Panel Report, *US – COOL*, para. 7.59.

---

reasons as to why, structurally, there is no such interdependence among the different measures identified by Brazil.

749.   First, the mere fact that at least four of the individual measures are part of the same import regime does not make them dependent on each other. Each one of the four measures could be terminated without affecting the operation of the other measures. Furthermore, as regards the self-sufficiency clause and the essential goods clause, while we share Brazil's understanding that these clauses seem to provide a legal basis to take trade-restrictive action, it remains unclear to us, whether and if so, how they are related to, and impact, the operation of the other four individual measures, or the import regime as a whole.

750.   Second, contrary to Brazil's assertion, we do not see the general prohibition as a consequence of the individual measures *operating together*. To us, to the extent we have found each one of these measures as having an actual or potential trade-restrictive effect, this effect does not arise out of or depend on any of the other measures. The "undue delay" measure, for example, by itself results in chicken meat and chicken products from Brazil not being permitted into Indonesia. This measure is not dependent on, or reinforced by any other measure.

751.   Indeed, from Brazil's point of view, as we understand it, as long as chicken meat and chicken products cannot be imported into Indonesia, it does not matter how many individual measures there are, what they are about and whether they relate to each other – the alleged unwritten measure still exists. Thus, there could be one individual measure or hundreds of them, they could be the ones already identified, different or new ones. In our view, this shows that the combined operation that Brazil alleges is not one that can be found in the design, structure or architecture of the various individual measures themselves.

752.   Therefore, we find that an examination of the structure, design and architecture of the different individual measures which Brazil identifies as the constitutive elements of the alleged general prohibition, does not show that they operate as part of a single measure and how such a single measure exists as distinct from its components.[880]

---

[880]   We note that the panel in *Indonesia – Import Licensing Regimes*, considered a measure that has some similarity with the alleged measure discussed here. In particular, we understand that measure to have been presented by the co-complainants as the interaction of seven individual measures some of which are almost identical predecessor versions of some of the ones at issue in the present case. We understand that panel to have considered the seven measures operating individually and as a whole, following the co-complainants characterization of the measures at issue. We note that, while some are identical, others of the seven measures are different from the ones discussed in this dispute; furthermore, the panel in that case identified certain compounded effects which directly resulted from the combined operation and interaction of the individual measures. The fact that our conclusion differs, may be explained by these differences as well as differences in the parties' argumentation. We further note that, in our understanding, that panel was not asked, and therefore did not make any findings, on the existence or non-existence of an unwritten measure. See Panel Report, *Indonesia – Import Licensing Regimes,* paras. 2.64 and 7.465.

753.   The above conclusion however does not mean that the existence of an unwritten measure cannot be proven by other means. We therefore turn to Brazil's next line of argument in support of its assertion.

7.10.4.2.4   Whether there is an overriding objective that binds together the constitutive elements

754.   Brazil has submitted evidence relating to its claim that there is an overriding policy objective that the unwritten measure is designed to implement. As noted above, Brazil describes the overriding policy objective as the "glue" that holds together the individual measures. Indonesia argues that some of the documents submitted by Brazil as evidence are inadmissible and otherwise submits that the evidence does not support the existence of the alleged measure. Indonesia argues that in the alternative, those pieces of evidence do not provide any meaningful support for Brazil's allegation that the general prohibition or overarching measure exists.[881]

755.   Like Indonesia, we understand the overriding policy objective to play a central role in Brazil's description of the measure. We recall that the standard to demonstrate the existence of the unwritten measure depends on what Brazil argues is the precise content of the measure.[882] Therefore, since Brazil submits that the policy objective is the "glue" of the various individual measures, Brazil has to prove that this is the case.

756.   We note that in *Argentina – Import Measures*, the complainants similarly attributed a central role to the policy objective pursued by the individual measures.[883] The Appellate Body in that case emphasized the central role of this objective in the panel's finding that there was an unwritten measure that operated as a single measure.[884]

757.   Accordingly, for the policy objective to be the "glue", it must be the rationale for the adoption of the individual measures that Brazil has identified (and possibly other existing measures that Brazil has not identified) *and* continue to be the reason for the adoption of any further trade-restrictive measures until that policy objective is abolished. In our view, Brazil needs to prove both these elements. With this in mind, we turn to assess the documents submitted by Brazil.

758.   Regarding the OECD reports submitted by Brazil, we note that only the report on Indonesia's agricultural policy, which is dated 2012, makes specific references to policy objectives pursued by Indonesia and to trade related measures applied to chicken meat and chicken products. The report, in one

---

[881]   See Indonesia's comment on Brazil's response to Panel question No. 70.
[882]   Appellate Body Reports, *Argentina – Import Measures*, para. 5.110.
[883]   Panel Reports, *Argentina – Import Measures*, para. 6.228.
[884]   Appellate Body Reports, *Argentina – Import Measures*, paras. 5.126 and 5.143.

place, mentions self-sufficiency as a priority in Indonesia's agricultural policy.[885] In other places the report describes non-tariff measures taken by Indonesia as "stringent", "used to control imports" and "implemented in a non-transparent" manner.[886]

759.   In assessing these references, we note that the OECD report is an outside perspective and is therefore, a secondary source of information. Furthermore, in our assessment, the above references are not sufficient to prove the role of an overriding policy objective as Brazil describes it in respect of the alleged unwritten measure. We observe that self-sufficiency as a policy objective does not necessarily imply the adoption of trade-restrictive measures. In our view, a Member may well pursue goals of self-sufficiency through means that are not WTO-inconsistent. Thus, showing that a Member pursues the policy of self-sufficiency, in and of itself, is not enough to prove that this policy has been implemented through an unwritten measure that consists in adopting trade-restrictive measures. While the OECD report does describe some trade-restrictive measures, it does not make any link between those and a policy goal of self-sufficiency. As noted above, in our view, Brazil is required to show evidence of this link.

760.   Regarding the five additional documents that Brazil has submitted at the Panel's second meeting, we first need to address Indonesia's objection that these documents have been submitted too late.[887] We note that Brazil has submitted these documents following a specific request from the Panel, which, in turn, was triggered by an argument that Brazil made in its responses to the Panel's questions following the first meeting. We take the view that given the circumstances, Brazil's submission of these documents was not too late pursuant to Paragraph 8 of our Working Procedures. We observe in this context that it is the Panel's prerogative to ask questions and scrutinize the parties' argumentation.[888]

761.   Turning to the content of the documents submitted, we note that one is a letter from the Director-General of livestock at the Ministry of Agriculture to the Brazilian Ambassador to Indonesia. As far as we can see, the letter is a follow up to the third in a series of bilateral meetings between Indonesia and Brazil. We also describe these bilateral meetings in section 7.7.2.2 above.[889] In the letter, the Indonesian Director-General declines Brazil's proposal for a sanitary certificate for poultry on the grounds that the Indonesian poultry industry is self-sufficient. We note that this evidence pertains to one of the six individual measures that Brazil has described as constitutive elements of the unwritten measure, namely,

---

[885]   See OECD Review of Agricultural Policies: Indonesia 2012 (Exhibit BRA-04), p. 22.
[886]   See OECD Review of Agricultural Policies: Indonesia 2012 (Exhibit BRA-04), pp. 138, 140, and 207.
[887]   See Indonesia's comment on Brazil's response to Panel question No. 70.
[888]   See Appellate Body Reports, *US – Zeroing (EC)*, para. 260; and *EC – Fasteners (China)*, para. 566.
[889]   See also Brazil's first written submission, para. 38.

the undue delay. In the context of discussing that measure, Brazil has submitted evidence of a statement by Indonesian authorities – subsequent to the one at issue here – that expresses the exact opposite, namely that exports of chicken products would be possible despite the domestic industry's efforts to become self-sufficient.[890] Thus, whether the letter is proof of self-sufficiency as the reason for the existence of the individual measures is doubtful. In addition, it has no evidentiary value for the continued existence of the alleged unwritten measure as we discuss further below.

762.   The other four documents that Brazil submitted following a request from the Panel are press articles. Like previous panels, we proceed with caution in assessing such press articles, mindful that they may not necessarily report facts in the most objective manner, but rather reflect opinions or the author's own interpretation of facts.[891] We note that the press articles date from 2012, 2015 and 2016. Two of them report on domestic overproduction of chicken as a consequence of a policy of self-sufficiency.[892] None of these articles, however, makes a link with trade-restrictive measures adopted on the importation of chicken. Their relevance, in our view, therefore, is very limited. The other two articles, both dated 2012, do make a link between a policy of self-sufficiency and trade-restrictive measures on chicken imports.[893] However the links made are either tenuous – not going beyond a reference to "protectionist policies on poultry"[894] – or speculative (creation of a "super body" that "could lead to greater curbs on imports and exports of staples").[895] In our view, they do not prove that the six individual measures that Brazil has identified as the constitutive elements of the alleged unwritten measure, have been adopted in order to implement a policy of self-sufficiency aimed at preventing imports of chicken.

---

[890]   Minutes of the CCA meeting of 15 and 16 September 2010 (Exhibit BRA-14), point 7.

[891]   See Panel Report, *Argentina – Import Measures*, paras. 6.69-6.71 (referring *inter alia* to Panel Reports, *Australia – Automotive Leather II*, fn 210 to para. 9.65; and *China – Intellectual Property Rights*, para. 7.629) (regarding news articles), and 6.78 (referring *inter alia* to Panel Reports, *EC – Approval and Marketing of Biotech Products*, para. 7.532; *Mexico – Taxes on Soft Drinks*, paras. 8.76-8.77; and *Turkey – Rice*, paras. 7.78-7.79 and fn 367) (regarding statements by government officials reported in the news).

[892]   Press notes reporting on a statement by Indonesian Agriculture Minister on exporting chicken. Available at: http://en.republika.co.id/berita/en/national-politics/16/09/03/ocxsnk414-indonesia-to-export-chicken-due-to-overproduction (Exhibit BRA-54); and News article about Indonesia's poultry policy.   Available   at: http://www.reuters.com/article/indonesia-poultry-policy-idUSL3N11Y1OE20150930 (Exhibit BRA-55).

893 See News article on a statement by the Head of the Food Security Agency of Indonesia's Ministry   of   Agriculture;   available   at: http://www.reuters.com/article/indonesia-food-idUSL4N09011D20121120 (Exhibit BRA-53) and Online article entitled: Indonesia aims for poultry and beef self-sufficiency (Exhibit BRA-56).

[894]   Online article entitled: "Indonesia aims for poultry and beef self-sufficiency" (Exhibit BRA-56).

[895]   News article on a statement by the Head of the Food Security Agency of Indonesia's Ministry of Agriculture; available at: http://www.reuters.com/article/indonesia-food-idUSL4N09011D20121120 (Exhibit BRA-53).

---

763.   Our assessment, thus, is that the documents submitted by Brazil do not sufficiently demonstrate that there is a link between a policy objective of self-sufficiency and the alleged specific trade-restrictive measures taken.

7.10.4.3   Whether Brazil has proven the specific nature of the measure in terms of future application

764.   There is a further issue with the evidence submitted by Brazil which concerns the third element of the test applicable to proving the existence of an unwritten measure, namely, the specific nature of the measure in terms of future application. The foregoing assessment of the evidence on the overriding policy objective submitted by Brazil mostly focuses on assessing the evidentiary value of what these documents state. What equally matters, in our view, is what these documents *do not* state. In fact, it is one thing to show evidence of a link between a policy objective of self-sufficiency and a specific trade-restrictive measure already taken (a link, which, as just stated, is not supported by the evidence on record), and it is another thing to show that the existence of this policy objective would also mandate the adoption of future trade-restrictive measures. As noted above, we believe that it is necessary to also demonstrate this latter element, insofar as the existence of an unwritten measure is not proven until it is proven that that measure has some form of application in the future.

765.   As the Appellate Body made clear in *Argentina – Import Measures*, the future application of an unwritten measure is part of its specific nature.[896] The Appellate Body clarified that an unwritten measure may vary in that it may be a rule or norm – that is, may have general and prospective application – or may be something other than a rule or norm.[897] The evidence necessary would depend on the specific nature of the measure as characterized by the complainant.[898]

766.   We note that Brazil has not indicated with sufficient particularity what it considers to be the nature of the challenged measure. In its response to a question from the Panel regarding the specific nature of the measure, Brazil submitted that the distinction between rules or norms and other unwritten measures such as ongoing conduct or concerted actions/practices was merely an "analytical tool[s] used to ascertain the existence of an unwritten measure".[899] In Brazil's view the distinction "does not change...the nature of the measure itself or the evidentiary threshold necessary to demonstrate its existence...".[900] We disagree on the basis of the Appellate Body's dictum referred to above.

767.   More generally, and, thus, irrespective of the specific nature of the measure, Brazil has not submitted any evidence that would support its contention that the measure exists and continues to exist for as long as chicken meat and

---

[896] Appellate Body Reports, *Argentina – Import Measures*, paras. 5.104-5.110.
[897] Appellate Body Reports, *Argentina – Import Measures*, paras. 5.107-5.108.
[898] Appellate Body Reports, *Argentina – Import Measures*, para. 5.110.
[899] Brazil's response to Panel question No. 5(c).
[900] *Ibid.*

chicken products cannot be imported into Indonesia. Thus, none of the documents discussed above, suggests an intention, going forward, to implement a possible policy objective of self-sufficiency through trade-restrictive measures.

768.   To sum up, the documents submitted by Brazil do not sufficiently demonstrate that there is a link between a policy objective of self-sufficiency and the specific trade-restrictive measures taken; much less do they show that there could be a future implementation of such a policy objective through trade-restrictive measures.

7.10.5   Conclusion

769.   In conclusion, we find that Brazil failed to make a *prima facie* case, because it did not demonstrate the existence of the alleged unwritten measure.

7.11   *Separate Opinion of One Panelist*

7.11.1   Introduction

770.   The fulfilment of a panel's function is best served by consensus decisions. Nevertheless, in exceptional circumstances, consensus may be unattainable requiring a panelist to express a separate opinion. In the case at hand, an important difference exists concerning the methodological approach to be followed regarding three of the measures at issue. The difference affects the sequence of the Panel's analysis and the examination by the Panel of these three measures. Consequently, respectfully I am unable to agree with the analysis and findings concerning these measures as set out in paragraphs 7.77 to 7.94 above and 7.103 to 7.452 above and the conclusions and recommendations set out in paragraphs 8.1(b); 8.1(c); and 8.1(d) iii to viii.

771.   In the current dispute, three of the measures challenged were amended twice after the request for the establishment of the panel. The measures concern (i) a limitation on importation of chicken cuts; (ii) a limitation on the destination allowed for imports of chicken meat; and (iii) the period for application and period of validity of import recommendations and import approvals.

772.   The two amendments were introduced through subsequent replacements of the entire regulations of the Minister of Agriculture (MoA) and of the Minister of Trade (MoT) that contain the legal framework applicable to imports of carcass, meat and processed products into Indonesia. Tables 1, 2 and 3 below show the changes adopted from the second to the third amendment (amended language bold and in italics).[901]

773.   Pursuant to these changes, it is my view that the Panel should start its analysis by addressing three questions: (1) What are the amended measures? (2) What is the Panel's jurisdiction over the amended measures? and (3) How does

---

[901]   The measures as they existed at the time of the panel request were not addressed by Brazil. Consequently, the case refers to the measures as amended the first and second time.

the Panel address an allegation by the respondent regarding "expiry of the original measures"? Thereafter, to the extent that the Panel determines that it has jurisdiction over the measure(s) as amended it should examine the amended measures in light of the claims made by the complainant.

7.11.2 What are the amended measures?

774.   In accordance with Article 3.3 of the DSU, the "measure" is the situation that *the complaining Member* considers impairs benefits accruing to it under the covered agreements. As explained by the Appellate Body[902], the measure "must be the source of *the alleged* impairment". Similarly, Article 7 of the DSU foresees that except if the parties agree otherwise, the identification and characterization of the measure to be examined by a panel is an exclusive right of the WTO Member requesting the establishment of a Panel. This right is limited by the requirements of Article 4 of the DSU on consultations and Article 6.2 of the DSU on specificity of the measures but the selection and characterization of the measure in dispute is the prerogative of the complainant.

775.   This principle applies to a situation where a complainant asks a panel to review an amended measure, suggesting that the measure to be reviewed is the measure that the complainant considers to be the "amended" source of the alleged impairment. The definition of the situation considered to impair benefits continues to be the prerogative of the complainant and is counterbalanced by the authority of the panel to decide whether the measure *as defined by the complainant* is within its jurisdiction. In addition, the exclusive right of the complainant to define the amended measure to be examined is subject to the legal basis set out in the panel request.

776.   In the case at hand, it is my understanding that Brazil, when referring to the amended measures requested the Panel to examine:

    a.   Concerning the limitation on imports of chicken cuts:

        i.   Article 7 paragraphs 2 and 3 of MoA 34/2016, which Brazil considers breach Article XI of the GATT 1994;

    b.   Concerning the limitation of imports to certain uses:

        i.   Articles 22(1), 31(1) and 32(3) of MoA 34/2016, which Brazil considers breach Article XI and Article III:4 of the GATT 1994.

    c.   Concerning the period for application and period of validity of import recommendations and import approvals:

        i.   Articles 21, 27 and 30 of MoA 34/2016, which Brazil considers that operating together breach Article XI of the GATT 1994 and Article 3.2 of the Agreement on Import Licensing Procedures.

---

[902]   Appellate Body Report, *United States — Gambling* para. 121.

7.11.3   Jurisdiction of the Panel over the amended measures

777.   To establish whether the Panel has jurisdiction over the amended measures, the Panel must review the content of the measures as described in the panel request vis-à-vis the content of the amended measures challenged by Brazil. The factual circumstances of the case provide additional elements that complement the analysis, in particular the overall structure of the legal framework, the fact that the amendments were adopted by a replacement of the entire MoA and MoT regulations with changes limited to the three measures covered by the dispute, and the timing of the changes which coincide with the Panel's proceedings.

778.   Pursuant to Articles 3.3, 3.4 and 6.2 of the DSU, the analysis concerning a panel's jurisdiction should focus on whether the subsequent measure is an "amendment" of the measure included in the panel's request. Questions to be considered include whether the amended measure is a modification of the original measure; whether there is a continuum between the original and the amended measure; whether they regulate the same subject. In addition, the panel should consider whether it can be reasonably concluded that the respondent (who controls the decision to amend the measure) was on notice that the amended measure would be referred to the panel. This is a due process consideration.

779.   In the current case three elements seem clear. First, the three amended measures are covered by the panel's request. This conclusion results from an analysis of the measures as described in the panel request and the content of the amended measures as challenged by Brazil. Each of the amended measures regulates the same subject as the original measure with only limited modifications. Further, in the request for the establishment of the panel, for each measure, Brazil includes a description of the measure followed each time by an indication that it includes amendments, replacements, related and implementing measures to the measures described. This express formulation gave notice to Indonesia that Brazil, as complainant, would request the Panel to review any amendments that Indonesia might make to the measures at issue during the period of the panel proceedings. When developing the modifications, Indonesia could have consulted with Brazil and the parties could have developed a mutually agreed solution and could have even have requested suspension of the work of the Panel. In the absence of such alternative actions, Indonesia could reasonably anticipate that Brazil would request the Panel to review any changes that Indonesia would make to the measures under consideration by the Panel.

780.   Second, the three amended measures remain three measures. *They did not become six or seven different measures.* Each amended measure is simply a modification of the original measure. Thus, the alleged limitation on imports of chicken cuts in its amended form comprises the list of allowed imports (Article 7(2) of MoA 34/2016) and the conditions set in Article 7(3) for non-listed products. The limitation on the destination allowed for imports refers to the enlarged list of uses (MoA 34/2016 Article 31(1)) together with the two new conditions requiring that an application for an import recommendation includes a

distribution plan identifying the would-be purchaser and that upon importation the importer files a weekly report indicating the purchaser of the goods (MoA Articles 22(1) and 32(3)). The alleged restriction resulting from the period of application and the period of validity of import recommendations and import approvals refers to an allegation of restriction based on the conditions operating together (MoA 34/2016 Articles 21, 27 and 30).

781.   Third, the jurisdiction of the Panel over the amended measures does not depend on whether the amended measure *fails to remove the original impairment*. The amended measures are each a modification of the respective original measure, regulating the same aspect of chicken imports into Indonesia covered by the Panel's jurisdiction. Each measure may contain elements that impair benefits either in a similar or different way to the original measure or the measure may contain no elements that impair benefits. It is the Panel's examination pursuant to its jurisdiction that allows it to determine whether one of three situations described above exist and whether there is a consequent impairment.

7.11.4   Relation between a panel's jurisdiction and an allegation of expiry

782.   Once jurisdiction is established, the Panel needs to examine *the amended measures* considering the claims and rebuttals by the parties and make findings and recommendations as appropriate. Jurisdiction is independent from an allegation by the respondent regarding expiry of the measure.

783.   An allegation of expiry should be considered as part of the analysis of the original measure, and only as a factual determination as to whether the legal instrument that incorporated the original measure has been revoked. Such is the case in the current dispute and therefore recommendations related to the original measures should not be made (measures included in MoA 58/2015 and MoT 5/2016).

784.   A second type of allegation of "expiry" whereby the respondent alleges that the original measure expired because the amended measure does not include the restriction embodied in the original measure would need to be dismissed. Such an allegation assumes that only measures that are contrary to the covered agreements can be the subject of examination by the Panel (acting pursuant to its jurisdiction). The argument seems to be that if a measure is amended and the original restriction eliminated, the WTO incompatibility is removed and the measure ceases to exist because it is no longer WTO-incompatible. This overlooks the fact that that the amended measure, as a matter of fact, exists because it is written in provisions incorporated in a legal instrument identified by the complainant and perceived by the complainant to be an alleged source of impairment.

7.11.5 Conclusions

785. It is my view, that the sequence of determining the content of the amended measure challenged, followed by a determination of jurisdiction over the measure is key to a clear and comprehensive examination by the panel.

786. An approach where the jurisdiction over an amended measure is only asserted after the panel determines that the measure (original) has not expired because the amended measure contains a similar restriction creates the risk that the panel focuses its examination on an issue that may no longer be the problem. Upon the amendment, the source of impairment is the measure *as amended* rather than the original measure. At that stage and to the extent that the complainant develops claims against the amended measure, the panel needs to examine the modified measure as defined by the complainant. This is important because it is possible that the amended measure resolves some problems while creating other problems. So long as the amended measure is covered by the panel's jurisdiction and the claim is covered by the legal basis identified in the panel request, the measure to be examined is the measure as amended.

787. In summary, it is my view that in the present case pursuant to the amendment of the measures and the allegation by Brazil that the amended measures are in breach of the provisions of the covered agreements indicated in the panel request, the Panel is required to determine whether it has jurisdiction over the amended measures (as defined by the complainant) and thereafter make findings and recommendations concerning *the measures as amended*. Altering this sequence with an examination of whether the "old measure" has expired because the "new measure removes the old problem" risks focusing the Panel's examination on a measure that is no longer the source of the alleged impairment. In addition, it risks changing the examination of the amended measure into an examination that does not consider the amended measure in its integrity and as identified by the complainant.

Table 1. Type of chicken meat and chicken products allowed to be imported

*Includes whole chicken and does not include chicken cuts

First amendment	Second amendment
MoA 58/2015	**MoA 34/2016**
Art.8 ...type of non-cattle carcass and processed products is included in attachment II*...	Art. 7(2) ...type of carcass, meat, and/or offal other than cattle including its processed products ...are listed in Annex II*... *(3) The type of carcass....not listed in.... Annex II* .... may still be granted recommendation as long as it meets the requirements of safe, healthy, wholesome and halal...*
MoT 5/2016	**MoT 59/2016**
Art. 7 The type of Animal and Animal product that can be imported shall be as per Appendix ... IV* Art. 10(1) To obtain approval to import ... submit application attaching Recommendation from Minister of Agriculture... Art. 10(2) To obtain approval ... attach: e) Recommendation of Min. of Agriculture ...for imports ...as per Appendix ...IV*.	Art. 7 (2) The types of Animal and Animal product which are limited for importation are as included in ...Annex III*... Art. 11(1) To obtain Import Approval... submit application attaching e) Recommendation from Minister of Agriculture for ...products listed ...in Annex III*... *Art. 29 Animal and animal product that are not contained in the attachment to this Minister Regulation may be imported after obtaining Import Approval ...by attaching recommendation referred to in Article 11...*

Table 2. Limitation on the destination of imports

First amendment	Second amendment
MoA 58/2015	**MoA 34/2016**
Art. 31(1) Intended use ... of carcass and meat ... is for hotels, restaurants, caterings, industries, and other particular purposes.	Art. 31(1) purpose of usage ...for carcass, meat, offal and /or its processes products *which required cold chain facility* ...hotels, restaurants, caterings, industries, *markets with cold chain facilities*.... Art. 22(1) Application of a Recommendation ...shall be enclosed with...: *(i) distribution plan ... in accordance to Format-2* *Art 32(3) Business Actors...which import...is required to submit a distribution report ...Format-4 every Thursday ...*

Table 3. **Application and validity periods for import recommendation and import approval**

First amendment	Second amendment
MoA 58/2015	**MoA 34/2016**
Art. 22 …must submit Recommendation application on 1st-31st Dec.; 1st–30 April; 1st-31st August. Art. 30(1) Validity period of the Recommendation …shall be… 1st Jan up to 30th April; 1st May up to 30th August; 1st Sept. up to 31 Dec.	Art.21 ….application for a Recommendation …*may be submitted at any time..* *Art 27. …within 3 months …submit an import approval …* Art. 30 …validity period of the Recommendation …*is for six months …*

8.   CONCLUSIONS AND RECOMMENDATIONS

788.   For the reasons set forth in this Report, the Panel concludes as follows:

a.   In respect of Indonesia's request for a preliminary ruling:

  i.   the Panel finds that the alleged general prohibition/overarching measure is properly within the terms of reference of the Panel, and in particular, that (a) Brazil's panel request provides a brief summary of the complaint sufficient to present the problem clearly, (b) the measure described in Brazil's first written submission is not altered to the point of falling outside the terms of reference of the Panel, and (c) the alleged general prohibition is properly identified in Brazil's panel request;

  ii.   the Panel finds that the panel request does not contain a challenge to the import licensing regime "as a whole", and such measure is therefore not within the terms of reference of the Panel;

  iii.   the Panel finds that Brazil's claims with regard to other prepared or preserved chicken meat are identified in Brazil's panel request and are therefore within the terms of reference of the Panel;

  iv.   the Panel takes note of Brazil's statement that it is not making any claims under Article 1 of the Agreement on Import Licensing Procedures and therefore sees no need to rule that Brazil is precluded from making such claims.

b.   In respect of the positive list requirement:

  i.   the Panel finds that the positive list requirement as enacted through MoA 58/2015 and MoT 05/2016 is inconsistent with Article XI of the GATT 1994;

      ii.   the Panel finds that the positive list requirement as enacted through MoA 58/2015 and MoT 05/2016 is not justified under Article XX(d) of the GATT 1994;

      iii.   the Panel considers that having found that the positive list requirement as enacted through MoA 58/2015 and MoT 05/2016 is inconsistent with Article XI of the GATT 1994 and is not justified under the general exception in Article XX(d) of the GATT 1994, it is not necessary to address Brazil's claim under Article 4.2 of the Agreement on Agriculture in order to secure a positive solution to this dispute;

      iv.   the Panel finds that the positive list requirement has not ceased to exist by virtue of the relevant provisions in MoA 34/2016 and MoT 59/2016;

      v.   the Panel finds that since the positive list requirement, as enacted through MoA 34/2016 and MoT 59/2016, continues to apply in the same manner as enacted through MoA 58/2015 and MoT 05/2016, the Panel's findings on Article XI and XX(d) of the GATT 1994, in respect of the measure as enacted through MoA 58/2015 and MoT 05/2016, also apply to this measure as enacted through MoA 34/2016 and MoT 59/2016.

   c.   In respect of the intended use requirement:

      i.   in respect of the intended use requirement as enacted through the relevant provisions in MoA 58/2015, the Panel finds that:

          1)   Article III:4 of the GATT 1994 is not applicable because of the absence of an equivalent domestic measure;

          2)   the intended use requirement is inconsistent with Article XI of the GATT 1994;

          3)   the intended use requirement is not justified under Article XX(b) or Article XX(d) of the GATT 1994;

          4)   having found that the intended use requirement is inconsistent with Article XI of the GATT 1994, it is not necessary to address Brazil's claim under Article 4.2 of the Agreement on Agriculture in order to secure a positive solution to this dispute;

      ii.   the intended use requirement has not ceased to exist by virtue of the amendments made to through the relevant provisions in MoA 34/2016;

iii. in respect of the intended use requirement as enacted through the relevant provisions in MoA 34/2016, the Panel finds that:

1) Article III:4 of the GATT 1994 is applicable, because there is an equivalent measure applied to like domestic products;

2) the intended use requirement with respect to its cold storage requirement is not inconsistent with Article III:4 of the GATT 1994,

3) the intended use requirement with respect to its enforcement provisions is inconsistent with Article III:4 of the GATT 1994;

4) the intended use requirement with respect to its enforcement provisions is not justified under the general exceptions in Article XX(b) or Article XX(d) of the GATT 1994.

5) having found that the intended use requirement with respect to its enforcement provisions is inconsistent with Article III:4 of the GATT 1994, it is not necessary to address Brazil's claim under Article XI:1 of the GATT 1994 and Article 4.2 of the Agreement on Agriculture in order to secure a positive solution to this dispute.

d. In respect of Indonesia's import licensing procedures:

i. the Panel finds that the positive list requirement is in the nature of an import licensing rule and is therefore not subject to the Import Licensing Agreement;

ii. the Panel finds that the intended use requirement is in the nature of an import licensing rule and is therefore not subject to the Import Licensing Agreement;

iii. the Panel finds that the application windows, the validity periods and the fixed licence terms, as enacted through MoA 58/2015 and MoT 05/2016, are inconsistent with Article XI:1 of the GATT 1994;

iv. the Panel finds that the application windows, the validity periods and the fixed licence terms, as enacted through MoA 58/2015 and MoT 05/2016, are not justified under Article XX(d) of the GATT 1994;

v. the Panel considers that having found that the application windows, the validity periods and the fixed licence terms, as enacted through MoA 58/2015 and MoT 05/2016, are inconsistent with Article XI of the GATT 1994, it is not necessary to address Brazil's claim under Article 4.2 of the

Agreement on Agriculture and Article 3.2 of the Import Licensing Agreement in order to secure a positive solution to this dispute;

vi.   the Panel finds that the application windows and the validity periods, as a single measure, have ceased to exist; the Panel thus refrains from making a recommendation in respect of this measure;

vii.   regarding the new validity period, as enacted through MoA 34/2016, the Panel finds that Brazil failed to demonstrate that this measure is inconsistent with Article XI:1 of the GATT 1994, Article 4.2 of the Agreement on Agriculture and Article 3.2 of the Import Licensing Agreement;

viii.   the Panel finds that because of the almost identical language in the relevant provisions governing the fixed licence terms, the Panel's findings on Article XI and XX(d) of the GATT 1994, in respect of this measure as enacted through MoA 58/2015 and MoT 05/2016, also apply to this measure as enacted through MoA 34/2016 and MoT 59/2016;

ix.   the Panel finds that Brazil failed to make a *prima facie* case that the following aspects of Indonesia's import licensing regime are WTO-inconsistent: (1) MoT's power to determine the amount of imported goods in the MoA Import Recommendation, as enacted through MoA 58/2015; and (2) the denial of import licences to secure price stabilization.

e.   In respect of the undue delay in the approval of the veterinary health certificate:

i.   the Panel finds that Indonesia has caused an undue delay in the approval of the veterinary health certificate inconsistent with Article 8 and Annex C (1)(a) of the SPS Agreement.

f.   In respect of the halal labelling requirements:

i.   the Panel finds that Brazil failed to demonstrate that Indonesia's implementation of its halal labelling requirements is inconsistent with Indonesia's obligations under Article III:4 of the GATT 1994.

g.   In respect of the transportation requirement:

i.   the Panel finds that Brazil failed to demonstrate that the direct transportation requirement, as enacted through Article 19(a) of MoA 34/2016, is inconsistent with Article XI:1 of the GATT 1994 and Article 4.2 of the Agreement on Agriculture.

h.   In respect of the general prohibition:

i.   the Panel finds that Brazil failed to make a *prima facie* case, because it did not demonstrate the existence of the alleged unwritten measure.

789.   Under Article 3.8 of the DSU, in cases where there is an infringement of the obligations assumed under a covered agreement, the action is considered *prima facie* to constitute a case of nullification or impairment. We conclude that, to the extent that the measures at issue are inconsistent with certain provisions of the GATT 1994 and the SPS Agreement, they have nullified or impaired benefits accruing to Brazil under those agreements.

790.   Pursuant to Article 19.1 of the DSU, the Panel, with the exception of the measure referred to in 8.1.d(vi) above, recommends that Indonesia bring its measures into conformity with its obligations under Articles III:4 and XI:1 of the GATT 1994 and Article 8 and Annex C(1)(a) of the SPS Agreement.

ANNEX A-1

WORKING PROCEDURES FOR THE PANEL

Adopted on 16 March 2016

1.   In its proceedings, the Panel shall follow the relevant provisions of the Understanding on Rules and Procedures Governing the Settlement of Disputes (DSU). In addition, the following Working Procedures shall apply.

General

2.   The deliberations of the Panel and the documents submitted to it shall be kept confidential except as communicated in the Panel report. Nothing in the DSU or in these Working Procedures shall preclude a party to the dispute (hereafter "party") from disclosing statements of its own positions to the public. Members shall treat as confidential information submitted to the Panel by another Member which the submitting Member has designated as confidential. Where a party submits a confidential version of its written submissions to the Panel, it shall also, upon request of a Member, provide a non-confidential summary of the information contained in its submissions that could be disclosed to the public.

3.   Upon indication from any party, at the latest on the first substantive meeting, that it shall provide information that requires protection additional to that provided for under these Working Procedures, the Panel shall, after consultation with the parties, decide whether to adopt appropriate additional procedures. Exceptions to this procedure shall be granted upon a showing of good cause.

4.   The Panel shall meet in closed session. The parties, and Members having notified their interest in the dispute to the Dispute Settlement Body in accordance with Article 10 of the DSU (hereafter "third parties"), shall be present at the meetings only when invited by the Panel to appear before it.

5.   Each party and third party has the right to determine the composition of its own delegation when meeting with the Panel. Each party and third party shall have the responsibility for all members of its own delegation and shall ensure that each member of such delegation acts in accordance with the DSU and these Working Procedures, particularly with regard to the confidentiality of the proceedings.

Submissions

6.   Before the first substantive meeting of the Panel with the parties, each party shall submit a written submission in which it presents the facts of the case and its arguments, in accordance with the timetable adopted by the Panel. Each party shall also submit to the Panel, prior to the second substantive meeting of

the Panel, a written rebuttal, in accordance with the timetable adopted by the Panel.

7.   A party shall submit any request for a preliminary ruling at the earliest possible opportunity and in any event no later than in its first written submission to the Panel. If Brazil requests such a ruling, Indonesia shall submit its response to the request in its first written submission. If Indonesia requests such a ruling, Brazil shall submit its response to the request prior to the first substantive meeting of the Panel, at a time to be determined by the Panel in light of the request. Exceptions to this procedure shall be granted upon a showing of good cause.

8.   Each party shall submit all factual evidence to the Panel no later than during the first substantive meeting, except with respect to evidence necessary for purposes of rebuttal, answers to questions or comments on answers provided by the other party. Exceptions to this procedure shall be granted upon a showing of good cause. Where such exception has been granted, the Panel shall accord the other party a period of time for comment, as appropriate, on any new factual evidence submitted after the first substantive meeting.

9.   Where the original language of exhibits is not a WTO working language, the submitting party or third party shall submit a translation into the WTO working language of the submission at the same time. The Panel may grant reasonable extensions of time for the translation of such exhibits upon a showing of good cause. Any objection as to the accuracy of a translation should be raised promptly in writing, no later than the next filing or meeting (whichever occurs earlier) following the submission which contains the translation in question. Any objection shall be accompanied by a detailed explanation of the grounds of objection and an alternative translation. Thereafter, the Panel will rule as promptly as possible on any objection to the accuracy of a translation.

10.   In order to facilitate the work of the Panel, each party and third party is invited to make its submissions in accordance with the WTO Editorial Guide for Panel Submissions attached as Annex 1, to the extent that it is practical to do so.

11.   To facilitate the maintenance of the record of the dispute and maximize the clarity of submissions, each party and third party shall sequentially number its exhibits throughout the course of the dispute. For example, exhibits submitted by Brazil could be numbered BRA-1, BRA-2, etc. If the last exhibit in connection with the first submission was numbered BRA-5, the first exhibit of the next submission thus would be numbered BRA-6.

Questions

12.   The Panel may at any time pose questions to the parties and third parties, orally or in writing, including prior to each substantive meeting.

Expert consultation

13.   Consistent with Article 13 of the DSU, Article 14.2 of the TBT Agreement and Article 11.2 of the SPS Agreement, the Panel may seek expert

advice from experts and from international organizations, as appropriate. In the course of the proceedings, and at the latest two weeks after the first written submission is received, the Parties should inform the Panel whether they consider that the Panel should consult with scientific or technical experts. Should the Panel decide to consult experts, it shall adopt additional working procedures.

Substantive meetings

14.   Each party shall provide to the Panel the list of members of its delegation in advance of each meeting with the Panel and no later than 5.00 p.m. the previous working day.

15.   The first substantive meeting of the Panel with the parties shall be conducted as follows:

a.   The Panel shall invite Brazil to make an opening statement to present its case first. Subsequently, the Panel shall invite Indonesia to present its point of view. Before each party takes the floor, it shall provide the Panel and other participants at the meeting with a provisional written version of its statement. In the event that interpretation is needed, each party shall provide additional copies to the interpreters. Each party shall make available to the Panel and the other party the final version of its statement, preferably at the end of the meeting, and in any event no later than 5.00 p.m. on the first working day following the meeting.

b.   After the conclusion of the statements, the Panel shall give each party the opportunity to ask each other questions or make comments, through the Panel. Each party shall have an opportunity to orally answer these questions. Each party shall send in writing, within a timeframe to be determined by the Panel, any questions to the other party to which it wishes to receive a response in writing. Each party shall be invited to respond in writing to the other party's questions within a deadline to be determined by the Panel.

c.   The Panel may subsequently pose questions to the parties. Each party shall then have an opportunity to answer these questions orally. The Panel shall send in writing, within a timeframe to be determined by it, any questions to the parties to which it wishes to receive a response in writing. Each party shall be invited to respond in writing to such questions within a deadline to be determined by the Panel.

d.   Once the questioning has concluded, the Panel shall afford each party an opportunity to present a brief closing statement, with Brazil presenting its statement first.

e. The Panel may, after consultation with the parties, set time limits for the opening statements; such time limits would be informed to the parties before the first substantive meeting.

16. The second substantive meeting of the Panel with the parties shall be conducted as follows:

a. The Panel shall ask Indonesia if it wishes to avail itself of the right to present its case first. If so, the Panel shall invite Indonesia to present its opening statement, followed by Brazil. If Indonesia chooses not to avail itself of that right, the Panel shall invite Brazil to present its opening statement first. Before each party takes the floor, it shall provide the Panel and other participants at the meeting with a provisional written version of its statement. In the event that interpretation is needed, each party shall provide additional copies to the interpreters. Each party shall make available to the Panel and the other party the final version of its statement, preferably at the end of the meeting, and in any event no later than 5.00 p.m. of the first working day following the meeting.

b. After the conclusion of the statements, the Panel shall give each party the opportunity to ask questions or make comments, through the Panel. Each party shall then have an opportunity to answer these questions orally. Each party shall send in writing, within a timeframe to be determined by the Panel, any questions to the other party to which it wishes to receive a response in writing. Each party shall be invited to respond in writing to the other party's questions within a deadline to be determined by the Panel.

c. The Panel may subsequently pose questions to the parties. Each party shall then have an opportunity to answer these questions orally. The Panel shall send in writing, within a timeframe to be determined by it, any questions to the parties to which it wishes to receive a response in writing. Each party shall be invited to respond in writing to such questions within a deadline to be determined by the Panel.

d. Once the questioning has concluded, the Panel shall afford each party an opportunity to present a brief closing statement, with the party that presented its opening statement first, presenting its closing statement first.

Third parties

17. The Panel shall invite each third party to transmit to the Panel a written submission prior to the first substantive meeting of the Panel with the parties, in accordance with the timetable adopted by the Panel.

18. Each third party shall also be invited to present its views orally during a session of this first substantive meeting, set aside for that purpose. Each third

party shall provide to the Panel the list of members of its delegation in advance of this session and no later than 5.00 p.m. the previous working day.

19.   The third-party session shall be conducted as follows:

a.   All third parties may be present during the entirety of this session.

b.   The Panel shall first hear the arguments of the third parties in alphabetical order. Third parties present at the third-party session and intending to present their views orally at that session, shall provide the Panel, the parties and other third parties with provisional written versions of their statements before they take the floor. In the event that interpretation is needed, each third party shall provide additional copies to the interpreters. Third parties shall make available to the Panel, the parties and other third parties the final versions of their statements, preferably at the end of the session, and in any event no later than 5.00 p.m. of the first working day following the session.

c.   After the third parties have made their statements, the parties may be given the opportunity, through the Panel, to ask the third parties questions for clarification on any matter raised in the third parties' submissions or statements. Each party shall send in writing, within a timeframe to be determined by the Panel, any questions to a third party to which it wishes to receive a response in writing. Each third party shall be invited to respond in writing to these questions within a deadline to be determined by the Panel.

d.   The Panel may subsequently pose questions to the third parties. Each third party shall then have an opportunity to answer these questions orally. The Panel shall send in writing, within a timeframe to be determined by it, any questions to the third parties to which it wishes to receive a response in writing. Each third party shall be invited to respond in writing to such questions within a deadline to be determined by the Panel.

Descriptive part

20.   The description of the arguments of the parties and third parties in the descriptive part of the Panel report shall consist of the executive summaries provided by the parties and third parties, which shall be annexed as addenda to the report. These executive summaries shall not in any way serve as a substitute for the submissions of the parties and third parties in the Panel's examination of the case.

21.   Each party shall submit an integrated executive summary of the facts and arguments as presented to the Panel in its written submissions and oral statements, in accordance with the timetable adopted by the Panel. This summary may also include a summary of responses to questions. The integrated executive summary shall not exceed 30 pages. The Panel will not summarize in

the descriptive part of its report, or annex to its report, the parties' responses to questions.

22.   Each third party shall submit an executive summary of its arguments as presented in its written submission and statement in accordance with the timetable adopted by the Panel. This summary may also include a summary of responses to questions, where relevant. The executive summary to be provided by each third party shall not exceed 6 pages.

Interim review

23.   Following issuance of the interim report, each party may submit a written request to review precise aspects of the interim report and request a further meeting with the Panel, in accordance with the timetable adopted by the Panel. The right to request such a meeting shall be exercised no later than at the time the written request for review is submitted.

24.   In the event that no further meeting with the Panel is requested, each party may submit written comments on the other party's written request for review, in accordance with the timetable adopted by the Panel. Such comments shall be limited to commenting on the other party's written request for review.

25.   The interim report, as well as the final report prior to its official circulation, shall be kept strictly confidential and shall not be disclosed.

Service of documents

26.   The following procedures regarding service of documents shall apply:

    a.   Each party and third party shall submit all documents to the Panel by filing them with the DS Registry (office No. 2047).

    b.   Each party and third party shall file 4 paper copies of all documents it submits to the Panel. Exhibits may be filed in 4 copies on CD-ROM, DVD, or USB stick and 3 paper copies. The DS Registrar shall stamp the documents with the date and time of the filing. The paper version shall constitute the official version for the purposes of the record of the dispute.

    c.   Each party and third party shall also provide an electronic copy of all documents it submits to the Panel at the same time as the paper versions, preferably in Microsoft Word format, either on a CD-ROM, a DVD, a USB stick or as an e-mail attachment. If the electronic copy is provided by e-mail, it should be addressed to *DSRegistry@wto.org*, with a copy to ****.****@wto.org, ****.****@wto.org, ****.****@wto.org, ****.****@wto.org, and ****.****@wto.org. If a CD-ROM, DVD, or USB stick is provided, it shall be filed with the DS Registry.

    d.   Each party shall serve any document submitted to the Panel directly on the other party. Each party shall, in addition, serve on all third parties its written submissions in advance of the first substantive meeting with the Panel. Each third party shall serve any document submitted to the Panel directly on the parties and all other third parties. Each party and third party shall confirm, in writing, that copies have been served as required at the time it provides each document to the Panel.

e.   Each party and third party shall file its documents with the DS Registry and serve copies on the other party (and third parties where appropriate) by 5.00 p.m. (Geneva time) on the due dates established by the Panel. A party may submit its documents to another party in electronic format only. With respect to third parties, a party or third party may submit its documents in electronic format only, unless a third party requests in writing to receive paper copies.

f.   The Panel shall provide the parties with an electronic version of the descriptive part, the interim report and the final report, as well as of other documents as appropriate. When the Panel transmits to the parties or third parties both paper and electronic versions of a document, the paper version shall constitute the official version for the purposes of the record of the dispute.

27.   The Panel reserves the right to modify these procedures as necessary, after consultation with the parties. The Panel will annex to its report these procedures.

ANNEX B

ARGUMENTS OF THE PARTIES

Contents		Page
Annex B-1	Integrated executive summary of the arguments of Brazil	4003
Annex B-2	Integrated executive summary of the arguments of Indonesia	4040

ANNEX B-1

INTEGRATED EXECUTIVE SUMMARY OF THE ARGUMENTS OF BRAZIL

I.   INTRODUCTION AND FACTUAL BACKGROUND

1.   For the past years Indonesia has implemented layer-upon-layer of a complex and intricate trade regulation that imposes several restrictions on the importation of Brazilian chicken meat and chicken products. First of all, not all types of chicken meat and chicken products are allowed to be imported into the country. Secondly, Indonesia prioritizes domestic food production and national food reserve over imports, as well as restricts imports to cases in which there are "shortages" in the domestic production. Thirdly, no imports are authorized for other uses than those previously allowed by the Indonesian legislation (hotels, restaurants, catering, industries, and other particular purposes), what means that imported products are not allowed in "wet markets" (traditional markets), which are estimated to correspond to 70% of the poultry market in Indonesia. Fourthly, Indonesia adopts a complex, non-transparent and arbitrary import licensing regime, which unduly restricts imports. Fifthly, Indonesia never presented any explanation for the ongoing delay of 7 years to undertake and complete the sanitary procedures required to import chicken meat and chicken products into Indonesia. As a matter of fact, the combined effects of these different trade, sanitary, and import licensing measures impose a general ban on Brazilian exports of chicken meat and chicken products.

2.   The products at issue in this dispute are referred by the following HS codes of the Gallus Domesticus species, as follows: 02.07. Meat and edible offal, of the poultry of heading 01.05, fresh, chilled or frozen - Of fowls of the species Gallus domesticus: 0207.11 (Not cut in pieces, fresh or chilled); 0207.12 (Not cut in pieces, frozen); 0207.13 (Cuts and offal, fresh or chilled); 0207.14 (Cuts and offal, frozen) and 16.02 Other prepared or preserved meat, meat offal or

blood - Of poultry of heading 01.05: 1602.32 (Of fowls of the species Gallus domesticus).

3.   Since 2009, Brazil has attempted through different channels to obtain access to the Indonesian market without success. Between 2009 and 2011, the private sectors of both countries tried to negotiate the sale of mechanically deboned chicken meat, but the required authorizations were never granted by the Indonesian authorities. In parallel, Brazil and Indonesia discussed the market access of Brazilian exports in several meetings of the Consultative Committee of Agriculture (CCA). In the Third Meeting of the CCA, on 4-5 May 2009, Brazil officially presented a proposal of health certificate for fresh poultry meat and for turkey and duck based on the guidelines of the OIE Terrestrial Code, but no official answer was ever received from the Indonesian Government. Also, during the Fourth Meeting of the CCA, on 15-16 September 2010, the Indonesian authorities indicated that they would evaluate the "possibility of opening" the chicken market. However, they pointed out that Indonesia was "self-sufficient" in these products (chicken), and therefore they would "prioritize" the imports of turkey and duck meat, which were never allowed as well. On the occasion, Brazilian authorities were informed that a sanitary inspection mission would be sent to the country, but it never happened nor any justification was given as to the reason the mission was not sent.

4.   Brazil raised several Specific Trade Concerns (STCs) in the WTO SPS Committee over the past years regarding the Indonesian restrictive legislation and failure to grant access to Brazilian exports of chicken meat and chicken products. Indonesia has never provided a satisfactory and WTO-consistent answer to Brazil's concerns. In light of this, in July 2014, Brazil presented a formal request for information based on Article 5.8 of the SPS Agreement. Indonesia limited itself to point out to several Indonesian legislations that would apply to imports of animal products. It did not present any sanitary reasons not to approve the health Certificates and not to send an inspection mission to Brazil. It also confirmed that no risk assessment for the Brazilian chicken meat and chicken products had ever been made. According to Indonesia, the "delay" (actually an absence of response) for the approval of the Veterinary Health Certificate was due to an allegedly Brazilian failure "to comply with the existing procedures and technical regulations" related to halal information.

5.   Indonesia's import regime for chicken meat and chicken products is established by the application of several laws, decrees and regulations, which are grounded on the basic premise that imports of chicken meat and chicken products shall only take place when the domestic supply is not sufficient. For the purpose of this Executive Summary, and considering that the pieces of legislation will be analyzed below, Brazil will not list them here.

6.   Brazil calls the Panel's attention, however, to Indonesia's continuous changes and amendments to its legislation in a manner that suggests a strategy to turn this litigation into a pursuit of a moving target. This poses particular problems. First, it may compromise the Member's ability to challenge the measures as the respondent could try to evade its obligations by simply

modifying the pertaining legislation. Second, it may affect what the Panel understands as its terms of reference. In this regard, Brazil submits that the matter before the Panel refers to "measures" and not to the legislation itself. The matter before the Panel covers the legal situation (i.e. the measures and its legal basis) identified by Brazil at its panel's request. The Panel is thus required to take into account the legal framework prevailing on the date of the establishment of the Panel, as well as any amendment introduced afterwards that affect this legal situation. This is particularly important in this case, because the changes have not served to correct the inconsistencies of Indonesian measures but rather to maintain the very same measures under a different guise, adding new layers of restrictiveness to this already extremely restrictive trade regime. It is to avoid this threat of legal insecurity when dealing with the so-called moving target that panels are required to primarily decide on the matter contained in the panel request, and, in light of the prospective relevance of its report in terms of implementation, to also evaluate the modifications occurred thereafter.

II.   PRELIMINARY RULING REQUEST

7.   With regard to Indonesia's preliminary ruling request, Brazil has demonstrated that its Panel request observed the obligations under Article 6.2 of the DSU On the issue of the Panel's terms of reference, Brazil demonstrated that the general prohibition described in Brazil's FWS preserves the same prohibitive nature and essence as the one identified in the panel request and is clearly within the scope of the Panel's terms of reference. Likewise, it was clearly established that all the products at issue in the dispute were properly identified in the panel request. The HS code used in both the panel request and in the FWS is exactly the same and corresponds in the official website of the World Customs Organization to "other prepared or preserved meat, meat offal or blood (of fowls of the species Gallus domesticus).

8.   Regarding Indonesia import licensing regime Brazil contended that in its panel request, it had addressed the restrictions and prohibitions laid out by the Indonesian import licensing regime, and identified that, as such, the regime is not consistent with Indonesia's commitments under the WTO. Finally, Brazil confirmed that it did not make any claim under Article 1 of the Agreement on Import Licensing. Brazil only addresses Article 1 in its FWS for the purpose of contextualization, as Article 1 informs both automatic import licensing (Article 2) and non-automatic import licensing (Article 3).

III.   MEASURES AT ISSUE

(1)   The general prohibition on the importation of chicken meat and chicken products

9.   Brazil considers that the combined interaction of several different individual measures challenged in the present dispute constitute an overarching measure that is, on its own, a violation of the Covered Agreements, regardless of

the specific impact of each of its constitutive elements. As such, it should be scrutinized by the Panel independently of and in addition to the analysis of claims regarding individual measures as "part of a holistic analysis", as indicated by the Appellate Body in *Argentina – Import Measures*. Even if one of the specific measures could be justified under WTO law, which could hardly be the case, the combined effects of the individual measures would still result in restrictive policies inconsistent with the Covered Agreements.

10.   Brazil highlighted that all the individual measures at stake in the current dispute were conceived to implement an official trade policy based on the overriding objective of restricting imports to protect domestic production. As the Appellate Body has recognized in *Argentina - Import Measures,* when different measures are framed for the fulfillment of a single overriding objective, the combined operation of these measures can be considered a single, self-standing measure whose consistency with the WTO agreements must be carefully scrutinized in order to effectively solve the dispute.

11.   Indonesia has put in place a set of measures which resulted in a *de jure* and a *de facto* prohibition on the importation of chicken meat and chicken products from Brazil. These measures are founded on the premise that the importation of animal products should be made only if domestic production was insufficient to fulfill the needs for the people's consumption. This restrictive overarching framework operates through the combined effect of several measures, as follows:

    ☐   Prohibition on the importation of types of chicken meat and chicken products which are not included in Indonesia's positive list of permitted imports, as explained below;

    ☐   Requirement related to the "insufficiency of local production", to be defined under the discretion of the Indonesian authorities: According to Law 18/2009 (Article 36(4)), "import of animal or livestock and animal product from overseas shall be made if domestic animal products and supply of livestock is insufficient to fulfill the need for the people consumption". Also Law 18/2012 (Article 36) clearly indicates that in the case of "staple food", which encompasses chicken meat and chicken products, Indonesia's Government should always prioritize domestic food production over food imports that should only be authorized as an exception. Thus, the lack of "sufficiency" of local production is currently a "requirement" for the importation of animal or livestock and animal products to Indonesia;

    ☐   Additional restrictions regarding the importation of essential and strategic goods, which include chicken meat and chicken products. According to Article 25(1) of Law 7/2014, Indonesia shall control the availability of essential goods in adequate quantities, of good quality, and at affordable prices. The control of prices and quantities is also implemented in accordance with Article 26(3) of

Law 7/2014, should Indonesian authorities understand that imports may affect the national production of strategic goods. The large margin of discretion of Indonesian authorities to confer a different treatment to imported chicken meat and chicken products, including prohibitions and/or restrictions to their importation in order to prioritize domestic products, is one of the major concerns of Brazil. This measure not only causes a high degree of unpredictability to international trade flows, but it also virtually allows Indonesian authorities to impede importation at any time, and for no specific reason;

☐ Restrictions on the use of imported chicken meat and chicken products, restricting the commercial opportunities for exporters to Indonesia, as explained below;

☐ Intricate and restrictive procedures for import licensing in Indonesia, which create unnecessary obstacles to trade, prohibiting the importation of chicken meat and chicken products, as explained below;

☐ Undue delay in the undertaking of the sanitary procedures required to allow Brazilian exports of chicken meat and chicken products into Indonesia, as explained below.

12.   The combined effects of the different Indonesian trade, licensing and sanitary measures impose a general ban on Brazilian exports of chicken meat and chicken products and have impeded Brazilian exports of the products at issue over the past seven years in a manner inconsistent with Indonesia's obligations. This general ban derives from and is implemented through the combined operation of several written regulations and procedures (and one omission, relating to the undue delay in examining and approving Brazil's proposal for a health certificate) conceived for the fulfillment of a single overriding objective – to protect Indonesia's domestic poultry industry – that is enshrined in Indonesia's legislation itself. Of particular relevance in this regard is Law 18/2009 ("Law on Husbandry and Animal Health"), whose Article 36(4) provides that imports of animal or animal products should only be authorized if domestic animal products and "supply or livestock are insufficient to fulfil the needs for the people's consumption".

13.   There is no doubt that the self-sufficiency policy is the overriding objective of Indonesia's unwritten ban on the importation of chicken meat and chicken products. Indeed, it is clear that this policy is the "glue", to use an expression coined by a third party that binds together all the individual components of the general ban and informs its implementation. Furthermore, in its current formulation, self-sufficiency is also an important component of the general measure, as it consists of a mandatory requirement that has to be applied by Indonesian authorities before imports are authorized. For instance, Law 18/2009 specifically provides in Article 36(4) that "import of animal or livestock

and animal product from overseas shall be made if domestic animal products and supply or livestock is insufficient to fulfil the need for the people consumption".

14.   During the panel's proceedings, Indonesia argued that Brazil has not met the threshold to demonstrate a causal link between the lack of chicken imports from Brazil and the import ban. It also argued that self-sufficiency is only a general principle governing its laws and regulations which has not had any practical effect on the importation of chicken into Indonesia. Based on these arguments, Indonesia insisted that Brazil has not demonstrated the existence of the general measure.

15.   Yet contrary to what Indonesia argues self-sufficiency is not simply a general objective within its legal framework with no practical effect. It is reflected in multiple Indonesian laws and regulations, permeates the formulation of all Indonesia's agricultural policies and has banned any kind of imports, not only from Brazil but from any other Member, at least since the enactment of Law 18/2009. The same policy is reinforced in other relevant legislation related to chicken imports, like Law 18/2012 (Article 36). Although the mentioned legal texts are sufficient to confirm that self-sufficiency should not be viewed solely as a "general principle", Brazil has submitted other pieces of evidence that shows that the self-sufficiency is indeed operative and has very noticeable trade effects. Finally, self-sufficiency has nothing to do with food security. In reality, the effects arising from this policy are quite the opposite: reduced access to food (chicken, in this case) and higher prices.

16.   More importantly, Brazil has clearly demonstrated that most of the constitutive elements of the General ban are described in written legal acts adopted by Indonesia, including the self-sufficiency policy objective of the import ban. This substantially reduces the evidentiary threshold borne by the complainant to demonstrate the existence of the challenged measure. In the current dispute, these legal acts, in conjunction with the undue delay, provide enough evidence of the existence of the measure. Brazil also clarified how these different elements operate together and, combined, result in an unwritten import ban. This ban operates either to decrease the market opportunities for imported chicken or to increase the costs and risks for exporters that intend to access the market, forming a thick, virtually impenetrable barrier to imports of any amount of chicken meat and chicken products from any source in the world.

17.   Brazil asks the Panel to make specific findings on the overarching measure in addition to those related to the individual restrictions. Each individual measure identified by Brazil remains a matter of concern and Brazil expects the Panel to make specific findings on them. However, although a finding of inconsistency on the individual measures may solve specific trade concerns, it would not dismantle the import ban system as whole, which is the main issue in this dispute. In terms of implementation, Indonesia could simply change the instruments through which the import ban is made effective. The fact that Indonesia's legislation is frequently modified suggests that this outcome is likely to happen.

(2) Prohibition on imports of chicken cuts and other prepared or preserved chicken meat ("positive list")

18.   MoA Regulation 58/2015 establishes in Articles 7 and 8 that "the types of non-cattle carcass and the processed product thereof … that can be imported are included in Appendix II ...", which only contemplates HS codes for chicken "not cut in pieces, fresh or chilled and frozen". This is also the case for MoT 05/2016, whose Article 7(2) establishes that the "types of animals and animal products that can be imported are listed in Annex II, III and IV which is an integral part of this regulation". Annex IV makes references to HS codes for chicken "not cut in pieces, fresh or chilled and frozen". Thus, as the HS codes for the other products at issue are not described in those appendices, they cannot be imported into Indonesia.

19.   Although Indonesia had argued the positive list no longer exists, as changes were introduced in this requirement by MoA Regulation 34/2016, MoT Regulation 05/2016 and MoT Regulation 37/2016, MoA Regulation 34/2016 and MoT Regulation 37/2016 still contain a list of animals and animal products that can be imported into Indonesia. HS Codes for chicken cuts and other prepared or preserved chicken meat are still not in the Annexes of both regulations. If the positive list requirement had been in fact terminated, there would be no need to have a list of products in the annexes of both Regulations in the first place. The fact that this list remains in force and that the relevant HS codes for the products at issue in this dispute are not included therein is in itself reliable evidence that the positive list requirement is still in place. Moreover, the fact that the importation of those products "may" be authorized under conditions which are not clear – that is, safe, healthy, wholesome, and halal – makes importation even more cumbersome and unpredictable. This uncertainty in itself is a restriction.

(3) Restrictions on the use of imported products ("intended use")

20.   The intended use requirement was provided for in Article 32(2) of MoA Regulation 139/2014 and consisted of "a limitation of the importation of chicken meat and chicken products to certain intended uses to meet the needs of "hotel, restaurant, catering, manufacturing, other special needs, and modern market" and maintained in subsequent legislation enacted by Indonesia (MoA Regulation 58/2015). After the first meeting with the Panel, Brazil learned that MoA Regulation 58/2015 was no longer in force and that the restriction on the intended uses was now contained in MoA Regulation 34/2016 and MoT Regulation 05/2016 (as amended by MoT Regulation 37/2016). In August, Indonesia enacted MoT Regulation 59/2016, replacing the previously amended MoT Regulation 05/2016.

21.   After all the aforementioned legislative changes, Indonesia now claims that the intended use requirement no longer exists because, under the current regime, frozen or chilled chicken meat and chicken products can be sold in any Indonesian market, provided it has a cold storage facility.

22.   Yet, the introduction of the expression "markets with cold chain facility" among the intended uses does not alter the prohibition in place. Instead of an outright prohibition as in the previous legislation, Indonesia enacted a tailor-made legislation with minor effects on the improvement of the competitive opportunities available for imported products. The market for imported chicken remains as niche markets, and the most relevant part of the marketplace continues to be allocated only for local producers.

23.   Moreover, MoA Regulation 34/2016 introduced additional features, which reinforces the restriction caused by the intended uses. For instance, it now requires importers, when applying for an Import Recommendation, to submit a distribution plan for the imported meat, which shall include in advance information on the type of meat, the quantity, the name and address of the establishments/buyers and the product's price. As expected, the list of buyers included in the distribution plan shall only be among those of the allowed intended uses. To reinforce compliance, the same Regulation requires importers to submit weekly distribution reports ("every Thursday") to confirm that the products were not redirected to other purposes. Importers appear to be now tied to the terms of the distribution plan and any deviation to it may subject to sanctions, including a one-year import suspension.

(4)   Indonesia's restrictive import licensing procedures

24.   The complex and burdensome Indonesian import licensing regime requires the importer to obtain various approvals, authorizations and recommendations, largely granted on the discretion of different authorities. Firstly, an importer has to obtain an Importer Identification Number (API-U, for chicken), which has a period of validity of 5 years, after which it has to be renewed. For that, the importer must submit a re-registration to the issuing agency at the latest 30 (thirty) business days after the period of 5 years. The business operator that holds an API-U is constrained to report about the import realization once every 3 months to the Head of Provincial Agency and to the Head of District/Municipal Agency having jurisdiction over the company's domicile. If a company fails to do so then the API-U shall be suspended. The API-U shall be revoked if it is suspended twice or if the company fails to perform the obligation to report the import realization (every 3 months) not later than 30 days as of the suspension date, submits untrue information or data in the document of application, breaches the provisions in the prevailing legislation in import sector, and abuses the document of import and the letters related to import. These possibilities of suspension and/or revocation of the API-U reinforce the control of the Indonesian authorities over the importation, what directly affects the importation of chicken meat and chicken products, increasing the lack of predictability of the regime and causing restrictions on market access.

25.   Secondly, after obtaining an API-U, an importer of chicken products must obtain a MoF Registration before the Director General of Customs and Excise. MoF Decree 454/2002 determines the need to hold a customs registration (SRP) valid in Indonesia's customs areas as a requirement for

undertaking customs activities in the importation. Thirdly, once the registration procedures are completed, the importer must apply for a MoA Import Recommendation, but only for products included in the list of authorized products to be imported. All the products not listed in these Appendices are therefore automatically banned from the Indonesian market, as they cannot be imported without this Recommendation. Fourthly, For the products that can obtain a MoA Import Recommendation, several requirements have to be fulfilled by the importer. Some of them, such as the Veterinary Control Number and the Livestock and Animal Health Registration Certificate or Business License require previous and complex *démarches*. Moreover, in order to obtain a MoA Import Recommendation, an importer must demonstrate, through a "statement letter with stamp duty affixed, accompanied with supporting document of the ownership of cold storage and refrigerated vehicle", and also prove – through an assignment letter or work contract – that it employs a veterinarian with competency to supervise the imported products. Besides that, importers of chicken meat and chicken products must also submit a letter of recommendation from the provincial livestock services office, which amounts to a certification that the importer has been supervised by the competent veterinarian. The provincial livestock services office has discretionary power to issue or not the letter of recommendation.

26.   Another requirement is the report of import realization from the previous period. The importer shall demonstrate that the transactions carried out during this period met the fixed terms established by previous MoA Import Recommendations related to business units, port of discharge, and type and origin of the goods covered by them.

27.   Indonesias regulation establish also that in order to obtain a Recommendation the importer must necessarily indicate the "intended use" for the products to be imported, which by itself is a requirement that imposes an important restriction on trade.

28.   The issuance of a MoA Import Recommendation "for meat and processed meat products" is under additional requirements, as supervision on the compliance of veterinary public health requirements shall be performed. It is not clear whether the authority responsible for issuing the MoA Import Recommendation is required to base the decision on the conclusions of the report of the veterinary public health supervisor.

29.   The requirements to obtain a MoA Import Recommendation are far from being the only problem.   After the MoA Import Recommendation is issued, no changes or amendments related to the country of origin, business unit of origin, port of discharge, type/category of product are allowed. If the importers, for any reason, modify any of these "fixed license terms", Indonesia regulations establishes that they shall be sanctioned by the "revocation of [his] recommendation" and the "denial of [his] next recommendation application".

30.   Moreover, the time window for imports is drastically reduced in Indonesia since they can only take place during the validity period of both the

MoT Import Approval and the MoA Import Recommendation, which now is 6 months each at maximum. During this short period, the importer must complete the entire import transaction authorized by both documents by loading, shipping, transporting, delivering, and clearing at the customs the imported goods.

31.   As it is the case for the MoA Import Recommendation, once the MoT Import Approval is issued, it cannot be modified. The importer who fails to comply with the "fixed license terms" is subject to several sanctions, including the revocation of the Approval and the impossibility of submitting new requests. Ff an Approval is revoked, the importer may only re-submit the application after 1 year.

32.   Even under the current regime established by MoA Regulation 34/2016 and MoT Regulation,59/2016 , these restrictive features of Indonesia´s import licensing regime – that were existent under MoA Regulation 139/2014; MoT Regulation 46/2013, MoA Regulation 58/2015 Regulation MoT 05/2016, recently modified have not been fundamentally altered. Although the seemly elimination of the application, windows could be considered a positive development, the validity period of Import Recommendation and of the Import Approval are still short (6 months), the positive list and the intended use, albeit in a different form are still and place and the fixed license terms have not experienced any change. Moreover, as import approvals can only be obtained after the issuance of an import recommendation and the application must be submitted within three months after the issuance of the corresponding Import Recommendation, an Import Approval cannot be obtained at "any time".These elements are part and parcel of the same import licensing regime, which means that their trade restrictiveness need to be assessed as if they were one single measure.

(5)   Undue delay with regard to the approval of sanitary requirements

33.   According to the Indonesian legislation (Articles 35 and 36 of MoA Regulation 58/2015), it is not possible to import chicken meat and chicken products into Indonesia without a health certificate approved by the country. As mentioned above, since 2009 Brazil has been striving to negotiate with Indonesia the terms of a veterinary certificate for poultry, in order to allow Brazilian exports of those products to enter the Indonesian market. The proposal was based on the international standards applicable and encompassed the sanitary requirements established by Indonesia's legislation. Indonesia has not provided a satisfactory clarification on the sanitary reasons why the Brazilian products were not allowed into Indonesia.

(6)   Restrictions on the transportation of imported products

34.   According to Article 20(a) of MoA Regulation 58/2015 (now replaced by Article 19(a) of MoA Regulation 34/2016), the transportation of carcass, meat and/or processed products shall be "conducted directly from the country of origin to the port of discharge within the territory of Indonesia". If the transportation is not direct, or, by any reason, a stop in a third country or port

during the transportation is necessary before the arrival at the port of destination, the products will not be allowed to be imported into Indonesia. Products will be refused even in the case of *force majeure* that may deviate the shipment to a third-country port for transit.

(7) Discriminatory implementation of halal labelling requirements

35.   Indonesia requires that all products that enter, circulate and are traded in the country must be certified halal. To that end all food products must be adequately labelled halal on the product's packaging. This legal requirement applies indistinctively to both imported and like domestic products. However, the implementation of this requirement is clearly discriminatory. While imported products have to comply with the labelling requirements before importing is authorized, domestic products are not subject to this strict requirement. According to a local expert, domestic producers, particularly in the wet market, do not generally attach any label or food packaging (i.e. do not follow the requirements stipulated by the relevant laws and regulations). In addition, only rarely does the Indonesian supervision authority check compliance with the halal labelling requirement in wet markets and non-official slaughterhouses. Brazil takes no issue with halal certification and labelling. It is concerned with the fact that Indonesia accords treatment less favorable to imported products.

IV.   LEGAL CLAIMS

1.   Claims related to border measures which create trade restrictions

36.   Indonesia adopts several measures which prohibit and/or restrict the importation of the products at issue. These measures, combined and individually, impose a general ban on the Brazilian products in violation of Article XI:1 of the GATT 1994 and Article 4.2 of the Agreement on Agriculture (AoA). Indonesia's import licensing procedures also amount to a non-automatic licensing regime whose application and administration causes trade-restrictive effects on imports in violation of Article 3.2 of the Agreement on Import Licensing Procedures (ILA).

1.1.   Relevant legal standard

(a)   Article XI:1 of the GATT 1994

37.   Article XI:1 encompasses "prohibitions" or "restrictions" which are made effective through "quotas", "import or export licenses" or any "other measures". The Panel in *India – Quantitative Restrictions* (para. 5.129) said that "the text of Article XI:1 is very broad in scope, providing for a general ban on import or export restrictions or prohibitions 'other than duties, taxes or other charges'" and "the term 'restriction' is also broad, as seen in its ordinary meaning, which is 'a limitation on action, a limiting condition or regulation'".

38.   In light of this broad scope, the fact that a measure does not totally prevent the imports or does not encompass the application of prohibited additional duties does not mean *per se* that there is no violation of that provision. The Appellate Body has indicated that the scope of Article XI:1 includes measures through which a prohibition or restriction is produced or becomes operative. Likewise, a violation of Article XI:1 may occur even when there is no specific threshold established limiting imports or exports. Actually, Article XI:1 does not require a showing of the measure's effects on trade volumes. A Member's regulation establishing, directly or indirectly, a "positive list" or certain binding "intended uses" would, in this sense, qualify as a quantitative restriction.

39.   A number of panels have considered the reference to "other measures" in Article XI:1 as a "broad residual category" which encompasses different types of measures instituted or maintained by a WTO Member with the ability to prohibit or restrict the importation of products. This broad category would encompass unwritten measures as well. In *Argentina – Import Measures* (para 6.248), the Panel found that the Trade-Related Requirements (TRRs measure), imposed by Argentina through the combined effect of different measures, fell within the meaning of "other measures", as provided for in Article XI:1 of the GATT 1994.

(b)   Article 4.2 of the Agreement on Agriculture

40.   Article 4.2 of the AoA establishes that Members "must not continue to apply measures covered by Article 4.2 from the date of entry into force of the WTO Agreement" ("maintain"), "must not introduce new measures 'of the kind' that it has not had in place in the past" ("resort to"), and "may not, at some later stage after the entry into force of the WTO, re-enact measures prohibited by Article 4.2 ("revert to"). The footnote 1 of Article 4.2 provides examples of these measures: quantitative import restrictions, variable import levies, minimum import prices, discretionary import licensing, non-tariff measures maintained through state-trading enterprises, voluntary export restraints and similar border measures other than ordinary customs duties. Brazil finds relevant the guidance of previous jurisprudence on the scope of the following terms: "quantitative import restrictions", "discretionary import licensing", and "similar border measures other than ordinary customs duties".

41.   With regard to the meaning of "quantitative import restrictions", the Panel in *Turkey – Rice* (para 7.120) considered that measures that affect the quantities of product that can be imported undoubtedly qualify as a quantitative import restriction, even when this effect is caused by the "lack of transparency and lack of predictability" of a Member's measure. The Panel in *Turkey – Rice* (para 7.133) also interpreted the expression "discretionary import licensing" as encompassing "the discretionary use by authorities in an importing country of the concession, or refusal to grant, a particular document which is necessary for the importation of a good, as an instrument to administer trade." As for the meaning of "similar border measures other than ordinary customs duties", the Appellate Body in *Chile – Price Band System* (para. 227) explained that an

inconsistency with Article 4.2 can be established when it is possible to identify border measures similar to the measures explicitly identified in footnote 1. The border measures listed in footnote 1 all "have in common the object and effect of restricting the volumes, and distorting the prices of imports of agricultural products in ways different from the ways that ordinary customs duties do". As the function of Article 4.2 and footnote 1 is "to enhance market access for agricultural products",[1] any measure which has the object and effect of restricting market access, limiting import volumes and distorting the prices of imports would be inconsistent with Article 4.2 of the AoA.

(c)   Article 3.2 of the Agreement on Import Licensing Procedures

42.   Article 1.1 of the ILA defines import licensing as the administrative procedures through which a business operator submits an import application or other documentation (other than that required for customs purposes) to the relevant administrative body as a prior condition for importation. Article 1.2 provides the general principle that should inform any licensing procedure: "Members shall ensure that the administrative procedures used to implement import licensing regimes are in conformity with the relevant provisions of GATT 1994 ... with a view to preventing trade distortions that may arise from an inappropriate operation of those procedures". This principle is also confirmed by Article 1.3 of ILA, which establishes a requirement that the rules for import licensing shall be neutral in "application and administered in a fair and equitable manner".

43.   The ILA also regulates two types of licensing procedures: automatic and non-automatic. Automatic import licensing is a procedure where approval of the application is granted in all cases, which means that the administrative authorities have no discretion to decide whether to grant or not the license. A non-automatic licensing regime is defined by exclusion, which means that in this case the importing country has the discretion to grant or not the import license. Normally, non-automatic licensing procedures are used when there is a restrictive condition in place on the imports, such as tariff rate quotas (TRQs), which gives rise to imports controls.

44.   Besides complying with the general principles established in Articles 1.2 and 1.3, Article 3.2 of the ILA provides, in relation to non-automatic licensing, that Members shall not establish licensing procedures that impose additional restrictions to those already caused by the underlying measure it implements. In order to assess a violation of Article 3.2, it is necessary to show a "decline in market share" and "a causal relationship between the licensing procedures and the trade distortion"[2] Moreover, Article 3.2 of ILA requires that the non-automatic licensing procedures shall not be more administratively burdensome than absolutely necessary to administer the measure they are used to implement.

---

[1]   Appellate Body Report, *Chile – Price Band System (21.5)*, para. 215.
[2]   Appellate Body Report, *EC – Poultry*, paras. 126-127.

Thus, the determination of this "measure" is crucial for the assessment of whether it is more burdensome or not than necessary in the context of this provision.

1.2   Legal analysis

(a)   The general prohibition is a border restriction inconsistent with Article XI:1 of the GATT 1994 and Article 4.2 of the Agreement on Agriculture

45.   Brazil submits that the combined effect of several different individual measures adopted by Indonesia in relation to chicken meat and chicken products amounts to a general prohibition on the importation of these products from Brazil. Combined, these measures constitute "prohibitions or restrictions other than duties, taxes or other charges made effective through quotas, import or export licenses or other measures" within the meaning of Article XI:1 of the GATT 1994. Indonesia has relentlessly created several obstacles to impede the importation of the products at issue through a comprehensive assortment of combined measures which established an institutional and procedural "wall" that has totally banned the importation of Brazilian chicken meat and chicken products. These measures reflect Indonesia's general policy objective of protecting the local production of chicken meat and chicken products in order to achieve self-sufficiency.

46.   In *Argentina – Import Measures,* the Panel and the Appellate Body dealt with a similar situation. The Panel established a framework of analysis in order to assess whether Argentina's unwritten measure had a limiting effect on imports and were affecting the competitive opportunities protected by Article XI:1. Firstly, it established that the measure at issue restricted market access. Secondly, that it created uncertainty as to an applicant's ability to import. Thirdly, the Panel concluded that the measure prevented companies to import as much as they desired or needed without regard to their export performance. Finally, it imposed a significant burden on importers that was unrelated to their normal importing activity.

47.   The Indonesian general prohibition on Brazilian imports of chicken meat and chicken products meets all these criteria. Indonesia only authorizes the importation of products specifically referred to in a "positive list" that does not include all the products at issue. And, even so, this importation shall only take place in case of insufficiency of local production and for very specific intended uses, which clearly restrict market access conditions. Market access is also limited by the fact that Indonesia has unduly delayed the approval of a health certificate that would allow Brazilian exports. Additionally, imports of chicken meat and chicken products are subject to a set of restrictive import licensing procedures that have created uncertainty to importers and imposed on them a significant burden which is unrelated to other importing controls, making importations extremely difficult. For all these reasons, the general prohibition on imports is inconsistent with Article XI:1 of the GATT 1994.

48.   The Panels in *India – Quantitative Restrictions* (paras. 5.241 – 5.242) and *Korea – Various Measures on Beef* (para 762) established that a measure that had been found to violate Article XI:1 was also to be considered in violation of Article 4.2 of the AoA, to the extent it applies to agricultural products. All the products at issue are undoubtedly covered by the AoA. Therefore Brazil submits that Indonesia's general prohibition on the importation of chicken meat and chicken products is also inconsistent with Article 4.2 of the AoA.

49.   Should the Panel opt to carry an independent analysis of Article 4.2, Brazil contends that the general prohibition clearly imposes a "quantitative import restriction" within the meaning of that provision. Combined, the individual measures adopted by Indonesia have the object and effect of restricting the volumes and distorting the prices of imports of agricultural products in ways different from the ways that ordinary customs duties do in the sense of the Appellate Body's understanding in *Chile – Price Band System*. Due to this general prohibition, Brazil has not been able to export chicken to Indonesia since 2009.

50.   In the case Indonesia's general prohibition is not found by the Panel to constitute a "quantitative import restriction", it still constitute a "similar border measure other than ordinary customs duties" within the meaning of footnote 1 of Article 4.2, as it has "characteristics in common with a quantitative import restriction" and limit opportunities for importation of the products at issue.

51.   Indonesia argued that to demonstrate a violation of Article 4.2 of the AoA, the complainant has the burden of establishing that the measure is not justified under Article XX of the GATT 1994 ("or other general, non-agriculture-specific provisions of the GATT").

52.   Brazil is puzzled by Indonesia's reasoning. The Appellate Body jurisprudence confirms exactly the opposite, i.e. that the burden to establish an affirmative defense under Article XX belongs to the respondent. Brazil fails to see how the nature of Article XX would be transformed from an affirmative defense (the burden of which lies with the respondent) into something else (whose inexistence the complainant should prove). Brazil is not aware of a single instance, in more than 20 years of WTO litigation and almost 70 years of dispute settlement including the GATT years, where the burden of proof under Article XX has been reversed from the responding party to the complainant. More broadly, Brazil ignores examples of panels or the Appellate Body requiring from a party – either party – to prove a negative, as Indonesia suggests Brazil is required to do. The reason is simple: it is a general principle of law that the party arguing the affirmative of a proposition has the burden to prove the basis and content of such proposition.

53.   Article 4.2 of the AoA requires the complainant to establish that the respondent maintains a measure of the kind which has been required to be converted into ordinary customs duties, such as, inter alia, quantitative import restrictions. It would be then to the respondent to demonstrate that the relevant measure is not maintained under any GATT exception. In the present dispute,

Brazil has established that Indonesia maintains restrictions on imports of chicken meat and chicken products covered by Article 4.2. Indonesia has never argued, much less demonstrated, that this measure is justified under Article XX of the GATT 1994 or any other general, non-agriculture-specific provisions of the GATT 1994, and Brazil has no information to the effect that this might be the case.

(b)   The individual measures are each a border restriction inconsistent with Article XI:1 of the GATT 1994 and Article 4.2 of the Agreement on Agriculture

(i)   Positive list

54.   Article XI:1 covers any measures which institute or maintain a "prohibition or restriction other than duties, taxes or other charges on the importation of any product". The impossibility of importation of the products not listed amounts to an import ban. Through the positive list, Indonesia maintains a prohibition other than "duties, taxes or other charges" equivalent to a zero quota which is incompatible with Article XI:1 of the GATT 1994.

55.   The positive list also amounts to a "quantitative import restriction" or a "similar border measure other than ordinary customs duties" and is inconsistent with Article 4.2 of the AoA. This measure undoubtedly contributes to restrict the volume of imports, to limit the quantities of the product that can be imported. Actually, it has prevented all imports of Brazilian chicken cuts and other prepared or preserved chicken meat, which constitutes the extreme type of "quantitative import restriction" prohibited by Article 4.2.

56.   The Panels in *India – Quantitative Restrictions* and *Korea – Various Measures on Beef* established that a measure that had been found to violate Article XI:1 was also to be considered in violation of Article 4.2 of the AoA to the extent it applies to agricultural products. Therefore, the positive list is inconsistent with Article 4.2 of the AoA.

57.   Should the Panel opt to carry out an independent analysis of Article 4.2, Brazil contends that this measure clearly imposes a "quantitative import restriction" within the meaning of that provision, as it has the object and effect of restricting the volumes, and distorting the prices of imports of agricultural products in ways different from the ways that ordinary customs duties do. In the case the positive list is not found to constitute a "quantitative import restriction", it constitutes a "similar border measure other than ordinary customs duties" within the meaning of footnote 1 of Article 4.2, as it has characteristics in common with a quantitative import restriction and limits the opportunities for importation.

58.   During the Panel's proceedings, Indonesia argued that the positive list requirement no longer exits. Brazil submits that the amendments introduced simply allow Indonesian authorities the discretionary power to determine which chicken products could receive a MoA Recommendation and a MoT Import

Approval. They do not ensure access to all types of chicken meat and chicken products, as required by Article XI:1 of the GATT 1994 and Article 4.2. In addition, the new pieces of legislation do not provide any guidance for importers in relation to what is to be regarded as "the requirements of safe, healthy, wholesome and halal". These changes not only kept in place the positive list, but also introduced new discretionary elements in the issuance of the import license.

(ii)   Intended use

59.   According to Indonesia's legislation, the chicken meat and chicken products that can be imported into Indonesia can only be destined to very specific uses. This measure has an important "limiting effect" on imports that falls squarely in the ambit of Article XI:1. As recognized by the Panel in *Colombia – Ports of Entry* (para. 7.240) any measures that have "implications on the competitive situation of an importer", creating uncertainties, affecting investment plans or restricting market access for imports is under the scope of this provision.

60.   As the Panel in *China – Raw Materials* (para 7.1081) established, to be considered a restriction it is not even necessary that the measure has an actual impact on trade flows. The very potential to limit trade is sufficient to constitute a restriction within the meaning of Article XI:1. Moreover, since this restriction is not applied for domestic products, by its very design and structure, this measure prevents "whole chicken, fresh or frozen" to have the same competitive opportunities than those granted to the domestic like products.

61.   The limitation on the intended uses, as well as the sanctions imposed for breaches of the original uses registered in the Recommendation, impose a limiting condition which adversely affects the market access to imported products in violation of Article XI:1.

62.   This restriction also amounts to a "quantitative import restriction" and is inconsistent with Article 4.2 of the AoA, as it contributes "to restrict the volume of imports" by limiting the quantities of product that can be imported, which is in contradiction of the very purposes of Article 4.2 of improving market access to agriculture products.

63.   In the case Indonesia's restriction on the intended use is not found to be a "quantitative import restriction", it still constitutes a "similar border measure other than ordinary customs duties" within the meaning of footnote 1 of Article 4.2 of the AoA, as it has "characteristics in common with a quantitative import restriction" and limits the opportunities for imports.

(iii)   Indonesia's restrictive import licensing procedures

64.   Several elements of the Indonesian import licensing regime impose unduly restrictions on the importation of chicken meat and chicken products. The positive list and the intended use requirements have already been demonstrated above to violate Article XI:1 of the GATT 1994 and Article 4.2 of the AoA. Brazil addresses below the negative effects of the limited application

windows, the short validity periods and the fixed license terms of the MoA Import Recommendation and the MoT Import Approval on the competitive opportunities for imports.

65.   Indonesia imposes limited (and short) application windows for importers to obtain authorization to import. Since the validity period itself of the Recommendations is also very limited (only 4 months), the importer has to apply for new Recommendations 3 times per year, at every new application window.

66.   Even with less than abundant factual evidence on how this system operates in practice, due to the *de facto* import ban on Brazilian products, there is no doubt that the limited application windows and validity periods have restricting effects on imports. Firstly, importers are not allowed to submit an application whenever a business opportunity occurs. Secondly, the system prevents, in practice, exports during the beginning of each validity period, as import transactions can only be carried out after the issuance of the MoA Import Recommendation and the MoT Import Approval. Considering also that shipments have to reflect exactly the terms of both authorizations, shipping operations can only be made after the commencement of the short 4-month validity period. For Brazil, this has a particular limiting effect, as the whole export procedures from Brazil to Indonesia are estimated to take on average 100 days, limiting the access to the Indonesian market to basically 20 days. In sum, there is a "dead zone" comprising most of the 4-month validity period during which no product can enter the Indonesian market. This implies also that exporters will not be able to dispatch more than one shipment of the products at each validity period.

67.   This limiting effect is aggravated by the fact that both authorizations have fixed terms. Once those documents are issued, no changes or amendments are allowed. By the time the importers apply for these authorizations, all information related to the covered transactions has to be precisely defined in advance, what is not in accordance with market practices. The importer who fails to comply with these "fixed license terms" is subject to several sanctions and its exports will be refused at the entry port. As no adjustments in the terms of the licensing can be made to respond to new business opportunities during the validity period, this requirement also impedes the importers to have the necessary flexibility to respond to changes in market conditions, thereby imposing a severe limitation on imports.

68.   Based on the findings in *Argentina – Import Measures*, Brazil submits that these aspects of the import licensing regime (limited application windows and validity periods, and fixed license terms) violate Article XI:1 because they (a) unduly restrict market access for Brazilian products; (b) create uncertainty as to an applicant's ability to import, which depends on the issuance of the import licenses to take all other necessary steps related to importation and also carry them out within the short 4-month validity period; and (c) impose a significant burden on importers that is unrelated to their normal importing activity.

69.   These elements of Indonesia's import licensing regime, together with the positive list, the intended use and the discretionary aspect of the import licensing regime also operate as a quantitative import restriction in the sense of footnote 1 of Article 4.2, as they represent a severe restriction on the volume of Brazilian exports, in blatant contradiction with the main objective of that agreement which is to enhance market access for agricultural products.

70.   In the case these aspects of Indonesia's license regime are not found to constitute a "quantitative import restriction", they still constitute a "similar border measure other than ordinary customs duties" within the meaning of footnote 1, as they are similar to a quantitative import restriction in a manner inconsistent with Article 4.2.

71.   Moreover, some requirements of Indonesia's import licensing regime, by their very design, encompass "the discretionary use by authorities of the concession or refusal to grant the documents required" for importation, such as those related to: (i) a letter of recommendation from provincial livestock services office; (ii) supervision on the compliance of veterinary requirements; and (iii) the stipulation of the "amount" to be imported per Business Player. As interpreted by the Panel in *Turkey-Rice*, these requirements fall squarely into the definition of "discretionary import licensing" of footnote 1 of Article 4.2.

72.   If the Panel does not consider these requirements as a "discretionary import licensing" under footnote 1, they still constitute a "similar border measure other than ordinary customs duties", as they are similar to discretionary import licensing within the meaning of footnote 1. For all the reasons above, Brazil submits that the aspects mentioned above of Indonesia's import licensing regime are inconsistent with Article 4.2 of the Agreement on Agriculture.

(iv)   Restrictions on the transportation of imported products

73.   As mentioned above, the transportation of carcass, meat and/or processed products shall be "conducted directly from the country of origin to the port of discharge within the territory of Indonesia". If the transportation is not straight to Indonesia or, by any reason (including *force majeure* events), it is necessary to stop in a third country or port before it arrives at the Indonesian port, then the products will not be allowed to be imported.

74.   This restriction has a clear "limiting effect" on the importation of the products at issue. Due to the long distance between Brazil and Indonesia, the vessels need at least one stop in a third country or port before going to the indicated port of entry in Indonesia. Since there are no direct vessel lines from Brazil to Indonesia, this requirement amounts to a virtual ban to Brazilian products. Even if it were possible to export from Brazil directly to Indonesia, this direct transportation requirement would largely increase the transportation costs of the Brazilian product and thus "discourage importation" which, according to the findings of the Panel in *Argentina – Import Measures*, is inconsistent with Article XI:1 of GATT 1994.

75.   This measure also clearly operates as a "quantitative import restriction" within the meaning of Article 4.2, as the costs and logistics involved in this direct transportation requirement discourages exports from distant countries, contributing, thus, to restrict the volume of imports. As Brazilian exports to Indonesia would take at least 100 days and would necessarily pass through third country ports, this requirement could not be fulfilled by Brazilian exporters, amounting to a complete ban of imports of Brazilian products in the Indonesian market, which cannot be justified under the Agreement on Agriculture.

76.   In the case Indonesia's direct transportation requirement is not found to be a "quantitative import restriction", it still constitutes a "similar border measure other than ordinary customs duties" within the meaning of footnote 1 of Article 4.2, as it has "characteristics in common with a quantitative import restriction" and limits opportunities for importation of chicken meat and chicken products. The Indonesian direct transportation requirement is inconsistent with the agricultural market access obligation of Article 4.2.

77.   During the Panel's proceedings, Indonesia has suggested that "direct" does not have its ordinary meaning, but may be used in the same manner as it is used in the airline industry. A direct flight is one that may make stops and pick up additional passengers but the original passengers do not leave the plane. Also, this requirement should be read in the context of the other provisions in the same Article, which would suggest that transit is, in fact, allowed.

78.   Firstly, the plain reading of Article 19(a) of MoA Regulation 34/2016 does not support the conclusion that transit would be allowed by the Indonesian authorities. There is not a logical connection (or any connection at all) identified in the specified provision that infers that the direct transportation requirement must be interpreted together with the provisions that regulate quarantine. This generates uncertainty to exporters and economic operators, as they may not have a legal remedy should their exports be prevented from entering Indonesia because they did not travel a direct route. Secondly, the way Indonesia has described its direct transportation requirement, as a flight that "makes stops and pick up additional passengers but the original passengers do not leave the plane", seems to imply that transshipment is not included in Indonesia's definition of transit. If this is the case, then the restrictions to transshipment is also a quantitative restriction inconsistent with Article XI:1 and 4.2 of the AoA. Finally, even if transit (and transshipment) is allowed in practice, the legal uncertainties generated by the murky language of Regulation Article 19(a) of MoA Regulation 34/2016 also amount to a quantitative restriction inconsistent with those Articles.

(c)   **Indonesia's import licensing procedures impose a border restriction inconsistent with the obligations under the Agreement on Import Licensing Procedures**

79.   Brazil takes issue with the following measures that restrict/prohibit imports of chicken meat and chicken products: (i) positive list of products allowed to be imported; (ii) intended uses; (iii) limited (and short) application

periods and validity periods of the MoA Import Recommendation and MoT Import Approvals; (iv) fixed license terms; and (v) discretionary import licensing. In addition of breaching Article XI:1 of the GATT 1994 and Article 4.2 of the AoA, these measures are also inconsistent with Article 3.2 of the ILA.

80.   The Panel in *EC – Bananas III* defined the two requirements that must be met in order to determine whether import licensing procedures are within the scope of Article 1.1 of the ILA: (i) the procedures should require the submission of an application or other documentation to the relevant administrative body; and (ii) the submission of an application or other documentation shall be a prior condition for importation.

81.   The Indonesian procedures meet the two criteria. Firstly, in order to obtain a MoA Import Recommendation and a MoT Import Approval, the importer must, among other steps, submit applications to different administrative bodies. Secondly, the submission of the application and the other required documents for the MoA Import Recommendation and MoT Import Approval are clearly a condition for the importation of the products at issue into Indonesia. Both applications are a prior condition for importation.

82.   The ILA allows for two types of licensing procedures: (i) automatic import licensing and (ii) non-automatic import licensing. Any licensing procedure that is not granted automatically or is subject to different limitations to apply and obtain a license should be considered a non-automatic licensing regime falling under the purview of Article 3.2 of ILA.

83.   The specific features of Indonesia's import licensing procedures, such as the limited application windows, short validity periods, fixed license terms, the positive list, the intended use requirements, are sufficient to demonstrate that import recommendations and approvals cannot qualify as an automatic procedure, as they are not "granted in all cases". Indonesia itself recognizes that its licensing procedures are aimed at addressing policy concerns (halal and sanitary requirements) what would suggest that such procedures are non-automatic. Also some aspects of this regime for chicken meat and chicken products are discretionary. Therefore, Indonesia's import licensing requirements are not automatic.

84.   In this context, and according to Article 3.2 of the ILA, to be consistent with WTO Agreements, the non-automatic procedures should be related to the implementation of a permissible trade restrictive measure; should not have trade restrictive effects additional to those caused by the imposition of the restrictive measure; should also correspond in scope and duration to the measure they are used to implement and should be no more administratively burdensome than absolutely necessary to administer the measure.

85.   This is not the case in Indonesia. Indonesia's import licensing procedures are not connected to a permissible restrictive measure. There is no persuasive connection between halal and sanitary concerns with the positive list requirement, the intended use requirement, the limited and short application periods and validity periods, the fixed license terms and the discretionary import

licensing procedures. Moreover, as Indonesia itself recognized there is a range of pre-market procedures in place to ensure that sanitary and halal requirements are fulfilled, such as: desk review to establish the sanitary conditions of the country of origin, import risk analysis, on-site visit inspections on business units and implementation of a halal assurance system, among others. Once these appropriate measures are implemented there are no grounds in WTO rules to submit the importation to the challenged measures.

86.   Even if Indonesia's procedures were applied to administer legitimate restrictions on imports, by its design, structure and operation the regime imposes restrictions on the importation far additional than those that would be required to implement the relevant restriction in violation of Article 3.2 of the ILA. Besides preventing importers from applying for licenses to products not included in the positive list and restricting applications for very limited intended uses, Indonesia prevents importers from obtaining licenses during most part of the year. These restrictions combined with the short validity period and the fixed license terms, imposes an unduly additional restriction on trade that severely affects Brazil's exports. Overall, there is a clear "causal relationship" between the licensing procedures and the fact that Brazil (or any other country in the world) has not exported chicken to Indonesia since 2009. Also, as there is no underlying permissible measure, the procedures do not correspond "in scope and duration" to any "measure" they are supposed to implement as required by the second sentence of Article 3.2. Finally, the lack of transparency and predictability of Indonesia's multi-layered import licensing procedures are more administratively burdensome than necessary to administer import procedures. Even assuming *in arguendo* that the controls were justified, the operation of the procedures is far from being simple, neutral in application and administered in a fair and equitable manner as required by Article 1 and 3.2 of the ILA.

87.   In respect to the standard of "no more administratively burdensome than absolutely necessary" in Article 3.2 of the ILA, Brazil understands that it is more stringent than that contained in Article XX of the GATT 1994. Firstly, different from the necessity test under the chapeau of Article XX, the second sentence of Article 3.2 of the ILA refers to burden ("no more burdensome"), and not to trade-restrictive. The trade-restrictiveness of the licensing procedures is examined under the first sentence of Article 3.2, which means that the second sentence must add to the obligations already contained under the first sentence. Secondly, the second part of the second sentence of Article 3.2 of the ILA contains the word "absolutely", which further limits the imposition of any burden on WTO Members in connection with the implementation of non-automatic licensing procedures.

88.   Similarly, the standard under Article 3.2 of the ILA is also not analogous to Article 2.2 of the TBT Agreement, which provides that "technical regulations shall not be more trade-restrictive than necessary to fulfil a legitimate objective taking account of the risks non-fulfilment would create". Under Article 2.2 of the TBT Agreement, the focus is on the proportionality between the trade-restrictiveness of the technical regulation (the measure) and the risks it seeks to

mitigate. By contrast, Article 3.2 of the ILA focuses on the burden of the implementation of the measure, not on its trade-restrictiveness. Therefore, even in situations where trade-restrictive or distortive effects cannot be substantiated, a non-automatic licensing regime can still violate Article 3.2 of the ILA if it is more burdensome than necessary.

89.   Indonesia also argued that of the five elements of its import licensing regime challenged by Brazil under Article 3.2 of the ILA, only the limited application and validy periods would fall under this agreement. The positive list and intended use do not fall under the ILA because they are substantive, rather than procedural import licensing requirements.

90.   Although the ILA distinguishes between administrative procedures (import licensing) and the substantive rules (the measures) these procedures are meant to administer, Brazil considers that this distinction does not apply in the present case. The dividing line between substantive and procedural requirements is somewhat blurred in relation to the challenged elements of Indonesia's import licensing regime. For instance, the positive list requirement establishes a quantitative restriction on the importation and could be considered a "substantive measure", though not permissible under WTO rules. Yet, it also obliges, as a prior condition for importation, the importer to submit documentation attesting that the products are included in positive list. In other words, there is also an administrative procedure attached to the implementation of the positive list requirement that falls squarely under the scope of the ILA.

91.   What makes it difficult to distinguish between procedural and substantive requirements is the fact that there is no clear permissible measure Indonesia's import licensing regime is meant to implement. Even if one considers the positive list requirement as the measure the administrative procedures are meant to implement, the question then becomes whether this requirement is permissible: as the positive list is in violation of Article XI:1 and Article 4.2, it cannot constitute a measure within the meaning of Article 3.2 of the ILA.

92.   Due to this specific feature of Indonesia's import licensing regime, there are several instances of grey zones where the requirements could be characterized both as substantive and procedural, and, in this sense, not only do they violate the substantive provisions of WTO Agreements, but also pertain to procedural provisions regulated by the ILA.

2.   Claims related to discriminatory treatment

2.1.   Relevant legal standard

93.   Article III:4 of the GATT 1994 enshrines the basic national treatment obligation which states that internal measures must not be applied so as to afford protection to domestic production. Viewed as a cornerstone of the WTO multilateral trading system, it encompasses the obligation to provide equality of competitive opportunities for both imported and like domestic products.

94.   The Appellate Body in *Korea – Various Measures on Beef* provided a reliable guidance to determine the existence of a violation of Article III:4. It ruled that three elements must be satisfied: (i) the imported and domestic products at issue must be "like products"; (ii) the measure at issue must be a "law, regulation, or requirement affecting their internal sale, offering for sale, purchase, transportation, distribution or use"; and (iii) the imported products are accorded "less favourable" treatment than that accorded to like domestic products.

95.   In what regards the first element, there is a reiterated understanding in WTO jurisprudence that if origin is the only factor distinguishing between imported and domestic products, there is no need to conduct a full likeness analysis using the traditional criteria set out in the GATT panel report in *Border Tax Measures*. In these cases, in which the foreign origin of the imported product is the sole distinctive element, the imported and domestic products are considered to be "like" for purposes of Article III:4, and the Panel need not go over the details of the competitive relationship between them.

96.   As for the second element, it must be established whether the measure could be viewed as a "law, regulation or requirement". Panels have agreed on the definition of "regulation" as any provision which is mandatory and applies across the board.[3] However, the core of the analysis is on the laws which "affect" the specific transactions, activities and uses mentioned in the provision. Thus, the word "affecting" is central to the analysis because it makes the link between the type of government action and the transactions, activities and uses relating to the like imported and domestic products in the marketplace.

97.   The Appellate Body has ruled that the word "affecting" has a broad scope of application and interpreted it as a measure which has "an effect on" something.[4] This understanding indicates that any law, regulation etc. that has "an effect on" the internal sale, offering for sale, purchase, transportation, distribution or use of the like products falls within the scope of Article III:4. Additionally, the word "affecting" has also been interpreted to cover not only measures which *directly* regulate the specific activities listed in Article III:4 but also any laws or regulations which might adversely modify the conditions of competition or create incentives or disincentives between the domestic and imported products.[5]

98.   With regard to the third element, the Appellate Body decided that to determine whether or not imported products are treated "less favourably" than like domestic products, it would be necessary to assess whether a measure

---

[3]   Panel Report, *China – Publications Audiovisual Products*, para. 7.1513. Panel Reports, *China – Auto Parts*, para. 7.239 (citing: GATT Panel Report on *Canada – FIRA*, para. 5.5; Panel Report, *India – Autos*, para. 7.181).

[4]   Appellate Body Report, *US – FSC (Article 21.5 – EC)*, para. 209-210.

[5]   Panel Reports, *China – Auto Parts*, para. 7.251; Panel Report, *China – Publications and Audiovisual Products*, para. 7.1450.

modifies the conditions of competition in the relevant market to the detriment of imported products.[6]

2.2. Legal Analysis

(a) The restrictions on the intended uses violates Article III:4

99. As previously detailed, MoA Regulation 58/2015 imposes restrictions on the possible uses of imported chicken meat and chicken products, while no such restrictions are imposed on domestic like products. Considering that the origin of products is the only distinguishing element for the imposition of this restriction, imported and domestic chicken meat and chicken products are "like" for the purposes of Article III:4 and that the Panel do not need to analyze the details of the competitive relationship between them.

100. Indonesia insists that imported frozen or chilled chicken and domestic fresh chicken are not like products and could not have the same treatment. Domestic products are offered for sale fresh while products imported from Brazil would necessarily be frozen. Brazilian chicken could not be offered for sale in markets not equipped with cold-chain systems, as Indonesia would not be able to ensure compliance with its sanitary and halal requirements.

101. Indonesia's arguments are groundless. Article 31(1) of MoA Regulation 58/2015 makes no reference whatsoever to "fresh", "frozen" or "chilled" products. This provision is applicable to all imported carcass and meat products, and the only distinctive criterion to restrict products to certain intended uses is the foreign origin of the product. Based on this understanding, no further analysis should be required to establish the likeness between imported and domestic chicken meat and chicken products, and there is a clear discrimination in the conditions of competition of imported and domestic like products in place in Indonesia.

102. However, if the Panel considers that a specific likeness analysis is deemed necessary, the determination of likeness under Article III:4 of the GATT is, fundamentally, a determination about the nature and extent of a competitive relationship between and among products. The application of the traditional four criteria of the GATT's *Border Tax Adjustments* is also not mandatory but simply a useful framework.

103. Indonesia has not provided any evidence to refute the assumption that the imported and domestic products would compete in the marketplace. As a matter of fact, Indonesia appears to agree with this argument when it affirmed that frozen-thawed chicken meat is similar to fresh meat once thawed and could be thus offered for sale as fresh meat after being thawed. Although limiting the

---

[6]   Appellate Body Report, *Korea - Various Measures on Beef*, para. 137; Appellate Body Report, *US – Tuna II (Mexico)*, para. 214.

discussion to fresh and thawed chicken meat, Indonesia concedes that the consumer would not, in practice, distinguish them.

104. First of all, the difference between the imported and domestic products at issue would depend only on the temperature conditions to which each one was subjected, something that does not change the relevant properties of the product. Secondly, even products that may present certain differences in physical characteristics, they may still be considered 'like' if the nature and extent of their competitive relationship justifies such a determination. Thirdly, freezing is a process capable of retaining the characteristics of chicken meat and chicken products, guaranteeing their quality and sanity and cannot be used to disqualify the likeness of the products at issue.

105. If Indonesia considers the restrictions as sanitary measures, Brazil understands that Indonesia would have to indicate what is its appropriate level of protection and whether a risk assessment was carried out to establish that the consumption of frozen or chilled products poses a higher risk to human health than fresh chicken. It has clearly not done so, limiting itself to assert, without scientific basis, that the freezing process may affect the basic characteristics of the product and therefore the analysis of likeness.

106. Finally, imported and domestic chicken are capable of serving the same or similar end-uses. Indonesia's arguments that its consumers would not perceive imported and domestic product as the same product because they could not be sure of the halalness of frozen or chilled product or of the quality of the products is simply self-serving and devoid of any credibility. Halal-consuming countries are amongst the major importers of halal frozen chicken. This discussion of whether or not there would be a risk of deceptive practices for the Indonesian consumer does not appear to square with the established analysis of likeness. This is a question of consumer information that could be easily solved, among other measures, by a label that would indicate that the imported chicken had been "previously frozen".

107. To determine whether the measure at issue falls within the scope of Article III:4, it is also necessary to establish whether it corresponds to "laws, regulations and requirements affecting internal sale, offering for sale, purchase, transportation, distribution or use". MoA Regulation 58/2015 is a legislation issued by Indonesia's Ministry of Agriculture, which is mandatory and applies across the board to all importers of chicken meat and chicken products. Also this restriction have "an effect on" the internal sale, offering for sale, distribution and use of the Brazilian chicken meat and chicken products in Indonesia and adversely modify the conditions of competition, favoring like domestic products. Firstly, it affects the uses available for the imported products. Secondly, it affects the internal sale and offering for sale of Brazilian chicken meat and chicken products. The restriction impedes direct access of consumers to Brazilian products through relevant distribution and retail channels, such as "wet markets", severely restricting the size of the Indonesian market and adversely shifting the balance of commercial opportunities towards like domestic products.

108. This restriction also results in less favourable treatment to imported product as it modifies the conditions of competition and accords like domestic products a *competitive advantage* in the market over like imported products. In *Korea – Various Measures on Beef* the Appellate Body confirmed the Panel's finding that the dual retail system for imported and domestic beef was inconsistent with Article III:4 because it modified the conditions of competition in the Korean food market to the detriment of imported products. The creation of a dual system, which required retailers to choose between the sale of imported or domestic beef, resulted in the sudden cutting off of access to normal distribution outlets, virtually excluding imported beef from the retail distribution channels through which domestic beef had normal access to Korean consumers. The main consequence of these restrictions was the imposition of a drastic reduction of commercial opportunity to reach, and hence to generate sales to, the same consumers served by traditional retail channels for domestic beef.

109. Brazil considers that the "less favourable treatment" under the present dispute is even more serious. Due to the restriction imposed by MoA Regulation 58/2015, even if imports from Brazil were allowed to enter into Indonesia, they could not reach the most important distribution channels in that country, where a the vast majority of food purchase occurs. The huge majority of consumers would not have access to Brazilian products. Thus, Indonesia's restrictions on the intended uses is inconsistent with Article III:4 of the GATT.

(b)   The halal labelling requirements violates Article III:4 of the GATT 1994

110. Brazil has demonstrated that imported and domestic chicken meat and chicken products are "like" because origin is the only distinguishing feature between these products. Brazil also demonstrated, and Indonesia has recognized, that Law 33/2014 and MoA Regulation 58/2015 are a "law, regulation or requirement" within the meaning of Article III:4.

111. Law 33/2014 provides for a five-year grace period for the full compliance with the labelling requirement. Even though this requirement is applicable for both imported and domestic halal products, Indonesian authorities do not conduct consistent surveillance concerning the implementation of halal labelling by domestic suppliers. It is very common for Indonesian consumers to find locally produced chicken meat and chicken products for sale without the halal label. This lack of surveillance is more evident in "wet markets", although it also occurs in other retail distribution channels such as modern markets. Therefore, while domestic products are not subject to strict control procedures, imports of chicken meat and chicken products must comply with the labeling requirements before importing is authorized. Without a halal label, Brazilian chicken meat and chicken products would not be able to access the Indonesian marketplace, even if the production process in Brazil strictly complies with the halal requirements imposed by Indonesia. This discriminatory treatment modifies the conditions of competition in the Indonesian marketplace. Not requiring that domestic like products comply with halal labelling tilts the balance in favour of local suppliers.

3. A measure can violate different WTO provisions simultaneously

Article XI:1 of the GATT and 4.2 of the AoA

112. Indonesia claims that a measure can violate only one WTO provision at a time. It insists that Article XI:1 of the GATT and Article 4.2 of the AoA are mutually exclusive provisions and that only Article 4.2 should apply to the measures at issue, since it is *lex specialis*. It also argues that in the case of Article 4.2 the complainant would have the burden to demonstrate not only that the measure is a restriction but also that is not justified under any of the exceptions in the GATT.

113. It is beyond any reasonable doubt that a measure can be inconsistent with more than one covered agreement simultaneously and that a Member is entitled to request for a panel to make findings on each one of these inconsistencies. The Panel's reasoning in *EC – Bananas III* can provide guidance to the understanding of what "conflict" means, based on the text of the General Interpretative Note to Annex I of the Agreement establishing the WTO. A legal conflict would occur in two situations: (i) first, clashes between obligations in the GATT and in the Annex 1A Agreements, where those obligations are mutually exclusive in the sense that a Member cannot comply with both obligations at the same time, and, second, (ii) when a rule in one agreement prohibits what a rule in another agreement explicitly permits. None of these situations relate to any of the alleged legal conflicts indicated by Indonesia.

114. There is no conflict between these Article XI:1 and 4.2. Actually, a violation of Article XI:1 would also entail a violation of Article 4.2. A measure that has a limiting effect on imports can entail a violation of both Articles. Indonesia attempt to convince the Panel that, differently from Article XI:1, the legal standard of Article 4.2 would require the complainant to bear the burden of showing that the challenged measure is not maintained under any of "other general, non-agriculture-specific provisions of GATT-1994", including its exceptions, such as Article XX, in order to make its prima facie case. Indonesia's construed legal standard not only makes no sense but is also contrary to all previous WTO jurisprudence which has determined that, in the case of affirmative defenses, the burden of proof remains with the party asserting the defense, not the opposite. To understand it otherwise would require the complainant not only to prove that there is a restriction prohibited under Article 4.2 but also that none of the multiple exceptions available in the GATT could justify the inconsistency of the measure at issue. This is simply unreasonable and would mean to prove a negative.

Article XI:1 of the GATT 1994, 4.2 of the AoA and 3.2 of the ILA

115. Indonesia also argues that the general prohibition cannot be, at the same time, incompatible with Article XI:1, Article 4.2 and Article 3.2 of the ILA. In Brazil's view, an import licensing formality or procedure can constitute a violation of Article XI:1 if it has a limiting effect on imports, what would also

entail a violation of Article 4.2, and can also violate Article 3.2 of the ILA. Members are required to administer non-automatic licensing in a manner which does not have additional trade-restrictive or trade-distortive effects on imports than those already caused by the imposition of the restriction itself. Indonesia's import licensing procedures are exactly the kind of measures that violate the first sentence of Article 3.2, as they reinforce the restrictions imposed by the country on the importation of chicken.

116.   The same argument is used by Indonesia in respect to the substantive requirements pertaining to the challenged import licensing regime. However, there are no grounds to consider that a licensing procedure cannot violate at the same time all those three Articles. As a third party has correctly reminded, if a Member imposes a consistent "restriction" through non-automatic licensing procedures, the ILA, including Article 3.2, applies to ensure that the permissible measure is not implemented through an overly restrictive or burdensome licensing procedure. Nevertheless, licensing requirements that in themselves impose a limitation or limiting condition on importation or have a limiting effect on trade also would fall within the scope of Article XI:1 of the GATT. The limiting effect on trade of Indonesia's import licensing regime cannot be disputed as not a single chicken has been able to enter the Indonesian market since 2009.

117.   More specifically, the positive list requirement has an important limiting effect on imports, in violation of both Article XI:1 and Article 4.2. Procedurally, requiring that the importer demonstrate that previous imports have complied with its declared intended use as a prior condition to obtain a new license is a violation of Article 3.2 of the ILA. As there is no permissible measure this requirement implements, any administrative procedure attached to the positive list is necessarily an additional restriction in the sense of Article 3.2 of the ILA. The same is true for the intended use requirement.

118.   As for the limited application windows, the short validity periods and the fixed license terms, Indonesia has not provided any defense to Brazil's claims regarding Article 3.2. It limited itself to say that Brazilian exporters have not obtained the Import Recommendation and Import Approval because they have not satisfied halal requirements. Yet, Indonesia has not explained how the limited application windows, the short validity periods and the fixed license terms are related to the observance of halal requirements. If there is no permissible measure non-automatic import licensing procedures are meant to implement, they are in violation of Article 3.2 of the ILA.

Article XI:1 and Article III:4 of the GATT 1994

119.   Finally, with regard to the intended used requirement, Indonesia argues that this requirement cannot be challenged under both Article III:4 and Article XI:1 of the GATT and that it should be viewed only as an internal measure, not a border measure, due to the alleged application of the Ad Note to Article III. According to Indonesia, although enforced at the border, this requirement applies also to domestic chicken. First, the intended use requirement has

different effects. It affects the process of importation itself: the importer will not have an import license if the imports do not contemplate one of the permitted intended uses. It also affects the conditions of competition once the product has entered the market. After customs clearance, the importer is not allowed to offer for sale the imported products to other distribution and retail channels than those listed in the import license. Therefore, the intended use requirement has different effects and violates both Article X1:1 and III:4. Second, the intended use requirement is not applicable in the same way to the domestic products. A shipment from Brazil to be used in a restaurant in Jakarta could not be directed to a traditional market (or even to another intended use, such as a hotel). However, if the same restaurant denies receiving chicken locally produced, the distributor can redirect it to another buyer, such as a hotel, restaurant or the traditional market. So, even the cold-chain requirement is not applicable in the same way to both imported and domestic products. Since there is not an "equivalent internal requirement", Ad Note to Article III is not applicable to the case. This is further demonstrated by Article 22(1) of MoA Regulation 34/2016 as it now requires importers, when applying for an Import Recommendation, to submit a distribution plan for the imported chicken, which, according to the template annexed to the legislation, shall include in advance information on the type of meat, the quantity, the name and address of the establishments/buyers and the product's price. Brazil considers that the importer is not only limited to the end-uses listed in the legislation but also to a pre-defined distribution plan within the allowed uses, preventing the importer from actually distributing the imported chicken meat and chicken product after the import operation occurs according to the best business offers it may be able to get.

120.   Regardless of the Panel's decision concerning the order of analysis and the exercise of judicial economy, nothing in the WTO rules prevents the Panel from making findings on each one of these inconsistencies challenged by Brazil. This would be particularly important in this case because of the shifting nature of Indonesia's legislation regarding the intended use requirement. In the absence of findings regarding the inconsistency of this measure both as a border measure and as an internal measure, Indonesia could continue to evade its obligations by simply reinforcing in new legislation the particular aspect of the intended used requirement that was not addressed by the Panel.

3.   Claims related to sanitary barriers

3.1.   Relevant legal standard: Article 8 and Annex C(1)(a) of the SPS Agreement

121.   Article 8 of the SPS Agreement provides that Members shall observe the provisions of Annex C in the operation of control, inspection and approval procedures regarding sanitary and phytosanitary measures. Annex C gives shape and content to Article 8 and a violation of the rules of Annex C necessarily entails a violation of Article 8.

122.   The most relevant provision of Annex C in the present dispute is Annex C(1)(a), which determines that "Members shall ensure, with respect to any procedure to check and ensure the fulfilment of sanitary or phytosanitary measures, that" […] "such procedures are undertaken and completed without undue delay".

123.   The relevant aspects in the interpretation of Annex C (1)(a) to be taken into account in the present dispute are (i) the identification of which are the "procedures designed to check and ensure" a sanitary measure; and (ii) the understanding that the term undue delay does not refer exclusively to a "delay", but also to an absence of formal response from the authorities when certain sanitary procedure was initiated before them.

124.   Concerning the first aspect, the term "procedure" is defined in the SPS Agreement in a manner as broad as possible. This interpretation has been upheld in several WTO cases.[7] The main feature to be established when ascertaining whether a certain procedure falls under the purview of Article 8 and Annex C(1)(a) is to determine that it "is aimed at 'checking and ensuring the fulfilment of sanitary or phytosanitary measures', and is undertaken in the context of 'control, inspection, or approval'". While Article 8 and Annex C list certain types of procedures as expressly falling within their ambit, the terms "including" in Article 8, and "include, inter alia", in footnote 7 to Annex C, clarify that the lists are illustrative.

125.   Previous WTO jurisprudence, in analyzing the term "procedures" as used in Annex A(1), upheld the understanding that "procedure" has to be interpreted in a wide sense. The panel report in *US-Animals* (para 7.40), stated that "the reference to 'procedures' in the second sentence of Annex A(1) is broad enough to encompass both procedures of general application as well as the specific implementation of a procedure in a particular instance."

126.   On the basis of these elements, the term "approval procedures" in both Article 8 and Annex C encompass "procedures applied to check and ensure the fulfilment of one or more substantive SPS requirements the satisfaction of which is a prerequisite for the approval to place a product on the market". The negotiation of an "International Veterinary Certificate" clearly constitutes a pre-marketing approval requirement.

127.   Concerning the second aspect, the term "undue delay" does not only refer to a "delay" *stricto sensu*, but also refers to occasions where there is no response at all from a Member's competent authority. This interpretation was clarified by the Panel in *EC – Biotech* (para 4.167), which found that the ordinary meaning of the term "delay" is "(a period of) time lost by inaction or inability to proceed". The requirement in Annex C(1)(b) of the SPS also provides context for this interpretation, particularly regarding the necessity for the competent authoritics

---

[7]   Panel Report, *US – Poultry (China)*, para. 7.363; Appellate Body Report *Australia – Apples*, para. 438; Panel Report, *US – Animals*, para. 7.68

to "promptly examine the completeness of the documentation" and to "inform the applicant in a precise and complete manner of all deficiencies". Moreover, in *EC–Biotech*, the Panel interpreted that "without undue delay" could adequately mean "without an unjustified loss of time". The Panel also stated that "[a]lthough Members are in principle allowed to take the time that is reasonably needed to determine with adequate confidence whether their relevant SPS requirements are fulfilled, they are also required to proceed with their SPS approval procedures as promptly as possible. Therefore, a Member is not allowed to freely decide when it will finish the undertaking and completion of the approval procedures. In cases in which there is a delay, the Member should ensure that it is not excessive or unwarranted and its causes are rightfully justified". Therefore, although possible in practice, a delay must be reasonable and cannot be unjustified and disproportionate. The absence of response naturally represents an unjustified and disproportioned delay in the sense of Article C(1)(a).

3.2 Legal Analysis: The undue delay of Indonesia to negotiate an "International Veterinary Certificate" with Brazil violates Article 8 and Annex C(1)(a)

128. The negotiation of an International Health Certificate is the first step undertaken by countries interested in the trade of animal products, including chicken. It is clear that the negotiation of a valid International Health Certificate is encompassed by the term "approval procedures" referred to by Article 8 and Annex C as it is a procedure "applied to check and ensure the fulfillment of one or more substantive SPS requirements the satisfaction of which is a prerequisite for the approval to place a product on the market".

129. The rule in Annex C(1)(a) determines that the competent sanitary authority must take the necessary steps to ensure that a sanitary procedure initiated before it is concluded. There is no defined deadline in Annex C(1)(a) and that the assessment of "undue delay" should be made on a case-by-case basis. In the present dispute, the complete lack of response after seven years of the first proposal is a clear evidence that Indonesian authorities have unjustifiably delayed the procedures to check and ensure the fulfillment of the sanitary requirements that would allow for the exportation of Brazilian products. By not answering, the Indonesian authorities violated Annex C(1)(a) of the SPS Agreement. Even where a proposal is inaccurate or does not contemplate all the necessary elements required by the Indonesian legislation, Indonesia must give a proper response in order to allow for the corrections and additions necessary. Annex C stems logically from Article 8 of the SPS Agreement. As the two provisions are intertwined, a breach of Annex C(1)(a) entails a breach of Article 8.

130. Indonesia attempted to justify its inaction by arguing that the lack of response is Brazil's own fault: Brazil did not present the appropriate documents and information related to the halal requirements related to two different business units. First, compliance with halal requirements has never been an issue for Brazil, which has had for several years its two main certification bodies duly

approved by Indonesia. Second, halal certification guards no connection with the conclusion of the sanitary procedures required by Indonesia. Halal certification is not a SPS procedure and should not be confounded with a sanitary requirement nor considered in a government-to-government sanitary approval process of an International Health Certificate. Indonesia does not dispute that halal certification is not covered by the scope of the SPS Agreement.

V. INDONESIA'S DEFENSES UNDER ARTICLE XX OF THE GATT

The intended use is not justified under Articles XX (b) and (d) of the GATT

131. Indonesia seeks to justify the intended use requirement under Article XX(b) of the GATT 1994, as it contributes to the protection of human life or health by eliminating the risk of freezing and thawing products for sale to consumers. It sustains that frequent thawing and freezing would increase microbial growth and facilitate product deterioration as this process would "mechanically damage the cell membranes and reduce water-holding capacity". However, there is no meaningful connection between limiting the sale of frozen chicken to places with cold chain facilities and the alleged objective pursued. First of all, if traditional markets have no cold storage, how is it possible that the chicken will be refrozen? Secondly, the freezing process is capable of ensuring that the meat will remain fresh for a longer period, as compared to the meat that has never been frozen. Indonesia would have more reasons to prohibit the sale of fresh chicken in markets without cold storage than prohibiting the sale of frozen chicken. Finally, Indonesia has offered no evidence to support its claims that food safety is the objective of the intended use requirement.

132. In any event, the intended use requirement is clearly not "necessary". There are less trade-restrictive measures which could satisfy Indonesia's appropriate level of protection, such as rules regulating the thawing of frozen chicken to be offered for sale and/or restricting the possibility of refreezing previously thawed chicken for sale in traditional markets. An outright prohibition of the sale of frozen chicken in those venues is in excess of the aim of protecting human life or health due to the alleged "risk of freezing and thawing products". Indonesia's assertions on this subject contradict the actual practice of its government. 9,000 tons of imported frozen meat from the United States was recently offered for sale in Indonesian traditional markets. Indonesia confirmed that the imported meat was sold frozen but did not inform whether it ensured that the products were exclusively kept in cold-chain systems at the points of sale. Given that these systems are normally not available in wet markets, it is improbable that the intended use requirement was duly enforced.

133. Indonesia also alleges that the intended use requirement is provisionally justified under the Article XX (d) because it is designed to secure compliance with Indonesia's laws and regulations on public health (namely, those setting out sanitary requirements), deceptive practices and customs enforcement. Indonesia has failed to provide any evidence that the measure contributes to the

enforcement of any particular law related to food safety. As noted by one of the third parties, there is no basis in the text, structure, or the legislative history of Law 18/2009 and Law 8/1999 to support the claim that this measure was designed to secure compliance with the food safety and consumer protection provisions cited by Indonesia. The recent decision to authorize the sale of imported frozen beef during Ramada at traditional markets demonstrates that the intended use requirement is only a protectionist tool. Similarly, Indonesia has not indicated whether there would not be any less trade-restrictive alternative measures to secure compliance with its laws and regulations. In any event, Indonesia has not demonstrated that the intended use respects the chapeau of Article XX of the GATT 1994.

The positive list is not justified under Article XX (d) of the GATT 1994

134.   Indonesia does not dispute the existence of a prohibition on the importation of chicken cuts. However, it tried to justify this prohibition on the basis of Article XX(d) of the GATT 1994, claiming that it "was necessary to secure compliance with Indonesia's laws and regulations dealing with halal food. According to Indonesia, its main concern has been that certain exporters may try to circumvent Indonesia's halal requirements by sourcing chicken parts from slaughterhouses that do not produce halal chicken, and passing them off as halal.

135.   Indonesia failed to demonstrate that this measure is necessary to secure compliance with its halal requirements. In reality, MoA Regulation 58/2015 (revoked by MoA Regulation 34/2016) and MoT Regulation 05/2016 (as altered by MoT 37/2016) do not impose the same restriction, for instance, in relation to the importation of cuts of lamb and goat, which should also comply with halal requirements. This exception demonstrates that Indonesia itself does not consider it necessary in all cases to restrict imports of cuts of animal products in order to ensure compliance with halal requirements. Moreover, there are less trade-restrictive alternative measures to guarantee the halalness of the products, for example, to implement certification procedures with foreign slaughterhouses seeking to export to Indonesia. Continuous certification procedures – which are a common feature of international trade of food products – would ensure the halalness of the products leaving the slaughterhouses and would also prevent deceptive practices with regard to the compliance with halal requirements. The positive list requirement cannot be justified under paragraph (d) of Article XX.

The limited application and validity periods are not justified under Article XX(d)

136.   Indonesia fraily attempts to justify the limited application and validity period under Article XX(d) of the GATT 1994 as a measure "designed to secure compliance with Indonesia's laws and regulations addressing halal, public health, as well as deceptive practices (consumer protection) and customs enforcement relating to halal and safety". It is difficult to see any connection between the limited application and validity periods with the observance of halal requirements. Moreover, compliance with halal and animal health requirements

can be obtained through much less trade-restrictive measures, such as proper certification procedures and verification, and information on trade flows can easily be obtained through other means.

The fixed license terms are not justified under Article XX (d) of the GATT 1994

137.   According to Indonesia, the fixed license terms "were designed to secure compliance with Indonesia's laws on halal and public health, as well as deceptive practices and customs enforcement relating to halal and food safety". Indonesia based its reasoning on the consideration that, allegedly, the fixed license terms "enable[s] the Government to monitor foreign trade and to facilitate customs enforcement. They provide an estimate of the volume of imports that would enter Indonesia at a particular port and at a given time so that the Government can best allocate its limited resources in order to expedite customs clearance". However, Indonesia had not explained how the fixed license terms bear any relation to the observance of halal or sanitary requirements. Secondly, according to Indonesia, "many of these terms are not as stringent", as "importers may identify more ports than they ultimately use, or higher quantities of import than they ultimately import". If this statement is accurate, one must wonder what actually the purpose of fixing the license terms is. The only purpose they can have is to serve as yet another trade restrictive tool to close the Indonesian market.

The halal labelling is not justified under Article XX of the GATT 1994

138.   Indonesia seeks to justify the implementation of its halal labelling certification procedures under subparagraphs (a) and (d) of Article XX of the GATT 1994. Under Article XX (a), Indonesia argues that "the halal requirements are necessary to protect public morals".

139.   Brazil does not challenge Indonesia's right to establish the halal requirements nor questions the fact that these requirements are necessary to protect its religious beliefs and public morals. As the world's leading exporter of halal chicken, Brazil is fully aware of the importance of respecting the different halal standards adopted by different Muslim countries. As required by Indonesia, halal slaughtering in Brazil is performed by the country's poultry slaughterhouses through manual slaughtering.

140.   Brazil contends that Indonesia did not provide any evidence to justify the "necessity" of the discrimination between domestic and imported chicken meat and chicken products to protect its public morals, as required by Article XX or how this discriminatory treatment contributes to further the public morals of the country. Also, even if it was possible to justify the discriminatory 5-year grace period halal certification and labeling requirements under subparagraph (a) of Article XX, this measure would not pass the test of the chapeau. Indeed, to the extent that the measure is only applicable to imported products, it is on its face a violation of Article III:4 of the GATT 1994.

141.   Furthermore, Indonesia tries to explain that halal labelling would be applicable only to packaged products and, therefore, because domestic chicken meat and chicken products are mainly sold in the traditional markets and are not necessarily packaged like imported products, then the halal label would not be mandatory for the domestic products. However, Indonesia's explanation forgets that Law 33/204 (article 38) does not make any reference with regard to the necessity to attach the halal label only to packaged products. Instead, it provides for three different possibilities to the attachment of the label: (i) in the package of the product; (ii) in a specific part of the product; and/or (iii) in a specific place of the product. That is, according to Indonesia legislation, packaging is not a reason to justify the discriminatory treatment.

142.   The same applies to the defense under paragraph (d) of Article XX. Indonesia has not provided any evidence that the challenged measures contribute to the enforcement of any particular law or regulation. It is not sufficient to simply asserts that "the implementation of halal requirements is 'necessary' to secure compliance with these domestic legal provisions" without providing any evidence or further clarification that would justify the discriminatory treatment against imported products.

VI.   CONCLUSION

143.   Brazil respectfully requests that the Panel find that:

(i)   Indonesia's general prohibition on the importation of chicken meat and chicken products is inconsistent with Article XI:1 of the GATT 1994 and Article 4.2 of the Agreement on Agriculture;

(ii)   Indonesia's prohibition on the importation of chicken cuts and other prepared or preserved chicken meat is inconsistent with Article XI:1 of the GATT 1994 and Article 4.2 of the Agreement on Agriculture;

(iii)   Indonesia's restrictions on the use of imported chicken meat and chicken products is inconsistent with Article XI:1 of the GATT 1994 and Article 4.2 of the Agreement on Agriculture;

(iv)   Indonesia's restrictive import licensing procedures is inconsistent with Article XI:1 of the GATT 1994, Article 4.2 of the Agreement on Agriculture, and Article 3.2 of the Agreement on Import Licensing Procedures;

(v)   Indonesia's restrictive transportation requirements for imported chicken meat and chicken products is inconsistent with Article XI:1 of the GATT 1994 and Article 4.2 of the Agreement on Agriculture;

(vi)   Indonesia's restrictions on the use of imported chicken meat and chicken products is inconsistent with Article III:4 of the GATT 1994;

(vii)   Indonesia's implementation of halal labelling requirements is inconsistent with Article III:4 of the GATT 1994; and

(viii)   Indonesia's undue delay with regard to the approval of sanitary requirements is inconsistent with Article 8 and Annex C of the SPS Agreement.

ANNEX B-2

INTEGRATED EXECUTIVE SUMMARY OF
THE ARGUMENTS OF INDONESIA

I.   INTRODUCTION

1.   This dispute raises fundamental issues as to how a WTO Member may properly structure its laws and regulations to promote food safety and ensure compliance with its religious requirements. Indonesia is home to the fourth largest population in the world with over 255 million citizens. It is home to the largest Muslim population in the world. Many devout Muslims in Indonesia consume only halal food, which means they are prohibited from consuming pork and other meat not slaughtered according to the Islamic Shar'ia, and from consuming products that have been in contact with non-halal foods. The burden falls heavily on the Indonesian Government to ensure that the food available to Muslim Indonesians conforms to halal requirements as well as to ensure that Indonesia's food supply is adequate and safe. Indonesia believes that these societal values are of the utmost importance. Indonesia also believes that it has struck the proper balance between protecting the religious principles of its citizens and respecting its WTO obligations.

2.   Brazil challenged Indonesia's laws and regulations relating to the importation of chicken meat and chicken products as a general prohibition (or overarching measure) on the importation of chicken meat and chicken products, as well as individual measures. The individual measures challenged by Brazil are: certain aspects of Indonesia's import licensing regime, including the positive list and intended use requirements; the alleged discriminatory implementation of halal labelling requirements; the alleged restrictions on the transportation of imported chicken products; and the so-called delays in the approval of sanitary requirements for the importation of chicken. Brazil appears to regard this dispute as an "open-and-shut case". It is not.

3.   Indonesia has no intention to ban, restrict or limit imports of chicken meat or chicken products from any country, including Brazil. Indonesia only wishes to ensure that chicken meat and chicken products are safe, healthy, wholesome and halal. Moreover, Indonesia is committed to further liberalize its trade by enacting measures that are fully consistent with Indonesia's legitimate interests in ensuring halal compliance, food safety and security, and safe and efficient customs and quarantine administration. In fact, Indonesia's efforts at further liberalization have resulted in the termination of some measures challenged by Brazil in these proceedings. Indonesia will address these issues in detail in this integrated executive summary.

4.   It is well known that complaining WTO Members engaging in WTO dispute settlement proceedings must meet high standards. These high standards

are reflected in the stringent requirements for a panel request, which must plainly connect the challenged measures with the provisions of the covered agreements claimed to have been infringed, so that the respondent is aware of the basis for the claims. In addition, the Appellate Body has noted that the requirement to make a *prima facie* case – made in the course of submissions to the panel – demands the same high standards. It stated that "the evidence and arguments underlying a *prima facie* case therefore must be sufficient to identify the challenged measure and its basic import, identify the relevant WTO provision and obligation contained therein, and explain the basis for the claimed inconsistency of the measure with that provision".[8] Furthermore, each factual assertion must be proven.[9]

5.   With all due respect, Indonesia is of the view that Brazil has not met these high standards in the course of these proceedings. As explained in greater detail below, Brazil has submitted many Indonesian laws and regulations to the Panel but has not properly identified the WTO-inconsistencies therein; it has cited several provisions in WTO agreements but has not explained the basis for the claimed inconsistency of the measure with those provisions. Brazil has also not always been clear as to whether it is challenging current or expired aspects of Indonesia's import licensing regime.[10]

6.   Moreover, throughout these panel proceedings (even at very late stages), Brazil made changes to the scope of its claim on the general prohibition/overarching measure, the import licensing regime and the halal labelling requirement. These constant changes result in a lack of clarity as to what Brazil is actually challenging in these proceedings and deprive Indonesia of the ability to defend itself properly. Furthermore, Brazil has challenged certain Indonesian measures under the incorrect WTO covered agreement and has also challenged the same aspects of the same measures under different WTO covered agreements, which have different obligations. Indonesia therefore considers that Brazil has not met its burden of proof to demonstrate that the measures it is challenging in these proceedings are inconsistent with Indonesia's WTO obligations. In addition, Brazil has not convincingly responded to Indonesia's arguments and evidence submitted with respect to each of these claims and it has not convincingly rebutted Indonesia's defences under Article XX of the GATT 1994, where applicable. Importantly, Brazil has not provided any relevant less-trade restrictive alternatives for the challenged measures.

7.   There are many weaknesses in Brazil's arguments and evidence with respect to each of the challenged measures. Indonesia submits that when a complainant fails to support its claims with adequate arguments and evidence, these claims must necessarily fail. A panel, in this situation, must find that the

---

[8]   Appellate Body Report, *US – Gambling*, para. 141.
[9]   Panel Report, *Argentina – Textiles and Apparel*, para. 6.35.
[10]   See, for example, Indonesia's opening statement at the second meeting, paras. 5-6 and Brazil's rebuttal submission, para. 155.

complainant failed to make its *prima facie* case of violation. Indeed, it is a well-settled principle of international law that a sovereign State's measure will be treated as consistent with that State's international obligations until proven otherwise.[11]

8.   Indonesia has submitted detailed legal arguments and comprehensive factual explanations with respect to its import licensing regime, including the intended use, positive list and transportation requirements; halal labelling and certification requirements. Indonesia has submitted charts detailing every step of the import licensing procedures, has explained fully the roles of the main government authorities involved in these procedures, and has clarified the scope and coverage of its own laws and regulations. Brazil has not fully engaged with, or properly responded to, any of these detailed legal arguments and factual explanations.

9.   Like many other active WTO Members, Indonesia is currently involved in several dispute settlement proceedings both as complainant and as respondent. Indonesia wishes to stress that the outcome of those disputes is not relevant for the conduct of this dispute. The outcome of this dispute must be determined on the strengths and weaknesses of the legal arguments and evidence put forward by both Brazil and Indonesia in this dispute. [12]

II.   INDONESIA'S REQUEST FOR A PRELIMINARY RULING

10.   Indonesia submitted its request for a preliminary ruling as an attachment to its first written submission. Indonesia considered that Brazil's panel request is problematic in several respects. With respect to the alleged general prohibition/overarching measure, Indonesia submitted that Brazil failed to provide a brief summary of the legal basis of the complaint sufficient to present the problem clearly as required by Article 6.2 of the Understanding on Rules and Procedures Governing the Settlement of Disputes (DSU), as it listed several elements of this measure, several Indonesia's legal instruments and several WTO provisions without making a connection between them.[13]

11.   Moreover, Indonesia noted that the alleged general prohibition/overarching measure described in Brazil's panel request does not correspond to the description of the alleged general prohibition/overarching measure in Brazil's first written submission. In its panel request, Brazil described this measure as a combined operation of *seven* individual measures resulting in the general prohibition on the imports of chicken. In its first written submission, Brazil decided to remove one such individual measure (halal labelling requirement) changing the scope of the general prohibition/overarching measure.

---

[11]   See, *inter alia*, Appellate Body Report, *US – Carbon Steel*, para. 157.
[12]   The information in this section is based on, *inter alia*, Indonesia's opening statement at the first meeting, paras. 3-4; and Indonesia's opening statement at the second meeting, paras. 2-8.
[13]   Indonesia's Request for a Preliminary Ruling under Article 6.2 of the DSU, paras. 1.14-1.28.

It then referred to this measure for the first time as an unwritten measure.[14] Similarly, Brazil failed to describe the objective of the alleged general prohibition/overarching measure in its panel request, but only referred to it in its first written submission. However, the objective of an alleged unwritten overarching measure plays a pivotal role in defining the measure at issue and, by not referring to it in the panel request, Brazil has not complied with the specificity requirements in Article 6.2 of the DSU.[15]

12.   Furthermore, Indonesia noted that Brazil's challenge to Indonesia's import licensing regime "as a whole" was not identified in its panel request, and was thus, outside the terms of reference of the Panel.[16] Along similar lines, Indonesia claimed that Brazil's challenge to an alleged import prohibition on other prepared or preserved chicken meat was not identified in Brazil's panel request and was therefore outside the terms of reference of the Panel.[17]

13.   Finally, Indonesia argued that, to the extent that Brazil was challenging Indonesia's measures under Article 1 of the Agreement on Import Licensing Procedures (Import Licensing Agreement), the Panel should refrain from entertaining such claims, as Article 1 was not mentioned in Brazil's panel request, and was thus outside the terms of reference of the Panel.[18]

III.   SYSTEMIC ISSUES ARISING IN THIS DISPUTE

A.   Brazil's Claim on the Alleged General Prohibition/Overarching Measure is a "moving target" for Indonesia and is not supported by relevant evidence

14.   Brazil submitted that Indonesia maintains "several prohibitions or restrictions on the importation of chicken meat and chicken products, which, combined, have the effect of a general prohibition on the importation of these products".[19] Brazil described this measure as an overarching measure/general prohibition comprising the following elements: the prohibition of the importation of non-listed products; prioritization of "national food" over "food import"; prohibitions or restrictions on imports of essential and strategic goods; limitations on chicken meat and chicken products to certain intended uses; alleged undue refusal to approve the health certificates for poultry products; alleged prohibitions and/or restrictions to importation through Indonesia's import licensing regime; and alleged import prohibition imposed through the halal

---

[14]   Brazil's first written submission, paras. 136-139.
[15]   Indonesia's Request for a Preliminary Ruling under Article 6.2 of the DSU, paras. 1.29-1.41. See also Indonesia's response to Panel Question No. 68.
[16]   Indonesia's Request for a Preliminary Ruling under Article 6.2 of the DSU, paras. 5.1-5.6.
[17]   Indonesia's Request for a Preliminary Ruling under Article 6.2 of the DSU, paras. 1.43-1.48.
[18]   Indonesia's Request for a Preliminary Ruling under Article 6.2 of the DSU, paras. 1.49-1.52.
[19]   See, Request for the Establishment of a Panel by Brazil, *Indonesia – Measures concerning the Importation of Chicken Meat and Chicken Products*, WT/DS484/8, 21 October 2015 (Brazil's panel request), pp. 1-2.

labelling requirements for imported chicken meat and chicken products.[20] In its first written submission, Brazil dropped the halal labelling requirement so that the description of the overarching measure/general prohibition then only included six elements.[21]

15.   Indonesia raised systemic concerns with respect to the manner in which Brazil described the alleged general prohibition/overarching measure and its challenge throughout these proceedings, as well as the inadequate nature and amount of evidence Brazil submitted to prove the existence of this measure. In *Russia – Tariff Treatment*, the panel acknowledged that if neither the respondent nor the panel were able to pin down the measure whose consistency with the covered agreements is contested, "[t]his could raise issues of due process".[22] Moreover, it is well-established in WTO jurisprudence that "the complaining party must 'present relevant arguments and evidence during the panel proceedings showing the existence of the measures, for example, in the case of challenges brought against unwritten measures'".[23] It is also generally acknowledged that a panel cannot lightly accept the complainant's assertion that the challenged unwritten measure exists.[24] This means that the evidentiary burden for a complainant challenging an unwritten measure must necessarily be higher than that arising from challenges to written measures, whose existence is not disputed.[25] Brazil has itself recognised this heightened burden.[26]

16.   With respect to the manner in which Brazil described the alleged general prohibition/overarching measure and its challenge, until the end of the Panel's proceedings, Brazil did not explain clearly what exactly it was challenging and on what basis. Brazil referred to the measure at issue as: "a general prohibition on the importations" of chicken meat and chicken products, "*de jure*" and "*de facto*" inconsistent with Indonesia's obligations; "a general proposition, concerted action or practice", an unwritten, overarching measure, distinct from its elements; and "on-going conduct" of "general and systematic application". In its panel request, Brazil stated that the measure at issue consists of *seven* prohibitions or restrictions, which are "combined" (i.e. interact and work in concert). In its first written submission, Brazil argued that the measure at issue consists of only *six* elements. In its other submissions, Brazil argued that the

---

[20]   Brazil's panel request, p. 2.
[21]   Brazil's first written submission, para. 74.
[22]   Panel Report, *Russia – Tariff Treatment*, paras. 7.291, 7.302.
[23]   See Panel Report, *Russia – Tariff Treatment*, para. 7.338 (citing Appellate Body Report, *US – Continued Zeroing*, para. 169).
[24]   See Panel Report, *Russia – Tariff Treatment*, paras. 7.348, 7.380. See also Appellate Body Report, *EC and certain member States – Large Civil Aircraft*, para. 792.
[25]   See Panel Report, *Argentina – Import Measures*, para. 6.323.
[26]   Brazil's rebuttal submission, para. 12. See these issues discussed in Indonesia's first written submission, paras. 96-109; Indonesia's opening statement at the first meeting, paras. 49-58; Indonesia's rebuttal submission, paras. 65-75; Indonesia's opening statement at the second meeting, paras. 10-21; Indonesia's responses to Panel Questions No. 5.c, 6-8, 68, 70; Indonesia's comments on Brazil's responses to Panel Questions No. 68, 70, and 71.

alleged general prohibition/overarching measure could consist of "six, seven or eight (or more, or fewer)" WTO-inconsistent measures. And then, in its response to Panel Question No. 5.a.v, Brazil suggested that other measures, in particular the direct transportation requirement, "could also be part of the general prohibition".[27]

17.   In its first written submission, Brazil specified the alleged objective of the general prohibition/overarching measure for the first time, and then expanded upon its argument in its opening statement at the first meeting of the Panel with the parties. In particular, Brazil clarified that "the combined interaction of different individual WTO-inconsistent measures constitutes an unwritten overarching measure and was conceived to implement an official trade policy based on the overriding objective of restricting imports to protect domestic production". Brazil referred to this policy as the requirement of "self-sufficiency". Brazil described the alleged requirement of "self-sufficiency" as the "overriding objective" and one of the elements of the measure at issue, as well as a "guiding principle". However, Indonesia explained that a measure and its objective are different concepts.[28]

18.   Indonesia acknowledges that a complainant has certain discretion to describe the measure it is challenging in the way it considers necessary. Nevertheless, Indonesia submits that once the complainant described the measure in one way, it is not free to stretch and squeeze its content throughout the panel proceedings. Doing so would compromise the ability of the respondent to prepare its defence, as in the present case. Moreover, given that the challenge to a rule or norm of "general and systematic application" is different from the challenge to a measure as applied, or as on-going conduct, or as an overarching measure, a complainant that has changed the description of the challenged measure, or the essence of its challenge to that measure, would have to start to make its *prima facie* case anew, possibly submitting additional evidence. Brazil has itself acknowledged that the description/characterization of the measure at issue by the complainant informs the evidence and arguments that are required to prove that the measure exists.[29]

19.   A clear and consistent description of the content of the challenged measure is especially important in circumstances where the measure is unwritten, as in the present dispute. By definition, the alleged general prohibition/overarching measure is not a measure set out in any laws, regulations

---

[27]   See Indonesia's response to Panel Question No. 6; Indonesia's rebuttal submission, para. 66 (citing *inter alia*, Brazil's first written submission, paras. 76, 173; Brazil's response to Indonesia's request for a preliminary ruling, para. 32).

[28]   Indonesia's rebuttal submission, para. 66; and Indonesia's comment on Brazil's response to Panel Question No. 68 (citing Brazil's first written submission, paras. 75 and 174; Brazil's opening statement at the first meeting, para. 11; and Brazil's responses to Panel Questions No. 5.b and 68).

[29]   Brazil's response to Panel Question No. 8.b (citing Appellate Body Report, *Argentina – Import Measures*, para. 5.107). See Indonesia's rebuttal submission, paras. 67-68; Indonesia's opening statement at the second meeting, paras. 10 and 11.

or official policy documents. It is rather a construction that Brazil has devised in order to cluster various otherwise distinct measures together to suggest that they supposedly advance a common objective. The very existence and the precise contours of the alleged overarching, unwritten measure are, therefore, uncertain, and should have been clearly established by Brazil.[30]

20.   With respect to the evidence that Brazil presented to prove that the measure at issue exists, the only pieces of evidence Brazil relied upon were: trade statistics showing the absence of imports of chicken into Indonesia from Brazil, and certain legal instruments in which some individual elements of the alleged general prohibition/overarching measure are established. Brazil did not provide any evidence showing *how* the alleged elements of the measure at issue *operate together*, as opposed to being merely individual unrelated "trade restrictions". Furthermore, Brazil did not prove its assertion that each of these elements was indeed established *with a view to achieving Indonesia's alleged objective of "self-sufficiency"*. Finally, Brazil failed to substantiate its assertion that the alleged general prohibition/overarching measure is applied in a *"general and systematic" manner*.[31]

21.   To be clear, Indonesia does not argue that the above elements must be demonstrated in each and every dispute involving unwritten measures. Brazil's evidentiary burden stems from its own characterization/description of the measure at issue in its panel request and its subsequent clarifications in the course of the Panel proceedings.[32]

22.   At the very end of these proceedings, in its response to a Panel's question following the second substantive meeting of the Panel with the parties, Brazil attempted to introduce additional pieces of evidence, such as a letter signed by Indonesia's Director General of Livestock, Ministry of Agriculture, and four news articles allegedly quoting Indonesian government officials. Indonesia requested the Panel to disregard these documents, as they constitute evidence-in-chief and, pursuant to paragraph 8 of the Working Procedures for this dispute, had to be submitted "no later than during the first substantive meeting". Most of the documents submitted were dated well before the deadline for submitting factual evidence, and were in Brazil's possession. Brazil did not even try to show good cause as to why it should be allowed to submit evidence-in-chief at that late stage. Instead, it argued that it was entitled to submit evidence-in-chief in response to a Panel's question.[33]

---

[30]   Indonesia's rebuttal submission, para. 69 (citing Appellate Body Report, *EC and certain member States – Large Civil Aircraft*, para. 792).
[31]   Indonesia's rebuttal submission, paras. 100-109; Indonesia's opening statement at the second meeting, para. 13.
[32]   See Indonesia's opening statement at the second meeting, para. 14 (citing Appellate Body Report, *Argentina – Import Measures*, para. 5.108; and Panel Report, *Russia – Tariff Treatment*, para. 7.296, footnote 448).
[33]   See Indonesia's comment on Brazil's response to Panel Question No. 70; and Brazil's comment on Indonesia's response to Panel Question No. 70.

23.   But even if those pieces of evidence were properly before the Panel, they do not provide any meaningful support for Brazil's allegation that the general prohibition/overarching measure exists. Brazil's evidence is contradictory and does not prove that the lack of imports of chicken meat and chicken products from Brazil into Indonesia is caused by the alleged requirement of self-sufficiency. On the contrary, as Indonesia demonstrated throughout these proceedings, the real reason for the lack of imports is Brazil's own failure to comply with Indonesia's import procedures. With respect to the news articles, they appear to contain "quotes" of Indonesian authorities taken out of context, and do not portray the accurate picture of the Indonesian market for chicken.[34]

24.   Based on these considerations, the fact that, even at the very end of the Panel proceedings, Brazil had not provided a clear description of the measure at issue and the nature of its challenge, and had not submitted adequate evidence demonstrating that this measure exists means that Brazil failed to make its *prima facie* case. Indeed, when various factual assertions of Brazil regarding the alleged content of the measure are assessed in a holistic manner, it becomes clear that the measure in the way it is described by Brazil in its different submissions does not even exist.[35]

B.   Brazil requests the Panel to make recommendations on measures that have expired

25.   In the course of the proceedings, Indonesia explained that some of the measures challenged by Brazil, namely, the intended use requirement, the positive list requirements, and certain aspects of Indonesia's import licensing regime, had expired. These new measures significantly liberalised the procedures and conditions to import chicken into Indonesia.

26.   Brazil claimed that the intended use requirement in MoA Regulation No. 139/2014 limited the importation and distribution of imported chicken to certain uses only, i.e. hotels, restaurants, catering, manufacturing, other special needs and modern markets).[36] Indonesia notes that this Regulation was modified by MoA Regulation No. 34/2016,[37] which terminated the intended use requirement. Article 31(1) of MoA Regulation No. 34/2016 now permits the sale of frozen chilled and chicken in any market where these products can be sold, i.e. any market with cold-chain facilities, including traditional markets.

27.   Brazil also challenged the positive list requirements, which prohibited the importation of chicken cuts that were not listed in the relevant annexes to MoA Regulation No. 139/2014 and MoT Regulation No. 46/2013.[38] MoA Regulation

---

[34]   Indonesia's comment on Brazil's response to Panel Question No. 70.
[35]   Indonesia's rebuttal submission, paras. 75 and 109.
[36]   Brazil's panel request, pp. 4 and 6.
[37]   Ministry of Agriculture Regulation No. 34/2016 Concerning Importation of Carcass, Meat, Offal and/or their Processed Products into the territory of the Republic of Indonesia (MoA Regulation No. 34/2016), Exhibit IDN-93.
[38]   Brazil's panel request, p. 4.

No. 139/2014 was modified by MoA Regulation No. 34/2016, and MoT Regulation No. 46/2013 was modified by MoT Regulation No. 59/2016, which terminated the positive list requirements. Pursuant to Article 7(3) of MoA Regulation No. 34/2016, importers can import *all* chicken products as long as they apply for an Import Recommendation and the imported products comply with the ASUH requirements (i.e. products are safe, healthy, wholesome and halal).

28.   Brazil also claimed that Indonesia's previous import licensing regime restricted the importation of chicken as importers had to apply for an Import Recommendation during a specific period (application period) that were valid for four months (validity period). Importers also had to specify the price, quantity, country of origin, port of entry and intended use of imported products without the ability to modify this information during the pertinent validity period (fixed-license terms).[39] As stated above, MoA Regulation No. 139/2014 was modified by MoA Regulation No. 34/2016, which further liberalised Indonesia's import regime. Article 21 of this Regulation terminated the application period and Article 30 extended the validity period of Import Recommendations from four to six months.

29.   During the second substantive meeting of the Panel with the parties, Brazil requested the Panel to review the WTO-consistency of these expired measures.[40]

30.   Indonesia notes that a panel can make only findings, but not recommendations with respect to measures that have expired.[41] Furthermore, even though Brazil's panel request covers "any amendments, replacements, related measures, or implementing measures", to the extent that the measure at issue was terminated by an amendment, the amendment necessarily changes the essence of the measure and, therefore, cannot be ruled upon. This approach finds support in WTO jurisprudence.[42] Thus, Indonesia submits that the provisions that terminate the positive list requirements, the intended use requirement and the application periods fall outside the Panel's terms of reference.

31.   That said, Indonesia submits that MoA Regulation No. 34/2016 and MoT Regulation No. 59/2016 can be used as evidence to confirm that the positive list requirements, the intended use requirement and the limited application periods expired.[43]

32.   Indonesia notes that the validity period requirement has not been terminated, but it was rather modified in Article 30 of MoA Regulation

---

[39]   *Ibid.*
[40]   See Brazil's response to Panel Question No. 66 and Brazil's comments on Indonesia's responses to the Panel Questions after the second meeting, paras. 1-5.
[41]   See Indonesia's response to Panel Question No. 149.
[42]   See Appellate Body Report, *Chile – Price Band System*, paras. 136-137; Panel Report, *China – Raw Materials*, para. 7.17; Panel Report, *India – Additional Import Duties*, paras. 7.62-7.63.
[43]   See a similar approach in Panel Report, *China – Raw Materials*, paras. 7.31, 7.33(b).

No. 34/2016. This provision, therefore, did not change the essence of the original measure. Indonesia submits that the Panel has jurisdiction to rule on the WTO-consistency of the validity period requirement in Article 30 of MoA Regulation No. 34/2016.[44]

33.　In the alternative, if the Panel were to find that it has jurisdiction over the expired measures, Indonesia submits that the current regime is WTO-consistent for the reasons explained in detail in its submissions.[45] Indonesia's defences under Article XX(b) and (d) of the GATT 1994 would apply, *mutatis mutandis*, to these measures.

C.　Brazil has challenged the same aspects of the same measures under different agreements

1.　Relationship between Article 4.2 of the Agreement on Agriculture and Article XI:1 of the GATT 1994

34.　Brazil challenged all measures at issue in this dispute, except Indonesia's halal labelling requirements and Indonesia's alleged failure to approve sanitary requirements, under both Article XI:1 of the GATT 1994 and Article 4.2 of the Agreement on Agriculture. In Indonesia's view, however, Article 4.2 of the Agreement on Agriculture applies to the exclusion of Article XI:1 of the GATT 1994. Both provisions regulate quantitative import restrictions. The products at issue (i.e. chicken meat and chicken products) are goods falling within the HS Codes listed in Annex 1 to the Agreement on Agriculture (i.e. HS0207 and HS 1602). Article 4.2 of the Agreement on Agriculture is, therefore, *lex specialis* vis-à-vis Article XI:1 of the GATT 1994.[46]

35.　Indonesia explained that, when read together, Article 4.2 and footnote 1 of the Agreement on Agriculture suggest that a complainant would not be able to make its *prima facie* case of inconsistency with Article 4.2 unless it establishes two elements: first, that the challenged measure is a "quantitative import restriction" or another type of restrictions listed, and, second, that this restriction is not "maintained under ... other general, non-agriculture-specific provisions of GATT 1994 [such as Article XX]". This is a threshold issue in order to determine whether the challenged measure is "of the kind which have been required to be converted into ordinary customs duties", and, therefore, "shall not [be] maintain[ed], resort[ed] to, or revert[ed] to" within the meaning of Article 4.2. In Indonesia's view, the difference between how the burden of proof is allocated between the complainant and respondent under Article 4.2 of the

---

[44]　See Indonesia's rebuttal submission, paras. 19-22. See also Indonesia's justification of the validity period and the fixed license terms in its response to Panel Questions No. 113, 114, 119, and 122 (covering the new regime as well).

[45]　See e.g., Indonesia's response to Panel Question No. 77, 88-91 and 113. See also Indonesia's comments on Brazil's responses to Panel Questions No. 77(d), 85, 86(b), 87, 90, 96, 99, 101 and 103.

[46]　See, *inter alia*, Indonesia's first written submission, paras. 66, 74; Indonesia's rebuttal submission, paras. 80, 84-85.

Agreement on Agriculture and Articles XI:1 and XX (General Exceptions) of the GATT 1994, respectively, gives rise to a conflict.[47]

36.   Pursuant to Article 21.1 of the Agreement on Agriculture and the General Interpretative Note to Annex 1A to the WTO Agreement, when a conflict exists, Article 4.2 prevails and applies to the exclusion of Article XI:1. Although the Appellate Body is yet to clarify the relationship between Article XI:1 and Article 4.2 and the allocation of the burden of proof under different elements of the latter provision, it has accepted in general, in a number of its decisions, that a conflict is possible.[48] The Appellate Body has understood the notion of "conflict" as covering situations in which rules and procedures under WTO covered agreements cannot be read as complementing each other.[49] Certainly, rules in different agreements that differ on such a fundamental issue as the allocation of the burden of proof cannot be considered as "complementing each other" – rather, they are "mutually exclusive".[50]

37.   The Appellate Body has explicitly confirmed this hierarchy between the Agreement on Agriculture and the GATT 1994, in particular between Article 4.2 and Article II:1(b) respectively, in *Chile – Price Band System*.[51] In *Turkey – Rice*, the panel expressed the same view with respect to the relationship between Article 4.2 and Article XI:1 by stating that "[t]he Agreement on Agriculture deals *more specifically* than the GATT 1994 with the prohibition on maintaining quantitative restrictions or quotas".[52]

38.   Brazil and a number of third parties in this dispute, in particular the European Union, New Zealand and the United States, argued that the burden of showing that the challenged import restriction meets the second element of the test in footnote 1 to Article 4.2 of the Agreement on Agriculture rests on the respondent.[53] The United States asserted that "[a]dopting Indonesia's interpretation would render a successful Article 4.2 claim nearly impossible".[54]

39.   Indonesia is not convinced by these arguments. If the drafters intended to create a general rule-exception relationship between the two elements of footnote 1 whereby the burden of satisfying the second element would be on the *respondent,* they would have used different, more explicit wording. For

---

[47]   Indonesia's first written submission, paras. 69-73; Indonesia's opening statement at the first meeting, paras. 23-24, 36; Indonesia's rebuttal submission, para. 81.
[48]   See, *inter alia*, Appellate Body Report, *EC – Export Subsidies on Sugar*, para. 221.
[49]   See Appellate Body Report, *Guatemala – Cement I*, para. 65.
[50]   See Indonesia's first written submission, paras. 67and 68; Indonesia's opening statement at the first meeting, paras. 28 and 29; Indonesia's response to Panel Question No. 49.
[51]   Appellate Body Report, *Chile – Price Band System*, para. 186 (see also paras. 187 and 190). See also Panel Report, *Peru – Agricultural Products*, paras. 7.19 and7.20.
[52]   Panel Report, *Turkey – Rice*, para. 7.48, emphasis added. The EC expressed the same view in that dispute in *ibid*, para. 7.47. See Indonesia's opening statement at the first meeting, para. 28.
[53]   Brazil's rebuttal submission, paras. 18-21; European Union's third party submission, paras. 23-24; New Zealand's third party submission, paras. 67-70; and United States' third party submission, paras. 57-58.
[54]   United States' third party submission, para. 58.

example, Article 3 of the TRIMS Agreement (titled "Exceptions") states explicitly that "[a]ll exceptions under GATT 1994 shall apply, as appropriate, to the provisions of this Agreement". Similar wording is used in Article 24.7 of the Agreement on Trade Facilitation. Furthermore, there are many examples of provisions in the covered agreements that convert exceptions under Article XX of the GATT 1994 into positive obligations, thereby shifting the burden of proof to the complainant, for example, Article 2.2 of the TBT Agreement. There are also many provisions in the covered agreements that require the complainant to demonstrate that certain exceptions do not apply, and, therefore, do not remove the inconsistency of the measure with the relevant positive obligation, for example, Article 2.4 of the TBT Agreement.[55]

40.   Indonesia further notes that, in an effort to avoid any conflict between Article 4.2 and Article XI:1, Brazil, Australia, the European Union and Canada suggested that both Articles apply "harmoniously" to the same type of quantitative import restrictions and that the "scope of measures prohibited could in principle be the same".[56] If the rules under Article 4.2 and Article XI:1 were the same, then one of them would be superfluous. This would go against the well-established principle of the effective treaty interpretation, pursuant to which "[a]n interpreter is not free to adopt a reading that would result in reducing whole clauses or paragraphs of a treaty to redundancy or inutility".[57]

41.   Finally, the United States and New Zealand suggested that the Panel begin its analysis with Article XI:1, and, in this way, it would not have to address the issue of conflict between Article XI:1 and Article 4.2.[58] Indonesia considers that the order of analysis suggested by these third parties would distort the fundamental due process rights of Indonesia, as it would bear the burden of proof in a situation where this burden is not envisaged by the applicable law. It is a well-established principle that panels are free to determine the order of analysis only to the extent that this determination would not "amount to an error of law", or "have repercussions for the substance of the analysis itself".[59]

2.   Relationship between the Agreement on Import Licensing, Article 4.2 of the Agreement on Agriculture and Article XI:1 of the GATT 1994

42.   Brazil challenges the same aspects of Indonesia's import licensing regime under Article 3.2 of the Licensing Agreement and Article 4.2 of the Agreement on Agriculture and Article XI:1 of the GATT 1994. These aspects are: (i)

---

[55]   Indonesia's opening statement at the first meeting, paras. 32-36.
[56]   See European Union's third party submission, para. 27. See also Brazil's rebuttal submission, para. 16; Australia's third party submission, para. 30; and Canada's third party submission, para. 58.
[57]   See Appellate Body Report, *US – Gasoline*, p. 20. See Indonesia's opening statement at the first meeting, paras. 37-38.
[58]   United States' third party submission, paras. 59-60; New Zealand's third party submission, para. 71.
[59]   Appellate Body Report, *Canada – Wheat Exports and Grain Imports*, para. 109. See Indonesia's opening statement at the first meeting, para. 39; Indonesia's response to Panel Question No. 49.

positive list requirements, (ii) intended use requirement, and (iii) limited application and validity periods.[60] Furthermore, in Question No. 128, the Panel asked Brazil to clarify whether Brazil is also challenging the fixed licence terms under Article 3.2 of the Licensing Agreement and "[i]f so, ... where this claim was developed in Brazil's submissions". In Indonesia's view, this claim, albeit included in Brazil's panel request, was not developed in Brazil's submissions, which means that Brazil failed to make its *prima facie* case with respect to this claim. This was confirmed by Brazil's response to this Question, in which it could not point to any passages in its first written submission and other submissions where it provided legal arguments and evidence in support for this claim.[61]

43.   Indonesia explained that the respective scopes of the application of the Import Licensing Agreement, on the one hand, and Article 4.2 of the Agreement on Agriculture and Article XI:1 of the GATT 1994, on the other hand, *are not the same*. Article XI:1 of the GATT 1994 and Article 4.2 of the Agreement on Agriculture establish certain *substantive rights and duties*, in particular the prohibition of quantitative import restrictions, whereas, according to Article 1.1 of the Licensing Agreement, the latter agreement regulates "administrative *procedures* used for the operation of import licensing regimes".[62] Indonesia explained that, among the measures challenged by Brazil under the Licensing Agreement, the only measure that actually falls within the scope of this agreement is the limited application and validity periods. This measure consists of *procedural requirements* that prescribe steps for obtaining the right to import chicken meat and chicken products into Indonesia. This view was shared by the European Union. Brazil, therefore, could not challenge the same measures under the Agreement on Import Licensing, and Article 4.2 of the Agreement on Agriculture and Article XI:1 of the GATT 1994.[63]

44.   In any event, in its submissions, Brazil failed to explain why the measures it challenged under Article 3.2 of the Licensing Agreement in fact constitute import licensing *procedures* that are *non-automatic*, and, therefore fall under Articles 1.1 and 3.2 of the Licensing Agreement. Furthermore, Brazil did not demonstrate how these measures are inconsistent with the specific legal obligations under Article 3.2.[64]

---

[60]   Brazil's first written submission, paras. 200, 228, 251. See Indonesia's rebuttal submission, para. 96.
[61]   Indonesia's comment on Brazil's response to Panel Question No. 128.
[62]   Footnote omitted, emphasis added.
[63]   See EU's response to Panel Question No. 7 addressed to third parties. See Indonesia's first written submission, paras. 75-80; Indonesia's responses to Panel Questions No. 48 and 49; Indonesia's rebuttal submission, para. 96.
[64]   Indonesia's responses to Panel Questions No. 48, 58-61; Indonesia's rebuttal submission, paras. 114-117; Indonesia's opening statement at the second meeting, paras. 24-36; Indonesia's comments on Brazil's responses to Panel Questions No. 124, 127.

3. Relationship between Article 4.2 of the Agreement on Agriculture, Article XI:1 and Article III:4 of the GATT 1994

45.   Another systemic issue arises from Brazil's approach of challenging the same aspects of the intended use requirement under both Article III:4 of the GATT 1994 (covering internal measures affecting competitive opportunities in the domestic market), and Article 4.2 of the Agreement on Agriculture and Article XI:1 of the GATT 1994 (covering border measures affecting competitive opportunities of imports).[65] The Panel's determination of whether the intended use requirement is an internal measure or a border measure is a threshold issue as the challenged aspect of the same measure cannot be a border measure and an internal measure at the same time.[66]

46.   Indonesia recalls that Note *Ad* Article III draws a clear distinction between internal and border measures. It provides that "any law, regulation or requirement of the kind referred to in paragraph 1 which applies *to an imported product and to the like domestic product* and is collected or enforced in the case of the imported product at the time or point of importation, is nevertheless to be regarded as ... a law, regulation or requirement of the kind referred to in paragraph 1, and is accordingly subject to the provisions of Article III" (emphasis added). This distinction was also clarified by the panel in *India – Autos*, which stated that what is targeted in Article XI:1 is exclusively restrictions which relate to the importation itself, and not to already imported products.[67]

47.   *Ad* Note to Article III presupposes an equivalent measure that applies to imported and like domestic products.[68] Article 22 and 23 of Minister of Agriculture Decree 306/1994 provide that frozen and chilled poultry meat is offered for sale in meat shops and supermarkets "equipped with cooler facilities (refrigerator and/or freezer)".[69] Thus, Minister of Agriculture Decree No. 306/1994 is a measure equivalent to the intended use requirement challenged by Brazil that applies to both imported and like domestic products,

---

[65]   Indonesia's first written submission, paras. 81-89; Indonesia's opening statement at the first meeting, paras. 41-47; and Indonesia's responses to Panel Questions No. 50-53 and 55.

[66]   See Appellate Body Report, *China – Auto Parts*, para. 139 (referring to Panel Report, *China – Auto Parts*, para. 7.105). See also GATT Panel Reports, *EEC – Parts and Components*, para. 5.4; *Greece – Import Taxes*, para. 5; *Canada – Gold Coins*, para. 49 and Panel Report, *Argentina – Hides and Leather*, para. 11.139.

[67]   The panel also explained that only in the very specific circumstance of state-trading enterprises involving a monopoly over both importation and distribution of goods, such as in the case of *Korea – Various Measures on Beef*, the traditional distinction between measures affecting imported products and measures affecting importation may be blurred. Panel Report, *India – Autos*, para. 7.221 and footnote 410 (citing Panel Report, *Korea – Various Measures on Beef*, para. 766).

[68]   See Panel Report, *EC – Asbestos, paras.* 8.91-8.95 (referring to GATT Panel Report, *US – Section 337 of the Tariff Act of 1930*); and Panel Report, *Argentina – Hides and Leather*, paras. 11.150 and 11.154.

[69]   Article 22(c) and Article 23 of the Minister of Agriculture Decree 306/1994 concerning slaughtering of poultry and handling of poultry meat and its by-products, Exhibit IDN-83.

namely chilled and frozen products. This brings the intended use requirement clearly within the scope of Article III:4 of the GATT 1994. It thus, does not fall under the scope of Article 4.2 of the Agreement on Agriculture or Article XI:1 of the GATT 1994.

IV. BRAZIL FAILS TO PROVE THAT THE CHALLENGED MEASURES ARE INCONSISTENT WITH INDONESIA'S WTO OBLIGATIONS

A. Alleged general prohibition/overarching measure

48. Indonesia recalls that Brazil challenged the so-called overarching measure/general prohibition as a "quantitative import restriction" inconsistent with Article XI:1 of the GATT 1994, and a "quantitative import restriction" or a "similar border measure" inconsistent with Article 4.2 of the Agreement on Agriculture.[70] As explained in Indonesia's submissions, Brazil failed to prove that the measure at issue exists in the way it is described by Brazil.[71]

49. Moreover, even if the Panel were to find otherwise, for the reasons already explained, Indonesia considers that, in the present dispute, Article 4.2 of the Agreement on Agriculture applies to the exclusion of Article XI:1 of the GATT 1994. In the context of its claim under Article 4.2, Brazil did not substantiate its assertions that a causal relationship exists between the alleged measure and the claimed trade distortion (i.e. the measure has a limiting effect), that the measure at issue constitutes a similar border measure, and that it is not "maintained under ... general, non-agriculture-specific provisions of GATT 1994 or of the other Multilateral Trade Agreements in Annex 1A to the WTO Agreement". In light of these deficiencies, Brazil failed to prove that the general prohibition/overarching measure – to the extent that Brazil established its existence (quod non) – is inconsistent with Article 4.2 of the Agreement on Agriculture.[72]

50. If, despite Indonesia's arguments, the Panel were nevertheless to address Brazil's claim under Article XI:1 of the GATT 1994, Brazil failed to prove that this measure is a quantitative import restriction inconsistent with this provision. This is because, as explained, Brazil failed to demonstrate that the general prohibition/overarching measure has a limiting effect.[73]

51. Thus, due to the highly abstract nature of Brazil's claim on the general prohibition/overarching measure, Indonesia submits that Brazil failed to make its

---

[70] Indonesia's first written submission, para. 94.
[71] Indonesia's first written submission, para. 109; Indonesia's rebuttal submission, paras. 98-109.
[72] Indonesia's first written submission, paras. 118-124.
[73] Indonesia's first written submission, paras. 125-127; Indonesia's opening statement at the first meeting, paras. 54-58.

prima facie case that this measure was inconsistent with both Article 4.2 of the Agreement on Agriculture and Article XI:1 of the GATT 1994.[74]

B. Halal Labelling Requirements

1. Brazil has not demonstrated that the halal labelling requirements are inconsistent with Indonesia's obligations under Article III:4 of the GATT 1994

52. Brazil challenged Indonesia's halal "labelling" requirements imposed through, *inter alia*, Law No. 33/2014 (Halal Law).[75]

53. Brazil claimed that Indonesia's halal "labelling" requirements violate Article III:4 of the GATT 1994. First, Brazil argued that Indonesia discriminated against Brazilian producers by granting a five-year grace period from the halal "labelling" requirement only to domestic products, but not to imported products. Brazil considered the certification requirements fell under labelling. Indonesia explained that what Brazil referred to as "labelling" was actually "certification".[76]

54. Indonesia enacted Law No. 33/2014 (Halal Law) to unify the halal assurance requirements under one instrument and to create new government bodies to guarantee halal product assurance, in coordination with the Indonesian Ulama Council (MUI). Article 4 of Law No. 33/2014 (Halal Law) provides that "products that enter, circulate and [are] traded in the territory of Indonesia must be certified halal". The Halal Product Assurance Organizing Agency (BPJPH) was the new agency formed by the Government to certify products as halal.[77] Article 67(1) provides that the "obligation of halal certification that circulate and [are] traded in the territory of Indonesia as intended in Article 4 comes into effect 5 (five) years from the [enactment] of this Law." Moreover, Article 64 provides that "the formation of the BPJPH .... must be formed no later than three years commencing from the [enactment] of this Law." Thus, it was expected that it would take three years to set up the BPJPH and another two years for the BPJPH to establish procedures before which its Halal Certification procedures would be mandatory.

55. However, the obligation for establishments to obtain halal certification was still required until the BPJPH was formed. Article 60 provides that "MUI still conducts its task in Halal Certification until BPJPH is formed." The requirement to obtain halal certification through the MUI, therefore, applied to both domestic and imported products throughout this grace period. It is only the BPJPH, as a body, that received the grace period. Indonesia submits that Brazil

---

[74] Indonesia's first written submission, para. 128.
[75] Brazil's panel request, p. 6.
[76] Indonesia's opening statement at the first meeting, paras. 113-115. Indonesia's opening statement at the second meeting, para 47.
[77] See Articles 1(5) to 1(11) of Law 33/2014 (Halal Law), Exhibit IDN-5.

has not established a *prima facie* case that the grace period constitutes discrimination with respect to the halal certification requirement.[78]

56.   Second, Brazil argued that the implementation of the halal labelling is discriminatory because Indonesian producers can sell chicken meat and chicken products without the halal label, whereas foreign products had to have a halal label. Indonesia recalls that for a violation of Article III:4 to be established, three elements must be satisfied: (i) the imported and domestic products at issue are "like products"; (ii) the measure at issue is a "law, regulation, or requirement" affecting the products' internal sale, offering for sale, purchase, transportation, distribution, or use", and (iii) the imported products are accorded "less favourable treatment" than that accorded to like domestic products.[79] Brazil has not satisfied these elements.

57.   Brazil argued that imported chicken meat and products were like domestic chicken meat and products.[80] Indonesia disagreed. Indonesia recalls that the determination of "likeness" under Article III:4 of the GATT 1994 is "…fundamentally, a determination about the nature and extent of a competitive relationship between and among products."[81] As the determination of likeness relates to the competitive relationship between domestic and imported products in the relevant *marketplace*,[82] a panel should base its analysis on the products that *actually* compete in the relevant market. For example, in Indonesia, *domestic fresh* chicken meat does not compete with *imported fresh* chicken meat because it would be virtually impossible for Brazil to import fresh chicken into Indonesia. Fresh chicken has a storage life of less than one day. A consignment from Brazil to Indonesia that is transported via marine cargo would take around 30 days, while transportation by air from São Paolo to Jakarta takes more than 45 hours and would be prohibitively expensive. Thus, in all likelihood, considering the distance, the transport time and the prohibitive transportation cost (if by air), Brazil would only import frozen chicken meat and products into Indonesia.[83] In contrast, domestic chicken meat is usually sold fresh in traditional markets.[84]

58.   Indonesia further explained that although, the end-uses of fresh and frozen products are similar for the ultimate consumer, the products at issue are not classified under the same HS-six-digit code and they have different products characteristics that affect heavily consumer tastes and habits in the Indonesian market.[85] Indonesia did not dispute that the halal labelling requirements are domestic regulations falling under Article III:4.

---

[78] See Indonesia's opening statement at the second meeting, paras. 46 and 47.
[79] Appellate Body Report, *Korea – Various Measures on Beef*, para. 133.
[80] Brazil's first written submission, para. 285.
[81] Appellate Body Report, *EC – Asbestos*, para. 99.
[82] Appellate Body Report, *EC – Asbestos*, para. 103 (emphasis added).
[83] Indonesia's first written submission, para. 149 and footnote 188.
[84] Indonesia's first written submission, para.159.
[85] Indonesia's first written submission, paras. 316-328.

59.   Brazil argued that imported chicken meat and products were accorded "less favourable treatment" than that accorded to like domestic products. Brazil relied on the text of Article 38 of Law No. 33/2014 (Halal Law), which provides that "halal labels must be affixed on (a) product's packaging; (b) specific part of the products, and/or (c) specific place of the product".[86] Indonesia explained although the Halal Law applies to a wide range of products including cosmetics, chemical products and consumer goods,[87] Government Regulation No. 69/1999 is the more specific regulation providing that halal labels do not need to be affixed to "food directly sold and packed before buyers". For example, it is common practice to sell *fresh* chicken without a halal label affixed directly on the product, but have the halal certificates for the products and for the slaughterman displayed at the point of sale in the traditional markets.[88] Thus, Indonesia requires halal compliance (albeit through different methods) for both frozen/chilled chicken sold in packages and for fresh chicken sold unpackaged. Therefore, there is no "less favourable treatment" accorded to imported chicken meat and products. In any event, at a late stage of the proceedings, Brazil stated that it "accepts Indonesia's contention that because Government Regulation 69/1999 is more specific it should prevail over Law 33/2014".[89] This means that Brazil's original arguments that Article 38 of Law No. 33/2104 requiring halal labels be placed on specific parts of fresh products prevailed over the exception in Government Regulation 69/1999 on "food directly sold and packed before buyers in a small number" are no longer valid.[90]

60.   Third, Brazil claimed that previously-frozen (thawed) chicken meat must be allowed to be sold as fresh chicken, i.e. unpackaged and unlabelled when sold before consumers in small quantities.[91] Indonesia argued that fresh, chilled and frozen chicken are not like products.[92] Moreover, there are legitimate grounds for distinguishing between the places where sellers can sell fresh chicken as compared to chilled/frozen products. These legitimate grounds are also reflected in the laws and regulations of other countries, notably Brazil itself and the Philippines.[93]

61.   In the light of the foregoing, Indonesia submits that Brazil has not made a *prima facie* case that the implementation of halal labelling requirements is inconsistent with Indonesia's obligations under Article III:4 of the GATT 1994. Brazil has not met its burden of proof and its claim should therefore be dismissed.

---

[86]   See Brazil's response to Panel Question No. 46.
[87]   See Article 1(1) of Law No. 33/2014 (Halal law).
[88]   See Indonesia's first written submission, paras. 316-328; Indonesia's response to Panel Question No. 43. See also Exhibit IDN-118.
[89]   See Brazil's response to Panel Question No.143.
[90]   See Indonesia's comment on Brazil's responses to Panel Question No. 143.
[91]   See Brazil's response to Panel Question No. 144.
[92]   Indonesia's comments on Brazil's responses to Panel Questions after the second meeting, paras. 62-66 and 120.
[93]   Indonesia's comments on Brazil's response to Panel Question No. 10..

2.   If the Panel were to find that the halal labelling requirements are inconsistent with Article III:4, this measure is justified under Article XX(a) and Article XX(d) of the GATT 1994

62.   If, however, the Panel were to find otherwise, Indonesia submits that the halal labelling requirements are justified under Article XX(a) and (d) of the GATT 1994. For a measure to be provisionally justified under Article XX(a) or Article XX(d) of the GATT 1994, a panel must conduct a two-step analysis. First, a panel must address whether the measure is designed and necessary "to protect public morals" or "to secure compliance with laws or regulations which are not inconsistent with the provisions of this Agreement", respectively. Then, a panel must address whether the application of the measure does not unjustifiably or arbitrarily discriminate among countries where the same conditions prevail or otherwise lead to a disguised restriction on international trade (the *chapeau*).

63.   With respect to the provisional justification under Article XX(a), Indonesia notes that the halal labelling requirements are "designed to protect public morals".[94] Indonesia recalls that the examination of whether a measure is designed to protect public morals is not "particularly demanding".[95] A measure will be designed to protect public morals if it is "not incapable of" protecting public morals.[96] The preamble of Law No. 33/2014 (Halal Law) makes clear that the halal requirements are designed to protect the religious principles of the majority Muslim population by guaranteeing that the products they are consuming are halal. The halal requirements are also "necessary to protect public morals" as they make a meaningful contribution to ensure that consumers are not misled as to what they are eating. In addition, the halal requirements are not trade-restrictive as they apply to all packaged products, whether domestic or imported. Indonesia submits that the relatively slight impact on packaged products is more than outweighed by the importance of the religious values Indonesia is attempting to protect through its halal labelling laws and regulations.

64.   With respect to the provisional justification under Article XX(d), Indonesia notes that the halal labelling requirements are "designed to secure compliance with laws and regulations" that are not inconsistent with the GATT 1994.[97] This is demonstrated by many textual linkages between the halal labelling requirements and the laws and regulations they seek to implement. In addition, the halal labelling requirements are "necessary to secure compliance with laws and regulations" that are not inconsistent with the GATT 1994 as they provide information to the consumer about the product he or she is consuming so

---

[94]   See Indonesia's first written submission, paras. 342-356; and Indonesia's opening statement at the first meeting, paras. 110-132.
[95]   Indonesia's opening statement at the first meeting, para. 117.
[96]   See Indonesia's opening statement at the first meeting, paras. 116-119. See also Appellate Body Report, *Colombia – Textiles*, para. 5.68.
[97]   See Indonesia's first written submission, paras.342-356 and Indonesia's opening statement at the first meeting, paras. 110-132.

that consumers are not misled as to what they are eating. In addition, they are not trade-restrictive as they apply to all packaged products, whether domestic or imported. If the Panel were nevertheless to consider these requirements as trade restrictive, Indonesia submits that the "relatively slight impact on imported products" is more than outweighed by the importance of the religious values Indonesia is attempting to protect through its halal labelling laws and regulations.

65.   Once a panel has weighed and balanced these different factors, it must then compare the challenged measure with possible alternative measures that achieve the same level of protection while being less trade-restrictive. The burden of submitting reasonably available alternatives lies with the complainant, Brazil. Brazil has never provided a less trade restrictive alternative to the halal labelling requirement.

66.   Turning to the *chapeau* of Article XX, it is well established that this provision is concerned with the manner in which the measure is applied. In undertaking an analysis under the *chapeau*, a panel must examine the design, architecture, and revealing structure of a measure.[98]

67.   Indonesia submits that the halal labelling requirements are not discriminatory as they apply to all packaged products, whether domestic or imported. If the Panel nevertheless were to find that discrimination exists because the halal labelling requirements apply only to packaged foods, Indonesia submits that there is a rational connection between the policy objective of protecting the religious beliefs of Indonesian Muslims not to eat non-halal products and informing them as to whether they are purchasing legitimate halal products. To be clear, the halal labelling requirements are not applied differently to countries in which the same conditions prevail. They are applied to all packaged products from all countries (including Indonesia) in a consistent manner.

68.   Finally, under the *chapeau* of Article XX, a measure must not constitute a disguised restriction on international trade, e.g., "concealed or unannounced restriction or discrimination in international trade".[99] The halal labelling requirements do not amount to a disguised restriction on international trade because the measures are transparent. The halal labelling requirements are published in, *inter alia*, Law 33/2014 (Halal Law) and Article 97 of the Law 18/2012 (Food Law).[100]

69.   In sum, Indonesia submits that the halal labelling requirements are not inconsistent with Article III:4 of the GATT 1994. If the Panel were to consider otherwise, Indonesia submits that this measure is justified under Article XX(a) and Article XX(d) of the GATT 1994.

---

[98]   Appellate Body Report, *Japan – Alcoholic Beverages II*, p. 29, DSR 1996:I, p. 120.
[99]   Appellate Body Report, *US – Gasoline*, p. 25.
[100] See Indonesia's opening statement at the first meeting, para. 131.

C.   Intended Use Requirement

1.   Brazil has not demonstrated that the intended use requirement is inconsistent with Indonesia's obligations under Article III:4 of the GATT 1994

70.   Brazil claimed that Indonesia's intended use requirement violated Article III:4 of the GATT. Indonesia recalls that for a violation of Article III:4 to be established, three elements must be satisfied: (i) the imported and domestic products at issue are "like products"; (ii) the measure at issue is a "law, regulation, or requirement affecting the products' internal sale, offering for sale, purchase, transportation, distribution, or use, and (iii) the imported products are accorded "less favourable treatment" than that accorded to like domestic products.[101] Brazil has not satisfied these elements.

71.   As discussed above, Indonesia explained that fresh, and frozen and chilled chicken are not "like products".[102] In addition, Indonesia noted that the intended use requirement was an internal measure imposed with respect to imported products at the moment of importation.[103]

(a)   Previous regime

72.   Before the enactment of MoA Regulation No. 34/2016, Indonesia required that frozen and chilled chicken meat and chicken products to be sold in industries, hotels, restaurants, catering, or be used for other specific purposes.[104] Article 22 and 23 of Minister of Agriculture Decree 306/1994 provide that domestic frozen and chilled poultry meat must be offered for sale in meat shops and supermarkets "equipped with cooler facilities (refrigerator and/or freezer)".[105] Such facilities had not been available in traditional markets. This intended use requirement aimed at ensuring that "frozen" or "chilled" chicken meat and products were not sold in markets that did not have proper cold-chain systems. It is generally recommended that frozen meat should ideally be thawed inside refrigerated facilities.[106] Indonesia must also ensure that previously frozen products were not thawed and refrozen.[107] It is noteworthy that Brazil shares

---

[101] Appellate Body Report, *Korea – Various Measures on Beef*, para. 133.
[102] See also Indonesia's first written submission, paras. 147-164.
[103] Indonesia's first written submission, paras. 81-89; Indonesia's opening statement at the first meeting, paras. 41-47; and Indonesia's responses to Panel Questions No. 50-53 and 55.
[104] See Section II.B.3 of Indonesia's rebuttal submission.
[105] Article 22(c) and Article 23 of the Minister of Agriculture Decree No. 306/1994, Exhibit IDN-83.
[106] See, *inter alia*, Exhibit IDN-85.
[107] Indonesia's first written submission, para. 134.

these same food safety concerns. In fact, Brazil requires thawing to be carried out in a refrigerated facility and prohibits the refreezing of thawed products.[108]

73.   Brazil argued that the intended use requirement meant that imports "could not reach the most important distribution channels" while domestic products "had open and free access to the 'wet markets'" "which represent around 70% of the Indonesian consumer market".[109] Indonesia explained that Articles 22 and 23 of Minister of Agriculture Decree 306/1994 provide that *all* frozen and chilled poultry meat must be offered for sale in meat shops and supermarkets "equipped with cooler facilities (refrigerator and/or freezer)". As a result, neither domestic nor imported frozen products had "open and free access to the 'wet markets'".

74.   Brazil argued that chicken products that had been imported for one intended use e.g. hotels, could not be redirected to another intended use, e.g. restaurants.[110] There is no basis for this assertion. Indonesia recalls that Article 31 of MoA Regulation No. 58/2015 provides that "intended use ... is for hotels, restaurants, caterings, industries, and other particular purposes". Article 38 (e) of the same Regulation provides that there would be sanctions for a breach of the intended use requirement. These sanctions apply when an importer directs the chicken products to a place other than those listed in Article 31. They do not apply when an importer redirects the products to another place listed in Article 31.[111]

(b)   Current regime

75.   Under the current regime, MoA Regulation No. 34/2016 terminated the intended use requirement by providing that frozen and chilled chicken meat can be sold in *any* market with cold-chain facilities, including traditional markets with cold chain facilities. This regulation also requires importers to provide a distribution plan and a distribution report. The distribution plan requires the importer to indicate an estimate of the products it intends to import and information with respect to potential buyers that must have cold-chain facilities available. The distribution report requires importers to submit information with respect to the actual imports and the actual buyers that are required to have cold-chain facilities available.

76.   Brazil argued that Indonesia simply replaced the term "modern markets" used in MoA Regulation No. 39/2014 with "markets with cold chain facilities" in MoA Regulation No. 34/2016. Brazil stated that "this seemingly more flexible formulation was, however, made more restrictive by the requirement [to] submit a "distribution plan" [and] "distribution reports" (every Thursday) so as to

---

[108]   See Article 1.1 of Brazil's Resolution No. 216/2004 on good practices for food services, Exhibit IDN-150 and Brazil's Normative Instruction DIVISA/SVS No. 4/2014 on good practices for commercial food establishments and food services, Exhibit IDN-151.
[109]   Brazil's first written submission, paras. 278-283 and 289.
[110]   Brazil's rebuttal submission, para. 55.
[111]   Indonesia's rebuttal submission, para. 141.

confirm that importers did not evade the previous plan". Indonesia explained that the term "markets with cold chain facilities" is a broader term, which includes, but is not limited to, "modern markets". Modern markets are characterized by offering a wide variety of products with a longer shelf life including pre-packaged and/or processed products, such as minimarkets, supermarkets, and hypermarkets. In contrast, "market with cold chain facilities" can be *any* market, including traditional markets, to the extent they have refrigerators, freezers or any other cold-chain facility. The difference between these two types of markets is critical. While MoA Regulation No. 34/2016 allows the sale of frozen/chilled products in traditional markets with cold chain facilities, the previous MoA Regulation No. 39/2014 did not.

77.   Brazil also argued that importers are now tied to the terms of the distribution plan submitted in the application process and any deviation may subject the importer to harsh sanctions.[112] Indonesia explained that importers are not tied to the terms of the distribution plan because they do not need to match the distribution report. Sanctions only apply when the importer fails to submit the required documents in the first place.[113] In addition, an equivalent requirement is applied to domestic producers when they apply for their meat distributor license.[114] This license requires that applicants disclose the delivery, type, area of the products, the report of sales for the last three months, as well as the meat distributor permit history.[115]

78.   Brazil argued that the distribution report served to confirm that chicken products that had been imported for one intended use, e.g. hotels, were not redirected to another intended use, e.g. restaurants, and any deviation would be subject to sanctions.[116] Indonesia notes that although there are enforcement provisions in Article 38 of MoA Regulation No. 34/2016, they apply only if the importer deviates from the terms listed in the Import Recommendation, i.e. if he sells at a market *without* a cold chain facility. Moreover, there is no sanction if the distribution plan does not match the distribution report. These sanctions only apply when the importer fails to submit the required documents in the first place.[117]

79.   In light of the above, Indonesia submits that the intended use requirement is not inconsistent with Article III:4 of the GATT 1994.

---

[112] Brazil's opening statement at the second meeting, para. 20.
[113] See Indonesia's response to Panel Question No. 88(a).
[114] See Requirements to obtain a Meat Distributor License, retrieved from: http://pelayanan.jakarta.go.id/site/detailperizinan/472, Exhibit IDN-131.
[115] *Ibid.*
[116] Brazil's opening statement at second meeting, para. 20.
[117] Indonesia's response to Panel Question 88(a).

2. **If the Panel were to find that the intended use requirement is inconsistent with Article III:4, this measure is justified under Article XX(b) and Article XX(d) of the GATT 1994**

80.   Should the Panel nevertheless consider otherwise, Indonesia demonstrated that this measure was justified under Article XX(b) and Article XX(d) of the GATT 1994.[118]

81.   To recall, for a measure to be provisionally justified under Article XX(b) or Article XX(d) of the GATT 1994, a panel must determine whether the measure is designed and necessary "to protect human health" or "to secure compliance with laws or regulations which are not inconsistent with the provisions of this Agreement", respectively. Following this determination, a panel must address whether the application of the measure complies with the requirement of the *chapeau* of Article XX.

82.   With respect to the provisional justification under Article XX(b), Indonesia noted that the intended use requirement is designed to, and necessary to, protect public health.[119] The intended use requirement is designed to protect public health, a value of the highest degree of importance,[120] as it prohibits the sale of frozen or chilled chicken in markets without cold-chain facilities. By doing so, the intended use requirement contributes to ensure that only safe chicken is sold in Indonesia. Indonesia has submitted several scientific articles[121] and regulations establishing food safety requirements from WTO Members[122] on the risks of (i) thawing frozen chicken meat at open-air temperatures, and (ii) refreezing products that had previously been frozen and then thawed at open-air temperatures. In addition, the intended use requirement is not trade-restrictive as it applied in an equivalent manner to both imported and domestic products.

83.   With respect to the provisional justification under Article XX(d), Indonesia notes that the intended use requirement is designed to, and necessary to, secure compliance with laws and regulations that are not inconsistent with the GATT 1994.[123] The intended use requirement is designed to ensure compliance with consumer protection laws and regulations. This is demonstrated by the textual linkages between the intended use requirement and the laws and regulations it seeks to implement. Indonesia notes that thawed chicken meat is deceptively similar to fresh chicken meat. The sanctions imposed in case of violation of the intended use requirement on sellers of imported products (that is,

---

[118] Indonesia's first written submission, paras. 179-216; Indonesia's opening statement at the first meeting, paras. 62-79.
[119] See Indonesia's first written submission, paras.342-356 and Indonesia's opening statement at the first meeting, paras. 110-132.
[120] Appellate Body Report, *EC – Asbestos*, para. 172.
[121] Exhibits IDN-54, IDN-55 and IDN-56.
[122] Exhibits IDN-84 and IDN-85.
[123] See Indonesia's first written submission, paras.342-356 and Indonesia's opening statement at the first meeting, paras. 110-132.

the revocation of the Import Recommendation)[124] contribute to the prevention of deceptive practices against consumers, as sellers will be reluctant to thaw frozen products and present them as fresh, in the light of the possible sanctions they may face. Indonesia submitted that the intended use requirement is not trade-restrictive as it applied in an equivalent manner to both imported and domestic products.

84.   Once a panel has weighed and balanced these different factors, it must then compare the challenged measure with possible alternative measures that achieve the same level of protection sought by the concerned Member, while being less trade-restrictive. Brazil provided "alternatives" that would not have achieved the specific objective and level of protection Indonesia sought with respect to the (now expired) intended use requirement, namely, to protect the public health of consumers by preventing frozen products from being thawed at tropical temperatures in open-air markets and to prevent consumers from being misled into buying thawed products believing they were fresh products. For example, Brazil's alternative of introducing a mandatory good hygienic practice (GHP) plan for establishments selling chicken meat is not a valid alternative as the Minister of Agriculture Decree No. 306/1994 already provides for good hygienic and sanitary practices. In addition, some of Brazil's alternatives became moot with the introduction of cold-chain facilities at the traditional markets. Nowadays, a consumer can buy a frozen product in a traditional market, keep it in a cold storage thermal bag, go home and put it safely in his freezer.

85.   Turning to the *chapeau* of Article XX, it is well established that discrimination under the *chapeau* is only possible "among countries where the same conditions prevail". In Indonesian traditional markets, chicken meat and products are mostly sold fresh and unpackaged. In contrast, imported products are frozen and packaged. Indonesia submitted that there is a different risk posed by frozen meat being thawed in open-air spaces compared to fresh meat that has been slaughtered a few hours before. Even if both products are exposed to tropical open-air conditions, fresh chicken meat does not have the excessive moisture conducive to bacteria growth as does frozen chicken. Therefore, there is no discrimination vis-à-vis imported products. Indonesia treats all frozen products in the same way, regardless of their origin, by preventing their sale in markets without proper cold-chain facilities.

86.   If the Panel were nevertheless to find that discrimination exists, Indonesia submits that there is a rational connection with the policy objective of protecting public health and ensuring compliance with food safety and consumer protection regulations. In addition, the intended use requirement does not constitute a disguised restriction on international trade as it is a transparent measure published in MoA Regulation No. 34/2016.[125]

---

[124]   Article 38(e) of the MoA Regulation No. 58/2015, Exhibit IDN-24.
[125]   Indonesia's first written submission, paras. 213-216; and Indonesia's opening statement at the first meeting, paras. 76-79.

87.   In sum, Indonesia submits that the intended use requirement is not inconsistent with Article III:4 of the GATT 1994. If the Panel were to consider otherwise, Indonesia submits its measure is justified under Article XX(b) and Article XX(d) of the GATT 1994.

D.   Positive List Requirements

88.   Brazil claims that the positive list requirements constitute a "prohibition or restriction" inconsistent with Article XI:1 of the GATT 1994. Brazil argues that this measure prohibits or restricts the importation into Indonesia of chicken meat and chicken products not included in the positive lists.[126]

89.   Under the previous regime, the positive list was introduced in response to an incident in 1999, where Tyson Foods of the United States sent a shipment of chicken cuts that was part halal and part non-halal. The Tyson incident was not an isolated incident. Rather, there were other instances that caused unrest among the majority Muslim community in Indonesia (87 per cent of the population) and led the Indonesian Government to take steps to ensure the integrity and halalness of all imported products.[127]

90.   Under the current regime, the Ministry of Trade and the Ministry of Agriculture have further liberalized Indonesia's trade policies with respect to the importation of chicken meat and chicken products. Under the current regime, neither the MoA nor the MoT Regulations provide for positive list requirements. Article 7(3) of MoA Regulation No. 34/2016 provides that chicken meat and chicken products that are not included in the relevant attachments to these Regulations may be imported in Indonesia as long as they meet the requirements of being safe, healthy, wholesome and halal (ASUH requirements).

91.   With respect to the current regime, Brazil argued that compliance with the ASUH requirements only provided an "abstract possibility of importation" and that the assessment of compliance with these requirements was "discretionary". Indonesia noted that the expression "may still be granted recommendation" is not used to express an "abstract possibility of importation", but rather the concrete conditions precedent that must be met prior to the granting of the Import Recommendation, i.e. that the importer: (i) applies for the Import Recommendation,[128] and (ii) complies with the ASUH requirements.

---

[126]   Brazil's first written submission, paras. 192-194. In addition, Brazil claimed that the positive list requirements constituted a "quantitative import restriction" or a "border measure similar to quantitative import restrictions" within the meaning of footnote 1 to Article 4.2 of the Agreement on Agriculture; and that this measure was also inconsistent with Article 3.2 of the Import Licensing Agreement. Brazil's first written submission, paras. 219-223, 251. Indonesia addressed the relationship between Article 4.2 of the Agreement on Agriculture, Article 3.2 of the Import Licensing Agreement and Article XI:1 of the GATT in other parts of this summary. Therefore, Indonesia addresses only Brazil's claim under Article XI:1.

[127]   Opening statement of Indonesia at the first meeting, para. 89. See Letter by Indonesia's Minster of Agriculture, Exhibit IDN-82; Letter by the US Secretary of Agriculture, Exhibit IDN-81.

[128]   See Article 4(3) of MoA Regulation No. 34/2016.

Moreover, Indonesia explained that there are objective criteria for the assessment of compliance with the ASUH requirements.[129] For example, compliance with Indonesia's halal requirements is assessed by customs officials through the inspection of the Halal Certificate.[130]

92.   Moreover, Brazil's concern that both "listed" and "non-listed" chicken meat and chicken products have to comply with ASUH requirements, but only "listed" chicken products enjoy certainty of being granted approval is without merit. The Annexes to MoA Regulation No. 34/2016 and MoT Regulation No. 59/2016 do not serve any purpose at this point in time. Indonesia has explained that pursuant to Article 2(b) of MoA Regulation No. 34/2016, the ASUH requirements apply to *all imported products*. In addition, ASUH as a comprehensive principle has existed since Animal Law No. 18/2009 was enacted. In addition, halal requirements date back to Law No. 6/1967 (previous Animal Law).[131] Safety requirements have applied ever since importation first took place. These safety and halal requirements continue to apply in accordance with, *inter alia*, MoA Regulation No. 34/2016.[132]

93.   To sum up, if an importer applies for an Import Recommendation and the imported products comply with the ASUH requirements (regardless of whether they are listed or not listed in the annexes to MoA Regulation No. 34/2016), the Import Recommendation will be granted.

94.   If the Panel were nevertheless to find that the positive list requirements are inconsistent with Article XI:1 of the GATT 1994, Indonesia justified this measure under Article XX(d) of the GATT 1994.[133]

95.   In its submissions, Indonesia identified specific laws with which the measure was designed to secure compliance. Furthermore, Indonesia showed that the positive list requirements were "designed to secure compliance with the relevant laws and regulations" by pointing to the textual linkages between the positive list requirements and the laws and regulations it seeks to secure compliance with. In addition, Indonesia submitted that the positive list requirements were "necessary to secure compliance with the relevant laws and regulations" as they prevented the circumvention of Indonesia's halal requirements.[134] Indonesia also considers that the importance of its objective and the existence of the contribution of the measure to the objective outweighed the relatively insignificant trade-restrictiveness of the measure. Nothing prevented Brazilian exporters from exporting to Indonesia whole carcasses of chicken, provided that Indonesia's halal requirements were fulfilled. Thus, in Indonesia's view, the measure is not highly trade restrictive.

---

[129] See Indonesia's response to Panel Question No. 77(a).
[130] Exhibit IDN-92(c).
[131] See Law of the Republic of Indonesia No. 6/1967 Concerning Basic Provisions on the Husbandry and Animal Health (previous Animal Law), Exhibit IDN-129.
[132] See Indonesia's response to Panel Question No. 77(a).
[133] Indonesia's first written submission, paras. 230-231.
[134] Indonesia's first written submission, para. 232.

96.   Indonesia further submitted that the positive list requirements were justified under the *chapeau* of Article XX. The *chapeau* of Article XX requires the measure not to be "applied in a manner which would constitute a means of arbitrary or unjustifiable discrimination between countries where the same conditions prevail, or a disguised restriction on international trade".[135] Indonesia applied the positive list requirements in a non-discriminatory manner to chicken meat and chicken products imported from all Members.[136] However, even if the Panel were to find that the positive list requirements accorded discriminatory treatment to imported chicken from Brazil, Indonesia submits that the discriminatory application of the measure is not unjustifiable or arbitrary. On the contrary, it is justifiable when considered in the light of the objective of the measure to secure compliance with Indonesia's halal requirements.[137] Put differently, the discrimination, to the extent that it existed, was necessary to achieve the measure's objective. Furthermore, again, the fact that there are important differences between the conditions that prevail in Indonesia and Brazil, namely that Indonesia is the country with the world's largest Muslim population, resolves any doubts as to whether the discriminatory treatment was arbitrary or unjustifiable. It was not.

97.   Finally, Indonesia submits that the question of whether the measure was a disguised restriction on international trade cannot be addressed in isolation from the analysis of the other elements of the *chapeau*.[138] The fact that the measure meets the requirements of the first two elements confirms that it is not a disguised restriction. In any event, the positive list requirements are a transparent regulation published in MoA Regulation No. 39/2014 and MoT Regulation No. 46/2013.

E.   Import Licensing Regime

1.   Most of Brazil's claims with respect to Indonesia's import licensing regime are repetitive, not supported by adequate evidence and arguments, or outside the Panel's terms of reference

98.   Brazil challenges almost identical elements of Indonesia's import licensing regime under Article XI:1 of the GATT 1994, Article 4.2 of the Agreement on Agriculture, and Article 3.2 of the Licensing Agreement. In particular, Brazil claims that the following elements of the import licensing regime "constitute restrictions on the importation of chicken meat and chicken products" that are inconsistent with both Article 4.2 of the Agreement on Agriculture and Article XI:1 of the GATT 1994: (i) the positive list requirements; (ii) the intended use requirement; (iii) the limited application and

---

[135]   Indonesia's first written submission, paras. 209-212.
[136]   Indonesia's first written submission, para. 233.
[137]   See Indonesia's first written submission, para. 210.
[138]   Appellate Body Report, *US – Gasoline*, p. 25.

validity periods; and (iv) the fixed license terms. The first two elements were also challenged as individual measures. With respect to these elements, Brazil simply incorporated by reference its arguments made in the context of its other claims.[139]

99.   In addition, in the course of these proceedings, Brazil raised a number of additional claims that were either unsubstantiated, or outside the Panel's terms of references. For example, Brazil claimed in the alternative, without providing adequate evidence and arguments, that the elements of Indonesia's import licensing regime at issue constitute "similar border measures other than ordinary customs duties" within the meaning of footnote 1 to Article 4.2 of the Agreement on Agriculture. Brazil did not make its *prima facie* case with respect to these claims.[140]

100.   Along the same lines, Brazil challenged the first, second and third elements of Indonesia's import licensing regime as inconsistent with Article 3.2 of the Licensing Agreement. However, Brazil did not explain adequately why these measures constitute "*non-automatic*" "import licensing *procedures*" within the meaning of Articles 1.1 and 3.1 of the Licensing Agreement, which is a threshold issue that must be addressed before analysing the consistency of a measure with Article 3.2. Furthermore, Brazil did not provide any arguments or evidence proving that the relevant aspects of Indonesia's import licensing regime are inconsistent Article 3.2, in particular they are "more administratively burdensome than absolutely necessary". Brazil's interpretation of Article 3.2 is based on an erroneous premise that, according to this provision, "a non-automatic procedure must be related to the implementation of a permissible 'trade restrictive measure', that is, a measure consistent with the relevant provisions of the WTO Agreement".[141] Brazil introduces this requirement into the legal tests under the first and second sentences of Article 3.2, and alleges that the challenged measures failed to satisfy this requirement.[142] However, Brazil did not explain from where it derived this additional requirement. Indeed, Indonesia demonstrated that Brazil's interpretation lacks any support in the text of Article 3.2, its context (in particular Article 1.1), negotiating history, and makes little sense from both a legal and a practical perspective. As stated clearly in Article 1.1, the Licensing Agreement disciplines administrative *procedures*, that is, import licensing, and is not concerned with a broader question of the WTO-consistency of the underlying measures those procedures seek to implement.[143]

---

[139] See Indonesia's first written submission, paras. 235-247; Indonesia's rebuttal submission, paras. 120-123 (citing Brazil's first written submission, paras. 200-201, 212, 228-231).
[140] Indonesia's rebuttal submission, para. 123.
[141] See Brazil's rebuttal submission, para. 117.
[142] Brazil's rebuttal submission, paras. 128 and 129.
[143] See Brazil's claim under Article 3.2 discussed in Indonesia's first written submission, paras. 76-80, 279-290; Indonesia's responses to Panel Questions No. 48, 57, 58, 59, 60; Indonesia's rebuttal

101.   Furthermore, as explained, in Question No. 128, the Panel asked Brazil to clarify whether Brazil is also challenging the fixed licence terms under Article 3.2 of the Licensing Agreement and, "[i]f so, ... where this claim was developed in Brazil's submissions". In its response, Brazil could not point to any passages in its first written submission, as well as other submissions, where it provided adequate legal arguments and evidence to develop this claim. Indonesia trusts that the Panel will find that Brazil failed to make its *prima facie* case with respect to the alleged inconsistency of the aforementioned measures with Article 3.2 of the Licensing Agreement.[144]

102.   In its response to Panel Question No. 15.b, Brazil stated generally that "[t]o the ... extent that MoT Regulation 87/2015 and MoT 05/2016 introduce additional requirements and procedures to obtain an import license whenever a product is considered a 'certain product', in the first case, or is a processed product coming from a country having a risk of spread of zoonosis, in the second, Brazil submits that these additional restrictions are also at issue in the present dispute". Brazil, however, failed to explain which specific measures it is challenging, under which specific provisions of the WTO covered agreements, and on what legal basis.[145]

103.   A number of Brazil's claims with respect to Indonesia's import licensing regime are not properly identified in Brazil's panel request and are, therefore, outside the Panel's terms of reference. In addition to Brazil's challenge to the regime "as a whole" already rejected by the Panel in its preliminary ruling, Brazil also challenged: (i) a letter of recommendation from provincial livestock services office; (ii) supervision on the compliance of veterinary public health requirements; and (iii) the alleged discretionary powers in determining "the amount in Recommendation per Business Player" under Article 27 of MoA Regulation No. 58/2015. Brazil claimed, *inter alia*, that these measures constitute "discretionary import licensing" within the meaning of footnote 1 to Article 4.2 of the Agreement on Agriculture.[146]

104.   However, even if the Panel were to find that it has jurisdiction over these claims, Indonesia demonstrated that Brazil's claims are without merit. The first two requirements do not constitute "licensing", and the second requirement does not even address the issue of importation. These measures cannot, therefore, be characterised as "import licensing". Furthermore, Brazil failed to demonstrate that the alleged licensing elements bestow any discretion on Indonesia's

---

submission, paras. 114-117; Indonesia's opening statement at the second meeting, paras. 22-36; Indonesia's comments on Brazil's responses to Panel Questions No. 124, 127.
[144]   Indonesia's comment on Brazil's response to Panel Question No. 128.
[145]   Indonesia's rebuttal submission, paras. 77-79, 118.
[146]   Indonesia's responses to Panel Questions No. 105.

authorities, as these measures are set out clearly in Indonesia's legislation and are based on transparent criteria.[147]

105.   Indonesia addresses below Brazil's claims that the limited application and validity periods and the fixed license terms are "quantitative import restrictions" within the meaning of Article 4.2 of the Agreement on Agriculture and Article XI:1 of the GATT 1994. The other claims with respect to Indonesia's import licensing regime are repetitive, not supported by adequate evidence and arguments, or outside the Panel's terms of reference.

2.   **Brazil has not demonstrated that the limited application and validity periods and the fixed license terms are inconsistent with Indonesia's obligations under Article 4.2 of the Agreement on Agriculture**

106.   As explained, Indonesia considers that, in the present dispute, Article 4.2 of the Agreement on Agriculture applies to the exclusion of Article XI:1 of the GATT 1994. In the context of its claim under Article 4.2, Brazil did not substantiate its assertion that the limited application and validity periods and the fixed license terms constitute a quantitative import restriction as these measures: "(a) unduly restrict market access for Brazilian products; (b) create uncertainty as to an applicant's ability to import...; and (c) impose a significant burden on importers that is unrelated to their normal importing activity". Brazil further argued that these measures create what Brazil calls a "dead zone", i.e. a period during which products cannot be imported into Indonesia. In its submissions, Indonesia has, however, demonstrated that, under both previous and current regimes, its import licensing procedures are fast and simple. Indeed, despite these measures, an importer could import the products at issue to Indonesia without interruption on terms it determined itself in its application for the Import Recommendation. For example, under the current regime, producers and importers can make their application for an Import Recommendation and an Import Approval at any time of the year to import within a six-month validity period. The flexibility is that an importer can apply for an infinite number of Import Recommendations and Import Approvals, at whichever point in time he wishes throughout the year. Brazil has not rebutted these arguments, or provided adequate evidence that Indonesia's import licensing regime indeed creates a "dead zone". To the extent that the alleged "dead zone" results from the way how Brazilian exporters operate, as Brazil's own evidence suggests, this dead zone cannot be attributed to any action or omission of Indonesia.[148]

107.   Moreover, Brazil did not provide any arguments or evidence showing that the above measures are not "maintained under ... general, non-agriculture-

---

[147]   See, inter alia, Indonesia's first written submission, paras. 267-275; Indonesia's responses to Panel Questions No. 12, 18 and 105; Indonesia's comment on Brazil's response to Panel Question No. 108.
[148]   See, inter alia, Indonesia's first written submission, paras. 250-259, 261-265 (citing Brazil's first written submission, paras. 202, 212, 228-231); Indonesia's rebuttal submission, paras. 9-22; Indonesia's comment on Brazil's response to Panel Question No. 103.

specific provisions of GATT 1994" within the meaning of footnote 1 of the Agreement on Agriculture.[149]

108.   In light of the foregoing, Brazil failed to prove that the limited application and validity periods and the fixed license terms are one of the measures listed in footnote 1 of the Agreement on Agriculture, and are not "maintained under ... general, non-agriculture-specific provisions of GATT 1994". Brazil thus failed to make its *prima facie* case that these measures are inconsistent with Article 4.2 of the Agreement on Agriculture.[150]

3.   Brazil has not demonstrated that the limited application and validity periods and the fixed license terms are inconsistent with Indonesia's obligations under Article XI:1 of the GATT 1994

109.   Should the Panel find that Article XI:1 of the GATT 1994 applies to the limited application and validity periods and the fixed license terms (*quod non*), as explained, these measures, under both previous and current regimes, do not have a limiting effect on imports. Brazil, therefore, failed to make its *prima facie* case of inconsistency with Article XI:1 of the GATT 1994.[151]

110.   Nevertheless, even if the Panel were to find otherwise, these measures are justified under Article XX(d) of the GATT 1994.[152]

4.   If the Panel were to find that the limited application and validity periods and the fixed license terms are inconsistent with Article XI:1, these measures are justified under Article XX(d) of the GATT 1994

111.   As explained, Article XX(d) of the GATT 1994 allows Members to apply measures that are "necessary to secure compliance with laws or regulations which are not inconsistent with the provisions of this Agreement, including those relating to customs enforcement, ... and the prevention of deceptive practices". Indonesia demonstrated that the limited application and validity periods and the fixed license terms are justified under Article XX(d), as these measures were designed to secure compliance with Indonesia's laws and regulations addressing halal requirements, public health, as well as deceptive practices (consumer protection) and customs enforcement relating to the halal requirements and food safety.[153]

112.   In particular, Indonesia identified certain laws with which the measures at issue ensure compliance, such as Law No. 18/2009 (Animal Law) as amended

---

[149]   Indonesia's first written submission, para. 277.
[150]   Indonesia's first written submission, para. 278.
[151]   See Indonesia's rebuttal submission, paras. 9-22, 126-127. See also Indonesia's first written submission, paras. 292-294.
[152]   Indonesia's rebuttal submission, para. 128.
[153]   See, inter alia, Indonesia's first written submission, paras. 295-300; Indonesia's opening statement at the first meeting, paras. 97-109; Indonesia's responses to Panel Questions No. 24, 27, 113-119, 121-122; Indonesia's comments on Brazil's responses to Panel Questions No. 120-123.

by Law No. 41/2014; Law No. 33/2014 (Halal Law); and Law No. 8/1999 (Consumer Protection Law). In this respect, Indonesia referred the Panel to the relevant provisions of these laws on food safety, halal requirements, and consumer deceptive practices. Furthermore, these laws are "not inconsistent with the provisions of [the GATT 1994]". It is a general principle that a Member's law is recognized to be WTO-consistent until proven otherwise. Brazil has not provided this proof.[154]

113.   Indonesia further explained how the application and validity periods and the fixed license terms contribute to securing compliance with these laws. At the outset, Indonesia noted that even though these measures are challenged as individual measures, they are the interrelated elements of Indonesia's import licensing regime for chicken. These measures are integral parts of Indonesia's comprehensive package of measures that aim at fulfilling the same objective. Although these measures *operating together* contribute to Indonesia's objective, it is difficult to segregate the *individual* contributions they make to Indonesia's objective.[155]

114.   With respect to the issue of contribution, Indonesia explained that it is a developing archipelagic country with vast territory, which imposes additional constraints on its ability to conduct expedient customs clearance operations, in particular for products that pose halal and safety risks, such as animal products. The application and validity periods and the fixed license terms seek compliance with Indonesia's relevant laws by facilitating the supervision by Indonesia's customs and quarantine officials over the importers' compliance with these laws at the time of importation. In other words, *the facilitation of supervision* is the immediate objective of these measures through which Indonesia seeks to achieve its ultimate objective of ensuring that animal products are safe, healthy, wholesome and halal; and that consumers are not deceived about these issues. For example, absent the limited validity period, one would not be able to estimate how many products of which particular type will be imported through which particular ports. Conversely, if Indonesia were to impose the validity period requirement without applying the fixed license terms requirement, it would have received information on the period of importation. However, it would not know, at least approximately, what quantity of which particular products would be imported and through which particular ports. In addition, importers submit arrival plans for imports on a monthly basis, which provide further information as to the quantity and the timing of the imports that will arrive at the specified ports. Thus, without these requirements, Indonesia would not be able to allocate a sufficient number of quarantine and customs officials to a particular port of entry to supervise an importer's compliance with halal and

---

[154]   See, inter alia, Indonesia's first written submission, paras. 297-298 (citing Appellate Body Report, *US – Carbon Steel*, para. 157); Indonesia's response to Panel Question No. 113.
[155]   Indonesia's response to Panel Question No. 113.

food safety requirements, as well as consumer protection. These measures, therefore, contribute to Indonesia's objective.[156]

115. In light of the foregoing, Indonesia considers that it has satisfied its burden of proof under Article XX(d) of the GATT 1994.[157]

116. Indonesia notes that Brazil did not propose any concrete alternative measures that are less-trade restrictive and make an equivalent contribution to Indonesia's objective. Brazil's so-called "alternatives" are vague and imprecise, and do not address the issue of supervision by Indonesia's customs and quarantine officials over the importer's compliance with Indonesia's relevant laws at the time of importation. Moreover, Indonesia already applies these measures. Brazil, therefore, failed to rebut Indonesia's defence under Article XX(d).[158]

117. Finally, Indonesia demonstrated that the limited application and validity periods and the fixed license terms are justified under the *chapeau* of Article XX. Indonesia applies these measures in a non-discriminatory manner to chicken meat and chicken products imported from all Members. In addition, there is no discrimination between imported and domestic like products, as Indonesian producers of the products at issue must comply with Indonesia's safety and halal requirements. Furthermore, even if these measures were found to accord discriminatory treatment to imports, Indonesia submits that this treatment is not unjustifiable or arbitrary. On the contrary, it is justifiable when considered in the light of the importance of Indonesia's objective to secure compliance with Indonesia's laws that address halal and public health, as well as the conditions that prevail in Indonesia. Finally, the fact that the measures at issue are not applied in a manner that constitutes a means of arbitrary or unjustifiable discrimination confirms that they are not a disguised restriction, as all elements of the test under the *chapeau* "may ... be read side-by-side [and] ... impart meaning to one another". In any event, these measures are published, and are, therefore, not "disguised".[159]

118. In light of the foregoing, even if the Panel were to find that the limited application and validity periods and the fixed license terms fall under Article XI:1 of the GATT 1994 (which they do not), these measures are, nevertheless, justified under both sub-paragraph (d) and the *chapeau* of Article XX of the GATT 1994.[160]

---

[156] See, inter alia, Indonesia's responses to Panel Questions No. 113, 115, 119.

[157] Indonesia's response to Panel Question No. 113.

[158] Indonesia's responses to Panel Questions No. 121, 122; Indonesia's comments on Brazil's responses to Panel Questions No. 121, 123.

[159] Indonesia's opening statement at the first meeting, paras. 107-109 (citing, inter alia, Appellate Body Report, *US – Gasoline*, p. 25).

[160] Indonesia's first written submission, para. 302.

F.   Alleged Delays in Approving Brazil's Veterinary Certificate

119.   Brazil claims that "Indonesia has consistently failed to undertake and complete the procedures to check and ensure the fulfillment of sanitary requirements necessary to authorize Brazilian exports of chicken meat and chicken products" thereby violating the requirements of Article 8 and Annex C(1)(a) of the Agreement on the Application of Sanitary and Phytosanitary Measures (SPS Agreement).[161] Brazil states it "has submitted in 2009 to Indonesia's authorities a proposal of an International [Veterinary] Certificate, which followed every single guideline from the World Organization for Animal Health".[162]

120.   Indonesia submits that Brazil has not obtained the "International Veterinary Certificate" because it has not submitted all the appropriate documentation. A letter from the Ministry of Agriculture, Directorate-General of Livestock and Animal Health Services dated 22 January 2013 indicates that the Director-General acknowledged the questionnaire of MFG-MARFRIG FRIGORIFICOS BRASIL S/A and COOPERATIVE CENTRAL AURORA ALIMENTOS, two Brazilian companies wishing to export beef, chicken meat and products to Indonesia.[163] The Indonesian government then informed Brazil that the application documents presented by the two Brazilian companies were at the stage of desk review. However, the submitted questionnaire only covered the food safety assurance system, and did not include information on halal practices in the exporting poultry slaughter house.[164] Therefore any delays experienced by Brazil are because they have not submitted the proper documentation, and should not be attributed to the Government of Indonesia.

121.   Indonesia does not dispute that negotiation of a Veterinary Certificate, which certifies that the country of origin is free of diseases or that exporters comply with safety requirements, may fall within the scope of Article 8 and Annex C of the SPS Agreement.[165] In Indonesia's view, the real question is whether Brazil has established that there was indeed a "delay" in the approval of the veterinary certificate for chicken meat and chicken products within the meaning of Article 8 and Annex C, and the delay, if were found to exist (*quod non*), is "undue". Indonesia understands the phrase "undue delay" as indicating that a delay in the approval procedure (i.e. "time lost by inaction" or "something

---

[161]   See Brazil's opening statement at the first meeting, para. 96. See also *Ibid.*, paras. 96-105; and Brazil's first written submission, paras. 294-315. Indonesia provided its interpretation of Article 8 and Annex C(1)(a) in, *inter alia*, its response to Panel Question No. 65.

[162]   Brazil's opening statement at the first meeting, para. 97. See also Brazil's first written submission, para. 35.

[163]   Letter from the Ministry of Agriculture to the Embassy of Brazil in Jakarta, 22 January 2013. Exhibit IDN-40.

[164]   *Ibid.*

[165]   Indonesia's response to Panel Question No. 65.

[that] is late or postponed")[166] can only result from a properly submitted application, which was not submitted in the case at hand. Furthermore, even if one were to interpret the term "delay" broadly as encompassing delays that were caused by applicants themselves (for example, applicants that failed to attach all required documents to their application), Indonesia submits that delays "attributable to action, or inaction, of an applicant" cannot properly be considered as "undue" (i.e. "[u]nwarranted or inappropriate"), as was confirmed by the panel in *EC – Approval and Marketing of Biotech Products*.[167] Such delays are, therefore, not inconsistent with Article 8 and Annex C of the SPS Agreement.

122. Indonesia submits that Brazil's claim is based on its erroneous interpretation of Article 8 and Annex C(1)(a) of the SPS Agreement, its total misunderstanding of Indonesia's import licensing regime, and the misleading presentation of facts underlying this claim. First, Brazil's argument that, under the SPS Agreement, sanitary procedures must be isolated from other procedures is legally incorrect. Indonesia submits that the determination of whether the delay in question is "undue" is not dependent upon the nature of the document that the applicant failed to submit as long as the document/requirement relates to the approval procedure. The Appellate Body and previous panels have confirmed that a wide range of measures, including those that are not themselves sanitary procedures, may fall within the scope of Article 8 and Annex C.[168]

123. The Appellate Body's statement that measures other than the sanitary procedures may infringe the requirements of Article 8 and Annex C must necessarily mean that the failure of an applicant to comply with additional legitimate requirements (e.g. to pay fees, or, *in casu*, to fill out the halal questionnaire) is relevant for the assessment of whether the alleged "undue delay" exists. For example, in the event of an applicant's failure to comply with these requirements, the delay cannot be attributed to governmental authorities conducting the approval procedure. Brazil has itself acknowledged that the term "procedures" in Article 8 and Annex C "is defined in the SPS Agreement *in a manner as broad as possible*".[169]

124. In addition, Brazil's argument has far-reaching practical implications. There may be legitimate reasons why a Member may wish to conduct a holistic assessment of the compliance by a particular establishment with sanitary requirements as well as other requirements. In its response to Panel Question No. 29, Indonesia explained that it would be inefficient to start the Document Desk Review process of the food safety assurance system of the business unit in

---

[166] See Panel Report, *EC – Approval and Marketing of Biotech Products*, para. 7.1495. See definition of "delay" in Oxford Dictionaries, Exhibit IDN-106.

[167] See Panel Report, *EC – Approval and Marketing of Biotech Products*, para. 7.1497.

[168] Appellate Body Report, *Australia – Apples*, para. 438. The broad scope of Article 8 and Annex C was also confirmed in Panel Report, *US – Poultry (China)*, para. 7.363; and Panel Report, *US – Animals*, paras. 7.67-7.68.

[169] Brazil's first written submission, para. 299, emphasis added.

Brazil and proceed to the field on-site inspection for food safety, if it is not known whether the business unit has a halal assurance system. To make separate trips to assess food safety and halal requirements separately would entail unnecessary costs for Indonesia, which is a developing country. This is why Indonesia treats the assessment of the food safety and halal requirements on a holistic basis.

125.   Furthermore, in its responses to Panel Questions No. 30, 32 and 37, Indonesia provided a detailed description of a four-step process for obtaining the approval of country of origin and business units. This process starts with the Desk Document Review, during which Indonesian authorities assess certain documents provided by Brazil and its business units, including: the questionnaire covering food safety and assurance system,[170] the halal questionnaire,[171] and the halal certificate approved by MUI or an Islamic body in Brazil recognized by the MUI.[172] Based on the results of the Desk Document Review, a field inspection will be undertaken to the proposed establishment (i.e. On-site Field Inspection in Country of Origin). At the following stage of Risk Analysis in Jakarta, Indonesia then analyses the reports to determine whether to approve or reject the application. The four-step process culminates with the conclusion of a bilateral agreement between the country of origin and Indonesia (Protocol)[173] which specifies the body in the country of origin responsible for the issuance of Veterinary Certificates at the regional or local level, certifying that meat exports will meet all veterinary and specific requirements determined by Indonesia. A model certificate is attached to the completed and signed Protocol between the country of origin and Indonesia.[174]

126.   Indonesia trusts that it has become clear that Brazil's proposal of an International Health Certificate was very premature and failed to meet the requirements under Indonesia's import licensing regime. A Veterinary Certificate can only be agreed upon at the very end of the four-step country of origin and business unit approval process, during the negotiations on the Protocol. It is in the Protocol that the approval of the permanent official veterinaries by a body in the country of origin can be established. However, Brazil has not reached this final stage of the approval process. In fact, Brazil's application is incomplete, and did not even trigger the Desk Document Review (i.e. the first step). The only document that Brazil has so far provided is the questionnaire covering food

---

[170]   See Questionnaire for Country of Origin on Food Safety, Exhibit IDN-101.
[171]   See Questionnaire for Business Unit on Food Safety and Halal Assurance System, Exhibit IDN-102.
[172]   See Form 2 to Questionnaire for Business Unit on Food Safety and Halal Assurance System, Exhibit IDN-102. See also Indonesia's response to Panel Question No. 30(a).
[173]   See Sample Protocol between the Directorate General of Livestock and Animal Health Services of the Ministry of Agriculture of the Republic of Indonesia and the Directorate General of XXX Concerning Establishment, Approval, and Inspection for Export of Meat, Meat Products and Milk Products from XXX to Indonesia, Exhibit IDN-115.
[174]   See Sample Health Certificate for Export of Beef from XXX to the Republic of Indonesia, Exhibit IDN-114.

safety and assurance system. There are other documents that are still to be submitted, including those establishing compliance with Indonesia's halal requirements. In its response to Question 4, Indonesia made clear that "[t]he delay of the approval for Brazil and its business units of slaughterhouse was due to failure in the application to comply with the existing procedures and technical regulations, stipulated by the Indonesian law", and "[t]he process of desk review was discontinued *because the Brazilian applications [were] not equipped with halal questionnaire*".[175]

127.   In the light of the above, Indonesia submits that Brazil's claim must be rejected in its entirety, as Brazil did not prove that there is any "delay" in the country of origin and business unit approval process, attributable to Indonesia within the meaning of Article 8 and Annex C(1)(a) of the SPS Agreement. Alternatively, should the Panel find otherwise, Brazil failed to prove that the delay is "undue".[176]

G.   Transportation Requirements

128.   Brazil alleges that Indonesia imposes restrictions on the transportation of imported products by requiring that the transportation of carcass, meat and/or processed products shall be "conducted directly from the country of origin to the port of discharge within the territory of [the Republic of] Indonesia".[177] It claims that the measure "clearly operates as a 'quantitative import restriction' within the meaning of Article 4.2 [of the Agreement on Agriculture] and Article XI:1 of the GATT 1994, and alleges that the measure restricts the volume of imports.[178]

129.   Indonesia submits that Brazil incorrectly understands the legal requirements related to the transportation of carcass, meat and/or processed products to Indonesia.

130.   Indonesia acknowledges that Article 20(a) of MoA 58/2015 refers to a direct transportation requirement from the country of origin to Indonesia.[179] However, this provision must be read in the context of the other provisions in the same Article, which provide for the application of animal quarantine measures. Article 20(b) requires that animal quarantine measures must be carried out at the country of origin, before the products are loaded on the conveyance. Article 20(c) of the same regulation provides that the "*transit* during importation shall

---

[175] Indonesia's responses to Brazil's information request under Article 5.8 of the SPS Agreement, Exhibit BRA-20, emphasis added.
[176] These issues are discussed in Indonesia's rebuttal submission, paras. 159-174; Indonesia's response to Panel Question No. 65.
[177] Brazil's first written submission, para. 239, citing Article 20(a) of MoA Regulation 58/2015, Exhibit IDN-24.
[178] Brazil's first written submission, paras. 214-217 and paras. 239-243.
[179] In this context, the term "direct" may be used in the same manner as it is used in the airline industry. A direct flight is one that may make stops and pick up additional passengers but the original passengers do not leave the plane. A "non-stop" flight does not make any stops at all. See: http://www.programmerinterview.com/index.php/assortment/whats-the-difference-between-a-nonstop-and-direct-flight/

be carried out pursuant to the animal quarantine laws and regulations". Thus, this provision acknowledges that transit during importation can take place as long as animal quarantine laws are respected. Article 20(e) requires that upon arrival at the port of discharge, further animal quarantine measures shall be performed or applied to the carcass, meat and/or processed products.

131. Animal quarantine requirements are regulated under Law 16/1992 on Animal, Fish and Plant Quarantine.[180] Recital (c) of the Considerations notes that "most of the pests and diseases of animals, fish and plants that are particularly injurious to [Indonesia's] biotic natural resources are not yet found in the Indonesian archipelago whereas a number of those that are already present are confined to certain islands".[181] Thus, Indonesia has concerns about pests and other organisms invading its territory, as do other countries that do not share contiguous borders. Article 5 of Law 16/1992 and Government Regulation 82/2000 on Animal Quarantine provides for animal quarantine requirements. Article 2 provides that all carrier media (or animal or non-animal products) must be equipped with health certificates issued by the authorized officials in the country of origin and the transit country. The definitions section provides that "transit is a temporary stop of [the means of transportation] in a harbour during a journey that brings in animals, material derived from animals, animal products and other things before arriving in the designated harbour." Part Three of Government Regulation 82/2000 is entitled "Transit" and provides, *inter alia*, in Article 34 that "in order to prevent quarantine animal pests entering [Indonesia] from a foreign country, transit shall only be approved at a designated place" and in Article 35 that the designated places for transit must have appropriate facilities.

132. Indonesia explained that imported products do not have to make the journey on a *non-stop* basis but on a *direct* basis.[182] It further explained that a breach of the "direct" transportation requirement would only occur if the vessel transporting the goods in question broke journey en route to Indonesia and the goods were imported and then re-exported from the transit country.[183]

133. In the light of the foregoing, it is factually incorrect for Brazil to argue that transit is not permitted during the transportation of chicken meat and chicken products from Brazil to Indonesia. As can be noted from the various laws and regulations discussed above, transit is permitted as long as it complies with Indonesia's animal quarantine regulations. Indeed, Format-1 for the Import Recommendation attached to MoA Regulation No. 58/2015 contains the following fields to be completed for importation: (a) tariff position, type/products category, country of origin and port of discharge; (b) name of

---

[180] Law No. 16/1992 on Animal, Fish and Plants Quarantine, Exhibit IDN–72.
[181] Recital (c) of Law No. 16/1992 on Animal, Fish and Plant Quarantine, Exhibit IDN–72.
[182] Indonesia's first written submission, para. 310.
[183] Indonesia's response to Panel question No. 39 after the first meeting.

business unit and establishment number; (c) *transit*, (d) intended use and (e) term of validity.[184]

134.   The European Union has noted that the existence of a prohibition to pass through third parties is factually disputed between Brazil and Indonesia.[185] Indonesia has submitted exhibits demonstrating that transit during importation has, in fact, occurred. Indonesia submitted an Import Declaration indicating that frozen, boneless beef was transited through Singapore before arriving at Tanjung Priok in Indonesia to demonstrate that transit was allowed by Indonesian authorities.[186] Indonesia also submitted a bill of lading and Import Declaration for another shipment that stopped in transit in a third country, namely Singapore, in September 2015.[187]

135.   In response to Indonesia's clarification of the so-called direct transportation requirement, Brazil merely stated "...if this is indeed the case, it is far from clear on the basis of Indonesia's trade regulations. It is actually a challenge to understand the notion of legal certainty argued by the Indonesian Government".[188] In Indonesia's view, this does not constitute a proper rebuttal.

136.   Brazil admits that it is unclear how transportation requirements operate in practice.[189] In *US – Carbon Steel*, the Appellate Body stated that "a party asserting that another party's municipal law, as such, is inconsistent with relevant treaty obligations *bears the burden of introducing evidence* as to the scope and *meaning* of such law to substantiate that assertion".[190] Brazil has not met this burden as it has not introduced any such evidence. Indonesia has explained the legal and administrative requirements for transportation of imports to Indonesia. The Appellate Body has endorsed the principle that a Member is normally well-placed to explain the meaning of its own law.[191]

137.   Brazil argues that Indonesia's description of its transportation requirements "*seems to imply*" that transhipment is not included in Indonesia's description of its transit requirements, and thus, in violation of Article XI:1 of the GATT 1994 and Article 4.2 of the Agreement on Agriculture."[192] Indonesia submits that Brazil's assertion is incorrect. Transhipment is the "transfer of a

---

[184]   MoA Regulation No. 58/2015, "Import Recommendation by Directorate General of Livestock and Animal Health", p. 27, Exhibit IDN-24.
[185]   European Union's third party submission, para. 52.
[186]   Import Declaration from Australia, Exhibit IDN-79.
[187]   See Indonesia's responses to Panel Questions No. 39 and 40; Bill of Lading and Import Declaration in Exhibit IDN-88.
[188]   Brazil's opening statement at the first substantive meeting, para. 107.
[189]   Brazil's rebuttal submission, para. 216.
[190]   Appellate Body Report, *US-Carbon Steel*, para. 157.
[191]   Appellate Body Report, *Thailand – Cigarettes (Philippines)*, footnote 253 endorsing para. 7.684 of the Panel Report, and referring to Panel Report, *China – Intellectual Property Rights*, para. 7.28. See also Panel Report, *EC – Trademarks and Geographical Indications*, para. 7.55.
[192]   Brazil's rebuttal submission, para. 219 (emphasis added).

shipment from one carrier, or more commonly, from one vessel to another.[193] Article 19(c) of Regulation 34/2016 explicitly allows for importation by way of transit or, in other words, a change in the vessel used to transport the goods.

138. In its rebuttal submission, Brazil in essence acknowledges that the requirement of direct transportation may in fact not exist, and that "transit (transhipment) is allowed in practice". It made a new claim, however, that restrictions on the transportation are caused by "the legal uncertainties generated by the murky language of Regulation Article 19(a) of MoA Regulation 34/2016".[194] Indonesia submits that this claim falls outside the Panel's terms of reference. In section II(ii) (third and tenth bullets) of its panel request, Brazil challenged "[r]estrictions on the transportation of imported products *by ...* requiring direct transportation from the country of origin to the entry points in Indonesia", as inconsistent, *inter alia*, with Article XI:1 of the GATT 1994. The preposition "by" indicates that the requirement of direct transportation was the only relevant cause of the alleged restrictions on the transportation of imported products.[195]

139. In the light of the foregoing, Indonesia submits that Brazil has not made a *prima facie* case to support its claim that the so-called direct transportation requirement violates Article XI:1 of the *GATT 1994* and Article 4.2 of the Agreement on Agriculture.[196]

V.   CONCLUSION

140. In the light of the foregoing, Indonesia requests the Panel to find that all of Brazil's claims are without merit and should be rejected

---

[193] See definition of transhipment in http://www.businessdictionary.com/definition/transshipment. html, last accessed on 03.10.2016 (emphasis added).
[194] Brazil's rebuttal submission, para. 222.
[195] Indonesia's response to Panel Question No. 139.
[196] See Indonesia's first written submission, paras. 303-311; Indonesia's response to Panel Question No. 139.

ANNEX C

ARGUMENTS OF THE THIRD PARTIES

ANNEX C-1

EXECUTIVE SUMMARY OF THE ARGUMENTS OF ARGENTINA

1.   Argentina takes part in this case due to its systemic interest in the correct and consistent interpretation and application of the covered agreements. This executive summary includes comments made by Argentina in its written submission, during the third party session and in its reply to the written questions by the Panel.

Brazil's claim of undue delay under article 8 and annex C(1)(a) of the SPS Agreement

2.	In Argentina's view, Article 8 of the SPS Agreement establishes an obligation to comply with the provisions contained in Annex C with regard to the operation of "control, inspection and approval procedures."

3.	Annex C(1) provides a general obligation to ensure that *any* procedure aimed t*o "check and* ensure the *fulfillment* of sanitary and phytosanitary measures" complies with the specific obligations in paragraphs (a) to (i). The use of the word *any* in this provision does not seem to limit the scope Article 8 and Annex C.

4.	The use of the term *inter alia* and *including* does not restrict the possibility of other procedures falling within their scope. All in all, article 8 and Annex C have a wide scope of application.

5.	In this context, Argentina considers that Brazil is correct in affirming that "the negotiation of the International Veterinary Certificate is a procedure designed to check and ensure the fulfillment of sanitary requirements" under Article 8 and Annex C(1) of the SPS Agreement, since the successful completion of this procedure is a prerequisite to allow the importation of Brazilian chicken meat and chicken products, and therefore it is subject to the obligations set forth in Article 8 and Annex C(1)(a).

6.	The negotiation of the International Veterinary Certificate is the only way available to obtain access to the Indonesian market and successful completion of this procedure is a prerequisite to allow the importation of chicken meat and chicken products.

7.	Argentina notes that there is uncontested evidence on the record that shows that both Brazil and Indonesia started and maintained periodical bilateral negotiations regarding the approval of the "Health Certificate" by the competent authorities of both countries for the importation of chicken meat and chicken products. Unlike the halal certificate, the "Veterinary" or "Health" Certificate serves mainly to check the compliance with several SPS requirements. In this regard, Argentina understands that the negotiation of the Veterinary Certificate is an approval procedure applied to comply with several of the objectives listed in Annex A(1) of the SPS Agreement and therefore falls within the definition of an SPS measure.

8.	Therefore, in making a determination under this procedure, Indonesia must comply with the pertinent obligations on "approval procedures" under Annex C(1) of the SPS Agreement.

9.	Second, Argentina believes that "the analysis of a claim under Article 8 and Annex C(1)(a) requires two steps. When intending to identify an undue delay under Article 8 and Annex C(1)(a), the complainant must establish first that there has been a "delay". Second, the complainant must establish that the delay was "undue."

10.   The first step for establishing that there has been a delay is to determine its existence. In this regard, "a determination of whether a delay exists should be made in light of the nature and complexity of the procedure to be undertaken and completed."

11.   A period of time lost because of the lack of response from a Member's competent authority in the negotiation of an International Veterinary Certificate, especially when there are available guidelines from the relevant international organization, can be considered as a "delay" incurred by that Member in the procedure.

12.   Argentina recognizes that the seven years delay alleged by Brazil could not be, in and of itself, conclusive as to whether Indonesia incurred in a delay. However, in light of the aforesaid and considering Brazil's evidence submitted for this claim, Argentina considers that in the present case there is a presumption of inactivity by Indonesia with regard to the negotiation of an International Veterinary Certificate, which acts as a strong indication that in such circumstances Indonesia may have incurred in a "delay".

13.   Regarding the second step, *i.e.* establishing that the existing delay is "undue", the Appellate Body defined "undue" as something "that ought not to be or to be done, inappropriate, unsuitable, improper, unrightful, unjustifiable" or "going beyond what is warranted or natural; excessive, disproportionate." It also explained that Annex C(1)(a) requires that relevant procedures are undertaken and completed with appropriate dispatch.

14.   Argentina considers that the term "undue delay" suggests that both the *reason* for the "delay" and its *duration* are relevant considerations for determining whether the delay is "undue" and therefore they must be analyzed taking special account on the proportionality between them. The proportionality between the reason and the duration of the delay has a central role in defining whether the delay is "undue". Such proportionality must be addressed always on a case-by-case basis, and in the context of the circumstances of each individual case.

15.   In the present case, according to the evidence submitted by Brazil, it can be inferred that Indonesia has not provided an adequate explanation that could justify its delay in the negotiation of the International Veterinary Certificate. Therefore, absent a proper justification by Indonesia, it can be considered that such delay was "undue".

16.   Argentina would like to highlight as well that Brazil is not challenging certain provisions of the Indonesian Regulations *as such*. According to Argentina's understanding, Brazil is challenging the undue delay of the Indonesian authorities to undertake and complete the sanitary procedures required to allow Brazilian imports of chicken meat and chicken products into Indonesia. Therefore, the measure at issue under this claim is Indonesia's undue delay and not the legal provision. As Indonesia explains in its submission, "any act or *omission* attributable to a WTO Member can be a measure of that Member for purposes of dispute settlement proceedings." Hence, in the present dispute

Brazil is challenging Indonesia's omission to undertake and complete the approval procedures, and not a particular provision of certain Regulation.

17. Even assuming, *arguendo*, that Brazil could be challenging certain provisions of the Indonesian legislation *as such* for the undue delay claim, Argentina notes that the defense presented by Indonesia is not clear or could have been exposed with a greater level of precision. At the beginning of its argument, Indonesia seems to be suggesting that Brazil's claim is incorrect because it addressed provisions of a wrong chapter of MoA Regulation 58/2015 (*i.e.* "Supervision" instead of "Import Procedures"). Argentina does not agree. While the title of the chapter of a Regulation does not always confine the scope of its provisions, Argentina considers that Article 33(1) provides that the performance of the "supervision" and/or "control" is precisely on the *veterinary public* health requirements. In turn, Article 36(4) details that these "requirements [...] are *the veterinary certificate* and halal certificate for the required product." Hence, in light of the findings of the Panel in *EC – Approval and Marketing of Biotech Products*, the application of these provisions ensure "the fulfillment of one or more *SPS* substantive requirements."

18. Indonesia seems to suggest that Brazil's claim is incorrect because it addressed the wrong legislation (*i.e.* "MoA Regulation 58/2015" instead of "Government Regulation 95/2012"). However, Argentina notes that, according to the evidence in the record, in 2014 – when Regulation 95/2012 was already in force - Indonesia informed Brazil that "the importation of poultry meat into Indonesia's territory is allowed as long as they meet the requirements stipulated in the Minister of Agriculture Regulation No. 84/2013" and when asked about the approval procedures for the Health Certificate for Brazilian poultry, Indonesia informed that "based on Minister of Agriculture Regulation No. 84/2013, the approval step for country and business unit will only be granted after desk review and on site review are completed." Argentina also notes that MoA Regulation 84/2013, which replaced MoA Regulation 50/2011, has been replaced by MoA Regulation 139/2014 which, in turn, has been replaced by MoA Regulation 58/2015, which is the regulation referred to by Brazil.

19. All these regulations are similar in their design, structure and even content. Therefore, despite the subsequent modifications of the legislation, the Sanitary Certificate requirement seems to be a permanent requirement which existed before Government Regulation 95/2012 went into force.

20. Argentina considers that the evidence in the record, including Indonesia's reply to Brazil questions pursuant to Article 5.8 of the SPS Agreement, does not establish that the importation requirements are addressed in Government Regulation 95/2012 and not in MoA Regulation 58/2015.

21. Furthermore, Indonesia provides an explanation of the stages of the approval procedure to import chicken meat and chicken products and affirms that any delays experienced by Brazil [in the approval procedure] are of its own doing. Argentina is puzzled with Indonesia's argument. Argentina notes that

Indonesia does not contend the existence of a delay in the procedure for approval to import chicken meat and chicken products. Rather, Indonesia tries to justify the existence of any delay in its approval procedure by attributing it to Brazil's failure to submit certain documentation regarding the *halal requirements*.

22.   Argentina agrees that delays attributable to action or inaction of an applicant cannot be held against the Member carrying out the procedure and that delays which "are justified in their entirety" by the Members' need "to determine with adequate confidence whether their relevant *SPS requirements* are fulfilled" should not be considered undue. However, this is not the case. Argentina considers that a "procedure applied to check and ensure the fulfillment of one or more substantive *SPS* requirements" should not be delayed by *non SPS* requirements. As Indonesia recognizes, "[t]he halal requirements are enforced for religious reasons, rather than to protect human health."

23.   In fact, the Panel in *EC – Approval and Marketing of Biotech Products* made exactly the same finding. According to the Panel, delays caused by measures which are not based on scientific evidence may be considered "undue". The Panel went further on by explicitly stating that "[t]his could be the case, for example, if a delay is caused by a request for additional information which *has nothing to do* with the issue of whether the relevant product meets the SPS requirements concerned". This seems to be exactly what Indonesia did, according to its own statements. The delay in the approval of the veterinary certificate was caused by an alleged failure to submit documentation regarding *halal requirements, i.e.*, information which "has nothing to do" with the issue of whether Brazilian chicken meat and products met the SPS requirements concerned.

24.   Indonesia asserts that the halal certificate requirement falls outside the scope of the SPS Agreement because "the information required for complying with halal requirements are completely different from sanitary or phytosanitary information provided by the business units to obtain the International Veterinary Certificate."

25.   Argentina believes that this argument does not help Indonesia's position. Argentina agrees that the halal requirement is not a sanitary or phytosanitary requirement. As a matter of fact, the parties in this dispute are also in agreement on this point. Argentina considers that this only reinforces the fact that, as mentioned before, Indonesia incurred in an undue delay by requiring a non SPS requirement to justify a delay in an SPS approval procedure.

Brazil's claim under Article 4.2 of the Agreement on Agriculture

26.   According to Indonesia, when presenting a claim of inconsistency of a given measure with Article 4.2, together with bearing the burden of showing that the measure falls within the scope of this provision, the complainant must show a "second element", *i.e.* that the measure at issue is not "maintained under [inter alia] ... other general, non-agriculture-specific provisions of GATT 1994 [such as Article XX]". Without providing at least some evidence or argumentation

addressing both of those elements, Indonesia believes that the complainant cannot make its *prima facie* case of inconsistency with Article 4.2.

27.   As many of the third parties in this dispute, Argentina disagrees with Indonesia's interpretation of the burden of proof under Article 4.2. Indonesia's arguments run counter not only with long standing WTO jurisprudence but also, if adopted, would result in an unreasonable burden for the complaining party.

28.   First, as it was made clear by the Panel in *India - Quantitative Restrictions*, the phrase "measures maintained under balance-of-payments provisions or under other general, non-agriculture-specific provisions of GATT 1994 or of the other Multilateral Trade Agreements in Annex 1A to the WTO Agreement" in footnote 1 constitutes an exception or an affirmative defense. Furthermore, the Panel in *Chile – Price Band System* explained that footnote 1 must be read "...as excluding from the scope of Article 4.2 those measures which Members are allowed to maintain in accordance with the provisions in GATT 1994 laying down *exceptions* to the general obligations of GATT 1994...". Indonesia recognizes such phrase as an exception. In its First Written Submission Indonesia states that "[a] number of panels have interpreted the latter phrase as excluding from the scope of Article 4.2 measures maintained under various *exceptions* set out in the GATT 1994...".

29.   As it is clear since *US – Wool Shirts and Blouses*, it is the burden of the defending party to invoke an exception or an affirmative defense. In fact, quoting *US – Wool Shirts and Blouses*, Indonesia itself recognizes that in the case of a provision which "...is in the nature of affirmative defense, [...] 'the burden of establishing such a defense should rest on the party asserting it', namely the respondent".

30.   Therefore according to well established WTO jurisprudence and Indonesia's own statements, it is clear that it is for the responding party to invoke the second phrase in footnote 1 as an affirmative defense or exception and submit evidence that a measure which falls under that footnote is not maintained under a general, non-agriculture-specific provision of the GATT.

31.   Furthermore, according to Indonesia, a party claiming a violation to Article 4.2 of the Agreement on Agriculture should show first that the measure falls within the category of measures specified in footnote 1. Then, for example, it should demonstrate that it is not maintained under *inter-alia*, article XII, article XIX, any of the sub-paragraphs a) to j) in article XX or the chapeau and even article XXI of the GATT. And this is only for the GATT. Not only the argumentative exercise would be almost endless for the complainant, but also such party would be required to submit arguments without knowing in advance which of the exceptions or affirmative defenses will be invoked by the responding party, if any.

32.   As the United States and the European Union stated in their written submissions, adopting Indonesia's interpretation would render a successful Article 4.2 claim either difficult or nearly impossible. In Argentina's opinion, Indonesia's interpretation is unreasonable and could, in effect, deter complaining

parties from pursuing claims under Article 4.2 due to the excessive burden they would face, depriving such provision of its role as one of the fundamental obligations in the Agreement on Agriculture.

The restrictions on intended use under Articles III:4 and XI:1 of the GATT 1994

33.   MoA Regulation 58/2015 is a mandatory legislation within the scope of Article XI:1. Within the import procedures set forth in Chapter III of the Regulation, Article 29(j) provides that all the recommendations issued for accepted applications shall at least contain the intended use, among other requirements. Hence, detailing the intended use is a condition for the issuance of the recommendation of importation.

34.   Furthermore, when defining the scope of the term "intended uses" for carcass and meat and processed products, Article 31 expressly limits these products to be used in hotels, restaurants, caterings, industries, particular purposes, and modern markets for processed products only. Therefore, there is a presumption that these restrictions may impose a condition for the importation of chicken meat and chicken products that is limiting, i.e. that has a limiting effect, in a manner inconsistent with the obligations under Article XI:1 of the GATT 1994.

35.   Also, in Argentina's view, the three elements as described in paragraph 263 of Brazil's First Written Submission could be the basis for a violation of GATT Article III:4. In the first place, the "intended use" that must be declared in the recommendation of importation following an online application is a condition that, according to the plain text of Regulation 58/2015 and its application by Indonesia, is not based in any other factor different from the origin of the product, *i.e.*, whether it is imported or domestic.

36.   Secondly, as above mentioned, the MoA Regulation is a mandatory legislation. Argentina considers that certain provisions of this Regulation have "an effect on" the use, internal sale and offering for sale of imported products. While Argentina is conscious of the fact that a broad interpretation of the term "to affect" does not necessary imply that any measure can fall within the scope of Article III:4 of the GATT 1994, it also believes that Brazil has identified the link of the MoA Regulation with the imported products so that it could be established that it affects the conditions of competition of the imported products on the Indonesian market in such a way that the domestic products are protected.

37.   Thirdly, regarding the less favourable treatment analysis, Argentina notes that this restriction does not seem to apply to domestic products. In this sense, Argentina considers that if certain requirements are imposed only on imported products, such as the "intended use" requirement, the mere existence of this requirement, applied only to imported products, may provide an indication that such products are treated less favourably.

38.   Argentina agrees with the EU in that Articles XI:1 and III:4 of the GATT 1994 contain different obligations and have each their own legal standard.

Article III is relevant for goods after that have cleared customs already, whereas Article XI:1 is relevant to assess measures that affect the actual importation of products. Without making reference to Article XI, Ad Note to Article III sheds some further light with respect to the application of Article III. According to this provision, a measure "enforced or collected in the case of an imported product at the time or point of importation" can be regarded as an internal measure. In that sense, for internal regulations applying to imported and like domestic products and enforced at the time of importation for the imported product, an analysis under Article III is prioritized.

39.   As the EU recalls, the condition for Article III to apply is that the imported product and the domestic product face the same (although not necessarily identical) requirement. Such a requirement is then an internal regulation, although enforced upon importation. As the Panel in *EC – Asbestos* explained, "... the word ... "and" in the English text ... [of Ad Note to Article III] implies in the first place that the measure applies to the imported product and to the like domestic product."

40.   However, Ad Note to Article III does not imply that when a measure is subject to Article III then Article XI cannot apply. In this regard, it must be recalled that in *India – Autos* the Panel considered that in certain circumstances a measure may have an impact (or effect) upon both the importation of products (Article XI) and the competitive conditions of imported products on the internal market (Article III).

41.   The Panel in *India – Autos* implied that, in the context of a specific measure and in the particular circumstances of a case, different effects of such measure may come under the purview of Article III and Article XI. That finding seemed to reflect in a later dispute in *Argentina – Import Measures*. In that case the Panel addressed a measure by which, among other requirements, companies were not allowed to import unless they increased the level of local content of domestic production through import substitution. The Panel found that the required increase of local content, either by purchasing from domestic producers or by developing local manufacture, had a direct limiting effect on imports, because economic operators were required to replace a specified amount of imports with domestic products in order to continue importing. The Panel found that this requirement, together with others, constituted a restriction on the importation of goods and thus rendered the measure inconsistent with Article XI:1 of the GATT 1994.

42.   Interestingly, in that case the Panel found that the same measure, with respect to the same local content requirement, modified the conditions of competition in the market to the detriment of imported products. Therefore, imported products were granted less favorable treatment than like domestic products within the meaning of Article III:4 of the GATT 1994. Accordingly, the measure, with respect to the local content requirement, was found to be inconsistent also with Article III:4 of the GATT 1994.

ANNEX C-2

EXECUTIVE SUMMARY OF THE ARGUMENTS
OF AUSTRALIA

AUSTRALIA'S VIEWS ON INDONESIA'S IMPORT LICENCING REGIMES

1.   Under various Indonesian laws identified by Brazil,[197] and by ourselves and other third parties in written submissions, Indonesia has in place the following measures to restrict imports of animal products:

   (a)   prohibition of chicken meat and chicken products not listed in its regulations.[198] This is in effect a positive list prohibition;

   (b)   restriction of importation other than for certain limited uses.[199] This includes rules preventing the sale of imported meat products in modern and traditional markets, which reduce the commercial opportunities for imported goods;

   (c)   limited licence validity periods and application windows. These prevent long term planning and contractual arrangements, impose additional costs on importers and exporters when the issuance of licences is delayed, and effectively prevent imports at the beginning and end of each import period;[200]

   (d)   fixed licence terms. These prevent importers from responding to any changes in the importing or exporting market during an import period;[201]

   (e)   restrictions on the transportation of imported animal products;[202] and

   (f)   strict enforcement of halal labelling requirements[203] when these same requirements are rarely enforced with regard to equivalent domestic products.

Australia considers that these measures constitute prohibitions and restrictions on importation inconsistent with Article XI:1 of the *General Agreement on Tariffs and Trade 1994* (GATT 1994) and Article 4.2 of the *Agreement on Agriculture*. To the extent that this Panel finds that the use, sale and distribution

---

[197]   Brazil's first written submission, paras. 49-56, 80-86, 172-189.

[198]   Brazil's first written submission, paras. 191-194.

[199]   Brazil's first written submission, paras. 195-199.

[200]   Brazil's first written submission, paras. 200-209.

[201]   Brazil's first written submission, paras. 210-213.

[202]   Brazil's first written submission, paras. 214-217.

[203]   Brazil's first written submission, paras. 136-139.

restrictions are internal measures, Australia considers that they are contrary to Article III:4 of the GATT 1994.[204]

2.   Australia agrees with Brazil that, to the extent the Panel considers that Indonesia's measures are non-automatic licensing procedures, they are also inconsistent with Article 3.2 of the *Agreement on Import Licensing Procedures*. As there is no underlying permissible restriction implemented by these licensing procedures, the trade-restrictive effects of these procedures, including their effect on long-term business planning and the flow of goods at the beginning and end of each import period, must be considered "additional". Furthermore, the procedures are clearly "more administratively burdensome than absolutely necessary" as there is no permissible measure that they administer.

INDONESIA'S CLAIMS REGARDING ITS MEASURES

3.   In our written submission, Australia disagreed with several claims made in Indonesia's first written submission. In Australia's view, Indonesia's assertions in regard to Article XI.1 of the GATT 1994 and Article 4.2 of the *Agreement on Agriculture*, and in regard to Article 4.2 of the *Agreement on Agriculture* and Article XX of the GATT 1994, are not supported by the text of the WTO covered agreements and are inconsistent with the findings of previous panels and Appellate Body reports.

4.   A number of disputes have considered claims made by Members under both Article XI:1 of the GATT 1994 and Article 4.2 of the Agreement on Agriculture. As outlined in Australia's written submission, the panels in *Korea - Beef* and *India - Quantitative Restrictions*, found that certain measures breached *both* Article XI:1 of the GATT 1994 and Article 4.2 of the *Agreement on Agriculture*.[205]

5.   As Australia outlined in paragraph 24 of its written submission, Australia agrees with Brazil that Indonesia's restrictions on imports of animal products are "measures of the kind which have been required to be converted into ordinary customs duties"[206] that are prohibited under Article 4.2 of the *Agreement on Agriculture*. These measures are also "quantitative import restrictions ... discretionary import licensing ... and similar border measures"[207] as identified in footnote 1 to Article 4.2 as specifically prohibited under Article 4.2. These measures are contrary to Article 4.2 as a result of the same limiting effects on imports that rendered them inconsistent with Article XI:1 of the GATT 1994. As previous panels have found, a breach of Article XI:1 of the GATT 1994 will also

[204] Brazil's first written submission, paras. 268-283.
[205] Panel Report, *Korea- Various Measures on Beef*, paras. 762 and 768. Panel Report, *India - Quantitative Restrictions*, paras. 5.238-5.242.
[206] Article 4.2, Agreement on Agriculture.
[207] Footnote 1 to Article 4.2, Agreement on Agriculture.

constitute a breach of Article 4.2 of the *Agreement on Agriculture*, where the measure is among those listed in footnote 1 to Article 4.2.[208]

6.　　Indonesia has also asserted that Article III:4 of the GATT 1994 and Article XI:1 of the GATT 1994 are mutually exclusive in their scope of application.[209] To date, these provisions have not been found by panels to be mutually exclusive. Given the systemic issues regarding the distinction between market access and domestic regulation, in Australia's view the Panel should carefully consider the classification of the measures at issue before reaching a conclusion. It is Australia's view that the Panel should examine the relationship between the two provisions in light of the manner in which Brazil has characterised its claims.

7.　　The Panel in *India – Autos* found that "there may be circumstances in which specific measures may have a range of effects".[210] The Panel went on to say that "[i]n appropriate circumstances [specific measures] may have an impact both in relation to the conditions of importation of a product and in respect of the competitive conditions of imported products on the internal market within the meaning of Article III:4".[211] For a Panel to find that a measure has "different effects" (i.e. definitive effect on importation, and then modifies the conditions of competition once the goods have entered the market), and therefore the measure may be both an internal measure and a border measure, will turn on the facts in dispute, and the scope of the measure under challenge. In *Brazil – Retreaded Tyres*, the Panel noted that "what is important in considering whether a measure falls within the types of measures covered by Art. XI:1 is the nature of the measure".[212] In Australia's view, the Panel should examine whether a measure can be assessed as a border measure and internal measure simultaneously in light of the manner in which Brazil has characterised its claims.

8.　　Australia notes that regulations that give effect to the measures at issue in this dispute have been frequently replaced. This has created continuing uncertainty and lack of transparency, without effecting any material change.[213] Australia considers that in order to "secure a positive solution to [a] dispute"[214] it is important that the Panel make rulings and recommendations on the measures at issue, irrespective of any changes to the regulations that Indonesia may have made, which do not actually effect any material change. In this regard, the Panel's characterisation of the measure will be important.

---

[208]　Panel Reports, *Korea – Various Measures on Beef*, para. 762 and *India – Quantitative Restrictions*, paras. 5.238-5.242.
[209]　Indonesia's first written submission, paras. 81-89.
[210]　Panel report, *India-Autos*, para. 7.296.
[211]　*Ibid.*
[212]　Panel report, *Brazil – Retreaded Tyres*, para. 7.372.
[213]　Brazil's first written submission, paras. 57-58.
[214]　Article 3.7 of the *Understanding on Rules and Procedures Governing the Settlement of Disputes* (DSU).

9.   In its first written submission, Indonesia asserts that regardless of whether its measures are found to be WTO-inconsistent under various agreements, the measures are nevertheless justified under Article XX of the GATT 1994.[215] Australia does not agree with Indonesia's claims that several of its measures can be justified under the exceptions in Articles XX(a), (b) and (d) of the GATT 1994. Indonesia provides no convincing evidence to support its claims that these measures are designed or "necessary" to achieve these objectives or that it has considered less trade-restrictive alternatives. Nor has Indonesia demonstrated it has equivalent measures in place to address any similar alleged risks posed by like domestic products. The Panel should therefore conclude that these measures do not meet the criteria in the Article XX exceptions, and also amount to "an arbitrary or unjustifiable discrimination between countries where the same conditions prevail, or a disguised restriction on international trade", contrary to the chapeau of Article XX.

CONCLUSION

10.   In conclusion, Australia considers that Indonesia's prohibitions and restrictions on imports of animal products are clearly inconsistent with Indonesia's WTO obligations under the GATT 1994, the *Agreement on Agriculture* and the *Agreement on Import Licencing Procedures*. In respect of the GATT 1994, Australia further considers that these measures cannot be justified under any of the exceptions in Article XX of the GATT 1994. Australia is further concerned that the measures at issue have been frequently amended to cause further uncertainty for importers and exporters, in order to achieve Indonesia's broader policy of self-sufficiency.

---

[215]   Indonesia's first written submission, paras. 179-192, 209-217, 232-234, 295-302, 342-355.

ANNEX C-3

EXECUTIVE SUMMARY OF THE ARGUMENTS
OF CANADA

I.   INTRODUCTION

1.   Canada intervenes in this dispute because of its systemic interest, as a major exporter of agricultural products, including animals and animal products, in the correct interpretation of Article XI:1 of the GATT 1994 and Article 4.2 of the *Agreement on Agriculture* (AoA).

II.   INDONESIA'S IMPORT CONTROL MEASURES

2.   The various laws and regulations maintained by Indonesia that make up its import control regime overlap in substance and appear to Canada to be designed to function as an integrated whole.

3.   Several of the measures at issue refer in some way to "insufficiency of local production" as a prerequisite for the approval of importation. Other measures appear to impose restrictions on the end use of imported chicken meat and products. There is also a positive list of goods that may be imported that seems to prohibit unlisted products from being imported. A multi-step approval process for the importation of chicken meat and products confers broad discretionary powers on decision-makers and appears to require that importers recomplete the process if they wish to continue to import products beyond the prescribed "validity term". Shipping requirements stipulate that carcasses, meat and/or processed products must be transported directly from the country of origin to their Indonesian port of destination. Finally, one measure at issue appears to require a valid International Veterinary Certificate as a pre-condition to importation.

III.   ARTICLE XI:1 OF THE GATT 1994

4.   Article XI:1 of the GATT 1994 lays down a general obligation to eliminate quantitative restrictions. In doing so, it reflects one of the basic principles animating the GATT 1994, that is, the idea that tariff measures are preferable to border measures that restrict trade volumes and distort prices. Thus, measures that prohibit or restrict the importation, exportation, or sale for export of products, other than duties, taxes or other charges, are inconsistent with the GATT 1994.[216]

---

[216]   Panel Reports, *India – Quantitative Restrictions*, paras. 5.128-5.129; *Colombia – Ports of Entry*, para. 7.233; and *Dominican Republic – Import and Sale of Cigarettes*, para. 7.248.

5.   The Appellate Body has observed that the use of the word "quantitative" in the title of the provision indicates that "Article XI [...] covers those prohibitions and restrictions that have a limiting effect on the quantity of a product being imported and exported."[217] However, the Appellate Body has also noted that Article XI:1 does not cover "every condition or burden placed on importation or exportation".[218] For a measure to fall within the scope of Article XI:1, it must "limit the importation or exportation of products".[219]

6.   The Appellate Body has also indicated that the phrase "made effective through" suggests that Article XI:1 covers, not only measures that set out prohibitions or restrictions, such as quantitative limits or quotas, but also measures "through which a prohibition or restriction is produced or becomes operative".[220] The Appellate Body has further stated that "in the context of import formalities or requirements, Article XI:1 requires an examination of whether those measures themselves produce a limiting effect on imports."[221]

7.   In addition, demonstrating that a measure has a limiting effect on imports does not require a complainant to produce evidence of actual trade effects. Rather, "such limiting effects can be demonstrated through the "design, architecture, and revealing structure of the measure at issue considered in its relevant context."[222] This is because Article XI:1 "protects competitive opportunities" rather than trade flows.[223]

8.   The Appellate Body has observed that the term "prohibition" is defined as a "legal ban on the trade or importation of a specified commodity."[224] This suggests that for a measure to constitute a "prohibition" it must proscribe all trade in the commodity in question.

9.   In contrast, the legal standard for determining whether a measure "restricts" imports considers: 1) the limiting effect of conditions placed on imports and 2) the negative effect on the condition of competitive opportunities of like imported goods.[225]

[217] Appellate Body Reports, *China – Raw Materials*, para. 320.
[218] Appellate Body Reports, *Argentina – Import Measures*, para. 5.217.
[219] *Ibid.*
[220] *Ibid.*, para. 5.218.
[221] Appellate Body Reports, *Argentina – Import Measures*, para. 5.245.
[222] *Ibid.*, para. 5.217.
[223] Panel Report, *Argentina – Hides and Leather*, para. 11.20.
[224] Appellate Body Reports, *China – Raw Materials*, para. 319.
[225] Panel Report, *Colombia – Ports of Entry*, para. 7.234.

A. The panel must properly characterize measures under Indonesia's Licensing Regime as restrictions or prohibitions

10. In Canada's view, various measures under Indonesia's import control regime appear to be designed to protect and promote the domestic chicken industry. Canada does not take a final position on the proper characterization of the various measures cited by Brazil, but notes that most of the measures at issue appear to fit more easily into the category of import restrictions under Article XI:1. Only the alleged delay in undertaking and completing the sanitary approval required to enable Brazilian exports of chicken meat and products seems to operate as a *de facto* general prohibition. This is because the alleged failure by Indonesia to undertake and complete the approval process has precluded imports of Brazilian chicken meat and products to Indonesia since 2009.

11. The panel in *Argentina – Import Measures* reiterated the meaning of "restriction" as interpreted by previous panels and the Appellate Body:

> The panel in *India – Quantitative Restrictions* also noted that the ordinary meaning of the term "restriction" is "a limitation on action, a limiting condition or regulation". The panel in *India – Autos* and the Appellate Body in *China – Raw Materials* endorsed this interpretation. The Appellate Body in *China – Raw Materials* added that the term "restriction" "refers generally to something that has a limiting effect".[226]

12. In *Colombia – Ports of Entry*, the panel reaffirmed the reasoning applied by the *India – Autos* panel that a "restriction" cannot mean merely "prohibitions" on imports since Article XI:1 covers both instances of restrictions and prohibitions on imports.[227] Likewise, a prohibition cannot mean only that restrictions on imports exist. This distinction should similarly be properly reflected in the panel's assessment of Brazil's claims since Brazil refers to both the general measure and the individual measures as operating to both limit imports of chicken meat and products *and* as a general prohibition on imports. This conflation of the terms 'prohibition' and 'restriction' has the potential to expand the meaning of the term "restriction" and the understanding of measures that constitute a restriction on imports. Such a conflation should be avoided.

13. Canada submits that the positive list maintained by Indonesia on permitted chicken meat and products appears to operate as a restriction rather than a complete prohibition under Article XI:1 as it only excludes from import certain subcategories of chicken meat and products.

---

[226] Panel Reports *Argentina – Import Measures*, para. 6.452. See also Panel Reports, *India – Quantitative Restrictions*, para. 5.129; *India – Autos*, paras. 7.269-7.270; and Appellate Body Reports, *China – Raw Materials*, para. 319.

[227] Panel Report, *Colombia – Ports of Entry*, para. 7.234.

14.   Canada agrees with Brazil that the design and structure of the import licensing system creates a procedural burden on importers and creates a disincentive to import, negatively affecting the conditions of competition and limiting imports.[228]

15.   Meanwhile, the possibility of additional restrictions being implemented pursuant to the discretion that is accorded to the Minister under Indonesia's chicken products and meat import regime can affect the business decisions of private actors to avoid imports. The panel in *Argentina – Import Measures* found that completely opaque and unfettered discretion exercised by governmental entities over import licenses creates uncertainty for importers of goods and is therefore a restriction that violates Article XI:1 of the GATT 1994.[229] Therefore, a measure that lacks criteria and provides overly broad discretion in determining if the required approvals will be granted, and consequently if the import licence will be issued, is likely to constitute an import restriction that is inconsistent with Article XI:1 of the GATT 1994.

B.   The panel must assess whether individual measures or the cumulative effects of measures operate as a *de facto* prohibition on imports of chicken meat and products

16.   The limiting effects on imports or the negative effects on the conditions of competition of imports under Article XI:1 of the GATT 1994 should be characterized as a "prohibition" only where the effects are so severe as to completely prevent the entry of any of the subject goods. Where an individual measure or the cumulative effect of numerous measures operates to create a *de facto* prohibition on imports, then those measures must be found inconsistent with Article XI:1 of the GATT 1994. Therefore, the Panel must consider whether the cumulative effect of the measures at issue operate as a *de facto* complete ban on chicken meat and products from Brazil.

17.   Both the delays in the veterinary certification and the direct transportation requirements for chicken meat and products appear to operate as a *de facto* prohibition on chicken meat and chicken imports from Brazil, even though the measures, on their face, do not prohibit imports of such products.

18.   Canada recalls that a prohibition has been defined as instituting a legal ban on a good. The legal standard applied by the Panel should maintain that threshold. Anything less than a "legal ban", whether *de facto* or *de jure,* should still be assessed as a restriction on imports.

---

[228]   Ministry of Trade Regulation 05/M-DAG /PER/1/2016, Exhibit BRA-03.
[229]   Panel Reports, *Argentina – Import Measures,* para. 6.467.

IV. ARTICLE 4.2 OF THE AOA: ANALYSIS OF PROHIBITED NON-TARIFF MEASURES

A. The legal standard to be applied

19.   Under Article 4.2 of the AoA, WTO Members are obliged not to maintain, resort to, or revert to any measures of the kind which have been required to be converted into ordinary customs duties.[230] Footnote 1 provides examples of measures captured by Article 4.2. If a WTO Member adopts or maintains a measure of the kind listed in Footnote 1, that Member violates Article 4.2.

B. Indonesia's Measures: Quantitative Import Restriction, Discretionary Import Licensing, or "Similar Border Measure"?

1. The domestic insufficiency condition

20.   Indonesia's framework legislation, as applied through its import licensing regime, only allows for the possibility of imports of chicken and chicken products when the government deems domestic production insufficient to satisfy the market. Furthermore, the laws and regulations establishing Indonesia's import licensing regime do not provide for explicit criteria by which the government is to determine domestic insufficiency. In Canada's view, this strongly suggests that Indonesia's "domestic insufficiency" condition operates as a quantitative import restriction. If, however, Indonesia's "domestic insufficiency" condition does not constitute a quantitative import restriction, it should also be assessed against the "discretionary import licensing" category. Should Indonesia's domestic insufficiency condition not fall squarely within the meaning of a quantitative import restriction or discretionary import licensing, it should also be evaluated to determine whether it falls within the meaning of a "similar border measure other than ordinary customs duties".

2. Strict application windows and short licence validity periods

21.   Indonesia's one-month application window for import recommendations and approvals directly preceding the three-month validity period for import licences limit the quantity of imports of chicken and chicken products for several weeks within each quarter of a given year. Should Indonesia's strict licence application windows and short licence validity periods not constitute *per se* quantitative import restrictions, given that they have the effect of limiting the quantity of imports of chicken and chicken products, they should be considered as "similar border measures other than ordinary customs duties".

---

[230] Article 4.2 of the Agreement on Agriculture, as contained in Annex 1A to the WTO Agreement (Article 4.2).

3. End-use restrictions

22.   Indonesia's end-use requirements for imports of chicken and chicken products prohibit their importation except for certain specific purposes, restricting access to the Indonesian market, either fully or partially. Indonesia's Schedules of Concessions under the GATT 1994 does not provide for such restrictions. Should Indonesia's end-use requirements not constitute *per se* quantitative import restrictions, given that they have the effect of restricting access to the Indonesian market, either fully or partially, they should be considered as similar border measures that are like or resemble the non-tariff measures listed in Footnote 1 to Article 4.2.

V.   CONCLUSION

23.   Canada invites the Panel to take the foregoing observations into account when assessing whether Indonesia's measures collectively and/or individually comply with the requirements of Article XI:1 of the GATT 1994 and Article 4.2 of the AoA.

ANNEX C-4

EXECUTIVE SUMMARY OF THE ARGUMENTS
OF THE EUROPEAN UNION

1.   The European Union intervenes in this case because of its systemic interest in the correct and consistent interpretation and application of the covered agreements and other relevant documents, and the multilateral nature of the rights and obligations contained therein, in particular the General Agreement on Tariffs and Trade 1994 (GATT 1994), the Agreement on Agriculture, the Agreement on Import Licensing Procedures (Import Licensing Agreement) and the Agreement on the Application of Sanitary and Phytosanitary Measures (SPS Agreement). This executive summary integrates comments made by the European Union in the Third Party Hearing on 14 July 2016 and in its reply to the written questions by the Panel of 2 August 2016.

2.   The case concerns a number of measures by Indonesia restricting the importation of chicken meat and chicken products. The European Union believes that the measures challenged by Brazil constitute quantitative restrictions within the meaning of Article XI:1 of the GATT 1994 and Article 4.2 of the Agreement on Agriculture. Their justification under Article XX of the GATT 1994 is implausible for most of them, and at least doubtful for the intended use requirement. The combined operation of various features of the Indonesian import licensing system, including applications to and documents issued by various authorities, very limited application windows and validity periods for import licences and fixed terms thereof is also problematic with regard to Article 3.2 of the Import Licensing Agreement. The main legal arguments made by the European Union in its submissions can be summarised as follows.

3.   On the scope of application of the various provisions at stake: The European Union does not see a conflict between the provisions of Article XI:1 of the GATT 1994 and Article 4.2 of the Agreement on Agriculture. For the purposes of the analysis in these proceedings, both provisions contain substantially similar obligations, especially with the same burden of proof as regards exceptions under Article XX of the GATT 1994. Hence, they apply concurrently to the measures at issue, with no mandatory order of analysis. Article 3.2 of the Import Licensing Agreement applies only to procedural restrictions (requirements of a formal, administrative nature), not to substantive restrictions (the import regime itself), which the non-automatic licensing procedure implements. Such procedural restrictions can be challenged concurrently under Article 3.2 of the Import Licensing Agreement and Article XI:1 of the GATT 1994[231], without a mandatory order of analysis.

---

[231]   See Appellate Body Report, *Argentina – Import Measures*, para. 5.244.

4.   On the alleged overarching measure of a "general import ban" on Brazilian chicken meat and chicken products, the European Union invites the Panel to consider all measures composing the overarching measures individually before examining the alleged overarching measure composed of these measures. In the European Union's view, in principle only components which are themselves non-compliant with WTO-law should be taken into account when assessing the existence of the overarching measure. The approach to be taken might however be different where (some of) the individual measures are inseparable from each other or from the overarching measure.

5.   The elements that a complainant must substantiate are attribution of the measure to the respondent, precise content and any additional features relevant to the specific type of measure at stake. What these additional features are depends on how the measure has been described or characterized by the complainant[232]. In the present case, following Brazil's description of the overarching measure, such additional feature consists in the fact that the individual measures, linked by virtue of the underlying policy objective of protecting domestic production, operate together so as to constitute a total import ban. It must result from the design and architecture of the overall system that it is more than the sum of the individual measures. Figuratively speaking, the overarching measure is like a "bouquet" of flowers, which by its composition and arrangement is obviously more than individual flowers lying around scattered on the floor. When considering whether individual components work together as a single measure distinct from its components, the Panel needs to carry out a holistic assessment of the entire system, with particular attention to the overall effects and the underlying policy objective. The underlying objective is a central element; it can be considered as the "glue" that glues the individual measures together into the overarching measure.

6.   On the question whether the intended use requirement falls under Article III:4 and XI:1 of the GATT 1994, the European Union invites the Panel to consider the design and architecture of the measure. By its design and architecture, the requirement seems to be a border measure falling under Article XI:1 of the GATT 1994 (rather than a "behind the border measure" falling under Article III:4 of the GATT 1994). The measure has a clear potential impact on trade volumes, and, in particular, the European Union has not seen evidence of equivalent domestic legislation restricting uses for domestic frozen meat in the same way as for imported frozen meat. Thus, the measure cannot be considered an internal measure pursuant to the Ad note to Article III of the GATT 1994[233] If Indonesia were to show that such truly equivalent internal regulation exists, the assessment would be different.

7.   For the so-called "likeness test" under Article III:4, the Panel should not apply mechanistically the different criteria developed by the case-law (physical

---

[232]   Appellate Body Report, *Argentina – Import Measures*, paras. 5.108, 5.110.

[233]   See Panel Report, *EC — Asbestos*, paras. 8.91-8.95.

properties, end-uses, consumers' tastes and habits and tariff classification). It should rather analyse which are the products that are in a competitive relationship at least in a certain segment of the market[234] It is crucial that the universe of products on both sides of the equation (imported and domestic) is exactly the same.

8.   With regard to an alleged undue delay of the competent authorities in undertaking and completing the approval procedures within the meaning of Article 8 and Annex C(1)(a) of the SPS Agreement, the European Union is of the opinion that the inaction of the applicants can only be relevant to justify that delay if it relates to the failure to submit documents or other evidence required in order to conduct the risk assessment or other controls designed to protect human, animal or plant life or health. The fact that domestic legislation makes the completion of a procedure under the SPS Agreement dependent on the satisfaction by the applicants of other requirements unrelated to the objectives of that Agreement should not, regardless of the nature of such requirements and of their eventual consistency with WTO obligations, justify of itself the inaction of the authorities competent for administering the SPS approval procedure.

---

[234] Appellate Body Reports, *EC-Asbestos*, paras. 101-103 (and cases cited therein); *Philippines — Distilled Spirits*, paras. 121, 220.

ANNEX C-5

EXECUTIVE SUMMARY OF THE ARGUMENTS
OF JAPAN

I.   THE RELATIONSHIP OF ARTICLE 4.2 OF THE AGREEMENT ON AGRICULTURE WITH ARTICLE XI:1 OF THE GATT 1994

1.   Although Indonesia argues that the "difference between how the balance is struck between Members' obligations and rights" under Article 4.2 of the Agreement on Agriculture, on the one hand, and Articles XI:1 and XX of the GATT 1994, on the other, "results in a conflict within the meaning of the Article 21.1" of the Agreement on Agriculture,[235] Japan disagrees with Indonesia's argument. Indonesia's interpretation is not supported by previous WTO jurisprudence in *Korea – Various Measures on Beef*[236] and *India – Quantitative Restrictions*,[237] which found that certain measures breached both Article 4.2 of the Agreement on Agriculture and Articles XI:1 of the GATT 1994. Further, there is no conflict between Article 4.2 of the Agreement on Agriculture and Article XI:1 of the GATT 1994. A complainant claiming a violation of Article 4.2 does not have to demonstrate that the challenged measure is not a measure maintained under other general, non-agriculture-specific provisions of the GATT 1994 or other Multilateral Trade Agreements in Annex 1A of the WTO Agreement, if the complainant chose not to challenge the measure under any other provisions or when a respondent chooses not to invoke any other provisions in its defense.

2.   In any case, in this dispute, the complainant invokes both Article 4.2 of the Agreement on Agriculture and Article XI:1 of the GATT 1994 and the Panel has the discretion to decide the order of analysis of these alleged violations.

II.   GENERAL PROHIBITION

3.   Brazil argues that six challenged measures, when combined, impose a general ban on imports of chicken meat and chicken products.[238] In its examination of this claim, the Panel should be guided by the Appellate Body's finding in *Argentina – Import Restrictions* that, in addition to attribution and precise content of the challenged measure that must be established in every WTO disputes, a complainant may be required to demonstrate "other elements, depending on the particular characteristics or nature of the measure being

---

[235] Indonesia FWS, para. 74.
[236] Panel Report, *Korea – Various Measures on Beef*, WT/DS161/169/R, July 31, 2000, para. 762.
[237] Panel Report, *India – Quantitative Restrictions*, WT/DS90/R, April 6, 1999, paras. 5.241-5.242.
[238] Brazil FWS, paras. 74-76.

challenged" [239] in proving the existence of a measure at issue. Japan also notes that, in *Argentina – Import Restrictions*, the Appellate Body stated that "a complainant challenging a single measure composed of several different instruments will normally need to provide evidence of how the different components operate together as part of a single measure and how a single measure exists as distinct from its components."[240]

4.   Further, Japan is of the view that, although the Panel may begin its assessment by considering the WTO-inconsistency of each element of the general prohibition, such assessment is not enough to reach a conclusion that the general prohibition is inconsistent with Indonesia's WTO obligation. This understanding is consistent with the panel's finding in *US-Export Restraints*, which stated that "[i]n considering whether any or all of the measures individually can give rise to a violation of WTO obligations, the central question that must be answered is whether each measure operates in some concrete way in its own right. By this we mean that each measure would have to constitute an instrument with a functional life of its own, i.e., that it would have to do something concrete, independently of any other instruments, for it to be able to give rise independently to a violation of WTO obligations." [241] This finding indicates that the general prohibition should exist as distinct from its elements, and it is such nature of the general prohibition which should be assessed in considering the WTO-consistency.

5.   In any case, the Panel should carefully assess the interaction and operation of each element of the general prohibition to decide whether the general prohibition exists and whether the combination of each element leads to a finding of WTO-inconsistency because the WTO-inconsistency of the general prohibition should not be found simply by combining multiple elements into a single measure.

III.   INTENDED USE

6.   Indonesia argues that Article III:4 of the GATT 1994, concerning internal measures, and Article XI:1 of the GATT 1994 and Article 4.2 of the Agreement on Agriculture, concerning border measures, are mutually exclusive and that only Article III:4 applies in this case. Japan submits that the Panel's decision to apply Article III:4 or Article XI:1 should be guided by the structure, design, and architecture of the challenged measure. While the intended use requirement imposed in this case is an import licensing requirement, which suggests the measure is subject to Article XI:1, if the Panel finds that a similar measure applies to Indonesia's domestic like products, application of Article III:4 would be appropriate.

---

[239] Appellate Body Report, *Argentina – Import Measures*, WT/DS438/444/445/AB/R, January 15, *2015*, para. 5.104

[240] *Ibid.*, para. 5.108

[241] Panel Report, *US – Export Restraints*, WT/DS194/R, June 29, 2001, para. 8.85.

IV. ARTICLE XI:1 OF THE GATT 1994

7.   Japan agrees with Brazil that any "prohibition" or "restriction" on importation may be considered a violation of Article XI:1 of the GATT 1994, if that restriction could have limiting effects on the importation of products of other Members.[242] Article XI:1 does not impose a high threshold with respect to the limiting effects that a measure must have to constitute a "restriction." Rather, limiting effects exist when a measure narrows opportunities for importation, thus limiting an imported product's ability to compete. [243][244]

8.   With regard to the means or features that may have "limiting effect" under Article XI:1, the panel in *Colombia – Ports of Entry* explained that "a number of GATT and WTO panels have recognized the applicability of Article XI:1 to measures which create uncertainties and affect investment plans, restrict market access for imports or make importation prohibitively costly, all of which have implications on the competitive situation of an importer", and that "these cases were based on the design of the measure and its potential to adversely affect importation."[245] Likewise, in *Argentina – Import Measures*, the panel found the DJAI procedure (in which an importer must file a DJAI (Advance Sworn Import Declaration) and obtain "exit" status to import goods into Argentina) had a limiting effect because "it: (a) restrict[ed] market access for imported products to Argentina as obtaining a DJAI in exit status is *not automatic*; (b) *create[d] uncertainty* as to applicant's ability to import; (c) d[id] *not allow* companies to import *as much as they desire or need* without regard to their export performance; and (d) *impose[d] a significant burden* on importers that is unrelated to their normal importing activity."[246] In short, prohibitions or restrictions to imports through basically any means violate Article XI:1.[247]

---

[242]   Panel Report, *Argentina – Import Measures*, WT/DS438/444/445/R, June 26, 2014, para. 6.363.
[243]   *E.g.*, Panel Report, *Argentina – Hides and Leather*, WT/DS155/R, February 16, 2001, para. 11.20, Panel Report, *India – Autos*, WT/DS146/175/R, December 21, 2001, paras. 7.269-7.270, and Panel Report, *Dominican Republic – Import and Sale of Cigarettes*, WT/DS/302/R, November 26, 2004, para. 7.261.
[244]   As presented in the Responses of Japan to Panel's Questions for the Third Parties Following the First Panel Meeting, Japan considers that the EU's argument stressing a *discernible quantitative dimension* of a measure puts too much weight on the quantitative aspect required for there to be a limiting effect. The EU's argument seems to entail an additional unnecessary burden of proving "a discernible quantitative dimension of the measure, in the form of a limiting effect on the quantity or value" for demonstrating a limiting effect under Article XI:1 of the GATT 1994.
[245]   Panel Report, *Colombia – Ports of Entry*, WT/DS366/R, April 27, 2009, para. 7.240.
[246]   Panel Report, *Argentina – Import Measures*, para. 6.474. (emphasis added) This finding was not reversed by the Appellate Body (*see* Appellate Body Report, *Argentina – Import Measures*, paras. 5.287-288).
[247]   Other examples are: the trade balancing condition as "an importer is not free to import as many restricted kits or components as he otherwise might so long as there is a finite limit to the amount of possible exports" (Panel Report, *India – Autos*, paras. 7.320-7.322.); and all of (i) the granting of licenses on "unspecified merits", (ii) making only government agencies eligible for licenses to import certain products, and (iii) restricting the entities that could obtain import licenses and the purpose for which they could do so, because they operated so that "certain imports may not be permitted" due to

9.   The following three considerations also support a broad understanding of the concept of "limiting effects" and accordingly of the term "restriction" in Article XI:1 of the GATT 1994:

(a)   a fundamental principle of the GATT 1994 is that trade-restrictive measures other than tariffs are prohibited unless expressly permitted under Article XI:2 or justified by the explicit exceptions in Article XX of the GATT 1994;

(b)   the measures that are excluded from the prohibition under Article XI:1 are specifically stipulated in Article XI:1 itself ("duties, taxes or other charges") and in Article XI:2, and thus all other measures with limiting effects were intended to be prohibited under Article XI:1; and

(c)   while application of a high threshold for the limiting effects could result in circumvention of GATT disciplines for measures without justifiable underlying policy objectives, it is not the case that legitimate trade-restrictions are unreasonably prohibited by a broad understanding of the concept of limiting effects because import restrictions which serve justifiable policy objectives could be justified under the general exceptions provided in Article XX of the GATT 1994 and thus properly addressed under the GATT disciplines.

V.   ARTICLE XX OF THE GATT 1994

10.   Finally, Japan invites the Panel to carefully assess Indonesia's claims under Article XX of the GATT 1994. In particular, Indonesia's arguments under Article XX (a), (b), and (d) should be carefully assessed as to whether the alleged objectives are specific enough, and whether the measures are designed for and are necessary to achieve these policy objectives listed in these provisions.

---

the product or the prospective importer at issue. (Panel Report, *India – Quantitative Restrictions*, paras. 5.125, 5.129, 5.137, 5.139, 5.140 and 5.142.)

ANNEX C-6

EXECUTIVE SUMMARY OF THE ARGUMENTS
OF NEW ZEALAND

INTRODUCTION

1.   Since 2009, Indonesia has enacted a series of laws and regulations that prohibit and restrict imports of agricultural products when domestic production is deemed sufficient to satisfy domestic demand. These instruments result in complex import licensing regimes that underpin a publicised government strategy to reduce imports to encourage domestic agricultural production in the hope of achieving self-sufficiency in food.

2.   In New Zealand's view, Indonesia's import regime is inconsistent with core WTO obligations. Specifically, as argued in *Indonesia — Importation of Horticultural Products, Animals and Animal Products* (DS477/DS478), New Zealand considers that several elements of Indonesia's import licensing regime for animal products (including chicken meat and chicken products) are inconsistent with Article XI:1 of the GATT 1994 and Article 4.2 of the Agreement on Agriculture.

I.   FACTUAL BACKGROUND

3.   Indonesia maintains an overarching framework of laws that underpin its import regimes for chicken and other animal products. In particular, Law 18/2009 as amended by Law 41/2014 (the Animal Law), Law 18/2012 (the Food Law), Law 7/2014 (the Trade Law) and Law 19/2013 (the Farmers Law) establish a framework through which imports of animal products are prohibited where domestic production is deemed sufficient to fulfil domestic demand. Pursuant to these laws, Indonesia has promulgated regulations through which additional prohibitions and restrictions on importation are made effective.

4.   As described above, there is substantial overlap between the measures at issue in this dispute and those challenged by New Zealand and the United States in DS477/DS478.[248] Specifically, the disputes challenge Indonesia's:

    a.   *"Positive list" prohibition* on unlisted animal products, which prohibits importation of animal products that are not listed in the relevant regulations;

---

[248] See New Zealand's request for the establishment of a panel, WT/DS477/9, circulated 24 March 2015 and the United States request for the establishment of a panel, WT/DS478/9, circulated 24 March 2015.

b.   *Restrictions on use, sale and distribution of imported animal products* (including chicken meat and chicken products), which prohibit all imported animal products from being imported for certain uses;

c.   Limited *application windows and validity periods* for MOA Import Recommendations and MOT Import Approvals, which provide that authorisation to import may only be applied for during limited application windows and is only valid for limited time periods;

d.   *Fixed licence terms* for MOA Import Recommendations and MOT Import Approvals, which prevent importers from importing, during a validity period, products of a different type, in a greater quantity, from another country, or through a different port than those specified in an MOA Import Recommendation and MOT Import Approval;

e.   Indonesia's *general prohibition on certain imports* which consists of the combined interaction of several different restrictive measures that collectively prohibit or restrict imports of animal products, including chicken meat and chicken products. New Zealand also considers that the *domestic insufficiency condition*, which forms part of the Indonesian import regime challenged by Brazil, constitutes a standalone restriction on importation.

5.   New Zealand considers that these measures constitute prohibitions and restrictions on importation inconsistent with Article XI:1 of the GATT 1994 and Article 4.2 of the Agreement on Agriculture.

6.   New Zealand notes that Indonesia's import regulations have changed frequently in recent years. However, many of the core trade-restrictive elements of its import regime, including those challenged by Brazil in this dispute, have not materially changed through these various iterations of the regulations. In light of these frequent changes to the *instruments* through which the *measures* at issue are made effective, New Zealand considers that it is important for this Panel to make rulings and recommendations on the *measures at issue,* irrespective of minor changes that may have been made to the *instruments* through which these measures are made effective.

II.   PROHIBITIONS AND RESTRICTIONS ON THE IMPORTATION OF ANIMAL PRODUCTS INCLUDING CHICKEN MEAT AND CHICKEN PRODUCTS

1.   Indonesia's restrictions on the importation of animal products

(a)   The positive list prohibition on unlisted animal products

7.   New Zealand agrees with Brazil's submission that animals and animal products that are not listed in the Appendices of MOA 58/2015 and MOT

5/2016 are prohibited from importation.[249] In addition to the specific HS Codes identified by Brazil in its first written submission, a number of other animal products are also prohibited from importation through this measure. Indonesia's regulations are clear that the carcass, meat, offal and processed products that can be imported are limited to those that are listed in the relevant appendices to MOA 58/2015 *and* MOT 5/2016. Products that are unlisted are ineligible to obtain MOA Import Recommendations and MOT Import Approvals, both of which are pre-requisites to importation.

8.   New Zealand does not consider that the positive list prohibition challenged by Brazil has been removed by MOT 37/2016. Indeed, MOT 37/2016 expressly acknowledges that products that are not listed must still obtain both an MOT Import Approval and an MOA Import Recommendation. However, unlike *listed* products, in respect of which the process for obtaining MOT Import Approvals and MOA Import Recommendations is set out in MOT 5/2016 and MOA 58/2015, there is no process by which MOT Import Approvals and MOA Import Recommendations for *unlisted products* can be obtained. This is because, based on New Zealand's understanding, MOA Import Recommendations and MOT Import Approvals cannot be obtained for such products.

(b)   Restrictions on use, sale and distribution of imported animal products

9.   As detailed in Brazil's submission, Indonesia's regulations prohibit importation of animal products other than for use in "hotels, restaurants, caterings, industries, and other particular purposes". The effect of this measure is that animal products are not permitted to be imported into Indonesia for any form of domestic use, or to be sold or distributed through consumer retail outlets. Importantly, it precludes certain imported animal products from being imported for sale at modern markets such as supermarkets and hypermarkets as well as traditional retail outlets. This substantially reduces the opportunities for imported products to reach Indonesian consumers who buy their household food products at these locations, and effectively precludes importation of certain animal products for domestic consumption.

10.   By prohibiting importation of products for certain uses, or from being sold or distributed through certain channels, the use and distribution restrictions have a limiting effect on the quantity or amount of product which can be imported and therefore constitute a "restriction" within the meaning of Article XI:1 of the GATT 1994 and a "quantitative import restriction" or "similar border measure" within the meaning of footnote 1 to Article 4.2 of the Agreement on Agriculture.

11.   New Zealand does not agree with Indonesia that Article XI:1 of the GATT 1994 and Article 4.2 of the Agreement on Agriculture "do not apply to

---

[249]   See Brazil's first written submission, paras. 99-103.

the intended use requirement". As explained above, Indonesia's restrictions on use, sale and distribution of imports of animals and animal products are imposed as a condition of importation *at the border*. Therefore, in New Zealand's view, these are the appropriate provisions for the Panel to commence its analysis of the consistency of the use, sale and distribution restriction.

12.   However, to the extent that the use, sale and distribution restriction is considered by the Panel to be an internal measure, New Zealand considers that it would be contrary to Article III:4 of the GATT 1994.

(c)   Limited application windows and validity periods

13.   The limited application windows and validity periods for MOA Import Recommendations and MOT Import Approvals described by Brazil restrict imports by limiting the time periods during which exports are able to access the Indonesian market. In addition, they require importers to determine well in advance, and then "lock in", the terms of importation (including the quantity, products, country of origin and port of entry), thereby further limiting market access for imports.

14.   The combination of the inability to import at the start of a validity period, along with the corresponding inability to export towards the end of a validity period means there is a "dead zone" during which products cannot be imported into Indonesia. The limited validity periods also create uncertainty and mean that importers are unable to enter into long-term contractual obligations with exporters, as importers cannot obtain the right to import product beyond the end of the upcoming validity period.

15.   New Zealand considers that limited application windows and validity periods have a limiting effect on the quantity of animal products that can be imported into Indonesia. As a consequence, the measure is contrary to Article XI:1 of the GATT 1994 and Article 4.2 of the Agreement on Agriculture. To the extent that the Panel finds that the limited application windows and validity periods are non-automatic licensing procedures, New Zealand considers that they are also inconsistent with Article 3.2 of the ILA.

(d)   Fixed licence terms

16.   New Zealand agrees with Brazil's submission that the "fixed licence terms" constitute a restriction on importation inconsistent with Article XI:1 of the GATT 1994 and Article 4.2 of the Agreement on Agriculture. Fixed licence terms "lock in" key terms of importation, including the quantity, type, country of origin and port of entry of the products that each importer may import during the relevant validity period.

17.   Fixed licence terms restrict imports by imposing quantitative limits on the amount of product that may be imported into Indonesia during each validity period. These restrictions are imposed through MOT Import Approvals, which specify the maximum quantity of products that may be imported during each validity period. By imposing a limitation on the quantity of products that are able

to be imported, fixed licence terms are inconsistent with Article XI:1 of the GATT 1994 and Article 4.2 of the Agreement on Agriculture.

2.   Indonesia's general prohibition on the importation of animals and animal products including the domestic insufficiency requirement

18.   New Zealand agrees with Brazil's statement that the "combined interaction of several different individual measures challenged in the present dispute constitute an overarching measure that is on its own a violation of the Covered Agreements".[250] In New Zealand's view, each of the individual trade-restrictive components of Indonesia's import licensing regime for animals and animal products constitutes an independent restriction on imports in violation of Article XI:1 of the GATT 1994 and Article 4.2 of the Agreement on Agriculture. However, these individual restrictions and prohibitions do not exist in a vacuum. Rather, each element of Indonesia's import licensing regime for animals and animal products also operates in conjunction to form an overarching trade-restrictive measure inconsistent with Article XI:1 of the GATT 1994 and Article 4.2 of the Agreement on Agriculture.

19.   New Zealand also agrees with Brazil's contention that "the individual measures at stake in the current dispute were conceived to implement an official trade policy based on the overriding objective of restricting imports to protect domestic production".[251] This underlying objective is reflected in multiple Indonesian laws, and permeates each individual component of Indonesia's import licensing regime. Indonesia's laws are explicit that imports of a range of products are prohibited when domestic production is deemed sufficient to meet domestic demand.

III.   ARTICLE XX OF THE GATT 1994

20.   Indonesia has sought to justify a number of its measures under Articles XX(a), (b) and (d) of the GATT 1994. New Zealand does not consider that any of the measures addressed in New Zealand's submissions in this dispute can be justified under these exceptions. In particular, New Zealand does not consider that Indonesia has demonstrated that the measures at issue are "necessary" to achieve the objectives specified by Indonesia in accordance with the relevant legal standards. New Zealand also considers that Indonesia has failed to demonstrate that its measures satisfy the chapeau to Article XX. New Zealand specifically comments on certain aspects of three measures in respect of which Indonesia has invoked Article XX defences.

---

[250] Brazil's first written submission, para. 74.
[251] Brazil's first written submission, para. 75.

1. The positive list is not justified under Article XX of the GATT 1994

21.   New Zealand considers that Indonesia has failed to demonstrate that the positive list is justified under Article XX(d) on the basis that it is necessary to secure compliance with "laws and regulations dealing with halal requirements ... deceptive practices ... and customs enforcement relating to halal".[252]

22.   New Zealand respects Indonesia's commitment to protect the right of its people to consume halal food. New Zealand emphasises, however, that the positive list does not determine an animal product's eligibility for importation based on its halal status. Rather, the positive list prohibits certain products irrespective of whether they conform to Indonesia's halal requirements. Accordingly, even if a product is certified as conforming to Indonesia's halal requirements, if it is not listed in the appendices to both MOA 58/2015 and MOT 5/2016, it is prohibited from importation.[253]

23.   New Zealand also emphasises the trade-restrictiveness of the measure - the positive list constitutes a complete prohibition on importation of certain products. There are clearly less trade restrictive measures available which would enable Indonesia's objectives to be satisfied, such as the existing requirement in Indonesia's laws for imports to have "rightful certificate" certifying that the products satisfy its halal standards.

2. The intended use requirement is not justified under Article XX of the GATT 1994

24.   In New Zealand's view, Indonesia has failed to demonstrate that the intended use requirement is justified under Articles XX(b) and (d) of the GATT 1994. New Zealand considers that the evidence before the Panel supports a conclusion that the measure is both unnecessary to achieve the objective of protecting human life or health or to secure compliance with laws and regulations regarding public health, deceptive practices and customs enforcement.

25.   New Zealand notes that the intended use requirement prevents the sale of all imported meat products in traditional markets, but does not appear to impose any comparable restrictions on the sale of domestically-produced products in these markets. New Zealand also emphasises that the substantial restrictiveness of the intended use requirement must be taken into account. The intended use requirement is highly restrictive and prevents imported animal products from reaching the majority of retail consumers in Indonesia.

---

[252] Indonesia's first written submission, paras. 229 - 234.
[253] See Brazil's first written submission, paras. 99 - 101.

3. Limited application and validity periods and fixed licence terms are not justified under Article XX of the GATT 1994

26. New Zealand considers that Indonesia has failed to demonstrate why limited application and validity periods and fixed licence terms are necessary for the objectives it specifies under Article XX(d) of the GATT 1994. New Zealand agrees that Indonesia has the right to take measures necessary to secure compliance with halal, food safety and customs laws. New Zealand does not agree that limiting the periods during which import licences can be obtained, and limiting the validity period of such licences, contribute towards, or is necessary for, the achievement of those objectives.

IV. LEGAL ISSUES RAISED IN INDONESIA'S FIRST WRITTEN SUBMISSION

1. Relationship between Article XI:1 of the GATT 1994 and Article 4.2 of the Agreement on Agriculture

27. Indonesia contends that there is a "conflict" between Article XI:1 of the GATT 1994 and Article 4.2 of the Agreement on Agriculture which renders Article XI:1 "not applicable law in the present dispute".[254] New Zealand disagrees with this proposition.

28. New Zealand notes that a number of disputes have considered claims made by Members under both Article XI:1 of the GATT 1994 and Article 4.2 of the Agreement on Agriculture. In none of those disputes have panels found a conflict between these two articles.[255] New Zealand considers Indonesia's suggestion of a conflict between these provisions an untenable interpretation that is not supported by the text of the provisions or extensive WTO jurisprudence.

29. Second, there is no "conflict" as New Zealand disagrees with Indonesia's contention that the legal standard under Article 4.2 of the Agreement on Agriculture places the burden on a complainant to establish that a measure is not maintained under a non-agriculture specific provision of the GATT 1994.

30. Furthermore, simply because the Agreement on Agriculture applies only to agricultural products and the GATT 1994 applies to all products (including agricultural products), this does not automatically render Article 4.2 of the Agreement on Agriculture the more specific provision in respect of import restrictions such as those at issue in the present dispute.

---

[254] Indonesia's first written submission, para. 74.
[255] See for example: Panel Report, Korea- Various Measures on Beef, paras. 762 and 768. Panel Report, India - Quantitative Restrictions, para. 5.242; Panel Report, US - Poultry (China), paras. 7.484 - 7.487.

2. Relationship between Article 4.2 of the Agreement on Agriculture and Article XX of the GATT 1994

31.   New Zealand does not agree with Indonesia's contention that a complainant has the burden of establishing that a measure is *not* maintained under general, non-agriculture-specific provisions of GATT 1994 or of the other Multilateral Trade Agreements in Annex 1A to the WTO Agreement. New Zealand considers that this novel argument is flawed. According to Indonesia, in order to demonstrate a violation of Article 4.2 of the Agreement on Agriculture, a complainant would not only have to demonstrate a *prima facie* violation of Article 4.2, but it would also have to posit and rebut possible defences under Article XX that a respondent might raise.

32.   There is no justification for shifting the well-established principle that a respondent bears the burden of demonstrating that a measure can be justified under Article XX. It would be contradictory if the same provision were an exception to Article XI:1 of the GATT 1994 and not an exception to the obligation under Article 4.2 of the Agreement on Agriculture. The character of the Article XX defences is as an exception and such character should be maintained.

ANNEX C-7

EXECUTIVE SUMMARY OF THE ARGUMENTS
OF NORWAY

I. THE APPLICABILITY OF BOTH THE GATT 1994 ARTICLE XI:1 AND ARTICLE 4.2 OF THE AGREEMENT ON AGRICULTURE WITH REGARD TO THE SAME MEASURE

1.   In its first written submission, Indonesia claims that the same aspects of the same measure may not be challenged under both the GATT 1994 Article XI:1 and Article 4.2 of the Agreement on Agriculture, as these provisions have different legal standards.[256] According to Indonesia, "by virtue of Article 21.[1] of the Agreement on Agriculture, Article 4.2 applies to measures challenged by Brazil to the exclusion of Article XI:1 of the GATT 1994".[257]

2.   Norway is puzzled by this argument. Like Australia argues in its third party submission, Norway asserts that Indonesia's claim lacks support in WTO jurisprudence, as it is clear that a measure can constitute a violation of both Article XI:1 of the GATT 1994 as well as of Article 4.2 of the Agreement on Agriculture. [258]

II. WHETHER LIMITED (AND SHORT) APPLICATION PERIODS AND VALIDITY PERIODS OF THE MINISTRY OF AGRICULTURE'S IMPORT RECOMMENDATION AND MINISTRY OF TRADE'S IMPORT APPROVAL AS WELL AS FIXED LICENSE TERMS CONSTITUTE RESTRICTIONS ON IMPORTS.

3.   Brazil argues in its first written submission that Indonesia's import licencing procedures constitute a "restriction" on importation in violation of the GATT 1994 Article XI:1 as well as the Agreement on Agriculture Article 4.2. According to Brazil, this is in particular due to; (i) the prohibition of applying for licences for the importation of chicken cuts and other prepared or preserved chicken meat due to their exclusion from the "positive lists" of the products allowed to be imported; (ii) the requirements related to the intended uses of imported chicken meat and chicken products; (iii) the limited (and short) application periods and validity periods of the MoA Import Recommendation

---

[256]   Indonesia's First Written Submission, paras. 65-74.
[257]   Indonesia's First Written Submission, para. 74.
[258]   Australia's Third Party Submission, para. 30, referring to Panel Report, *Korea – Various Measures on Beef*, para. 762 and Panel Report, *India – Quantitative Restrictions*, paras. 5.241-5.242.

and MoT Import Approvals; and (iv) the fixed licence terms.[259] Norway wishes to offer its observations on the latter two elements.

4.   Indonesia asserts that "[t]he mere fact that importers must reapply periodically for the new Import Recommendation and the Import Approval does not, in and of itself, mean that the measure at issue is a quantitative restriction".[260] Norway agrees that the covered agreements do not oblige Members to apply automatic import licencing. However, if the application windows and the validity periods are limited to the extent that they create obstacles which have a "limiting effect" on trade, they will also constitute a restriction which fall under the scope of both Article XI:1 of the GATT 1994 and Footnote 1 of Article 4.2 of the Agreement on Agriculture.

5.   As regards the fixed licence terms, Indonesia holds that "importers determine their own terms of importation" according to this requirement, which in turn does not have any limiting effect on imports. Indonesia refers to the fact that "the terms of import licenses – including the type, quantity, country of origin, and port of entry – are at the complete discretion of the importers themselves". Hence, Indonesia argues that "[t]he terms of importation listed on import license applications are, therefore, not measures that are 'instituted or maintained' by Indonesia. They fall outside the scope of Article 4.2, as they are determined by private parties".[261] We assume that Indonesia would use the same argument with regard to scope of Article XI:1 of the GATT 1994.

6.   Indonesia's argument appears to rely on the fact that the regime provides that importers initially define the terms by setting out in their import licence applications the specific type of products to be imported, quantity, the country of origin of the products, and the port of entry through which the products will enter Indonesia. However, Indonesia here fails to point to the *measure* at issue, as it is the fact that the licence term, once defined by the importers, are *fixed*, and *may not be altered* during a term that constitutes the restriction.

7.   Previous panels have found that measures imposing the same kind of limits as those found in Indonesia's import regime violate GATT 1994 Article XI:1. For instance, the panel in *Colombia - Ports of Entry* concluded that restrictions limiting imports from Panama to two ports of entry in Colombia limit "competitive opportunities", and consequently had a limiting effect on imports arriving from Panama contrary to Article XI:1.[262] Furthermore, in *India – Autos*, the panel found that a measure which in reality has the consequence that an importer would not be "free to import [as much] as he otherwise might" constituted a restriction.[263] Hence, Norway agrees with Brazil that the fact that the importers are prevented from responding to changes in market conditions

---

[259]   Brazil's First Written Submission, para. 200.
[260]   Indonesia's First Written Submission, para. 257.
[261]   Indonesia's First Written Submission, para. 262.
[262]   Panel Report, *Colombia - Ports of Entry*, para. 7.274.
[263]   Panel Report, *India – Autos*, para. 7.320.

will have a limiting effect on trade. Moreover, Norway notes that importers may experience a need to respond to other factors that normally affect importation during the validity periods, as well as taking into consideration factors related to importation that they did not predict at the start of the validity period. Being prevented from doing this can restrict the volume of imports. The measure challenged is therefore not *the terms of importation as they are determined by private parties*, as put by Indonesia,[264] but rather the measure limiting what importers may import.

8.   The importers being "free to alter their terms of importation from one license application to the next"[265] does not change the fact that this limitation has a limiting effect in a set term. Moreover, one must also bear in mind that import opportunities as regards availability of products etc. may change from one term to another. It is not given that what a company has the "desire and ability to export"[266] at one point in time would also be desired and available months later.

III.   THE TERM "RESTRICTION" IN ARTICLE XI:1 OF THE GATT 1994

9.   It is clear from WTO jurisprudence that the term "restriction" in the GATT 1994 Article XI:1 should be interpreted as something that has a "*limiting effect*".[267] In establishing this, the Appellate Body has stated this can be "demonstrated through the design, architecture, and revealing structure of the measure at issue".[268] In Norway's view, the Panel in this dispute should not deviate from this test. We are not convinced that "*discernible quantitative dimension*", as suggested by the European Union, would be a correct expression of this test.

---

[264]   Indonesia's First Written Submission, para. 262.
[265]   Indonesia's First Written Submission, para. 263.
[266]   Panel Report, *India – Autos*, para. 7.268.
[267]   See, e.g. Appellate Body Reports, *China - Raw Materials*, para. 319; *Argentina - Import Measures*, para. 5.217.
[268]   *Ibid.*

ANNEX C-8

EXECUTIVE SUMMARY OF THE ARGUMENTS
OF PARAGUAY[269]

1.   Mr. Chairman and distinguished Members of the Panel, Paraguay would like to thank the Panel and the Secretariat for their work in this dispute and for the opportunity to present our views today.

2.   Paraguay is a third party in these proceedings, mainly because of our systemic interest in the interpretation of the WTO Agreements. We would like to stress the importance that this matter reverts for landlocked developing countries, like ours.

3.   In that context, we would like to underscore the key role that Article XI of the GATT 1994 plays for the multilateral trading system, as it establishes a general prohibition on the use of quantitative restrictions. Similar measures generate losses, and thus, have distortive effects for international trade. Often, they create systems that are not transparent and increase the trade costs for exporters and importers, especially from developing countries.

4.   With regard to the interpretation and application of Article XI of the GATT, the WTO jurisprudence has set certain parameters that we would like to recall in our brief statement. First and foremost, the scope of this provision has repeatedly been understood in a wide manner. Indeed, the broad scope of the term "restriction" has been reaffirmed in the GATT and the WTO jurisprudence. It is also clear from previous cases that not only de jure, but also de facto restrictive measures are covered by this provision.

5.   We would also like to stress the standard of review. Complainants are not required to demonstrate trade effects attributable to the challenged measure. Panels have repeatedly stated that GATT Article XI reflects the obligation to safeguard the competitive opportunities for imported products, and, consequently, all complainants need to show is that a measure operates as a quantitative restriction without incurring the additional obligation to also show that the measure at hand is responsible for the reduced volume of trade.

6.   It follows that panels dealing with GATT Article XI must focus their work on the design, structure and architecture of the challenged measures, and inquire into whether they may affect the importation of products by restricting market access. This could be the outcome of, for example, increased trade costs, as a result of the adoption of more complicated procedures.

7.   Finally, we would like to refer to the panel's letter of 3 June 2016 regarding Oman and Qatar's request to participate as third parties in this dispute.

---

[269]   Paraguay has requested that it's oral statement serves as executive summary.

Paraguay welcomes the panel's decision, and the consideration given to the experience that these WTO Members have in dispute settlement cases.

8.   As noted by the panel, the DSU allows the WTO adjudicating bodies to exercise a certain margin of discretion when dealing with issues, that have not been explicitly addressed in the body of the DSU. When doing so nevertheless, panels and the Appellate Body must always observe due process. In this specific case, we agree with the panel that that due process rights of the parties have not been affected, and we are of the opinion that this type of deliberations will help those WTO Members, that have limited experience in dispute settlement, in better understanding the rules and procedures.

9.   With that, we conclude our statement and thank the panel for its attention.

ANNEX C-9

EXECUTIVE SUMMARY OF THE ARGUMENTS OF QATAR[*]

I.   INTRODUCTION

1.   Mr. Chairman and distinguished Members of the Panel, the State of Qatar appreciates this opportunity to appear before you today as a third party to the dispute *Indonesia – Measures Concerning the Importation of Chicken Meat and Chicken Products* (DS484). Qatar is of the view that the Panel's resolution of the dispute should be, first and foremost, respectful of the religious and moral choices of each Member. Qatar will thus limit its intervention to the important questions relating to the halal-labelling obligations imposed by Indonesia.

2.   Brazil claims that the halal-labelling requirements violate the National Treatment obligation of GATT Article III:4 because Indonesia accords to imported chicken meat and chicken products treatment less favorable with respect to the implementation and enforcement of its halal requirements as it does to like domestic products.

3.   Indonesia argues that there is no violation of the National Treatment obligation because (1) imported "chilled" or "frozen" chicken products are not "like" domestic "fresh" chicken as predominantly sold in the wet markets and (2) the treatment accorded to imported products is no less favorable when compared with like domestic products, as soon as the entire regulatory regime applicable to domestic products is appropriately taken into account. In addition, Indonesia argues that the halal-labelling requirements do not and cannot apply to fresh chicken but apply only to packaged, chilled or frozen chicken, whether domestically produced or imported.

4.   Furthermore, Indonesia argues that any violation is in any case justified under the General Exceptions of GATT Article XX a) and d), given that the halal requirements are necessary to protect public morals and necessary to secure the enforcement of domestic laws that are not otherwise WTO inconsistent.

5.   Qatar would like to take this opportunity to address a few systemic considerations raised by Brazil's challenge in this particular case.

6.   First, it should be entirely within the discretion of each Member to impose product-related requirements that are necessary to ensure respect for the religious considerations and preferences of each Member. Religious requirements are part of public morals and should not be set aside or challenged based on economic or trade-related considerations. In *EC – Seal Products*, the Appellate Body acknowledged that "Members should be given some scope to define and apply for themselves the concept of public morals according to their

---

[*]   Qatar has requested that it's oral statement serves as executive summary.

own systems and scales of values."[1] Qatar considers that this acknowledgement must be given meaning, not only in the specific context of a defense under GATT Article XX but also when examining the consistency of measures with a Member's basic WTO obligations. One must be careful not to confuse permissible measures adopted for religious reasons with impermissible measures imposed so as to afford protection to domestic products.

7.   Second, Brazil confirms that it is not challenging the halal requirements as such but only their practical application by Indonesia. In particular, as noted by Indonesia, Brazil has recognized that it "takes no issue with regard to the fulfillment of the halal certification and labelling, as required by the Indonesian legislation."[2] However, Qatar is of the view that a panel should pay particular attention in the context of a "de facto" challenge of this kind to avoid a false positive. A "de facto" claim of violation arguably concerns only the application and implementation of the requirement in question. But the distinction between application, implementation and enforcement of a requirement based on religion and public morals would be difficult and could easily become in fact a challenge of the requirement itself.

8.   Third, Qatar considers that an important distinction must be made between products produced in a manner respectful of religious considerations and requirements in the country that imposes such requirements, on the one hand, and products imported from a country where these religious considerations and requirements are not applicable. For example, respect for halal-related requirements is part and parcel of Muslim countries' culture, thus justifying perhaps less need for additional inspection and verification of products produced domestically. The fact that stringent requirements relating to inspection and verification apply in particular to imported products from non-Muslim countries is thus not a protectionist measure but simply a reflection of this religious reality. Although it may not be necessary to demonstrate that the measure is driven by protectionist intentions, the complete absence of any evidence suggesting that a measure on its face is origin neutral nevertheless violates the National Treatment obligation and in Qatar's view it must play an important role in the context of the Panel's examination.

9.   Fourth, and related to the above points, the mere fact that there are certain differences in the manner in which domestic and imported products are treated should not lead to the immediate conclusion that less favorable treatment is accorded. It must be demonstrated that the measure in question has adversely affected the conditions of competition for imported products. Qatar would like to suggest that the Panel closely examines the arguments and evidence cited by Brazil in support of its claim of less favorable treatment, with particular attention to the specific circumstances of the Indonesian market.

---

[1]   Appellate Body Report, *EC – Seals Products*, para. 5.199.
[2]   Indonesia's first written submission, para. 352 referring to Brazil's first written submission, para. 139.

II. CONCLUSION

10.   This dispute raises a number of very important and systemic issues that concern the essence of the freedom to regulate for religious reasons.

11.   The key question when it comes to Brazil's challenge of Indonesia's halal requirements and their application in practice, is whether it has been demonstrated that these measures were imposed and applied so as to afford protection or whether the practical differences between domestic and imported products explain any differences in the treatment of these products. It needs to be examined whether the conditions of competition have been distorted so as to afford protection to domestic products.

12.   Public morals and religious requirements are not merely relevant considerations to justify a violation. In Qatar's view, they also play an important role when examining whether a violation exists in the first place. In addition, when examining whether a violation can be justified for reasons related to religion and public morals, Qatar considers that considerable deference should be given to Members. It is our view that it should be the prerogative of each member to regulate on the basis of public morals and extensive latitude should be allocated to their right to do so.

ANNEX C-10

EXECUTIVE SUMMARY OF THE ARGUMENTS
OF THE UNITED STATES

I. INDONESIA'S IMPORT LICENSING MEASURES ARE INCONSISTENT WITH ARTICLE XI:1 OF THE GATT 1994 AND ARTICLE 4.2 OF THE AGREEMENT ON AGRICULTURE

1.   Indonesia's import licensing regime for animals and animal products imposes impermissible "restrictions" and "prohibitions" within the meaning of Article XI:1 of the GATT 1994. "Restriction," as used in Article XI:1, refers to "[a] thing which restricts someone or something, a limitation on action, a limiting condition or regulation," i.e., "to something that has a limiting effect." "Prohibition" refers to a "legal ban on the trade or importation of a specified commodity." Thus, Article XI:1 establishes a "general ban on import or export restrictions or prohibitions" other than duties, taxes, or other charges. Article XI:1 does not require a complaining party to demonstrate quantitatively that a measure has adversely impacted the overall volume of imports. The Appellate Body affirmed this interpretation in *Argentina – Import Measures*, finding that a measure's limitation on action or limiting condition on importation "need not be demonstrated by quantifying the effects of the measure at issue; rather, such limiting effect can be demonstrated through the design, architecture, and revealing structure of the measure at issue considered in its relevant context."

2.   Indonesian regulation MOT 46/2013, as amended, and MOA 139/2014, as amended, list all the types of animals and animal products "that can be imported" into Indonesia. Numerous types of animals and animal products are not listed in the appendices to these regulations, including chicken cuts and parts (frozen and fresh or chilled). Applications for Recommendations or Import Approvals to import animals or animal products that are not listed in the appendices of *both* regulations will not be granted. And importers are prohibited from importing animals and animal products not specified on a valid Recommendation and Import Approval. Indonesia's positive list of animals and animal products that can be imported, and its consequent ban on importation of any products not included on that list, thus constitutes a "prohibition" in breach of Article XI:1 of the GATT 1994.

3.   Indonesia also requires, as a condition for importation, that animals and animal products be imported only for certain specific uses. This restriction varies in scope depending on the product at issue, but for all imported products, the permitted uses do not include retail sale in traditional Indonesian markets, where Indonesians purchase the vast majority of their meat. Specifically, importers of the animal products listed in Appendix II to MOT 46/2013 and MOA 139/2014 (non-bovine animals, meat, and offal) are only eligible to obtain a Recommendation from the Ministry of Agriculture if they indicate on their

application a permitted use, including sale in manufacturing, hotels, restaurants, catering, or other limited purposes, or for sale in modern markets (i.e., supermarkets and convenience stores, but not in traditional markets). Thus, Indonesia impermissibly precludes importers from importing non-bovine animals, meat, and offal for commercially important purposes. The use requirements are, therefore, a limitation on action or limiting condition on importation constituting a "restriction" in breach of Article XI:1.

4.   Next, Indonesia's application window and validity period requirements create a period of several weeks at the end of one validity period and the beginning of another during which products *cannot* be exported to Indonesia. Specifically, Import Approvals are issued four times a year for a single three-month validity period and can be applied for only during the month preceding the start of a period; they cannot be submitted in advance. Further, Import Approvals are not issued until after the import period has begun, and exporters cannot ship until they receive the approval. Moreover, all animals and animal products imported during a validity period must arrive in Indonesia and clear customs prior to the end of the period. This means that exporters must stop accepting orders and shipping to Indonesia up to several weeks before the end of the period, depending on the time it takes to transport products to a port, ship them to Indonesia, and clear customs. Consequently, depending on their origin, there is a window of time of up to several weeks at the end of each period when Indonesian importers seeking to import animals or animal products are *precluded* from doing so due to the structure of the application window and validity period requirements. These requirements are a limitation on action or limiting condition on importation, and therefore constitute a "restriction" in breach of Article XI:1 of the GATT 1994.

5.   Indonesia also limits the imports of animals and animal products to products of the type, quantity, country of origin, and port of entry listed on the Recommendations and Import Approvals granted at the beginning of that period. Importation of any animals and animal products without permits covering their type, quantity, country of origin, and port of entry is prohibited. But once an import period begins, importers cannot apply for new permits to import different or additional products, or for products shipping from, or into, a new location. Thus imports are strictly limited to the products specified on outstanding permits. Importers that do not comply with this requirement are subject to sanctions, including revocation of their Recommendations and ineligibility for future Recommendations and revocation of their Import Approvals, and any goods not in compliance with the requirement will be re-exported at the importer's expense. Once a period begins, therefore, importers cannot make changes based on market or other developments that may be necessary to meet current demand, whether because certain products are no longer needed, because new or additional products are needed due to the unavailability or insufficiency of the original orders, or even due to changed circumstances regarding the importer itself. The type, quantity, country of origin, and port of entry requirement imposed through Recommendations and Import Approvals is,

therefore, a limitation on action or limiting condition on importation, and thus constitutes a "restriction" within the meaning of Article XI:1.

6. Finally, Indonesia's domestic insufficiency requirement explicitly places a limiting condition on imports by conditioning all importation of animals and animal products on the insufficiency of domestic products to meet Indonesian consumers' needs. The requirement thus severely limits the opportunities for importation, in that imported products are given market access only if, and to the extent that, domestic supply is deemed insufficient to satisfy domestic needs. The lack of transparency and predictability in the implementation of the domestic insufficiency requirement itself has an additional limiting effect on imports. Therefore, the requirement is a "restriction" within the meaning of Article XI:1 of the GATT 1994.

7. For the same reasons these measures breach Article XI:1 of the GATT 1994, they also breach Article 4.2 of the Agreement on Agriculture.

8. Indonesia's import licensing restrictions for animals and animal products are "measures of the kind which have been required to be converted into ordinary customs duties" within the meaning of Article 4.2 of the Agreement on Agriculture. Footnote 1 to Article 4.2 provides that such measures include, *inter alia*, "quantitative import restrictions," "minimum import prices," and "similar border measures" other than ordinary customs duties. Where a measure constitutes a "prohibition or restriction" (other than duties, taxes or other charges) in breach of Article XI:1 of the GATT 1994, that measure also would run afoul of the prohibition in Article 4.2 on Members maintaining agricultural measures of the kind listed in footnote 1. The United States considers that Indonesia's import licensing measures therefore breach Article 4.2 for the same reasons they breach Article XI:1 of the GATT 1994. When a measure concerning agricultural products has been found inconsistent with Article XI:1 of the GATT 1994, previous panels have found that the measure would also be inconsistent with Article 4.2 of the Agreement on Agriculture.

II. A COMPLAINANT NEED NOT SHOW THAT A MEASURE DOES NOT FALL WITHIN AN ARTICLE XX EXCEPTION TO DEMONSTRATE A BREACH UNDER ARTICLE 4.2

9. Footnote 1 of Article 4.2 of the Agreement on Agriculture provides that the scope of Article 4.2 does not extend to measures maintained under "general, non-agriculture-specific provisions of the GATT 1994," which include Article XX. Indonesia asserts that to make a *prima facie* case that a challenged measure is inconsistent with Article 4.2, the complainant bears the burden to show that a measure *does not* fall within one of the exceptions of Article XX.

10. In the United States' view, adopting Indonesia's interpretation would render a successful Article 4.2 claim nearly impossible. Taking Indonesia's interpretation to its logical conclusion means that a complainant must present arguments and evidence to prove a negative; that is, none of the measures at issue are maintained under the ten sub-articles of Article XX or under other

general, non-agricultural-specific provisions of the GATT 1994 or of the other WTO multilateral trade agreements. Indeed, Indonesia has not cited to any previous panel or Appellate Body reports that found that the complainant must prove that a measure is not maintained under Article XX or any other WTO provision in its Article 4.2 *prima facie* case. In fact, the panel in *India – Quantitative Restrictions* indicated that it is the respondent who must prove that the exceptions in footnote 1 apply. Such an interpretation is also consistent with previous panel and Appellate Body findings indicating more generally that the party that invokes a justification under Article XX of the GATT 1994 bears the burden to demonstrate that the inconsistent measures come within its scope.

11.   In any event, the United States notes that the Panel need not reach Indonesia's novel legal interpretations, because Brazil has raised claims under both Article XI:1 of the GATT 1994 and Article 4.2 of the Agreement on Agriculture. If the Panel begins its analysis with Article XI:1, followed by an examination of Indonesia's defenses under Article XX, and if the Panel were to find that each measure breaches Article XI:1 and that Indonesia has made out an affirmative defense for any measure, then the Panel would not need to reach the issue raised by Indonesia under footnote 1 to Article 4.2 at all because that provision would not apply.

III.   INDONESIA'S REQUEST FOR A PRELIMINARY RULING

12.   A close examination of the panel request suggests that Brazil has presented its claim against Indonesia's "general prohibition" in a manner consistent with Article 6.2 of the DSU. In section I of its panel request, Brazil identified a single measure consisting of seven components, each described narratively in detail. Brazil went on to list the five legal instruments through which the single measure is maintained below the narrative description. Finally, Brazil listed 15 provisions of the WTO agreements with which it considered the single measure to be inconsistent, including the aspect of each of those provisions Brazil was invoking. That is, the single measure was identified and then connected with each of the WTO provisions with which Brazil claimed that measure to be WTO inconsistent. Thus, Brazil has sufficiently identified the single measure and the legal bases for its claims to bring the matter within the Panel's terms of reference.

13.   Questions of whether Brazil has demonstrated that such a measure exists in Indonesia, or whether the identified measure breaches any of the 15 WTO provisions, are substantive issues to be resolved by the Panel on the merits. Identification of the objective of a measure also is not required for purposes of Article 6.2. To the extent the objective of a measure is relevant to the ultimate resolution of a substantive claim, that issue would be resolved by the panel on the merits.

EXECUTIVE SUMMARY OF US THIRD PARTY
ORAL STATEMENT

IV.   INDONESIA'S DEFENSES UNDER GATT ARTICLE XX

14.   Indonesia first seeks to justify its intended use requirement under Article XX(b) by arguing that it is necessary to protect human life or health. Setting aside the second step of showing compliance with the chapeau to Article XX, to make out preliminarily a defense under Article XX(b), Indonesia must show that two elements of its text are met: (1) that the challenged measure's objective is "to protect human, animal or plant life or health" and (2) that the measure is "necessary" to the achievement of its objective. In the context of an exception for a measure that would otherwise be WTO-inconsistent, a measure may be viewed as "necessary" when it is indispensable, or nearly so.

15.   Indonesia specifically asserts that the intended use requirement prevents food spoilage and protects the public health by "ensur[ing] that frozen products are not sold in markets without a proper cold chain." However, Indonesia has offered no evidence – from either the text, structure, or the legislative history of the Ministry of Agriculture and the Ministry of Trade regulations – to show that food safety is, in fact, the objective (or one of the objectives) in pursuit of which the intended use requirements were imposed. Therefore, there would not appear to be an evidentiary basis for the Panel to find that the first element of the Article XX(b) defense has been met. With respect to the "necessary" element, Indonesia has also failed to show how prohibiting the importation of non-beef animal products, including poultry meat and products, for sale in traditional markets contributes to the objective of food safety. Specifically, the intended use requirement in the MOA Regulation at issue only prohibits the sale of *imported* frozen meat in traditional markets; it does not address the sale of *domestic* frozen meat at all.

16.   In addition to Article XX(b), Indonesia also attempts to justify the intended use requirement under Article XX(d), arguing that it is necessary to secure compliance with Indonesia's laws on food safety and consumer protection, in particular Law 18/2009 on Animals and Law 8/1999 on Consumer Protection. Although the MOT and MOA regulations "noted" Law 18/2009 and Law 8/1999 in their preambulatory sections, there is no support in the text, structure, or the legislative history of legal instruments that shows that the intended use requirement was *designed* to secure compliance with the food safety and consumer protection provisions cited by Indonesia.

17.   More importantly, Indonesia has failed to show that the intended use requirement is necessary to secure compliance with the legal provisions it identified. With respect to the food safety laws, Indonesia has not explained how barring the importation of poultry products for sale at traditional markets contributes to securing compliance with Articles 58 and 59 of Law 18/2009, which relate to the requirement on the government to regulate animal products

for food safety within its authority and the requirement for importers to obtain import permits. And with respect to compliance with the consumer protection law, Indonesia argues that the intended use requirement prevents vendors in traditional markets from selling thawed frozen meat as fresh meat. However, as discussed above, the intended use requirement does not address domestic frozen meat at all, making any contribution to securing compliance with consumer deception provisions negligible.

18.   Indonesia also asserts that its positive list requirement, which prohibits the importation of any product not listed in its regulations, is justified under Article XX(d), because it is designed – and necessary – to secure compliance with its laws on halal as well as consumer protection and customs enforcement laws related to halal. Again, however, Indonesia has failed to sufficiently support its defense. The entirety of its argument consists of (1) listing the provisions regarding veterinary certificates, halal certification, and the requirement to provide truthful product information, and (2) concluding that it can be "hardly disputed" that the positive list requirement is designed to secure compliance with those laws. Indonesia has offered only its own characterization of the objective, without evidence or even argumentation in support; this is insufficient to meet its burden under the first element of the Article XX(d) test.

19.   With respect to the first element, Indonesia provides no evidence or explanation to show that the positive list is designed to secure compliance with halal and related laws. Even aside from Indonesia's failure to establish the first element, however, Indonesia cannot demonstrate that the positive list is necessary to secure compliance with its law on halal and consumer protection and customs enforcement laws related to halal, because the positive list simply bans the importation of any poultry meat and poultry products not listed in the import licensing regulations, regardless of whether they comply with Indonesia's halal requirements.

20.   In seeking to justify the limited application window and validity periods and the fixed license term requirements under Article XX(d), Indonesia appears to have adopted the same approach it took with respect to the positive list requirement. That is, it lists a myriad of food safety, halal, and consumer protection laws, and concludes summarily that "it can hardly be disputed" that its import licensing measures are designed to secure compliance with those provisions. Again, Indonesia has not offered any evidence or explanation from the text, structure, or legislative history on *whether* or *how* these two measures are designed to secure compliance with halal and other legal requirements. Such a showing is clearly insufficient to succeed under the first element of Article XX(d).

21.   Indonesia also has failed to explain sufficiently how the limited application window and validity periods and the fixed license term requirements are necessary to secure compliance with the food safety, halal, and consumer protection provisions it has identified. Instead, Indonesia asserts that these requirements "enable[] government officials to monitor foreign trade" by making the importers reapply for permits periodically. As examples, Indonesia argues

that these requirements address the problems of "overstatement of anticipated import volume" and customs enforcement at the various ports of entry. None of these arguments and examples relate to the food safety, halal, and consumer protection provisions that Indonesia cited.

V. THE LEGAL STANDARDS REGARDING BRAZIL'S "GENERAL PROHIBITION" CLAIM

22.   The United States would also like to offer initial views on Brazil's identification of a "general prohibition" in Indonesia on the importation of poultry meat and poultry products, as well as the legal standards applicable to Brazil's demonstration of the existence of such a measure.

23.   First, with respect to identification, the DSU does not specify in detail the types of measures that complainants may identify in a panel request. The DSU requires that the measure be "taken by another Member" and suggests that a measure would normally be capable of "impair[ing]" "benefits accruing to it directly or indirectly under the covered agreements" and would normally be capable of being withdrawn in the absence of a mutually agreed solution. Once the complainant identifies a specific measure in the panel request, this measure forms part of the "matter" referred to the Dispute Settlement Body under Article 7.1 of the DSU and that the DSB tasks the panel with examining to assist the DSB in carrying out its responsibilities under the DSU.

24.   Second, with respect to proving the existence of the challenged measure, the United States recalls that the burden is on the complainant to demonstrate the existence of a measure. This requirement on the complainant is the same whether the measure is written or unwritten. Due to the nature of an unwritten measure, however, a larger volume of evidence may be required to prove the existence of an unwritten measure while a written measure may often be identified solely by reference to its publication.

25.   In *Argentina – Import Measures*, the Appellate Body found that a panel should look to "the specific measure challenged and how it is described and characterized by a complainant" to determine "the kind of evidence it is required to submit and the elements it must prove to establish the existence of the measures challenged." The Appellate Body further noted that, in a dispute in which the complainant has characterized the measure as a single, unwritten measure composed of different instruments, the complainant may need to "provide evidence of how different components operate together as part of a single measure and how a single measure exists as distinct from its components."

26.   Therefore, the Panel may find that the "general prohibition" challenged by Brazil exists if Brazil brings forward evidence that such a prohibition exists "as distinct from" the individual measures constituting that prohibition, as identified by Brazil in its panel request.

UNITED STATES - MEASURES CONCERNING THE IMPORTATION, MARKETING AND SALE OF TUNA AND TUNA PRODUCTS

Recourse to Article 22.6 of the DSU by the United States

Decision by the Arbitrator
WT/DS381/ARB

Circulated on 25 April 2017

TABLE OF CONTENTS

LIST OF APPENDIXES

LIST OF ANNEXES

ANNEX A

WORKING PROCEDURES OF THE ARBITRATOR

Contents		Page
Annex A-1	Working Procedures of the Arbitrator	4267
Annex A-2	Procedures of the Arbitrator Concerning Business Confidential Information	4272
Annex A-3	Additional Working Procedures of the Arbitrator on Partially Open Meetings	4274

ANNEX B

ARGUMENTS OF THE PARTIES

Contents		Page
Annex B-1	Executive summary of the arguments of Mexico	4279
Annex B-2	Executive summary of the arguments of the United States	4291

CASES CITED IN THIS REPORT

Short Title	Full Case Title and Citation
Brazil – Aircraft (Article 22.6 – Brazil)	Decision by the Arbitrators, *Brazil – Export Financing Programme for Aircraft – Recourse to Arbitration by Brazil under Article 22.6 of the DSU and Article 4.11 of the SCM Agreement*, WT/DS46/ARB, 28 August 2000, DSR 2002:I, p. 19
Canada – Aircraft Credits and Guarantees (Article 22.6 – Canada)	Decision by the Arbitrator, *Canada – Export Credits and Loan Guarantees for Regional Aircraft – Recourse to Arbitration by Canada under Article 22.6 of the DSU and Article 4.11 of the SCM Agreement*, WT/DS222/ARB, 17 February 2003, DSR 2003:III, p. 1187
Canada – Patent Term	Appellate Body Report, *Canada – Term of Patent Protection*, WT/DS170/AB/R, adopted 12 October 2000, DSR 2000:X, p. 5093

Short Title	Full Case Title and Citation
Canada – Renewable Energy / Canada – Feed-in Tariff Program	Panel Reports, *Canada – Certain Measures Affecting the Renewable Energy Generation Sector / Canada – Measures Relating to the Feed-in Tariff Program*, WT/DS412/R and Add.1 / WT/DS426/R and Add.1, adopted 24 May 2013, as modified by Appellate Body Reports WT/DS412/AB/R / WT/DS426/AB/R, DSR 2013:I, p. 237
EC – Bananas III (US) (Article 22.6 – EC)	Decision by the Arbitrators, *European Communities – Regime for the Importation, Sale and Distribution of Bananas – Recourse to Arbitration by the European Communities under Article 22.6 of the DSU*, WT/DS27/ARB, 9 April 1999, DSR 1999:II, p. 725
EU – Biodiesel (Argentina)	Appellate Body Report, *European Union – Anti-Dumping Measures on Biodiesel from Argentina*, WT/DS473/AB/R and Add.1, adopted 26 October 2016
EC – Hormones	Appellate Body Report, *EC Measures Concerning Meat and Meat Products (Hormones)*, WT/DS26/AB/R, WT/DS48/AB/R, adopted 13 February 1998, DSR 1998:I, p. 135
EC – Hormones (Canada) (Article 22.6 – EC)	Decision by the Arbitrators, *European Communities – Measures Concerning Meat and Meat Products (Hormones), Original Complaint by Canada – Recourse to Arbitration by the European Communities under Article 22.6 of the DSU*, WT/DS48/ARB, 12 July 1999, DSR 1999:III, p. 1135
EC – Hormones (US) (Article 22.6 – EC)	Decision by the Arbitrators, *European Communities – Measures Concerning Meat and Meat Products (Hormones), Original Complaint by the United States – Recourse to Arbitration by the European Communities under Article 22.6 of the DSU*, WT/DS26/ARB, 12 July 1999, DSR 1999:III, p. 1105
EC and certain member States – Large Civil Aircraft	Appellate Body Report, *European Communities and Certain Member States – Measures Affecting Trade in Large Civil Aircraft*, WT/DS316/AB/R, adopted 1 June 2011, DSR 2011:I, p. 7
Japan – DRAMs (Korea)	Appellate Body Report, *Japan – Countervailing Duties on Dynamic Random Access Memories from Korea*, WT/DS336/AB/R and Corr.1, adopted 17 December 2007, DSR 2007:VII, p. 2703
US – 1916 Act (EC) (Article 22.6 – US)	Decision by the Arbitrators, *United States – Anti-Dumping Act of 1916, Original Complaint by the European Communities – Recourse to Arbitration by the United States under Article 22.6 of the DSU*, WT/DS136/ARB, 24 February 2004, DSR 2004:IX, p. 4269
US – Continued Suspension	Panel Report, *United States – Continued Suspension of Obligations in the EC – Hormones Dispute*, WT/DS320/R and Add.1 to Add.7, adopted 14 November 2008, as modified by Appellate Body Report WT/DS320/AB/R, DSR 2008:XI, p. 3891
US – Continued Suspension	Appellate Body Report, *United States – Continued Suspension of Obligations in the EC – Hormones Dispute*, WT/DS320/AB/R, adopted 14 November 2008, DSR 2008:X, p. 3507
US – Continued Zeroing	Panel Report, *United States – Continued Existence and Application of Zeroing Methodology*, WT/DS350/R, adopted 19 February 2009, as modified as Appellate Body Report WT/DS350/AB/R, DSR 2009:III, p. 1481
US – COOL (Article 21.5 – Canada and Mexico)	Panel Reports, *United States – Certain Country of Origin Labelling (COOL) Requirements – Recourse to Article 21.5 of the DSU by Canada and Mexico*, WT/DS384/RW and Add.1 / WT/DS386/RW and Add.1, adopted 29 May 2015, as modified by Appellate Body Reports WT/DS384/AB/RW / WT/DS386/AB/RW

Short Title	Full Case Title and Citation
US – COOL (Article 22.6 – United States)	Decisions by the Arbitrator, *United States – Certain Country of Origin Labelling (COOL) Requirements – Recourse to Article 22.6 of the DSU the United States*, WT/DS384/ARB and Add.1 / WT/DS386/ARB and Add.1, circulated to WTO Members 7 December 2015
US – FSC (Article 22.6 – US)	Decision by the Arbitrator, *United States – Tax Treatment for "Foreign Sales Corporations" – Recourse to Arbitration by the United States under Article 22.6 of the DSU and Article 4.11 of the SCM Agreement*, WT/DS108/ARB, 30 August 2002, DSR 2002:VI, p. 2517
US – Gambling (Article 22.6 – US)	Decision by the Arbitrator, *United States – Measures Affecting the Cross-Border Supply of Gambling and Betting Services – Recourse to Arbitration by the United States under Article 22.6 of the DSU*, WT/DS285/ARB, 21 December 2007, DSR 2007:X, p. 4163
US – Offset Act (Byrd Amendment) (Brazil) (Article 22.6 – US)	Decision by the Arbitrator, *United States – Continued Dumping and Subsidy Offset Act of 2000, Original Complaint by Brazil – Recourse to Arbitration by the United States under Article 22.6 of the DSU*, WT/DS217/ARB/BRA, 31 August 2004, DSR 2004:IX, p. 4341
US – Oil Country Tubular Goods Sunset Reviews (Article 21.5 – Argentina)	Appellate Body Report, *United States – Sunset Reviews of Anti-Dumping Measures on Oil Country Tubular Goods from Argentina – Recourse to Article 21.5 of the DSU by Argentina*, WT/DS268/AB/RW, adopted 11 May 2007, DSR 2007:IX, p. 3523
US – Tax Incentives	Panel Report, *United States – Conditional Tax Incentives for Large Civil Aircraft*, WT/DS487/R and Add.1, circulated to WTO Members 28 November 2016 (appealed by the United States 16 December 2016)
US – Tuna II (Mexico)	Panel Report, *United States – Measures Concerning the Importation, Marketing and Sale of Tuna and Tuna Products*, WT/DS381/R, adopted 13 June 2012, as modified by Appellate Body Report WT/DS381/AB/R, DSR 2012:IV, p. 2013
US – Tuna II (Mexico)	Appellate Body Report, *United States – Measures Concerning the Importation, Marketing and Sale of Tuna and Tuna Products*, WT/DS381/AB/R, adopted 13 June 2012, DSR 2012:IV, p. 1837
US – Tuna II (Mexico) (Article 21.5 – Mexico)	Panel Report, *United States – Measures Concerning the Importation, Marketing and Sale of Tuna and Tuna Products – Recourse to Article 21.5 of the DSU by Mexico*, WT/DS381/RW, Add.1 and Corr.1, adopted 3 December 2015, as modified by Appellate Body Report WT/DS381/AB/RW
US – Tuna II (Mexico) (Article 21.5 – Mexico)	Appellate Body Report, *United States – Measures Concerning the Importation, Marketing and Sale of Tuna and Tuna Products – Recourse to Article 21.5 of the DSU by Mexico*, WT/DS381/AB/RW and Add.1, adopted 3 December 2015
US – Upland Cotton (Article 21.5 – Brazil)	Panel Report, *United States – Subsidies on Upland Cotton – Recourse to Article 21.5 of the DSU by Brazil*, WT/DS267/RW and Corr.1, adopted 20 June 2008, as modified by Appellate Body Report WT/DS267/AB/RW, DSR 2008:III, p. 997
US – Upland Cotton (Article 22.6 – US I)	Decision by the Arbitrator, *United States – Subsidies on Upland Cotton – Recourse to Arbitration by the United States under Article 22.6 of the DSU and Article 4.11 of the SCM Agreement*, WT/DS267/ARB/1, 31 August 2009, DSR 2009:IX, p. 3871
US – Upland Cotton (Article 22.6 – US II)	Decision by the Arbitrator, *United States – Subsidies on Upland Cotton – Recourse to Arbitration by the United States under Article 22.6 of the DSU and Article 7.10 of the SCM Agreement*, WT/DS267/ARB/2 and Corr.1, 31 August 2009, DSR 2009:IX, p. 4083

EXHIBITS REFERRED TO IN THIS REPORT

Panel Exhibit	Title
MEX-02	Sebastien Pouliot, "Methodology and Measurement of Losses to the Mexican Tuna Industry from the U.S. Dolphin-Safe Labelling Measure" (06 July 2016)
MEX-04	U.S. ITC, "Tuna: Customs Value by HTS Number and Customs Value for All Countries - U.S. Imports for Consumption", Monthly data for 2002-2015, available online at: https://dataweb.usitc.gov/
MEX-06	Atuna, "Tuna Species Guide" (2016), available online at: http://www.atuna.com/index.php/en/tuna-info/tuna-species-guide
MEX-15	Nielsen, "Item Rank Report – Seafood- Tuna – Shelf stable" (12-week and 52-week reports ending 24 October 2015)
MEX-21	USDA, FAS, "Ecuador: Ecuador's Tuna Fish Industry Update" (26 August 2015), available online at: http://www.fas.usda.gov/data/ecuador-ecuadors-tuna-fish-industry-update.
MEX-24	Ley de los Impuestos Generales de Importacion y de Exportacion (*Tarifa*), Capitulo 16 (excerpt) Mexican Official Gazette (18 June 2007)
MEX-36	Business Confidential Information (BCI)
MEX-45	(BCI)
MEX-63	Public Opinion Strategies, National Survey Methodology (Oct. 16, 2010)
MEX-68	Harmonized Tariff Schedule of the United States, Supplement 1, Ch. 16 (July 1989), available online at: http://www.usitc.gov/tata/hts/archive/8910/1989_supplement_index.htm
MEX-71	Public Opinion Strategies, Dolphin Safe National Survey
MEX-72	NOAA Fisheries, Tuna/Dolphin Embargo Status Update, available online at: http://www.nmfs.noaa.gov/pr/dolphinsafe/embargo2.htm
MEX-80	NMFS data supporting Figure 1 in the first written submission (pg. 43)
MEX-100-f	R code to calculate own-price elasticities of demand for canned yellowfin tuna and canned generic tuna
MEX-106	BCI
MEX-119	International Trade Commission, Tuna: Competitive Conditions Affecting the U.S. and European Tuna Industries in Domestic and Foreign Markets, USITC Publication 2339, December 1990
USA-01	The Dolphin Protection Consumer Information Act (DPCIA) 16 U.S.C. §1385 (2011)
USA-02	Dolphin Safe Tuna Labelling Regulations, 50 C.F.R. § 216, Subpart H (2016)
USA-07	Amanda Hamilton et al., Forum Fishery Agency (FFA), *Market and Industry Dynamics in the Global Tuna Supply Chain* (2011)
USA-08	Fu-Sung Chiang et al., "Will American Consumers Pay More for Eco-Friendly Canned Tuna? Estimating US Consumer Demand for Canned Tuna Varieties using Scanner Data", Elsevier Editorial system™ for Ecological Economics (publication pending 2016)

Panel Exhibit	Title
USA-10	BCI
USA-17	"52-week Canned Tuna Sales, Summed by Type" (based on Exhibit MEX-15)
USA-18	Sam Roe & Michael Hawthorne, "How Safe is Tuna?" *Chicago Tribune*, Dec. 13, 2005
USA-22	"U.S. Tuna Cannery Receipts" (data collected from NMFS TTVP database)
USA-36	"Imports of Canned Tuna from All Countries Individually – 2010 – 2015" (data drawn from NOAA U.S. Foreign Trade, http://st.nmfs.noaa.gov/commercial-fisheries/foreign-trade/)
USA-38	BCI
USA-40	"Dolphin Statements from Retailers" (2016)
USA-41	BCI
USA-43	IATTC, Doc. IAATTC-90-04a: Tunas, Billfishes and Other Pelagic Species in the Eastern Pacific Ocean in 2015 (June 2016)
USA-52	IATTC, Resolution C-16-02: Harvest Control Rules for Tropical Tunas (July 2016)
USA-55	Simon Board, University of California, Los Angeles, "Partial Equilibrium: Positive Analysis" (2009)
USA-62	"U.S. Imports of Tuna Product from the World and Mexico" (data collected from U.S. Census Bureau, Economic Indicators Division, https://dataweb.usitc.gov/)
USA-77	IATTC, Resolution C-13-01: Multiannual Program for the Conservation of Tuna in the Eastern Pacific Ocean During 2014-2016 (June 2013)
USA-81	U.S. Model
USA-87	James Joseph, FAO, Managing Fishing Capacity of the World Tuna Fleet (2003)
USA-90	Crown Prince, Yellowfin Tuna, http://www.crownprince.com/cpn-yellowfin-tuna.htm (Sept. 18,2016)
USA-93	Sustainable Seas, "Products and Online Shopping", http://online-store.sustainableseas.com/online-products.html (accessed Sept. 18, 2016)
USA-96	"U.S. Cannery Purchases of YF, Total and Share" (data drawn from NMFS database)
USA-111	Roger L. Core et al., ITC, *Competitive Conditions in the U.S. Tuna Industry* (1986)
USA-114	Liam Campling et al., Pacific Island Countries, The Global Tuna Industry and the International Trade Regime – A Guidebook (2007)
USA-142	Wesley W. Parks et al., "U.S. Trade in Tuna for Canning, 1987," 52 Marine Science 14 (1990)
USA-144	Prices of EU Imports of Tuna Product in 2015
USA-148	Remington Research Group, National Public Opinion Survey (2016)
USA-150	"U.S. Calculation of Average Willingness to Pay"
USA-175	"Share of Grocery Sales by the Top 20 Retailers" (data provided by USDA Economic Research Services)
USA-199	"European Union Prices of Yellowfin Imports, by Type" (data drawn from EuroStat)

ABBREVIATIONS USED IN THIS REPORT

Abbreviation	Description
2013 Final Rule	Enhanced Document Requirements to Support Use of the Dolphin Safe Label on Tuna Products; Final Rule 78 Fed. Reg. 40997 (July 9, 2013)
AIDCP	Agreement on the International Dolphin Conservation Program
AIDS	Almost ideal demand system
BCI	Business confidential information
CFR	Code of Federal Regulations
DMLs	Dolphin Mortality Limits
DPCIA	Dolphin Protection Consumer Information Act
DSB	Dispute Settlement Body
DSU	Understanding on Rules and Procedures Governing the Settlement of Disputes
GATT 1994	General Agreement on Tariffs and Trade 1994
EII	Earth Island Institute
ETP	Eastern Tropical Pacific
FAO	United Nations Food and Agriculture Organization
IATTC	Inter-American Tropical Tuna Commission
NAFTA	North American Free Trade Agreement
NMFS	National Marine Fisheries Service
NOAA	National Oceanic and Atmospheric Administration
NTB	Non-tariff barrier
OLS	Ordinary least squares
RPT	Reasonable Period of Time
St	Short tons
TBT Agreement	Agreement on Technical Barriers to Trade
UPC	Universal Product Code
USFDA	United States Food and Drug Administration
USITC	United States International Trade Commission
Vienna Convention	Vienna Convention on the Law of Treaties, Done at Vienna, 23 May 1969, 1155 UNTS 331; 8 International Legal Materials 679
WCPO	Western and Central Pacific Ocean
WLS	Weighted least squares
WTO	World Trade Organization

1. INTRODUCTION

1.1 Prior Proceedings

1.1 On 13 June 2012, the Dispute Settlement Body (DSB) adopted the original Appellate Body report in this dispute, together with the report of the original panel as modified by the Appellate Body. In so doing, the DSB adopted the Appellate Body's finding that the Tuna Measure at issue in the original proceedings (the original Tuna Measure)[1] was inconsistent with Article 2.1 of the Agreement on Technical Barriers to Trade (TBT Agreement).[2]

1.2   On 2 August 2012, Mexico and the United States informed the DSB that additional time was required to discuss a mutually agreed reasonable period of time for the United States to implement the recommendations and rulings of the DSB.[3] On 17 September 2012, Mexico and the United States informed the DSB that they had agreed on a reasonable period of time of 13 months from 13 June 2012. The reasonable period of time expired on 13 July 2013.[4] On 9 July 2013, the United States published in its *Federal Register* a legal instrument entitled "Enhanced Document Requirements to Support Use of the Dolphin Safe Label on Tuna Products" (the 2013 Final Rule). According to the United States, the 2013 Final Rule constituted the measure taken to comply with the DSB recommendations and rulings pursuant to Article 21.5 of the Understanding on Rules and Procedures Governing the Settlement of Disputes (DSU). The United States referred to the Tuna Measure as amended by the 2013 Final Rule as the "amended dolphin safe labelling measure", the "amended tuna measure", or the "amended measure".[5] In this Decision, we refer to this measure as the 2013 Tuna Measure.

1.3   Mexico considered that the 2013 Final Rule failed to bring the United States into compliance with the DSB recommendations and rulings. On 2 August 2013, Mexico and the United States informed the DSB of their Agreed Procedures under Articles 21 and 22 of the DSU.[6] Subsequently, on 14 November 2013, the DSB, at Mexico's request, established a panel under Articles 6 and 21.5 of the DSU, Article 14 of the TBT Agreement, and Article XXIII of the General Agreement on Tariffs and Trade 1994 (GATT 1994). On 14 April 2015 , that panel found that the United States had not brought its

---

[1]   The "original Tuna Measure" consisted of: the Dolphin Protection Consumer Information Act of 1990, codified in *United States Code*, Title 16, Section 1385 (DPCIA); *United States Code of Federal Regulations* (CFR) Title 50, Sections 216.91 and 216.92 (the original implementing regulations); and a ruling by a US Federal Appeals Court in *Earth Island Institute v Hogarth*, 494 F.3d 757 (9th Cir. 2007) (*Hogarth* Ruling).

[2]   Appellate Body Report, *US – Tuna II (Mexico)*, para. 407(b).

[3]   Communication from Mexico and the United States concerning Article 21.3(c) of the DSU, WT/DS381/16).

[4]   Agreement under Article 21.3(b) of the DSU, WT/DS381/17).

[5]   Panel Report, *US – Tuna II (Mexico) (Article 21.5 – Mexico)*, para. 1.13; Appellate Body Report, *US – Tuna II (Mexico) (Article 21.5 – Mexico)*, para. 6.8.

[6]   WT/DS381/19. The parties agreed, *inter alia*, that, in the event that the DSB, following a proceeding under Article 21.5 of the DSU, ruled that a measure taken to comply either did not exist or was inconsistent with a WTO covered agreement, Mexico could request authorization to suspend the application of concessions or other obligations under the covered agreements to the United States pursuant to Article 22 of the DSU, and the United States would not assert that Mexico was precluded from obtaining such authorization on the ground that the request was made outside the 30-day time-period specified in Article 22.6 of the DSU.

measure into compliance, and that the "amended tuna measure" was inconsistent with Article 2.1 of the TBT Agreement and Articles I:1 and III:4 of the GATT 1994.[7] The Appellate Body upheld those findings, albeit largely on the basis of different reasoning.[8] The Appellate Body report and the panel report as modified by the Appellate Body were adopted by the DSB on 3 December 2015.

1.2 Request for Arbitration and Arbitration Proceedings

1.4   On 10 March 2016, Mexico requested authorization from the DSB to suspend concessions to the United States in the amount of USD 472.3 million annually. On 22 March 2016, the United States objected to Mexico's proposed level of suspension. At the DSB meeting of 23 March 2016, the DSB took note that, the United States having objected to Mexico's proposed level of suspension on 22 March 2016, the matter had been referred to arbitration as required by Article 22.6 of the DSU.[9] At the same meeting, the United States informed the DSB that, on 22 March 2016, the US National Oceanic and Atmospheric Administration (NOAA) had issued a new rule modifying the dolphin safe labelling measure (the 2016 Rule). According to the United States, this Rule "directly addressed issues raised by both the Appellate Body and the compliance [p]anel".[10] In this Decision, the Arbitrator refers to the Tuna Measure as modified by the 2016 Rule as the 2016 Tuna Measure.

1.5   The chairperson of the original panel was not available for the arbitration proceedings. On 22 April 2016, Mexico requested the Director-General to appoint a replacement. The Arbitrator was thus composed as follows:

Chairperson: Mr Stefán Haukur Jóhannesson

Members: Ms Mary Elizabeth Chelliah

                 Mr Franz Perrez

1.6   An organizational meeting was held on 25 May 2016 to discuss procedural aspects of the arbitration proceedings. After consulting with the parties, on 7 June 2016, the Arbitrator adopted its Working Procedures together with Additional Working Procedures concerning Business Confidential Information (BCI). For the reasons explained below[11], after consulting with the parties, the Arbitrator modified its Working Procedures on 3 August 2016. The Arbitrator adopted a timetable for the proceedings on 14 June 2016. In response to a request by the United States for a preliminary ruling, the Arbitrator, after consulting with the parties, modified the timetable for the proceedings on 18 August 2016.

---

[7]   Panel Report, *US – Tuna II (Mexico) (Article 21.5 – Mexico)*, paras. 8.2-8.5.
[8]   Appellate Body Report, *US – Tuna II (Mexico) (Article 21.5 – Mexico)*, para. 8.1.
[9]   WT/DSB/M/376, p. 10.
[10]   WT/DSB/M/376, p. 9.
[11]   See below, Section 2.

1.7   In accordance with the timetable and Working Procedures adopted by the Arbitrator, on 6 July 2016, Mexico submitted a communication explaining its methodology for calculating the proposed level of suspension (Mexico's Methodology Paper). The United States filed its written submission, including a request for a preliminary ruling, on 3 August 2016. Mexico filed its written submission, including a response to the United States' request for a preliminary ruling, to the Arbitrator on 31 August 2016. On 7 September 2016, the Arbitrator sent to the parties written questions concerning the United States' request for a preliminary ruling. The Arbitrator also sent written questions concerning the merits of the case to the parties on 14 September 2016. The parties responded to these questions in writing on 30 September 2016.

1.8   The Arbitrator issued its conclusion in respect of the United States' request for a preliminary ruling on 11 October 2016. That conclusion and the reasons underpinning it are set out in Section 3 below.

1.9   The Arbitrator held its substantive meeting with the parties on 25 and 26 October 2016. Prior to the meeting, on 28 September 2016, the Arbitrator had sent additional written questions to the parties. The parties responded to these questions in writing on 9 November 2016. The parties submitted comments on each other's responses on 16 November 2016.

1.10   This Decision is structured as follows. In Section 2, we address two procedural issues, namely the treatment of BCI and the partially open meeting of the Arbitrator with the parties. Section 3 deals with the United States' request for a preliminary ruling concerning the relevant measure, also outlining the Arbitrator's mandate in these proceedings. In Section 4, we examine the appropriate counterfactual and time-period for our analysis. Then, in Section 5, we move to the assessment of the proposed level of suspension, examining: (a) Mexico's proposed model for determining the level of nullification or impairment; and (b) the United States' proposed model for determining the level of nullification or impairment. Based on this examination, we proceed to conduct our own assessment of the level of nullification or impairment in Section 6. Our conclusion and decision on the level of suspension of concessions or other obligations is contained in Section 7.

2.   PROCEDURAL MATTERS

2.11   In this Section of its Decision, the Arbitrator deals with two procedural matters arising in these proceedings. First, we briefly explain our treatment of BCI. Second, we discuss the United States' request to partially open the Arbitrator's meeting with the parties.

2.1   Treatment of BCI

2.12   At the Arbitrator's organizational meeting held on 25 May 2016, both parties requested that the Arbitrator adopt additional working procedures to protect the confidentiality of BCI submitted in the course of the proceedings. As indicated in the preceding Section, the Arbitrator adopted such additional working procedures on 7 June 2016.

2.13   The Additional Working Procedures of the Arbitrator Concerning Business Confidential Information (Additional Working Procedures) are annexed to this Decision.[12] They (a) define BCI for the purposes of these proceedings[13]; (b) provide that each party shall clearly indicate the presence of BCI in its submissions[14]; and (c) limit access to, and permissible use of, BCI submitted in the course of the proceedings.[15]

2.14   Additionally, paragraph 7 of the Additional Working Procedures provides that "[t]he Arbitrator shall not disclose BCI, in its Decision or in any other way, to persons not authorized under these procedures to have access to BCI". Importantly, the paragraph goes on to state that although the Arbitrator may "make statements of conclusion drawn from such information", the parties shall be provided with an opportunity to ensure that all BCI has been redacted from the Decision prior to its circulation to the WTO membership. This paragraph forms the "legal basis"[16] on which the Arbitrator has redacted statements of BCI from the public version of its Decision. In drafting and redacting this Decision, we have strived to "ensure that an appropriate balance is struck between the need to guard against the risk of harm that could result from the disclosure of particularly sensitive information, on the one hand, and the integrity of the adjudication process … and the rights of and systemic interests of the WTO membership at large, on the other hand".[17] We have also tried to "ensure that the public version of [our Decision] circulated to all Members of the WTO is understandable".[18] Having said that, it is also important to note that the technical nature of these arbitration proceedings has meant that the Arbitrator has had to have reference to evidence classified as BCI more frequently than may be usual in panel proceedings.

2.15   Accordingly, the text of the version circulated to Members is identical to the text of the confidential version issued to the parties, with the exception of passages that disclose BCI. Such passages were replaced by "[[xxx]]".

---

[12]   Annex A-2.

[13]   Paragraph 2 of the Additional Working Procedures defines BCI as "any information that has been designated as such by the party submitting the information and that is not available in the public domain and the release of which could reasonably be considered to cause or threaten to cause harm to an interest of the person or entity that supplied the business information to the party".

[14]   Additional Working Procedures Concerning Business Confidential Information, Annex A-2, paras. 3 and 4.

[15]   Additional Working Procedures Concerning Business Confidential Information, Annex A-2, para. 5.

[16]   Appellate Body Report, *US – Tuna II (Mexico) (Article 21.5 – Mexico)*, para. 5.4.

[17]   Appellate Body Report, *US – Tuna II (Mexico) (Article 21.5 – Mexico)*, para. 5.3; Appellate Body Report, *EC and certain member States – Large Civil Aircraft*, Annex III, Procedural Ruling of 10 August 2010, para. 15.

[18]   Appellate Body Report, *Japan – DRAMS (Korea)*, para. 279.

2.2   Partially Open Meeting of the Arbitrator with the Parties

2.2.1   Procedural background

2.16   At the Arbitrator's organizational meeting, the United States proposed a change to the working procedures to allow the Arbitrator's substantive meeting to be publicly observed. The United States noted that two prior Article 22.6 arbitrators had already held such meetings, including in a dispute involving Mexico as a party. In the United States' view, meetings opened for public observation enhance understanding of the system and promote confidence in its objectivity and professionalism.

2.17   Mexico indicated that it was not in a position to accept open meetings in this dispute. Mexico recalled that even in those disputes where it did not object to open meetings, it had indicated that this was without prejudice to its systemic position on public observation of meetings in dispute settlement proceedings. Mexico also noted that the meetings in the original and first round of compliance proceedings in this dispute were not open for public observation.

2.18   The United States then indicated that it was not asking the Arbitrator to mandate the opening of the meeting over Mexico's objection. The United States asked instead that the Arbitrator make arrangements to allow the United States to make its statements in public. The United States argued that it was possible for it to disclose its own statements and at the same time to maintain the confidentiality of Mexico's statements.

2.19   Mexico responded that it could not accept that the United States would be allowed to lift the confidentiality of its own statements to the Arbitrator, as the DSU was clear that meetings are confidential, except if all parties agree otherwise. In Mexico's view, the Arbitrator should therefore reject the United States' request.

2.20   Through a joint communication with the parallel compliance panels in this dispute, we informed the parties that we considered ourselves to have the authority to authorize the United States to lift the confidentiality of its statements at the meeting with the parties. We further indicated that any public observation of the meeting would be through delayed viewing (delayed closed-circuit television broadcasting), to ensure that the confidentiality of Mexico's statements would not be breached. The parties were informed that the reasons supporting this determination would be elaborated later by the Arbitrator in its Decision and by the Panels in their Reports.[19]

2.21   After consulting the parties, on 3 August 2016 we made appropriate adjustments to paragraph 3 of our Working Procedures.[20] Invoking that paragraph, the United States requested us to adopt additional working procedures to facilitate the lifting of the confidentiality of the United States'

---

[19]   Panels' and Arbitrator's letter of 29 July 2016.
[20]   See Annex A-1.

statements at the Arbitrator's meeting. On 18 October 2016, after consulting the parties we adopted additional working procedures on partially open meetings.[21]

2.22　We held our substantive meeting with the parties on 25 and 26 October 2016. After completing the process of redacting the video-recording of the Arbitrator's meeting in accordance with the additional working procedures, at Mexico's request we held a preview screening of the redacted video-recording for the parties on 12 December 2016, which both parties attended. The public broadcast of the redacted video-recording of the Arbitrator's meeting took place on 16 December 2016.

2.2.2　Merits of the United States' request for a partially open meeting

2.23　The Arbitrator notes that this is the first dispute in which a party has requested that a WTO adjudicator organize a partially open meeting with the parties. An identical request was made by the United States in the parallel compliance panel proceedings in this dispute. Much of the exchange between the parties on the merits of the United States' request took place in the context of the compliance panel proceedings. Although the parties did not specifically request that their relevant communications to the compliance panels be incorporated into the arbitration record, it was clear to the Arbitrator and was understood by the parties that their arguments to the compliance panels would and should be taken into account also by the Arbitrator.[22] For the better understanding of our decision on the United States' request, we therefore provide below a general summary of the parties' respective positions as developed for the most part in the compliance panel proceedings.

2.24　The United States observes that it seeks to exercise its right to disclose to the public its own statements at the Arbitrator's meeting, and that it requests the Arbitrator to facilitate this disclosure by adopting appropriate procedures. The United States submits that its request is supported by the Appellate Body report in *US – Continued Suspension*. According to the United States, the Appellate Body in that dispute agreed that each party has the right to maintain the confidentiality of its own statements and therefore provided each party and third party a possibility to lift the confidentiality of their statements at the Appellate Body's hearing. The United States notes that it is possible to protect Mexico's right to maintain the confidentiality of its statements while also protecting the United States' right to disclose its own statements to the public.

2.25　Mexico considers that Appendix 3 of the DSU applies *mutatis mutandis* to arbitration proceedings and indicates that deliberations must be kept confidential. Mexico recalls in this connection that it was a third party in *US –*

---

[21]　See Annex A-3.
[22]　As indicated, the Arbitrator and compliance panels informed the parties at the same time of their view that they had the power to authorize one party to lift the confidentiality of its statements.

Continued Suspension, and that it was among the Members that criticized the approach taken in that dispute at the DSB meeting at which the panel and Appellate Body reports were adopted. Mexico notes that unlike in that dispute, in this dispute there has been no agreement by the parties on holding a public meeting. In Mexico's view, there is in the present dispute a relationship of confidentiality between the parties and the Arbitrator, not between each party and the Arbitrator. Mexico is aware that the United States' request leaves it to each party to decide for itself whether to lift the confidentiality of its statements. Nevertheless, in Mexico's view, proceeding as the United States requests would affect the rights of Mexico and those of other Members that have systemic concerns about open meetings. Mexico submits in this regard that acceding to the United States' request could force other Members to accept open meetings because otherwise only one party's views are ventilated. Mexico suggests that the DSU already gives the United States the possibility to make its statements available on the USTR's website, as is its practice. Mexico considers that the United States' right to disclose its own positions and statements to the public does not have to be exercised through an open meeting. Mexico submits, finally, that the Appellate Body in *EU – Biodiesel (Argentina)* declined the European Union's request to allow public observation of the oral hearing, noting that the other party expressed a preference against doing so.

2.26   Mexico is therefore of the view that the Arbitrator should deny the United States' request for a partially open meeting. Mexico also clarifies that it is not prepared to waive its right to confidentiality and therefore designates all information submitted by it in this dispute as confidential. Mexico considers that all statements and documents are confidential until the Arbitrator's Decision is circulated.

2.27   The Arbitrator begins by noting that numerous WTO adjudicators, including the Appellate Body, panels and Article 22.6 arbitrators, have on request opened meetings with parties for public observation in their entirety, except for any parts of meetings during which BCI was addressed.[23] If a WTO adjudicator has the power to accede to a request to fully open a hearing or meeting with the parties, then *a fortiori* it must in principle also have the power to go less far, including by opening only parts of a meeting with the parties.

2.28   The meetings with parties in previous WTO dispute settlement proceedings that have been opened for public observation in their entirety have been opened with the agreement of all parties. At those fully open meetings, the parties were authorized to disclose not only statements of their own positions, but also statements of the positions of the other party or parties. The situation in the present proceedings is different, however. The United States is seeking authorization to disclose statements of its own positions only.

---

[23]   The United States in this dispute is not seeking authorization to disclose BCI to the public. Indeed, the United States has requested the Arbitrator to adopt additional working procedures for the protection of BCI.

2.29   We observe in this regard that, according to Article 18.2 of the DSU, nothing in the DSU precludes a party "from disclosing statements of its own positions to the public".[24] According to the Appellate Body, this provision allows a party to forego confidentiality protection in respect of statements of its own positions.[25] The Appellate Body has further confirmed that Article 18.2 of the DSU covers not just statements in written form, but also oral statements and responses to questions at Appellate Body hearings.[26] The same holds true, in our view, for oral statements and responses given at meetings of panels and Article 22.6 arbitrators. We further observe that Article 18.2 of the DSU does not stipulate that a party may disclose its statements only once, or only after any meetings of a WTO adjudicator with the parties.[27]

2.30   Mexico nevertheless considers that we cannot authorize the United States to forego confidentiality protection in respect of its statements of its own positions, except with Mexico's agreement. Mexico bases this contention on the Appellate Body's procedural ruling in *EU – Biodiesel (Argentina)*.[28] In our view, Mexico's reliance on this procedural ruling is misplaced. In *EU – Biodiesel (Argentina)*, the Appellate Body rejected a unilateral request by the European Union that the Appellate Body conduct a fully open hearing even though Argentina was not supportive of that request.[29] As we have said, this is not the situation we are facing, since the United States in this dispute requests authorization to disclose statements of its own positions, not those of Mexico.[30]

2.31   Mexico further seems to consider that in respect of meetings or hearings, the DSU protects the confidentiality of the relationship between the parties taken as a group and a WTO adjudicator, rather than between each of the parties and a WTO adjudicator. We note, however, that Article 18.2 of the DSU gives each party individually the right to disclose statements of its own positions. Where a fully open meeting is to be held, it is clear that all parties need to request

---

[24]   We note that the immediate context of Article 18.2 of the DSU suggests that it relates to statements of positions made to panels or the Appellate Body. However, we consider that the provisions of Article 18.2 of the DSU are also applicable, at least by analogy, to the present proceedings under Article 22.6 of the DSU.

[25]   Appellate Body Report, *US – Continued Suspension*, Annex IV, paras. 4 and 11.

[26]   Appellate Body Report, *US – Continued Suspension*, Annex IV, para. 4.

[27]   As we address below, Article 18.2 of the DSU does not mean that we must automatically authorize the United States to disclose to the public an oral statement of its own positions made during our meeting. Indeed, we recall in this respect that even if we were to deny the United States' request, the United States could still exercise its right to disclose statements of its own positions in a different form or on a different occasion.

[28]   Mexico refers to Appellate Body Report, *EU – Biodiesel (Argentina)*, Annex D-2 (procedural ruling of 11 July 2016).

[29]   Appellate Body Report, *EU – Biodiesel (Argentina)*, Annex D-2, paras. 2 and 3.

[30]   We emphasize that we are not suggesting that a fully open meeting could be conducted in the absence of an agreement between the parties. Nor is this the position of the United States in this dispute. Indeed, the United States initially sought Mexico's agreement to conduct a fully open Arbitrator's meeting. When Mexico expressed its opposition, the United States did not pursue its proposal. The United States proceeded instead to request that we allow the United States to disclose statements of its own positions at our meeting.

authorization to disclose the statements of their own positions that they wish to make at the meeting. This does not imply, however, that one party can simply veto another party's request that it be authorized to disclose statements of its own positions. Indeed, this is also the approach taken by the Appellate Body in respect of third parties participating in its hearings. Although the Appellate Body has referred to a relationship of confidentiality between "the third participants"[31] and itself, it has authorized those third parties that so wished to lift the confidentiality of their statements at the hearing, despite objections by other third parties.[32] Thus, the Appellate Body did not impose an inflexible "all-or-none" rule for the lifting of confidentiality. In our view, this approach is equally appropriate in respect of the relationship between the parties and a WTO adjudicator. Indeed, it would be incongruous to permit third parties to forego confidentiality protection in respect of their statements (in those disputes where the parties have requested the same) even as other third parties wish to hold on to that protection, but to withhold that same opportunity from a party merely because another party objects to the granting of such an opportunity.

2.32   Mexico has also referred to Article 14.1 of the DSU and Paragraph 3 of Appendix 3 of the DSU, which provide that panel "deliberations" are to be confidential. Although we have no difficulty accepting that these provisions are relevant, at least by analogy, to Article 22.6 of the DSU proceedings, we do not agree that they imply that the United States cannot be authorized to lift the confidentiality of its statements. These provisions relate to a panel's internal work, not the meetings with the parties and third parties.[33] Moreover, just like the Appellate Body, panels have authorized third parties that so wished to lift the confidentiality of their statements even as some third parties objected.[34] This approach necessarily assumes that Article 14.1 of the DSU does not prescribe closed panel meetings with parties or third parties.

2.33   In our view, the confidentiality of panel meetings is covered by Paragraph 2 of Appendix 3 of the DSU, which says that panels shall meet in closed session. However, this paragraph forms part of those provisions from which panels may depart pursuant to Article 12.1 of the DSU, after consulting the parties and provided that such departure is not contrary to another provision of the DSU.[35] In any event, Paragraph 2 in our view does not preclude a party or third party from foregoing confidentiality protection for its statements at a meeting, provided that another party or other third parties can maintain confidentiality

---

[31]   Appellate Body Report, *US – Continued Suspension*, Annex IV, para. 6.
[32]   Appellate Body Report, *US – Continued Suspension*, Annex IV, paras. 1 and 11.
[33]   We note that in *US – Continued Suspension*, the Appellate Body used the term "deliberations" in the same sense, in relation to the internal work of the Appellate Body. Appellate Body Report, *US – Continued Suspension*, Annex IV, para. 8. See also Panel Report, *US – Continued Suspension*, para. 7.49.
[34]   See, for instance, *US – Tax Incentives*, para. 1.20; *Canada — Feed-In Tariff Program/Canada – Renewable Energy*, para. 1.9; *US – COOL (Article 21.5 – Canada and Mexico)*, para. 1.10; and *US – Continued Zeroing*, para. 1.9.
[35]   Panel Report, *US – Continued Suspension*, paras. 7.46-7.47.

protection for their statements. Indeed, as already explained, this is the approach followed by those panels that held partially open third party sessions. We consider that Paragraph 2, when applied by analogy, permits the same approach in the present proceedings with regard to the parties.

2.34   In the light of the foregoing, we consider that in principle we have the power to authorize the United States to disclose statements of its own positions (but not those of Mexico) to the public through a partially open Arbitrator's meeting, even if Mexico opposes the United States' request. However, it does not follow that we must automatically grant the United States' request. We thus turn to set out below the main considerations that underpin our decision to grant the United States' request in these proceedings.

2.35   Although the United States has an autonomous right to disclose statements of its own positions to the public, that right is not absolute. In the context of this dispute, it notably finds its limitation in Mexico's right *not* to have statements of its own positions disclosed by the United States during any public parts of the Arbitrator's meeting.[36] Mexico indicated in this regard that it wished to maintain the confidentiality of its own positions and information submitted to the Arbitrator. It is therefore necessary to provide for a review process prior to any public viewing of a partially open meeting, to allow the Arbitrator and the parties to ensure that any statements disclosed by the United States do not inadvertently disclose, directly or indirectly, statements of Mexico's positions. It follows from these considerations that we can authorize the United States to disclose in a partially open meeting only those parts of its statements that do not disclose statements of Mexico's positions, and that we must therefore reserve the right to appropriately redact the statements that the United States wishes to be open for public observation.[37]

2.36   A further limitation arises from the requirements of due process. These requirements mean that all parties must be given the opportunity to lift the confidentiality of statements of their own positions at partially open meetings. In these proceedings, Mexico chose not to avail itself of that opportunity. Further, the implementation of any additional working procedures for partially open meetings, including the associated redaction process, must not impair the ability of any party that opposes partially open meetings to present its case or defence effectively.

2.37   We note, in addition, Mexico's argument that if a partially open meeting is conducted, viewers will by definition be exposed to only one party's statements. In our view, however, this does not compromise due process. First, a party that does not wish its statements at a WTO adjudicator's meeting to be

---

[36]   Consistent with paragraph 1.1(c) of our Additional Working Procedures on Partially Open Meetings, we use the term "positions" in this Section of our Decision to encompass also the exhibits submitted and the arguments put forward by a party.

[37]   We note that this type of redaction is already routinely undertaken in open meetings whenever the statements made by the parties or third parties address BCI.

open for public observation is not thereby deprived of the possibility to otherwise disclose statements of its positions to the public. More importantly, Article 18.2 of the DSU already allows each party to disclose statements of its own positions to the public independently of whether another party does the same. A partially open meeting thus does not create a new situation. The media, for instance, can (and does) already report to the public based on statements of only one party's positions where only that party has made available its statements on its government's website. Finally, we recall that in disputes where the meetings with the parties were opened for public observation, both the Appellate Body and panels have authorized third parties that so wished to lift the confidentiality of their statements at the relevant hearing or third-party session. Under this practice, it is accepted that viewers of those meetings are exposed to the views of only some third parties, even though the Appellate Body and panels are required to take all third parties' views into account.[38]

2.38   Another factor that in our view should be taken into account when assessing a request for a partially open meeting is the importance, articulated in Article 3.3 of the DSU, of the prompt settlement of disputes. This suggests to us that the conduct of a partially open meeting should not significantly delay a WTO adjudicator's proceedings. In our view, one way to fulfil this objective is to devise additional working procedures governing partially open meetings that put appropriate emphasis on workability and efficiency.

2.39   In addition, we must bear in mind our primary duty, which is to carefully assess the matter before us and resolve the dispute between the parties. Partially open meetings impose a greater burden on a WTO adjudicator than fully open meetings, owing to the need to make sure that there is no disclosure of statements of any party that wishes to maintain the confidentiality of its statements. In deciding whether to authorize a request for a partially open meeting, it therefore appears appropriate that a WTO adjudicator assess at the outset whether it has access to the requisite resources, in technical, logistical and human terms, to conduct a partially open meeting and any associated redaction process. Otherwise, the conduct of a partially open meeting could potentially have an adverse impact on the proper discharge of the adjudicative function and could thus also be detrimental to due process or the prompt settlement of disputes.

2.40   We note, finally, the Appellate Body's view that any authorization to forego the confidentiality protection for statements of a party's or third party's positions must not undermine the integrity of the adjudicative function. The Appellate Body has already clarified in this regard that the mere fact of permitting public observation of a meeting does not have an adverse impact on the integrity of the adjudicative function.[39]

---

[38]   See, for instance, Article 10.1 of the DSU.
[39]   Appellate Body Report, *US – Continued Suspension*, Annex IV, paras. 7 and 10.

2.41   In sum, it is in our view permissible for a WTO adjudicator to authorize a request for a partially open meeting if the conduct of such a meeting does not impair or interfere with (a) a non-disclosing party's right to confidentiality protection of statements of its own position, (b) due process, (c) the prompt settlement of disputes, or (d) the careful and efficient discharge, or the integrity, of the adjudicative function. Beyond that, we consider that it falls within the sound discretion of each WTO adjudicator considering a request for a partially open meeting to decide whether it is appropriate in the particular circumstances of its case to accede to that request.[40] We observe in this respect that the rejection of such a request by a WTO adjudicator would not in and of itself deprive the requesting party of its right to disclose statements of its own positions to the public, since it would still have available to it other ways of exercising that right.

2.42   Guided by the foregoing considerations, in the present proceedings we devised additional working procedures in consultation with the parties that we think fully protect Mexico's right to confidentiality protection, satisfy the requirements of due process, and are sufficiently workable and efficient to safeguard the promptness of dispute settlement and the proper discharge and integrity of our adjudicative function.[41]

2.43   In granting the United States' request we notably also took into account the following three circumstances. First, the present dispute concerns the protection of dolphins and thus a conservation-related measure. In this kind of dispute, even a partially open meeting is apt to enhance understanding of, and confidence in, the WTO dispute settlement process.[42] Second, there was in these proceedings only one relatively short substantive meeting with the Arbitrator that was requested to be partially opened for public observation. Third, the parallel conduct of a second round of compliance panel proceedings in this dispute required the assembly of a substantial Secretariat support team. We were thus in a position where we could conduct a partially open meeting and carry out the associated redaction process without this compromising our substantive work.

2.44   On the basis of these considerations, we therefore concluded that in the particular circumstances of this case it was, on balance, appropriate for us to accept the United States' request that it be permitted to disclose through public viewing the statements of its own positions made during the Arbitrator's meeting. Our authorization was subject to the dual condition that the public viewing take the form of delayed (rather than simultaneous) viewing, and that

---

[40]   See Appellate Body Report, *EC – Hormones*, para. 154.

[41]   See Annex A-3, in particular paras 3.4, 4.1-4.9.

[42]   The United States indicated that it was pursuing these objectives in requesting the opening of our meeting. We also note in this connection that in our additional working procedures, at paragraph 4.2, we have sought to avoid unnecessary discontinuity in the delayed viewing by inviting the United States to structure its statements in such a way as to separate those statements that disclose statements of positions of Mexico. See Annex A-3.

any parts of the meeting opened for public observation not disclose statements of Mexico's positions and hence be subject to redaction prior to the public viewing as necessary.

3. UNITED STATES' REQUEST FOR A PRELIMINARY RULING CONCERNING THE RELEVANT MEASURE

3.1 Procedural Background

3.45   On 3 August 2016, the United States submitted, in its written submission to the Arbitrator, a request for a preliminary ruling. The request concerned Mexico's identification of the 2013 Tuna Measure as the proper basis for the Arbitrator's assessment of the level of nullification or impairment.

3.46   Mexico responded to the United States' request for a preliminary ruling in its own written submission to the Arbitrator, which it filed on 31 August 2016. Additionally, after consulting with the parties, the Arbitrator modified its timetable on 18 August 2016 to provide for additional submissions from the parties on the issues raised by the United States' request. Pursuant to this modification, the Arbitrator sent questions to the parties concerning the United States' request on 7 September 2016. The parties responded to these questions in writing on 14 September 2016. The parties submitted comments on each other's responses on 21 September 2016. Additionally, the United States and Mexico each provided additional comments on the request for a preliminary ruling on 21 and 28 September 2016 respectively.

3.47   On 11 October 2016, the Arbitrator issued its conclusion on the United States' request for a preliminary ruling. The Arbitrator indicated that it would provide the reasons supporting its conclusion at the end of the proceedings, in the Arbitrator's Decision. The Arbitrator also indicated that both the conclusion and the reasons supporting it would form an integral part of the Arbitrator's Decision in this matter.[43]

3.2 Issue

3.48   In its first written submission, the United States requested the Arbitrator to make a preliminary ruling that the relevant measure for the purposes of these arbitration proceedings is the Tuna Measure as amended by the 2016 final rule (i.e. the 2016 Tuna Measure), rather than the 2013 Tuna Measure. According to the United States, Mexico has effectively asked the Arbitrator to determine some past level of nullification or impairment, and therefore seeks authorization to suspend concessions regardless of whether there is currently (i.e. under the 2016 Tuna Measure) any nullification or impairment. In the view of the United States,

---

[43]   Communication from the Arbitrator, para. 1.1.

this approach has no legal basis, and indeed is contrary to the relevant provisions of the DSU.[44]

3.49   Mexico requests the Arbitrator to reject the United States' request for a preliminary ruling. According to Mexico, the Arbitrator should use the 2013 Tuna Measure to calculate the level of nullification or impairment. In Mexico's view, it would be neither legally permissible nor systematically desirable to use the 2016 Tuna Measure.[45] Additionally, Mexico argues that the United States' request represents an effort to "improperly conflate the Arbitrator's mandate in this Article 22.6 arbitration with the claims at issue in the second round of Article 21.5 proceedings" that are being held in parallel.[46]

3.50   The Arbitrator notes that the question raised by the United States' request is whether, in these proceedings, the Arbitrator should assess the level of nullification or impairment caused by the 2013 or the 2016 Tuna Measure. As this issue bears directly on our mandate, and as it raises certain issues about Article 22.6 of the DSU that has not been directly ruled on by any previous arbitrator, a detailed examination is in order.

3.3   Text and Context of Article 22.6 of the DSU

3.51   The Arbitrator begins its analysis by looking at the text and context of Article 22.6 of the DSU, which is the provision under which the United States has brought these arbitration proceedings.[47]

3.52   Article 22.6 of the DSU relevantly provides as follows:

> When the situation described in paragraph 2 occurs, the DSB,
> upon request, shall grant authorization to suspend concessions or
> other obligations within 30 days of the expiry of the reasonable
> period of time unless the DSB decides by consensus to reject the
> request. However, if the Member concerned objects to the level of
> suspension proposed, or claims that the principles and procedures
> set forth in paragraph 3 have not been followed where a
> complaining party has requested authorization to suspend
> concessions or other obligations pursuant to paragraph 3(b) or (c),
> the matter shall be referred to arbitration.

3.53   Other paragraphs of Article 22 of the DSU form part of the immediate context of Article 22.6 and are therefore also relevant to our analysis. Article 22.1 of the DSU relevantly provides that:

---

[44]   United States' written submission, paras. 42 and 50.

[45]   Mexico's written submission, para. 4.

[46]   Mexico's written submission, para. 19.

[47]   Pursuant to Article 3.2 of the DSU, we are required to apply the customary rules of interpretation of public international law. We must therefore interpret DSU provisions in accordance with the ordinary meaning to be given to their terms in their context and in the light of the object and purpose of the relevant treaty. See e.g. Appellate Body Report, *Canada – Patent Term*, para. 54.

Compensation and the suspension of concessions or other obligations are temporary measures available in the event that the recommendations and rulings are not implemented within a reasonable period of time.

3.54   Article 22.2 of the DSU, to which explicit reference is made in the first sentence of Article 22.6, provides as follows:

If the Member concerned fails to bring the measure found to be inconsistent with a covered agreement into compliance therewith or otherwise comply with the recommendations and rulings within the reasonable period of time determined pursuant to paragraph 3 of Article 21 [of the DSU], such Member shall, if so requested, and no later than the expiry of the reasonable period of time, enter into negotiations with any party having invoked the dispute settlement procedures, with a view to developing mutually acceptable compensation. If no satisfactory compensation has been agreed within 20 days after the date of expiry of the reasonable period of time, any party having invoked the dispute settlement procedures may request authorization from the DSB to suspend the application to the Member concerned of concessions or other obligations under the covered agreements.

3.55   Article 22.4 of the DSU provides that:

The level of the suspension of concessions or other obligations authorized by the DSB shall be equivalent to the level of the nullification or impairment.

3.56   Article 22.7 of the DSU relevantly provides that:

The arbitrator acting pursuant to paragraph 6 shall not examine the nature of the concessions or other obligations to be suspended but shall determine whether the level of such suspension is equivalent to the level of nullification or impairment.

3.57   Finally, Article 22.8 of the DSU relevantly provides that:

The suspension of concessions or other obligations shall be temporary and shall only be applied until such time as the measure found to be inconsistent with a covered agreement has been removed, or the Member that must implement recommendations or rulings provides a solution to the nullification or impairment of benefits, or a mutually satisfactory solution is reached.

3.58   According to the United States, Articles 22.4 and 22.7 of the DSU make clear that an arbitrator is to determine whether there is equivalence between the proposed level of suspension and the level of nullification or impairment at the time the DSB authorizes the suspension of concessions, rather than whether the proposed level of suspension is equivalent to the level of nullification or impairment caused by a past measure or at some point in the past. In support of this view, the United States refers to the phrasing of Article 22.4 of the DSU, noting in particular the use of an imperative command ("shall be") in relation to "the" level of nullification. The United States also emphasizes that neither Article 22.4 nor Article 22.7 of the DSU refers to a past period of time. In the view of the United States, if the Members of the WTO had intended the level of nullification or impairment to be fixed at a specific point in the past, such as the expiry of the reasonable period of time (RPT), the text would have specified the relevant point in time.[48]

3.59   The United States further submits that Article 22.8 of the DSU provides contextual support for its view that the relevant measure in an arbitration proceeding is that version of the measure that exists at the time of the arbitration and the suspension of concessions, rather than the version that existed at some earlier point in time. According to the United States, the issue under Article 22.8 is the measure as it currently exists, if indeed a measure does still exist, and not some measure that existed in the past.[49]

3.60   Mexico disagrees with the United States' text-based arguments. According to Mexico, the United States interprets Articles 22.4 and 22.7 of the DSU in isolation from the other provisions of Article 22. In Mexico's view, a proper, holistic reading of Article 22 of the DSU makes clear that the procedures provided for in that Article all flow from the same triggering event, that is, the failure of a Member to come into compliance with adverse DSB recommendations and rulings within the applicable deadline. In Mexico's view, this fact leads to the conclusion that the measure at issue in arbitration proceedings is the measure that existed at the expiry of the applicable deadline, in this case, the expiry of the RPT on 13 June 2013.[50]

3.61   Additionally, in response to the United States' argument that Article 22.7 of the DSU contains no reference to a past period of time, Mexico notes that Article 22.7 refers to the principles and procedures set forth in Article 22.3 that a complaining Member must apply in considering what concessions or other obligations to suspend in case of the responding Member's non-compliance with adverse DSB recommendations and rulings. Mexico observes that Article 22.3(a) sets forth the general principle that the complaining party should first seek to suspend concessions or other obligations with respect to the same sector(s) as that in which the panel or Appellate Body has found a violation or other nullification or impairment. According to Mexico, this wording explicitly addresses a past situation, rather than a present one, and clearly links the suspension of concessions to the nullification or impairment found by a panel or the Appellate Body sometime in the past, i.e. prior to the suspension.[51]

3.62   The Arbitrator notes the text of Article 22.6 of the DSU, which states that "[w]here the situation in paragraph 2 [of Article 22] occurs", the DSB shall,

---

[48]   United States' written submission, paras. 43-45; response to Arbitrator question No. 2.
[49]   United States' written submission, para. 45.
[50]   Mexico's comments on the United States' response to Arbitrator question No. 6.
[51]   *Ibid.*

within 30 days of the expiry of the reasonable period of time, grant authorization to suspend concessions. Article 22.6 of the DSU further stipulates that if the Member against whom suspension of concessions is sought objects to the proposed level of suspension, the matter "shall be referred to arbitration". The text of Article 22.6 does not specify which measure should form the basis of the request for, or authorization of, suspension of concessions. The text of Article 22.6, therefore, at least when read in isolation, does not clearly support either the United States' or Mexico's position.

3.63   Given that Article 22.6 of the DSU explicitly refers to "the situation" described in Article 22.2, that latter provision clearly provides relevant context for the interpretation of Article 22.6. To recall, the text of Article 22.2 provides in relevant part that in a situation where a Member fails to bring a measure previously found by to be inconsistent with the covered agreements into compliance therewith, and where no satisfactory compensation is agreed within 20 days of the expiry of the applicable RPT, the complaining Member may request authorization from the DSB to suspend concessions or other obligations. The "situation" referred to in Article 22.6 thus occurs where (a) a Member has failed to bring a measure into compliance with the covered agreements before the expiry of the applicable RPT; and (b) the parties have failed to agree on satisfactory compensation.

3.64   Read together, Articles 22.2 and 22.6 of the DSU thus establish that a complaining Member may seek authorization to suspend concessions in situations where the responding Member has failed, within the RPT, to bring into conformity a measure that has previously been found to be inconsistent with the covered agreements. It is therefore the continued WTO-inconsistency of the original or a compliance measure (where a compliance measure was taken within the RPT) at the time the RPT expires that forms the basis for any request for authorization to suspend concessions.[52] In turn, a request for authorization to suspend concessions typically triggers a request for arbitration under Article 22.6. There is thus a close connection between an Article 22.6 arbitration and the WTO-inconsistent original measure, or a WTO-inconsistent compliance measure, which existed at the time of expiry of the RPT. Or to put it another way, the origin of, and impetus for, arbitration proceedings under Article 22.6 can be traced back to a WTO-inconsistent measure that existed when the RPT expired, which is either the same original measure that has previously been found to be WTO-inconsistent or a WTO-inconsistent compliance measure taken subsequently (but prior to the expiry of the RPT).

3.65   As noted above, Article 22.4 of the DSU provides that "[t]he level of the suspension of concessions or other obligations authorized by the DSB shall be

---

[52]   This is also confirmed by Article 22.1, whose first sentence provides that "[c]ompensation and suspension of concessions or other obligations are temporary measures available in the event that the recommendations and rulings [in respect of the relevant original or compliance measure] are not implemented within a reasonable period time".

equivalent to the level of the nullification or impairment". We do not read either the reference to "the" level of the suspension of concessions or the use of the phrase "shall be" as indicating that an arbitrator's assessment must be based on the most recent version of the measure in question. Indeed, the unqualified reference to "the level of the nullification or impairment" must be interpreted taking into account the surrounding paragraphs of Article 22 of the DSU, and in particular Article 22.2, which by implication refers to the original or a compliance measure that existed at the time of expiry of the RPT. Consequently, and bearing in mind the principle in Article 3.8 of the DSU that "[i]n cases where there is an infringement of the obligations assumed under a covered agreement, the action is considered *prima facie* to constitute a case of nullification or impairment", the reference in Article 22.4 to "the level of the nullification or impairment" must in our view be construed to mean the level of nullification or impairment caused by the WTO-inconsistent original or compliance measure[53] that existed at the time of expiry of the RPT.[54]

3.66   Additionally, Article 22.3 of the DSU, and in particular Article 22.3(a), supports our interpretation of Article 22.6. As Mexico notes, Article 22.3(a), which concerns what concessions or other obligations may be suspended, provides that "the complaining party should first seek to suspend concessions or other obligations with respect to the same sector(s) as that in which the panel or Appellate Body has found a violation or other nullification or impairment". This provision closely links past findings concerning the inconsistency of a measure and a Member's right to suspend specific concessions or other obligations. It requires, as a default rule, identity between the sector(s) affected by the nullification or impairment caused by a WTO-inconsistent measure and the sector(s) in which a Member requests to suspend concessions or other obligations. It is therefore clear to us that the measure that forms the basis of a Member's request to suspend concessions is the WTO-inconsistent original or compliance measure that existed at the time of expiry of the RPT.

3.67   The United States contends that Article 22.8 of the DSU provides support for its interpretation of Article 22.6. We note, however, that Article 22.8 refers to a stage in the WTO dispute settlement process that is reached, if at all, after an Article 22.6 arbitrator has completed its task (if an arbitration has been requested). It is true that Article 22.8 sets out an ongoing obligation on a Member that has suspended concessions to terminate the suspension as soon as the measure found to be inconsistent has been removed or an alternative solution has been reached. In that sense, Article 22.8 is concerned with the "present"[55]

---

[53]   By "WTO-inconsistent original or compliance measure", we mean a measure that is the subject to adverse DSB recommendations and rulings.

[54]   In our view, the same interpretation must be given to Article 22.7. Thus, we consider that the "level of nullification or impairment" referred to in Article 22.7 is the level of nullification or impairment caused by the WTO-inconsistent original or compliance measure that existed at the time of expiry of the RPT.

[55]   United States' written submission, para. 45.

situation and hence with the most recent compliance measure that may be in place. But Article 22.8 does not suggest or imply that, in determining the permissible level of suspension of concessions, an arbitrator should look to the most recent version of the measure in question that exists at the time that an Article 22.6 arbitration is initiated. Moreover, our interpretation of Article 22.6 sits comfortably with Article 22.8 of the DSU. As we see it, Article 22.8 serves to ensure that if and when the WTO-inconsistent original or compliance measure that existed at the time of expiry of the RPT is removed – and the responding Member may do this, for instance, by adopting a new compliance measure – any suspension of concessions applied by the complaining Member will be terminated.

3.68   In sum, our view is that, when read in the light of its context, the text of Article 22.6 of the DSU mandates an arbitrator to assess the level of nullification or impairment caused by the WTO-inconsistent original measure (where no compliance measure was subsequently taken), or a subsequent WTO-inconsistent compliance measure, that was in existence at the time of expiry of the RPT. This measure may or may not be the most recent version of the relevant measure.

3.69   In the present proceedings, the measure to which this interpretation directs us is the 2013 Tuna Measure, and not the 2016 Tuna Measure. The 2016 Tuna Measure is not yet subject to any panel or Appellate Body findings, and so it is not a measure that has been found to be WTO-inconsistent. Moreover, the 2013 Tuna Measure, not the 2016 Tuna Measure, was the version of the Tuna Measure in force at the time the RPT expired. Accordingly, the 2016 Tuna Measure could not and did not bring the Tuna Measure into compliance by the time the RPT expired, and it therefore should not form the basis of the Arbitrator's assessment of the level of nullification or impairment in these proceedings.

3.4   Previous Arbitration Decisions

3.70   The United States argues that its request for a preliminary ruling is supported also by the findings of previous arbitrators.

3.71   Mexico argues that the decisions cited by the United States are "inapposite".[56]

3.72   The Arbitrator notes that the United States cited to three arbitration decisions in support of its position: *EC – Bananas III*, *US – Upland Cotton*, and *Brazil – Aircraft*. We will consider each of these cases to determine whether they support an interpretation of Article 22.6 that is different to the one we have outlined above.

---

[56]   Mexico's written submission, Section II.C.

3.73   We begin with the arbitrator's decision in *EC – Bananas III*. According to the United States, this decision confirms that the task of an arbitrator acting under Article 22.6 is to look at the measure in question as it currently exists, and not the measure in some earlier form. In particular, the United States refers to the following passage from the arbitrator's decision:

> [W]e could resort to the option of measuring the level of nullification or impairment on the basis of our findings in the original dispute, as modified by the Appellate Body and adopted by the DSB. To do that would mean to ignore altogether the undisputed fact that the European Communities has taken measures to revise its banana import regime. That is certainly not the mandate that the DSB has entrusted to us.[57]

3.74   In the United States' view, this statement indicates that the arbitrator assessed the level of nullification or impairment caused by the most recent version of the measure at issue, even though an earlier version of the measure had been ruled on by the panel and Appellate Body.[58]

3.75   Mexico rejects the United States' interpretation of the arbitration decision in *EC – Bananas III*. It argues that the particular dilemma faced by the arbitrator in that case does not arise in the present proceedings, and accordingly the Arbitrator in the present proceedings should not follow the approach in that case. In particular, Mexico notes that unlike in the present proceedings, in *EC – Bananas III* the compliance panel proceedings on the amended version of the measure at issue[59] had not yet been resolved when the matter was referred to arbitration.[60] This, in the view of the arbitrator in that case, raised a serious concern, because "authorization by the DSB of the suspension of concessions or other obligations presupposes the existence of a failure to comply with the recommendations or rulings contained in panel and/or Appellate Body reports as adopted by the DSB".[61] In the absence of such adverse DSB recommendations and rulings, the arbitrator decided to take upon itself the task of determining preliminarily the WTO-consistency of the amended measure before calculating

---

[57]   Decision by the Arbitrator, *EC – Bananas III (US) (Article 22.6 – EC)*, para. 4.7.
[58]   United States' written submission, para. 46.
[59]   In *EC – Bananas*, two compliance panels, one requested by the European Communities and one requested by Ecuador – were established on 12 January 1999. On 14 January 1999, the United States requested the DSB to authorize it to suspend concessions against the European Communities under Article 22 of the DSU. At the DSB meeting held on 25 January-1 February 1999, the European Communities objected to the level of suspension proposed by the United States on the ground that it was not equivalent to the level of nullification or impairment of benefits suffered by the United States and claimed that the principles and procedures set out in Article 22.3 of the DSU had not been followed. In response, the DSB decided on 29 January 1999, prior to the conclusion of the compliance panel proceedings, to submit the matter to arbitration of the original panel in accordance with Article 22.6 of the DSU.
[60]   Mexico's written submission, para. 31.
[61]   Decision by the Arbitrator, *EC – Bananas III (US) (Article 22.6 – EC)*, para. 4.4.

the level of nullification or impairment that it caused.[62] In Mexico's view, such an approach is inappropriate where, as in the present dispute, adverse DSB recommendations and rulings concerning the United States' failure to comply already exist. According to Mexico, the Arbitrator should base its calculations on the measure that is the subject of those existing adverse DSB recommendations and rulings.[63]

3.76   We agree with Mexico that the circumstances in *EC – Bananas III* were different to those we face in these proceedings. Most importantly, in *EC – Bananas III* the arbitrator faced a situation where it might have had to determine the level of nullification or impairment in the absence of DSB recommendations and rulings that the European Communities had failed to bring its measure into compliance within the applicable RPT. This, according to the arbitrator, would have put the arbitrator in a difficult position because "we cannot fulfil our task to assess the *equivalence* between the two levels before we have reached a view on whether the revised EC regime is, in light of our and the Appellate Body's findings in the original dispute, fully WTO-consistent".[64] In other words, the arbitrator considered that an analysis of the WTO-consistency of the measure taken to comply was a prerequisite to the assessment of the level of nullification or impairment, because if the measure taken to comply had in fact brought the European Communities into compliance within the RPT, there would, legally speaking, have been no nullification or impairment to assess. Accordingly, the arbitrator decided that it would analyse the WTO-consistency of the measure taken to comply, and only then, if it found that measure to be WTO-inconsistent, proceed to assess the level of nullification or impairment caused by that measure.

3.77   In adopting this approach, the arbitrator emphasized that the DSB, when referring the matter to arbitration, noted that there "remains the problem of how the Panel and the Arbitrators would coordinate their work", and charged the arbitrator with finding "a logical way forward".[65] The arbitrator stated that its decision to analyse the WTO-consistency of the measure taken to comply was, in its view, the most logical way forward.[66]

3.78   We are not faced with the "problem" identified by the DSB in *EC – Bananas III*, and accordingly do not consider it necessary or appropriate to follow the approach devised by the arbitrator in that case as a "logical" solution. Unlike in *EC – Bananas III*, the present arbitration takes place in response to DSB recommendations and rulings that the 2013 Tuna Measure failed to bring the United States into compliance within the RPT. There is therefore no uncertainty in this case regarding whether the measure taken by the United States within the RPT to comply with its WTO obligations – the 2013 Tuna

---

[62]   Decision by the Arbitrator, *EC – Bananas III (US) (Article 22.6 – EC)*, para. 4.8.
[63]   Mexico's written submission, para. 31.
[64]   Decision by the Arbitrator, *EC – Bananas III (US) (Article 22.6 – EC)*, para. 4.8.
[65]   Decision by the Arbitrator, *EC – Bananas III (US) (Article 22.6 – EC)*, para. 4.9.
[66]   *Ibid.*

Measure – is WTO-inconsistent. Consequently, we do not find ourselves in a situation where we must either analyse ourselves the WTO-consistency of the 2013 Tuna Measure or else "ignore altogether"[67] the fact that the United States revised its Tuna Measure in 2013.

3.79   The fact that the United States has since made further changes to the Tuna Measure (so that it now constitutes the 2016 Tuna Measure) does not place us in a situation comparable to that in *EC – Bananas III*. The mere fact that the United States has made additional changes to the Tuna Measure is not sufficient grounds for concluding that the United States has come into compliance.[68] Rather, we agree with Mexico that the existing adverse DSB recommendations and rulings remain in effect until such time as there are new, overriding panel and/or Appellate Body findings that have been adopted by the DSB or a mutually agreed solution has been notified to the DSB.[69] Moreover, the decision in *EC – Bananas III* in our view does not stand for the proposition that every time a responding Member adopts a new compliance measure and asserts compliance while arbitration proceedings under Article 22.6 are underway, the arbitrator must analyse the WTO-consistency of the new measure. A careful review of the facts and circumstances surrounding that arbitration decision reveals that at most it can support the proposition that such an analysis may be warranted if there have been no prior DSB recommendations and rulings that the responding Member has failed to bring itself into compliance within the RPT. As explained, in this case, there have been such adverse DSB recommendations and rulings.

3.80   In sum, unlike in *EC – Bananas III*, the DSB in this case has already determined that the measure taken by the United States to comply (the 2013 Tuna Measure) is WTO-inconsistent. Because of these existing adverse DSB recommendations and rulings, the issue does not arise in this case whether as arbitrators acting under Article 22.6 we could and should undertake our own evaluation of the WTO-consistency of the 2013 Tuna Measure. Further, there are (as yet) no overriding panel and/or Appellate Body findings that have been

---

[67]   Decision by the Arbitrator, *EC – Bananas III (US) (Article 22.6 – EC)*, para. 4.7.

[68]   Appellate Body Report, *US – Continued Suspension*, para. 317.

[69]   In support of this position, Mexico relies on the Appellate Body's statement in *US – Continued Suspension* that "until the removal of the European Communities' inconsistent measure was determined through WTO dispute settlement, the United States' and Canada's authorization to suspend concessions did not lapse" (Appellate Body Report, *US – Continued Suspension*, para. 403). The United States argues that this statement is irrelevant, because the Appellate Body in that case was addressing the situation where the DSB had already authorized the suspension of concessions and the issue was at what point that DSB authorization would terminate. Although the United States is correct that the Appellate Body in *US – Continued Suspension* did not address the specific issue before us, in our view similar considerations apply with respect to DSB recommendations and rulings concerning the WTO-inconsistency of a measure taken to comply. Thus, just as a statement by a Member that it has come into compliance does not cause the expiry of an existing DSB authorization to suspend concessions (see Appellate Body Report, *US – Continued Suspension*, para. 317), so also such a statement would not affect the continued validity of DSB recommendations and rulings concerning the WTO-inconsistency of a measure taken to comply.

adopted by the DSB, or a notified mutually agreed solution, concerning the 2016 Tuna Measure that could have affected the continued validity of the adverse DSB recommendations and rulings concerning the 2013 Tuna Measure. We therefore conclude that the arbitrator's decision in *EC – Bananas III* does not support the United States' view that we should base our assessment on the 2016 Tuna Measure.

3.81   We now turn to the arbitrator's decision in *US – Upland Cotton*. According to the United States, the arbitrator in that case rejected a request by Brazil as the complaining party for authorization to take countermeasures in relation to a measure that had been withdrawn before the arbitration proceedings (but after the expiry of the RPT), reasoning that such an authorization would necessarily exceed the current level of nullification or impairment. In the United States' view, Mexico's position that the proper basis for the Arbitrator's assessment is the 2013 Tuna Measure "directly contravenes" the approach taken by the arbitrator in that case because the 2013 Tuna Measure was withdrawn and replaced by the 2016 Tuna Measure.[70]

3.82   Mexico argues that the decision in *US – Upland Cotton* is not relevant to these arbitration proceedings. In particular, Mexico notes that, in that case, the United States withdrew the WTO-inconsistent "Step 2 subsidy" after the expiry of the RPT but prior to the compliance panel proceedings and subsequent arbitration under Article 22.6 of the DSU. Mexico observes that the compliance panel declined to make a finding in respect of this withdrawn subsidy, and that accordingly there were never any DSB recommendations or rulings pursuant to Article 21.5 that the United States had failed to bring the Step 2 subsidy into compliance. In Mexico's view, the situation in the present proceedings is completely different: here, there exist clear DSB recommendations and rulings pursuant to Article 21.5 that the United States failed to bring its Tuna Measure into compliance prior to the expiry of the RPT.

3.83   In our view, the situation facing the arbitrator in *US – Upland Cotton* was markedly different to the one we face. In *US – Upland Cotton*, Brazil agreed that the Step 2 subsidy had been withdrawn by the United States, albeit after the expiry of the RPT.[71] Accordingly, it was undisputed that, by the time of the compliance proceedings, which preceded the arbitration proceedings, the subsidy had been withdrawn. Brazil sought a finding from the compliance panel that the United States had acted inconsistently with the covered agreements by failing to withdraw the subsidy prior to the expiry of the RPT, but it did not argue that the subsidy continued to exist.[72]

---

[70]   United States' written submission, para. 46.
[71]   Panel Report, *US – Upland Cotton (Article 21.5 – Brazil)*, paras. 9.57 and 9.65.
[72]   Panel Report, *US – Upland Cotton (Article 21.5 – Brazil)*, para. 9.57.

3.84   In the present dispute, the United States argues that the 2013 Tuna Measure is no longer in existence.[73] Mexico, however, has never conceded that the Tuna Measure has ceased to exist. To the contrary, it argues that the Tuna Measure continues to exist and, in its 2016 version, remains inconsistent with the covered agreements. It is pursuing its claims in respect of the 2016 Tuna Measure in compliance panel proceedings. Accordingly, a central circumstance that was present in *US – Upland Cotton* – the agreement by the parties that the Step 2 subsidy had ceased to exist prior to the compliance panel proceedings, albeit after the expiry of the RPT – is not present in the dispute before us.

3.85   Further, as Mexico notes, the compliance panel in *US – Upland Cotton* decided not to make any findings concerning the period between the expiry of the RPT and the withdrawal of the Step 2 subsidy.[74] Brazil did not appeal that decision.[75] Accordingly, there were no adverse DSB recommendations and rulings pursuant to Article 21.5 of the DSU with respect to the Step 2 subsidy.[76] In the absence of such recommendations and rulings, the arbitrator in *US – Upland Cotton* found that there was no "legitimate basis" for the imposition of countermeasures in respect of that measure. Additionally, the arbitrator found that, because it was undisputed that the Step 2 subsidy had been withdrawn, it would be inappropriate to authorize the suspension of concessions given that the purpose of such suspension is precisely to induce compliance.[77]

3.86   In the present dispute, we are not faced with the same situation. There are adverse DSB recommendations and rulings in respect of the measure taken by the United States to comply, i.e. the 2013 Tuna Measure. Additionally, there is no agreement between the parties that the Tuna Measure has subsequently been brought into compliance, nor are there any more recent panel and/or Appellate Body findings that have been adopted by the DSB. The adverse DSB recommendations and rulings covering the 2013 Tuna Measure therefore continue to provide a valid basis for the suspension of concessions. Consequently, we do not find it appropriate to follow the approach taken by the arbitrator in *US – Upland Cotton* in respect of the Step 2 Subsidy.

3.87   Finally, we turn to the arbitrator's decision in *Brazil – Aircraft*. The United States observes that in that case, the arbitrator found that it needed to take into account the results of the separate, ongoing compliance proceedings under Article 21.5 of the DSU before it could reach a conclusion under Article 22.6. According to the United States, the same approach should be adopted by the Arbitrator in the present proceedings.[78]

---

[73]   United States' written submission, para. 42; United States' response to Arbitrator question No. 1; United States' comments on Mexico's responses to Arbitrator questions.

[74]   Panel Report, *US – Upland Cotton (Article 21.5 – US I)*, para. 9.71.

[75]   Decision by the Arbitrator, *US – Upland Cotton (Article 22.6 – US I)*, para. 3.20.

[76]   *Ibid.*

[77]   Decision by the Arbitrator, *US – Upland Cotton (Article 22.6 – US I)*, para. 4.62.

[78]   United States' written submission, paras. 52-53.

3.88   Mexico rejects the United States' reliance on *Brazil – Aircraft*. According to Mexico, in that case, as in *EC – Bananas III*, there were no prior adverse DSB recommendations and rulings pursuant to Article 21.5 in respect of the measure taken to comply. Rather, Mexico observes, the arbitration and the first round of compliance proceedings ran in parallel. It is in that context that the arbitrator decided to take the outcome of the compliance panel proceedings into account in its assessment of the level of nullification or impairment.[79]

3.89   We agree with Mexico that the facts in *Brazil – Aircraft* were similar to those in *EC – Bananas III*, inasmuch as there were no existing adverse DSB recommendations and rulings pursuant to Article 21.5 at the time the arbitrator began its work. There were therefore no existing recommendations and rulings on whether the responding party had failed to bring its measure into compliance before the expiry of the RPT, which failure, as we have explained above, is the event that allows the complaining party to have recourse to the procedures in Article 22 of the DSU.

3.90   To recall, in the present dispute there are existing DSB recommendations and rulings that the United States failed to bring its measure into compliance prior to the end of the RPT. Moreover, as we mentioned above, given that Mexico contests the United States' claim that the 2016 Tuna Measure brought the United States into compliance, the DSB recommendations and rulings that the 2013 Tuna Measure failed to bring the United States into compliance within the RPT continue to provide a valid basis for the suspension of concessions and hence remain relevant for purposes of these arbitration proceedings.

3.91   For the reasons given above, we consider that the arbitration decisions cited by the United States do not support the United States' position. Those decisions dealt with circumstances that were different from those in this dispute. Notably, they dealt with circumstances in which there were no DSB recommendations and rulings that the responding party had failed to bring its measure into compliance within the reasonable period of time. Consequently, we conclude that the decisions cited by the United States do not contradict our text-based interpretation of Article 22.6.

3.5   Additional Considerations

3.92   Both parties raise a number of additional issues concerning the proper interpretation of Article 22.6 of the DSU and its application in this dispute. These issues are: (a) the possible systemic consequences of granting the United States' request for a preliminary ruling; (b) whether denying the United States' request for a preliminary ruling would result in the authorization of a punitive or retroactive suspension of concessions; (c) the relevance of the bilateral sequencing agreement agreed between Mexico and the United States; and (d) the

---

[79]   Mexico's written submission, para. 33.

date on which the 2016 Tuna Measure entered into force, and the legal relevance of that fact. The Arbitrator will consider these issues in turn.

3.5.1 Possible systemic consequences of granting the United States' request

3.93   Mexico argues that granting the United States' request for a preliminary ruling would render Article 22 of the DSU ineffective.[80] According to Mexico, an Article 22.6 arbitration that is based on the DSB recommendations and rulings on a preceding round of Article 21.5 proceedings must not be influenced or delayed by the claims and issues before a new Article 21.5 compliance panel established to determine the WTO-consistency of a new compliance measure. Otherwise, the result would be an endless loop that could indefinitely preclude the right to suspend concessions or other obligations pursuant to Article 22. In Mexico's view, a Member maintaining a WTO-inconsistent measure could then delay the resolution of a meritorious complaint by introducing amendments each time the complaining Member sought to enforce its rights under Article 22 following a round of Article 21.5 proceedings. This, in Mexico's view, would render Article 22 meaningless.[81]

3.94   The United States submits that, in a situation like the one envisaged by Mexico where there is an Article 22.6 arbitration and a new compliance measure, one option would be to allow the threshold issue of compliance to be resolved through compliance panel proceedings before any assessment of the level of nullification or impairment. The United States points out, however, that the issue of compliance could also be resolved by an arbitrator acting under Article 22.6 of the DSU. Thus, modifications made to a measure could be taken into account by the arbitrator, and would not necessarily require that the arbitration be delayed until the end of additional compliance proceedings under Article 21.5 of the DSU.[82]

3.95   Mexico responds that nothing in the DSU authorizes an arbitrator to deal with compliance issues, and that to allow an arbitrator to address such questions could affect the rights and obligations of WTO Members, because, for example, arbitrations are not subject to appeal.[83]

3.96   The Arbitrator notes that the existence of Article 21.5 as a separate provision suggests that generally, compliance issues should be dealt with separately from the assessment of the level of nullification or impairment, by a compliance panel. Nevertheless, in at least one previous dispute, an arbitrator acting under Article 22.6 has considered issues of compliance in the course of

---

[80]   Mexico's written submission, para. 19.
[81]   Mexico's written submission, para. 27; letter to the Arbitrator of 3 June 2016.
[82]   United States' response to Arbitrator question No. 3; letter to the Arbitrator of 3 June 2016, paras. 10 and 19.
[83]   Mexico's comments on the United States' response to Arbitrator question No. 3.

assessing the level of nullification or impairment.[84] As we have explained, however, the circumstances facing that arbitrator were unusual, and the arbitrator itself stated that it would consider issues of compliance in view of the DSB's specific request that it find a "logical way forward".[85] We have already pointed out above that our circumstances are different. Notably, we are not in a situation where we either have to analyse the WTO-consistency of the 2016 Tuna Measure, or else be prepared to make an assessment of the level of nullification or impairment in the absence of DSB recommendations and rulings that the United States had failed to bring its Tuna Measure into compliance within the applicable RPT. We therefore do not consider it appropriate in this dispute to follow the approach taken by that other arbitrator.

3.97   With respect to the systemic concern expressed by Mexico, we think it is valid. As Mexico notes, the interpretation of Article 22.6 of the DSU advocated by the United States seems to imply that whenever a compliance measure subject to adverse DSB recommendations and rulings is further modified and the responding party claims to have come into compliance, and an Article 22.6 arbitration is subsequently conducted, a new assessment of compliance becomes necessary before the DSB can authorize any suspension of concessions. If, in a situation such as ours where an Article 22.6 arbitration is conducted, new compliance panel proceedings under Article 21.5 needed to be undertaken every time a measure already found to be inconsistent at the expiry of the RPT were modified and compliance was claimed, this could very substantially delay, and in theory effectively thwart, a complaining party's efforts towards obtaining DSB authorization to suspend concessions. This is because it would then presumably be necessary to delay or suspend an Article 22.6 arbitration until after completion of compliance proceedings. If, following such proceedings, there were new adverse panel and/or Appellate Body findings that were adopted by the DSB, the arbitration would resume, subject to possible further delay if yet another modification of the measure occurred in the meantime and compliance were claimed. Such an outcome would not, in our view, be consistent with the DSU's objectives of preserving the rights of Members[86], including complaining Members, and promoting the prompt settlement of disputes.[87]

3.98   Besides the general systemic concern about the United States' interpretation of Article 22.6, we note that Mexico has in any event firmly opposed any delay to the arbitration proceedings or their suspension until the completion of the parallel compliance panel proceedings.

3.99   In the light of the foregoing, it is in our view appropriate in the circumstances of this dispute to undertake a prompt assessment of the level of nullification or impairment on the basis of the 2013 Tuna Measure and leave the

---

[84]   Decision of the Arbitrator, *EC – Bananas III (US) (Article 22.6 – EC)*.
[85]   See above, para. 3.33.
[86]   Article 3.2 of the DSU.
[87]   Article 3.3 of the DSU.

analysis of the WTO-consistency of the 2016 Tuna Measure to the two compliance panels established to undertake that precise task.

3.5.2 Whether denying the United States' request for a preliminary ruling would result in the authorization of a retroactive or punitive suspension of concessions

3.100 The United States argues that denying its request for a preliminary ruling could result in the Arbitrator's Decision leading to the DSB authorizing a suspension of concessions that is retroactive and/or punitive. The United States argues that this is so because, if the Arbitrator based its assessment on the 2013 Tuna Measure, it would be ignoring the fact that the 2016 Tuna Measure is, in the United States' view, WTO-consistent and therefore does not cause any nullification or impairment. According to the United States, nothing in the DSU allows such retroactive or punitive remedies.[88]

3.101 As the Arbitrator has noted, the WTO-consistency of the 2016 Tuna Measure is not an issue that will be analysed in these proceedings, and accordingly the Arbitrator takes no position on the United States' argument that the 2016 Tuna Measure causes no nullification or impairment. We would note, though, that even if the United States were correct on that point, this would not mean that, in assessing the nullification or impairment caused by the 2013 Tuna Measure, we would be inviting the DSB to authorize retroactive or punitive remedies.

3.102 What Mexico seeks in these arbitration proceedings is a prospective remedy, in response to the United States' failure to implement the adverse DSB recommendations and rulings regarding the 2013 Tuna Measure, that extends from the date of the expiry of the RPT. Mexico does not seek a retroactive remedy that extends from a date prior to the expiry of the RPT. The fact that Mexico is only now requesting authorization to suspend concessions, some three years after the expiry of the RPT, is due to the interference in the timeline of the first compliance proceedings and Mexico's agreement, pursuant to the United States-Mexico Sequencing Agreement, not to request authorization to suspend concessions until after those compliance proceedings. That delay, however, does not turn Mexico's request into a request for retroactive remedies properly-so-called, since Mexico is still only seeking to retaliate as from the date when the United States should have come into compliance.

3.103 Nor do we agree that Mexico is seeking authorization to suspend concessions in a punitive manner. As we understand the United States' argument, a punitive remedy would be one where, contrary to Article 22.4 of the DSU, a Member suspends concessions at a level higher than the level of nullification or impairment caused by the relevant measure. However, consistent with Article 22.4 of the DSU, Mexico in these proceedings is seeking to impose a level of

---

[88] United States' comments on Mexico's responses to Arbitrator questions.

suspension that it considers is "equivalent" to the level of nullification or impairment caused by the 2013 Tuna Measure. We have already explained the reasons why we believe that this Measure is the appropriate basis for our assessment of the level of nullification or impairment.

3.104 In this connection, we observe that, because of the existence of parallel compliance panel proceedings concerning the 2016 Tuna Measure, it is conceivable that, after Mexico has received DSB authorization to suspend concessions on the basis of this Decision, the compliance panels may find that the 2016 Tuna Measure brings the United States into compliance. If (following any appeal) the DSB were to adopt that finding, Mexico pursuant to Article 22.8 of the DSU would need to promptly terminate any suspension of concessions that it might have applied after receiving the DSB's authorization in these proceedings. Mexico itself acknowledges this.[89] A DSB finding that the 2016 Tuna Measure brought the United States into compliance would not, however, render any preceding suspension of concessions retroactive, since the relevant point of reference is, as noted, the date of expiry of the RPT, and not the date on which the 2016 Tuna Measure was put in place. Nor would such a DSB finding render any preceding suspension of concessions punitive, because that DSB finding of WTO-consistency would itself have effect only from the date of its own adoption.

3.105 Finally, we note the United States' observation that once the DSB has granted authorization for a particular level of suspension, there is no mechanism to modify that level to take account of the results of subsequent compliance proceedings.[90] In making this point, the United States seems to envisage a situation where the outcome of the compliance proceedings is that the 2016 Tuna Measure is WTO-inconsistent, but causes less nullification or impairment than the 2013 Tuna Measure.[91]

3.106 We note that we do not face the situation envisaged by the United States. As we see it, our task in these proceedings is limited to assessing the level of nullification or impairment caused by the 2013 Tuna Measure, and we cannot speculate about the outcome of the second round of compliance panel proceedings in this dispute. We therefore do not find it either necessary or appropriate to further address the issue identified by the United States.[92]

---

[89] Mexico's written submission, para. 42; response to Arbitrator question No. 11.

[90] United States' comments on Mexico's responses to Arbitrator questions.

[91] We observe that, at least in principle, the situation envisaged by the United States could also be inverted: Article 21.5 proceedings could result in a finding that a new compliance measure causes more nullification or impairment than a previous one. In such circumstances, the issue raised by the United States – whether and how it would be possible to adjust the authorized level of suspension – could also arise.

[92] We note our agreement with the United States that the DSU does not explicitly address whether and how it would be possible to adjust the authorized level of suspension or the applied level of suspension. A detailed interpretative analysis would therefore be warranted. Any such analysis should in our view begin by examining whether it is correct to assume, as the United States appears to do, that a downward adjustment of the level of suspension would be required if a second

3.5.3 Relevance of the sequencing agreement between Mexico and the United States

3.107 Both parties have made reference in their arguments to the bilateral sequencing agreement between Mexico and the United States.[93] Neither party, however, has alleged a violation of that agreement. In particular, the United States has not suggested that proceeding with these arbitration proceedings on the basis of the 2013 Tuna Measure would somehow breach the sequencing agreement.[94] Accordingly, in the Arbitrator's view, it is not necessary in these proceedings either to interpret that agreement or to consider whether we would have jurisdiction over any claim thereunder.

3.5.4 The date on which the 2016 Tuna Measure entered into force, and the legal relevance of that fact

3.108 Finally, we note that both parties have made arguments and responded to questions concerning the date of entry into force of the 2016 Tuna Measure. The parties disagree about whether that Measure was in force at the time this dispute was referred to arbitration.[95]

3.109 In the Arbitrator's view, it is not necessary in these proceedings to determine whether the 2016 Tuna Measure was in force when this dispute was referred to arbitration. Even if, as the United States contends, the 2016 Tuna Measure was in force when this dispute was referred to arbitration, that would not modify our conclusion that the measure on which we should base our assessment of the level of nullification or impairment is the 2013 Tuna Measure. As we have explained above, it was through the 2013 Tuna Measure that the United States failed to come into compliance with its WTO obligations before the expiry of the RPT. That first compliance measure is the subject of still valid adverse DSB recommendations and rulings. Moreover, there is no agreement between the parties that the 2016 Tuna Measure has brought the United States into compliance.[96] In these circumstances, the date of entry into force of the 2016 Tuna Measure does not affect the outcome of our assessment of the level of nullification or impairment.

---

compliance panel proceeding confirmed that a new compliance measure taken by the responding Member presents fewer WTO-inconsistent aspects than a previous compliance measure and thus achieves partial (but still only partial) compliance, and therefore presumably causes a lower level of nullification or impairment. We take no position on this issue.

[93] WT/DS381/19.

[94] The United States has noted that the sequencing agreement does not bind the Arbitrator. United States' letter to the Arbitrator of 3 June 2016, fn. 6.

[95] United States' written submission, para. 48; response to Arbitrator question Nos. 14 and 15; Mexico's written submission, para. 26; response to Arbitrator question Nos. 14 and 15.

[96] In our view, if for instance a compliance measure subject to adverse DSB recommendations and rulings were subsequently withdrawn, and if such withdrawal were recognized by the complaining party as having brought the responding party into compliance and removed the nullification or impairment caused, then the date of that withdrawal, and particularly whether it was effected before or after an Article 22.6 arbitration, may be a factor for an Article 22.6 arbitrator to consider.

3.6 Conclusion

3.110 For all of the reasons given above, the Arbitrator concludes that the relevant measure for the purposes of these arbitration proceedings is the 2013 Tuna Measure, which is the subject of specific adverse DSB recommendations and rulings. We therefore reject the United States' request for a preliminary ruling that we find the relevant measure to be the 2016 Tuna Measure.

3.111 What we must and therefore will assess in the present Article 22.6 arbitration is the level of nullification or impairment caused by the 2013 Tuna Measure. As already noted, we will not determine the WTO-consistency of the 2016 Tuna Measure (even if we could do so), nor will we assess the level of nullification or impairment (if any) caused by the 2016 Tuna Measure.

4. THE APPROPRIATE COUNTERFACTUAL AND TIME-FRAME

4.112 Having dealt with a number of preliminary issues, the Arbitrator now turns to the merits of these arbitration proceedings. We recall that our task is to determine whether the level of suspension of concessions requested by Mexico is equivalent to the level of nullification or impairment caused by the 2013 Tuna Measure. We begin our analysis by assessing the appropriate counterfactual on the basis of which we should base our calculation of the nullification or impairment.

4.1 The Appropriate Counterfactual

4.113 As mentioned in Section 3 above, our mandate under Article 22.7 of the DSU is to determine whether the proposed level of suspension of concessions is equivalent to the level of nullification or impairment sustained by Mexico as a result of the United States' failure to bring the Tuna Measure into compliance.[97] To discharge this mandate, we will first have to determine the level of nullification or impairment caused by the 2013 Tuna Measure, which was the measure existing at the time of the expiry of the RPT, and then compare that to the level of suspension of concessions proposed by Mexico.

4.114 Neither Article 22.6 nor any other provision of the DSU prescribes a particular methodology for the determination of the level of nullification or impairment. Conceptually, the level of nullification or impairment caused by the United States' failure to comply with the DSB recommendations and rulings represents the difference between the value of trade (if any) in Mexican tuna products that occurred despite the WTO-inconsistent US measure, typically calculated for one year, and the value of trade that would have occurred, over the course of one year, had the United States complied with the DSB recommendations and rulings. The key issue, therefore, is how to determine

---

[97] Decision by the Arbitrator, *US – 1916 Act (EC) (Article 22.6 – US)*, para. 4.5; Decision by the Arbitrator, *US – Gambling (Article 22.6 – US)*, para. 2.6.

what the value of Mexico's exports of tuna products to the United States would have been, over the course of one year, had the United States complied with the DSB recommendations and rulings by the expiry of the RPT.

4.115 It is well established that it is for the responding party to choose how to implement DSB recommendations and rulings.[98] Consequently, there is no prescribed manner of complying; the responding party may choose to withdraw the measure at issue in its totality or appropriately modify its WTO-inconsistent aspects. The implication of this principle for Article 22.6 arbitration proceedings is that the arbitrator does not always know what form implementation would have taken had the responding party implemented the DSB recommendations and rulings. As a result, in past arbitration proceedings, arbitrators have found it necessary to base their decisions on a so-called "counterfactual". In this context, a counterfactual refers to a hypothetical scenario that describes what would have happened in terms of trade flows had the responding party implemented the DSB recommendations and rulings.[99]

4.116 Prior dispute settlement practice establishes that the legal standard that a scenario must meet for it to constitute an appropriate counterfactual for purposes of Article 22.6 proceedings is that of *plausibility* and *reasonability*. In *US – Gambling*, for instance, the arbitrator emphasized that it was important for the counterfactual to reflect accurately the nature and scope of the benefits that were being nullified or impaired by the measure at issue.[100] The arbitrator observed that a counterfactual does not necessarily need to reflect the most likely compliance scenario, as counterfactuals always involve an inherent degree of uncertainty because they represent a hypothetical scenario.[101] The counterfactual should, however, reflect at least a plausible or "reasonable" compliance scenario.[102]

---

[98] Appellate Body Report, *US – Oil Country Tubular Goods Sunset Reviews (Article 21.5 – Argentina)*, para. 184.

[99] A counterfactual approach was used in several past arbitration proceedings. In *EC – Bananas III*, the arbitrator compared the value of relevant EC imports from the United States under the actual banana import regime with their value under a hypothetical WTO-consistent regime (a "counterfactual" situation). (Decision by the Arbitrator, *EC – Bananas III (US) (Article 22.6 – EC)*, para. 7.1). In *Canada – Aircraft (Article 22.6 – Canada)*, the arbitrator noted how past arbitrators had used a "counterfactual approach", comparing the existing situation with that which would have occurred "had implementation taken place as of the expiration of the reasonable period of time". (Decision by the Arbitrator, *Canada — Aircraft Credits and Guarantees (Article 22.6 – Canada)*, para. 3.21). In *EC – Hormones*, the arbitrator based its analysis on what the complaining party's exports of the relevant product to the responding party would have been had the latter withdrawn the measure at the end of the RPT. (Decision by the Arbitrator, *EC – Hormones (Canada) (Article 22.6 – EC)*, para. 38). In the recent *US – COOL* arbitration, the arbitrator also decided to use a counterfactual that assumed that the COOL measure was withdrawn at the end of the RPT. (Decision by the Arbitrator, *US – COOL (Article 22.6 – US)*, para. 6.32).

[100] Decision by the Arbitrator, *US – Gambling* (Article 22.6 – US), para. 3.25.

[101] Decision by the Arbitrator, *US – Gambling* (Article 22.6 – US), paras. 3.26.

[102] Decision by the Arbitrator, *US – Gambling* (Article 22.6 – US), paras. 3.27.

4.117 In the present arbitration proceedings, Mexico initially proposed a counterfactual under which the WTO-inconsistent discrimination caused by the 2013 Tuna Measure would be eliminated.[103] In Mexico's view, this counterfactual could manifest itself in two ways (hereafter Mexico's "two scenarios").

a. In one scenario, the United States would eliminate the disqualification of tuna caught by setting on dolphins from the dolphin-safe label such that Mexican tuna products would not be treated differently from tuna products of any other country.[104] Under this scenario, Mexican tuna products would qualify for the US dolphin-safe label.

b. In the other scenario, the United States would apply the same eligibility criteria, certification requirements, and tracking and verification requirements to all tuna, regardless of where it is harvested. Mexico contends that, under this scenario, the majority of tuna products from all countries, including Mexico and the United States, would not be eligible for the dolphin-safe label.[105]

4.118 The United States proposed a different counterfactual. Its counterfactual assumes that the Tuna Measure would be withdrawn. The United States underlined in this regard that it is up to the responding party to decide how to implement DSB recommendations and rulings. The United States further pointed out that past arbitrators have indicated that the normal counterfactual for calculating the level of nullification or impairment is withdrawal of the measure.[106]

4.119 Although the parties initially proposed counterfactuals that were not the same, later in the proceedings, Mexico stated that "[t]he counterfactual proposed by the United States – withdrawal of the measure entirely – is consistent with removing the discrimination", and explained that "provided that reasonable assumptions and projections are used, Mexico would accept the U.S. counterfactual under which the [T]una [M]easure is withdrawn."[107]

4.120 We note that both parties agree that the withdrawal of the Tuna Measure would constitute an appropriate counterfactual. For our part, we also consider that withdrawal of the measure is an appropriate counterfactual in these proceedings, for two reasons. First, as mentioned, in most past Article 22.6 arbitrations, the counterfactual used was the withdrawal of the WTO-

---

[103] Mexico's methodology paper, para. 19.
[104] Mexico's written submission, para. 47.
[105] Mexico's written submission, para. 50.
[106] United States' written submission, para. 69.
[107] Mexico's opening statement at the substantive meeting with the parties, para. 8.

inconsistent measure.[108] Second, the withdrawal of the Tuna Measure would indisputably be WTO-consistent.

4.121 On the basis of these considerations, we decide to base our calculation of the level of nullification or impairment caused by the 2013 Tuna Measure on a counterfactual under which the 2013 Tuna Measure has been withdrawn by the time of the expiry of the RPT. In other words, as part of our assessment of the level of nullification or impairment, we will determine what the value of Mexico's exports of canned yellowfin to the United States would have been, over the course of one year, had the United States withdrawn the 2013 Tuna Measure at the expiry of the RPT.

4.2   The Appropriate Time-Frame

4.122 Having identified the appropriate counterfactual for the calculation of the level of the nullification or impairment, we now proceed to examine the time-frame that will form the basis of that calculation.

4.123 Mexico argues that the Arbitrator should look at the short-term impact of the counterfactual.[109] The United States also finds the short-term assessment to be appropriate[110], although it argues that Mexico's model reflects a hybrid time-frame that is somewhere between short-term and long-term.[111]

4.124 We note that it is undisputed between the parties that it is appropriate to assess the counterfactual on a short-term basis. We also note that there seems to be no disagreement between the parties on what a short-term assessment entails. It is understood to be an assessment covering a time-period within which the process of adjustment by producers, consumers and owners of factors of

---

[108] In *US – COOL*, the arbitrator's counterfactual assumed that the COOL measure was withdrawn at the end of the RPT. (Decision by the Arbitrator, *US – COOL (Article 22.6 – US)*, para. 6.32). In *US – Gambling*, the arbitrator did not find it unreasonable to assume that compliance might have been achieved through the removal of the specific source of discrimination identified by the Appellate Body. (Decision by the Arbitrator, *US – Gambling (Article 22.6 – US)*, para. 3.58). In *US – Offset Act (Byrd Amendment)*, the arbitrator's core rationale was that the trade effect of the measure could be estimated to be the nullification or impairment that the requesting parties have suffered as a result of the measure not having been withdrawn. (For instance, Decision by the Arbitrator, *US – Offset Act (Byrd Amendment) (Brazil) (Article 22.6 – US)*, para. 3.147). In *Canada – Aircraft Credits and Guarantees*, the arbitrator stated that the key issue was whether the withdrawal of subsidies by Canada by 20 May 2002, i.e. the date of the expiry of the reasonable period of time, would have resulted in a change in Air Wisconsin's future purchases. (Decision by the Arbitrator, *Canada – Aircraft Credits and Guarantees (Article 22.6 – Canada)*, para. 3.22). In *US – FSC*, the arbitrator decided to assess the proposed suspension of concessions at the time the United States should have withdrawn the prohibited subsidy at issue, in 2000. (Decision by the Arbitrator, *US – FSC (Article 22.6 – US)*, para. 2.15). In *EC – Hormones (US)*, the arbitrator estimated what the annual prospective US exports of hormone-treated beef products to the European Communities would have been if the latter had withdrawn the ban. (Decision by the Arbitrator, *EC – Hormones (US) (Article 22.6 – EC)*, para. 38).
[109] Mexico's written submission, para. 111.
[110] United States' response to Arbitrator question No. 60.
[111] *Ibid.*

production to the withdrawal of the 2013 Tuna Measure has not been fully completed. Accordingly, any investments that canneries could be assumed to make in the long-term in response to the withdrawal of the 2013 Tuna Measure are not taken into account in a short-term assessment.[112]

4.125 There is no rule in the DSU prescribing the time-frame for the determination of the level of nullification or impairment. Past Article 22.6 arbitration decisions indicate that the period of time for the arbitrator's determination of the level of nullification or impairment is usually the period that follows the end of the RPT.[113] In this regard, we also share the parties' view that a short-term assessment of the withdrawal of the 2013 Tuna Measure would be appropriate in these proceedings. In our view, the impact of the withdrawal of the Measure would be best captured in the period immediately following the withdrawal. Developments in the long-run would be less likely to be linked to withdrawal.

4.126 However, the parties disagree on specific one-year period for which we should calculate the level of nullification or impairment. Mexico contends that the appropriate period would be the first full calendar year following the expiry of the RPT, i.e. 2014.[114] The United States contends that it would be more appropriate to use the most recent data available, which is from calendar year 2015.[115] The United States argues that since there has been a consistent trend of declining tuna consumption in the United States over the past 15 years, any calculation based on 2014 data would overstate the level of nullification or impairment.[116] In the United States' view, in determining the appropriate one-year period, the Arbitrator should also take into account for which period the available data would provide the most accurate determination of the level of nullification or impairment, and would best capture the state of the canned tuna market.[117] According to the United States, the Arbitrator should therefore base its determination on calendar year 2015, because there is better data available for that year.[118]

---

[112] Mexico's written submission, para. 111; United States' response to Arbitrator question No. 60..

[113] In *US – COOL*, the arbitrator decided to follow a counterfactual under which the COOL measure was withdrawn at the end of the RPT. (Decision by the Arbitrator, *US – COOL (Article 22.6 – US)*, para. 6.32). Also, the arbitrator in *US – Upland Cotton* found that the choice of marketing year 2005, which represented the first moment at which the United States should have removed the adverse effects of the subsidies or withdrawn the subsidies, was in principle appropriate. (Decision by the Arbitrator, *US – Upland Cotton (Article 22.6 – US II)*, para. 4.118).

[114] Mexico's methodology paper, para. 16; Mexico's written submission, para. 136.

[115] United States' response to Arbitrator question No. 59; written submission, para. 5.

[116] *Ibid.*

[117] United States' response to Arbitrator question No. 135.

[118] According to the United States, the most detailed data on prices on the record – Exhibit MEX-15, the US exhibits based on Exhibit MEX-15, Exhibit USA-144 (on import prices of canned yellowfin and other canned tuna in the EU), and Exhibit USA-10 (BCI) cover 2015 (as well as 2014). See United States' response to Arbitrator question No. 135.

4.127 Mexico responds that the trends described by the United States in consumption and production have no immediate relevance to the calculation of the level of nullification or impairment.[119] Mexico also argues that the United States has not established that 2014 is an inappropriate period for assessing the level of nullification or impairment.[120]

4.128 In our view, given that 2014 is the calendar year that immediately follows the expiry of the RPT, it is the most appropriate one-year period to assess the short-term impact of the withdrawal of the 2013 Tuna Measure. With regard to the United States' argument that data is lacking for 2014, we note that the parties have submitted a significant amount of data for both 2014 and 2015. In particular, for 2014, there are many exhibits providing information on retail sales of tuna products in the US market.[121] Moreover, overall, we have received more data for 2014 than for 2015.

4.129 As for the United States' argument that the year 2014 is "unrepresentative" because of the decline in the consumption of tuna products, we agree with Mexico that whether or not 2014 is representative against the background of a long-term trend is not necessarily relevant to our task in these proceedings. Our task is to assess the level of nullification or impairment caused by the United States' failure to bring the 2013 Tuna Measure into compliance by the expiry of the RPT. Consistent with the views of the parties, we do this by assessing, *inter alia*, the impact in the short-term that the withdrawal of that Measure by the end of the RPT would have had. Seen in this light, 2014 is plainly the first full year that follows the expiry of the RPT and for which data is available. We also note that the United States should have been in compliance during all of 2014. We do not therefore agree that assessing the level of nullification or impairment caused over the course of that year could properly be said to overstate the level of nullification or impairment caused by the United States' failure to come into compliance by the expiry of the RPT.

4.130 The United States claims that no event occurred that made the year 2015 unrepresentative of the level of nullification or impairment caused by the 2013 Tuna Measure.[122] However, we consider that the evidence on the record does not point to any particular event that makes the year 2014 inappropriate for assessing the level of nullification or impairment.

4.131 In the light of the foregoing, we conclude that it is appropriate in these proceedings to assess the level of nullification or impairment caused by the 2013 Tuna Measure for the year 2014, which is the year immediately following the expiry of the RPT given to the United States to comply with the DSB recommendations and rulings.

---

[119] Mexico's written submission, para. 138.
[120] Mexico's comments on United States' response to Arbitrator question No. 135.
[121] See, for example, Exhibits USA-175, USA-38 (BCI) and USA-41 (BCI).
[122] United States' response to Arbitrator question No. 135.

5.   **PROPOSED MODELS FOR ASSESSING THE LEVEL OF NULLIFICATION OR IMPAIRMENT**

5.132   In the preceding Section, we determined that the counterfactual on which we should base our calculation of the level of nullification or impairment is the withdrawal of the Tuna Measure. We have also explained that the time-frame for our analysis should be the 2014 calendar year. We now turn to the economic model that we should use to calculate the export value Mexico would have enjoyed in the counterfactual situation, that is, had the Tuna Measure been withdrawn prior to the expiry of the RPT. Precisely because the model will influence our calculation of how much tuna Mexico *would* have exported had the Tuna Measure been brought into compliance by the expiry of the RPT, our choice of economic model is crucial.

5.133   In this Section, we will review the economic model proposed by Mexico. We will then consider the model proposed by the United States. In doing so, we will first describe the models proposed by each party. We will then critically consider the reasonableness of the assumptions underlying those models, based on the evidence before us. Once we have discussed and analysed both models, we will determine whether we are able to use either of these models as the basis for our calculations, or whether we need to develop an alternative model of our own to calculate the nullification or impairment caused by the 2013 Tuna Measure.

5.1   Mexico's Proposed Model for Determining the Level of Nullification or Impairment

5.1.1   Description of Mexico's model

5.134   Mexico maintains that the annual level of nullification or impairment caused by the 2013 Tuna Measure, measured by the estimated amount of export losses to Mexico, is USD 472.3 million.[123] This amount results from calculations based on a calibrated partial equilibrium model of the US and Mexican canned tuna markets.[124] In short, Mexico's model consists of a set of equations purporting to describe the market for canned tuna in the United States and Mexico by defining (a) the demand for canned tuna in the United States and Mexico, respectively, (b) the supply of canned tuna in the United States and Mexico, respectively, and (c) the market equilibrium conditions in the US and Mexican markets for canned tuna.[125]

5.135   Mexico's model separates the canned tuna products into two groups, namely, "generic tuna" and "yellowfin". "Generic tuna" is considered to be a composite category that covers all canned tuna currently offered for sale in the

---

[123] Mexico's methodology paper, para. 17.
[124] Mexico's methodology paper, para. 27.
[125] Mexico's methodology paper, paras. 20-40; Exhibit MEX-02, pp. 4-27.

US market. This includes mainly skipjack, with albacore and tongol also being commonly offered for sale. The model assumes that generic tuna is of lower quality than yellowfin.[126] The model therefore also assumes that if canned generic tuna and canned yellowfin were offered at the same price, a large majority of consumers would purchase canned yellowfin rather than canned generic tuna.[127]

5.136 In Mexico's model, the demand for canned tuna in the US market is derived by aggregating individual consumer demand for yellowfin and generic tuna. In the model, consumer preferences are modelled using a choice model, which, in Mexico's view, is standard in economics.[128] When parameterizing the demand for yellowfin and generic tuna, Mexico assumes that (a) half of all US consumers are willing to pay more than a USD 2/kg premium for yellowfin over generic tuna and half are willing to pay less; (b) Mexican and US consumers have the same preferences; and (c) the intensity of demand is the same for yellowfin and generic tuna (that is, at a given price, consumers buy the same total amount of canned tuna independently of whether they prefer yellowfin or generic tuna). Mexico contends that the demand for canned tuna is calibrated using a "conservative approach"[129] under which it is assumed that the mean willingness to pay for yellowfin is lower than the premium currently observed.[130]

5.137 With regard to the supply of generic tuna, in its baseline model, Mexico assumes that world supply of generic tuna is infinitely elastic.[131] As for Mexico's supply of canned yellowfin, it is perfectly elastic up to a certain quantity and then becomes perfectly inelastic, reflecting that Mexico's capacity to can yellowfin tuna is fixed in the short-run. In this regard, Mexico notes that in 2014 Mexican canneries operated with a single day shift, and that Mexico's production could therefore be easily expanded using imported yellowfin tuna. In the model, the maximum supply of exports of canned yellowfin is determined by the total production in Mexico, that is, production from Mexican as well as imported yellowfin tuna.[132] The model is solved assuming that Mexico would import yellowfin to produce canned tuna for domestic consumption in order to replace some of the canned yellowfin that would be exported to the United States.[133]

5.138 Mexico's model assumes that because transportation costs between Mexico and the United States are small, and because of preferences under the North American Free Trade Agreement (NAFTA), the withdrawal of the Tuna Measure would give Mexico a significant advantage in its exports of canned

---

[126] Mexico's methodology paper, para. 32.
[127] Mexico's methodology paper, para. 35.
[128] *Ibid.*
[129] Mexico's methodology paper, para. 36.
[130] *Ibid.*
[131] Mexico's methodology paper, para. 33.
[132] Mexico's methodology paper, para. 39.
[133] Mexico's methodology paper, para. 42.

yellowfin to the United States.[134] Therefore, Mexico assumes that it would be the only exporter of yellowfin tuna to the United States.

5.139 Mexico's model yields a calculated total of USD 495 million worth of canned yellowfin exports from Mexico to the United States in 2014. The value of actual exports of Mexican canned tuna to the United States in 2014 was USD 22.65 million. The model deducts the value of actual exports from the value of total exports, and finds nullification or impairment in the amount of USD 472.3 million per year.[135]

5.140 Table 12 of Exhibit MEX-02 contains a summary of the most salient results of Mexico's model. They are reproduced below:

Solutions of Mexico's model		
	United States	Mexico
Consumption of yellowfin tuna (metric tonnes)	63,568	21,932
Consumption of generic tuna (metric tonnes)	230,746	51,199
Price of yellowfin tuna ($/kg)	7.84	7.79
Price of generic tuna including tariff and charge ($/kg)	5	5.32
Exports of yellowfin tuna (metric tonnes)	0	63,568
Imports of yellowfin tuna (metric tonnes)	63,568	20,000
Exports of generic tuna to the U.S. (metric tonnes)	0	0
Imports of generic tuna from other countries (metric tonnes)	53,340	28,199
Note: Mexico assumes that the United States produces 177,350 metric tonnes of canned tuna as observed in 2014. Source: Exhibit MEX-02		

5.1.2   United States' arguments regarding Mexico's model

5.141 The United States presents two sets of arguments regarding Mexico's model, one concerning the choice of the model, the other concerning the assumptions made under the model. Specifically, the United States contends that Mexico's election to use a partial equilibrium model is inappropriate because sufficient data do not exist to construct a correctly specified model. Further, the United States contends that Mexico's model is based on certain incorrect assumptions concerning US consumer demand and the potential supply of canned yellowfin from Mexico, the United States, and other WTO Members.[136] In this Section, we describe the United States' arguments on Mexico's choice of the model. We discuss the United States' arguments regarding the assumptions under Mexico's model, in the following Section.

5.142 With regard to the choice of the model, the United States contends that partial equilibrium models are often used to calculate the impact of a policy change by generating a picture of a defined market through a series of simplifying assumptions. The United States submits that where a partial equilibrium analysis is used to model the removal of a particular non-tariff

---

[134]   Mexico's methodology paper, para. 41.
[135]   Mexico's methodology paper, para. 43.
[136]   United States' written submission, para. 80.

barrier (NTB), the generally-accepted method is to calculate a tariff equivalent, or "price wedge", of the NTB and then model its removal.[137] For the United States, these types of models produce meaningful results when they are set up to solve for the issue at hand, using relevant variables that are based on actual data or reasonable assumptions, something that the United States says Mexico's model does not do.[138]

5.143 The United States argues that the generally accepted way to use a partial equilibrium analysis would be to determine the value of the US dolphin-safe label and model the effect of its removal on the equilibrium price and quantity of Mexican tuna products sold to the United States. The United States submits, however, that determining the value of the dolphin-safe label would require detailed data on US purchases of tuna products with and without the dolphin-safe label, including store-by-store sales of tuna by type, i.e. albacore, yellowfin, and light tuna, accounting for product characteristics such as pouched versus canned, water versus oil, and flavoured, and including information on the timing of sales and whether sales were made at promotional values.[139]

5.144 For the United States, it appears to be undisputed that this level of data concerning the US tuna product market is not available.[140] The United States argues that Mexico's dataset does not include retail level data that would allow a comparison between particular types of labelled and unlabelled tuna products, necessary to estimate the value of the dolphin-safe label, and that Mexico's dataset does not have data on sales and purchases of the same type of tuna products (by species, form, and pack, at least) sold with and without the dolphin-safe label or on whether tuna was sold at a promotional value. Mexico's dataset, in the United States' view, does not allow for any comparison of labelled and unlabelled tuna product, or even store-by-store analysis of the price difference between comparable yellowfin and non-yellowfin tuna products. The United States contends that all of these issues result in Mexico being unable to calculate the price wedge necessary for an accurate partial equilibrium model.[141]

5.1.3   Arbitrator's analysis of Mexico's model

5.145 Mexico's model is based on many assumptions regarding the state of the market for tuna products in the world, in the United States, and in Mexico. For purposes of our assessment, we find it useful to group them into three main assumptions, namely, first, that the Tuna Measure has restricted the supply of canned yellowfin from Mexico to the US market; second, that US consumers have a preference for canned yellowfin and US retailers would sell Mexican canned yellowfin after the withdrawal of the Tuna Measure; and third, that

---

[137]   United States' written submission, para. 83.
[138]   United States' written submission, para. 81.
[139]   United States' written submission, para. 84.
[140]   United States' written submission, para. 85.
[141]   *Ibid.*

Mexican producers would supply all of the increased consumption of canned yellowfin in the US[142] market following the withdrawal of the Tuna Measure.

5.146 In this Section, we address these assumptions in turn. In our assessment of a given assumption, we first describe the assumption, then highlight the United States' arguments with respect to that assumption, and present our assessment of the assumption. The assumptions underlying Mexico's model can be found in Exhibit MEX-02.

5.147 With respect to the legal standard governing our assessment of the assumptions underlying Mexico's model, we note, and agree with, the statement of the arbitrator in *US – Gambling* that if the estimation of the level of nullification or impairment requires certain assumptions to be made, "such assumptions should be reasonable, taking into account the circumstances of the dispute".[143] We also find relevant the finding made in several arbitration proceedings that assumptions should be based on "credible, factual, and verifiable information".[144] We will therefore be guided by these principles in our assessment of the assumptions on which Mexico's model is based.

5.1.3.1 The Tuna Measure has restricted the supply of canned yellowfin from Mexico into the US market

5.148 The first assumption underlying Mexico's model is that the Tuna Measure has restricted the supply of canned yellowfin from Mexico to the United States. Mexico acknowledges that there is currently some consumption of canned yellowfin in the US market.[145] It contends, however, that such consumption is insignificant, and that Mexican exports of yellowfin to the US market may be considered as *de minimis*.[146] In Mexico's view, the Tuna Measure has caused a decline in the supply of canned yellowfin to the United States because the Measure excludes supply from an important region located close to the United States.[147]

5.149 The United States disagrees with Mexico, and contends that the Tuna Measure does not stop Mexican canned tuna from entering the US market. For the United States, the Tuna Measure "is neither a *de facto* nor a *de jure* prohibition on the sale of canned yellowfin in the United States".[148] In support of this assertion, the United States notes that dolphin-safe canned yellowfin is sold

---

[142] The first and second assumptions, taken together, imply that when the Tuna Measure is withdrawn, there will be increased consumption of canned yellowfin in the US market.

[143] Decision by the Arbitrator, *US – Gambling (Article 22.6 – US)*, para. 3.30.

[144] Decision by the Arbitrators, *US – COOL (Article 22.6 – US)*, para. 4.5; *US – 1916 Act (EC) (Article 22.6 – US)*, para. 5.54; see also Decision by the Arbitrator, *EC – Hormones (US) (Article 22.6 – EC)*, para. 41.

[145] Mexico's written submission, para. 173 (referring to Exhibit USA-17).

[146] Mexico's response to Arbitrator question No. 87.

[147] Mexico's response to Arbitrator question No. 72.

[148] United States' opening statement at the meeting of the Arbitrator, para. 10.

in the US market, but in relatively small quantities, because demand for yellowfin is weak.[149] Consequently, the United States argues that withdrawing the measure would not alter the supply of canned yellowfin. The United States also contends that the evidence on the record points to a lack of demand, not of supply, as the reason for the currently low levels of canned yellowfin consumption in the United States.[150]

5.150 The Arbitrator notes that the record shows, and both parties agree, that the current level of canned yellowfin consumption in the US market is low.[151] The evidence on the record shows that "yellowfin products... make up only [[xxx]]% of volume sales"[152], and canned yellowfin made up 1.2% of all reported sales by weight and 1.5% by value, during the period from October 2014 to October 2015.[153] The parties disagree, however, as to the reasons for this low level of consumption. In particular, they disagree on whether the Tuna Measure might have resulted in a decline in consumption.

5.151 In support of its argument that the Tuna Measure restricted the supply of canned yellowfin from Mexico to the United States, Mexico refers to the decline in the volume of Mexican exports of canned yellowfin into the United States, and the increase in the price of that product in the US market, following the adoption of the Tuna Measure in 1990. With regard to import volumes, the parties agree that import volumes have declined since the adoption of the Tuna Measure. However, they, disagree on the reasons for this decrease. With regard to the evolution of prices in the US market, the parties disagree significantly on how prices behaved after the introduction of the Tuna Measure, and in particular as to whether they increased.

5.152 In reviewing the assumption that the Tuna Measure has restricted the supply of canned yellowfin from Mexico into the US market, we will evaluate these two aspects in turn. In our view, a decline in the volume of US yellowfin imports, and an increase in their price, would tend to support the proposition that the Tuna Measure has had a restrictive effect on US imports of canned yellowfin from Mexico. With this in mind, we now turn to our assessment of the evolution of the volume of exports from Mexico to the United States and the price of canned yellowfin in the US market following the adoption of the original Tuna Measure.

---

[149] United States' response to Arbitrator question No. 65.
[150] United States' opening statement at the meeting of the Arbitrator, para. 12.
[151] Mexico's written submission, para. 173 (referring to Exhibit USA-17); United States' written submission, para. 23 (referring to referring to Exhibits USA-10 (BCI) USA-17).
[152] Exhibit USA-10 (BCI).
[153] Exhibits MEX-15 and USA-17.

                5.1.3.1.1   Evolution of the volume of canned
                                      yellowfin exports from Mexico to
                                      the United States

5.153 At the outset, we note that both parties agree that there has been a pronounced decrease in the volume of canned yellowfin into the United States from the late 1980s. The parties disagree, however, as to the reasons that caused that decrease.[154]

5.154 We note that, according to the data presented in Exhibit USA-79, the average volume of tuna product exports from Mexico to the United States for the period 1975-1980 was 9,664,954 kg; and in the period 1986-1989, the volume was 9,646,266 kg. There were no imports in the period 1981-1985, presumably because of a US embargo on tuna products from Mexico. Following the adoption of the original Tuna Measure, the volume of exports from Mexico fell from 13,060,153 kg in 1989 to 2,781,159 kg in 1990. The volume of exports has never again reached pre-1990 levels. The average volume of Mexico's exports in the period 1990-2014 was 3,469,210 kg.

5.155 We are aware that these data pertain to tuna products in general[155], and not only to canned yellowfin. We note, however, that, as indicated in a United States International Trade Commission (USITC) report presented as Exhibit MEX-119, Mexico's tuna harvest prior to the adoption of the Tuna Measure was predominantly composed of yellowfin.[156] We therefore find the data presented in Exhibit USA-79 to be relevant to our assessment.

5.156 Additionally, we note that (a) in the late 1980s, Mexico's exports to the United States were mainly fresh yellowfin, whereas the Mexican industry subsequently underwent an important transformation such that it is now vertically integrated and able to export canned tuna products; (b) the Mexican industry has essentially abandoned the fresh tuna market[157]; and (c) the Mexican tuna production industry cans most of the yellowfin harvested by Mexican fishing vessels. As a result of these factors, the nature of the product exported from Mexico to the United States has changed significantly since the adoption of the Tuna Measure, from fresh to canned tuna. In other words, prior to the adoption of the Tuna Measure, Mexico primarily exported fresh rather than canned tuna. We recall that the question before us at this stage of our analysis is whether the Tuna Measure had the effect of restricting exports of canned tuna to

---

[154] Mexico's response to Arbitrator question No. 158; Mexico's comments on United States' response to Arbitrator question No. 158; United States' response to Arbitrator question No. 158; United States' comments on Mexico's response to Arbitrator question No. 158.

[155] Fresh, frozen, prepared and canned. Exhibit USA-79.

[156] The USITC report states that "[y]ellowfin was the leading species of tuna caught by the Mexican tuna fleet in 1989, accounting for about 79 per cent of the catch that year." Exhibit MEX-119, p. 5-20. We also note that the NMFS import data presented by Mexico, in Exhibit MEX-80, shows that the share of yellowfin in Mexico's overall exports of fresh tuna to the United States in the period 1986-1989 was 81% in volume (31,341,390 kg out of a total of 38,585,064 kg).

[157] Mexico's written submission, para. 148.

the United States. However, in our assessment, we focus on the evolution of the volume of fresh and frozen yellowfin exports from Mexico to the United States following the adoption of the Tuna Measure, and not on the volume of canned yellowfin exports. This is so because we do not have data on the volume of canned yellowfin exports from Mexico to the United States in this period. Accordingly, and to the extent possible, we use the evolution of the volume of exported fresh and frozen Mexican tuna as a proxy for the evolution of the volume of exported canned Mexican tuna.

5.157 We also note that, in parallel with the decreasing trend observed in the volume of tuna exports from Mexico to the United States following the introduction of the original Tuna Measure, the volume of yellowfin purchases by US canneries also declined. We note that the United States recognizes that US canneries' receipts for yellowfin tuna have declined "dramatically" since the late 1980s.[158] The United States provides the following graphs (where "YF" indicates yellowfin), which illustrate this decline:

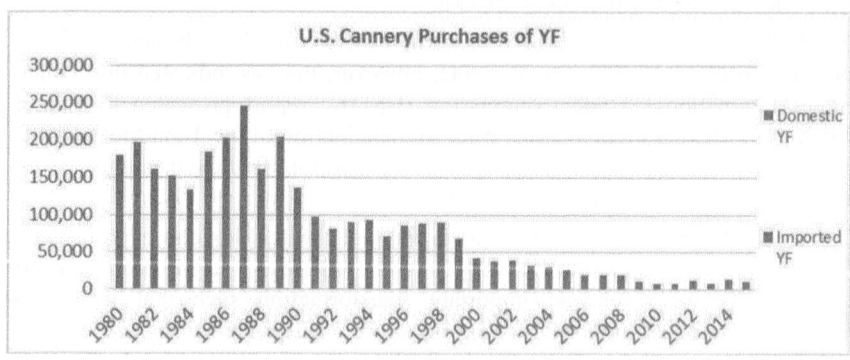

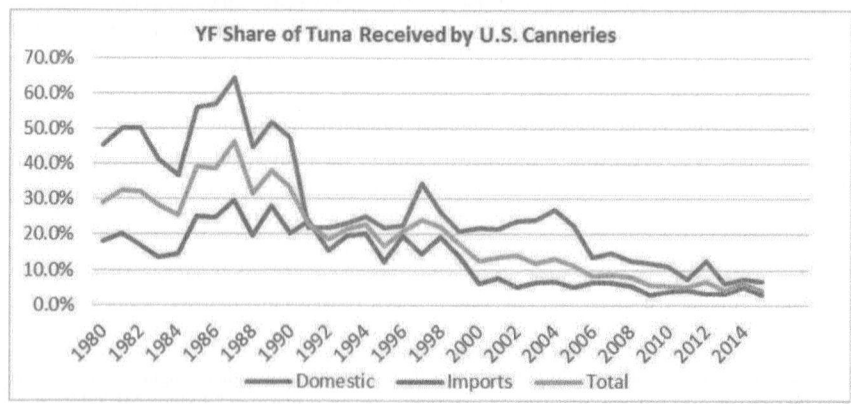

Source: Exhibit USA-96.

---

[158] United States' response to Arbitrator question No. 51.

5.158 These graphs, together with Exhibit USA-96[159], show that US canneries' purchases of imported yellowfin declined from an average of 71,595 short tons (st) in the period 1985-1989 to 43,723 st in the period 1990-1994, representing a decrease of 38.9%. Similarly, US canneries' purchases of domestic yellowfin declined from an average of 127,729 st in the period 1985-1989 to 55,981 st in the period 1990-1994, representing a decrease of 56.17%. We note that this decline in US canneries' receipts started in 1990, coinciding with the adoption of the original Tuna Measure, and continued to decline throughout the period 1990-2014.

5.159 There is thus an important correlation between the adoption of the original Tuna Measure, on the one hand, and the decline in volume of yellowfin purchases by US canneries and exports of tuna from Mexico, on the other hand. Having identified a decline in the volume of exports of tuna from Mexico to the United States and a parallel decline in the US canneries' receipts of yellowfin, we now turn to the parties' diverging arguments regarding the reasons for this decline.

5.160 The United States maintains that, in addition to the above-mentioned trends, consumption of canned yellowfin was also declining in the same period. According to the United States, this decline in consumption of canned yellowfin in the US market shows that the decline in exports from Mexico and US cannery purchases of yellowfin was due to limited demand rather than limited supply. Additionally, the United States notes that the decline in Mexican exports and US cannery purchases of yellowfin did not occur suddenly, as it would have had there been a severe supply restriction, but over a period of decades.[160] The United States submits that rather than stemming from limitations in supply, the decreased exports and cannery purchases can be attributed to declining consumer demand as well as the decision by the "big three" US tuna companies not to process tuna caught by setting on dolphins.[161] Additionally, the United States claims that the decline in US cannery purchases of yellowfin in the early 1990s was due not to consumers substituting consumption of canned yellowfin for fresh yellowfin, but rather to developments in US consumer preferences and other factors, including (a) growing consumer preference in the late 1980s and early 1990s (and continuing today) for tuna not caught by setting on dolphins; (b) growing consumer preference for albacore as a premium product; (c) consumer preference for the cheapest canned tuna; and, (d) health considerations.[162]

---

[159] This exhibit contains data on US cannery purchases of yellowfin, in short tons, for the period 1980 to 2015.
[160] United States' response to Arbitrator question No. 51.
[161] United States' response to Arbitrator question No. 158.
[162] *Ibid.*

5.161 Mexico, for its part, argues that it is well established that the US tuna fishing fleet moved away from the ETP to the Western and Central Pacific in the late 1980s and early 1990s, and that this led to the creation and growth of cannery operations in American Samoa. Mexico also contends that the price of yellowfin rose following the imposition of the tuna measure, and that this price increase made yellowfin uneconomical for use by US canneries for canning.[163] Thus, in Mexico's view, the decline in cannery purchases of yellowfin does not reflect a shift in US consumer preference away from yellowfin towards albacore or skipjack. Rather, it reflects a shift in readily available supplies from ETP-caught yellowfin to WCPO-caught skipjack and the increasing cost of canned yellowfin.[164]

5.162 In the Arbitrator's view, the reasons for the decline in the volume of the United States' imports from Mexico and canneries' purchases of yellowfin are not fully clear. While the data and graphs discussed above clearly show that there was a decline in the volume of United States' imports from Mexico and US canneries' purchases of yellowfin following the adoption of the original Tuna Measure, there is also evidence suggesting that part of that decline may have been due to the dolphin-safe policies adopted by US tuna canning companies, rather than to the Tuna Measure itself. For example, a 1992 USICT report states that "the US canners, led by StarKist, announced in April 1990 that they would no longer buy tuna from domestic or foreign suppliers who refused to certify that the tuna was 'dolphin-safe'".[165] Nevertheless, in our view, the sharpness of the decline in both imports of tuna from Mexico and purchases of yellowfin by US canneries following the adoption of the Tuna Measure in 1990 suggests that the adoption of the Tuna Measure was the main reason for the declining trend. This sharpness is very clear with respect to the United States' imports of tuna from Mexico. With regard to the US cannery purchases of yellowfin, we note that there was a decline from 1987 to 1988, prior to the adoption of the Tuna Measure, that this was followed by an increase from 1988 to 1989, and that the decline that started in 1990 has not changed course in any significant way.

5.163 Further, we are not persuaded by the United States' interpretation of this declining trend as being the result of a sharp change in consumer preferences, particularly given that the most substantial part of the decline came on the heels of the adoption of the Tuna Measure. We do not find plausible the argument that such a sudden and sharp decline in imports can be explained by an equally sudden and sharp change in consumer preferences. In our view, it is unusual to observe consumer preferences undergoing an important discrete change, as suggested by the United States. Although we do not rule out that this might be possible, in our view the United States has not submitted evidence sufficient to establish the existence of such a change in this case.

---

[163] Mexico's response to Arbitrator question No. 158.
[164] Mexico's comment on the United States response to Arbitrator question No. 158.
[165] Exhibit MEX-73, p. 3-10.

5.164 We therefore conclude that, following the adoption of the original Tuna Measure, there was an important decline in the volume of US imports of yellowfin tuna from Mexico and purchases of yellowfin by US canneries. The Arbitrator now turns to consider the evidence relating to the price of yellowfin on the US market following the adoption of the Tuna Measure.

5.1.3.1.2   Evolution of yellowfin prices in the US market

5.165 The Arbitrator begins by noting the parties' agreement that if the Tuna Measure reduced the supply of canned yellowfin in the United States, the price in the US retail market for such products would be expected to increase.[166] Unfortunately, there is no evidence on the record on historical prices of canned yellowfin in the US market and, consequently, we have to rely on the evidence presented by the parties on import prices for fresh or frozen yellowfin to assess the possible effects that the Tuna Measure might have had on retail prices of canned yellowfin. In this regard, Mexico asserts that it is "nearly impossible to find a time series data for yellowfin tuna"[167], and notes that it did not find price data for "canned yellowfin tuna at retail or wholesale"[168]. Mexico argues that the only source for price data regarding the United States concerns frozen tuna.[169]

5.166 Before proceeding to our analysis of the price data on the record, we note Mexico's reference to Exhibit USA-10 (BCI) in support of its argument that the Tuna Measure restricted the supply of canned yellowfin from Mexico to the United States. Mexico contends that this Exhibit shows that the price of canned yellowfin in the US market is high because raw yellowfin is expensive, and that it is due to these high prices that consumption is low.[170] The United States disagrees with Mexico's interpretation of Exhibit USA-10 (BCI) and argues that the excerpt cited by Mexico explains that yellowfin generally sells at [[xxx]].[171] For the United States, Exhibit USA-10 (BCI) confirms that the main driver for the limited consumption of yellowfin in the United States is [[xxx]].[172]

5.167 We note that Exhibit USA-10 (BCI) contains a market review for yellowfin products prepared by a US tuna canning company. It mentions that growth of yellowfin products in the US shelf stable seafood segment has been [[xxx[173],]] and states that these types of products are [[xxx]].[174] Additionally, we

---

[166] Mexico's response to Arbitrator questions No. 17 and 72; United States' opening statement at the meeting of the Arbitrator, para. 17.
[167] Mexico's response to Arbitrator question No. 72.
[168] *Ibid.*
[169] *Ibid.*
[170] Mexico contends that Exhibit USA-10 (BCI) explains that consumption of yellowfin is limited by the higher cost of yellowfin and that US tuna producer [[xxx]] stated that: [[xxx]]. Mexico submits that [[xxx]] also stated that [[xxx]]. Mexico's written submission, paras. 125-126.
[171] United States' response to Arbitrator question No. 130.
[172] *Ibid.*
[173] Exhibit USA-10 (BCI) p. 3.
[174] Exhibit USA-10 (BCI) p. 4. [[xxx]].

note that the Exhibit states that [[xxx]].[175] In our view, when the relevant parts of the Exhibit are taken as a whole, it is reasonable to conclude that the market review suggests that the cost associated with the production of yellowfin products is [[xxx]] and that this can in turn be explained by [[xxx]].

5.168 Therefore, in our view, although Exhibit USA-10 (BCI) seems to lend some support to Mexico's argument, we do not interpret it to show that the Tuna Measure restricted the supply of canned yellowfin from Mexico to the United States. This is mainly because Exhibit USA-10 (BCI) is not concerned with the impact of the Tuna Measure on the supply of canned yellowfin from Mexico, but rather with providing a description of the trends in the US canned tuna market. Further, we note that this market review does not cover the period when the original Tuna Measure was adopted, and therefore provides no information as to how the market for tuna products reacted to the adoption of that Measure. We therefore turn to the rest of the evidence on the record regarding prices in order to assess the impact that the Tuna Measure may have had on the evolution of yellowfin prices in the US market.

5.169 At the outset, we observe that the parties have presented arguments on how the impact of the Tuna Measure, in particular on prices, might be different depending on the level of the market that is analysed, e.g. harvesting, canning, or wholesaling of tuna products, and depending on the type of the particular tuna product under review, e.g. frozen, fresh, or canned tuna. In this connection, we note that Mexico maintains that when assessing prices for yellowfin tuna and the effect of the Tuna Measure, it is important to understand at what stage of the supply chain the prices are measured. According to Mexico, the immediate effect of the Tuna Measure can be described as a shift to the left of the supply curve for canned yellowfin to the United States, because the Tuna Measure "effectively banned"[176] tuna harvested from an important source of inexpensive yellowfin. For Mexico, the loss of an inexpensive source of yellowfin resulted in an increase in the cost of supply of canned yellowfin to the US market. A second effect of the Tuna Measure, according to Mexico, is a decrease in the demand for frozen yellowfin from the ETP because that tuna is "no longer welcome on the US market, the largest market in the world for canned tuna".[177] This is so because, as a consequence of the Tuna Measure, the US tuna fishing fleet moved out of the ETP region and US canneries stopped accepting tuna of ETP origin.[178] To show how the impact of the adoption of the Tuna Measure might differ depending on the production stage, Mexico refers to a 1992 Report of the USITC that shows that prices of frozen tuna in the US market fell between 1990

---

[175] Exhibit USA-10 (BCI) p. 10.
[176] Mexico's response to Arbitrator question No. 72.
[177] *Ibid.*
[178] *Ibid.*

and 1992[179] although, in Mexico's view, the prices of canned yellowfin went up in the same period.[180]

5.170 We note that Exhibits MEX-79 and MEX-104 contain price data relevant to our analysis. Exhibit MEX-79 contains a graph showing the price of US imported tuna from 1980 to 2014. Mexico explains that this Exhibit illustrates US import prices for fresh and frozen tuna, and argues that it shows that the price of frozen yellowfin significantly differed from the price of skipjack and albacore as of the beginning of the 1990s.[181] Exhibit MEX-104 contains data on the price of tuna landings[182] for several species, including yellowfin, from 1980 to 2014. In Mexico's view, like Exhibit MEX-79, Exhibit MEX-104 provides price information on fresh and frozen yellowfin landings in the United States between 1980 and 2014. In Mexico's view, the data in Exhibit MEX-104 shows that the price of yellowfin was higher than that of other tuna species, including albacore and skipjack, in the years immediately before and after the introduction of the Tuna Measure, and that the price of yellowfin started deviating from the prices of albacore and skipjack after the introduction of the Tuna Measure.[183] In Mexico's view, this indicates that, following the introduction of the Tuna Measure, yellowfin became relatively more expensive than skipjack or albacore.

5.171 The United States does not consider that Exhibits MEX-79 and MEX-104 support Mexico's position. Importantly, the United States draws a distinction between the price for fresh and frozen yellowfin, on the one hand, and the price of cannery-grade yellowfin[184], on the other hand, and contends that the price of the former is not a good proxy for the latter.[185] With respect to Exhibit MEX-79, the United States notes that the last major cannery that bought yellowfin to can in the United States was closed in 2001.[186] The United States argues that, as from 2001, US canneries only processed tuna loins, as opposed to whole fish, to produce canned tuna. Therefore, in the view of the United States, after this period there is no relationship between the price of fresh and frozen yellowfin and the price of cannery-grade yellowfin.

5.172 The United States also disagrees with Mexico about the relevance to our inquiry of the price data presented in Exhibit MEX-79. With regard to the data for the period prior to 2001, the United States contends that the price data presented in this Exhibit do not pertain exclusively to cannery-grade yellowfin,

---

[179] Mexico's response to Arbitrator question No. 72 (referring to Exhibit MEX-73).
[180] Mexico's response to Arbitrator question No. 72 (referring to Exhibit MEX-74).
[181] Mexico's response to Arbitrator question No. 153.
[182] We understand "fish landings" to indicate the volume and value of fish landed and sold at the dock, usually in pounds (or other weight measurement) and ex-vessel dollar value of fish caught and sold. See http://www.st.nmfs.noaa.gov/commercial-fisheries/commercial-landings/landings-background/index (last accessed on 13 February 2017).
[183] Mexico's response to Arbitrator question No. 153.
[184] We understand "cannery-grade yellowfin" to be the particular yellowfin tuna or tuna product that is used to produce canned yellowfin.
[185] United States' response to Arbitrator question No. 153.
[186] United States' response to Arbitrator question No. 153 (referring to Exhibit USA-192).

and therefore overstates the prices of cannery grade yellowfin.[187] As for the price data after 2001, the United States underlines the fact that such data bears no relationship to the raw material (loins, not the entire yellowfin tuna) that US canneries use to produce canned yellowfin. Consequently, the United States argues that the prices reported in Figure 1 of Exhibit MEX-79 reflect the changing composition of US yellowfin imports, and not an increase in the price of cannery-grade yellowfin.[188] The United States submits that the data in Exhibit MEX-104 is similarly unhelpful to the Arbitrator's analysis.[189]

5.173 As noted above, Exhibit MEX-79 presents a graph illustrating fresh and frozen yellowfin prices, presented in Exhibit MEX-80. The same graph has been presented by Mexico in a way that shows the annual trends in prices, as follows:[190]

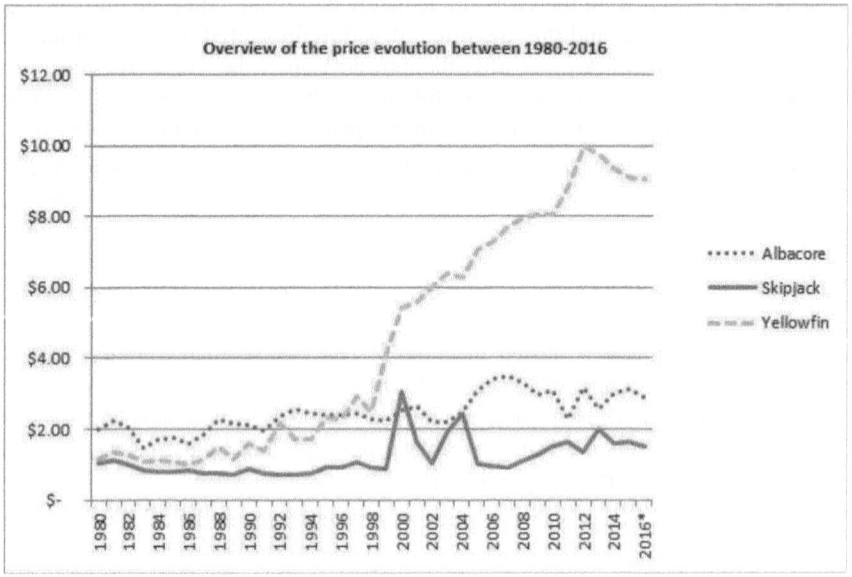

* Data for 2016 covers period until August.

Source: Exhibits MEX-79 and 80.

5.174 In our view, the relevant period to assess the effects that the Tuna Measure might have had on the prices of yellowfin is the years following its introduction in 1990. The graph shows that prices for fresh and frozen yellowfin remained more or less stable from 1980 to 1990 and increased in the early

---

[187] United States' comments on Mexico's response to Arbitrator question No. 158.
[188] United States' response to Arbitrator question No. 153.
[189] United States' comments on Mexico's response to Arbitrator question No. 153.
[190] Mexico's response to Arbitrator question No. 153.

1990s, especially when compared with the stable trends in the prices of albacore and skipjack. We note, however, that after the adoption of the Tuna Measure, the prices did not increase particularly quickly, and that the above graph does not show a significant spike in prices immediately after the introduction of the Tuna Measure.

5.175 We further note that, as Mexico also acknowledges[191], from 1990 to 1992 prices of fresh and frozen yellowfin decreased before starting to increase again. The United States argues that this trend contradicts Mexico's assertion that cannery-grade yellowfin prices increased in the US market after the adoption of the Tuna Measure.[192] Mexico, however, argues that the Tuna Measure decreased demand for frozen yellowfin from the ETP, thereby causing a decrease in its price.[193]

5.176 In our view, the decline in the prices of fresh and frozen yellowfin from 1990 to 1992 does not necessarily undermine Mexico's argument that the Tuna Measure had a restrictive effect.[194] Simply put, this observed decline might reflect short-term price adjustments following the adoption of the Tuna Measure. This is explained by the fact that, since US canneries were no longer buying frozen yellowfin of ETP origin, the demand for frozen yellowfin went down, so did its price. Indeed, the 1992 USITC report also indicates that, around the time of the adoption of the Tuna Measure, US canneries substituted large yellowfin of ETP origin with small yellowfin and skipjack, and that "[t]he supply of [large] yellowfin declined, but demand declined even more; thus, the price dropped by 18 percent immediately after the dolphin-safe announcement in April 1990".[195] Such decline in the demand for and price of large yellowfin of ETP origin may thus well have disrupted the link between the evolution of the price of frozen yellowfin from the ETP and the price of canned yellowfin in the US market, at least temporarily. Furthermore, we note that the decline from 1990 to 1992 was followed by a steady increase in the following decade. In our view, it is reasonable to assume that it took some time for large yellowfin (that could no longer be sold to the United States) to find other buyers. This may account for the price decline observed between 1990-1992.

5.177 Turning now to the United States' argument that the price data contained in Exhibit MEX-79 relates to fresh and frozen tuna rather than cannery-grade tuna, we note that this argument differentiates between two periods, i.e. before and after 2001. As far as the period before 2001 is concerned, we understand the United States to contend that the prices presented in this Exhibit do not pertain exclusively to cannery-grade yellowfin. However, we understand that the raw material for producing canned tuna is typically frozen tuna, and thus there is a

---

[191] Mexico's response to Arbitrator question No. 72 (referring to Exhibit MEX-73).
[192] United States' comment on Mexico's response to Arbitrator question No. 153.
[193] Mexico's response to Arbitrator question No. 72.
[194] Mexico's response to Arbitrator question No. 72 (referring to Exhibit MEX-74).
[195] Exhibit MEX-73, p. 2-10.

relationship between frozen and cannery-grade yellowfin.[196] Indeed, the United States seems to agree with the proposition that that there is a connection between frozen and cannery grade tuna[197], and has acknowledged that "[p]rior to 2000, there is some relationship"[198] between the prices of cannery-grade yellowfin and frozen yellowfin. Moreover, our understanding is that the prices presented in Exhibit MEX-79 cover all yellowfin, including cannery-grade. The United States has not argued that the product scope of this Exhibit for the years before 2001 *excludes* cannery-grade yellowfin. Therefore, we find the prices presented in this Exhibit for the period prior to 2001 to be relevant to our inquiry.

5.178 As for the period from 2001, the United States argues that in this period US canneries exclusively used loins, as opposed to whole fish, to produce canned tuna products, and that therefore the prices in Exhibit MEX-79, which pertain to whole fish, bear no relationship to the prices of the tuna used by canneries. In our view, the evolution of prices in the 2000s is not relevant for our inquiry, as it is too far away from the date of adoption of the Tuna Measure. Accordingly, we need not determine whether the price data from this period related to whole fish rather than loins.

5.179 Turning to the other Exhibit presented by Mexico containing price data relevant to our analysis, Exhibit MEX-104, we note that it presents data on the prices of fresh and frozen yellowfin landings on an annual basis. Mexico presented this data in a graph, which we reproduce below:[199]

---

[196] Mexico's response to Arbitrator question No. 153.
[197] The United States argues that "...the fatal flaw in the exhibit is that, from 2000 onwards, it depicts exclusively imports of fresh and frozen yellowfin for direct consumption" and that "[c]onsequently, since 2000, the data in the exhibit refer entirely to imports of sashimi grade fresh and frozen yellowfin for the direct consumption market". United States' comments on Mexico's response to Arbitrator question No. 153.
[198] United States' comments on Mexico's response to Arbitrator question No. 158.
[199] Mexico's response to Arbitrator question No. 153.

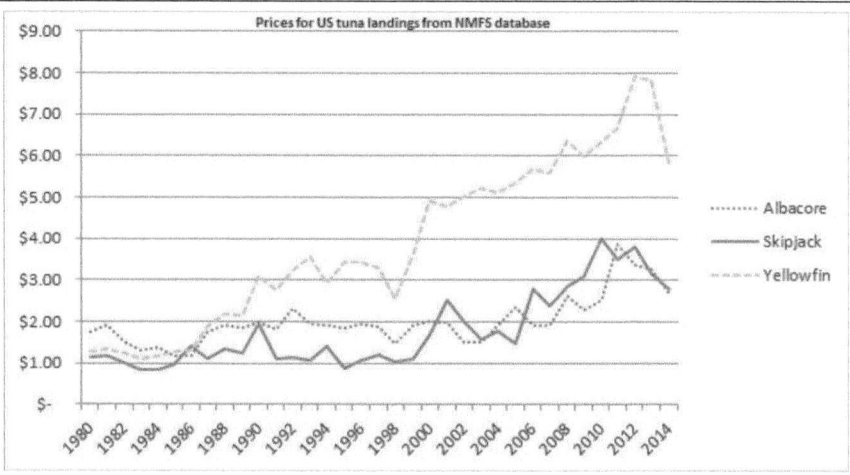

5.180 This graph shows that, similar to the trends observed in Exhibit MEX-79, yellowfin tuna landing prices increased in the years after the adoption of the Tuna Measure, continuing a trend that began a few years earlier. Furthermore, and importantly, this graph shows that the prices of yellowfin landings started deviating from those for albacore and skipjack at around the time of the adoption of the Tuna Measure. Specifically, the price of yellowfin increased while the price of albacore and especially skipjack decreased. Thus, after the introduction of the Tuna Measure, there was an increase in the relative price of yellowfin tuna as compared to the prices of albacore and skipjack. This suggests to us that the relative competitiveness of yellowfin was negatively affected by the Tuna Measure, as it became relatively more expensive than skipjack or albacore. As a result, canneries would have faced increased costs in the canning of yellowfin and this might, in turn, have created the incentives for canneries to substitute yellowfin for less-expensive skipjack or albacore tuna.

5.181 The United States contends that the prices of frozen yellowfin remained stable between the early- and mid-1990s following the adoption of the Tuna Measure. In this connection, it has presented evidence, in Exhibit USA-205, which, in its view, contradicts the price evidence submitted by Mexico. Exhibit USA-205 contains the following graph:

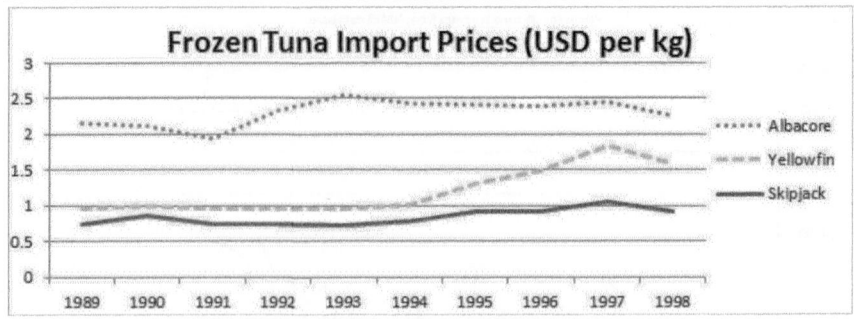

Source: Exhibit USA-205, reporting data from US Census Bureau.

5.182 At the outset, we note that this graph shows only the prices of frozen yellowfin, whereas the evidence presented by Mexico covers the prices of both fresh and frozen yellowfin. We also note that although, as the United States argues, this graph shows that the prices of frozen yellowfin remained stable until the mid-1990s, it also shows that such prices increased significantly thereafter. In this connection, we recall Mexico's argument that, to the extent that no increase was observed in yellowfin prices in the US market following the adoption of the Tuna Measure, this could be explained by the fact that the US canneries started importing lower quality yellowfin.[200] Support for this argument is found in the USITC report cited in paragraphs 5.24 and 5.31 above, which states:

> [T]he shift by some foreign and most U.S. fishermen from the large-yellowfin fishery to the fisheries for skipjack and small yellowfin entails an effective decline in average unit value received by the fishermen, even if canner-contracted prices by fish category do not change. That is, small tuna of any one species receive a lower price from the canner than do large tuna of the same species because the processing costs for the former exceed those for the latter.[201]

5.183 As pointed out above, we are of the view that the decline from 1990 to 1992 does not change the fact that prices followed a generally increasing trend as from 1990. The fact that frozen yellowfin prices did not go up following the adoption of the Tuna Measure may in our view be explained by short-term price adjustments. The excerpt from the USITC report shows that, in that period, US canneries started substituting large yellowfin with skipjack and small yellowfin. In our view, the price increase that could have been expected for frozen yellowfin was counterbalanced by this fact. We also find it reasonable to consider that, as the demand for cheaper small yellowfin increased, eventually

---

[200] Mexico's comment on the United States' response to Arbitrator question No. 153.
[201] Exhibit MEX-73, p. 3-18.

the price of frozen yellowfin also started increasing, as shown by the graph provided by the United States.

5.184 To sum up, we note that both the data presented by Mexico on the price of fresh and frozen yellowfin and the data presented by the United States on the price of frozen yellowfin show a generally increasing trend in the price of fresh and frozen yellowfin in the years after the introduction of the Tuna Measure. Such trend is apparent in Mexico's data since 1992, after a price decrease between 1990 and 1992, and in the United States' data since 1994, after a stable pattern between 1990 and 1994. Considering the data submitted by Mexico and the United States together, we note that they are consistent in showing a trend of non-decreasing yellowfin prices from 1994 onwards. The fact that the price of frozen yellowfin may not have increased immediately after the adoption of the Tuna Measure in 1990 can be explained by short-term price adjustments, as mentioned above. The trend of non-decreasing yellowfin prices from 1994 onwards is in our view consistent with the notion that the Tuna Measure restricted the supply of Mexican yellowfin in the US market.

5.1.3.1.3   Conclusion

5.185 We have found that, following the adoption of the Tuna Measure, the volume of tuna exports from Mexico to the United States and US cannery purchases of yellowfin declined. This is consistent with the view that the Tuna Measure had a restrictive effect on the supply of Mexican yellowfin into the United States. Moreover, prices in the US market for fresh or frozen yellowfin increased, or at the very least remained stable, in the years immediately after the introduction of the Tuna Measure. This too is consistent with the view that the Tuna Measure had a restrictive effect. We therefore conclude that the assumption that the Tuna Measure restricted the supply of canned yellowfin from Mexico to the United States is reasonable. However, we do not consider that the Tuna Measure is tantamount to an import ban, as Mexico has suggested.[202]

5.1.3.2   US Consumers have a preference for canned yellowfin and US retailers would sell Mexican canned yellowfin after the withdrawal of the Tuna Measure

5.186 The second assumption underlying Mexico's model is that US consumers have a preference for canned yellowfin, and that US retailers would sell Mexican canned yellowfin after the withdrawal of the Tuna Measure. Mexico maintains that, following the withdrawal of the Tuna Measure, Mexican producers would be able to inform US consumers about the real nature of their fishing methods. As a result of this, the misconception about setting on dolphins would be

---

[202] Mexico's written submission, para. 172.

corrected and the US consumers' real preferences for yellowfin would be revealed to the market. In this situation, canned yellowfin produced from tuna caught by setting on dolphins would be supplied in the market as a product like canned yellowfin caught by other methods. Given this additional supply, the price of canned yellowfin would fall and its consumption in the US market would increase.

5.187 The second assumption is based on two main arguments, one concerning consumer preferences, the other concerning US retailers' willingness to sell Mexican canned yellowfin. The Arbitrator examines each of these in turn.

5.1.3.2.1   US consumers' preferences

5.188 With regard to the first argument concerning consumer preferences, we begin by noting that the parties disagree on certain issues. One point of disagreement pertains to the fishing method by which tuna is caught. In this regard, we note that Mexico argues, and the United States agrees, that if the Tuna Measure were withdrawn, Mexican producers would be able to use a label containing the words "dolphin-safe". Indeed, the United States submits that Mexican tuna products produced consistently with the rules of the Agreement on the International Dolphin Conservation Program (AIDCP) would likely be able to be marketed as "AIDCP-certified dolphin-safe" or similar.[203] However, the United States also notes that if the Tuna Measure were withdrawn, it would be reasonable to expect that producers and retailers of tuna products not produced from setting on dolphins would seek to differentiate their products from tuna products produced from setting on dolphins, including by marketing their products in ways that Mexican producers could not.[204]

5.189 Mexico claims that US consumers would distinguish between tuna products made from unregulated and regulated setting on dolphins.[205] In this connection, Mexico argues that the Tuna Measure does not correctly inform US consumers about the impact on dolphins of fishing techniques used in the production of tuna products that are currently allowed to carry the dolphin-safe label. Following the withdrawal of the Tuna Measure, Mexican producers would be able to use an "AIDCP-certified dolphin-safe" or "AIDCP-compliant setting on dolphins" label on their products, and "market misconceptions regarding unregulated fishing methods and AIDCP-compliant fishing methods [would] be immediately corrected".[206] This, in Mexico's view, would educate US consumers about dolphin-safe fishing methods and have an effect on the consumption of canned yellowfin in the United States.

---

[203]   United States' response to Arbitrator question No. 57.

[204]   United States' written submission, para. 123.

[205]   We understand Mexico to use the term "regulated setting on dolphins" to refer to setting on dolphins in compliance with AIDCP rules.

[206]   Mexico's written submission, para. 76.

5.190 According to the United States, US consumers distinguish between tuna caught by setting on dolphins on the one hand, and by other fishing methods on the other hand. According to the United States, consumers do not, as Mexico argues, distinguish between regulated and unregulated setting on dolphins.[207] In other words, while Mexico contends that the AIDCP-compliant setting on dolphins label would inform US consumers that this method is harmless to dolphins and that, as a result, consumers would buy Mexican canned yellowfin, the United States maintains that US consumers would not buy tuna products made from tuna caught by setting on dolphins regardless of whether the affected dolphins were set on in compliance with AIDCP rules. The United States argues that there is no evidence to support Mexico's contention in this regard.[208]

5.191 Both parties have submitted survey results to support their positions in this connection. Mexico submitted two surveys, in Exhibit MEX-63 and MEX-71. The survey presented in Exhibit MEX-63 was conducted in 2010 by Public Opinion Strategies. It shows that when asked what "dolphin-safe" means, 59% of interviewees said that it means that no dolphins were injured or killed in the course of capturing tuna, whereas 10% said it means that dolphins were not encircled and then released in the capture of the tuna.[209] The survey also asked the interviewees whether, if they learned that under a series of international dolphin conservation agreements in place since 1993 dolphin mortalities in the ETP had declined from more than 150,000 per year throughout the 1980s to less than 200 each year since 1993, they would consider those agreements to be working towards the conservation of dolphins. In response, 71% of the interviewees said yes, and 14% said no.

5.192 The survey presented in Exhibit MEX-71 was also conducted by Public Opinion Strategies, but dates from 2016. It shows that while one third of Americans interviewed "look for" the dolphin-safe label when buying canned tuna, another one third do not.[210] It also shows that one quarter of Americans interviewed specifically "inspect" tuna cans to find a dolphin-safe label before adding it to their shopping cart, while 6% do not.[211] Finally, it shows that 52% of Americans interviewed think that "dolphin-safe" means that no dolphins were injured or killed in the capture of the tuna, while 14% think that it means that dolphins were not encircled and then released in the capture of the tuna.[212]

5.193 In Exhibit USA-148, the United States submitted a survey conducted by Remington Research Group in 2016. The survey results show that 50% of interviewees considered that tuna caught by intentionally chasing and capturing dolphins should not be labelled as "dolphin-safe" even if that method does not kill or seriously injure dolphins. 74% of the interviewees also said that they

---

[207] United States' response to Arbitrator question No. 133.
[208] *Ibid.*
[209] Exhibit MEX-63, p. 2.
[210] Exhibit MEX-71, p. 3.
[211] Exhibit MEX-71, p. 4.
[212] Exhibit MEX-71, p. 6.

would not buy canned tuna produced from tuna caught by such a method. In response to a question as to what should be the definition of dolphin-safe for tuna, 39% of the interviewees said it should mean that no dolphins were intentionally killed or seriously injured or intentionally chased and captured in catching tuna, 27% said it should mean that no dolphins were intentionally chased and captured in catching the tuna, and 17% said it should mean that no dolphins were killed or seriously injured in catching the tuna.[213]

5.194 We note that the three surveys show a mixed picture of the extent to which US consumers perceive the dolphin-safe label as referring to catching tuna by setting on dolphins rather than to a fishing method that does not kill or seriously injure dolphins. We also note that due to the difference in the questions asked in these surveys, they are not fully comparable. Moreover, in the absence of general US census data against which we could compare the survey sample sizes, it is not clear to us whether the survey samples accurately represent US census demographics in terms of population age, ethnicity, or educational attainment. Accordingly, we are not persuaded that it would be appropriate to attach weight to these surveys.

5.195 We accept the United States' position that it adopted the Tuna Measure in response to growing public awareness about the well-being of dolphins and the preservation of marine mammals in general. However, we do not necessarily interpret this to mean that US consumers predominantly interpret the dolphin-safe label as indicating that a labelled product was not produced using tuna caught by setting on dolphins. It is therefore not apparent to us that US consumers would not buy Mexican canned yellowfin after the withdrawal of the Tuna Measure, if Mexican producers were then able to use a label showing that their methods are AIDCP-certified dolphin-safe. We find both parties' arguments on this issue, and their reliance on the mentioned survey results, to be unpersuasive and decline to adopt them as presented.

5.196 The second disagreement between the parties with regard to consumer preferences pertains to the characteristics of yellowfin as opposed to other species of tuna. Mexico argues in this respect that canned yellowfin, like canned albacore, is a premium tuna product. Mexico submits that US consumers would therefore pay a premium for canned yellowfin, and that canned yellowfin, if priced competitively, would sell in significant quantities in the US market. In support of this argument, Mexico provides empirical evidence that consumers prefer yellowfin over generic tuna, including albacore. This evidence shows that consumers are willing to pay a premium to buy yellowfin.[214]

5.197 The United States disagrees with Mexico. It considers that the demand for canned yellowfin is limited because US consumers dislike its taste, texture, and colour, compared with albacore.[215] In addition, the United States submits that

---

[213] Exhibit USA-148, p. 2.
[214] Exhibit MEX-02, table 7 on p. 20.
[215] United States' written submission, para. 23.

while yellowfin is indeed sold partly as a gourmet product, it is often sold as "light" tuna, which is a term used to refer to yellowfin canned with skipjack.

5.198 Based on the evidence on the record, we consider reasonable Mexico's assumption that yellowfin, sold on its own (rather than as "light" tuna), is a premium product. In this regard, we note that the United States recognizes the existence of a premium segment in the canned tuna market. That segment is currently being served with albacore tuna and, to a significantly lesser extent, yellowfin tuna.[216] We also note the United States' recognition that canned yellowfin can be considered a premium or gourmet product in some circumstances.[217]

5.199 Regarding consumer preferences, the United States further asserts that one reason why producers combine yellowfin and skipjack together and sell it as "light tuna", rather than selling cans of 100% yellowfin, is to lower the mercury level per can of yellowfin and thus produce a safer product that is consistent with US Food and Drug Administration (USFDA) food safety regulations. The United States contends that US consumers are concerned about mercury levels in light tuna products composed of large tuna, namely yellowfin, as compared to the mercury levels of light tuna products composed of skipjack.[218]

5.200 In response to the United States' argument, Mexico submits that although US consumers are sensitive to the mercury content of tuna, the mercury level in yellowfin is not higher than that in other large tuna species, such as albacore. Therefore, in Mexico's view, consumers would buy Mexican canned yellowfin.

5.201 We note that the evidence presented in Exhibit MEX-64 shows that mercury levels in yellowfin and albacore are almost identical. Even accepting that US consumers may be sensitive to the mercury content of tuna products and may not be willing to buy products with high mercury levels, we also note that canned albacore, which contains the almost the same levels of mercury as yellowfin, is widely consumed in the United States. This, in our view, undermines the United States' argument that US consumers would refrain specifically from buying canned yellowfin because of its mercury level.

5.202 Based on the foregoing, we agree with Mexico's argument that US consumers have a preference for canned yellowfin.

5.1.3.2.2   US retailers' willingness to sell Mexican canned yellowfin

5.203 Mexico's second argument is that US retailers would carry Mexican canned yellowfin following the withdrawal of the Tuna Measure. The United States disagrees, and argues that US retailers are sensitive to consumer demand

---

[216] United States' written submission, paras. 20-23.
[217] United States' written submission, paras. 22 and 102; response to Arbitrator question No. 143.
[218] United States' response to Arbitrator question No. 54.

and that they therefore would only sell tuna products not produced from tuna caught by setting on dolphins.[219]

5.204 At the outset, we note that there is evidence on the record suggesting that at least some US retailers would be willing to sell canned yellowfin from Mexico if it were eligible to receive a dolphin-safe label. Exhibit MEX-36 (BCI) contains an affidavit dated 2010 from [[xxx]], attesting to several facts relevant to our analysis. In particular, the affidavit mentions that [[xxx]]. Notably, the exhibit also contains an e-mail from [[xxx]]. The e-mail closes by stating that [[xxx]].

5.205 Further, we note that in a three-week period in 2003 when, because of modifications made to the US law, Mexican producers had an opportunity to export canned yellowfin to the United States carrying a dolphin-safe label, some US retailers accepted to sell that product. In this regard, Exhibit MEX-45 (BCI) contains an affidavit supplementing the affidavit contained in MEX-36 (BCI). It states that in January 2003, following a change by the US government on the definition of dolphin safe, [[xxx]]. In February of the same year, [[xxx]]. In our view, Exhibits MEX-36 (BCI) and MEX-45 (BCI) lend support to Mexico's argument, in that they demonstrate that there are US retailers who have indicated that they would sell Mexican canned yellowfin after the withdrawal of the Tuna Measure, when such products would be eligible to carry a dolphin-safe label.

5.206 We note, however, that the United States argues that many of the companies engaged in the sale of tuna products in the US market have agreements with the Earth Island Institute (EII) and adhere to EII's dolphin-safe standard, which excludes tuna caught by setting on dolphins.[220] In particular, the United States argues that the dolphin safe policies of the companies that have the largest market share in the United States[221] confirm that US retailers are sensitive to the demands of their consumers and are committed not to sell tuna products containing tuna caught by setting on dolphins.[222] The United States contends that it is aware of written statements to that effect from retailers accounting for [[xxx]]% of the retail market and [[xxx]]% of all canned tuna consumption.[223] In addition, the United States notes a statement by Walmart indicating that none of the tuna major brands it sells produce products from tuna caught by setting on dolphins, and that purchasing decisions are governed by Walmart's new sustainability policy, rather than by whether the tuna product qualifies for the dolphin safe label under the US measure. The United States concludes, that including Walmart, the retailers covered by statements account for [[xxx]]% of the US retail market share, and [[xxx]]% of total US consumption.[224]

---

[219] United States' written submission, para. 33.
[220] United States' written submission, paras. 31-32.
[221] United States written' submission, para. 33 (referring to Exhibit USA-38 (BCI)).
[222] United States written' submission, para. 33 (referring to Exhibit USA-40).
[223] United States written' submission, para. 33 (referring to Exhibit USA-38 (BCI) and USA-41 (BCI)).
[224] United States written' submission, para. 35.

5.207 Mexico responds that these statements were "manufactured"[225] by the United States solely for the purposes of these arbitration proceedings, and alleges that the retailers were pressured into stating that they would not sell Mexican tuna products. In Mexico's view, therefore, these statements do not have important evidentiary value.[226] With respect to the statement by Walmart in particular, Mexico notes that this statement does not mention setting on dolphins, but refers rather to the sustainability of different fishing methods. Mexico therefore considers that Walmart's statement does not support the United States' argument.[227]

5.208 The statements presented by the United States pertain to 15 companies and are found in Exhibit USA-40. Of these 15 statements, 14 indicate, either explicitly or by reference to the EII standards, that the relevant company commits not to sell tuna products obtained from setting on dolphins. The statement by Walmart, however, contains no reference to setting on dolphins, and states instead that Walmart's policy is to sell tuna products obtained from sustainable fisheries.

5.209 Mexico questions the relevance of some of these statements, many of which were prepared years ago.[228] Indeed, some of these statements were made in 1999, 2007, or 2011, which was prior to the expiry of the RPT granted to the United States to comply with the DSB recommendations or rulings, while others were made in 2015 or 2016. The United States acknowledges that some of the statements are older than others, but contends that the five retailers that signed statements predating the expiry of the RPT continue to be in EII's list of approved dolphin-safe retailers, which was last updated in December 2015.[229] Mexico does not dispute this contention.

5.210 Based on the evidence on the record, we find reasonable the United States' contention that certain US retailers would not change their dolphin-safe policies and would continue to refrain from offering for sale Mexican canned yellowfin made from tuna caught by setting on dolphins, even if the Tuna Measure were withdrawn. In particular, we accept that companies that have made commitments to EII would not begin purchasing tuna products made from tuna caught by setting on dolphins if the Tuna Measure were withdrawn. Certainly, we are not persuaded that they would abandon their dolphin-safe policies in the short-term. We would add that, in our view, Mexico has not substantiated its allegation that the statements were manufactured solely for the purposes of these proceedings.

5.211 The situation in respect of Walmart is less clear. The Walmart statement refers to Walmart's Canned Tuna Policy and indicates that this policy was

---

[225] Mexico's written submission, para. 15 and Section III.B.2.a.(2)(b).
[226] Mexico's written submission, para. 77.
[227] Mexico's written submission, para. 79.
[228] Mexico's written submission, para. 85.
[229] United States' response to Arbitrator question No. 146(c).

released in May 2015, that is to say, on a date well after the end of 2014, which is the year for which we are assessing the level of nullification or impairment.[230] As we have no information on Walmart's purchasing policy in 2014, it would not be appropriate in our view to make assumptions on the basis of that new policy regarding Walmart's purchasing policy in 2014.

5.212 Even disregarding this, we note that the focus of Walmart's statement is the sustainability of the relevant fishery, as evidenced in particular through participation in a recognized sustainability programme.[231] Walmart's 2015 canned tuna purchasing policy as reflected in the statement submitted to us does not explicitly commit Walmart not to purchase Mexican tuna products without a dolphin-safe label. Similarly, the purchasing policy does not explicitly commit Walmart not to purchase tuna products produced from tuna caught by setting on dolphins. Moreover, the excerpt from Walmart's purchasing policy provided to us is ambiguous as to the precise requirements or circumstances in which tuna products would be considered sustainable. In particular, it is not clear to us what the different sustainability programmes listed by Walmart require or entail, and whether any of those programmes requires canned tuna to be "dolphin-safe", and if so, whether this would necessarily exclude tuna products produced from setting on dolphins.[232] Therefore, even considering this statement, we are unable to determine on the basis of this statement alone whether the United States is correct in suggesting that Walmart would not offer for sale Mexican canned yellowfin made from tuna caught by setting on dolphins, even if the Tuna Measure were withdrawn.

5.213 Mexico has submitted an affidavit from July 2016 [[xxx]]. The statement provides no information regarding when this exchange took place, and so we cannot assume that it concerns 2014 and draw inferences concerning that year.[233] [[xxx]].

---

[230] Exhibit USA-40, p. 16.

[231] Walmart's canned tuna policy requires all canned tuna suppliers to source from fisheries that: (a) comply with International Sustainable Seafood Foundation (ISSF) sustainability conservation measures, including those adopted in collaboration with relevant tuna RFMO and from vessels that are registered on the Pro-active Vessel Register (PVR); (b) Manage a program in accordance with the Principles of Credible Sustainability Programs developed by The Sustainability Consortium (third party review must be commissioned and provided upon request) or certified as sustainable using Marine Stewardship Council (MSC); (c) use better management fishing practices as validated through chain of custody (e.g. pole and line, free-school sets); or (d) actively work toward certification or involved in a Fisheries Improvement Project (FIP) that has definitive and ambitious goals, measurable metrics and time bound milestones.

[232] While we have some evidence concerning the requirements for sustainability certification under the Marine Stewardship Council, no evidence has been submitted concerning the contents of the International Sustainable Seafood Foundation programme, or concerning whether eligibility for the dolphin-safe label may be of relevance under a Fisheries Improvement Project or in the context of "better management fisheries practices".

[233] Reading Exhibit MEX-106 (BCI) together with Exhibit MEX-36 (BCI), which contains an earlier affidavit by the same person, it appears that the relevant exchange may have taken place in 2008.

5.214 Moreover, the fact that Walmart may not have been purchasing Mexican canned yellowfin is not, in our view, a reason to think that it would not purchase such products if the Tuna Measure were withdrawn and Mexican canned yellowfin were eligible to be labelled as "dolphin-safe" in the US market.

5.215 For the reasons given above, we conclude that the information before us does not allow us to conclude that Walmart would not offer for sale canned yellowfin if the Tuna Measure were withdrawn and Mexican producers therefore had the ability to use a "dolphin-safe" label. Consequently, we do not consider it appropriate to include Walmart's [[xxx]]% market share in the total market share of retailers who, following the withdrawal of the Tuna Measure, would not offer Mexican canned yellowfin for sale. Based on the evidence before us, we therefore accept that US retailers accounting for 26.9% of total US consumption of tuna products would not commercialize Mexican canned yellowfin even after the withdrawal of the Tuna Measure. The remainder of US retailers, which account for 73.1%[234] of total US consumption of tuna products, are retailers in respect of which we have no evidence suggesting that they would not offer for sale Mexican canned yellowfin after the withdrawal of the Tuna Measure.[235]

5.216 Based on the foregoing, we consider that there is no reason to assume that US retailers would not sell Mexican canned yellowfin after the withdrawal of the Tuna Measure, except those retailers accounting for 26.9% of total consumption of tuna products with respect to whom evidence on the record suggests that they would not sell tuna caught by setting on dolphins regardless of whether it carried a dolphin-safe label.

5.1.3.2.3   Conclusion

5.217 Based on the above considerations, we consider reasonable the second assumption underlying Mexico's model, namely, that US consumers have a preference for canned yellowfin, and that there is no reason to assume that US retailers would not sell Mexican canned yellowfin after the withdrawal of the Tuna Measure, except those that made statements to the contrary, as explained above. We also note that the evidence on the record shows that the share of yellowfin in US cannery receipts was 34% in the period 1980-1989[236], prior to the adoption of the Tuna Measure. This, in our view, lends support to our finding that the second assumption is reasonable.

---

[234] 73.1% is equal to the sum of Walmart's [[xxx]]% market share and the [[xxx]]% market share of other US retailers that have not, *ex ante*, ruled out the possibility of selling Mexican canned yellowfin after the withdrawal of the Tuna Measure.

[235] We note that while the United States argued that [[xxx]]% of the retailers are committed to selling only "dolphin safe" tuna product and will not carry tuna product produced from setting on dolphins, this figure refers to 2015. According to USA-41 (BCI), for the year 2014, the corresponding number is [[xxx]]% and Walmart's market share is [[xxx]]%.

[236] Exhibit USA-22 revised.

5.1.3.3   Mexican producers would supply all of the increased consumption of canned yellowfin in the US market following the withdrawal of the Tuna Measure

5.218 The third assumption underlying Mexico's model is that, following the withdrawal of the Tuna Measure, Mexico will be the sole supplier of canned yellowfin in the US market.[237] In Mexico's view, this assumption is "strongly supported by market realities".[238] The United States disagrees with this assumption, and submits that both US and foreign canneries that currently supply the US market with canned yellowfin would compete with Mexican producers to satisfy any increased demand for canned yellowfin in the US market.[239]

5.219 Before proceeding to an assessment of the specific arguments underlying this aspect of Mexico's model, we find it useful to clarify the exact nature of Mexico's contention. Specifically, we need to assess whether Mexico's argument is (a) that in the counterfactual situation, i.e. where the United States withdraws the Tuna Measure, suppliers from countries other than Mexico (US canneries and canneries from third countries) would not supply canned yellowfin to the US market), or (b) whether Mexico recognizes that there *would or may* be such supply, but chooses to disregard it for the purposes of modelling the counterfactual (for instance, because in Mexico's view the volume of supply from countries other than Mexico would be very small).

5.220 At the outset, we note that in Mexico's model, the United States does not import canned yellowfin from third countries (i.e. countries other than Mexico). Indeed, equation 20 in Exhibit MEX-02 says that yellowfin tuna consumed in the United States comes from Mexico.[240] This suggests that Mexico might be arguing that, after the withdrawal of the Tuna Measure, Mexico would be the only supplier of canned yellowfin in the US market. We asked Mexico to help us clarify its position. In response, Mexico indicated that it agreed with the United States' argument that "yellowfin tuna is produced elsewhere in the world and that US canneries do not operate at full capacity".[241] However, Mexico argues that the share of canned yellowfin currently being imported into the United States from countries other than Mexico is 1.2% of the overall consumption of tuna products in the United States. Moreover, Mexico argues that this share would not be affected by the withdrawal of the Tuna Measure because the import of such products into the US market is not limited by the Tuna Measure. Mexico further contends that the non-Mexican yellowfin currently being imported into the US market sells at a price higher than that at which Mexico would supply its

---

[237] Exhibit MEX-02, p. 30.
[238] Mexico's written submission, para. 175.
[239] United States' written submission, para. 112.
[240] Exhibit MEX-02, p. 30.
[241] Mexico's response to Arbitrator question No. 18.

canned yellowfin after the withdrawal of the Tuna Measure.[242] According to Mexico, these two factors (current small supply and high price) mean that, if anything, the supply of canned yellowfin from other sources "would be even smaller with the removal of the tuna measure[]" than it is currently.[243] Thus, in Mexico's view, "the inclusion of the global supply of canned yellowfin tuna into the model would have a marginal negative impact on the level of nullification or impairment".[244] Mexico argues that, for modelling purposes, the supply of non-Mexican canned yellowfin can be excluded in calculating the level of nullification or impairment caused to Mexico by the Tuna Measure.[245]

5.221 Based on these clarifications, we understand Mexico's argument to be that although there *is* currently some limited supply of canned yellowfin from US canneries and third countries, and although such supply would or at least may remain in the market after the withdrawal of the Tuna Measure, Mexico's model need not account for it because the volume of that supply is small, and will become even smaller following the withdrawal of the Tuna Measure. In the light of this, Mexico considers it appropriate, for modelling purposes, to treat Mexico as the sole supplier of canned yellowfin in the US market, as this assists in simplifying the calculation of the alleged level of nullification or impairment. Accordingly, we understand Mexico's argument to be that although in the counterfactual situation Mexico would not be the *sole* supplier of yellowfin in the US market following the withdrawal of the Tuna Measure, but rather the *dominant* supplier, for modelling purposes Mexico considers it acceptable to ignore other suppliers and treat Mexico as though it would be the sole supplier.

5.222 Given Mexico's argument, the issue that the third assumption raises is whether it is reasonable to assume that Mexico would be the dominant supplier of canned yellowfin to the United States following the withdrawal of the Tuna Measure. If we find that it would, we will then discuss whether it is also appropriate, in Mexico's model, to disregard other sources of canned yellowfin (US canneries and imports from third countries), treating Mexico as the sole supplier of canned yellowfin in the US market.

5.223 Mexico's assumption that it would be the dominant supplier of canned yellowfin to the US market after the withdrawal of the Tuna Measure is based on three arguments: (a) the Mexican canning industry would be competitive in the US canned yellowfin market *vis-à-vis* US canneries and other foreign canned yellowfin suppliers; (b) no other potential large supplier is affected by the Tuna Measure, and unaffected suppliers would not be incentivized to sell canned yellowfin to the United States after the withdrawal of the Tuna Measure; and (c) Mexico could and would import canned yellowfin from other countries in the

---

[242] Mexico's response to Arbitrator question No. 123.
[243] *Ibid.*
[244] *Ibid.*
[245] *Ibid.*

region to meet its own domestic demand. We will assess each of these arguments in turn.

5.1.3.3.1   The Mexican canning industry would be competitive in the US canned yellowfin market *vis-à-vis* US canneries and other countries exporting canned yellowfin to the United States

5.224 Mexico argues that it has an important cost advantage in the canned yellowfin market over other countries. According to Mexico, the factors underpinning this cost advantage include (a) the installed processing capacity in Mexico; (b) the vertical integration of the Mexican canned tuna industry; (c) Mexico's strategic location near the fishing zones and as a neighbour to the United States; (d) the inexpensive labour cost in Mexico; and (e) duty-free access to the US market by virtue of being a signatory to NAFTA.[246]

5.225 Mexico also asserts that although it is competitive in the canned yellowfin markets of developed countries such as the European Union and the United States, tariff rate quotas limit exports to the European Union[247], while the Tuna Measure restricts exports to the United States.[248] In respect of the EU market, Mexico elaborates further by pointing out that its exports of canned yellowfin to the EU market are subject to several constraints, including (a) a tariff rate quota comprising an over-quota tariff of 24% and an in-quota tariff of 6.8% for a volume in 2014 of between 8500 and 9000 tonnes; (b) higher transportation costs than some of Mexico's main competitors; (c) the existence of a large, established supply of yellowfin from the fleets of Spain, Italy, Portugal, and France; (d) unlimited duty-free treatment accorded by the European Union to certain other countries; and (e) subsidies provided by the European Union and its member States to the EU fleets. Mexico further explains that its exports to South American markets are limited because of the large, established supply of tuna in those markets, in particular, from the Ecuadorian fleet.[249] Thus, in Mexico's view, any current limitations of its supply of canned yellowfin to foreign markets do not indicate any inherent lack of competitiveness.

5.226 In response to Mexico, the United States argues that Mexico's assertion about the competitiveness of its canned yellowfin industry is contradicted by the evidence on the record.[250] The United States contends that Ecuador has almost all of the advantages that Mexico asserts give it a cost advantage, but has greater

---

[246]   Mexico's written submission, para. 175.
[247]   Mexico's response to Arbitrator question No. 85.
[248]   Mexico's response to Arbitrator question No. 149.
[249]   Mexico's response to Arbitrator question No. 85.
[250]   United States' response to Arbitrator question No. 66 (referring to Mexico's written submission, paras. 129, 148).

capacity than Mexico to take advantage of economies of scale. In this regard, the United States refers, in particular, to the fact that Ecuador has installed processing capacity, a semi-vertically integrated canning industry, is located near the relevant fishing zones, and has a relatively inexpensive, productive labour force.[251]

5.227 The United States further submits that Thailand has many of the advantages that Mexico claims, and in particular that Thailand benefits from close proximity to the Western and Central Pacific Ocean (WCPO). The United States contends that fish is the most significant component in the cost of canned tuna and Thailand's dominance in the canning industry makes it a global leader in canning-grade frozen skipjack and yellowfin.[252] According to the United States, Thailand is also better placed than any industry in the world to take advantage of economies of scale in processing and canning due to the high concentration of processing facilities around Bangkok.[253] The United States also argues that Thailand has a low-cost, highly productive labour force, which is about 7% more productive, per metric ton of production, than Ecuador's.[254] The United States contends that other WCPO countries, such as the Philippines and China, also benefit from many of the advantages enjoyed by Thailand, including installed processing capacity, strategic location near fishing zones, and a low-cost, high productivity workforce.[255]

5.228 The United States also notes that Mexico exports very little canned tuna to the European and South American markets. According to the United States, these small export volumes suggest deficiencies in Mexico's competitiveness in those markets.[256] For the United States, Mexico's failure to compete in the European Union is particularly notable given the European consumer preference for yellowfin and the fact that there is no EU-wide measure equivalent to the US Tuna Measure.[257] The United States recognizes that, owing to its NAFTA membership, Mexican tuna products have a tariff advantage *vis-à-vis* most other imported canned tuna products in the US market. However, the United States contends that this tariff advantage has a limited impact on Mexico's overall competitiveness in the US market for canned yellowfin.[258] The United States argues that Mexico has provided no evidence suggesting that duty-free access

---

[251] United States' response to Arbitrator question No. 66 (referring to Exhibits MEX-21 and USA-07).
[252] United States' response to Arbitrator question No. 66 (referring to Exhibits USA-07 and MEX-02).
[253] United States' response to Arbitrator question No. 66 (referring to Exhibits USA-114).
[254] *Ibid.*
[255] United States' response to Arbitrator question No. 66.
[256] United States' response to Arbitrator question No. 55.
[257] United States' response to Arbitrator question Nos. 55 and 149; opening statement at the meeting of the Arbitrator, para. 34.
[258] United States' response to Arbitrator question No. 142.

under NAFTA counterbalances the significant competitive advantages of the existing major suppliers to the US market.[259]

5.229 Additionally, the United States asserts that Mexico's exports of canned yellowfin to the EU market also benefit from preferential tariff treatment, compared to many other major canned tuna producing countries, including Thailand, China, Indonesia, Vietnam, and Senegal. The United States does not dispute the existence of the tariff rate quota in the EU market, but argues that Mexico has never come close to fulfilling its tariff rate quota in prepared tuna (i.e. canned tuna and tuna loins) exports.[260] According to the United States, the fact that Mexico is unable to compete with those other exporting countries in the EU market despite its tariff advantage, which the United States says is larger than its NAFTA tariff advantage in the US market, proves that Mexico is not a competitive supplier of canned yellowfin. The United States infers from this that Mexico would not be the only supplier of canned yellowfin to the US market in the event of the withdrawal of the Tuna Measure, as Mexico's model assumes.[261]

5.230 The issue we need to consider is whether Mexico would be sufficiently competitive *vis-à-vis* other suppliers of canned yellowfin in the US market, in a way that would support the argument that Mexico would in the short-term become the dominant supplier of canned yellowfin in the US market following the withdrawal of the Tuna Measure.

5.231 We begin our analysis of this issue by considering whether Mexican canned yellowfin would be competitive *vis-à-vis* US canned yellowfin. In this connection, we note that, as far as the Mexican industry's competitiveness *vis-à-vis* the US canneries is concerned, both parties agree that US vessels would not return to the ETP in order to set on dolphins. Further, since US canneries are not vertically integrated and currently produce the majority of their tuna product from tuna caught by non-US vessels, as acknowledged by the United States[262], they would have to purchase yellowfin from other fleets fishing in the WCPO and elsewhere that catch substantial quantities of yellowfin. Given the distance of those regions from the United States, it is plausible that such purchases would command higher prices compared to the Mexican producers' prices, which, in turn, would increase the production costs of US canneries. This, in our view, means that the Mexican canning industry would enjoy a competitive advantage *vis-à-vis* the US canneries.

5.232 We now turn to Mexico's argument regarding its industry's competitiveness *vis-à-vis* the suppliers from third countries. To assess the merits of Mexico's argument about the competitiveness of the Mexican canning industry in the US market, we would ideally need information on the costs of production of Mexican producers relative to their competitors from third

---

[259] United States' response to Arbitrator question No. 66.
[260] United States' comment on Mexico's response to Arbitrator question No. 85.
[261] *Ibid.*
[262] United States' response to Arbitrator question No. 66.

countries. Such information, however, is not on the record. In our view, Mexico's argument that its canning industry is vertically integrated and, therefore, faces lower production costs is not by itself sufficient to support Mexico's claim. Other suppliers, such as Ecuador, are in fact also vertically integrated.[263]

5.233 However, as regards market access conditions to the US market, Mexico's close geographical proximity to the United States and the fact that it has duty-free access to the US market as a NAFTA member[264] in our view provide Mexico with a crucial dual advantage relative to its competitors. In this context, we do not consider that the United States' argument that "the fact that Mexico is unable to compete with [Indonesia, Vietnam, Senegal and China] in the EU market, despite a tariff advantage that is *larger* than its NAFTA tariff advantage in the U.S. market" provides a basis to ignore Mexico's tariff preference in the US market and its proximity to the United States.[265] In other words, Mexico enjoys an advantage in the US market that it does not enjoy in the EU market, especially regarding geographical proximity.

5.234 As for the United States' argument regarding the inability of Mexico's canning industry to compete in markets such as the European Union or South American countries[266], we accept that it may in principle be appropriate for the Arbitrator to make such horizontal comparisons in ascertaining Mexico's competitiveness in the US market. In our view, however, the circumstances in those markets, which Mexico refers to and we note in paragraph 5.94 above, distinguish such markets from the US market, and counsel against drawing conclusions from the situation observed in those other markets. Therefore, we do not consider it appropriate to attach weight to Mexico's allegedly limited competitiveness in such other markets.

5.235 On the basis of the above, our view is that Mexico does have a competitive advantage in the US market *vis-à-vis* other foreign canned yellowfin producers.

5.236 In sum, we find plausible the argument that the Mexican industry would be competitive *vis-à-vis* the US canneries after the withdrawal of the Tuna Measure mainly because the Mexican industry is vertically integrated whereas the US canneries buy yellowfin from WCPO and other distant countries at considerable transport costs. Additionally, given Mexico's important advantage stemming from its geographical proximity to the United States and the tariff preference resulting from its NAFTA membership, we also find plausible the argument that the Mexican industry would be competitive *vis-à-vis* other

---

[263] See, for instance, Exhibit USA-07, p. 29.
[264] The United States' MFN duty rate is 35% for tuna products in oil, and 6% for those in water. Exhibit MEX-05. We note that the United States agrees that NAFTA membership provides a tariff advantage. See United States' response to Arbitrator's Question No. 142.
[265] United States' comment on Mexico's response to Arbitrator question No. 85.
[266] United States' response to Arbitrator question No. 55.

suppliers of canned yellowfin. For these reasons, we find plausible Mexico's argument that it will, in the short-term, be competitive *vis-à-vis* other suppliers of canned yellowfin in the US market after the withdrawal of the Tuna Measure.

5.1.3.3.2   No other potential large supplying country is affected by the Tuna Measure, and unaffected supplying countries would not be incentivized to sell canned yellowfin after the withdrawal of the Tuna Measure

5.237   Mexico argues that there are no potential important suppliers of canned yellowfin to the United States other than Mexico that are affected by the Tuna Measure, and that only exports of canned tuna from Mexico would increase in a significant way after the withdrawal of the Measure. Mexico contends that the market forces that have so far prevented exports of greater quantities of canned yellowfin from other countries would not be affected by the withdrawal of the Measure. In Mexico's view, the same market forces would also continue to operate in such a way as to stop US canneries from increasing their production of canned yellowfin after the withdrawal of the Tuna Measure.[267]

5.238   While Mexico recognizes that canned yellowfin tuna could be produced by the United States if the US fleet were to move back into the ETP to catch yellowfin in response to the withdrawal of the Tuna Measure, Mexico argues that this would not be feasible in the short-run because US vessels are not equipped to catch yellowfin by setting on dolphins in the ETP. Even if it were feasible for US boats to move back into the ETP, fishing in the ETP would not be profitable.[268]

5.239   Mexico acknowledges that yellowfin is produced elsewhere in the world and that US canneries are not operating at full capacity, but contends that this is not relevant to the Arbitrator's analysis. For Mexico, the relevant question is whether the Tuna Measure currently prevents these countries from exporting canned yellowfin to the United States and thus whether the withdrawal of the Measure would increase their exports to the United States.[269] Mexico argues that suppliers of canned yellowfin located in South East Asia are not currently impacted by the Tuna Measure because the Measure affects only the countries that harvest tuna by setting on dolphins in the ETP.[270] Additionally, Mexico recognizes that there are a few Central and South American countries that harvest tuna in the ETP, but argues that those countries would not be able to

---

[267] Mexico's written submission, para. 174.
[268] Mexico's written submission, para. 176.
[269] Mexico's response to Arbitrator question No. 18.
[270] Mexico's response to Arbitrator question No. 18; opening statement at the meeting of the Arbitrator.

compete with Mexico's producers of canned yellowfin because they have small production capacities, are located further from the United States, and their exports are subject to US import tariffs. Mexico also underlines the fact that the United States maintains embargoes on imports of yellowfin products from Belize, Bolivia, Colombia, Honduras, Nicaragua, Panama, Vanuatu, Venezuela, and Peru, as these countries have chosen not to seek an "affirmative finding" from the US Department of Commerce that they are in compliance with the AIDCP requirements. This, in Mexico's view, shows that any export response by other countries to the withdrawal of the Tuna Measure would be minor.[271]

5.240 The United States submits that countries that fish and process tuna in the WCPO region could supply canned yellowfin to the US market. The United States explains that the WCPO is the most important source of yellowfin in the world, including yellowfin produced for canning, and that the United States imports substantial amounts of canned tuna from all of the WCPO producers, including Thailand, Vietnam, the Philippines, and Indonesia, which together accounted for 79% of all canned tuna imported into the United States between 2010 and 2015.[272] The United States submits that it already imports canned yellowfin from these and other tuna producing countries.[273] The fact that the United States does not import more canned yellowfin is, therefore, due to a lack not of supply but of demand. Finally, regarding Mexico's arguments concerning the US fleet, the United States agrees with Mexico that it is reasonable to consider that US vessels would not return to the ETP in order to set on dolphins. However, the United States contends that the reason for this is not because US canneries "are not set up" to process ETP yellowfin, but rather because such canneries would not purchase tuna products produced from tuna caught by setting on dolphins because US consumers do not want such product.[274]

5.241 In assessing Mexico's argument about the possible export response by other countries to the withdrawal of the Tuna Measure, the Arbitrator finds it important to note that, in small quantities[275], canned yellowfin is already sold in the US market.[276] We recall that the share of yellowfin in the total consumption of tuna products in the US market is 1.2%. In examining whether countries other than Mexico would also export canned yellowfin to the United States following the withdrawal of the Tuna Measure, we find it useful to separate those countries into two groups: (a) countries that already supply canned yellowfin to the US

---

[271] Mexico's response to Arbitrator question No. 18 (referring to NOAA Fisheries, Tuna/Dolphin Embargo Status Update, Exhibit MEX-72).
[272] United States' response to Arbitrator question No. 66 (referring to Exhibit USA-36).
[273] United States' response to Arbitrator question No. 66 (referring to Exhibits MEX-15, USA-10 (BCI) and USA-90).
[274] United States' response to Arbitrator question No. 66.
[275] Mexico's response to Arbitrator question No. 150; United States' comments on Mexico's response to Arbitrator question No. 150.
[276] Exhibits MEX-15, USA-10 (BCI), USA-36, USA-93 and USA-96; United States' response to Arbitrator question No. 157.

market, and (b) countries that do not currently supply canned yellowfin to the US market.

5.242 Regarding the countries whose products are already sold in the US market, Mexico argues that the market forces that currently limit the amount of their exports to the United States would remain the same following the withdrawal of the Tuna Measure.[277] This aspect of Mexico's argument would be reasonable if the current price of canned yellowfin in the US market were higher than or equal to the price generated by Mexico's model. That is, if the price generated by Mexico's model is higher than the prevailing price in the US market, the producers of other countries would tend to increase their exports to the United States. For Mexico to become the dominant supplier in the US market, it is necessary that the price of canned yellowfin decrease with Mexico's entry into the US market following the withdrawal of the Tuna Measure.

5.243 We note that the parties have not submitted information on the 2014 prices of canned yellowfin. Only some indirect evidence has been provided using 2015 export prices to the European Union.[278] Not only do we not have clear information on the price of wholesale yellowfin in the United States in 2014, it is also not clear to us how the quality of the canned yellowfin that Mexico's model assumes will be sold to the United States compares to the quality of the canned yellowfin currently sold in the US market. We observe, however, that, as noted above, it can reasonably be expected that Mexico would increase its exports of canned yellowfin to the United States following the withdrawal of the Tuna Measure. Such an increase in the supply of canned yellowfin would most likely decrease the price of this product in the US market. In such a situation, producers from other countries would not have any incentive to increase their exports to the United States. If anything, such a development would potentially decrease the exports from such countries. We therefore find this aspect of Mexico's assumption to be reasonable.

5.244 Regarding the effect of the withdrawal of the Tuna Measure on canned yellowfin suppliers whose products are not currently sold in the US market, we note that Mexico itself recognizes that countries that harvest tuna in the ETP would be affected by the withdrawal of the Measure.[279] Countries that can reasonably be expected to be affected by the withdrawal of the Tuna Measure are those that harvest yellowfin in the ETP by setting on dolphins and that, consequently, are not eligible for the dolphin-safe label in the US market. This group includes 11 countries: Belize, Bolivia, Colombia, Ecuador, El Salvador, Guatemala, Nicaragua, Panama, Peru, Vanuatu, and Venezuela. Of these 11

---

[277] Mexico's written submission, para. 174.

[278] United States' response to Arbitrator question No. 138; oral statement at the meeting with the Arbitrator, paras. 31-33.

[279] Mexico's response to Arbitrator question No. 18 (referring to NOAA Fisheries, Tuna/Dolphin Embargo Status Update, Exhibit MEX-72). See also fn. 44, Mexico's written submission: "other countries are affected by the tuna measure. But as discussed by Mexico before, it is not expected that they will be able to export canned yellowfin tuna on the U.S. market once the measure is removed".

countries, seven, i.e. Colombia, Ecuador, Guatemala, Mexico, Nicaragua, Panama, and Venezuela[280], were granted dolphin mortality limits (DMLs)[281] during the period 2012-2014, and eight had requested DMLs for the period 2015-2017.[282] While we are mindful of Mexico's argument that the United States maintains an embargo on imports of yellowfin tuna products from some of these countries, we note that Mexico itself recognizes that Ecuador and Guatemala harvest yellowfin by setting on dolphins, with no embargo being imposed by the United States on yellowfin from these countries. Therefore, the withdrawal of the Tuna Measure would likely encourage Ecuador and Guatemala, at least, to seek to expand their exports of canned yellowfin to the United States. However, the capacity of these two countries to export to the United States yellowfin caught by setting on dolphins and eligible to receive the AIDCP dolphin-safe label is limited. Each of these countries had only one vessel with a DML in 2014.[283] Further, neither of these countries benefit from preferential access to the US market. Therefore, we do not consider that they could in the short-term significantly increase their exports of canned yellowfin to the United States after the withdrawal of the Tuna Measure.

5.245 On this basis, we find plausible Mexico's argument that unaffected supplying countries would not be incentivized to sell canned yellowfin – and that affected suppliers would not contribute significantly to an increase in supply of canned yellowfin – to the US market after the withdrawal of the Tuna Measure.

> 5.1.3.3.3   Mexico would import canned yellowfin from other countries in the region to meet its own domestic demand

5.246 Mexico's model assumes that nearly all of Mexico's production of canned yellowfin will be exported to the United States and that Mexico will import the equivalent of 20,000 metric tonnes of canned yellowfin from other ETP countries in order to meet its domestic demand for canned yellowfin.[284] The United States disagrees with Mexico's argument, and maintains that the only ETP country that could provide this much yellowfin to Mexico is Ecuador, and it is not clear why Ecuador would prefer selling its yellowfin to Mexico rather than canning and exporting it to the United States itself.[285] The United States also

---

[280]   Exhibit USA-200.
[281]   We understand that in order to be eligible to receive the AIDCP dolphin-safe label, the vessel that harvests the tuna must have a DML. Thus, only tuna caught by those types of vessels could eventually compete with Mexican canned yellowfin in the US market.
[282]   Colombia, Ecuador, Guatemala, Mexico, Nicaragua, Panama, the United States and Venezuela. Exhibit USA-160.
[283]   Mexico's response to Arbitrator question No. 80.
[284]   Exhibit MEX-02, pp. 28-29.
[285]   United States' written submission, para. 118.

argues that Mexico could not make such purchases without causing an increase in yellowfin prices.[286]

5.247 In our view, Mexico would not necessarily need to purchase all of its imported yellowfin from a single ETP country, i.e. Ecuador. Indeed, Table 10 in Exhibit MEX-02 shows that the combined capacity of other ETP countries is greater than Ecuador's. We do not, however, need to deal with this argument because we reject Mexico's argument for reasons explained below.

5.248 We do not find Mexico's argument persuasive. To justify this assumption, Mexico would need to show either that one or more ETP countries would catch 20,000 metric tonnes in addition to the quantity currently harvested, or that one or more ETP countries would be willing to sell 20,000 metric tonnes of their yellowfin to Mexico rather than destine it for internal consumption or sell it to other countries.

5.249 In the first scenario, it is not clear whether catching the corresponding additional quantity of yellowfin tuna in the ETP would be allowed under other international rules, such as the IATTC, which regulates catches of tuna species in the ETP, monitors and takes corrective action if they rise above sustainable levels.[287]

5.250 In the second scenario, we do not understand how the market price could remain the same if certain suppliers decided to sell their product to Mexican canneries and not to the canneries in those countries to which they normally export. In this regard, we find it important to note that 20,000 metric tonnes represents a significant amount, given that the total equivalent quantity of canned yellowfin harvested in the ETP region from which Mexico intends to source its imports of yellowfin[288] was 55,388 metric tonnes in the year 2014.[289] In percentage terms, 20,000 metric tonnes amounts to 36% of total production from the mentioned ETP region. In our view, if Mexico were to purchase as significant a share as this, it would cause an increase in Mexico's import prices. Depending on the magnitude of such a price increase, Mexican producers might choose to sell part or all of their canned yellowfin in the Mexican market rather than exporting to the US market. Mexico submits that the United States has not demonstrated why Mexico's assumption about the availability of 20,000 metric tonnes of yellowfin from the South American countries is invalid.[290] In our view, however, it is for Mexico to demonstrate the validity of its own assumption before we would expect the United States to refute that assertion. Mexico has not done so.

5.251 Based on these considerations, we do not find plausible Mexico's argument that it could import the equivalent of 20,000 metric tonnes of canned

---

[286] United States' comments on Mexico's response to Arbitrator question No. 80.
[287] United States' written submission, para. 117, referring to Exhibits USA-43 and USA-52.
[288] See Exhibit MEX-02, table 10.
[289] Exhibit MEX-02, table 10.
[290] Mexico's comments on the United States' response to Arbitrator question No. 141.

yellowfin from other ETP countries in order to meet its domestic demand for canned yellowfin.

5.1.3.3.4   Conclusion

5.252 As we have explained, the third assumption underlying Mexico's model is based on three arguments, namely, (a) that the Mexican producers would be competitive *vis-à-vis* the US canneries and producers from other countries, (b) that no country other than Mexico would be significantly incentivized to export canned yellowfin to the United States after the withdrawal of the Tuna Measure, and (c) that Mexico would buy the equivalent of 20,000 metric tonnes of canned yellowfin from other ETP countries to meet the domestic demand for canned yellowfin in Mexico.

5.253 We find the first argument to be plausible mainly because of Mexico's geographical proximity to the US market and the tariff-free treatment that it enjoys as a NAFTA member. We have also agreed with the argument that the withdrawal of the Measure would not lead to a significant increase in the volume of exports to the United States of canned yellowfin from countries other than Mexico. In this regard, we have noted that the situation of countries that already export canned yellowfin to the United States would not change after the withdrawal of the Tuna Measure. As for the two ETP countries that might be affected by the withdrawal of the Tuna Measure, namely, Ecuador and Guatemala, we have noted that because their capacity is limited, they would not be in a position to significantly increase their exports to the United States in the short-term. However, we do not find plausible the third argument underlying this assumption, namely, that Mexico could import the equivalent of 20,000 metric tonnes of canned yellowfin from other ETP countries to meet its domestic demand for canned yellowfin. Mexico has not demonstrated to us that in the short-term there could be excess supply in the ETP which would allow Mexico to purchase the equivalent of 20,000 metric tonnes of canned yellowfin, without increasing the catch level in that region, or the price of fresh and frozen yellowfin in a way that would undermine Mexico's competitiveness *vis-à-vis* other countries that could supply the US market.

5.254 In the light of these findings, we conclude, overall, that Mexico's third assumption, which implies that it would be the dominant supplier of canned yellowfin in the US market following the withdrawal of the Tuna Measure, is a reasonable one. We consider that the fact that Mexico would be competitive *vis-à-vis* US canneries and suppliers from third countries, coupled with the fact that the third-country suppliers would not be incentivized to significantly increase their exports of canned yellowfin to the United States following the withdrawal of the Tuna Measure, supports this conclusion, even if we do not find plausible Mexico's argument about purchasing the equivalent of 20,000 metric tonnes of canned yellowfin. In our view, Mexico would still be the dominant supplier of canned yellowfin in the US market in the short-term even if it were not able to import the equivalent of 20,000 metric tonnes of canned yellowfin from the other ETP countries.

5.255 Having found that it is reasonable to assume that Mexico would be the dominant supplier of canned yellowfin to the United States after the withdrawal of the Tuna Measure, the next question is whether it is also appropriate that Mexico, for modelling purposes, disregards the supply of canned yellowfin from other sources and in its model treats Mexico as the sole supplier of that product to the United States, in order to facilitate the actual calculation of the level of nullification or impairment. For reasons explained in Section 6.2.2 below, we find this approach to be appropriate in calculating the level of nullification or impairment.

5.1.3.4   Conclusion on Mexico's proposed model

5.256 In the preceding paragraphs, we have described and critically analysed Mexico's proposed model. We have found that many but not all of the assumptions on which the model is based are reasonable. Therefore, we consider that it could, in principle, be appropriate for us to base our calculation on Mexico's model, provided that we respecified those assumptions that we have found to be unreasonable.

5.257 Before we could do so, however, we must examine the alternative model proposed by the United States, to determine whether it constitutes a reasonable or superior alternative to the model proposed by Mexico.

5.2   United States' Proposed Model for Determining the Level of Nullification or Impairment

5.2.1   Description of the model

5.258 The United States uses a model which examines Mexico's historical share in the US tuna products market prior to the adoption of the Dolphin Protection Consumer Information Act (DPCIA) and compares actual US imports from Mexico of tuna products with the 2013 Tuna Measure in place to the level of imports that would occur if the Measure were withdrawn. The United States contends that this approach is consistent with that taken by past arbitrators as well as with the evidence on the record.[291] According to the model presented by the United States, the level of nullification or impairment suffered by Mexico in the present case is between USD 8.5 and USD 21.9 million.[292]

5.259 The United States' model can be described as a five-step methodology geared towards calculating the hypothetical US imports of Mexican tuna products in the counterfactual scenario[293]:

    a.   The United States identifies Mexico's share in US imports of tuna products prior to the adoption of the DPCIA;

---

[291]   United States' written submission, para. 125.
[292]   United States' written submission, para. 137.
[293]   United States' written submission, paras. 124-137; Exhibit USA-81.

b.   it applies those percentages to current US imports of tuna products;

c.   it multiplies the projected import volumes by the average price of imported tuna products, excluding Mexican tuna products;

d.   it discounts the results from the previous step in order to account for the alleged current US consumer preference for tuna products produced from fishing methods other than setting on dolphins over tuna products produced from setting on dolphins; and

e.   it subtracts the value of Mexico's actual imports from the figure calculated in the previous step.

5.260 Regarding the first step, the United States explains that it identified exports of tuna products from Mexico to the United States in the period 1987-1989 and calculated Mexico's export share by volume, which amounted to 3.9%, with a historical high of 5.8% in 1987.[294] The United States considers 3.9% to be a reasonable estimate of what Mexico's annual share of US imports of tuna products would be in the absence of the Tuna Measure, and 5.8% to represent the highest possible share of potential imports that could be affected by the Tuna Measure. The United States explains that its approach uses Mexico's share in US imports of the covered products during the relevant historical period rather than absolute quantities of imports[295], and that although using Mexico's historical share of all tuna imports, rather than just tuna products, may overestimate the level of nullification or impairment, the resulting estimate is likely very close to Mexico's historical share in the US imports of tuna products.[296]

5.261 Regarding the second step, the United States explains that it applies the percentages obtained in the first step to current US imports of tuna products based on average annual imports of tuna products for 2013-2015.[297] The United States argues that during this three-year period, it imported on average 251,011 metric tonnes of tuna products, and that assigning Mexican tuna products a 3.9% share of imports at this level suggests that US imports of Mexican tuna products would be approximately 9,789 metric tonnes per year, and that at 5.8%, US imports of Mexican tuna products would be 14,559 metric tonnes a year.[298]

5.262 In the third step, the United States multiplies the projected quantity of Mexico's exports of tuna products by the average import price of tuna products from the world, excluding Mexico, for the period 2013-2015[299], resulting in an annual value of US imports of Mexican tuna products of USD 51.8 million,

---

[294] United States' written submission, para. 130. We note that the United States contends that using an average is preferred in cases like this as it smooths year-to-year anomalies and gives a more accurate picture of Mexico's market share during the relevant period.
[295] United States' written submission, para. 128.
[296] United States' written submission, para. 129.
[297] United States' written submission, para. 131 (referring to Exhibits USA-62 and USA-81).
[298] United States' written submission, para. 131.
[299] United States' written submission, para. 132.

based on a 3.9% share in overall US imports of tuna products, and USD 77.1 million, based on a 5.8% share in those imports. The United States explains that excluding imports from Mexico from the calculation of the average price of tuna products has the virtue of accounting for any price difference between Mexican tuna products and other tuna products due to the ineligibility of the Mexican product for the dolphin-safe label.[300]

5.263 In the fourth step, the United States discounts the figures obtained thus far to reflect its contention that producers and retailers would continue to differentiate tuna products produced from fishing methods other than setting on dolphins from tuna products produced from tuna caught by setting on dolphins.[301] The United States argues that these preferences are revealed in the commitments that many companies serving the US market have made to the EII not to produce, hold, or sell tuna products produced from setting on dolphins and that, as these commitments do not depend on the content of US law, they would not likely change even if the Tuna Measure were withdrawn.[302] According to the United States, retailers that account for [[xxx]]% of total consumption of tuna products in the US market have such policies. The United States introduces this discount in its model by multiplying the estimated value of imports of Mexican tuna products, the figure resulting from the third step, by 0.53 to reflect the market share available to tuna products produced from setting on dolphins.[303] This leads to a result of USD 27.45 million based on a 3.9% share in overall US imports of tuna products, and USD 40.8 million, based on a 5.8% share in those imports.

5.264 In the fifth step, the United States subtracts the value of current US imports of Mexican tuna products from the value of imports from Mexico that would have occurred in the counterfactual situation. Using the average actual value of US imports of Mexican tuna products for 2013-2015 produces a result, which, the United States argues, constitutes its estimate of the level of nullification or impairment, of USD 8.5 million, based on a 3.9% share in overall US imports of tuna products, and an upward bound of USD 21.9 million, based on a 5.8% share in those imports.[304]

5.2.2   Mexico's arguments on the United States' model

5.265 Mexico argues that the market-based approach proposed by the United States is flawed and underestimates losses suffered by Mexico because of the Tuna Measure.[305] For Mexico, the historical figures used in the United States' model are not indicative of the levels of imports in the case of the withdrawal of

---

[300]   *Ibid.*
[301]   United States' written submission, para. 134.
[302]   United States' written submission, para. 135.
[303]   United States' written submission, para. 136.
[304]   United States' written submission, para. 133.
[305]   Mexico's written submission, para. 177.

the Tuna Measure because these import volumes occurred more than 25 years ago, at a time when market conditions were very different from those observed in 2014.[306] Mexico considers that the historical market share approach suggested by the United States leads to a flawed counterfactual because market conditions prevailing at the time of adoption of the Tuna Measure in 1990 were not the same as the conditions in 2014.[307]

5.266 Mexico presents several reasons why the market conditions have changed between the period 1987-1989 and 2014. First, Mexico argues that the United States maintained a trade embargo on imports of Mexican tuna from 1980-1986 and that when the United States lifted the embargo, it pressured Mexico to agree to "voluntarily" restrain exports to the United States.[308] Second, Mexico contends that the 1987-1989 period does not correspond to what would be observed following the withdrawal of the Tuna Measure in 2014 because Mexican firms now have much better access to the US market due to Mexico's membership in NAFTA. In particular, Mexico notes that while the applicable duty rate in the 1987-1989 period was 35% for tuna products in oil and 12.5% for tuna products not in oil, as a NAFTA member, Mexico can now export canned tuna to the United States free of customs duties.[309] Third, Mexico submits that the US market was essentially emptied of canned yellowfin in 2014, while during 1987-1989 the market for canned yellowfin was occupied by US domestic production.[310] Mexico underlines that competition in the canned yellowfin market was "stiff"[311] in the 1987-1989 period and that prior to the enactment of the Tuna Measure in 1990, US canneries processed large quantities of yellowfin from domestic and imported sources. Mexico argues that in this period, canned yellowfin tuna produced by US companies competed with Mexican canned tuna in the US market, and limited the presence of Mexican canned tuna in the US market. However, Mexico submits that the US fleet has since moved out of the ETP, and that the US canning industry has changed so significantly that it is no longer capable of processing large quantities of yellowfin from the ETP.[312] In Mexico's view, it follows from these reasons that the market segment in which Mexico specializes is currently not occupied, and that it can therefore be expected that Mexico's market share after the withdrawal of the Tuna Measure will be much larger than what it was in the 1987-1989 period.[313]

5.267 Mexico also contends that the United States' model does not control for the shifts that have been made in Mexico's production from raw and frozen tuna

---

[306] Mexico's written submission, para. 178
[307] Mexico's written submission, paras. 177 and 178.
[308] Mexico's written submission, para. 179.
[309] Mexico's written submission, para. 180 (referring to Exhibit MEX-68).
[310] Mexico's response to Arbitrator question No. 112.
[311] Mexico's written submission, para. 181.
[312] *Ibid.*
[313] Mexico's response to Arbitrator question No. 112.

to canned tuna products. Mexico notes in particular that the fact that Mexico exported a certain quantity of raw yellowfin to the United States in the period 1987-1989 does not mean that Mexico would export the same quantity of canned yellowfin to the United States in 2014, because it has since modernized its boats and canning facilities. Mexico submits that the shift in production has implications on production costs that are not taken into account in the United States' model and argues that the Mexican canned tuna industry is now vertically integrated, making it even more cost-efficient. For these reasons, Mexico contends that it would export much higher quantities of canned yellowfin to the United States than its exports of raw yellowfin in 1987-1989.[314]

5.2.3   Arbitrator's analysis

5.268 As we did before with Mexico's model, we will, in this Section, identify and assess the main assumptions underlying the United States' model. The United States' model rests on two main assumptions: (a) that US imports of tuna products from Mexico in the period 1987-1989 provide a reasonable basis to estimate the quantity of US imports of tuna products from Mexico in 2014, and (b) that even if the Tuna Measure were withdrawn, some of the retailers in the US market would still not carry Mexican canned yellowfin due to the fact that they have made commitments not to produce, hold, or sell tuna products produced from setting on dolphins. We will assess each of these assumptions in turn.

5.2.3.1   US imports of tuna products from Mexico in the period 1987-1989 provide a reasonable basis to estimate the quantity of US imports of tuna products from Mexico in 2014

5.269 To recall, in the first step of its methodology, the United States uses the value of US imports of tuna products from Mexico in the 1987-1989 period and calculates Mexico's share, by volume, in overall US imports of such products.[315] The United States considers the resulting figures to be a reasonable estimate of what Mexico's annual share of US imports of tuna products would be in the absence of the Tuna Measure.[316] In contrast, as we mentioned in Section 5.2.2 above, Mexico contends that the approach taken by the United States is not instructive of the levels of imports in the scenario where the Tuna Measure is withdrawn, because these import volumes were observed more than 25 years ago, at a time when market conditions were very different from those observed in 2014.[317] The gist of Mexico's argument is that because a proper counterfactual keeps everything but the measure of interest constant, and because market

---

[314] *Ibid*.
[315] United States' written submission, para. 130.
[316] *Ibid*.
[317] Mexico's written submission, para. 178.

conditions when the tuna measure was enacted in 1990 were not the same as in 2014, the United States' approach is flawed.[318]

5.270 The issue before us with respect to the first assumption is whether the market conditions in the period 1987-1989 were sufficiently similar to the conditions in 2014 such that the volume of exports of tuna products from Mexico to the United States in 1987-1989 represents "a reasonable estimate"[319] for what the volume of Mexico's exports of canned yellowfin to the United States in 2014 would have been in the event of withdrawal of the Tuna Measure.[320]

5.271 In response to Mexico's arguments regarding the United States' methodology, the United States argues that neither the fact that there were voluntary export restraints during the period mentioned by Mexico, nor the fact that Mexico is now a signatory to NAFTA, renders the United States' methodology inappropriate for calculating of the level of nullification or impairment caused to Mexico.[321] Regarding the first point, the United States contends that while the United States and Mexico agreed to certain voluntary export restraints on Mexico's total exports of tuna and tuna products to the United States, Mexico's actual exports of such products to the United States were below the agreed level in each of the three years during which the restraints were in place.[322] Regarding the second point, the United States argues that data on Mexico's pre- and post-NAFTA exports of other seafood products to the United States, as well as data on other countries' exports of canned tuna to the United States, demonstrate that Mexico's share in the overall US imports of tuna products would not be significantly different in 2014 from its share in the 1987-1989 period simply because NAFTA came into effect.[323] The United States also contends that the structure of the US market has been remarkably consistent over the past 25 years, and that changes in the Mexican tuna industry (away from exporting loins towards exporting canned products) do not suggest that Mexico's overall share in the United States' tuna product imports would be affected. Rather, in the United States' view, Mexican producers would simply export a higher value product, since the overall capacity of Mexico's tuna industry is essentially unchanged from the late 1980s.[324]

5.272 The United States further submits that its model controls for certain other factors mentioned by Mexico, namely, the location and capacity of US canneries and the capacity of Mexican canneries, by using Mexico's market share of all

---

[318] Mexico's written submission, paras. 177 and 178.
[319] United States' written submission, para. 130.
[320] *Ibid.*
[321] United States' response to Arbitrator question No. 56.
[322] United States' response to Arbitrator question No. 56 (referring to Exhibits USA-111 and USA-142).
[323] United States' response to Arbitrator question No. 56.
[324] United States' response to Arbitrator question No. 155.

tuna products as the baseline.[325] The United States argues that Mexico has not explained the "many other reasons" allegedly showing that the 1987-1989 period was different from 2014,[326] despite the fact that US tuna products imports have been remarkably consistent over the past 25 years.

5.273 We note that there is a difference of approximately 25 years between the period 1987-1989 and the year 2014, which is the year for which we determine the level of nullification or impairment in these proceedings. We consider this gap to be too substantial to justify the United States' reliance on this historical comparison. We do not find reasonable the assumption that the state of the world in the period 1987-1989 was sufficiently similar to 2014 to justify such a comparison. We are not saying that for a comparison to be reasonable the time periods compared must in all cases be very close. However, where the periods compared are as distant as they are in the US model, we would expect a persuasive explanation why such a comparison is reasonable, despite the very substantial gap. On balance, we are not persuaded by the explanations provided by the United States. For example, the United States argues that trends in imports of other seafood products from Mexico and of canned tuna from other countries "suggest that the fact that 1987-1989 pre-date NAFTA does not render the US counterfactual inappropriate"[327]. In our view, however, this argument does not suffice to justify such a comparison. For this argument to amount to a *prima facie* showing, we would have expected the United States to demonstrate, for instance, that these other US seafood products markets behaved similarly to the US tuna products market before the Tuna Measure, and that they have been facing similar types of market changes since. In our view, given the substantial gap between these two periods, significant changes would have occurred in the market, including, but not limited to, those referred to by Mexico, for instance the fact that the Mexican tuna industry is now vertically integrated and that Mexico is a signatory of the NAFTA. We are not convinced that all such changes have been described and adequately controlled for in the US model.

5.274 We therefore do not find it reasonable to base our calculation of the level of nullification or impairment on a comparison between Mexico's shares in overall US imports of tuna products in the 1987-1989 period and 2014.

---

[325] United States' oral statement at the meeting with the Arbitrator, para. 65.
[326] United States' oral statement at the meeting with the Arbitrator, para. 65 (referring to Mexico's written submission, para. 182).
[327] United States' response to Arbitrator question No. 56.

5.2.3.2   Some of the retailers in the US market would
           still not carry Mexican canned yellowfin due to
           the fact that they have made commitments not
           to produce, hold, or sell tuna products
           produced from setting on dolphins

5.275 The second assumption underpinning the US model is that even if the
Tuna Measure were withdrawn, some of the retailers in the US market would
still not carry Mexican canned yellowfin because they have made commitments
not to produce, hold, or sell tuna products produced from setting on dolphins.

5.276 We have examined this argument presented by the United States in
assessing Mexico's methodology in Section 5.1.3.2.2 above, and concluded that
it was reasonable to assume that US retailers representing 26.9%[328] of all tuna
product sales in the US market would not carry Mexican canned yellowfin even
if the Tuna Measure were withdrawn. For the same reasons, we find it
reasonable to assume that some retailers would not carry Mexican canned
yellowfin even after the Tuna Measure has been removed.

5.2.3.3   Conclusion on the United States' proposed
           model

5.277 For the foregoing reasons, we decline to use the US model in our
assessment of the nullification or impairment in these proceedings. We will,
however, incorporate elements of the United States' assumption that some of the
retailers in the US market would still not carry Mexican canned yellowfin
because of their commitments, in our calculation of the level of nullification or
impairment.

5.3   Overall Conclusion

5.278 In the preceding paragraphs, the Arbitrator has addressed the models that
Mexico and the United States have submitted, as well as the assumptions
underpinning them. In this process, we have described both models and
highlighted the main concerns we have.

5.279 To recall, Mexico presents a calibrated partial equilibrium model of the
US and Mexican canned tuna markets.[329] It consists of a set of equations
purporting to describe the US and Mexican tuna markets by defining (a) the
demand for canned tuna in the United States and Mexico, respectively, (b) the
supply of canned tuna in the United States and Mexico, respectively, and (c) the
market equilibrium conditions in the US and Mexican markets for canned
tuna.[330] We note that Mexico's model is underpinned by three main assumptions,

---

[328] As explained in para. 5.84, 26.9% reflects the total share of consumption covered by retailers'
statements ([[xxx]]% minus Walmart's market share [[xxx]]%).
[329] Mexico's methodology paper, para. 27.
[330] Mexico's methodology paper, paras. 20-40; Exhibit MEX-02, pp. 4-27.

namely, that (a) the Tuna Measure has restricted the supply of canned yellowfin from Mexico into the United States; (b) that US consumers have a preference for canned yellowfin and US retailers would sell Mexican canned yellowfin after the withdrawal of the Tuna Measure; and (c) that Mexican producers would supply all of the increased consumption of canned yellowfin in the US market following the withdrawal of the Tuna Measure. We found that, on the whole, these assumptions are reasonable, although we are not convinced by some of Mexico's intermediate arguments, in particular its arguments that (a) all US retailers would be willing to sell canned yellowfin imported from Mexico and (b) Mexico would export all of its canned yellowfin to the United States and import yellowfin from other producing countries to produce canned yellowfin for its domestic consumption.

5.280 With respect to the United States' model, we recall that that model is based on Mexico's historical share in the US tuna products market prior to the adoption of the Tuna Measure. It compares actual US imports from Mexico of tuna products with the Tuna Measure in place with the level of imports, that would occur if the Measure were withdrawn. We have explained above that the United States' model would not be a reasonable basis for our calculation of the level of nullification or impairment caused by the 2013 Tuna Measure because it bases Mexico's share in the US tuna market on historical data that goes too far back into the past.

5.281 Thus, for the reasons given above, we conclude that both of the models proposed by the parties have shortcomings. Accordingly, in our view, neither model, at least as initially presented by the parties, provides an appropriate basis for our calculation of the level of nullification or impairment caused by the 2013 Tuna Measure.

5.282 Assessing the two models in comparative terms, we recall that the fundamental difference between Mexico's and the United States' arguments is that Mexico is of the view that the Tuna Measure restricted the supply of canned yellowfin from Mexico to the United States, whereas the United States maintains that the decline in supply has been due to weak demand for canned yellowfin in the US market. As we have explained, we think that the evidence on the record tends on the whole to support Mexico's assertion that the Tuna Measure has restricted the supply of yellowfin tuna to the US market. We also agree with Mexico that the evidence demonstrates the existence of demand in the US market for canned yellowfin, and establishes that Mexico would be a competitive supplier of canned yellowfin. Accordingly, it would in our view be possible to base our calculation on a modified version of Mexico's model, that is, a version of Mexico's model that replaces those assumptions we have not found to be reasonable with other assumptions that we think better reflect the counterfactual on which we base our assessment.

5.283 We recall that, in assessing the level of nullification or impairment caused by the 2013 Tuna Measure, we are not bound to base our calculation on either Mexico's or the United States' model. We could, in principle, attempt to develop an alternative model that would more accurately represent our understanding of the relevant counterfactual.

5.284 The most plausible alternative approach would be the so-called "price wedge method", whereby one would first determine the tariff equivalent of the US dolphin-safe label, and then model the effect of its removal on the equilibrium price and quantity of Mexican canned tuna products sold in the United States.[331] However, as both parties acknowledge, the data on the record does not allow the Arbitrator to apply the price wedge approach, because the data does not allow for a comparison between the price of labelled and unlabelled tuna products.[332]

5.285 As we are unable to develop an alternative model, and because we find the theory underlying Mexico's model more convincing than the theory underlying the United States' model, we will base our calculation on a respecified version of Mexico's model.

5.286 In practical terms, this means that we will use a partial equilibrium model to calculate the level of nullification or impairment. Partial equilibrium models are used to calculate the equilibrium price and quantity in a certain market. Market demand and supply curves are constructed on the basis of consumer preferences and income, production technology, input costs, and conditions of competition, among other factors.[333] The equilibrium price and quantity of the goods at issue in the specific market are found by equating supply and demand.[334]

5.287 As the United States also recognizes, "partial equilibrium models are often used to show the impact of a policy change, which is modelled as an exogenous change in supply or demand, as appropriate".[335] In the case at hand, the parties have proposed to calculate the level of nullification or impairment as the export loss, i.e. the difference between the counterfactual level of exports of canned tuna (in the case of the withdrawal of the 2013 Tuna Measure) and the actual level of exports, with both levels being determined for the year 2014. A partial equilibrium model can therefore be used to analyse the impact of the withdrawal of the Tuna Measure – which, in economic terms, can be conceived of as an exogenous shift in supply – on Mexico's exports of canned tuna to the United States. Indeed, as discussed above, the Arbitrator considers reasonable Mexico's assumption that the Tuna Measure has restricted Mexico's supply of canned yellowfin to the US market and therefore finds it reasonable to model the counterfactual as a shift to the right of the supply curve of canned yellowfin

---

[331] United States' written submission, paras. 84 and 86.
[332] United States' written submission, paras. 81-87; response to Arbitrator question No. 62; Mexico's written submission, para. 172.
[333] Exhibit USA-55, p. 3.
[334] Exhibit USA-55, p. 8.
[335] United States' written submission, para. 83.

from Mexico to the United States, reflecting the expected increase in supply under the counterfactual.

5.288 In conclusion, it is the Arbitrator's view that, if appropriately implemented, the partial equilibrium modelling approach proposed by Mexico is a reasonable methodology to estimate the export losses caused by the Tuna Measure. Accordingly, in the following Section we will calculate the level of nullification or impairment on the basis of a respecified partial equilibrium model.

6. THE ARBITRATOR'S OWN DETERMINATION OF THE LEVEL OF NULLIFICATION OR IMPAIRMENT

6.289 The Arbitrator now turns to its own assessment of the level of nullification or impairment caused by the 2013 Tuna Measure. In particular, we will begin by examining the demand and supply function of canned tuna products in Mexico and in the United States and the parametrization of the model. Subsequently, we will discuss our calculation of the level of nullification or impairment and discuss the reasonableness of the result in the light of the issues raised by the parties during the proceedings.

6.1 Demand for Canned Tuna

6.290 The Arbitrator begins by examining the demand and supply function of canned tuna products in Mexico and in the United States. We note first that a preliminary decision to take when defining the demand function in a market is how to model consumer preferences among different varieties of goods. To simplify the model and allow for its numerical simulations, different varieties of a good (in this case, different varieties of canned tuna) may need to be treated as a composite good.

6.1.1 Modelling consumers' choices across different varieties of canned tuna

6.291 As we have explained above in our description of Mexico's model, Mexico constructs the demand for canned tuna in the United States assuming that consumers take their decisions as to how much yellowfin to consume at a given price of yellowfin, taking into consideration the price of generic tuna (an aggregate of all other types of tuna) and their preferences for yellowfin.

6.292 We specify the demand for canned tuna in both the United States and Mexico based on Mexico's quality differentiation model.[336] Consumers choose between two products, canned yellowfin and canned generic tuna. We define the former as canned tuna that includes 100% yellowfin, in chunk or any other form.

---

[336] Exhibit MEX-02, pp. 11-33.

We define the latter as canned tuna that either does not include yellowfin or includes yellowfin mixed with other tuna, such as skipjack, in which case the canned tuna product is not made of 100% yellowfin.[337]

6.293 The United States argues that Mexico's use of the choice (or hedonic) model to model consumer demand for the product is incorrect, and that the standard way to model consumer demand for a product that is already on the market would be the almost ideal demand system (AIDS) model.[338] Even though the AIDS model is used extensively in the economic literature as a way to test and calibrate demand (and indeed, Mexico refers to several studies using the AIDS model to estimate elasticity for canned tuna), we consider it more appropriate to model demand for canned tuna with the choice model in these proceedings, for several reasons. First, as recognised in the literature, in its simple static form, the AIDS model does not provide a fully satisfactory explanation of consumers' behaviour.[339] Second, as Mexico argues, the AIDS model "is an empirical model of demand ... typically used to estimate elasticities of demand (own-price, cross-price and income)".[340] However, the AIDS model "cannot provide information about consumers' valuation of different tuna species".[341] It is therefore not clear to us how the AIDS model could be used in the context of our model, taking into account the data on the record. Accordingly, in our view, the appropriate model is the hedonic model, which is used in Mexico's methodology paper.

6.1.2   Aggregation across tuna species

6.294 The United States further argues that it is wrong to aggregate light meat tuna, such as skipjack, and albacore, in the same composite good. We recall in this regard that, in Mexico's model, there are two types of canned tuna products: yellowfin and generic. This distinction is based on assumed quality differences between higher quality yellowfin and lower quality generic tuna, broadly defined to include skipjack, albacore and tongol.[342]

6.295 In the view of the United States, Mexico errs in aggregating demand for albacore and light tuna.[343] The United States asserts that "Mexico could have justified its aggregation of skipjack and albacore in one (or both) of two ways, either with Hicks' Composite Commodity Theorem, as Mexico has tried to do, or with the Leontief-Sono separability assumption. However, neither of these holds

---

[337]   We note that Mexico argues that the type of tuna that Mexico would export to the United States under the counterfactual is canned tuna that includes 100% yellowfin (see Mexico's response to Arbitrator question No. 83, para. 57).

[338]   United States' written submission, footnote 165 (referring to Exhibit USA-8).

[339]   A. Deaton and J. Muellbauer (1980), "An Almost Ideal Demand System," *American Economic Review* 70(3): 312–326.

[340]   Mexico's response to Arbitrator question No. 34.

[341]   *Ibid.*

[342]   Exhibit MEX-02, p. 11.

[343]   United States' response to Arbitrator question No. 64.

in this instance".[344] In the United States' view, the US tuna product market is made up of a variety of products – not only "yellowfin" and "generic" as Mexico assumes.[345] The market has a low-end portion, composed of "light tuna" – a mixture of skipjack, yellowfin, tongol, and/or big-eye tuna – and a high-end portion, dominated by "white tuna" (i.e. albacore).[346] According to the United States, albacore is more similar to canned premium yellowfin than to generic light tuna.[347] Consequently, albacore and generic light tuna do not fall into the category of products that – according to the Leontief-Sono separability condition – can properly be aggregated into a composite commodity *vis-à-vis* yellowfin. According to the United States, this is because the marginal rate of substitution between skipjack and albacore is not independent of yellowfin.[348]

6.296 With regard to the requirements of the Hicks' composite commodity theorem, the parties agree that the aggregation of tuna species such as skipjack and albacore in a single composite good is valid if the conditions stated in the theorem hold, i.e. if the prices of the group of aggregated goods change proportionally.[349] The parties disagree, however, on whether the Hicks' composite commodity theorem is satisfied in this case.

6.297 Mexico argues that the theorem is indeed satisfied in this case. In Mexico's view, the demand for canned generic tuna and the demand for canned albacore tuna respond in the same way (i.e. shifting to the left) to the decline in the price of canned yellowfin. According to Mexico, this is true even though the two types of product are of different qualities.[350] Mexico further refers to the results of an academic study showing that both skipjack and albacore are substitute goods for yellowfin (both have positive cross price elasticities with respect to yellowfin).[351]

6.298 By contrast, the United States argues that the conditions of the theorem are not met. This is because there is evidence from the above-mentioned academic study of statistically significant substitution elasticities between albacore and skipjack, and because "the price of canned albacore and all other canned tuna imports (a reliable proxy for skipjack) do not always move in the same direction, let alone proportionally, to the price of all canned tuna imports".[352]

---

[344] United States' comments on Mexico's response to Arbitrator question No. 86.
[345] United States' written submission, para. 102.
[346] *Ibid.*
[347] United States' response to Arbitrator question No. 64.
[348] United States' response to Arbitrator question No. 64; comments on Mexico's response to Arbitrator question No. 86, para. 53.
[349] Mexico's response to Arbitrator question No. 86; United States' comments on Mexico's response to Arbitrator question No. 86.
[350] Mexico's response to Arbitrator question No. 38 (referring to Exhibit USA-8).
[351] Mexico's response to Arbitrator question No. 86.
[352] United States' comments on Mexico's response to Arbitrator question No. 86.

6.299 We understand that there may be reasons for a more detailed disaggregation of the model for the calculation of the level of nullification or impairment. However, a model with individual demand for canned skipjack and canned albacore would be significantly more complex and less transparent than a model with non-yellowfin products aggregated into a single composite commodity.[353] Furthermore, while the parties acknowledge that albacore and yellowfin are both premium products, the evidence on the record indicates that US consumers have also been paying a premium for canned yellowfin as compared to canned albacore, and not only as compared to skipjack.[354] We further note that the price data in Exhibit US-214 actually show a significant co-movement of the prices of albacore and skipjack in the period 1989-2015 (although admittedly not in every single year). In the light of this evidence on the record, and accounting for the potential repercussions of working with a more complex and less transparent model, we consider it reasonable to simplify the modelling of the US canned tuna market by assuming that it is made up of two product types: generic tuna and yellowfin.

6.300 Having determined that we can model the demand for canned tuna in both the United States and Mexico as a consumer decision between two products, canned yellowfin and canned generic tuna, we now proceed to specify the demand equations. As further detailed in equations 1, 2, 3 and 4 in Appendix 1 to this Decision, the demand for each canned tuna product (yellowfin or generic) in each country[355] depends on the price of the product[356]; preferences for yellowfin versus generic tuna[357]; and two parameters, the demand intensity and the elasticity of demand.[358] In the United States, the demand for each canned tuna product (yellowfin or generic) also depends on a third parameter, namely the share of US retailers that would sell Mexican canned yellowfin. We now proceed to discuss all the determinants of the demand for canned tuna in the two countries, starting with the distribution of preferences.

6.1.3   Distribution of preferences and its functional form

6.301 Consumer preferences for yellowfin versus generic tuna depend on how much a consumer prefers yellowfin to generic tuna, relative to how much higher is the price of yellowfin than the price of generic tuna.[359] All consumers with a

---

[353] Mexico's response to Arbitrator question No. 38.

[354] Mexico's response to Arbitrator question No. 79.

[355] Respectively, Q_{yus} for the demand for yellowfin in the United States in equation 1; Q_{gus} for the demand for generic in the United States in equation 2; Q_{ymx} for the demand for yellowfin in Mexico in equation 3; and Q_{gmx} for the demand for generic in Mexico in equation 4.

[356] Respectively, p_{yus} for the price of yellowfin in the United States; p_{gus} for the price of generic in the United States; p_{ymx} for the price of yellowfin in Mexico; and p_{gmx} for the price of generic in Mexico.

[357] Respectively, the functions $H(\cdot)_{us}$ for the United States and $H(\cdot)_{mx}$ for Mexico.

[358] The demand intensities are denoted A_{us} and A_{mx} for the United States and Mexico, respectively. The demand elasticity is the parameter η.

[359] Exhibit MEX-02, pp. 11-13.

"willingness to pay" for yellowfin below the price premium for yellowfin (p, defined as $p_y - p_g$) will only purchase generic tuna. All consumers with a "willingness to pay" for yellowfin above the price premium p will only purchase yellowfin. The share of consumers purchasing generic tuna, $H(\cdot)$, and the share of consumers purchasing yellowfin, $1 - H(\cdot)$, will therefore depend on the price premium p, that is $H(\cdot) = H(p)$.

6.302 Mexico assumes, both for US and Mexican consumers, a logistic distributional form for the function $H(p)$.[360] Accordingly, the function $H(p)$ is equal to $\left(\dfrac{1}{1 + e^{\frac{\mu - y}{s}}}\right)$, where $e(\cdot)$ is the exponential function. With this specification, $H(p)$ is increasing in the price premium p (i.e., the larger the price premium, the larger the share of consumers that will purchase generic tuna). Furthermore, it depends on two parameters: the mean and median willingness to pay (henceforth, "mean willingness to pay") for canned yellowfin over canned generic tuna among consumers (μ), and a scale parameter (s), which determines the dispersion of the distribution (the larger s, the more dispersed the distribution).

6.303 We accept the assumption that the function $H(p)$ can be parameterized with a logistic functional form, both in the case of US consumers and in the case of Mexican consumers, for the following three reasons. First, the United States argues that a logistic function does not describe the US distribution of willingness to pay for tuna, because many US consumers show a high sensitivity to price. This is shown, according to the United States, by the fact that nearly half of all US sales of canned tuna are at discounted (sale) prices.[361] Mexico counters this argument by contending that there is nothing in the logistic distribution that impedes the demand for canned yellowfin being sensitive to its price.[362] We agree with Mexico on this point. Second, the United States contends that an exponential distribution for US consumers' willingness to pay should be adopted.[363] However, the United States does not offer a compelling argument for using an exponential distribution to model US consumers' preferences.[364] Third, the parties agree that by manipulating the logistic functional form, the willingness to pay can easily be parameterized based on actual consumption shares $H(p)$ and $1 - H(p)$ observed in the United States and in Mexico in 2014. We will follow the procedure suggested by the parties when assigning parameter values to μ for the United States and Mexico.

6.304 The scale parameter of the logistic distribution and the mean willingness to pay are parameters (not variables to be solved for) of the model. We therefore need to assign values to them (that is, "parameterize" them).

---

[360] Exhibit MEX-02, p. 14 (referring to equation 8 therein).
[361] United States' written submission, para. 105.
[362] Mexico's response to Arbitrator question No. 37.
[363] United States' response to Arbitrator question No. 71.
[364] Mexico's response to Arbitrator question No. 102.

6.1.3.1   Parameterization of the scale parameter of the
           logistic distribution

6.305 Mexico proposes to use $s = 1$, arguing that this is common in the empirical literature for logistic regression models.[365] Mexico provides sensitivity analysis showing that the higher the scale parameter s, the larger the export loss.[366] The United States disagrees, arguing that Mexico has presented no evidence to explain the basis for parameterizing $s = 1$ and asserts that a scale parameter equal to 1 concentrates the majority of consumers close to the centre of preference.[367] We are not persuaded that the latter is a problem, and we note that the United States does not suggest a different s. We therefore accept the parameterization $s = 1$, both in the United States and in Mexico.

6.1.3.2   Parameterization of the mean willingness to
           pay

6.306 To parameterize the mean willingness to pay μ, Mexico initially assumed a value of USD 2/kg, both for the United States and for Mexico. Mexico submitted that there is no reason to believe that preferences for canned tuna should differ across the two countries.[368] We disagree with this contention because, as the United States contends, "Mexican and U.S. consumer preferences differ both in general terms and in specific preferences for food products".[369] In what follows, we proceed to parameterize the mean "willingness to pay" for the United States and Mexico based on the observed yellowfin shares in the overall consumption of canned tuna in 2014.

6.1.3.2.1   Willingness to pay in the United
             States

6.307 To justify the assumed value of USD 2/kg for the mean willingness to pay, Mexico initially argued that it was following a conservative approach, assuming that the mean willingness to pay for canned yellowfin was much lower than an econometrically-estimated premium.[370] The United States asserts that the USD 2/kg value assigned by Mexico to the mean willingness to pay for canned yellowfin over generic tuna products is a mere assumption and divorced from the reality of the US market.[371] Despite this disagreement, the parties agree that canned yellowfin only represented a share of 1.2% of the US canned tuna market

---

[365] Mexico's response to Arbitrator question No. 92.
[366] Exhibit MEX-02, p. 46 (referring to Figure 5 therein).
[367] United States' comments on Mexico's response to Arbitrator question No. 92, para. 70; written submission, para. 90.
[368] Mexico's written submission, para. 160.
[369] United States' written submission, para. 100.
[370] Exhibit MEX-02, p. 20.
[371] United States' written submission, para. 104.

in 2014.[372] Thus, at our substantive meeting with the parties, the United States proposed a method to parameterize the mean willingness to pay with simple algebraic manipulations of the logistic functional form for the function $H(p)$, based on yellowfin's 1.2% share in overall canned tuna product consumption in 2014 and an econometrically-estimated price premium.[373]

6.308 We accept the methodology proposed by the United States to parameterize the mean willingness to pay in the United States. Since parameterization is meant to reflect the *status quo*, that is, the current conditions, we consider it reasonable to use all available information – and in particular, the share of canned yellowfin in total US tuna product consumption – when assigning parameter values. Mexico accepts the approach[374], and we are therefore proceeding in a manner that is consistent with the parties' views on this issue.

6.309 Since, as explained above, μ is chosen as the solution to the equation, $\mu = s \cdot \ln\left[\dfrac{1-H(p)}{H(p)}\right] + p$, the determination of the price premium p is crucial to the determination of μ. To determine the value of p, Mexico proposes a hedonic regression model, in which the dependent variable is the price of canned tuna in the United States, expressed in USD per kilogram, and the explanatory variables are its attributes (size, form, type of container, flavour, pack and salt content).[375] Mexico relies on scanner data for canned tuna by Universal Product Code and presented in Exhibit MEX-15 (the Nielsen data). These data come in two sets, a 12-week period and a 52-week period dataset. Both datasets contain a breakdown of total sales, number of units sold, and average price per US region (East North Central, East South Central, Middle Atlantic, Mountain, New England, Pacific, South Atlantic, West North Central and West South Central).

6.310 Mexico estimates the premium for canned yellowfin sold in the United States using the coefficient on the dummy variable "yellowfin", i.e., a variable equal to 1 if the canned tuna is yellowfin, and zero if it is not. This variable captures all attributes of canned yellowfin (other than size, form, type of container, brand, region etc.) that differ from generic tuna but that are not controlled for in the regression model.[376]

---

[372] Mexico's response to Arbitrator question No. 150; United States' comments on Mexico's response to Arbitrator question No. 150.

[373] The United States' methodology in this respect is to solve equation (8) in Exhibit MEX-02 (p. 14) for the variable μ, yielding $\mu = s \cdot \ln\left[\dfrac{1-H(p)}{H(p)}\right] + p$, where p is the econometrically-estimated price premium; $H(p) = 0.988$ (since the share of canned yellowfin in the United States, $1 - H(p)$, is 0.012); and s is assumed to be equal to 1. See Exhibit USA-150.

[374] See Mexico's opening statement at the meeting of the Arbitrator, para. 45; Mexico's response to Arbitrator question No. 121.

[375] Exhibit MEX-02, pp. 16-17.

[376] Exhibit MEX-02, p. 19.

6.311 We note that the parties disagree on four issues regarding the econometric estimation of the price premium. First, Mexico deletes observations where the quantity sold is zero.[377] Second, Mexico proposes two alternative econometric specifications for each of the two datasets: ordinary least squares (OLS) and weighted least squares (WLS). The WLS method uses the number of units sold as weights in the regression, such that the more the units of a product sold, the more the product's weight in the regression model.[378] Third, Mexico estimates an additional premium for yellowfin because it is offered in more desirable forms than generic tuna.[379] Fourth, the United States submits that it is necessary to adjust the econometrically estimated premium for a mark-up from import to retail.[380]

6.312 Regarding the first issue, namely the deletion of observations where the quantity sold is zero, the United States notes that the need to remove over 60% of observations due to lack of sales demonstrates that the dataset is not representative of the entire market.[381] Mexico disagrees, arguing that "several of these [canned tuna] products were not sold at the time when the data were collected and may not have been sold for years. The quantities for these products appear as zero".[382] When a product is not sold, there is no recorded price, and it is impossible to include zero quantity observations in the regressions. Therefore, the deletion of zero quantity observations is, in Mexico's view, "the only way to proceed" and "a necessity rather than a matter of choice".[383] We find Mexico's position reasonable because there is no way to include missing data in a regression. We therefore follow Mexico's position in our assessment.

6.313 Concerning the second issue, namely the regression methodology, Mexico argues that the WLS regressions are to be preferred to the OLS regressions for two reasons: first, if the number of units sold is not used as weight, the high-priced generic tuna biases down the estimated premium for canned yellowfin; and second, the WLS regressions have a much better fit (higher R-squared) than the OLS regressions.[384] The United States argues that using the OLS regressions "is standard unless there is reason to think that the data observations are measured with varying degrees of precision and/or data are heteroskedastic, and Mexico advances no such reason".[385] At our substantive meeting with the parties, the United States expressed the view that – if a

---

[377] Exhibit MEX-02, p. 18.
[378] *Ibid.*
[379] See Exhibit MEX-02, pp. 18-19; Mexico's comments on the United States' response to Arbitrator question No. 141.
[380] United States' response to Arbitrator question No. 141.
[381] United States' written submission, para. 104.
[382] Mexico's response to Arbitrator question No. 49.
[383] Mexico's response to Arbitrator question Nos. 49 and 50.
[384] Exhibit MEX-02, p. 20.
[385] United States' response to Arbitrator question No. 71, footnote 289. In econometrics, the concept of heteroscedasticity (from Ancient Greek *hetero* "different" and *skedasis* "dispersion") refers to the presence of different variances across sub-groups of the error term of a regression.

weighted regression approach should be used at all – the weights in the WLS regression ought to be in terms of volumes (kilograms) rather than number of units sold.[386] Moreover, the United States argues that it is standard in economics to take the square root of a variable on which a regression is weighted.[387]

6.314 We asked Mexico whether the large differences in coefficient estimates between OLS and WLS obtained by Mexico could reflect model misspecification. Mexico replied that such differences do not reflect model misspecification, but that "[an OLS] regression that considers all products equally will yield very different results than a weighted regression when some products sell thousand times more than others".[388] Moreover, Mexico argues that "weighted regression should be used if a census parameter estimate is desired"[389], as is the case of the regression for the premium paid for canned yellowfin in Mexico's methodology. Since both parties eventually presented WLS regressions (although with different weighting variables), we will also use WLS regressions in our calculations.

6.315 With regard to the United States' contention that the square root of weights should be used in weighted regressions, Mexico argues that this is incorrect.[390] The United States asserts that, while Stata software automatically takes the square root of the weighted variable when performing a WLS regression, the software used by Mexico (R) does not automatically take the square root.[391] We note, however, that: (a) we could replicate with alternative software, namely Stata, all the regressions that Mexico estimated, without taking the square root of the weighting variable, with the R software; and (b) the results of our own WLS regressions are identical when estimated with the R software and when estimated with the Stata software, always using the variable itself, rather than its square root, as weights. We therefore reject the United States' argument that, while the Stata software automatically takes the square root of the weighted variable in a WLS regression, the R software does not. Accordingly,

---

[386] This is because, according to the United States, the purpose of the analysis is to study the price of tuna by weight, not by number of units sold, and the units vary substantially by size (can size, as well as packs of 4 or more). See United States' comments on Mexico's response to Arbitrator question No. 100.

[387] United States' comments on Mexico's response to Arbitrator question No. 100.

[388] Mexico's response to Arbitrator question No. 100.

[389] Mexico's response to Arbitrator question No. 100, citing A. C. Cameron and P. K. Trivedi (2009), *Microeconometrics Using Stata*, College Station (TX): Stata Press (Exhibit MEX-115). As explained in Exhibit MEX-115, p. 107, census parameter estimates give more weights to oversampled groups in the population.

[390] In Mexico's comments on the United States' response to Arbitrator question No. 131, Mexico explains that it is possible to produce WLS estimators by multiplying the dependent and the independent variables of a regression model by the square root of the regression weights. But regression packages in common statistical software programs (e.g., R or Stata) make this unnecessary. Weighting in these regression packages requires specifying the weights as the weighting variable itself, rather than as its square root.

[391] United States' comments on Mexico's response to Arbitrator question No. 100.

we estimate WLS regressions with the weighting variable itself, rather than its square root, as weights.

6.316 With regard to the United States' argument that the weights in the WLS regression ought to be in terms of volumes (kilograms) rather than number of units sold, Mexico also estimates WLS regressions using the total volume sold (measured in kilograms) as weight, as suggested by the United States.[392] Since both parties propose estimations with volume weights, we also use such weights.

6.317 Concerning the third issue, namely the additional "form" premium for yellowfin, Mexico calculates that US consumers have paid USD 1.18/kg more for yellowfin because it is offered in more desirable forms than generic tuna.[393] Mexico suggests that the estimated form premium should be added to the coefficient on the yellowfin dummy to get an estimated value of the price premium.[394] This is because "[t]he form in which tuna is canned reflects the characteristics of the tuna meat and it cannot always be chosen by canneries, as it depends on the species and the size of tuna caught".[395] The United States disagrees with this argument, noting that the form premium "has no place in the calculation of the level of nullification or impairment. Mexico exports only chunk products to the United States and is no longer even asserting that they would export a higher-quality product under the counterfactual".[396] In our view, a premium for the form should be added, for the following reasons.

6.318 First, there is evidence on the record indicating that yellowfin, especially large yellowfin, is better suited and more likely to be canned in the form of solid or fillet than generic tuna. This is confirmed by a report by the United Nations Food and Agriculture Organization (FAO) explaining that "[m]ost of the commercial [yellowfin] catch is used for canning and fish over 10 kg are considered prime raw material for this purpose"[397], as well as by the Tuna Species Guide from Atuna.com, which reports that "the large size of the yellowfin makes it well fit for solid packaging in cans".[398] Tuna fished in the ETP falls in this category of tuna because it is large.[399] In addition, Exhibit MEX-02 shows that the percentage of yellowfin canned in the form of fillet (20.5%) is much larger than the percentage of generic tuna in that form (2%).[400]

---

[392] Mexico's response to Arbitrator question No. 79.

[393] See Exhibit MEX-02, p. 19. The premium for the form is estimated, both for yellowfin and generic tuna, in comparison with the chunk form.

[394] See Mexico's response to Arbitrator question No. 121; Mexico's comments on the United States' response to Arbitrator question No. 141.

[395] Exhibit MEX-02, p. 18.

[396] United States' comments on Mexico's response to Arbitrator question No. 121.

[397] Exhibit USA-87, p. 9.

[398] Exhibit MEX-06, p. 6.

[399] The United States reports that "[I]n 2015, for example, the average weight of the yellowfin tuna caught in the WCPO, the ETP, and the Indian Ocean was 18.9 kg., 13.9 kg., and 45.8 kg per fish. Dolphin sets in the ETP also tend to produce large yellowfin (the average weight per fish was 21.4 kg in 2015)" [footnotes omitted] (United States' response to Arbitrator question No. 151).

[400] See Exhibit MEX-02, Table 6, p. 19.

6.319 Furthermore, we believe that the counterfactual does not need to be restricted by the assumption that Mexico would continue to export to the United States tuna in the form it currently exports (chunk). The evidence on the record shows that Mexico produces and exports "Ventresca" (tuna belly, a gourmet cut of tuna in solid form) in olive oil.[401] Although Mexico does not currently export this product to the United States[402], we find it reasonable to assume that Mexico could potentially export canned tuna in fillet or solid form. The form premium is computed using the share of each form in the total volumes sold in the US market.

6.320 Concerning the fourth issue, namely whether the econometrically-estimated premium should be adjusted for a mark-up from import to retail, the United States argues that while the level of nullification or impairment should be based on the premium calculated using import prices (a proxy of the price paid to the exporter in Mexico), Mexico wrongly calculates the premium at retail prices.[403] In so doing, the United States argues, Mexico overestimates the premium for canned yellowfin at importation.[404] The United States asserts that "[i]n general, the mark-up from import to retail is based on the price of the product and is higher for gourmet products because these have fewer close substitutes and are purchased by consumers who have lower marginal utility of income".[405] In support of this argument, the United States cites Exhibit USA-174, which shows that in 2007 the retail mark-up for imported fish and seafood was 29%.

6.321 Mexico explains that its methodology applies at the wholesale level. Since only retail data are available, Mexico assumes that the wholesale to retail mark-up is the same for canned generic and for canned yellowfin tuna.[406] In Mexico's view, this is a reasonable assumption because the mark-up reflects costs and there is no reason to think that costs are different for canned yellowfin and generic tuna. According to Mexico, it costs the same to take canned yellowfin and canned generic tuna from wholesale to retail because these canned products are of similar sizes and weights.[407] Furthermore, Mexico argues that even "if there were a reason to make adjustments to the model because of an unaccounted-for mark-up, the material in Exhibit USA-174 does not offer the information necessary to perform such a correction"[408], because it is unclear how data in Exhibit USA-174 have been calculated, and the original source (of which Exhibit USA-174 is an excerpt) is not publicly available.

---

[401] Mexico's response to Arbitrator question No. 78.
[402] United States' comments on Mexico's response to Arbitrator question No. 78.
[403] United States' response to Arbitrator question No. 141.
[404] *Ibid.*
[405] *Ibid.*
[406] Exhibit MEX-02, p. 16.
[407] See Exhibit MEX-02, p. 16; Mexico's comments on United States' response to Arbitrator question No. 141.
[408] Mexico's comments on United States' response to Arbitrator question No. 141.

6.322 We agree with the United States that the canned tuna prices on which the calculation of the level of nullification or impairment should be based are the prices paid to the exporter in Mexico[409], and that the value added on services rendered in the United States should be excluded from the relevant price in the calculations. In this regard, we note that Mexico's model is indeed calibrated at wholesale prices and that Mexico uses retail prices only to estimate the price premium. We understand that the key issue is whether the wholesale to retail mark-up differs between yellowfin and generic tuna. We agree with Mexico that, insofar as the mark-up reflects transportation costs, it is reasonable to assume that they mainly depend on volume and weight and are unlikely to depend on the value of the specific can of tuna. We also understand that other factors can affect the mark-up, which can depend on price, for example, when markets are not perfectly competitive. However, the evidence on the record does not allow us to assess whether these circumstances exist in this case. On this basis, we consider reasonable Mexico's assumption that the mark-up is approximately the same for canned yellowfin and generic tuna. We therefore reject the United States' contention that the econometrically estimated premium should be adjusted for a mark-up from wholesale to retail.

6.323 The only remaining issue to discuss is whether to rely on the 12-week or the 52-week dataset in our calculations. The parties have not discussed this specific issue. Both datasets have unique observations by Universal Product Code and region. The difference between the two is the timespan for the average of all variables across Universal Postal Codes and regions. The 12-week dataset uses an average over the 12 weeks ending on 24 October 2015; the 52-week dataset uses an average over the 52 weeks ending on 24 October 2015. We prefer the estimations based on the 52-week dataset, for three reasons: first, the longer timespan used to average variables implies that the resulting averages are less sensitive to the economic cycle; second, the 52-week dataset covers two months of 2014 – the first calendar year following the expiry of the RPT and the year for which we have chosen to calculate the level of nullification or impairment – while the 12-week dataset only covers the year 2015; and third, the

---

[409] We note that this is consistent with the approach taken by previous arbitrators to focus on "trade forgone", i.e. lost exports: "In this sense, our task of estimating nullification and impairment is very different from that of a panel examining the WTO conformity of certain measures. Once a panel has found a WTO inconsistency, it can presume – pursuant to Article 3.8 of the DSU – that the inconsistency has caused nullification and impairment. On that ground the panel can give redress to the winning party under Article XXIII of GATT 1994 or corresponding provisions in other WTO agreements. What normally counts for a panel are competitive opportunities and breaches of WTO rules, not actual trade flows. A panel does not normally need to further assess the nullification and impairment caused; it can presume its existence. We, in contrast, have to go one step further. We can take it for granted here that the hormone ban is WTO inconsistent. What we have to do is to estimate the nullification and impairment caused by it (and presumed to exist pursuant to Article 3.8 of the DSU). To do so in the present case, we have to focus on trade flows. We must estimate trade foregone due to the ban's continuing existence beyond 13 May 1999." Decision by the Arbitrator, *EC – Hormones (Canada) (Article 22.6 – EC)*, para. 41. See also Decision by the Arbitrator, *US – 1916 Act (EC) (Article 22.6 – US)* para. 5.24.

number of observations N is approximately 10% larger in the 52-week dataset (N_{52} = 3379) than in the 12-week dataset (N_{12} = 3009).

6.324 To summarize, we find it appropriate in the circumstances of this dispute to estimate econometrically the price premium using WLS, with weights given by the total volume sold (measured in kilograms), in the 52-week dataset, assuming the same mark-up from wholesale to retail for yellowfin and generic tuna. Our estimated coefficient for the yellowfin dummy, which represents the price premium of yellowfin relative to all other tuna, after controlling for a full set of dummy variables for form, brand, container, flavour, pack, salt and region, is equal to 3.76 (standard error equal to 0.51). Then, we add the form premium, also calculated using the 52-week dataset and WLS with volumes as weights, of 0.85. Therefore, the total premium of yellowfin plus the form is 4.61.

6.325 It follows that, for the United States, using our econometrically estimated price premium (p) of 4.61, a value of 1 - $H(p)$ of 1.2% and a value of s equal to 1 in the equation $\mu = s \cdot \ln\left[\dfrac{1-H(p)}{H(p)}\right] + p$, we parameterize the mean willingness to pay in the United States, μ_{us}, to be equal to 0.199.

6.1.3.2.2   Willingness to pay in Mexico

6.326 To parameterize the mean willingness to pay in Mexico, μ_{mx}, we follow the same procedure as the one used above for μ_{us}, considering that the parties agree on this procedure and on the calibration result.[410]

6.327 Mexico estimates a price premium for canned yellowfin in 2014 in Mexico equal to USD 1.10/kg.[411] Mexico further estimates the following consumption shares in Mexico: $H(p)$ (share of generic tuna consumption in Mexico) equal to 29,585/87,929 (33.65%) and $1 - H(p)$ (share of yellowfin consumption in Mexico) equal to 58,344/87,929 (66.35%). Using these values in the formula proposed by the United States for the calculation of the mean willingness to pay, which we have already used for the United States, yields

$\mu = s \cdot \ln\left[\dfrac{1-H(p)}{H(p)}\right] + p = \ln\left(\dfrac{58344}{29585}\right) + 1.1 = 1.78$. Therefore, in keeping with both

parties' views, we calibrate μ_{mx} = 1.78.

6.1.4   Parameterization of the demand intensity

6.328 Mexico calibrates the US aggregate demand intensity parameter A_{us} assuming that, in the *status quo*, the consumption of canned yellowfin in the United States is low enough to be considered *de minimis*. Under this assumption, the share of the United States' consumption of canned generic tuna, $H(p)$, is equal to 1, and the demand equation for canned generic tuna in the United States

---

[410] Mexico's response to Arbitrator question No. 121.
[411] Exhibit MEX-02, p. 27.

can be written as $Q_{dgus} = A_{us} p_{gus}^{\eta}$. Solving this equation for A_{us}, using the average observed price of imported canned tuna of USD 5/kg in 2014, a value of total US consumption of canned tuna of 330,264 metric tonnes and a price elasticity η = -1, the aggregate demand intensity parameter A_{us} computed by Mexico is 1,651,320,000.[412]

6.329 In order to take into consideration the small share of yellowfin consumption in the United States, we slightly modify these calculations and assume $H(p)$ to be equal to 0.988 in the equation $Q_g = A_{us} H(p) p_g^{\eta}$. Using the same values for p_g (equal to 5) and for η (equal to -1) as the ones used by Mexico, we obtain a (slightly higher) calibrated value for A_{us}, equal to 1,671,376,518.

6.330 To calibrate the aggregate demand intensity parameter A_{mx}, for Mexico, we cannot use the same approach used to calibrate A_{us}. This is because a product can be sold as yellowfin in Mexico if the pack contains at least 40% yellowfin. The resulting mixing of tuna species in canned tuna makes it impossible to isolate prices for yellowfin and generic tuna in Mexico.[413] In this connection, we rely on the methodology used by Mexico, noting that this methodology is not contested by the United States. We therefore assume that A_{mx} equals 443,162,161.[414]

6.1.5 Parameterization of the elasticity of demand

6.331 Mexico uses an elasticity of demand η equal to -1 in the equation $q_{j=} a p_j^{\eta}$ for both the US and Mexican markets and for both canned yellowfin and generic tuna. Mexico argues that this value is in the upper range of elasticities reported

---

[412] See Exhibit MEX-02 (referring to equation (12), p. 16).

[413] See Exhibit MEX-02, p. 26.

[414] Mexico calibrates A_{mx} solving a system of three equations: the demand equations for yellowfin and generic tuna in Mexico, respectively $Q_{dymx} = A_{mx}(1 - H(p))_{mx} p_{ymx}^{\eta}$ and $Q_{dgmx} = A_{mx} H(p)_{mx} p_{gmx}^{\eta}$ and an equation that models the average price of canned tuna in Mexico as a weighted average of the price of yellowfin and generic tuna, with weights given by consumption shares: $\overline{p}_{mx} = (1 - H(p))_{mx} p_{ymx} + H(p)_{mx} p_{gmx}$. We note that to solve the system of three equations described above, it is necessary to transform the observed average retail price of USD 5.58 per kg into a wholesale price. Using data for 2014 from Exhibit MEX-20, Mexico estimates the mark-up between wholesale and retail prices as the coefficient on a dummy variable taking value one if the marketing level is wholesale, and zero if the marketing level is retail, in an OLS regression controlling for brand dummies, product dummies, region dummies and month dummies (Exhibit MEX-02, p. 27). Since the coefficient on the "wholesale" dummy is estimated at -0.54, Mexico subtracts this value from the observed average retail price of USD 5.58 per kg, obtaining an estimated wholesale price $\overline{p}_{mx}$ = USD 5.04 per kg. Using this value, along with with Q_y = 58,344 metric tonnes, Q_g = 29,585 metric tonnes, a resulting consumption share for canned yellowfin $(1 - H(p))$ of 66.35%, and a resulting consumption share for canned generic $(H(p))$ of 33.65% in the system of three equations, yields a solution for A_{mx} equal to 443,162,161 (Exhibit MEX-02, pp. 26-27).

in the literature.[415] The United States contends that both yellowfin and skipjack have particularly elastic demand.[416] However, Mexico has shown mathematically that the assumption of unitary price elasticity for the individual demand for canned tuna is not incompatible with higher values (in absolute values) of the price elasticities of aggregate demand for generic tuna and canned yellowfin.[417] We therefore accept this argument by Mexico and use the parameterization $\eta = -1$.

6.1.6   Accounting for some US retailers not commercializing Mexican canned yellowfin

6.332 Having established that there is evidence on the record suggesting that a subset of US retailers, representing a fraction $1-\alpha = 1 - 73.1\% = 26.9\%$ of consumption of canned tuna products in the United States, would not purchase Mexican canned yellowfin harvested by setting on dolphins, we proceed to modify the US market shares for canned yellowfin and for canned generic tuna.

6.333 Both the United States and Mexico propose a method we could use to adjust the demand for canned yellowfin if a segment of retailers is not willing to sell tuna caught by setting on dolphins. The United States removes a share $1-\alpha$ of tuna consumption from the US yellowfin intensity of demand parameter and adds it to the consumption of generic tuna.[418] Mexico modifies the market shares of canned yellowfin and generic tuna consumption as $\alpha(1 - H(\cdot))$ and $1 - \alpha(1 - H(\cdot))$, respectively, in the demand equations for canned yellowfin and for canned generic tuna.[419]

6.334 The United States submits that Mexico's methodology in this respect produces estimates of the level of nullification or impairment that are not materially different from those produced applying the United States' approach.[420] On this basis, we accept the modification suggested by Mexico in our determination of the level of nullification or impairment.

6.2   *Supply of Canned Tuna*

6.2.1   The counterfactual

6.335 As discussed above, we consider that withdrawal of the Tuna Measure is the appropriate counterfactual for the calculation of the level of nullification or

---

[415] Exhibit MEX-02, p. 15.

[416] United States' written submission.

[417] Mexico's written submission, para. 143.

[418] United States' response to Arbitrator question No. 141.

[419] That is, the aggregate demand for canned yellowfin in the United States becomes $Q_y = A\big[\alpha(1 - H(\cdot))\big]p_y^{\eta}$, and the aggregate demand for canned generic tuna in the United States becomes $Q_g = A\big[1 - \alpha(1 - H(\cdot))\big]p_g^{\eta}$. See Mexico's responses to Arbitrator question No. 146.

[420] United States' comments on Mexico's response to Arbitrator question No. 146.

impairment in these proceedings. We also consider reasonable Mexico's assumption that the Tuna Measure has restricted Mexico's supply of canned yellowfin to the US market. Therefore, we model the counterfactual as a shift to the right of the supply curve of yellowfin to the United States.

6.336 In the following paragraphs, we describe how we model and parametrize the supply of canned yellowfin and generic tuna in the United States and in Mexico[421], and how we reflect the shift of the supply of tuna products in the definition of the counterfactual.

6.2.2   Export supply of canned yellowfin

6.337 Following Mexico's modelling approach, we model the counterfactual as a shift of Mexico's supply of canned yellowfin. Although, as noted above, the Tuna Measure constitutes a restriction on imports, rather than an import ban, given the small share that canned yellowfin had in the US tuna product market in 2014 and that only a small portion of that small share was supplied by Mexico, for simplicity, we specify the model as if Mexico did not export canned yellowfin to the United States in 2014. Specifically, we note that in 2014 canned yellowfin represented only 1.2% of the United States' consumption of tuna products. Of this share, only a small percentage was accounted for by Mexican exports. It therefore seems to us to be a reasonable approximation of reality to specify the model as if no canned Mexican yellowfin was imported into the US market in 2014.

6.338 Following the withdrawal of the Tuna Measure, Mexico would be able to supply canned yellowfin tuna to the US market. Under the counterfactual, Mexico would be supplying canned yellowfin at a lower price than that currently prevailing in the US market given its competitive advantage. Therefore, Mexico would be the dominant supplier of canned yellowfin to the United States.[422] Countries other than Mexico currently supply canned yellowfin to the US market in small quantities, and would likely continue to do so. Further, as we noted in paragraph 5.113 above, Ecuador and Guatemala would also seek to expand their exports of canned yellowfin to the United States after the withdrawal of the Tuna Measure. Indeed, we understand that consumers like having access to a range of canned tuna products, and that one or more varieties of canned yellowfin, including gourmet products in olive oil, could therefore maintain a certain share of the US market even in the presence of a more competitive supplier of canned yellowfin. However, empirical models built to simulate the impact of a policy change need to strike a balance between tractability and transparency on the one hand and reasonableness of the assumptions on the other. In order to build a

---

[421]   We denote by Q_{ymx} Mexican production of canned yellowfin; $Q_{ymx\,exp}$ Mexican exports of canned yellowfin; $Q_{ymx\,imp}$ Mexican imports of canned yellowfin; Q_{gmx} Mexican production of canned generic; Q_{gus} US production of canned generic; and $Q_{gus\,imp}$ US imports of canned generic. See equations 5, 6, 7, 9, 11 and 12 in Appendix 1 to this Decision.

[422]   See Section 5.1.3.3 above.

model where suppliers of canned yellowfin other than Mexico retain a small share of the US market following the removal of the Tuna Measure, Mexico's model would need to be substantially restructured[423] and much more information (such as information on marginal costs across countries and substitution possibilities across products) would be required.[424]

6.339 In our view, in the specific circumstances of this case, given that the production capacity of ETP countries that would be directly affected by the withdrawal of the Tuna Measure is small, and that we are assessing the short-run effect of such withdrawal, it is reasonable to approximate market conditions by assuming that there would be no additional supply of canned yellowfin into the US market by other ETP countries following the removal of the Tuna Measure. As far as existing suppliers of canned yellowfin are concerned, we are of the view that, given that they currently only represent a small share (1.2%) of the US market for canned tuna, modelling their exports would further complicate the model without significantly affecting the calculations of the level of nullification and impairment. We acknowledge that, as we have explained above, under the counterfactual Mexico would not fully displace exports of existing suppliers that benefit from long-term relationships with retailers and renowned brands. However, we choose not to model the presence of such existing suppliers in the market because they only have a small share of the market and therefore inclusion of their export volume would not, in our view, meaningfully affect the outcome of our calculations. Furthermore, as we have already explained, so long as Mexico is a cheaper source of canned yellowfin, we believe that it is unlikely that existing exporters would react to the withdrawal of the Tuna Measure by exporting at a lower price to match the price at which Mexico would export to the United States. Therefore, in what follows, we will only model the supply of canned yellowfin into the US market from Mexico.

6.340 Having decided to model the counterfactual as a shift of Mexico's supply of canned yellowfin into the US market, we move to the next step of our analysis, namely, the determination of the shape of Mexico's supply curve. Depending on the value of the export supply elasticity, the supply curve may be flat, positively sloped or vertical. Like Mexico, we consider it reasonable to assume that the export supply of canned yellowfin to the United States is infinitely elastic (flat) until a threshold quantity, beyond which the supply of canned yellowfin becomes perfectly inelastic (vertical). However, unlike Mexico, we set this threshold equal to Mexico's production in 2014. We explain the rationale for our approach in the following paragraphs.

---

[423]   United States' response to Arbitrator question No. 131.
[424]   *Ibid.*

6.2.2.1   Export supply elasticity for yellowfin

6.341 The United States contests Mexico's assumption of an infinitely elastic supply curve, and argues that this assumption is "unsupported and incorrect".[425] Unlike the United States, we do not understand Mexico's assumption to imply that Mexico could produce an infinite amount of canned yellowfin without incurring any additional marginal costs.[426] Rather, the way it is presented, Mexico's assumption holds true only up to a threshold: the current level of canned tuna production.[427]

6.342 We also disagree with the United States' claim that "Mexico presents no evidence justifying the decision to model Mexico's supply of canned yellowfin as perfectly elastic until a point and then perfectly inelastic".[428] In fact, Mexico justifies its modelling assumption on the basis of the small share that yellowfin has in the overall tuna products consumption in the United States.[429] In Mexico's general formulation, the elasticity of supply of canned yellowfin to the United States will be equal to the ratio between the elasticity of the world supply of canned yellowfin and the US share in the world production of canned yellowfin.[430] Although the record contains no data on world production of canned yellowfin, and therefore it is not possible to calculate the US share in that production, this share is likely to be small. In fact, US consumption of canned yellowfin represents only 2.7% of Mexico's production.[431] It would therefore be logical to consider that, if all world supply of canned yellowfin were taken into consideration, the United States would represent an even lower share of that consumption.

6.343 Moreover, we disagree with the United States' argument that in modelling the supply of canned yellowfin as very elastic, Mexico "appears to acknowledge that there is not, in fact, a restriction on the supply of canned yellowfin to the U.S. market, and, therefore, no reason why the demand observed in the market currently does not reflect actual U.S. consumer demand".[432] In our view, the assumption that Mexico's supply of canned yellowfin to the US market is perfectly elastic does not necessarily contradict the assumption that the supply of canned yellowfin into the US market is currently restricted. As Mexico acknowledges[433], it is correct that the United States is fully integrated into the global canned yellowfin market, and most likely it is also correct that the United States imports from countries whose fleets are the top harvesters of yellowfin in the WCPO. However, the evidence on the record shows that the price at which

---

[425]   United States' written submission, para. 116.
[426]   *Ibid.*
[427]   Mexico's written submission, para. 141.
[428]   United States' comments on Mexico's response to Arbitrator question No. 115.
[429]   Mexico's response to Arbitrator question No. 115.
[430]   *Ibid.*
[431]   *Ibid.*
[432]   United States' comments on Mexico's response to Arbitrator question No. 115.
[433]   Mexico's response to Arbitrator question No. 123.

canned yellowfin is currently supplied into the US market is higher than that of other types of tuna.[434] Therefore, it is possible that, although potentially infinitely elastic, the current supply of dolphin safe canned yellowfin is set at a high price, thus yielding low levels of consumption.

6.344 Furthermore, as noted above in connection with our description of Mexico's model, we are of the view that Mexico's duty-free access to the United States under NAFTA rules as well as Mexico's proximity to the United States and the consequent lower transportation costs provide Mexico with a significant advantage in the US market for canned tuna products. It is therefore reasonable to expect that if the Tuna Measure were to be withdrawn and Mexico were to export canned yellowfin to the US market, canned yellowfin would be available in the US market at a cheaper price than the actual 2014 prices.

6.345 Finally, we find plausible Mexico's characterization of the counterfactual export supply to the United States whereby once the threshold quantity, Q_{ymx} (which corresponds to Mexico's production capacity of canned yellowfin in 2014)[435], has been reached, the supply curve becomes vertical, i.e. perfectly inelastic. This is consistent with our decision in the context of these proceedings to focus our analysis on the short-run effects of the withdrawal of the Tuna Measure.

6.2.2.2 Mexican production capacity of canned yellowfin

6.346 As calculated by Mexico, we set the value of Q_{ymx} equal to the Mexican production capacity in 2014, i.e. 65,342 metric tonnes. This value has been computed as carcass weight net of exports plus the imports for production, using 2014 data.[436] We consider this to be a plausible approach, and note that the United States does not contest it.

6.347 We set Mexican imports (Q_{ymx_imp}) from other ETP countries equal to zero. This is despite Mexico's assumption that it would be able to import an additional quantity equivalent to 20,000 metric tonnes of canned yellowfin from other ETP countries and process it in Mexican canneries, for domestic consumption.[437] Mexico claims that it would be able to expand its production capacity without incurring increased marginal costs. Mexico has explained that this is because Mexican canneries operated in 2014 with a single day shift.[438] According to Mexico, the increase in production would take place at constant marginal costs because it "would come from an increase in production time in

---

[434] Mexico's response to Arbitrator question No. 119; Mexico's response to Arbitrator question No. 153; Exhibit USA-10 (BCI).
[435] Exhibit MEX-02, p. 22.
[436] Calculations using the data from Table 8 on p. 24 of Exhibit MEX-02 yield: (144,650-16,870+2,560)*0.525-3,091=65,342 metric tonnes. Mexico approximates this amount to 65,500 metric tonnes. We do not follow this approach as there is no need for such approximation.
[437] Exhibit MEX-02, p. 22 and Exhibit MEX-02, Table 11, p.32.
[438] Exhibit MEX-02, p. 22, 29; Mexico's written submission, para. 142.

existing facilities".[439] Mexico claims that "as shown in Table 10 of [Exhibit] MEX-02, the catch of yellowfin tuna from other ETP countries is plentiful enough to provide a quantity equivalent to 20,000 metric tonnes of canned yellowfin tuna to Mexico".[440] Table 10 in Exhibit MEX-02 shows that in 2014 total yellowfin catch of selected ETP countries was around 55,300 metric tonnes (equivalent quantities canned). According to this data, ETP countries would export 36% of their catch to Mexico. However, in our view, and as we have explained above, Mexico has not convinced us that this assumption (that it would import an additional quantity equivalent to 20,000 metric tonnes of canned yellowfin from other ETP countries and process it in Mexican canneries, for domestic consumption) is reasonable.

6.348 First, Mexico has not shown how much yellowfin each of these ETP countries consumes and would be able to export. There is no evidence on the record indicating that other ETP countries can and would increase their supply of yellowfin to Mexico by an amount equivalent to 20,000 metric tonnes of canned tuna. In contrast, the United States has submitted evidence showing that the catch of tuna in the ETP is limited under international rules, and that current levels of tuna catch cannot be increased by any significant amount. The catch of tuna species in the ETP is regulated by the IATTC, which monitors catches and takes corrective action if they rise above sustainable levels. The latest IATTC report suggested that "yellowfin tuna was in an overfished state".[441] Therefore, we find it reasonable to assume that the IATTC would take action if the catch of yellowfin in the ETP were to increase substantially. Indeed, the IATTC Resolution C-13-01 declared a yearly 62-day closure period for the large purse seine fishery in the ETP for 2014-2016.[442] Furthermore, we note that "at the 2016 meeting of the IATTC, the Commission adopted interim harvest control rules for yellowfin tuna that would trigger measures to reduce catch".[443] We therefore find persuasive the United States' contention that there is a limited quantity of yellowfin available in other ETP countries.[444]

6.349 Second, even if an excess supply of yellowfin existed in the other ETP countries, it is not clear to us why other countries in the region, such as Ecuador, which can currently export yellowfin to the United States using the dolphin-safe label, would not already import such excess supply in order to process it, consume it domestically and/or increase exports of dolphin-safe tuna to the United States.

6.350 Finally, we are of the view that setting Mexican imports from other ETP countries equal to zero is consistent with the setup of the model. As discussed above, it is a simplified model where the impact of the withdrawal of the Tuna

---

[439] Exhibit MEX-02, p. 22.
[440] Mexico's response to Arbitrator question No. 45.
[441] United States' written submission, para. 117 (referring to Exhibit USA-43).
[442] United States' written submission, para. 117 and footnote 231 (referring to Exhibit USA-77).
[443] United States' written submission, para. 117.
[444] United States' comments on Mexico's response to Arbitrator question No. 115.

Measure on ETP countries that may potentially be affected by the Measure (e.g. Guatemala and Ecuador) is not taken into account because their potential additional export supply of yellowfin is limited by their own production capacity in 2014. In particular, we recall that in 2014, Ecuador and Guatemala each had only one vessel with a DML[445] that caught tuna by setting on dolphins. This argument is used also by Mexico to support its assumption that other ETP countries that may potentially be affected by the Tuna Measure can only marginally change the export volumes.[446] In our view, however, if Mexico's argument about importing the equivalent of 20,000 metric tonnes of canned yellowfin for domestic consumption were accepted, it would be necessary to extend the same assumption to other ETP countries. For example, we would also need to allow that Ecuador could import more for domestic consumption. Therefore, we agree with the United States that removing these additional 20,000 metric tonnes equivalent of canned yellowfin from the model "would partly account for the fact that other countries, including Ecuador, could produce canned yellowfin".[447]

6.2.3   Export supply of generic tuna

6.351 As foreseen in Mexico's model, we assume that canned generic tuna is produced domestically in the United States and Mexico, and that any excess demand is fulfilled by imports from the rest of the world. Mexico's model sets the United States' domestic production of canned generic tuna (Q_{gus}) equal to 177,351 metric tonnes.[448] This value is uncontested by United States. We set the Mexican production of canned generic tuna (Q_{gmx}) equal to 23,000 metric tonnes. This value has been computed by Mexico as carcass weight net of exports plus the import for production[449] and is uncontested by the United States.

6.352 The world export supply of canned generic tuna to the United States is defined in Mexico's model as:

$$Q_{gw\_exp} = \left(\frac{Pgw}{\beta}\right)^{\varepsilon} \quad \text{where } Q_{gw\_exp} = Q_{gus\_imp} = Q_{dgus} - Q_{gus} \text{ is US excess demand}$$

for canned generic tuna; β is a measure of the intensity of supply; p_{gw} is the price

---

[445] Exhibit USA-200. See para. 5.113.
[446] Mexico's response to Arbitrator question No. 18.
[447] United States' response to Arbitrator question No. 131.
[448] Exhibit MEX-02, Tables 1 and 2, p. 5. The value is obtained from Exhibit MEX-03.
[449] Exhibit MEX-02, Table 8, p. 24. 23,000 = (17,771-7,090+29,467)*0,525+1,860. The approximation does not affect the estimated level of nullification or impairment.

of generic tuna; and ε is the elasticity of export supply.[450] We now discuss how ε and p_{gw} are parametrized.[451]

6.2.3.1 Elasticity of export supply of canned generic tuna

6.353 The shape of the world supply curve of canned generic tuna depends on the value assigned to the ε parameter. The correct parametrization of ε is an issue between the parties because the export supply elasticity that a country faces depends on the country's size in the global market. Thus, if the United States were a "small country"[452] in the world tuna market, its consumption choices would not affect the world price of canned tuna. Hence, ε would be large and the United States would face a perfectly elastic (flat) world supply curve. In contrast, if the United States were a large country relative to the world tuna market, it would affect the world price of canned tuna. In this case, the ε parameter would take a finite value. The world supply curve would be imperfectly elastic and positively sloped.

6.354 Thus, the first issue we must resolve is whether the United States' tuna market is small or large relative to the world market for canned tuna. The evidence on the record is contradictory on this point. Mexico asserts that "[t]he United States production and consumption of tuna are small shares of the global tuna market" because its production and consumption of tuna account, respectively, for almost 6.72% and 7.83% of the world tuna harvest.[453] Arguing that these shares are small, Mexico initially modelled the world supply for canned generic tuna to the United States as very elastic.[454] In particular, Mexico set the parameter ε equal to 100000000000.[455]

6.355 Conversely, the United States asserts that it is "by far the single biggest consumer of canned tuna, representing 19 percent of world consumption".[456] Given this share, the United States claims that it "is the single greatest influence

---

[450] See Mexico's written submission, para. 163. Mexico expresses the equation as $Q_{gwexp} = Bp_{gw}^{e}$.

We use $\beta \equiv B^{\frac{1}{x}}$ for consistency with the notation in Exhibit MEX 100-f and in Appendix 3 to our Decision.

[451] Q_{gwexp} and β are endogenous variables.

[452] In the economic terminology, a country is "small" when it is assumed not to affect the world price.

[453] Exhibit MEX-02, p. 7. 6.72% is computed as the ratio of the total US supply of fresh and frozen tuna for canning in 2014 (258,258 metric tonnes) and the world harvest of tuna (4.3 million metric tonnes). Conversely, 7.83% is the ratio of the total US consumption of canned tuna in 2014 (330,264 metric tonnes) and the world harvest of tuna (4.3 million metric tonnes).

[454] Exhibit MEX-02, Figure 1, p. 9.

[455] Exhibit MEX 100-f, line 89.

[456] United States' written submission, para. 15. Exhibit USA-07 shows that the United States consumes 600,000 metric tonnes of canned tuna compared to the 3,137,500 metric tonnes consumed globally. According to Exhibit USA-8, p. 5, "[t]he US is the world's largest consumer of canned tuna (as a country, the European Union is higher as a block)."

on the global market for canned tuna"[457] and that it would not face a perfectly elastic world supply curve. However, the United States does not provide an indication of what would be the correct figure for the export supply elasticity. In response to the United States' assertion that the United States does not face infinite export supply elasticity in the market for canned generic tuna, Mexico proposes alternative results based on two different calibrations of the export supply elasticity, with the export supply elasticity equal to 1 or 10, respectively.[458]

6.356 In order to select a value for ε, we have proceeded as follows. First, we calculated the size of each country's market in the world tuna market in terms of their trade shares.[459] We extracted data on imports of canned tuna from the UN Comtrade database using WITS. We used the 2012 HS classification and took into account HS codes 160414, i.e. "Fish preparations; tunas, skipjack and Atlantic bonito (sarda spp.), prepared or preserved, whole or in pieces (but not minced)", and 160419, i.e. "Fish preparations; fish prepared or preserved, whole or in pieces (but not minced), n.e.c. in heading No. 1604".[460] On the basis of these two HS codes, we find that Mexico's imports account for only 0.32% of global imports of canned tuna, while the United States accounts for 12.65% of those imports. These percentages are equal to 0.34% and 15.29% for Mexico and the United States, respectively, using the HS code 160414 only, as done by the United States.[461] These results suggest that while Mexico is likely to behave like a "small country" in the global tuna market, the United States is likely to be a "large country" in the global tuna market, facing finite export supply elasticity.

6.357 Second, in the absence of a specific value for the elasticity of supply produced by the parties, we have looked at the existing economic literature for guidance. A peer reviewed study published in an international journal[462] provides estimates for the export supply elasticity for the product category of "preserved and prepared fish" (HS heading 1604 – a wider category than tuna products) across several countries, ranging between 0 and 10 with an average equal to 2.2. In particular, the estimate for the export supply elasticity faced by the United States is equal to 2.61. Guided by this evidence, we find it reasonable to use a value of $\varepsilon = 2.61$ in our model. This number also falls within the range of parameter values used by Mexico for the world supply of generic tuna to the

---

[457] United States' written submission, para. 15.
[458] Mexico's written submission, paras. 166 (when assuming $\varepsilon = 1$) and 164 (when assuming $\varepsilon = 10$). See also Mexico's response to Arbitrator question No. 46, para. 83 and Tables 4 and 5 therein.
[459] S.M. Suranovic (2010), *International Trade Theory and Policy*, Chapter 90-3 (retrieved from http://internationalecon.com/Trade/Tch90/T90-3.php) suggests that the share of country imports or exports in the world market should be used to determine the relative size of a country.
[460] These two HS codes are referred to in Table 9 of Exhibit MEX-02, p.25.
[461] United States' response to Arbitrator question No. 67, Table entitled "U.S. Imports of Canned Tuna in 2015".
[462] C. Broda, N. Limao and D.E. Weinstein (2008), "Optimal Tariffs and Market Power: the Evidence," *American Economic Review* 98(5): 2032-2065.

United States in its simulations (namely, 1 and 10).[463] We note, in addition, that we have tested the sensitivity of our simulation results to alternative values of the export supply elasticity, including the assumption of a perfectly elastic supply. The results are only marginally affected. We are therefore confident that our estimate of the level of nullification or impairment is robust to alternative assumptions on the supply elasticity of generic tuna.

6.2.3.2 World price of canned generic tuna

6.358 Data for the calibration of the world price of generic tuna, p_{gw}, comes from Table 3 in Exhibit MEX-02. The parameter p_{gw} is computed as the ratio between total import value and import quantity. As such, it is the average unit value across all listed countries. The specific value of parameter p_{gw} is equal to 4.30 USD/kg. This value is not contested by the United States.

6.3 Other Parameters of the Model: Duty Rates, Transport Costs and Charges

6.359 All other parameters of the model are set as in Mexico's model, because the data provided by Mexico are uncontested.

6.360 We set the duty rate for the United States' imports of canned tuna (d_{us}) at 12.5%. This figure, uncontested by the United States, is computed as the ratio between the duty value (USD 83,778) and the total value of imports (USD 667,178) in 2014.[464] We set the duty rate for Mexico's imports of canned tuna (d_{mx}) at 20%.[465] We set the transport costs between the United States and Mexico (t) at USD 0.05/kg.[466] These are computed as the ratio of the costs of insurance and freight (USD 305) and the import quantities (5657 metric tonnes).[467] Finally, we compute the charges for the United States' imports (t_{us}) as the average charge for all imports of canned tuna, i.e. USD 0.16/kg.[468] Mexico asserts that "[g]iven the proximity of the U.S. and Mexican markets and that these countries both import skipjack from South-East Asia, the same import charge is applied to U.S. and Mexican imports".[469] Therefore, we also set the charges for Mexico's imports, t_{mx}, at USD 0.16/kg. Table 1 below summarizes all parameter values in our model.

---

[463] Mexico's written submission, paras. 164-166.
[464] Exhibit MEX-02, Table 11, p. 32. The value is obtained from Exhibit MEX-04.
[465] Exhibit MEX-02, Table 11, p. 32. The value is obtained from Exhibit MEX-24.
[466] Exhibit MEX-02, p. 7 and Table 11, p. 32.
[467] Exhibit MEX-02, p. 7 and Table 3, p. 6.
[468] Exhibit MEX-02, Table 11, p. 32. The value is obtained from Exhibit MEX-04. See also Mexico's response to Arbitrator question No. 90.
[469] Exhibit MEX-02, p. 31.

Table 1. Exogenous variables and parameters

Variable	Value
US production of canned generic tuna, Q_{gus} (metric tonnes)	177,350
US consumption of canned tuna, $cons_{us}$ (metric tonnes)	330,264
Share of canned generic tuna consumption in the United States, H_{us} (%)	98.8
Average price of canned tuna in the United States, p_{us} (USD/kg)	5
Mexican production of canned yellowfin tuna, Q_{ymx} (metric tonnes)	65,342
Mexican production of canned generic tuna, Q_{gmx} (metric tonnes)	23,000
Mexican consumption of canned yellowfin tuna, $cons_{mxy}$ (metric tonnes)	58,344
Mexican consumption of canned generic tuna, $cons_{mxg}$ (metric tonnes)	29,585
Share of canned generic tuna consumption in Mexico, H_{mx} (%)	33.65*
Average price for canned tuna in Mexico, p_{mx} (USD/kg)	5.04
Mexican imports of canned yellowfin tuna, $Q_{ymx\ imp}$ (metric tonnes)	0
Transportation costs between Mexico and the United States, t (USD/kg)	0.05
World price of generic tuna, p_{gw} (USD/kg)	4.30
Duty rate for Mexican imports of tuna, d_{mx} (%)	20
Duty rate for US imports of tuna, d_{us} (%)	12.5
Charge for Mexican imports of tuna, t_{mx} (USD/kg)	0.16
Charge for US imports of tuna, t_{us} (USD/kg)	0.16
Share of US retailers willing to sell Mexican canned yellowfin tuna, α (%)	73.1
Shape parameter of the logistic distribution, s	1
Price elasticity of demand for canned tuna, η	-1
Price elasticity of export supply of canned generic tuna, ε	2.61
US demand intensity parameter, A_{us} (USD million)	1,671.37
Mexican demand intensity parameter, A_{mx} (USD million)	443.162
Mean willingness to pay for canned yellowfin tuna in the United States, μ_{us}	0.199
Mean willingness to pay for canned yellowfin tuna in Mexico, μ_{mx}	1.78

* $H_{mx} = cons_{mxg}/(cons_{mxg} + cons_{mxy}) = 29,585/(29,585+58,344)$

6.4   Calculation of the Level of Nullification or Impairment

6.361 The results of the endogenous variables in the model are summarized in Table 2.[470]

---

[470] Appendix 1 presents the theoretical model we used for the simulation. Appendix 2 provides the Stata do file used for econometric estimations of the price premium. Appendix 3 provides the R codes for solving the model.

Table 2. Results

	United States	Mexico
Consumption of yellowfin (metric tonnes)	28,077	37,265
Consumption of generic (metric tonnes)	311,622	38,752
Price of yellowfin (USD/kg)	6.67	6.62
Price of generic (USD/kg)	4.76	5.07
Exports of yellowfin (metric tonnes)	0	28,077
Imports of yellowfin (metric tonnes)	28,077	0
Exports of generic (metric tonnes)	0	0
Imports of generic (metric tonnes)	134,272	15,752
Export value of canned tuna to the United States (million USD)	0	185.88

6.362 We consider it crucial that the counterfactual price of yellowfin in the United States is lower than the actual 2014 price. As noted above, we do not know the price level for canned yellowfin in the US market in 2014. However, the United States argues that the US import price of canned yellowfin exported from the European Union could provide a good proxy for the wholesale price of canned yellowfin. This is because at higher import prices several exporters of yellowfin to the European Union would divert their exports to the US market.[471]

6.363 In this connection, the United States argues that in 2015, the European Union imported nearly 77,000 metric tonnes of canned yellowfin at an average price of USD 5.31/kg.[472] After adjusting for duty rates and charges on US canned tuna imports estimated equal to USD 0.85/kg, this price would corresponds to USD 6.16/kg.[473] In response, Mexico notes that the price used by the United States pertains to 2015, while the counterfactual year is 2014. Mexico also notes that the value of the US dollar compared to the Euro increased by 20% from 2014 to 2015. Thus, Mexico contends that the value of USD 5.31/kg in 2015 is equivalent to USD 6.35/kg in 2014 (USD 5.31/kg*1.195). Furthermore, Mexico adjusts the value of total US tariffs and charges in 2015 (USD 0.85/kg) to 2014, obtaining USD 1.02/kg (USD 0.85/kg * 1.195). Adding this estimated value of tariffs and charges in 2014 to the estimated price of canned yellowfin in 2014 (USD 6.35/kg) yields a total export price to the United States, after adjustments for exchange rate movements and US tariffs and charges, of USD 7.37/kg in 2014.[474]

---

[471] United States' opening statement at the meeting of the Arbitrator, para. 32.

[472] United States' opening statement at the meeting of the Arbitrator, para. 31.

[473] As argued by Mexico, Exhibit USA-144 is not detailed, but it seems from its last page that the total of US tariff and charges was USD 0.85/kg in 2015 (see Mexico's response to Arbitrator question No. 124).

[474] Mexico's response to Arbitrator question No. 124.

6.364 As shown in Table 2 above, we estimate a counterfactual price of canned yellowfin in the United States of USD 6.67/kg. We note that this is clearly below the price estimated in Mexico's model (USD 7.84/kg[475]) and the counterfactual 2014 import price adjusted as proposed by Mexico (USD 7.37/kg), and only slightly above the reference price submitted by the United States for 2015 (USD 6.16/kg). We note, however, that the evidence on the record shows a fall in the EU import prices of frozen yellowfin for processing – which, as argued by the United States, are "consistent with the global cannery-grade yellowfin price"[476] – between 2014 and 2015.[477] Therefore, in all likelihood, the price of canned yellowfin that prevailed in the US market was higher in 2014 than in 2015. From this, we can conclude with reasonable confidence that we solve for a price decrease. This is consistent with the modelled increase in the supply of canned yellowfin to the United States.

6.365 As regards the level of nullification or impairment resulting from our model and its endogenous variables, we recall that the level of nullification or impairment in these proceedings is the difference between the value of total canned tuna exports estimated under the counterfactual and the value of Mexico's actual exports of canned tuna to the United States, with both levels being calculated for the year 2014. Under the counterfactual, we estimate the value for total exports in 2014 of canned tuna from Mexico to the United States (all of it being canned yellowfin) to be equal to USD 185.88 million. The value of Mexican canned tuna actually exported to the United States in 2014 was USD 22.65 million. Taking the difference between the total value of exports of canned tuna from Mexico to the United States under the counterfactual and the total value of actual exports in 2014, we find that Mexico's estimated trade loss in 2014 amounted to USD 163.23 million.

7.   CONCLUSION AND AWARD

7.366 For the reasons set out above, the Arbitrator determines that the level of nullification or impairment of benefits accruing to Mexico as a result of the 2013 Tuna Measure is USD 163.23 million per annum. Therefore, in accordance with Article 22.4 of the DSU, Mexico may request authorization from the DSB to suspend concessions or other obligations as indicated in document WT/DS381/29 at a level not exceeding USD 163.23 million per annum.

---

[475] See Exhibit MEX-02, Table 12, p. 33.
[476] United States' response to Arbitrator question No. 153.
[477] See Exhibit USA-199, showing that the EU import prices of frozen yellowfin for processing decreased from USD 2.85/kg to USD 2.10/kg (a 26.3% decrease) between 2014 and 2015.

ECONOMIC APPENDIXES

APPENDIX 1

EQUATIONS OF THE ARBITRATOR'S MODEL

Equation 1: US demand for canned yellowfin tuna

$$Q_{dyus} = A_{us}\alpha(1 - H(p))_{us}\,p^{\eta}_{yus} = A_{us}\alpha\left(\frac{e^{\frac{\mu - (p_{yus} - p_{gus})}{s}}}{1 + e^{\frac{\mu - (p_{yus} - p_{gus})}{s}}}\right)p^{\eta}_{yus}$$

Equation 2: US demand for canned generic tuna

$$Q_{dgus} = A_{us}\left[1 - \alpha(1 - H(p))_{us}\right]p^{\eta}_{gus} = A_{us}\left[1 - \alpha\left(\frac{e^{\frac{\mu - (p_{yus} - p_{gus})}{s}}}{1 + e^{\frac{\mu - (p_{yus} - p_{gus})}{s}}}\right)\right]p^{\eta}_{gus}$$

Equation 3: Mexican demand for canned yellowfin tuna

$$Q_{dymx} = A_{mx}(1 - H(p))_{mx}\,p^{\eta}_{ymx} = A_{mx}\left(\frac{e^{\frac{\mu - (p_{ymx} - p_{gmx})}{s}}}{1 + e^{\frac{\mu - (p_{ymx} - p_{gmx})}{s}}}\right)p^{\eta}_{ymx}$$

Equation 4: Mexican demand for canned generic tuna

$$Q_{dgmx} = A_{mx}(H(p))_{mx}\,p^{\eta}_{gmx} = A_{mx}\left(\frac{1}{1 + e^{\frac{\mu - (p_{ymx} - p_{gmx})}{s}}}\right)p^{\eta}_{gmx}$$

Equation 5: Mexican export supply of canned yellowfin tuna

$$Q_{ymx\_exp} = Q_{dyus} = Q_{ymx} + Q_{ymx\_imp} - Q_{dymx}$$

Equation 6: US import demand of canned generic tuna

$$Q_{gus\_imp} = Q_{gus} - Q_{dgus}$$

Equation 7: World price of canned generic tuna

$$P_{gw} = \frac{\beta}{Q_{gus\_imp}^{1/\varepsilon}}$$

Equation 8: US price of canned generic tuna

$$P_{gus} = (1+d_{us})P_{gw} + t_{us}$$

Equation 9: Mexican price of canned generic tuna

$$P_{gmx} = \begin{cases} (1+d_{us})P_{gw} + t_{mx} & if & Q_{gmx\_exp} = 0 \\ P_{gus} - t & if & Q_{gmx\_exp} > 0 \end{cases}$$

Equation 10: US price of canned yellowfin tuna (arbitrage condition)

$$P_{yus} = P_{ymx} + t$$

Equation 11: Mexican exports of generic tuna to United States

$$Q_{gmx\_exp} = max\{0, Q_{dgmx} - Q_{gmx}\}$$

Equation 12: Mexican imports of generic tuna from other countries

$$Q_{gmx\_imp} = max\{0, Q_{gmx} - Q_{dgmx}\}$$

APPENDIX 2

STATA DO FILE FOR ECONOMETRIC
ESTIMATION OF PRICE PREMIUM

```
clear all
cap log close
set more off, perm

global WD "USE YOUR OWN DIRECTORY " /*  Working directory  */
cd "$WD"


******************************************************************************
*  Preliminary dataset construction                        *
{

quietly   {

foreach k in 12 52  {

insheet using Nielsen_`k'_week.csv, clear

/*    These CSV datasets are created in lines 168-169 of R file "Arbitrator_construction_12week_52week_Nielsen_csv_datasets". This
is
      mutuated from lines 1-169 of Exhibit "MEX-100-b - US Nielsen data.R"
*/

foreach var of varlist  brand_ form_ container_ flavor_ pack_ salt_ region_   {

    unique `var'
    vallist `var', sort
    tab `var', g(`var'_cat)

                                    }
                                    *  `var'


save Arbitrator_`k'weeks_temp, replace


            }
            *  `k'


        }
        *  quietly ends here

}
******************************************************************************


******************************************************************************
*  Arbitrator's determination if premium for the form NOT considered       *
{

local controls

    foreach m in 12 52           {

    use Arbitrator_`m'weeks_temp, replace

    foreach k in volume n_units   {

        reg   price_`m'*cat*   yellowfin  `controls' [aweight = `k'_`m']
        scalar beta_yf_`m'_`k' = _b[yellowfin]
        scalar mu_`m'_`k' = _b[yellowfin] + ln((1/(1-.012))-1)*1
        scalar list beta_yf_`m'_`k' mu_`m'_`k'

                }
                *  `k'
```

```
                          }
                        *  `m'


*********************************************************
*  Calculation of mu_US                       *
{

scalar      NO_mu_52_volume           = (mu_52_volume)
scalar list NO_mu_52_volume

scalar      NO_mu_52_avg_volume_units  = (mu_52_volume + mu_52_n_units)/2
scalar list NO_mu_52_avg_volume_units

scalar      NO_mu_avg_12_52_n_units    = (mu_12_n_units + mu_52_n_units)/2
scalar list NO_mu_avg_12_52_n_units

scalar      NO_mu_avg_12_52_volume     = (mu_12_volume + mu_52_volume)/2
scalar list NO_mu_avg_12_52_volume

scalar      NO_mu_avg_overall          = (mu_12_volume + mu_52_volume + mu_12_n_units + mu_52_n_units)/4
scalar list NO_mu_avg_overall

}
*********************************************************


}
*****************************************************************************


*****************************************************************************
*  Arbitrator's determination if premium for the form IS considered      *
{

*********************************************************
*  Preliminary construction              *
{

        foreach m in 12 52                            {

        foreach k in volume n_units                      {

        foreach x in form  /*brand container flavor pack salt region */   {


        preserve

        use Arbitrator_`m'weeks_temp, replace

        bysort yellowfin: egen total_`k'_`m'_temp = total(`k'_`m')
        bysort yellowfin form_: egen total_`k'_`m'_form_temp = total(`k'_`m')
        g share_`k'_`m' = total_`k'_`m'_form_temp / total_`k'_`m'_temp
        keep yellowfin form_ share*
        duplicates drop
        reshape wide share_`k'_`m', i( form_) j(yellowfin)
        ren share_`k'_`m'0 sh_`k'_other
        ren share_`k'_`m'1 sh_`k'_yfin

        foreach j of varlist sh*     {

        replace `j' = 0 if missing(`j')

                          }
                        *  `j'

        save temp_`m'_form_`k'_shares, replace

        restore

                          }
                        *  `x'

                          }
                        *  `k'
```

```
                                     }
                               *  `m'

********************************************************************
*   Calculation of "form premium" (12-week dataset, volume weight)    *
{

use Arbitrator_12weeks_temp, replace

**************************************************************
*   Shares from "temp_12_form_volume_shares.dta" dataset      *
{

g other_share_Iform2      =   0.0016170
g other_share_Iform3      =   0.0005138
g other_share_Iform4      =   0.0003206
g other_share_Iform5      =   0.0032770
g other_share_Iform6      =   0.2617792
g other_share_Iform7      =   0.0000251

g yfin_share_Iform2       =   0.1838225
g yfin_share_Iform3       =   0.0000000
g yfin_share_Iform4       =   0.0033019
g yfin_share_Iform5       =   0.0000000
g yfin_share_Iform6       =   0.2088498
g yfin_share_Iform7       =   0.0000000

}
**************************************************************

local controls

drop *__*
ren pack_size size_pack
tostring region, replace

renvars, subs(container ctn)

        foreach x in form        {

            encode `x', g(encoded_`x')
            tab `x' encoded_`x'

                        }
                   *  `x'

xi:   reg   price_12   i.brand i.form i.ctn i.flavor i.pack i.salt i.region yellowfin `controls' [aweight = volume_12]
est store Arbitrator

forvalues k = 2(1)7    {

   g beta_Iform`k' = _b[_Iform__`k']

                }
           *  `k'

g form_premium_12 =   beta_Iform2*(yfin_share_Iform2 - other_share_Iform2)   + ///
            beta_Iform3*(yfin_share_Iform3 - other_share_Iform3)   + ///
            beta_Iform4*(yfin_share_Iform4 - other_share_Iform4)   + ///
            beta_Iform5*(yfin_share_Iform5 - other_share_Iform5)   + ///
            beta_Iform6*(yfin_share_Iform6 - other_share_Iform6)   + ///
            beta_Iform7*(yfin_share_Iform7 - other_share_Iform7)
sum form_premium_12

scalar define form_premium_12_volume = r(mean)
scalar list form_premium_12_volume

}
**********************************************************************


**********************************************************************
*   Calculation of "form premium" (52-week dataset, volume weight)    *
{

use Arbitrator_52weeks_temp, replace
```

Decision by the Arbitrator

```
****************************************************************
*   Shares from "temp_52_form_volume_shares.dta" dataset      *
{

g other_share_Iform2    =   0.0015417
g other_share_Iform3    =   0.0003065
g other_share_Iform4    =   0.0003542
g other_share_Iform5    =   0.0027262
g other_share_Iform6    =   0.2634644
g other_share_Iform7    =   0.0000080

g yfin_share_Iform2     =   0.1823488
g yfin_share_Iform3     =   0.0000000
g yfin_share_Iform4     =   0.0034064
g yfin_share_Iform5     =   0.0000000
g yfin_share_Iform6     =   0.1990382
g yfin_share_Iform7     =   0.0000000


}
****************************************************************

local controls

drop *__*
ren pack_size size_pack
tostring region, replace

renvars, subs(container ctn)

    foreach x in form       {

        encode `x', g(encoded_`x')
        tab `x' encoded_`x'


            }
            * `x'

xi:    reg    price_52   i.brand i.form i.ctn i.flavor i.pack i.salt i.region yellowfin `controls' [aweight = volume_52]
est store Arbitrator

forvalues k = 2(1)7    {

  g beta_Iform`k' = _b[_Iform__`k']


            }
            * `k'

g form_premium_52 =    beta_Iform2*(yfin_share_Iform2 - other_share_Iform2)    + ///
            beta_Iform3*(yfin_share_Iform3 - other_share_Iform3)   + ///
            beta_Iform4*(yfin_share_Iform4 - other_share_Iform4)   + ///
            beta_Iform5*(yfin_share_Iform5 - other_share_Iform5)   + ///
            beta_Iform6*(yfin_share_Iform6 - other_share_Iform6)   + ///
            beta_Iform7*(yfin_share_Iform7 - other_share_Iform7)
sum form_premium_52

scalar define form_premium_52_volume = r(mean)
scalar list form_premium_52_volume


}
****************************************************************


****************************************************************
*   Calculation of "form premium" (12-week dataset, n_units weight)   *
{

use Arbitrator_12weeks_temp, replace

****************************************************************
*   Shares from "temp_12_form_n_units_shares.dta" dataset     *
{

g other_share_Iform2    =   0.00215040
g other_share_Iform3    =   0.00019197
g other_share_Iform4    =   0.00041838
```

```
g other_share_Iform5       =   0.00813812
g other_share_Iform6       =   0.22235054
g other_share_Iform7       =   0.00003278

g yfin_share_Iform2        =   0.20729758
g yfin_share_Iform3        =   0.00000000
g yfin_share_Iform4        =   0.00568317
g yfin_share_Iform5        =   0.00000000
g yfin_share_Iform6        =   0.21372929
g yfin_share_Iform7        =   0.00000000


}
*****************************************************************

local controls

drop *__*
ren pack_size size_pack
tostring region, replace

renvars, subs(container ctn)

        foreach x in form          {

            encode `x', g(encoded_`x')
            tab `x' encoded_`x'


                    }
                    *  `x'

xi:   reg   price_12   i.brand i.form i.ctn i.flavor i.pack i.salt i.region yellowfin `controls' [aweight = n_units_12]
est store Arbitrator

forvalues k = 2(1)7   {

    g beta_Iform`k' = _b[_Iform__`k']


                }
                *  `k'

g form_premium_12 =    beta_Iform2*(yfin_share_Iform2 - other_share_Iform2)   + ///
                beta_Iform3*(yfin_share_Iform3 - other_share_Iform3)   + ///
                beta_Iform4*(yfin_share_Iform4 - other_share_Iform4)   + ///
                beta_Iform5*(yfin_share_Iform5 - other_share_Iform5)   + ///
                beta_Iform6*(yfin_share_Iform6 - other_share_Iform6)   + ///
                beta_Iform7*(yfin_share_Iform7 - other_share_Iform7)
sum form_premium_12

scalar define form_premium_12_n_units = r(mean)
scalar list form_premium_12_n_units


}
*********************************************************************


*********************************************************************
*   Calculation of "form premium" (52-week dataset, n_units weight)    *
{

use Arbitrator_52weeks_temp, replace

*********************************************************************
*   Shares from "temp_52_form_n_units_shares.dta" dataset      *
{

g other_share_Iform2       =   0.00198908
g other_share_Iform3       =   0.00012039
g other_share_Iform4       =   0.00045978
g other_share_Iform5       =   0.00672650
g other_share_Iform6       =   0.22540790
g other_share_Iform7       =   0.00001032

g yfin_share_Iform2        =   0.20455195
g yfin_share_Iform3        =   0.00000000
g yfin_share_Iform4        =   0.00582262
g yfin_share_Iform5        =   0.00000000
```

```
g yfin_share_Iform6    =  0.20176426
g yfin_share_Iform7    =  0.00000000


}
****************************************************************

local controls

drop *__*
ren pack_size size_pack
tostring region, replace

renvars, subs(container ctn)

     foreach x in form      {

        encode `x', g(encoded_`x')
        tab `x' encoded_`x'

                }
                * `x'

xi:   reg   price_52   i.brand i.form i.ctn i.flavor i.pack i.salt i.region yellowfin `controls' [aweight = n_units_52]
est store Arbitrator

forvalues k = 2(1)7    {

   g beta_Iform`k' = _b[_Iform__`k']

              }
              * `k'

g form_premium_52 =   beta_Iform2*(yfin_share_Iform2 - other_share_Iform2)   + ///
              beta_Iform3*(yfin_share_Iform3 - other_share_Iform3)   + ///
              beta_Iform4*(yfin_share_Iform4 - other_share_Iform4)   + ///
              beta_Iform5*(yfin_share_Iform5 - other_share_Iform5)   + ///
              beta_Iform6*(yfin_share_Iform6 - other_share_Iform6)   + ///
              beta_Iform7*(yfin_share_Iform7 - other_share_Iform7)
sum form_premium_52

scalar define form_premium_52_n_units = r(mean)
scalar list form_premium_52_n_units


}
*********************************************************************


*********************************************************************
*   Calculation of average form premia                    *
{


scalar    form_premium_52_avg_volume_units   = (form_premium_52_volume + form_premium_52_n_units)/2
scalar list   form_premium_52_avg_volume_units

scalar    form_premium_avg_12_52_volume    = (form_premium_12_volume + form_premium_52_volume)/2
scalar list   form_premium_avg_12_52_volume

scalar    form_premium_avg_overall       = (form_premium_12_volume + form_premium_52_volume +
form_premium_12_n_units + form_premium_52_n_units)/4
scalar list   form_premium_avg_overall



}
*********************************************************************


}
*****************************************************


*****************************************************
*   Calculation of mu_US                   *
{

scalar    YES_mu_52_volume          = (mu_52_volume + form_premium_52_volume)
```

```
scalar list    YES_mu_52_volume

scalar         YES_mu_52_avg_volume_units    = NO_mu_52_avg_volume_units + form_premium_52_avg_volume_units
scalar list    YES_mu_52_avg_volume_units

scalar         YES_mu_avg_12_52_volume    = NO_mu_avg_12_52_volume + form_premium_avg_12_52_volume
scalar list    YES_mu_avg_12_52_volume

scalar         YES_mu_avg_overall    = NO_mu_avg_overall + form_premium_avg_overall
scalar list    YES_mu_avg_overall

}
*******************************************************

}
**********************************************************************************


**********************************************************************************
*   Erase temp files                              *
{

foreach k in *temp*.dta              {

    local myfiles: dir . files "*`k'*", respectcase
    foreach file of local myfiles {
        capture rm  "`file'"
        }
    *

                          }
                          *  `k'

}
**********************************************************************************
```

APPENDIX 3

R FILES FOR SOLVING THE MODEL

MODEL FUNCTIONS

```
###############################################
### Return the correct distribution function ###
###############################################

pdist_US <- function(premium, mu, s){

  if(dist_US == "logistic"){return(plogis(premium, location = mu, scale = s))}

}

pdist_MX <- function(premium, mu, s){

  if(dist_MX == "logistic"){return(plogis(premium, location = mu, scale = s))}

}


######################################
### Function for interior solution ###
######################################

func_interior <- function(theta){

  ############################
  ### Equations of the model ###
  ############################

  #World price of generic tuna (world supply - from Mexico's submission)
  pgw_func <- function(qgusimp){
    as.numeric(theta["beta_us"]*qgusimp^(1/theta["epsilon"]))
  }

  #US price of yellowfin - arbitrage between US and Mexico
  py_func <- function(pymx){as.numeric(pymx + theta["t"])}

  #US price of generic tuna
  pgus_func <- function(qgusimp){as.numeric(pgw_func(qgusimp)*(1+theta["dus"]) + theta["tus"])}

  #MX price of generic tuna
  pgmx_func <- function(qgusimp){as.numeric(pgw_func(qgusimp)*(1+theta["dmx"]) + theta["tmx"])  }

  #US demand for yellowfin
  qdyus_func <- function(pymx, qgusimp){
    as.numeric(theta["Aus"]*a_share*(1-pdist_US(py_func(pymx) - pgus_func(qgusimp), theta["mu_us"],
theta["s_us"]))*py_func(pymx)^theta["eta"])
  }

  #US demand for generic tuna
  qdgus_func <- function(pymx, qgusimp){
    as.numeric(theta["Aus"]*(1-a_share*(1-pdist_US(py_func(pymx) - pgus_func(qgusimp), theta["mu_us"],
theta["s_us"])))*pgus_func(qgusimp)^theta["eta"])
  }

  #MX demand for yellowfin
  qdymx_func <- function(pymx, qgusimp){
    as.numeric(theta["Amx"]*(1-pdist_MX(pymx - pgmx_func(qgusimp), theta["mu_mx"], theta["s_mx"]))*pymx^theta["eta"])
  }

  #MX demand for generic tuna
  qdgmx_func <- function(pymx, qgusimp){
    as.numeric(theta["Amx"]*pdist_MX(pymx - pgmx_func(qgusimp), theta["mu_mx"],
theta["s_mx"])*pgmx_func(qgusimp)^theta["eta"])
  }
```

```
}

#########################
### Equations to solve ###
#########################

#Quantity of generic tuna in U.S. (from Mexico's submission)
qg_sol_func <- function(pymx, qgusimp){
  as.numeric(qgusimp + theta["Qgus"] - qdgus_func(pymx, qgusimp))
}

#Quantity of yellowfin tuna
qy_sol_func <- function(pymx, qgusimp){
  as.numeric(theta["Qymx"] - qdymx_func(pymx, qgusimp) - qdyus_func(pymx, qgusimp))
}

#Objective function
obj_func <- function(x){
  pymx <- x[1]
  qgusimp <- x[2]
  y <- numeric(2)
  #Objective function
  y[1] <- qg_sol_func(pymx, qgusimp)
  y[2] <- qy_sol_func(pymx, qgusimp)
  #Return vector of functions
  y
}

#Square function to solve - for corner solution on qgusimp = 0
obj_func_2 <- function(pymx){
  as.numeric((qy_sol_func(pymx, 0))^2)
}

###############
### Solutions ###
###############

sol <- nleqslv(c(7, 80000000), obj_func, control = list(cndtol = 1e-16))
print(sol$message)

pymx_sol <- as.numeric(sol$x[1])
qgusimp_sol <- as.numeric(sol$x[2])

#Return solutions for all variables in a vector
vec_sol <- c(Qdymx = qdymx_func(pymx_sol, qgusimp_sol),
        Qdgmx = qdgmx_func(pymx_sol, qgusimp_sol),
        Qdyus = qdyus_func(pymx_sol, qgusimp_sol),
        Qdgus = qdgus_func(pymx_sol, qgusimp_sol),
        Qymx_exp = max(0, theta["Qymx"] - qdymx_func(pymx_sol, qgusimp_sol)),
        Qymx_imp = max(0, qdymx_func(pymx_sol, qgusimp_sol) - theta["Qymx"]),
        Qgmx_exp = max(0, theta["Qgmx"] - qdgmx_func(pymx_sol, qgusimp_sol)),
        Qgmx_imp = max(0, qdgmx_func(pymx_sol, qgusimp_sol) - theta["Qgmx"]),
        Qgus_imp = max(0, qdgus_func(pymx_sol, qgusimp_sol) - max(0, theta["Qymx"] - qdgmx_func(pymx_sol, qgusimp_sol)) -
theta["Qgus"]),
        pymx = pymx_sol,
        pgmx = pgmx_func(qgusimp_sol),
        pyus = py_func(pymx_sol),
        pgus = pgus_func(qgusimp_sol))

  return(vec_sol)

}

######################################
### Function for corner solution  ###
######################################

func_corner <- function(theta){

  #(Re)calculate Mexico's domestic production - corner solution on exports of yellowfin tuna
  qymx_dom <- theta["Qymx"] - ymx_imp

  #########################
  ### Equations of the model ###
  #########################
```

Decision by the Arbitrator

```
#World price of generic tuna (world supply - from Mexico's submission)
pgw_func <- function(qgusimp){
  as.numeric(theta["beta_us"]*qgusimp^(1/theta["epsilon"]))
}

#US price of generic tuna
pgus_func <- function(qgusimp){as.numeric(pgw_func(qgusimp)*(1+theta["dus"]) + theta["tus"])}

#MX price of generic tuna
pgmx_func <- function(qgusimp){as.numeric(pgw_func(qgusimp)*(1+theta["dmx"]) + theta["tmx"])}

#US demand for yellowfin
qdyus_func <- function(pyus, qgusimp){
  as.numeric(theta["Aus"]*a_share*(1-pdist_US(pyus - pgus_func(qgusimp), theta["mu_us"], theta["s_us"]))*pyus^theta["eta"])
}

#US demand for generic tuna
qdgus_func <- function(pyus, qgusimp){
  as.numeric(theta["Aus"]*(1-a_share*(1-pdist_US(pyus - pgus_func(qgusimp), theta["mu_us"],
theta["s_us"])))*pgus_func(qgusimp)^theta["eta"])
}

#MX demand for yellowfin
qdymx_func <- function(pymx, qgusimp){
  as.numeric(theta["Amx"]*(1-pdist_MX(pymx - pgmx_func(qgusimp), theta["mu_mx"], theta["s_mx"]))*pymx^theta["eta"])
}

#MX demand for generic tuna
qdgmx_func <- function(pymx, qgusimp){
  as.numeric(theta["Amx"]*pdist_MX(pymx - pgmx_func(qgusimp), theta["mu_mx"],
theta["s_mx"])*pgmx_func(qgusimp)^theta["eta"])
}

#########################
### Equations to solve ###
#########################

#Quantity of generic tuna in U.S. (from Mexico's submission)
qg_sol_func <- function(pyus, qgusimp){
  as.numeric(qgusimp + theta["Qgus"] - qdgus_func(pyus, qgusimp))
}

#Quantity of yellowfin tuna
qy_sol_func <- function(pyus, qgusimp){
  as.numeric(qymx_dom - qdyus_func(pyus, qgusimp))
}

#Objective functions
obj_func <- function(x){
  pyus <- x[1]
  qgusimp <- x[2]
  y <- numeric(2)
  #Objective function
  y[1] <- qg_sol_func(pyus, qgusimp)
  y[2] <- qy_sol_func(pyus, qgusimp)
  #Return vector of functions
  y
}

#Mexican consumption of yellowfin tuna equals its imports
obj_func_mx <- function(pymx, qgusimp){
  #Objective function
  y <- qdymx_func(pymx, qgusimp) - ymx_imp
  #Return vector of functions
  y^2
}

#Square function to solve - for corner solution on qgusimp = 0
obj_func_2 <- function(pymx){
  as.numeric((qy_sol_func(pymx, 0))^2)
}

###############
### Solutions ###
###############
```

```
sol <- nleqslv(c(pyus = 7, qgusimp = 80000000), obj_func, control = list(cndtol = 1e-16))
print(sol$message)

pyus_sol <- as.numeric(sol$x[1])
qgusimp_sol <- as.numeric(sol$x[2])

#Solve for Mexican price of yellowfin
pymx_sol <- optimize(obj_func_mx, c(2,10), qgusimp = qgusimp_sol, tol = .Machine$double.eps^2)$minimum

#Return solutions for all variables in a vector
vec_sol <- c(Qdymx = ymx_imp,
        Qdgmx = qdgmx_func(pymx_sol, qgusimp_sol),
        Qdyus = as.numeric(qymx_dom),
        Qdgus = qdgus_func(pyus_sol, qgusimp_sol),
        Qymx_exp = max(0, qymx_dom),
        Qymx_imp = max(0, ymx_imp),
        Qgmx_exp = max(0, theta["Qgmx"] - qdgmx_func(pymx_sol, qgusimp_sol)),
        Qgmx_imp = max(0, qdgmx_func(pymx_sol, qgusimp_sol) - theta["Qgmx"]),
        Qgus_imp = max(0, qgusimp_sol),
        pymx = pymx_sol,
        pgmx = pgmx_func(qgusimp_sol),
        pyus = pyus_sol,
        pgus = pgus_func(qgusimp_sol))

  return(vec_sol)


}

#############################################################
### Function to select solution depending on corner solution ###
#############################################################

sol_func <- function(gamma){
  ifelse(func_interior(gamma)["Qymx_exp"] <= 65500000, return(func_interior(gamma)), return(func_corner(gamma)))


}

##############################
### Function to solve model ###
##############################

model_solution <- function(x, lambda, vec_US, vec_MX){

  ###########################################
  ### Calibration of US demand and supply ###
  ###########################################

  #Demand intensity parameter
  Aus <- as.numeric(vec_US["cons_US"]/(Hus*(vec_US["p_US"]^x["eta"])))

  #Supply intensity parameter
  beta_us <- as.numeric(lambda["pgw"]/(vec_US["cons_US"]-vec_US["Qgus"])^(1/x["epsilon"]))

  #########################################################
  ### Calibrate Mexican demand              ###
  #########################################################

  MX_func <- function(py){
    py <- py[1]
    #
    pg <- function(py){
      (vec_mx["p_mx"] - (1-vec_mx["Hmx"])*py)/vec_mx["Hmx"]
    }

    y1 <- vec_mx["cons_MXy"]/vec_mx["cons_MXg"] - ((1-pdist_MX(py - pg(py), x["mu_mx"], x["s_mx"]))/pdist_MX(py - pg(py),
x["mu_mx"], x["s_mx"]))*(py/pg(py))^x["eta"]

  return(y1^2)
  }

  pymx <- optim(c(5.4), MX_func, method = "Brent", lower = 4.00, upper = 8, control = list(abstol = .Machine$double.eps))$par
  #pymx

  #Find value for pg
  pgmx <- (vec_mx["p_mx"] - (1-vec_mx["Hmx"])*pymx)/vec_mx["Hmx"]
```

```
#Find value for A
Amx <- as.numeric(vec_mx["cons_MXy"])/((1-pdist_MX(pymx - pgmx, x["mu_mx"], x["s_mx"]))*pymx^x["eta"]))
#Amx

##################
### Solve model ###
##################

sol <- sol_func(c(x, lambda, Aus = Aus, Amx = Amx, beta_us = beta_us, Qgus = as.numeric(vec_US["Qgus"])))

#Return vector of solutions and parameters of calibration
return(c(sol, Aus_cal = Aus, Amx_cal = Amx, beta_us = beta_us, pymx_cal = pymx, pgmx_cal = pgmx))

}
```

MODEL SOLUTIONS

```
#Clear memory of all objects
rm(list = ls())

#Load library for numerical optimizer
library(nleqslv)
library(stringr)

################################
### Set the working directory ###
################################

setwd("USE YOUR OWN DIRECTORY") #use "/" rather than "\"

##################################################################
### Load the R file with model equations and numerical solutions ###
##################################################################

source("Arbitrator Final - Model functions.R")

##############################
### Parameter for US demand ###
##############################

vec_US <- c(Qgus= 177350000,
        cons_US = 330264000,
        p_US = 5)

##################################
### Parameter for Mexican demand ###
##################################

vec_mx <- c(cons_MXy = 58344000,
        cons_MXg = 29585000,
        p_mx = 5.04,
        Hmx = 29585000/(29585000+58344000))

########################
### Model parameters ###
########################

ymx_imp <- 0

vec_cal <- c(Qymx = 65342000 + ymx_imp,
        Qgmx = 23000000,
        t = 0.05,
        pgw = 4.30,
        dmx = 0.20,
        dus = 0.125,
        tmx = 0.16,
        tus = 0.16)

############################
### Choice of distribution ###
############################

dist_US <- "logistic"

dist_MX <- "logistic"


#################################
### Adjustment for lack of access ###
#################################

a_share <- .731   #26.9% of US retailers will not sell Mexican yellowfin
Hus <- .988     #Since we parameterize Aus with observed consumption share of 1.2% for yellowfin"


########################################################
### Vector of parameters for demand and supply equations ###
########################################################
```

```
s_logis <- 1

vec_par <- c(eta = -1,
        epsilon = 2.610382,
        mu_us = .19906683,
        mu_mx = 1.779089,
        s_us = s_logis,
        s_mx = s_logis)


##################
### Solve model ###
##################

sol <- model_solution(vec_par, vec_cal, vec_US, vec_mx)

#Make table of results
results <- data.frame(array(NA,c(8,2)))
colnames(results) <- c("US", "Mexico")
rownames(results) <- c("Cons_y", "Cons_g", "Price_y", "Price_g", "Exp_y", "Imp_y", "Exp_g", "Imp_g")

results["Cons_y", "US"] <- sol["Qdyus"]
results["Cons_g", "US"] <- sol["Qdgus"]
results["Price_y", "US"] <- sol["pyus"]
results["Price_g", "US"] <- sol["pgus"]
results["Exp_y", "US"] <- 0
results["Imp_y", "US"] <- sol["Qdyus"]
results["Exp_g", "US"] <- 0
results["Imp_g", "US"] <- sol["Qgus_imp"]
results["Aus", "US"] <- sol["Aus_cal"]

results["Cons_y", "Mexico"] <- sol["Qdymx"]
results["Cons_g", "Mexico"] <- sol["Qdgmx"]
results["Price_y", "Mexico"] <- sol["pymx"]
results["Price_g", "Mexico"] <- sol["pgmx"]
results["Exp_y", "Mexico"] <-sol["Qymx_exp"]
results["Imp_y", "Mexico"] <- ymx_imp
results["Exp_g", "Mexico"] <- 0
results["Imp_g", "Mexico"] <- sol["Qgmx_imp"]
results["Amx", "Mexico"] <- sol["Amx_cal"]


######################
### Table of results ###
######################

results

library(xlsx)
write.xlsx(results, file = "Arbitrator Final - Model results.xlsx")

##########################
### Calculate export losses ###
##########################

exp_value <- as.numeric(sol["Qymx_exp"]*(sol["pyus"]-vec_cal["t"]) + sol["Qgmx_exp"]*sol["pgmx"])
exp_value/1000000
exp_value - 22650000 -> nullification


###################################################
### Arbitrator's determination of nullification or impairment ###
###################################################

nullification/1000000
```

ANNEX A

WORKING PROCEDURES OF THE ARBITRATOR

Contents		Page
Annex A-1	Working Procedures of the Arbitrator	4267
Annex A-2	Procedures of the Arbitrator Concerning Business Confidential Information	4272
Annex A-3	Additional Working Procedures of the Arbitrator on Partially Open Meetings	4274

ANNEX A-1

WORKING PROCEDURES OF THE ARBITRATOR

Adopted on 7 June 2016

Modified on 3 August 2016

1.   In its proceedings, the Arbitrator shall follow the relevant provisions of the Understanding on Rules and Procedures Governing the Settlement of Disputes (DSU). In addition, the following Working Procedures shall apply.

General

2.   The deliberations of the Arbitrator and the documents submitted to it shall be kept confidential. Nothing in the DSU or in these Working Procedures shall preclude a party to the dispute (hereafter "party") from disclosing statements of its own positions to the public. Business Confidential Information (BCI), as defined in the Arbitrator's Additional Procedures Concerning Business Confidential Information, shall be submitted and treated in accordance with those Additional Procedures.

3.   The Arbitrator shall conduct its internal deliberations in closed session. The parties shall be present at meetings only when invited by the Arbitrator to appear before it. The Arbitrator may, upon request by a party, authorize that party to lift the confidentiality, by way of delayed viewing, of its own statements made during the Arbitrator's meeting with the parties. Such lifting of confidentiality will be authorized only where it does not impair or otherwise interfere with either the rights of the other party or the integrity and promptness of the dispute settlement process. Moreover, such lifting of confidentiality shall

be in accordance with additional working procedures, to be adopted by the Arbitrator after consulting with the parties. A request that the Arbitrator adopt additional working procedures to facilitate this lifting of confidentiality shall be made to the Arbitrator no fewer than six weeks before the meeting where the statements in question will be delivered.

4.   Each party has the right to determine the composition of its own delegation when meeting with the Arbitrator. Each party shall have responsibility for all members of its own delegation and shall ensure that each member of such delegation acts in accordance with the DSU and these Working Procedures, particularly with regard to the confidentiality of the proceedings.

Submissions

5.   Mexico shall transmit to the Arbitrator and to the United States a communication explaining the basis for its request, including the methodology and data supporting it, in accordance with the timetable adopted by the Arbitrator.

6.   Each party to the dispute shall also transmit to the Arbitrator a written submission in which it presents the facts of the case and its arguments, in accordance with the timetable adopted by the Arbitrator.

7.   A party shall submit any request for a preliminary ruling at the earliest possible opportunity and in any event no later than in its written submission to the Arbitrator. If the United States requests such a ruling in its written submission to the Arbitrator, Mexico shall submit its response to the request in its written submission. If Mexico requests such a ruling in its written submission to the Arbitrator, the United States shall submit its response to the request prior to the substantive meeting, at a time to be determined by the Arbitrator in light of the request. Exceptions to this procedure shall be granted upon a showing of good cause.

8.   Each party shall submit all factual evidence to the Arbitrator no later than in its written submission, except with respect to evidence necessary for purposes of rebuttal, answers to questions or comments on answers provided by the other party. Exceptions to this procedure shall be granted upon a showing of good cause. Where such exception has been granted, the Arbitrator shall accord the other party a period of time for comment, as appropriate, on any new factual evidence submitted after the substantive meeting.

9.   Where the original language of exhibits is not a WTO working language, the submitting party shall submit a translation into the WTO working language of the submission at the same time. The Arbitrator may grant reasonable extensions of time for the translation of such exhibits upon a showing of good cause. Any objection as to the accuracy of a translation should be raised promptly in writing, preferably no later than the next filing or meeting (whichever occurs earlier) following the submission which contains the translation in question. The Arbitrator may grant reasonable extensions of time for the filing of such objection upon a showing of good cause. Any objection

shall be accompanied by a detailed explanation of the grounds of objection and an alternative translation.

10.   In order to facilitate the work of the Arbitrator, each party is invited to make its submissions in accordance with the WTO Editorial Guide for Submissions, as relevant and to the extent that it is practical to do so.

11.   To facilitate the maintenance of the record of the dispute and maximize the clarity of submissions, each party shall sequentially number its exhibits throughout the course of the proceedings. For example, exhibits submitted by Mexico could be numbered MEX-1, MEX-2, etc. If the last exhibit in connection with the first submission was numbered MEX-5, the first exhibit of the next submission thus would be numbered MEX-6.

Questions

12.   The Arbitrator may at any time pose questions to the parties, orally or in writing, including prior to the substantive meeting.

Substantive meeting

13.   Each party shall provide to the Arbitrator the list of members of its delegation in advance of each meeting with the Arbitrator and no later than 5.00 p.m. the previous working day.

14.   The substantive meeting of the Arbitrator with the parties shall be conducted as follows:

    a.   The Arbitrator shall invite the United States to make an opening statement to present its case first. Subsequently, the Arbitrator shall invite Mexico to present its point of view. Before each party takes the floor, it shall provide the Arbitrator and other participants at the meeting with a provisional written version of its statement. Each party shall make available to the Arbitrator and the other party the final version of its statement, preferably at the end of the meeting, and in any event no later than 5.00 p.m. on the first working day following the meeting.

    b.   After the conclusion of the statements, the Arbitrator shall give each party the opportunity to ask each other questions or make comments, through the Arbitrator. Each party shall then have an opportunity to answer these questions orally. Each party shall send in writing, within a timeframe to be determined by the Arbitrator, any questions to the other party to which it wishes to receive a response in writing. Each party shall be invited to respond in writing to the other party's written questions within a deadline to be determined by the Arbitrator.

    c.   The Arbitrator may subsequently pose questions to the parties. Each party shall then have an opportunity to answer these questions orally. The Arbitrator shall send in writing, within a timeframe to be determined by it, any questions to the parties to which it wishes to receive a response in writing. Each party shall be invited to respond in writing to such questions within a deadline to be determined by the Arbitrator.

d.   Once the questioning has concluded, the Arbitrator shall afford each party an opportunity to present a brief closing statement, with the United States presenting its statement first.

Executive summaries

15.   The description of the arguments of the parties in the Decision of the Arbitrator shall consist of executive summaries provided by the parties, which shall be annexed as addenda to the decision. These executive summaries shall not in any way serve as a substitute for the submissions of the parties in the Arbitrator's examination of the case.

16.   Each party shall submit an executive summary of the facts and arguments as presented to the Arbitrator in its written submissions and oral statements, in accordance with the timetable adopted by the Arbitrator. Each such executive summary shall not exceed 15 pages. The Arbitrator will not summarize in a descriptive part, or annex to its decision, the parties' responses to questions.

Service of documents

17.   The following procedures regarding service of documents shall apply:

a.   Each party shall submit all documents to the Arbitrator by filing them with the DS Registry (office No. 2047).

b.   Each party shall file five (5) paper copies of all documents it submits to the Arbitrator. However, when exhibits are provided on CD-ROMS/DVDs, four (4) CD-ROMS/DVDs and two (2) paper copies of those exhibits shall be filed. The DS Registrar shall stamp the documents with the date and time of the filing. The paper version shall constitute the official version for the purposes of the record of the dispute.

c.   Each party shall also provide an electronic copy of all documents it submits to the Arbitrator at the same time as the paper versions, preferably in Microsoft Word format, either on a CD-ROM, a DVD or as an e-mail attachment. If the electronic copy is provided by e-mail, it should be addressed to DSRegistry@wto.org, with a copy to ***.***@wto.org, ***.***@wto.org, ***.***@wto.org, ***.***@wto.org, and ***.***@wto.org. If a CD-ROM or DVD is provided, it shall be filed with the DS Registry.

d.   Each party shall serve any document submitted to the Arbitrator directly on the other party. Each party shall confirm, in writing, that copies have been served as required at the time it provides each document to the Arbitrator.

e.   Each party shall file its documents with the DS Registry and serve copies on the other party by 5.00 p.m. (Geneva time) on the due dates established by the Arbitrator. A party may submit its documents to another party in electronic format only, subject to the recipient party's prior written approval and provided that the Arbitrator's Secretary is notified.

f. The Arbitrator shall provide the parties with an electronic version of its decision, as well as of other documents as appropriate. When the Arbitrator transmits to the parties both paper and electronic versions of a document, the paper version shall constitute the official version for the purposes of the record of the dispute.

Modification of Working Procedures

18. The Arbitrator reserves the right to modify these procedures as necessary, after consultation with the parties.

ANNEX A-2

PROCEDURES OF THE ARBITRATOR CONCERNING BUSINESS CONFIDENTIAL INFORMATION[1] (DS381)

Adopted on 7 June 2016

1.   These procedures apply to any business confidential information (BCI) that a party submits to the Arbitrator.

2.   For the purposes of these procedures, BCI is defined as any information that has been designated as such by the party submitting the information and that is not available in the public domain and the release of which could reasonably be considered to cause or threaten to cause harm to an interest of the person or entity that supplied the business information to the party.

3.   No person may have access to BCI except a member of the Secretariat or the Arbitrator, a party's employee participating in the dispute, and a party's outside advisor for purposes of this dispute. However, an outside advisor is not permitted access to BCI if that advisor is an officer or employee of an enterprise engaged in the production, export, or import of tuna or tuna products. When a party provides BCI to an outside advisor who is an employee or officer of an industry association of such enterprises, that party shall obtain written assurances from such advisor that he or she has read and understands these procedures and will not disclose any BCI in contravention of these procedures.

4.   A party obtaining access to BCI as a result of the BCI being submitted in this dispute shall treat it as confidential, i.e. shall not disclose that information other than to those persons authorized to receive it pursuant to these procedures. Each party shall have responsibility in this regard for its employees as well as any outside advisors for the purposes of this dispute. BCI obtained under these procedures may be used only for the purpose of providing information and argumentation in this dispute.

5.   A party submitting or referring to BCI in a document shall mark the cover and each page of the document to indicate the presence of BCI in the document as follows: BCI shall be placed between double brackets (for example, [[xx,xxx.xx]]). The cover and the top of each page of the document shall contain the notice "Contains Business Confidential Information". Any BCI that is submitted in electronic form shall be clearly marked with the phrase "Contains BCI" on a label on the storage medium, and clearly marked with the phrase "Contains BCI" in the electronic file name.

---

[1]   These procedures are adopted according to, and are an integral part of, the Arbitrator's Working Procedures of 7 June 2016.

6.   The parties and the Arbitrator shall store all documents containing BCI so as to prevent unauthorized access to such information.

7.   The Arbitrator shall not disclose BCI, in its decision or in any other way, to persons not authorized under these procedures to have access to BCI. The Arbitrator may, however, make statements of conclusion drawn from such information. Before the Arbitrator makes its decision publicly available, the Arbitrator shall give each party an opportunity to ensure that the decision does not contain any information that it has designated as BCI.

ANNEX A-3

ADDITIONAL WORKING PROCEDURES OF
THE ARBITRATOR ON PARTIALLY
OPEN MEETINGS

Adopted on 18 October 2016

Having regard to paragraph 3 of the Arbitrator's Working Procedures, and having received a request from the United States for the adoption of additional working procedures to facilitate the lifting of the confidentiality of its statements at the Arbitrator's meeting with the parties, the Arbitrator has, after consulting with the parties, adopted the following Additional Working Procedures:

1.   DEFINITIONS

1.1   For the purposes of these Additional Working Procedures:

a.   "Disclosing party" means any party that wishes to lift the confidentiality of its statements at the Arbitrator's meeting with the parties;

b.   "Non-disclosing party" means any party that wishes to maintain the confidentiality of its statements at the Arbitrator's meeting with the parties;

c.   "Statement" means:

i.   A party's opening oral statement;

ii.   A party's closing oral statement;

iii.   A party's oral responses to questions from the Arbitrator concerning (a) issues of law; and (b) the disclosing party's own exhibits, arguments, or positions (referred to in these Working Procedures as a "paragraph 1.1(c)(iii) question");

excluding, however, any part or section of those items that discloses, directly or indirectly, the exhibits, arguments, or positions of a non-disclosing party. Any part or section of the items that discloses, directly or indirectly, the exhibits, arguments, or positions of a non-disclosing party shall, prior to the delayed viewing, be redacted in accordance with the procedures provided for in Section 4 of these Additional Working Procedures.

d.   "Delayed viewing" means the broadcasting by the WTO Secretariat, after the conclusion of the Arbitrator's meeting with the parties, of the statements of disclosing parties that have been recorded and redacted in accordance with Sections 3 and 4 of these Additional Working Procedures.

2.   GENERAL

2.1   Disclosure by a disclosing party of its statements at the Arbitrator's meeting with the parties shall be by way of delayed viewing. The viewing shall be in a room inside the WTO Secretariat building. It will be open to officials of WTO Members and Observers, and, upon registration with the Secretariat, to accredited journalists, accredited representatives of non-governmental organizations, and other interested persons, including members of the public. The names of all persons registered to attend the delayed viewing will be shared with the parties. To this effect, the Secretariat will place a notice on the WTO website, informing the public of the delayed viewing and including a link through which members of the public can register to attend. The notice shall specify: (a) that the names of all persons registered to attend the delayed viewing will be shared with the parties; and (b) that no person attending the delayed viewing is allowed to use electronic devices to record any portion of the broadcast.

2.2   The date of the delayed viewing will be decided by the Arbitrator after consulting with the parties. The redacted recording will be broadcast once, simultaneously in English and Spanish.

3.   RECORDING OF STATEMENTS

3.1   In accordance with the usual practice of the WTO, the audio of the entirety of the Arbitrator's meeting with the parties (including the floor recording and interpretation) shall be recorded and entered into the dispute record.

3.2   The entirety of a disclosing party's opening and closing oral statements shall be video recorded, except as provided for in paragraph 3.7.

3.3   A disclosing party's oral responses to paragraph 1.1(c)(iii) questions shall also be video recorded, except as provided for in paragraph 3.4. A disclosing party shall advise the Arbitrator, prior to responding to a paragraph 1.1(c)(iii) question, if its response to that question discloses, directly or indirectly, the exhibits, arguments, or positions of a non-disclosing party.

3.4   To facilitate the implementation of paragraph 3.3:

    a.   The Arbitrator shall, when it sends advance questions to the parties, indicate which questions it considers meet the definition in paragraph 1.1(c)(iii) of these Additional Working Procedures.

    b.   Either disputing party shall promptly inform the Arbitrator if it considers (a) that a question indicated by the Arbitrator as meeting the definition in paragraph 1.1(c)(iii) does not meet that definition; or (b) that a question not indicated by the Arbitrator as meeting the definition in paragraph 1.1(c)(iii) meets that definition. The Arbitrator, after hearing the views of the other disputing party, will decide whether the question meets the definition in paragraph 1.1(c)(iii).

    c.   Spontaneous questions asked by the Arbitrator during the course of the meeting shall not be recorded.

3.5   The video recording foreseen under paragraphs 3.2 and 3.3 shall be entered into the dispute record.

3.6   The video recording foreseen under paragraphs 3.2 and 3.3 shall be made from a single camera. The camera shall be set at the same position, zoom, and focus throughout the meeting.

3.7   In addition to the video recording foreseen under paragraphs 3.2 and 3.3, a secondary video recording, using a separate video recording channel but captured from the video camera referenced in paragraph 3.6 will be made of the entirety of the Arbitrator's meeting with the parties for back-up purposes. Except where the primary video recording is technically defective, this secondary video will not be used when the Secretariat compiles the video for the delayed viewing, and will be deleted once the procedures provided for in Section 4 of these Additional Working Procedures have been completed.

3.8   A disclosing party shall advise the Arbitrator prior to addressing its own or another party's BCI in its statements. When a disclosing party so advises, both video recordings will be discontinued for the relevant portion of the statement, after which the video recordings will be resumed. At the conclusion of a disclosing party's statement, the Arbitrator will ask the non-disclosing party to confirm that none of its own BCI was disclosed during the video recorded portion of the statement. In the interests of ensuring an efficient meeting, a disclosing party is invited to structure its statements so as to first deliver a non-BCI portion before delivering a portion that contains BCI.

4.   REDACTION OF RECORDED STATEMENTS

4.1   In order to ensure, pursuant to paragraph 3 of the Arbitrator's Working Procedures, that disclosure by a disclosing party of its statements at the Arbitrator's meeting with the parties does not impair or otherwise interfere with either the rights of a non-disclosing party or the integrity and promptness of the dispute settlement process, statements recorded pursuant to Section 3 of these Additional Working Procedures shall be redacted as described in this Section prior to delayed viewing.

4.2   A disclosing party shall indicate, in the final written version of its opening and closing oral statements, which paragraphs disclose, directly or indirectly, the exhibits, arguments, or positions of a non-disclosing party. For example, a disclosing party could use the following phrases in the final written version of its opening and closing oral statements: *Beginning of discussion of [non-disclosing party]'s submissions* and *End of discussion of [non-disclosing party]'s submissions*. Paragraphs that disclose, directly or indirectly, the exhibits, arguments, or positions of a non-disclosing party shall be redacted from the video recording. In order to avoid unnecessary discontinuity in the delayed viewing, a disclosing party is invited to structure its statements in such a way as to separate those statements that disclose, directly or indirectly, the exhibits, arguments, or positions of a non-disclosing party.

4.3   Pursuant to paragraph 3.3 of these Additional Working Procedures, where a response to a paragraph 1.1(c)(iii) question discloses, directly or indirectly, the exhibits, arguments, or positions of a non-disclosing party, that response shall be redacted from the video recording.

4.4   Following the conclusion of the Arbitrator's meeting with the parties, the Arbitrator will review the recorded statements and the final written versions of a disclosing party's opening and closing oral statements. Using the paragraph numbers contained in the final written version of a disclosing party's opening and closing oral statements, the Arbitrator will identify to the disputing parties any paragraphs additional to those identified by the disclosing party pursuant to paragraph 4.2 that, in the Arbitrator's view, disclose, directly or indirectly, the exhibits, arguments, or positions of a non-disclosing party. These paragraphs will be redacted from the video recording, except as provided for in paragraph 4.7.

4.5   Following the conclusion of the Arbitrator's meeting with the parties, the Arbitrator will review the video recording of a disclosing party's oral responses to paragraph 1.1(c)(iii) questions. The Arbitrator will identify to the disputing parties, by reference to the question number, any responses additional to the responses identified by the disclosing party pursuant to paragraph 3.3 of these Additional Working Procedures that, in the Arbitrator's view, disclose, directly or indirectly, the exhibits, arguments, or positions of a non-disclosing party. These responses will also be redacted from the video recording, except as provided for in paragraph 4.7.

4.6   If a non-disclosing party considers that any part of the video-recorded statements not identified by a disclosing party (pursuant to paragraphs 4.2 and 4.3 of these Additional Working Procedures) or redacted by the Arbitrator (pursuant to paragraph 4.4 or 4.5 of these Additional Working Procedures) discloses, directly or indirectly, the exhibits, arguments, or positions of a non-disclosing party, that party may bring such part of the video-recorded statements to the attention of the Arbitrator (through the Secretariat) and the disclosing party. Such notification should be made within a deadline to be specified by the Arbitrator, and should identify the particular paragraph of the relevant opening or closing statement (or, where relevant, third party statement), or the particular response by question number, and indicate how, in the view of the notifying party, it discloses, directly or indirectly, the exhibits, arguments, or positions of a non-disclosing party. Before the Arbitrator makes a decision regarding any identified issue, the disclosing party will be afforded an opportunity to explain where appropriate why, in its view, the identified part of the video-recorded statements does not disclose, directly or indirectly, the exhibits, arguments, or positions of a non-disclosing party.

4.7   If a disclosing party considers that any part of the video-recorded statements redacted by the Arbitrator (pursuant to paragraph 4.4 or 4.5 of these

Additional Working Procedures) does not disclose, directly or indirectly, the exhibits, arguments, or positions of a non-disclosing party, that party may bring such part of the video-recorded statements to the attention of the Arbitrator (through the Secretariat) and the non-disclosing party. Such notification should be made within a deadline to be specified by the Arbitrator, and should identify the particular paragraph of the relevant opening or closing statement (or, where relevant, third party statement), or the particular response by question number, and indicate how, in the view of the notifying party, it does not disclose, directly or indirectly, the exhibits, arguments, or positions of a non-disclosing party. Before the Arbitrator makes a decision regarding any identified issue, the non-disclosing party will be afforded an opportunity to explain where appropriate why, in its view, the identified part of the video-recorded statements does disclose, directly or indirectly, the exhibits, arguments, or positions of a non-disclosing party.

4.8   The Arbitrator is mindful of the need to ensure the promptness of the dispute settlement process. Therefore, in the interests of ensuring the workability and efficiency of these Additional Working Procedures, where a paragraph of a disclosing party's opening or closing oral statements, or a disclosing party's response to a paragraph 1.1(c)(iii) question, is found to disclose, directly or indirectly, the exhibits, arguments, or positions of a non-disclosing party, the entire paragraph or response will be redacted, even if the paragraph or response also contains content that does not disclose, directly or indirectly, the exhibits, arguments, or positions of a non-disclosing party.

4.9   If either party requests to view the redacted video recording prior to the delayed viewing, the Arbitrator will invite both parties to attend a preview session, accompanied by a representative of the Secretariat, on the premises of the WTO. The preview session will be held on a date to be determined by the Arbitrator in consultation with the parties.

4.10   The Arbitrator retains the right to modify these procedures after consulting with the parties.

ANNEX B

ARGUMENTS OF THE PARTIES

Contents		Page
Annex B-1	Executive summary of the arguments of Mexico	4279
Annex B-2	Executive summary of the arguments of the United States	4291

ANNEX B-1

EXECUTIVE SUMMARY OF THE ARGUMENTS OF MEXICO

1.   Mexico's methodology paper demonstrates that the amended 2013 Tuna Measure (Tuna Measure) in place at the expiration of the reasonable period of time (RPT) on 13 July 2013 has caused significant monetary losses to the Mexican tuna industry from reduced export revenues. Because the United States has not brought the Tuna Measure into conformity with its obligations, Mexico is seeking authorization to suspend concessions in the amount of USD $472.3 million.

2.   Under Article 22.4 of the Understanding on Rules and Procedures Governing the Settlement of Disputes (DSU), the level of suspension must be "equivalent to the level of the nullification or impairment". In the present case, the Arbitrator's mandate under Articles 22.6 and 22.7 of the DSU is to determine whether the proposed level of the suspension of concessions requested by Mexico is equivalent to the level of the nullification or impairment of benefits accruing to Mexico as a result of the United States' failure to bring its WTO-inconsistent Tuna Measure into compliance. To determine the level of benefits to suspend, Mexico has compared the actual circumstances of the U.S. market for Mexican tuna products during 2014 (first calendar year after the expiration of the RPT on 13 July 2013) to a counterfactual in which the WTO-inconsistent discriminatory aspects of the original and amended Tuna Measure were eliminated. The difference between those circumstances is the amount of the nullification or impairment caused by the amended Tuna Measure.[1]

---

[1]   The relevant data is more readily available on a calendar year basis and 2014 is the most immediate calendar year following the end of the RPT. This approach is consistent with Mexico's approach in the Article 22.6 arbitration in *US – COOL* where the RPT expired on 23 May 2013 and the baseline year for Mexico's and the arbitrator's analysis was calendar year 2014.

3.   Mexico's methodology and calculations are based on a calibrated partial equilibrium model of the American and Mexican canned tuna markets. The calculations assume a counterfactual for 2014 where there is no measure for the labeling of tuna as "dolphin-safe" that discriminates in a WTO-inconsistent manner between Mexican tuna products and tuna products from the United States and other countries.

4.   The structure of Mexico's model to calculate the level of nullification or impairment is as follows. First, demand equations for tuna products in the United States and Mexico are derived based on consumers' preference for yellowfin tuna and generic tuna (all other tuna) and consumption values in 2014. Second, supply equations for canned yellowfin tuna and canned generic tuna to the United States and Mexico are derived based on observed supply in 2014. Third, the model finds the market equilibrium under the counterfactual where the Tuna Measure is removed. The model's solution yields increased exports of Mexican canned yellowfin tuna products to the United States. Under this counterfactual, based on values observed for 2014, Mexico exports a total of USD $495 million (63,568 metric tonnes x USD $7.79/kg) of canned tuna to the United States. Trade loss for Mexico is calculated by deducting from the aforementioned figure the actual value of exports of Mexican canned tuna to the United States in 2014 (USD $22.65 million), which gives rise to an amount of USD $472.3 million annually.

5.   In response, the United States proposes a "market-based approach" that builds on the comparison, on a prospective basis, of the U.S. imports from Mexico of tuna product with the measure in place to the level of imports that would occur if the measure were withdrawn. The approach used by the United States is flawed in many ways. For example, the U.S. calculations are based on data from the late 1980s. The amount of time elapsed is too long to make the late 1980s a proper counterfactual for 2014 as markets for canned tuna have very much changed since then. Further, the U.S. methodology assumes that retailers accounting for 46.4 percent of the U.S. market for tuna products will not purchase and offer for sale Mexican tuna products because the tuna was caught using the AIDCP-certified dolphin encirclement fishing method.[2] In addition, the United States assumes that 100 percent of tuna products from all other sources will be able to use the dolphin-safe label.[3] All of these assumptions are incorrect.

6.   Mexico's methodology paper need only present a counterfactual that is "plausible" or "reasonable". It is not for an arbitrator to speculate on what might have been the "most likely" scenario of compliance by the Member concerned;[4]

---

[2]   U.S. written submission, paras. 135-136.
[3]   U.S. written submission, paras. 71, 76 and 123.
[4]   *US - Gambling (Article 22.6 - US)*, paras. 3.26 ("We do not consider that the proposed counterfactual must necessarily reflect the 'most likely' scenario of compliance by the Member concerned. ... It is not for us to speculate on what might have been the 'most likely' such scenario") and 3.56 ("whether the scenario at issue is the 'most likely' ... is not pertinent as such in our determination").

rather, a counterfactual should reflect at least a "plausible" or "reasonable" compliance scenario.[5] For the United States to merely present an alternative methodology, scenario or period (i.e., 2015) is insufficient to rebut the level of nullification or impairment in Mexico's methodology paper. In *US – COOL*, the Arbitrator stated that "[i]n the absence of a demonstration that the proposing party's methodology is incorrect, the mere submission of an alternative methodology would not meet the objecting party's burden of proof".[6] This standard is consistent with the burden of proof applied in other arbitrations, including *EC – Hormones (US) (Article 22.6 – EC)*, *EC – Bananas III (Ecuador) (Article 22.6 – EC)* and *US – 1916 Act (EC) (Article 22.6 – US)*.

7.   Thus, the United States bears the initial burden of establishing a *prima facie* case that the level of suspension of benefits requested by Mexico is not in accordance with the requirements of the DSU. The United States has failed to discharge its burden. There are significant mischaracterizations and misinterpretations of economic concepts in the United States' criticisms of Mexico's methodology, and also legal errors in the alternative methodology that the United States proposes. Mexico's comprehensive analysis is the appropriate approach under the circumstances, and it has been properly applied to accurately estimate the level of nullification and impairment caused by the amended Tuna Measure. The United States' incorrect criticisms and flawed alternative "market-based approach" that relies on historical levels of U.S. imports of Mexican tuna and tuna products prior to 1990 (1987-1989) are therefore insufficient to establish a *prima facie* case that Mexico's methodology is inconsistent with DSU Article 22.4. Thus, there is no basis to reject the use of 2014 as the period of reference in Mexico's methodology paper or to use the United States' projections.

8.   In the event that the Arbitrator disagrees and finds instead that the United States has established a *prima facie* case, in whole or in part, then Mexico submits that even if the alternative counterfactual proposed by the United States is used, the level of nullification or impairment will not change, provided that reasonable assumptions are made under that counterfactual. That counterfactual assumes a scenario whereby Mexican tuna products can use the AIDCP-certified dolphin-safe label, and all other tuna products can use a dolphin-safe label provided that it is accurate and does not deceive U.S. consumers. The level of the nullification or impairment estimated by Mexico will be no lower, and possibly higher, under the U.S. counterfactual.[7]

---

[5]   *US - Gambling (Article 22.6 - US)*, paras. 3.26-3.27 and 3.56.

[6]   Decisions by the Arbitrators, *US – COOL*, para. 4.12.

[7]   In its description of the history in paragraph 11 of its written submission, the United States omits to mention that the United States maintained a *complete embargo* on imports of Mexican yellowfin tuna products from 1999 until 2000, although the embargo had been found inconsistent with the United States' GATT obligations in 1991. *US – Tuna (Mexico) (GATT)*. The United States also omits that, in connection with the creation of the AIDCP, in the 1995 Panama Declaration the United States committed to revise the definition of "dolphin-safe" in the tuna measure to match that of the AIDCP.

The measure to be analyzed is the 2013 Tuna Measure

9.   As the Arbitrator confirmed, its sole mandate in this arbitration is to either confirm or determine the appropriate level of suspension for the purposes of Article 22 of the DSU with respect to the 2013 Tuna Measure. This is consistent with the provisions of the DSU and the *Understanding between the United States and Mexico regarding Procedures under Articles 21 and 22 of the DSU*,[8] since the arbitration is based on the DSB's recommendations and rulings pursuant to Article 21.5 in the first compliance proceeding, specifically with regard to the nullification and impairment sustained by Mexico as a result of the United States' failure to bring the tuna measure, as amended by the 2013 Final Rule, into compliance before the expiry of the RPT on 13 July 2013.[9] Thus, Mexico's model is based on the 2013 Tuna Measure.

Appropriateness of Mexico's Partial Equilibrium Model

10.   The partial equilibrium model presented by Mexico is fully consistent with the proposed counterfactual for the calculation of the export losses to Mexico. A simulation using a partial equilibrium model is the proper method to employ given the data available and the amount of time since the adoption of the tuna measure. Mexico follows a state-of-the-art approach in its simulation.[10] Simulations in partial equilibrium models have been used in previous disputes at the WTO (e.g., *US – Upland cotton*, *US – COOL*). The partial equilibrium model of Mexico focuses very precisely on the issue at hand, which is the modification of the Tuna Measure in a manner that is consistent with WTO obligations.

11.   Mexico's partial equilibrium model captures the essential features of the canned tuna market in the United States and Mexico. The production of canned

---

See Panel Report, *US – Tuna II (Mexico)*, paras. 2.35–2.39. Moreover, the United States sought to implement that commitment until the Hogarth court ruling in 2007. See Panel Report, *US – Tuna II (Mexico)*, paras. 4.23–4.24 and 7.332. Mexico reaffirms that its tuna industry has been improperly blocked from the U.S. market for over 25 years. Mexico also notes that the United States incorrectly states that Mexico initiated the WTO proceedings in 2009; Mexico initiated the proceedings in 2008, shortly after the United States indicated it was giving up on implementing its commitment. WT/DS381/1 (28 Oct. 2008).

[8]   Understanding between the United States and Mexico regarding Procedures under Articles 21 and 22 of the DSU, *US – Tuna II (Mexico)*, WT/DS381/19 (7 Aug. 2013).

[9]   Recourse to Article 22.2 of the DSU by Mexico, *Tuna II (Article 22.2 – Mexico)*, p. 2 ("As required by Article 22.4 of the DSU, the level of suspension of concessions proposed by Mexico is equivalent on an annual basis to the level of the nullification or impairment of benefits accruing to Mexico under the covered agreements due to the United States' failure to bring its Tuna measure into compliance by 13 July 2013 or to otherwise comply with the recommendations and rulings of the DSB in *United States – Measures Concernin the Importation, Marketing and Sale of Tuna and Tuna Products*"); Dispute Settlement Body, Minutes of Meeting (13 May 2016), WT/DSB/M/376, para. 7.6 ("Mexico's request for the suspension of concessions complied with all of the requirements under Article 22.2 of the DSU, in particular the failure by the United States to comply with the DSB's recommendations and rulings within the reasonable period of time").

[10]   See Exhibit US-57 p. 139.

tuna in Mexico is mostly specialized in the production of canned yellowfin tuna, which is of higher quality than the average tuna quality consumed in the United States.

12.   The partial equilibrium model is calibrated to data observed for 2014. As such, it captures the state of the market in 2014 and incorporates in the demand curves relative preferences and substitution between generic tuna and yellowfin tuna and income, and it incorporates in the supply curves input prices, production technology and expectations. Equilibrium prices and quantities are found at the intersection of demand and supply curves.

Supply and demand equations for the U.S. Market

13.   Mexico's model is based on the total supply of canned tuna to the United States observed in 2014. At the margin, the price of canned tuna in the U.S. market is determined by the world supply of canned tuna to the United States. The world supply of canned tuna to the United States is assumed perfectly elastic in Mexico's model because the United States is a relatively small market for canned tuna but this can be adjusted.[11]

14.   The total U.S. import cost of canned tuna products (which is the sum of the import value, the duties and the charges, divided by the import quantities) in 2014 was on average USD $5.00/kg, significantly more than the import cost of tuna from Mexico, which was USD $4.06/kg. The supply of canned tuna to the United States under the Tuna Measure is for what is labeled as "generic" tuna in Mexico's methodology paper. Generic tuna is a composite category that includes all canned tuna currently offered in the United States. This is mostly skipjack, but it also includes albacore and tongol. This generic tuna is of an overall lower quality than Mexican canned yellowfin tuna.

15.   With regard to the demand for tuna products, the total consumption of canned tuna in the United States in 2014 was 330,264 metric tonnes. As mentioned before, most of that canned tuna is generic tuna, with marginal volumes of canned yellowfin tuna products. However, this does not mean that there is no demand for canned yellowfin tuna in the United States.

16.   Yellowfin tuna products are superior in quality to generic tuna products because they offer a more desirable solid pack for canning with a firm and mild tasting meat. The model recognizes the quality difference between generic and yellowfin tuna. The model assumes that consumers can purchase two types of canned tuna: generic and yellowfin. The results of an econometric analysis show that U.S. consumers have been paying a significant premium for canned yellowfin tuna. If generic tuna and yellowfin tuna are offered at the same price, almost all consumers will purchase yellowfin tuna over generic tuna. Consumers' preferences are modeled using a choice model that is standard in economics. Demand equations for canned generic tuna and canned yellowfin tuna are

---

[11]   The R code in Exhibits MEX-100-f and MEX-100-g allows for adjusting the world supply of canned generic tuna to the United States.

derived by aggregating individual consumers' demand for yellowfin and generic tuna. The demand model is calibrated using a conservative approach in which it is assumed that the mean willingness to pay for yellowfin tuna is lower than the premium currently observed.

17.　　Contrary to the United States' explanation that the weak consumption of yellowfin tuna in the United States is a consequence of a weak demand, there is strong demand for canned yellowfin tuna in the United States. Observed small consumption volumes of canned yellowfin tuna reflect the intersection of the demand and the supply for that product. Because, under the Tuna Measure, canned yellowfin tuna is supplied at a high cost to the United States, the U.S. demand for canned yellowfin tuna meets the supply to the United States of canned yellowfin tuna at a small volume. Mexico has put forward evidence of an increase in the price of raw yellowfin tuna paid by U.S. canneries. The decline in U.S. cannery receipts for yellowfin tuna is a consequence of the Tuna Measure, was not caused by U.S. consumers valuing yellowfin tuna less, and reflects world market conditions for yellowfin tuna products.[12]

18.　　Although the United States argues that consumers are not willing to pay a premium for canned yellowfin tuna, Mexico's methodology paper provides significant evidence that U.S. consumers are willing to pay such a premium. This premium is reflected in the data. If consumers were not willing to pay a premium for canned yellowfin tuna, as it is currently selling for a high price, there would be no consumption of yellowfin tuna in the United States. In Mexico's model, albacore tuna is bundled together with all other canned tuna. The regression model provides evidence that U.S. consumers are willing to pay a premium for canned yellowfin tuna versus the average (generic) canned tuna consumed in the United States. This is the appropriate way to provide evidence of willingness to pay for canned yellowfin tuna because it is consistent with the construction of the model. The regression model provides the necessary information to support that there is a premium for yellowfin tuna.[13]

19.　　Another argument that the United States claims as evidence that there is little demand for yellowfin tuna is that some yellowfin tuna is mixed with skipjack in light tuna. However, for the model in Mexico's methodology paper, the mixing of yellowfin tuna or albacore tuna in light meat tuna is not problematic. 100 percent canned yellowfin tuna is the product that Mexico would export to the United States and is of higher quality than the yellowfin tuna mixed into light tuna. The model is calibrated for canned yellowfin tuna that is marketed as such, versus all other (generic) canned tuna. Whether the generic

---

[12]　The shift of the U.S. fleet out of the ETP/away from yellowfin and to the Western and Central Pacific/to skipjack in the late 1980's and early 1990's closely mirrors the decline in consumer consumption of canned tuna in the U.S. market. It is reflective of the declining quality of generic tuna with the removal of yellowfin from the supply chain.

[13]　See Tables 5, 6 and 7 of Mexico's methodology paper (Exhibit MEX-2).

canned tuna contains some yellowfin or not is captured in the value of the mean premium.

20.   The United States has also raised the issue that yellowfin contains more mercury than skipjack tuna, hence depressing the demand for yellowfin tuna. However, according to the U.S. government itself, the mercury content in albacore tuna is essentially the same as in yellowfin tuna.[14] With increased U.S. consumption of canned albacore tuna since the adoption of the Tuna Measure and with its consumption occupying nearly a third of the U.S. canned tuna market by volume, it is clear that mercury is not a primary concern of a large segment of U.S. consumers. Thus, mercury issues do not have a material impact on purchases of yellowfin tuna products in the U.S. market.

21.   Mexico's methodology model does not assume any shift in demand. The increased consumption for canned yellowfin tuna in the United States comes from a decline in the price that comes from an increase in supply from the introduction of supplies of canned yellowfin tuna from Mexico. In this regard, an elastic demand for yellowfin tuna products explains why the consumption of yellowfin increases substantially with the decline of the price of yellowfin tuna in the United States. An elastic demand means that consumption is sensitive to changes in the price of a good. The modification of the Tuna Measure under the counterfactual yields a decline in the price of yellowfin tuna products in the United States. Because the demand for yellowfin tuna products is elastic, even a small decline in the price of canned yellowfin tuna yields a large increase in the consumption of canned yellowfin tuna. Thus, as the price of yellowfin canned tuna declines, many consumers naturally switch from the consumption of canned generic tuna to the consumption of canned yellowfin tuna, namely, the modification of the Tuna Measure would bring about a significant decline in the price of canned yellowfin tuna in the United States and hence a very large increase in consumption because the demand is elastic.

22.   U.S. consumer preferences for the "dolphin safe" label today, and at the time of the expiry of the RPT, are shown in a September 2016 consumer survey submitted by Mexico.[15] According to this survey, a majority of Americans believe that "dolphin safe" means that no dolphins were injured or killed in the course of capturing tuna, and that the definition of "dolphin safe" should be that no dolphins were injured or killed in the course of capturing tuna.[16] Moreover, an overwhelming number of adults believe that it is important to have environmentally-sustainable seafood products that ensure the health of the whole ecosystem, including dolphins, and not just the health of dolphins in particular.[17] Thus, if the tuna measure permitted U.S. consumers to be fully informed of the

---

[14]   See U.S. Food and Drug Administration, "Mercury Levels in Commercial Fish and Shellfish (1990-2010)", available online at http://www.fda.gov/Food/FoodborneIllnessContaminants/ Metals/ucm115644.htm (Exhibit MEX-64).
[15]   Public Opinion Strategies, Dolphin Safe National Survey (Exhibit MEX-71).
[16]   Ibid., pp. 6 and 8.
[17]   Ibid., p. 14.

dolphin protection and environmental virtues of AIDCP-compliant fishing and the disadvantages of alternative fishing methods, they would prefer tuna products containing tuna caught in the manner used by the Mexican tuna fleet.

23.   Contrary to the argument of the United States, the model in Mexico's methodology paper captures the necessary market realities of the U.S. canned tuna market to properly calculate the level of nullification or impairment. These market realities include differentiation in the canned tuna market and U.S. consumers' willingness to pay a premium for canned yellowfin tuna over canned generic tuna.

Supply and demand equations for the Mexican Market

24.   Regarding Mexican supply, the counterfactual considers that the Mexican tuna industry produces canned tuna using domestically caught yellowfin and skipjack, as well as yellowfin tuna imported for canning. That is, Mexican production capacity is not limited by domestic catch under the counterfactual and allows for imports of unprocessed yellowfin tuna from other ETP countries. Mexican canneries operated in 2014 with a single day shift. This means that production could easily be expanded using imported yellowfin tuna. The export volume to the United States is limited to yellowfin tuna caught by the Mexican fleet and canned yellowfin tuna made from imported tuna is consumed in Mexico.

25.   The United States incorrectly describes Mexico's model when stating that "Mexico has a completely elastic supply curve (i.e., Mexican industry could supply an unlimited quantity of canned yellowfin at no increasing marginal cost)."[18] As Mexico has explained, the supply curve of canned yellowfin tuna by Mexican canneries is initially perfectly elastic, but for a quantity equal to the Mexican production of yellowfin tuna in 2014 it becomes perfectly inelastic. The model assumes that Mexican canneries could increase production by importing yellowfin tuna from other countries. Furthermore, the model assumes a constant marginal cost (perfectly elastic supply) for the Mexican production of canned yellowfin tuna up to the assumed production capacity where it increases to infinity (perfectly inelastic supply).

26.   The demand for canned tuna in Mexico is modeled in the same way as the demand for canned tuna in the United States. It is calibrated based on consumption observed in 2014.

Model Solution

27.   Imports from Mexico are cost competitive compared to other imports because of geographic proximity to the U.S. market and lower customs duties. Thus, modifications of the tuna measure would bring new inexpensive supplies of canned yellowfin tuna from Mexico into the U.S. market. Accordingly, the

---

[18]   U.S. written submission, para. 88.

removal of the tuna measure is appropriately modeled as a shift to the right of the supply of canned yellowfin tuna on the United States market.

28.   The broad geographic scope of the sources of supply for U.S. production and imported products encompasses the many regions in which dolphins are killed and seriously injured during tuna fishing operations. Other than Mexico, there are a few Central and South American countries that harvest tuna in the ETP. However, these countries have small production capacities and could not compete with Mexico's canned yellowfin tuna products because they are located further from the United States and these countries have chosen not to seek an "affirmative finding" from the Department of Commerce that they are in compliance with the AIDCP.[19] This means that an export response by other countries to modifications to the Tuna Measure would be small and that only Mexico's exports to the United States would be significantly impacted by the removal of the tuna measure. Similarly, because imports from all other ocean regions have been permitted to use the dolphin-safe label without independent observer monitoring or comprehensive tracking and verification systems, no tuna products from those other regions have been affected by the Tuna Measure, and therefore they would also not be affected by the withdrawal of the Tuna Measure.

29.   The model shows that because transportation costs between Mexico and the United States are small, the removal of the tuna measure would yield large exports of Mexican canned yellowfin tuna to the United States.

30.   Arbitrage between Mexico and the United States causes the price of canned yellowfin tuna to equalize between the two countries once transportation costs are accounted for. The model is solved assuming that Mexico imports yellowfin tuna products that are canned domestically for domestic consumption to replace some of the canned yellowfin tuna exported to the United States. Other Central and South American countries harvest tuna in the ETP. The proximity of these countries to Mexico means a low cost of transporting tuna to Mexico. Many vessels would directly unload their catch in Mexico.

31.   Under the counterfactual considered in Mexico's methodology paper, tuna products made from tuna caught by other fleets can be sold on the Mexican domestic market. The scenario considered assumes that Mexico would import from other ETP countries the equivalent of tuna for producing 20,000 metric tonnes of canned yellowfin tuna. With this Mexican import volume of yellowfin tuna, nearly all of the yellowfin tuna harvested and canned by Mexican firms to be exported to the United States. Other ETP countries are not in a position to compete with Mexico in the U.S. market for canned yellowfin tuna. This is because of Mexico's competitive advantage from its nearby location, its large production capacity, its low marginal cost and its access to the U.S. market free of import tariffs. It is also because most of the tuna products from other ETP

---

[19] NOAA   Fisheries,   Tuna/Dolphin   Embargo   Status   Update,   available   at http://www.nmfs.noaa.gov/pr/dolphinsafe/embargo2.htm (Exhibit MEX-72).

countries are completely banned by other U.S. measures from exporting yellowfin tuna products to the United States. Mexican imports of yellowfin tuna from other ETP countries are a natural outcome of economic forces operating under the removal of the Tuna Measure.

32.   The model finds that with the removal of the tuna measure, 21.5 percent of U.S. consumption of canned tuna would be from canned yellowfin tuna imported from Mexico. This is a reasonable market share given the low production costs for canned tuna in Mexico, the absence of duties for U.S. imports of canned tuna from Mexico and the small transportation cost for canned yellowfin tuna given the proximity of Mexico to the United States. Moreover, in 1987, canned yellowfin tuna occupied at a minimum 22 percent of the consumption of canned tuna in the United States.[20] With the removal of the tuna measure, a similar market share would be observed with the difference that canned yellowfin tuna would be produced in Mexico rather than in the United States before the adoption of the tuna measure.

33.   Under Mexico's counterfactual, Mexico exports a total of USD $495 million (63,568 metric tonnes x USD $7.79/kg) of canned tuna to the United States. Therefore, deducting from this figure the actual value of exports of Mexican canned tuna to the United States in 2014 (USD $22.65 million) yields a trade loss to Mexico of USD $472.3 million annually.

The United States' Market-Based Approach is unreliable

34.   Apart from employing a counterfactual that is not correctly defined, the "market-based approach" proposed by the United States is flawed and underestimates losses from the tuna measure to Mexico.

35.   The calculation of the United States is based on the historical import volumes of canned tuna from Mexico before the adoption of the tuna measure. However, these historical figures are not instructive of the levels of imports if the Tuna Measure were withdrawn. A proper counterfactual keeps everything but the measure of interest constant. It is obviously not the case that market conditions when the original tuna measure was enacted in 1990 are the same as in 2014. For instance, the United States maintained a trade embargo on imports of Mexican tuna from 1980 to 1986, which arose from a dispute over the scope of territorial waters and fishing rights. Therefore, the period immediately following the termination of the embargo is not representative of open market conditions.

36.   In addition, the reference of the United States concerning Mexico's share of U.S. imports of tuna products of 3.9 percent on a weight basis for the 1987-89 period[21] does not correspond to what would be observed with the removal of the Tuna Measure in 2014. Indeed, Mexican firms now have a much better access to the U.S. market than in the period between 1987 and 1989 because Mexico is a

---

[20]   Mexico's Response to Arbitrator's question 119.
[21]   U.S. written submission, para. 130.

signatory of North American Free Trade Agreement (NAFTA). Therefore, Mexico can export canned tuna to the United States free of duties. Moreover, the Mexican canned tuna industry has developed since the adoption of the tuna measure to increase its production and become much more cost competitive, including by building canneries devoted exclusively to producing tuna products. In addition, unlike the 1987 to 1989 period, the market conditions for canned yellowfin tuna observed in 2014 have left the U.S. market almost empty of canned yellowfin tuna.

37.   The United States' assumption that retailers accounting for 46.4 percent of the U.S. market for tuna products will not purchase and offer for sale Mexican tuna products because the tuna was caught using the AIDCP-certified dolphin encirclement fishing method[22] is incorrect. The United States' assumption is incorrectly based on the premise that the dolphin-safe label itself has no value because the market is only concerned with the narrow question of whether or not dolphins were encircled in the process of harvesting the tuna. This is contradicted by the findings of the Panels and Appellate Body in the prior proceedings. Besides, the United States' premise depends almost exclusively on information and activities related to Earth Island Institute (EII) which refers to historic "unregulated" dolphin encirclement and ignores the AIDCP dolphin-safe requirements and the success of the Mexican fleet in protecting dolphins for over twenty years. Furthermore, the letters submitted by the United States as "evidence" to demonstrate that U.S. retailers would not carry Mexican tuna products are unreliable since they rather demonstrate that the United States is "shaping" consumer expectations in the market to comport with its outdated perspective on dolphin mortalities in the ETP large purse seine fishery. In fact, the United States has mischaracterized the content of most of the letters, and the current policies of the great majority of the retailers as published on their websites actually suggest that they would carry Mexican products. The published policies of the retailers are much more compelling evidence of the retailers' policies that the letters submitted by the United States.

38.   As part of its counterfactual, the United States endorses EII's purported dolphin-safe program, arguing in effect that if the United States were to withdraw the Tuna Measure, EII should be viewed as controlling use of the dolphin-safe label. However, the Arbitrator should not base the counterfactual on the United States' speculation about whether a new label might be created by a non-governmental entity and whether it could convince retailers that such a label would be more meaningful than the AIDCP dolphin-safe label. Indeed, if the United States were to withdraw the measure entirely, the AIDCP dolphin-safe label would become the only official dolphin-safe label in the U.S. market, and, in particular, the only label endorsed by the U.S. government through its role in the AIDCP. Mexico also submitted evidence demonstrating that major

---

[22]   U.S. written submission, paras. 135-136.

suppliers and retailers use tuna sources that are not authorized by EII, showing that EII does not have the market power attributed to it by the United States.

39.   The United States also bases its counterfactual on the assumption that 100 percent of tuna products from all other sources will be able to use the dolphin-safe label.[23] Under the United States' proposed counterfactual, the U.S. Federal Trade Commission (FTC) consumer labelling rules apply generally and all tuna products would be able to use a dolphin-safe label provided that such label is accurate so that consumers are not deceived. Thus, tuna products from the United States and other countries would be able to use a dolphin-safe label provided that such a label is accurate so that U.S. consumers are not deceived. However, it would not be reasonable to assume that consumers and retailers, let alone the FTC, would accept that a "dolphin-safe" label could be used on tuna products containing tuna that was caught in a fishing set or gear deployment in which dolphins were killed or seriously injured, and/or in circumstances where it is impossible to verify that the product contains only tuna that was caught in a dolphin-safe manner. Thus, some form of mechanism will have to be put in place by tuna product suppliers so that dolphin-safe claims can be verified. The implementation of such procedures will take time and will involve costs. Some suppliers will invest the time and money to adopt and implement, others will not. Accordingly, it is unreasonable for the United States to assume that 100 percent of the tuna products containing tuna caught outside the ETP will immediately be eligible to use a dolphin-safe label.

Conclusion

40.   For the reasons explained in Mexico's methodology paper (based on the detailed econometric analysis) and in its submission, Mexico reaffirms its requested authorization to suspend concessions equal to USD $472.3 million annually, which is the level of the nullification or impairment resulting from the failure of the United States to comply with the recommendations and rulings of the DSB and bring the Tuna Measure into consistency with the covered agreements after the expiry of the RPT. If the Arbitrator disagrees with some of the assumptions of Mexico's model, Mexico invites the Arbitrator to use the R code submitted by Mexico to calculate the amount of nullification or impairment under the assumptions it considers reasonable.

---

[23]   U.S. written submission, paras. 71, 76 ("all tuna product that currently qualifies as dolphin safe would continue to qualify for the label") and 123.

ANNEX B-2

EXECUTIVE SUMMARY OF THE ARGUMENTS
OF THE UNITED STATES

SUMMARY OF U.S. WRITTEN STATEMENT

1.   Mexico's Methodology Paper dramatically overestimates the level of nullification or impairment attributable to the U.S. dolphin safe labeling measure. In lieu of Mexico's fatally flawed model, the United States puts forward an approach based on levels of U.S. imports from Mexico prior to the adoption in 1990 of the original Dolphin Protection Consumer Information Act (DPCIA). Such a historical, market-based approach is the most appropriate in the light of the available data and is consistent with the approach taken by past Article 22.6 arbitrators.

I.   THE U.S. TUNA PRODUCT MARKET

2.   The measure at issue is the U.S. dolphin safe labeling measure for tuna products.[1] The measure sets out the minimum conditions under which tuna product may be marketed as "dolphin safe." The U.S. canned tuna product market is an approximately $1.5 billion market. Eighty percent of the market is served by three companies: Bumblebee, Chicken of the Sea, and StarKist ("the big three"), which produce tuna product from U.S. and foreign canneries. About half the U.S. market is supplied by canneries located in the United States and its territories.

A.   U.S. Consumer Preferences for Tuna Product

3.   U.S. consumers of canned tuna have definite preferences with respect to price, taste, texture, and whether the tuna product was produced in a dolphin safe manner, in particular that it was not produced from the intentional encirclement of dolphins. There is no overriding demand for tuna product produced from yellowfin tuna as Mexico claims, and U.S. consumers are disinclined to purchase tuna product produced by setting on dolphins. Therefore, demand for Mexican canned tuna is low, irrespective of the U.S. dolphin safe labeling requirements.

---

[1]   "Tuna product" refers to a "food item which contains tuna and which has been processed for retail sale, except perishable sandwiches, salads, or other products with a shelf life of less than 3 days." In other words, "tuna product" is tuna that has undergone some processing and is not sold as "fresh" tuna. In light of the fact that much of the other processed products are ultimately processed into canned tuna, much of the data in the literature regarding "tuna product" focuses on canned tuna rather than the other smaller-volume tuna products.

1.   U.S. Consumer Preference for Less Expensive Tuna Product

4.   The U.S. canned tuna market is "characterized by high volume and low margins." Since the advent of canned tuna in the 1900s, it has been considered a low cost and practical source of protein for the U.S. consumer. The literature indicates that there is a "psychological limit" for U.S. consumers against paying more than $1 for a can of tuna. Consistent with that proposition is the fact that as the per can cost approaches $1, U.S. demand for canned tuna weakens.

2.   U.S. Consumers Preference for Canned Albacore

5.   Although the U.S. market is generally characterized by high volume, low value products, some tuna products are sold at a premium. In the canned market, that differentiation occurs largely between premium canned albacore, which is sold as "white" tuna, and discount canned tuna, which is sold as "light" tuna and generally contains skipjack tuna, alone or in combination with other species. Under U.S. Food and Drug Administration (FDA) regulations, canned tuna can be labeled "white meat" if it is 100 percent albacore, while tuna product produced from other species generally qualifies for the "light meat" label. Canned tuna can also be labeled by species – albacore, skipjack, yellowfin, etc. – if it is 100 percent composed of that species.

6.   U.S. consumers have a preference for canned albacore over tuna product containing other tuna species due to albacore's mild flavor, firm texture, and light color. Many U.S. consumers are willing to pay a price premium for albacore, as shown by the fact that the average retail price for canned albacore is $5.32 a pound, while the average retail price for skipjack is $3.17 a pound. Exhibit MEX-15 shows that sales of canned albacore accounted for 29 percent of canned tuna sales during the covered period by weight but 40 percent by value. This preference for albacore is distinct from consumer preferences in other countries, as the U.S. market consumes 19 percent of global production of canned tuna overall but 55-60 percent of world consumption of albacore.

3.   Weak U.S. Consumer Demand for Canned Yellowfin

7.   Dolphin safe tuna product sold in the United States can be, and is, produced from yellowfin. Such tuna product is either sold as "yellowfin" or as "light tuna." Canned yellowfin can command a higher price within the gourmet market, but demand is limited, and so much of the canned yellowfin produced for the U.S. market is labeled as "light tuna" – often canned with skipjack – rather than as "yellowfin." A 2005 investigation found that only about half the cans of yellowfin are labeled as such, and industry officials explained that vessels producing for the U.S. market catch more yellowfin than can be sold as a gourmet product. Canned yellowfin has long been marketed to U.S. consumers as "light meat," and that practice continues today.

8.   Another factor dampening demand for yellowfin tuna product is consumer concerns regarding mercury in canned tuna. Mercury is present in marine creatures, particularly in the larger predators, such as albacore and

yellowfin, and to a lesser extent in smaller fish, such as skipjack. One of the reasons that producers process yellowfin and skipjack together and sell it as "light tuna," rather than selling cans of 100 percent yellowfin, is to lower the per can mercury level of canned yellowfin and produce a safer product that is consistent with FDA regulations.

9.   U.S. cannery receipts tell a consistent story of weak demand for canned yellowfin. In 1987, when the U.S. fleet was still operating in the ETP, 46.1 percent of U.S. cannery receipts were yellowfin. But the next year, yellowfin's share dropped to 31.6 percent. Between 1991 and 1999, the percentage was between 17.3-24.3 percent (with albacore increasing to 33.8 percent by 1999 and skipjack constituting about half of the total). In the 2000s, the share of yellowfin continued to drop. Since 2009, the share of yellowfin has been below 7 percent, while the share of albacore has been above 35 percent and the share of skipjack has been above 46 percent.

10.   These low percentages of yellowfin being processed by U.S. canneries do not indicate lack of availability of dolphin safe yellowfin. Market data show that about 40 percent of the yellowfin-labeled canned tuna was produced by the big three brands, all of which sell only dolphin safe products. This suggests that if there were greater demand for canned yellowfin, the market would have met that demand. The fact that the tuna industry has instead produced less and less canned yellowfin over the last few decades indicates how weak U.S. consumer demand for canned yellowfin is, even where that tuna product is marketed as "dolphin safe."

4.   Weak Demand for Canned Tuna Produced from Setting on Dolphins

11.   It is established that U.S. consumers prefer dolphin safe tuna product and that this "sensitiv[ity]" is driven by a desire not to purchase tuna produced from setting on dolphins. As the original panel discussed, in the 1980s, in reaction to purse seine vessels killing tens to hundreds of thousands of dolphins in the ETP every year, one NGO, Earth Island Institute (EII), led a media campaign to raise consumer awareness of the issue. This campaign produced significant results, as the big three and other companies changed their purchasing policies in April 1990 to not purchase tuna from vessels that set on dolphins. These policies remain in place today because canned tuna produced from the intentional harassment and capture of dolphins remains an important issue for consumers. As the original panel noted, these policies "suggest[] that the producers themselves assume that they would not be able to sell tuna products that do not meet dolphin-safe requirements, or at least not at a price sufficient to warrant their purchase."

12.   The most engaged actor on the dolphin safe issue is EII. EII has its own standard for "dolphin safe," which includes a prohibition on setting on dolphins. Companies that agree to adhere to the EII dolphin safe standard, pay a licensing fee, and otherwise promise to comply with EII requirements, can use the EII label. EII reportedly has commitments from 90 percent of all tuna companies to, *inter alia*, not produce, hold, or sell tuna product produced from setting on

dolphins. In general, EII has certified compliance of upstream companies, such as producers and distributors. EII has agreements with 159 processing and fishing companies in 51 countries and territories. All major exporting and importing countries are represented. For the United States, 53 companies have agreements with EII, including many of the largest players in the U.S. market. The vast majority of tuna product sold at retail in the United States passes through at least one of these companies, the major exception being Mexican tuna product.

13.   In light of the fact that EII's focus is primarily on upstream companies, the United States contracted a leading market research firm to provide specific data as to the retail market, which accounts for about 70 percent of all sales of canned tuna. Based on that list, the United States reviewed the evidence as to dolphin safe policies of the companies that have the largest share of the U.S. market. This evidence confirms the thrust of the EII data, *i.e.*, that major U.S. retailers are sensitive to the demands of their consumers, and, as such are committed to selling only "dolphin safe" tuna product and will not carry tuna product produced from setting on dolphins. In addition, the United States is aware of a statement by Walmart, the leading seller of tuna product in the United States, stating that all major brands it sells are not produced from setting on dolphins and that purchasing decisions are governed by Walmart's sustainability policy, rather than whether the tuna product qualifies for the dolphin safe label under the U.S. measure.

14.   As demonstrated and reinforced by these policies, there is no demand for Mexican tuna product in this segment of the market. Further, this lack of demand relates to the substance of Mexico's fishing practices not the measure at issue. Including Walmart, the retailers covered by statements account for 66 percent of retail market share, 46.4 percent of total consumption.

2.   The Supply of Tuna to the U.S. Tuna Product Market

15.   The United States is the largest consumer of canned tuna, with an estimated 19 percent share of the global market. Approximately 50-55 percent of the canned tuna supplying the U.S. market is produced by U.S. processors, using U.S.-caught tuna and imported tuna for canning. The other 45-50 percent of the market is supplied by canned tuna imports. The top exporters of canned tuna product to the United States are Thailand, Ecuador, Vietnam, the Philippines, and Indonesia, which together account for 93 percent of canned tuna imports into the United States.

II.   THE LEVEL OF SUSPENSION OF CONCESSIONS PROPOSED BY MEXICO IS NOT EQUIVALENT TO THE LEVEL OF NULLIFICATION OR IMPAIRMENT

16.   Pursuant to Article 22.6 of the DSU, the United States objected to Mexico's proposed level of suspension of concessions because that proposed level is not equivalent to the level of nullification or impairment attributable to

the measure. Article 22.4 of the DSU is explicit and requires that the "level of suspension of concessions or other obligations authorized by the DSB shall be equivalent to the level of nullification or impairment." Mexico's calculations suffer from conceptual flaws and methodological errors that result in estimates of the level of nullification or impairment that are not accurate and inconsistent with Article 22.4 of the DSU.

A.   Mexico Has Proposed Incorrect Counterfactuals

17.   Mexico describes its proposed counterfactual as one where "the WTO-inconsistent discriminatory aspects of the original and amended Tuna Measure were eliminated." However, a Member has discretion as to how to implement DSB recommendations and rulings. Further, past WTO arbitrators have indicated that the normal counterfactual for calculating nullification or impairment is withdrawal of the measure. There is no precedent for an arbitrator choosing a counterfactual that based on a complainant's theory of compliance that is not related to the DSB recommendations and rulings. Withdrawal of the measure is thus the appropriate counterfactual.

B.   Mexico's Model Is Fundamentally Flawed and Overstates of the Level of Nullification or Impairment

18.   Mexico's proposed level of $472.3 million dramatically overstates the level of nullification or impairment because it is calculated using a deeply flawed economic model.

1.   Mexico's Model Is Not Appropriate in Light of Available Data

19.   In this context, the generally accepted way to use partial equilibrium analysis would be to determine the value of the U.S. dolphin safe label and model the effect of its removal on the equilibrium price and quantity of Mexican tuna product sold in the United States. To determine the value of the dolphin safe label would require detailed data on U.S. purchases of tuna product with and without the dolphin safe label, including store-by-store sales of tuna by type, accounting for product characteristics, and including information on the timing of sales and whether sales were made at promotional values. It appears to be *undisputed* that this level of data concerning the U.S. tuna product market is not available. Mexico's dataset does not include retailer-level data that would allow the comparison between particular types of labeled and unlabeled tuna product that would be necessary to estimate the value of the dolphin safe label.

20.   Mexico's partial equilibrium model thus does not seek to measure the value of the U.S. dolphin safe label and the effect of its removal. Rather, Mexico's model asks a wholly different question, namely what is the demand for canned yellowfin tuna in the U.S. market if one assumes: 1) canned yellowfin's access to the U.S. market is so severely restricted that current consumption is not indicative of demand; 2) U.S. consumers have a strong preference for canned yellowfin tuna (including produced by setting on dolphins) over all other canned tuna; and 3) Mexico is the only possible supplier of canned yellowfin tuna to the

U.S. market. Mexico's model is simply not an appropriate model to use for this case given the available data and also because Mexico's assumptions have no basis in the real world.

2. Mexico's Model Is Based on Incorrect Assumptions and Is Fundamentally Flawed as a Result

21. Mexico's model is defined by a series of demand equations and that are specified almost entirely based on assumptions. Specifically, the model is based on the assumptions that: (1) yellowfin tuna product has been so restricted in its entry into the U.S. market that current consumption levels have no relationship to demand; (2) the Mexican and U.S. tuna product markets constitute a single market with an identical consumer preference for yellowfin tuna product; (3) Mexico is the only possible supplier of yellowfin tuna product to the U.S. market; and (4) Mexico has a completely elastic supply curve. Each of the four key assumptions is incorrect, and Mexico's model results in an inflated level of nullification or impairment.

a. There Is No Pent-Up Demand for Canned Yellowfin

22. Mexico's model is premised on the assumption that canned yellowfin tuna has been almost entirely barred from the U.S. market such that the current U.S. consumption of canned yellowfin does not reflect demand. The model then disregards all evidence of U.S. consumer preferences, as reflected in actual consumption, and derives demand based on assumptions. But the underlying assumption is incorrect: dolphin safe yellowfin canned tuna *is* sold in the U.S. market but it is sold in small quantities because demand is weak.

23. Contrary to Mexico's assumptions, there are numerous other sources of canned yellowfin in the U.S. market that are not adversely affected by the U.S. dolphin safe labeling measure and thus are available on an unrestricted basis. For example, all of the "big three" companies sell all-yellowfin dolphin safe tuna products in the United States. Other tuna processors also sell canned yellowfin on the U.S. market. Indeed, from 2010-2015, dolphin safe yellowfin accounted for between 4.3 and 6.7 percent of the tuna processed by U.S. canneries. U.S. canneries sourced this dolphin safe yellowfin from both U.S. vessels and foreign vessels.

24. If demand for canned yellowfin tuna were strong, dolphin safe canned yellowfin would sell in higher quantities given the available supply of yellowfin caught in a dolphin safe manner, but that is not the case. Sales of tuna products containing 100 percent yellowfin are dwarfed by sales of albacore and lightmeat tuna. Further, much of the dolphin safe yellowfin produced for the U.S. market is not marketed as "yellowfin" at all, but sold (often combined with skipjack) as "lightmeat". There is simply not sufficient demand for even the amount of dolphin safe yellowfin currently available. In this regard, Mexico's evidence suggests the same is true for *non-dolphin safe* canned yellowfin, since Exhibit MEX-15 indicates that both leading Mexican brands, Tuny and Dolores, market "chunk light" products in the United States.

25.   The absence of demand for yellowfin tuna product is further confirmed by the fact that the decline in the quantity and share of the yellowfin processed by U.S. canneries continued after the measure went into effect. The share of tuna processed by U.S. canneries made up by yellowfin was already falling before the DPCIA was enacted – from 46.1 percent in 1987 to 33.2 percent in 1990 – and fell to 23.0 percent in 1991. Instead of stabilizing at that level, however, (or rising back to the earlier level), the share of tuna processed by U.S. canneries represented by yellowfin has steadily fallen. Mexico's story of the measure operating as a supply restriction does not explain this continued decline in yellowfin's share of the U.S. cannery receipts.

26.   Thus, Mexico's model is based on the assumption of an unsatisfied demand for canned yellowfin that is contradicted by the evidence. U.S. consumers have access to canned yellowfin, both dolphin safe and non-dolphin safe, but the data prove that they do not demand the product enough for canneries to increase supply or even to market all of the yellowfin they have as such. There is, therefore, no reason to think that U.S. consumption of yellowfin would increase if the U.S. measure were removed and Mexican producers could market their canned yellowfin as "dolphin safe." Thus, the assumption upon which Mexico's model is premised is false.

b.   The U.S. and Mexican Markets Are Not One Market with a Strong Preference for Canned Yellowfin

27.   Another factor driving the outcome of Mexico's model is its assumption that the United States and Mexico constitute a single market with a strong preference for canned yellowfin. The model sets the willingness to pay for yellowfin, distribution of willingness to pay, and the elasticity of demand for tuna equal across the two countries. This leads to a result that is almost entirely driven by the percentage of consumption between the two countries, because the "intensity of demand" parameter is the only variable that differs between the U.S. and Mexican demand equations. However, Mexico's assumption is incorrect, and, consequently, the parameters of Mexico's model relating to U.S. demand are all inaccurate.

28.   *First*, there is no reason to believe that Mexican and U.S. consumers have the same preferences concerning canned tuna. Mexican and U.S. consumer preferences for food products often differ. For example, Mexican and U.S. consumers have different preferences concerning chicken meat, with U.S. consumers preferring white meat and Mexican consumers preferring dark meat. Preferences are also different with respect to cheeses and fruits and vegetables.

29.   Mexico submits no evidence substantiating its assertion that "[t]here is no reason for U.S. consumers to have a different appreciation for canned yellowfin tuna than Mexican consumers." The fact that 17 percent of Americans are Hispanic suggests that some part of that 17 percent of the U.S. population may have preferences similar to Mexican consumers but does not support the idea that U.S. consumers *generally* have the same preferences as Mexican consumers. Indeed, the fact that Hispanic Americans are regarded as a subgroup with

distinct preferences suggests that the opposite is true. Further, the evidence indicates that U.S. and Mexican consumers differ in their willingness to purchase tuna product produced from setting on dolphins.

30.   *Second*, the assumption that U.S. consumers have a strong preference for canned yellowfin vis-à-vis canned "generic" tuna is also refuted by the available evidence. The U.S. tuna product market is made up of a variety of products – not "yellowfin" and "generic." The low-end portion of the market is composed of light tuna and is heavily influenced by cost. The high-end portion of the market is dominated by albacore. Some products labeled yellowfin also fall into the high-end portion of the market, although demand for such products is low because U.S. consumers do not prefer it to canned albacore.

31.   Mexico has provided no evidence in support of its assumption that U.S. consumers have a preference for yellowfin tuna over all other types of canned tuna. Indeed, Mexico's model does not even acknowledge the existence of albacore and its popularity with U.S. consumers, despite the fact that Exhibit MEX-9 states that albacore is an important premium tuna product on the U.S. market. Further, Exhibit MEX-29 relates to Mexican consumer preferences rather than to U.S. consumer preferences. Pinsa and Marindustrias, the two leading Mexican tuna product companies mentioned in the exhibit, may market only yellowfin as a premium product, but many companies focused on the U.S. tuna product market, including the "big three" companies, have one or more premium albacore products, as well as sometimes premium yellowfin products.

32.   Further, the $2 per kg value assigned to the mean willingness to pay for canned yellowfin over "generic" tuna is divorced from the reality of the U.S. market. Mexico suggests that this figure is conservative in light of a regression analysis that suggested an estimated premium on yellowfin tuna of $1.13-$4.67 per kg, yet Mexico acknowledges that the data is not available "to calibrate the distribution of preference for canned yellowfin tuna versus canned generic tuna." Mexico also asserts, in contradiction to its price premium assumption, that "canned yellowfin tuna is priced to compete with other canned tuna products." Further, the regression does not properly represent the price premium for yellowfin, as, *inter alia*, the data is not detailed enough to do a proper analysis and the regression does not account for albacore.

33.   The assumption of a logistic distribution of willingness to pay, for which Mexico provides no justification, is also inconsistent with the reality of the U.S. market. A logistic distribution means that half of consumers are willing to pay more than the mean premium and half are willing to pay less. This does not describe the U.S. distribution of willingness to pay for tuna, where many consumers show a high sensitivity to price, as shown by the fact that nearly half of all sales of canned tuna are at discounted (sale) prices, suggesting that consumers are unwilling to pay full price, let alone a premium. A recent study found that yellowfin and skipjack have particularly elastic demand such that consumers will decrease consumption of these types of canned tuna by more than a proportional amount as prices rise.

34.   Thus, the key assumptions underlying the demand side of Mexico's model are not supported by the evidence. The demand parameters set based on those assumptions are, therefore, also incorrect. Specifically: (i) Equations 1 and 2 are wrong in assuming a market in which all premium product is yellowfin; (ii) Equation 3 is wrong in establishing a mean willingness to pay of $2 per kg. for yellowfin over all other tuna products; (iii) the intensity of demand parameter introduced in Equation 5 wrongly assumes that the only difference between the U.S. and Mexican markets is the quantity of tuna consumed; and (iv) the logistic distribution assumed in Equation 8 is inappropriate because it ignores the fact that tuna sales are highly sensitive to price and, therefore, willingness to pay is not distributed in this manner. These equations are central to Mexico's model and, consequently, Mexico's model is critically flawed.

c.   **Mexico Is Not the Only Supplier of Canned Yellowfin**

35.   Another key assumption underlying Mexico's model is that Mexico is the only potential supplier of yellowfin tuna product to the U.S. market. Mexico assumes that, once the alleged latent demand for yellowfin has been awakened, only Mexican producers will be able to respond to it. Mexico asserts that U.S. canneries could not increase production and that Mexico is the only supplier of yellowfin tuna product to the U.S. market. These assumptions are incorrect.

36.   *First*, yellowfin tuna is caught and processed throughout the world; Mexico is not the sole supplier. The data presented in Exhibit MEX-15 shows that at least 30 different brands from North America, Europe, Asia, and South America marketed all-yellowfin tuna products in the U.S. market. Similarly, U.S. cannery receipts show that U.S. canneries purchase from U.S. vessels and import yellowfin each year for processing. Data from regional fisheries management organizations (RFMOs) similarly show that many countries' vessels harvest yellowfin.

37.   *Second*, if there were a sudden increase in U.S. demand for canned yellowfin, the Mexican industry would not be the only one to respond. U.S. canneries are not operating at full capacity, and there is no reason to think that other tuna industries in other countries could not also increase production. In particular, canneries in Thailand and Ecuador – the two largest exporters of canned tuna to the United States – are operating at about 80 and 70 percent capacity. Consequently, there is every reason to believe that the tuna processing industries in these countries would increase production to meet any increased U.S. demand for canned yellowfin.

38.   Thus, Mexico's assumption that only the Mexican tuna industry could respond to any change in U.S. demand for yellowfin is incorrect. In reality, both U.S. canneries and the foreign canneries that currently supply the U.S. market with yellowfin and other tuna product would compete to satisfy any new U.S. demand. Consequently, Equation 20, the parameter imposing that assumption on the U.S. market, and Mexico's model as a whole are fundamentally flawed.

d.   Mexican Canneries Do Not Have the Ability to Increase Production Without Any Impact on Marginal Cost

39.   Mexico's model assumes that Mexico has the ability to increase production of canned yellowfin without increasing marginal cost. This assumption is incorrect because (1) the United States is a sufficiently important consumer of canned tuna that a shift in demand of the size Mexico envisions would affect world prices of cannery grade yellowfin; and (2) Mexico could not import large quantities of yellowfin from other ETP fishing nations at no increased cost.

40.   On the second point, the supply of yellowfin in the ETP is not unlimited and an increase of the kind Mexico assumes would encounter hard supply constraints. Catches of tuna in the ETP are regulated by the IATTC, and the latest IATTC report found that recent fishing mortality rates are slightly below the MSY level, suggesting that yellowfin tuna was in an overfished state. This suggests that the IATTC would take action if catches of yellowfin in the ETP increased substantially. Indeed, at the 2016 meeting of the IATTC, the Commission adopted interim harvest control rules for yellowfin tuna that would trigger measures to reduce catch.

41.   Mexico's assumption that it could import additional yellowfin for canning without any increased cost is particularly flawed. Mexico claims that it would import from other ETP fishing countries the 20,000 additional mt. of yellowfin that its processors would need to serve the Mexican market, given the increased exports to the United States. Ecuador is the only country that could supply that volume, but Ecuador has its own tuna processing industry. It was the second largest producer of canned tuna as of 2008 and is the second largest exporter (by value) of canned tuna to the United States. Yet Mexico's model assumes that if the U.S. measure were changed so as to unleash a latent demand for canned yellowfin, the Ecuadorian industry would not try meet this demand itself, but instead would sell the less valuable raw/frozen input to Mexico so that the Mexican industry could reap the profits of producing a processed product.

42.   Thus, Mexico's assumption of a perfectly elastic supply curve based on its ability to import yellowfin for canning without limit and without any effect on its price, reflected in Equations 20 and 22, is not reasonable. Relatedly, Mexico's assumption of a constant price of yellowfin supply and other tuna product, reflected throughout its model, is also incorrect. These assumptions are both central to Mexico's model and, therefore, the model itself is deeply flawed.

III.   THE APPROPRIATE CALCULATION OF THE LEVEL OF NULLIFICATION OR IMPAIRMENT

A.   The Appropriate Counterfactual Is Withdrawal of the Measure

43.   A Member has discretion as to how to implement DSB recommendations, and past WTO arbitrators have indicated that the normal counterfactual is withdrawal of the measure. The United States uses this counterfactual to

calculate the level of nullification or impairment. Under this counterfactual, it is reasonable to conclude that all tuna product currently meeting the dolphin safe labeling requirements, as well as tuna product produced from setting on dolphins consistent with the AIDCP, could be sold with some label suggesting it is "dolphin safe." It is also reasonable to conclude that producers and retailers of tuna product not produced from setting on dolphins will continue to seek to differentiate their product from tuna product produced from setting on dolphins. Finally, it is reasonable to conclude that the commitments made to EII or directly to customers by the vast majority of producers, distributors, exporters, importers, and retailers that serve the U.S. tuna product market to not produce, hold, or sell tuna or tuna product produced from setting on dolphins would remain in place.

B.   A Market-Based Approach Is the Appropriate Method of Calculating the Level of Nullification or Impairment

44.   In light of the evidence available, the most appropriate methodology to calculate the level of nullification or impairment would be to compare, on a prospective basis, the U.S. imports from Mexico of tuna product with the measure in place to the level of imports that would occur if the measure were withdrawn. This approach, which examines Mexico's historical market share of the U.S. tuna product market prior to the adoption of the DPCIA, is both consistent with the approach taken by past Article 22.6 arbitrators as well as the evidence on this record.

45.   Where relevant data were available, previous arbitrators have used historical trade data to determine the level of nullification or impairment. Such an approach is appropriate here. Prior to 1990, there was no dolphin safe labeling measure or other instrument addressing dolphin safety concerns. As such, levels of Mexican exports to the United States prior to 1990 during years when there was no measure and market access was not limited are instructive as to the levels of imports from Mexico that might exist if the measure were withdrawn. The U.S. model, therefore, uses Mexican exports during the three years preceding 1990 (1987-1989).

46.   The U.S. approach uses Mexico's share of U.S. tuna imports during the relevant period rather than absolute quantities of imports for two reasons. First, U.S. consumption of tuna product has declined since the period before the DPCIA was adopted, and a volume-based approach would not account for this decline. Second, data on imports of "tuna product," as such, is only available beginning in 1989. It is preferable not to base a historical analysis on data from a single year, as that year may not be representative. The U.S. model therefore uses Mexico's share of imports of all tuna (*i.e.*, tuna products and fresh tuna) during the three years prior to 1990. This may overestimate the level of nullification and impairment, but is likely very close to Mexico's historical share of tuna product imports because: (1) tuna product is a substantial subset of the "all tuna" category, accounting for between 90.3 and 98.0 percent of U.S. imports of all tuna, by volume, since 1989; and, (2) Mexico's share of U.S.

imports of tuna product in 1989 (3.8 percent) was very close to Mexico's share of U.S. imports of all tuna (3.4 percent).

47.   On this basis, the United States identified U.S. imports of tuna from Mexico in the three years prior to 1990 and calculated Mexico's market share, by volume, which was 3.9 percent. The United States also notes that in 1987 Mexico's import share reached its high of 5.8 percent. Thus, 3.9 percent is a reasonable estimate of what Mexico's annual share of U.S. imports of tuna product would be in the absence of the U.S. measure, and 5.8 percent represents the highest possible level of potential imports that could be affected by the U.S. measure (without taking into account U.S. consumer preferences for tuna product not produced from setting on dolphins).

48.   Next, to establish a range of U.S. imports of Mexican tuna product that could be expected under the counterfactual, the United States applied both percentages to current U.S. imports of tuna product based on average annual imports for 2013-2015. Over this period, the United States imported, on average, 251,011 mt. of tuna product per year. Assigning Mexican products a 3.9 percent share of imports at this level suggests that U.S. imports of Mexican tuna product would be approximately 9,789 mt. per year. At Mexico's historical high import share of 5.8 percent, U.S. imports of Mexican tuna product would be 14,559 mt. a year.

49.   To establish the value of U.S. imports of Mexican tuna product under the counterfactual, the United States multiplied the projected quantity of Mexican tuna product imports by the average import price of tuna products from the world, excluding Mexico, for 2013-2015. Excluding imports from Mexico from the calculation of the average price of tuna product accounts for any price difference between Mexican tuna product and other tuna product due to the ineligibility of Mexican product for the label. Based on this calculation, the annual value of U.S. imports of Mexican tuna product under the counterfactual would be $51.8 million, based on a 3.9 percent share of tuna product imports, and $77.1 million, based on a 5.8 percent share.

50.   From this projected value of U.S. imports of Mexican tuna product under the counterfactual, it is necessary to subtract the value of current U.S. imports of Mexican tuna product to identify how much higher such imports would be if the U.S. measure were withdrawn. Using the average actual value of U.S. imports of Mexican tuna product for 2013-2015 produces a result of $32.9 million, based on a 3.9 percent import share, and an upward bound of $58.1 million, based on Mexico's historical high import share.

C.   Results of the Market-Based Approach Must Be Discounted to Account for U.S. Preferences to Arrive an Accurate Level of Nullification or Impairment

51.   As noted above, this market-based approach does not take into account the current U.S. consumer preference for tuna product produced from fishing methods other than setting on dolphins. In light of this fact, and the fact that

under the counterfactual producers and retailers would still be able differentiate products produced from fishing methods other than setting on dolphins from products produced from setting on dolphins, the figures listed in the preceding section should be discounted to arrive at an accurate level of nullification or impairment.

52.   The market impact of this consumer preference can be found in the commitments that the many companies serving the U.S. market have made to EII. These commitments do not depend on the content of U.S. law and likely would not change if the measure were withdrawn. It is difficult to estimate how much of the U.S. market is covered by commitments to EII, although *90 percent* is a reasonable estimate, since about 90 percent of tuna companies globally have made commitments to EII. At a minimum, the discount must reflect the policies of individual retailers on the record. Retailers accounting for 46.6 percent of total U.S. tuna product consumption have policies not to sell tuna product produced by setting on dolphins or policies that are not affected by the dolphin safe labeling measure. It is necessary, therefore, to reduce by that amount the projections of Mexican exports of tuna product to the United States under the counterfactual. To do so, the U.S. model, after calculating the estimated value of imports of Mexican tuna product, multiplied that figure by 0.53, to reflect the market share available to tuna product produced from setting on dolphins, before subtracting the value of Mexico's actual imports.

53.   Thus, the level of nullification or impairment, adjusted for consumer preferences, would amount to $8.5 million, using the average actual value of U.S. imports of Mexican tuna product for 2013-2015, and $21.9 million, using Mexico's historical high import share.

V.   CONCLUSION

54.   The United States requests that the Arbitrator find that the level of suspension of concessions requested by Mexico is in excess of the appropriate level of nullification or impairment. The more appropriate level would be about $8.5 to $21.9 million per year.

SUMMARY OF U.S. OPENING STATEMENT

55.   The question in this proceeding is whether Mexico's request for authorization to suspend concessions is "equivalent" to the level of nullification or impairment caused by the measure, and if not, then what the equivalent level is. The United States has shown that Mexico's request is not consistent with the requirements of the DSU. As a result, it is appropriate to move to the second part of the question. The U.S. analysis and calculations show that the level of nullification or impairment should be no more than $8.5 to $21.9 million per year.

I. MEXICO'S MODEL IS FUNDAMENTALLY FLAWED AND IS NOT CAPABLE OF ACCURATELY ESTIMATING THE LEVEL OF NULLIFICATION AND IMPAIRMENT

56. The evidence shows that the three critical assumptions underlying Mexico's model are all incorrect and that Mexico's calculation of nullification or impairment is grossly inflated.

A. The Measure Does Not Ban the Sale of Canned Yellowfin in the United States

57. One of the key assumptions underlying Mexico's model is that the U.S. measure "effectively bans" sales of canned yellowfin in the United States. Based on this assumption, Mexico estimates the level of nullification or impairment by modeling the introduction of a hypothetical new product in the U.S. market, instead of modeling the removal of the labelling standards. In doing so, Mexico ignores the data on actual U.S. imports and consumption of canned yellowfin and derives demand for the product based on incorrect assumptions.

58. The U.S. measure is neither a *de facto* nor a *de jure* prohibition on the sale of canned yellowfin. Many countries around the world catch and process yellowfin. Yellowfin is the second most produced tuna species, by volume, in the global tuna industry. The majority of this catch is by purse seine vessels and destined for the global canned market. Exhibit MEX-15 shows that U.S.-produced and imported canned yellowfin products are sold in the U.S. market. Mexico also exports canned tuna to the United States. Mexico was the sixth largest source of U.S. canned tuna imports in 2014-2015, accounting for 3.6 percent of all canned tuna imports, by volume. Mexico's share of U.S. imports of canned tuna is consistent with Mexico's share of U.S. imports of other major seafood products, such as shrimp, crab, and sardines.

59. Further, evidence proves that a lack of demand, not lack of supply, is responsible for the fact that canned yellowfin accounts for only 1-2 percent of U.S. canned tuna consumption. *First*, yellowfin accounted for a larger share of U.S. cannery receipts in the 1980s than it does today, but during that time it largely was sold not as "yellowfin," but, combined with skipjack, as "light tuna." Thus, the fact that U.S. canneries used to purchase more yellowfin does not mean that there ever was strong demand for all-yellowfin products. *Second*, the steady decline in U.S. cannery purchases of yellowfin over the last three decades confirms the lack of U.S. consumer demand for canned yellowfin. *Third*, the behavior of tuna producers in the U.S. market, in supplying increasing quantities of albacore products while canning yellowfin with skipjack as light tuna, also confirms the lack of U.S. consumer demand for yellowfin. *Fourth*, the rise of U.S. wholesale and retail tuna prices during the early 1990s refutes Mexico's claim that the decline in U.S. cannery yellowfin purchases was caused by the measure restricting supply.

60. There are several factors that have driven down demand for canned yellowfin, including: (1) yellowfin is the only type of tuna caught in association

with dolphins, which U.S. consumers strongly do not prefer; (2) growing preference for albacore; and, (3) a preference for light tuna containing exclusively or primarily skipjack, which has a lower mercury content than yellowfin and is less expensive. Thus, the evidence refutes Mexico's claim that the U.S. measure effectively bars sales of canned yellowfin in the U.S. market. Consequently, the decision to disregard existing consumer data and to derive a demand function based entirely on the assumption of a tremendous unobserved preference for canned yellowfin is wrong.

B.   Mexico Is Not the Only Possible Supplier of Canned Yellowfin

61.   Another major assumption underlying Mexico's model is that Mexico is the only possible supplier of canned yellowfin to the U.S. market, or the only possible supplier of low cost canned yellowfin. Based on this assumption, Mexico's model equates "canned yellowfin" with Mexican canned tuna exports to the United States and ignores all other potential sources of canned yellowfin. In reality, however, Mexico is not the supplier of a unique product, either canned yellowfin or "low cost" canned yellowfin, and U.S. consumers *do not* have a preference for Mexican canned yellowfin over all other types of canned tuna.

62.   As already explained, Mexico is far from the only source of cannery grade yellowfin, and the U.S. tuna product market is deeply integrated into the global tuna industry. A significant amount of tuna purchased by U.S. canneries has been caught by foreign flagged vessels, and imports account for nearly half of all canned tuna on the U.S. market. The sources of U.S. tuna product imports include Members whose fleets are among the top harvesters of yellowfin and Members that purchase tuna from the top harvesters of yellowfin. Not surprisingly, numerous tuna companies, both U.S. and foreign, market all- or partly-yellowfin products in the U.S. market. Thus there are many current suppliers of canned yellowfin to the U.S. market that have the capacity to supply significantly more canned yellowfin if U.S. demand were greater.

63.   Mexico now acknowledges this is the case, but claims that only Mexican canned yellowfin would enter the U.S. market on the grounds that: 1) Mexico is a unique producer of low-cost yellowfin; and 2) there is "no reason" that if the scenario Mexico models comes to pass that the domestic and foreign competitors of Mexico would increase their production of canned yellowfin for the U.S. market. The evidence on the record proves otherwise.

64.   *First*, Mexico presents no evidence regarding the cost of production of its industry or the industries of other Members to prove that the Mexican industry is the lowest cost producer of canned yellowfin. In fact, the available evidence indicates that this is not the case. Other countries have much greater advantages in terms of low-cost tuna processing. Mexico's claim is also contradicted by the fact that its model assumes that Ecuadorian yellowfin is interchangeable with Mexican yellowfin and by the fact that Mexican products are not currently the least expensive canned yellowfin products on the U.S. market.

65.   *Second,* Mexico is wrong when it claims that there is "no reason" that, if the scenario Mexico models comes to pass, other domestic and foreign tuna industries would not increase sales canned yellowfin on the U.S. market. The basis of Mexico's claim is that other producers would not be affected by the removal of the U.S. measure, but this is not what Mexico modeled. Mexico modeled the introduction of a new product for which there is significant, untapped consumer demand, such that the product sells at a higher price and in much greater quantities than canned yellowfin does. The U.S. import price generated by Mexico's model is significantly higher than the current import price of Mexican canned tuna and of canned tuna from other countries that produce canned yellowfin. It is also significantly more than the current average EU import price for canned yellowfin. It is simply unreasonable to assume, as Mexico does, that all producers of canned yellowfin would not react to the dramatically increased demand assumed in Mexico's model by increasing production of that product for the U.S. market.

66.   In short, the available evidence contradicts Mexico's claim that it is the only possible supplier of canned yellowfin, low cost or otherwise, to the U.S. market. Thus, the decision to equate U.S. imports of canned yellowfin with Mexican canned tuna exports is wrong and cannot be used to accurately calculate the level of nullification and impairment in this dispute.

C.   Mexico's Demand Equations Are Incorrect

67.   Mexico used a choice model to depict demand in the U.S. and Mexican markets but derived the demand equations based entirely on assumptions rather than on the highly disaggregated consumer-level data or academic studies that would normally be used to construct such a model. The evidence proves that the assumptions Mexico made are incorrect.

68.   *First,* Mexico's assumption that the United States and Mexico are a single market, in which consumers have the same preferences, is contradicted by the evidence. The evidence shows that U.S. and Mexican consumers have different preferences concerning many different food products, including canned tuna. For example, U.S. consumers have a distinct preference for canned albacore that Mexican consumers do not share, and Mexican consumers have a much stronger preference for canned yellowfin. Also, U.S. consumers have demonstrated a preference for tuna not caught by setting on dolphins that seems to be absent among Mexican consumers. Finally, Mexico's claim that Mexican canned tuna is a gourmet product that is "competitively-priced" with "generic" products and that, therefore, U.S. consumers could not possibly *not* prefer it, is incorrect. In fact, the Mexican canned yellowfin products sold on the U.S. market are not gourmet products and are not priced competitively with bargain-end products.

69.   *Second,* Mexico's unsubstantiated assumption that U.S. demand for canned tuna is represented by a logistically distributed $2 per kg. mean willingness to pay for canned yellowfin over other types of canned tuna is inconsistent with a properly structured consumer choice model and refuted by the evidence on the record. Mexico asserts that its assumption of a $2 per kg.

mean willingness to pay a premium for yellowfin is conservative because it is less than the premium calculated using its weighted OLS regression. But Mexico ignores the fact that the $2 per kg. is *more* than the premium calculated using the OLS regressions. Scaling the distribution function such that 6.6 percent of consumers are willing to pay a premium of $4.65 per kg. is wrong regardless because only 1-2 percent of consumers are paying the current premium. Also, the fact that nearly half of all canned tuna in the United States is sold on sale confirms that the logistic distribution Mexico chose is not accurate for the U.S. market. Finally, the import prices of yellowfin tuna products in the EU demonstrate that, if U.S. demand for yellowfin were such that the United States would import 63,568 metric tons of canned yellowfin if the U.S. import price rose to $7.84 per kg., many countries other than Mexico would supply the product.

70.   *Third*, Mexico's "intensity of demand" parameter is inconsistent with the appropriate use of a consumer choice model and is contradicted by the evidence. In Mexico's model, all consumer preferences other than the preference for yellowfin are represented by a single variable that reflects total consumption in the United States and Mexico. Because this is essentially the only variable that differs between U.S. and Mexican demand, it is the main factor driving the outcome of the model. This is inconsistent with the appropriate use of a choice model, as a properly specified model would derive demand for products based on the product characteristics valued by consumers. Further, Mexico's use of the intensity of demand parameter is inconsistent with the evidence, since it is not correct that the entire U.S. canned tuna market represents the market for canned yellowfin. Only 1-2 percent of all consumption of canned tuna is yellowfin, and at most only 6 percent of consumers, according to Mexico's own consumer survey, even look for canned yellowfin. But Mexico's use of the demand intensity parameter assumes that the U.S. market for canned *yellowfin* is the same as the U.S. market for *all canned tuna*. In reality, the fact that the U.S. market for all canned tuna is larger than the Mexican one does not mean that the U.S. market for canned yellowfin is proportionally as large. That is why, to accurately reflect demand, a model must be based on economic data, not unreasonable assumptions.

II.   THE U.S. MODEL PROVIDES A REASONABLE ESTIMATE OF THE LEVEL OF NULLIFICATION AND IMPAIRMENT

71.   The United States has presented a model that provide a reasonable estimate of the level of nullification and impairment, and Mexico has not shown that the period prior to 1990 is inappropriate to use to estimate Mexico's market share if the measure were withdrawn.

72.   *First*, the agreement between the United States and Mexico concerning U.S. imports of Mexican tuna between 1987 and 1989 did not restrict imports during the period. In only one year, 1987, did U.S. imports of Mexican tuna product come close to the agreed level. In 1988 and 1989, U.S. imports from

Mexico were only 29.7 and 47.5 percent of the agreed levels. Additionally, evidence of Mexico's share of U.S. imports of all tuna product during the period prior to the 1980 embargo confirms that Mexico's import share for 1987-1989 was representative of Mexico's share in the absence of any measure affecting Mexican exports to the United States.

73.   *Second*, the available evidence suggests that NAFTA would not make a significant difference in Mexico's market share of U.S. imports of tuna product. Trends in Mexico's market share of the products most similar to tuna product reveal that NAFTA did not have a large or long-lasting effect on Mexico's import share. Mexico's share of U.S. crab, shrimp, and sardine imports all rose in the years following NAFTA (although noting close to the *2,056 percent* increase in Mexico's share of canned tuna imports predicted by Mexico's model), but all later declined to pre-NAFTA levels (all except sardines within 5 years of NAFTA coming into force). Data on U.S. imports of canned tuna from other countries that have experienced a change in tariff treatment also suggests that using Mexico's pre-NAFTA market share is not unreasonable.

74.   *Third*, the location and capacity of U.S. canneries and the capacity of Mexican canneries are controlled for by using Mexico's market share of all tuna as the baseline. In the 1980s, when there were more U.S. canneries in the EPO region and Mexico's canning capacity was lower, Mexico exported tuna loins and frozen tuna to the U.S. market. As Mexico's canning industry developed, the balance of Mexico's exports shifted towards canned tuna. The U.S. model controls for shifts in the balance of Mexico's exports to the United States by using Mexico's historical share of imports of all tuna to estimate Mexico's share of tuna product imports in the absence of the measure, while multiplying the estimated quantity of imports from Mexico by the higher price of all tuna product rather than the lower price of raw tuna for canning.

75.   In conclusion, the U.S. model is consistent with models used in previous arbitrations and generates a reasonable outcome. Mexico has not shown that this is not the case. Thus, the level of nullification and impairment of $8.5 to $21.9 million per year is appropriate.

UNITED STATES - ANTI-DUMPING AND COUNTERVAILING MEASURES ON LARGE RESIDENTIAL WASHERS FROM KOREA

Arbitration under Article 21.3(c) of the DSU

Award of the Arbitrator
WT/DS464/RPT[*]

Circulated on 13 April 2017

Parties:

Korea

United States

Arbitrator:

Claudia Orozco

TABLE OF CONTENTS

Page

[*] As of 13 April 2017, for ease of reference, awards of arbitrators under Article 21.3(c) of the DSU will bear the symbol WT/DS[number]/RPT.

ABBREVIATIONS USED IN THIS AWARD

Abbreviation	Description
Anti-Dumping Agreement	Agreement on Implementation of Article VI of the General Agreement on Tariffs and Trade 1994
Appellate Body Report	Appellate Body Report, *United States – Anti-Dumping and Countervailing Measures on Large Residential Washers from Korea*, WT/DS464/AB/R
DPM	Differential Pricing Methodology
DSB	Dispute Settlement Body
DSU	Understanding on Rules and Procedures Governing the Settlement of Disputes
GATT 1994	General Agreement on Tariffs and Trade 1994
Panel Report	Panel Report, *United States – Anti-Dumping and Countervailing Measures on Large Residential Washers from Korea*, WT/DS464/R
RSTA	Korea's Restriction of Special Taxation Act
Samsung	Samsung Electronics Co., Ltd
SCM Agreement	Agreement on Subsidies and Countervailing Measures
Section 123 proceeding	Proceeding pursuant to Section 123(g) of the Uruguay Round Agreements Act, Public Law No. 103-465, 108 Stat. 4831, codified as *United States Code*, Title 19, Section 3533(g)
Section 129 proceeding	Proceeding pursuant to Section 129(b) of the Uruguay Round Agreements Act, Public Law No. 103-465, 108 Stat. 4837, codified as *United States Code*, Title 19, Section 3538(b)
T-T	transaction-to-transaction
URAA	Uruguay Round Agreements Act
USDOC	United States Department of Commerce
USTR	United States Trade Representative
Washers anti-dumping investigation	USDOC [A-580-868] Antidumping Duty Investigation of Large Residential Washers from the Republic of Korea
Washers countervailing	USDOC [C-580-869] Countervailing Duty Investigation of Large

Abbreviation	Description
duty investigation	Residential Washers from the Republic of Korea
W-T	weighted average-to-transaction
WTO	World Trade Organization
W-W	weighted average-to-weighted average

CASES CITED IN THIS AWARD

Short Title	Full Case title and citation
Argentina – Hides and Leather (Article 21.3(c))	Award of the Arbitrator, *Argentina – Measures Affecting the Export of Bovine Hides and the Import of Finished Leather – Arbitration under Article 21.3(c) of the DSU*, WT/DS155/10, 31 August 2001, DSR 2001:XII, p. 6013
Brazil – Retreaded Tyres (Article 21.3(c))	Award of the Arbitrator, *Brazil – Measures Affecting Imports of Retreaded Tyres – Arbitration under Article 21.3(c) of the DSU*, WT/DS332/16, 29 August 2008, DSR 2008:XX, p. 8581
Canada – Pharmaceutical Patents (Article 21.3(c))	Award of the Arbitrator, *Canada – Patent Protection of Pharmaceutical Products – Arbitration under Article 21.3(c) of the DSU*, WT/DS114/13, 18 August 2000, DSR 2002:I, p. 3
Chile – Price Band System (Article 21.3(c))	Award of the Arbitrator, *Chile – Price Band System and Safeguard Measures Relating to Certain Agricultural Products – Arbitration under Article 21.3(c) of the DSU*, WT/DS207/13, 17 March 2003, DSR 2003:III, p. 1237
China – GOES (Article 21.3(c))	Award of the Arbitrator, *China – Countervailing and Anti-Dumping Duties on Grain Oriented Flat-Rolled Electrical Steel from the United States – Arbitration under Article 21.3(c) of the DSU*, WT/DS414/12, 3 May 2013, DSR 2013:IV, p. 1495
Colombia – Ports of Entry (Article 21.3(c))	Award of the Arbitrator, *Colombia – Indicative Prices and Restrictions on Ports of Entry – Arbitration under Article 21.3(c) of the DSU*, WT/DS366/13, 2 October 2009, DSR 2009:IX, p. 3819
Colombia – Textiles (Article 21.3(c)	Award of the Arbitrator, *Colombia – Measures Relating to the Importation of Textiles, Apparel and Footwear – Arbitration under Article 21.3(c) of the DSU*, WT/DS461/13, 15 November 2016
EC – Export Subsidies on Sugar (Article 21.3(c))	Award of the Arbitrator, *European Communities – Export Subsidies on Sugar – Arbitration under Article 21.3(c) of the DSU*, WT/DS265/33, WT/DS266/33, WT/DS283/14, 28 October 2005, DSR 2005:XXIII, p. 11581
EC – Tariff Preferences (Article 21.3(c))	Award of the Arbitrator, *European Communities – Conditions for the Granting of Tariff Preferences to Developing Countries – Arbitration under Article 21.3(c) of the DSU*, WT/DS246/14, 20 September 2004, DSR 2004:IX, p. 4313
Japan – DRAMs (Korea) (Article 21.3(c))	Award of the Arbitrator, *Japan – Countervailing Duties on Dynamic Random Access Memories from Korea – Arbitration under Article 21.3(c) of the DSU*, WT/DS336/16, 5 May 2008, DSR 2008:XX, p. 8553
US – 1916 Act (Article 21.3(c))	Award of the Arbitrator, *United States – Anti-Dumping Act of 1916 – Arbitration under Article 21.3(c) of the DSU*, WT/DS136/11, WT/DS162/14, 28 February 2001, DSR 2001:V, p. 2017

Short Title	Full Case title and citation
US – Continued Zeroing	Appellate Body Report, *United States – Continued Existence and Application of Zeroing Methodology*, WT/DS350/AB/R, adopted 19 February 2009, DSR 2009:III, p. 1291
US – COOL (Article 21.3(c))	Award of the Arbitrator, *United States – Certain Country of Origin Labelling (COOL) Requirements – Arbitration under Article 21.3(c) of the DSU*, WT/DS384/24, WT/DS386/23, 4 December 2012, DSR 2012:XIII, p. 7173
US – Countervailing Measures (China) (Article 21.3(c))	Award of the Arbitrator, *United States – Countervailing Duty Measures on Certain Products from China – Arbitration under Article 21.3(c) of the DSU*, WT/DS437/16, 9 October 2015
US – Offset Act (Byrd Amendment) (Article 21.3(c))	Award of the Arbitrator, *United States – Continued Dumping and Subsidy Offset Act of 2000 – Arbitration under Article 21.3(c) of the DSU*, WT/DS217/14, WT/DS234/22, 13 June 2003, DSR 2003:III, p. 1163
US – Shrimp II (Viet Nam) (Article 21.3(c))	Award of the Arbitrator, *United States – Anti-Dumping Measures on Certain Shrimp from Viet Nam – Arbitration under Article 21.3(c) of the DSU*, WT/DS429/12, 15 December 2015
US – Softwood Lumber V (Article 21.5 – Canada)	Appellate Body Report, *United States – Final Dumping Determination on Softwood Lumber from Canada – Recourse to Article 21.5 of the DSU by Canada*, WT/DS264/AB/RW, adopted 1 September 2006, DSR 2006:XII, p. 5087
US – Stainless Steel (Mexico)	Appellate Body Report, *United States – Final Anti-Dumping Measures on Stainless Steel from Mexico*, WT/DS344/AB/R, adopted 20 May 2008, DSR 2008:II, p. 513
US – Stainless Steel (Mexico) (Article 21.3(c))	Award of the Arbitrator, *United States – Final Anti-Dumping Measures on Stainless Steel from Mexico – Arbitration under Article 21.3(c) of the DSU*, WT/DS344/15, 31 October 2008, DSR 2008:XX, p. 8619
US – Washing Machines	Appellate Body Report, *United States – Anti-Dumping and Countervailing Measures on Large Residential Washers from Korea*, WT/DS464/AB/R and Add.1, adopted 26 September 2016
US – Washing Machines	Panel Report, *United States – Anti-Dumping and Countervailing Measures on Large Residential Washers from Korea*, WT/DS464/R and Add.1, adopted 26 September 2016, as modified by Appellate Body Report WT/DS464/AB/R
US – Zeroing (Japan)	Appellate Body Report, *United States – Measures Relating to Zeroing and Sunset Reviews*, WT/DS322/AB/R, adopted 23 January 2007, DSR 2007:I, p. 3

1. INTRODUCTION

1.1   On 26 September 2016, the Dispute Settlement Body (DSB) of the World Trade Organization (WTO) adopted the Appellate Body Report[1] and the Panel Report[2] in *United States – Anti-Dumping and Countervailing Measures on Large*

---

[1]   WT/DS464/AB/R.
[2]   WT/DS464/R.

Residential Washers from Korea. This dispute concerns Korea's challenge of certain methodologies used by the United States in anti-dumping investigations and administrative reviews, as well as certain anti-dumping and countervailing measures imposed by the United States on imports of large residential washers from Korea. The Panel and the Appellate Body found the measures at issue to be inconsistent with various provisions of the Agreement on Implementation of Article VI of the General Agreement on Tariffs and Trade 1994 (Anti-Dumping Agreement), the Agreement on Subsidies and Countervailing Measures (SCM Agreement), and the General Agreement on Tariffs and Trade 1994 (GATT 1994).

1.2   At the meeting of the DSB held on 26 October 2016, the United States indicated its intention to implement the DSB's recommendations and rulings in this dispute, and stated that it would need a reasonable period of time in which to do so.[3]

1.3   By letter dated 9 December 2016, Korea informed the DSB that its consultations with the United States on the reasonable period of time for implementation pursuant to Article 21.3(b) of the Understanding on Rules and Procedures Governing the Settlement of Disputes (DSU) had not resulted in an agreement. Korea therefore requested that the reasonable period of time be determined through binding arbitration pursuant to Article 21.3(c) of the DSU.[4]

1.4   On 21 December. 2016, the United States and Korea sent a joint communication to the Chairman of the DSB and requested that it be circulated to WTO Members.[5] In the communication, the United States and Korea indicated their agreement that, "in the event an arbitration under Article 21.3(c) of the DSU is requested, it shall be completed no later than 60 days after the date of the appointment of an arbitrator, unless the arbitrator, following consultation with the parties, considers that additional time is required."[6] The United States and Korea also confirmed that any award of the arbitrator, including an award not made within 90 days after the adoption of the recommendations and rulings of the DSB, would be deemed to be an award of the arbitrator for the purposes of Article 21.3(c) of the DSU.

1.5   By letter dated 22 December 2016, Korea informed the Director-General of the WTO that consultations with the United States had not led to mutual agreement on an arbitrator. Korea therefore requested the Director-General to appoint an arbitrator pursuant to footnote 12 to Article 21.3(c) of the DSU. After consulting with the parties, the Director-General appointed me as the Arbitrator on 12 January 2017.

1.6   On 12 January 2017, the United States sent a letter requesting that the due date for the United States' submission be no earlier than 27 January 2017, in

---

[3]   WT/DSB/M/387, para. 2.3.
[4]   WT/DS464/13.
[5]   WT/DS464/14.
[6]   *Ibid.*

light of expected difficulties in preparing that written submission due to office closures relating to the United States Presidential Inauguration on 20 January 2017, as well as a federal public holiday on 16 January 2017.

1.7   On 16 January 2017, I informed the parties of my acceptance of the appointment as Arbitrator, and invited Korea to comment on the United States' letter of 12 January 2017. On 18 January 2017, Korea indicated that it did not intend to comment on the United States' letter and that it thereby expressed no objection to the United States' request. On 19 January 2017, I transmitted to the parties a Working Schedule identifying the dates for the filing of the parties' written submissions and the date for the hearing.[7]

1.8   On 20 January 2017, I received a letter from Korea requesting modification of the deadline for the filing of Korea's written submission from Friday, 3 February 2017 to Monday, 20 February 2017, and modification of the date of the hearing from 16 February 2017 to a few days later. Korea identified several reasons for its request in respect of its filing deadline. Korea pointed out that, in previous Article 21.3(c) arbitrations, the submissions of the implementing and complaining Members have been due 7 and 14 days, respectively, after the arbitrator's acceptance of the appointment. Korea expressed due process concerns arising from the fact that, under the Working Schedule, the United States had been given 11 days for its submission while Korea's submission was due 7 days thereafter. Korea added that its ability to prepare its submission was also reduced by virtue of Korea's national holidays for the Lunar New Year from 27-30 January 2017. Korea supported its request to postpone the date of the hearing with reference to its participation in expert sessions and panel meetings in the dispute *Korea – Import Bans, and Testing and Certification Requirements for Radionuclides* (DS495) in mid-February 2017.

1.9   On 20 January 2017, I invited the United States to comment on Korea's request. On 24 January 2017, the United States indicated that it had no objection to Korea's request to extend the deadline for the filing of its written submission, provided that the hearing date be extended in a corresponding way so as to preserve a period of at least two weeks between that deadline and the date of the hearing in order to allow the United States sufficient time to consider Korea's submission in preparing for the hearing. Accordingly, the United States requested that any extension of the date for the filing of Korea's written submission be accompanied by an extension of the date for the hearing until at least 6 March 2017.

1.10   On 24 January 2017, I sent the parties a revised Working Schedule, pursuant to which the United States filed its written submission on 2 February 2017, Korea filed its written submission on 20 February 2017, and the hearing

---

[7]   The Working Schedule of 19 January 2017 indicated that the written submission of the United States should be filed on 27 January 2017, the written submission of Korea should be filed on 3 February 2017, and the hearing would be held on 16 February 2017.

was held on 9 March 2017. At the hearing, I indicated that, in light of the parties' requests to postpone the dates for the filing of their written submissions and for the hearing, the Award would be issued by 13 April 2017.

2. ARGUMENTS OF THE PARTIES

2.1   Annexes A and B to this Award contain the executive summaries of the parties' submissions. Certain details of the parties' arguments are further described below, insofar as they are relevant to the analysis.

3. REASONABLE PERIOD OF TIME

3.1   Introduction

3.1   I have been appointed by the Director-General, at the request of Korea, to determine the "reasonable period of time" pursuant to Article 21.3(c) of the DSU for the United States to implement the recommendations and rulings of the DSB in *United States – Anti-Dumping and Countervailing Measures on Large Residential Washers from Korea*.

3.2   The United States requests 21 months as the reasonable period of time for implementation of the DSB's recommendations and rulings in this dispute.[8]

3.3   Korea requests that the reasonable period of time be either 6 or 8 months, depending on the precise means of implementation.[9]

3.4   This section sets out the mandate of the arbitrator under Article 21.3(c) of the DSU in light of the text of the DSU. It then identifies the specific measures that the United States is required to bring into conformity with the recommendations and rulings of the DSB. Finally, it analyses the factors affecting the determination of the reasonable period of time in this dispute, including the means of implementation, the steps in the implementation process, and circumstances particular to this dispute that the parties allege should be taken into account in reaching the determination.

3.2   Mandate of the Arbitrator Under Article 21.3(c) of the DSU

3.5   Article 21.3 of the DSU provides, in relevant part:

> If it is impracticable to comply immediately with the recommendations and rulings [of the DSB], the Member concerned shall have a reasonable period of time in which to do so. The reasonable period of time shall be:
>
> ...

---

[8]   United States' submission, para. 8.
[9]   Korea's submission, para. 8.

(c)   a period of time determined through binding arbitration within 90 days after the date of adoption of the recommendations and rulings. In such arbitration, a guideline for the arbitrator should be that the reasonable period of time to implement panel or Appellate Body recommendations should not exceed 15 months from the date of adoption of a panel or Appellate Body report. However, that time may be shorter or longer, depending upon the particular circumstances. (fns omitted)

3.6   Accordingly, the mandate of the arbitrator is to determine the time period within which the implementing Member is to comply with the recommendations and rulings of the DSB. Article 21.3(c) establishes as a guideline that such period should not exceed 15 months and recognizes that, "depending upon the particular circumstances" of the dispute, the period "may be shorter or longer".

3.7   In determining the period of time that is reasonable in light of the particular circumstances of a dispute, the arbitrator should bear in mind the provisions of the DSU that provide context to Article 21.3(c), in particular Article 21.1, which establishes that "prompt compliance" with the DSB's recommendations and rulings is essential "to ensure effective resolution of disputes", and the introductory clause of Article 21.3, which foresees a reasonable period of time for implementation when it is "impracticable to comply immediately". Both provisions indicate the importance of compliance in as short a period as possible when immediate compliance is not practicable.

3.8   Further, in determining the reasonable period of time, the means of implementation available to the Member concerned is a relevant factor. Determining this period of time thus requires consideration of how that Member proposes to implement under its municipal law.[10] Previous awards have indicated that, while the Member concerned has discretion in choosing the means of implementation that it deems most appropriate, the means of implementation chosen must be apt in form, nature, and content to bring the Member into compliance with its WTO obligations.[11] Previous awards have also indicated that, if the action that the implementing Member proposes to take seeks to achieve objectives unrelated to the DSB's recommendations and rulings, or forms part of a wider reform of that Member's municipal law, then these considerations cannot justify a longer implementation period for the WTO dispute.[12] At the same time, the mandate under Article 21.3(c) of the DSU is

---

[10]   Award of the Arbitrator, *Japan – DRAMs (Korea) (Article 21.3(c))*, para. 26. See also Award of the Arbitrator, *US – COOL (Article 21.3(c))*, para. 68.

[11]   See Awards of the Arbitrators, *Colombia – Textiles (Article 21.3(c))*, para. 3.4; *US – Countervailing Measures (China) (Article 21.3(c))*, para. 3.3; *China – GOES (Article 21.3(c))*, para. 3.2; and *Colombia – Ports of Entry (Article 21.3(c))*, para. 64.

[12]   See Awards of the Arbitrators, *Colombia – Textiles (Article 21.3(c))*, paras. 3.36 and 3.41; *Colombia – Ports of Entry (Article 21.3(c))*, paras. 64 and 85; *EC – Export Subsidies on Sugar (Article 21.3(c))*, para. 69; and *EC – Tariff Preferences (Article 21.3(c))*, para. 31.

limited to determining the period of time within which it would be reasonable to expect implementation of the recommendations and rulings of the DSB to occur, and does not involve deciding on the content of the implementation needed, nor a determination of the consistency with the covered agreements of the measure that the Member envisages to adopt in order to comply. The latter question, should it arise, is to be addressed in proceedings conducted pursuant to Article 21.5 of the DSU.[13]

3.9   Pursuant to the last sentence of Article 21.3(c), the "particular circumstances" of a dispute may affect the reasonable period of time, making it "shorter or longer". Previous arbitrators have observed that the objective of "prompt compliance" in Article 21.1 of the DSU calls for the implementing Member to utilize the flexibilities available within its legal system in implementing the relevant recommendations and rulings of the DSB.[14] An implementing Member is not, however, expected to utilize "extraordinary procedures" to bring its measure into compliance.[15]

3.10   Finally, with regard to the burden of proof, it is well established that the implementing Member bears the overall burden of proving that the time period requested for implementation constitutes a "reasonable period of time".[16] However, this does not "absolve" the complaining Member of its duty to provide evidence supporting why it disagrees with the period of time proposed by the implementing Member, and to substantiate its view that a shorter period of time for implementation is reasonable.[17]

3.3   *Measures to Be Brought Into Conformity*

3.11   The parties agree that the scope of the United States' implementation obligations in this dispute is defined by the recommendations and rulings of the DSB, as set forth in section 6 of the Appellate Body Report, together with

---

[13]   See Awards of the Arbitrators, *Colombia – Textiles (Article 21.3(c))*, para. 3.6; *US – Shrimp II (Viet Nam) (Article 21.3(c))*, para. 3.3; *US – Countervailing Measures (China) (Article 21.3(c))*, para. 3.4; and *Japan – DRAMs (Korea) (Article 21.3(c))*, para. 27.

[14]   See Awards of the Arbitrators, *Colombia – Textiles (Article 21.3(c))*, paras. 3.51-3.53; *US – Shrimp II (Viet Nam) (Article 21.3(c))*, para. 3.5; *US – Countervailing Measures (China) (Article 21.3(c))*, para. 3.5; *China – GOES (Article 21.3(c))*, para. 3.4; *US – Stainless Steel (Mexico) (Article 21.3(c))*, para. 42; *Brazil – Retreaded Tyres (Article 21.3(c))*, para. 48; *Japan – DRAMs (Korea) (Article 21.3(c))*, para. 25; and *US – Offset Act (Byrd Amendment) (Article 21.3(c))*, para. 64.

[15]   See Awards of the Arbitrators, *US – Countervailing Measures (China) (Article 21.3(c))*, para. 3.5; *China – GOES (Article 21.3(c))*, para. 3.4; *US – COOL (Article 21.3(c))*, para. 70; *US – Stainless Steel (Mexico) (Article 21.3(c))*, para. 42; *Brazil – Retreaded Tyres (Article 21.3(c))*, para. 48; *Japan – DRAMs (Korea) (Article 21.3(c))*, para. 25; and *US – Offset Act (Byrd Amendment) (Article 21.3(c))*, para. 74.

[16]   See Awards of the Arbitrators, *US – Countervailing Measures (China) (Article 21.3(c))*, para. 3.6; *China – GOES (Article 21.3(c))*, para. 3.5; *Canada – Pharmaceutical Patents (Article 21.3(c))*, para. 47; *US – 1916 Act (Article 21.3(c))*, para. 33; and *EC – Tariff Preferences (Article 21.3(c))*, para. 27.

[17]   See Award of the Arbitrator, *Colombia – Ports of Entry (Article 21.3(c))*, para. 67.

paragraph 8.1 of the Panel Report.[18] At the hearing, the parties agreed that the measures to be brought into conformity with the covered agreements could generally be summarized as follows[19]:

a. In respect of certain methodologies used by the United States Department of Commerce (USDOC) in anti-dumping investigations:

  i. aspects of the Differential Pricing Methodology (DPM) used to determine whether to apply the weighted average-to-transaction (W-T) methodology; and

  ii. aspects of the methodologies used to calculate the margin of dumping when applying the W-T methodology.

b. In respect of the *Washers* anti-dumping investigation[20]:

  i. the USDOC's determination to apply the W-T methodology on the basis of:

  - its identification of a pattern of export prices which differ significantly among different purchasers, regions or time periods; and

  - its explanation as to why such differences could not be taken into account by the methodologies that are normally to be used; and

  ii. the USDOC's calculation of the margin of dumping.

c. In respect of the *Washers* countervailing duty investigation[21]:

  i. the USDOC's determination that Article 10(1)(3) of Korea's Restriction of Special Taxation Act (RSTA) is *de facto* specific, in particular:

  - the original and remand determinations that Samsung Electronics Co., Ltd (Samsung) received subsidies in disproportionately large amounts; and

  - the USDOC's failure to take account of the duration and economic diversification factors referred to in the final sentence of Article 2.1(c) of the SCM Agreement; and

  ii. the manner in which the USDOC calculated the *ad valorem* subsidization rate for Samsung, in particular:

---

[18] Parties' responses to questions at the hearing.
[19] See also United States' submission, para. 3 and Korea's submission, paras. 16-20.
[20] USDOC [A-580-868] Antidumping Duty Investigation of Large Residential Washers from the Republic of Korea.
[21] USDOC [C-580-869] Countervailing Duty Investigation of Large Residential Washers from the Republic of Korea.

- the test applied to ascertain whether the tax credits bestowed under Articles 10(1)(3) and 26 of the RSTA were tied to particular products and the failure to take account of certain evidence submitted by Samsung that was potentially relevant to the assessment of a possible tie between the tax credits claimed by Samsung and the products manufactured by its digital appliance business unit; and

- the presumptive attribution of tax credits received by Samsung under Article 10(1)(3) of the RSTA to Samsung's domestic production without assessing all the arguments and evidence submitted by interested parties and other relevant facts surrounding the bestowal of such tax credits.

3.12   With respect to the measures described above, the Panel and the Appellate Body found: (i) certain aspects of the USDOC's anti-dumping methodologies to be inconsistent "as such" with Articles 2.4.2, 2.4, and 9.3 of the Anti-Dumping Agreement, and Article VI:2 of the GATT 1994; (ii) certain actions by the USDOC in the *Washers* anti-dumping investigation to be inconsistent "as applied" with Articles 2.4.2 and 2.4 of the Anti-Dumping Agreement; and (iii) certain actions by the USDOC in the *Washers* countervailing duty investigation to be inconsistent "as applied" with Articles 2.1(c) and 19.4 of the SCM Agreement, and Article VI:3 of the GATT 1994.[22]

3.4   *Factors Affecting the Determination of the Reasonable Period of Time*

3.13   The United States indicates that a reasonable period of time to implement the DSB's recommendations and rulings in this dispute is 21 months.[23] The United States argues that this period is necessary due to the "number and magnitude of modifications to the challenged measures, the procedural requirements under U.S. law, the complexity of the issues involved, and the current resource demands and constraints on the USDOC".[24] According to the United States, it requires a three-phase process: one in respect of each of the three sets of measures identified in paragraph 3.11 above. The United States explains that it requires a proceeding pursuant to Section 123(g) of the Uruguay Round Agreements Act (URAA)[25] to address the "as such" findings of inconsistency concerning the DPM and the use of the W-T methodology in

---

[22]   See Panel Report, para. 8.1; and Appellate Body Report, paras. 6.1-6.16.
[23]   United States' submission, para. 13.
[24]   United States' submission, para. 8.
[25]   Uruguay Round Agreements Act, Public Law No. 103-465, 108 Stat. 4831, codified as *United States Code*, Title 19, Section 3533(g).

investigations and assessment proceedings.[26] A second and a third proceeding, each pursuant to Section 129(b) of the URAA[27], are needed to address the "as applied" findings relating to the *Washers* anti-dumping investigation and the *Washers* countervailing duty investigation, respectively.[28] In addition, the United States asserts that the Section 129 proceeding concerning the *Washers* anti-dumping investigation cannot be commenced until it has partially completed the Section 123 proceeding because the Section 123 proceeding will develop the revised approaches and methodologies to be applied in the Section 129 proceeding.[29]

3.14   Korea questions the time requested for preparatory work and the need to undertake a Section 123 procedure to address the "as such" findings. Korea contends that, taking into account "the number and complexity of the issues involved, and the administrative procedures that the United States must undergo in order to implement revisions to its measures", the United States should reasonably be able to implement all of the DSB's recommendations and rulings through proceedings under Section 129 within 6 months.[30] Even if a Section 123 proceeding were to be undertaken to implement the "as such" recommendations and rulings, Korea maintains that all three proceedings could be completed within a maximum of 8 months.[31]

3.15   The parties agree that, notwithstanding that the United States will conduct more than one proceeding, a single reasonable period of time should be determined. The parties also agree that two Section 129 proceedings are needed – one to implement the recommendations and rulings concerning the *Washers* anti-dumping investigation and one to implement the recommendations and rulings concerning the *Washers* countervailing duty investigation – and that they can be conducted separately and independently from each other. The parties disagree, however, on: (i) whether a Section 123 proceeding is necessary; and therefore whether any additional time that such a proceeding may entail should

---

[26]   United States' submission, para. 4.

[27]   Uruguay Round Agreements Act, Public Law No. 103-465, 108 Stat. 4837, codified as *United States Code*, Title 19, Section 3538(b).

[28]   United States' submission, para. 4. Although the United States refers to these proceedings as "Phase I"; "Phase II"; and "Phase III", such categorization may be taken to imply that the phases are to be conducted sequentially. This, however, would be misleading, as the United States itself envisages that there would be some overlap in time among them. Accordingly, this Award refers to: (i) the proceeding pursuant to Section 123(g) of the URAA proposed to address the "as such" findings of inconsistency with the Anti-Dumping Agreement and the GATT 1994 as the "Section 123 proceeding"; (ii) the proceeding pursuant to Section 129(b) of the URAA proposed to address the "as applied" findings of inconsistency with the Anti-Dumping Agreement as the "Section 129 anti-dumping proceeding" or the "Section 129 anti-dumping redetermination"; and (iii) the proceeding pursuant to Section 129(b) of the URAA proposed to address the "as applied" findings of inconsistency with the SCM Agreement as the "Section 129 countervailing duty proceeding" or the "Section 129 countervailing duty redetermination".

[29]   United States' submission, para. 26.

[30]   Korea's submission, para. 8.

[31]   *Ibid.*

be taken into account in determining the reasonable period of time; (ii) the extent to which a Section 123 proceeding could be conducted simultaneously with the Section 129 anti-dumping proceeding; and (iii) the amount of time reasonably needed to conduct each of the three proceedings.

3.16   The analysis below first addresses the parties' disagreement with respect to the means of implementing the "as such" recommendations and rulings. Second, it examines the parties' arguments concerning the specific steps that must be taken by the United States under the different proceedings, including the extent to which a Section 123 proceeding could be conducted simultaneously with the Section 129 anti-dumping proceeding. Third, it analyses the particular circumstances of this dispute alleged by the parties to be relevant to the determination of the reasonable period of time.

3.4.1   Means of implementation

3.17   While the parties agree that separate proceedings are required for implementing the DSB's recommendations and rulings relating to the anti-dumping measures and those relating to the *Washers* countervailing duty investigation, they disagree on the means to implement the "as such" recommendations and rulings relating to the DPM and the application of the W-T methodology. Korea argues that implementation can and should be undertaken through a Section 129 proceeding rather than a Section 123 proceeding.[32] Specifically, Korea states that modification of the relevant anti-dumping methodologies does not require "formal rulemaking or legislation" and can be achieved through a Section 129 proceeding.[33] Korea points out that the existing methodologies were developed within the framework of specific anti-dumping investigations.[34] Further, Korea maintains that a Section 129 proceeding is a "more efficient" means of implementation[35], and refers to the awards of the arbitrators in *US – Stainless Steel (Mexico)* and *Argentina – Hides and Leather* for the proposition that, where multiple means of implementation are available, the reasonable period of time should be based on the shortest possible time period.[36] In Korea's view, Section 129 constitutes a flexibility available to the United States that should be exercised in order for the United States to implement its obligations in the shortest possible period of time.[37]

3.18   At the hearing, Korea indicated that, notwithstanding the views expressed in its submission, Korea has "no problem" with the United States pursuing a Section 123 proceeding. Korea nevertheless stressed that the amount of time

---

[32]   Korea's submission, paras. 30-38.
[33]   Korea's submission, para. 33.
[34]   Korea's submission, para. 32.
[35]   Korea's submission, para. 36.
[36]   Korea's submission, para. 35 (referring to Awards of the Arbitrators, *US – Stainless Steel (Mexico) (Article 21.3(c))*, para. 53; and *Argentina – Hides and Leather (Article 21.3(c))*, para. 47).
[37]   Korea's submission, paras. 34 and 38.

sought by the United States is excessively long and unjustified, and that both the Section 123 and Section 129 anti-dumping proceedings could be undertaken simultaneously.

3.19   For its part, the United States asserts that a Section 123 proceeding is appropriate to address the "as such" findings concerning the anti-dumping measures. The United States indicates that "Section 123 is a legal instrument that generally governs changes in [the USDOC's] practice when a panel or the Appellate Body finds the practice to be inconsistent with the URAA" while Section 129 "sets out the procedures regarding individual proceedings".[38] The United States highlights that Korea challenged the DPM as a practice and that the Panel found that the DPM is a rule or norm of general and prospective application. For the United States, it is therefore appropriate to consider the DPM a practice.[39] The United States also argues that, taking account of the "number and magnitude" of the "as such" findings by the Panel and the Appellate Body, it has determined that a Section 123 proceeding, rather than legislative change, is the most practical way to implement these obligations.[40]

3.20   In addressing this issue, it is important to recall, from paragraph 3.8 above, that an implementing Member has discretion in choosing its means of implementation as long as the means chosen is apt in form, nature, and content to bring the Member into compliance with its WTO obligations.

3.21   In the current dispute, the Panel found the DPM and the USDOC's methodology for applying the W-T comparison to be measures that could be challenged "as such" in WTO dispute settlement on the basis of a finding that they are rules or norms of general and prospective application.[41] The Panel considered that the evidence before it demonstrated that the DPM "represents a policy choice [by the USDOC] that extends well beyond the mere repetition of the methodology in certain specific cases" and is thus applicable in all cases.[42]

3.22   Further, the text of Section 123(g)(1) explicitly indicates that, "[i]n any case in which a dispute settlement panel or the Appellate Body finds in its report that a regulation or practice of a department or agency of the United States is inconsistent with any of the Uruguay Round Agreements, that regulation or practice may not be amended, rescinded, or otherwise modified in the implementation of such report unless and until" the relevant steps set forth under Section 123(g) have been followed.

---

[38]   United States' response to questions at the hearing. Section 123 proceedings are "often used to amend or modify an agency regulation or practice" while Section 129 proceedings are "used to amend or modify an action taken in a particular proceeding". (United States' submission, fn 17 to para. 4)

[39]   United States' response to questions at the hearing.

[40]   *Ibid.*

[41]   Panel Report, paras. 7.97-7.117 and fn 321 to para. 7.173.

[42]   Panel Report, para. 7.115. See also para. 7.110; and Appellate Body Report, paras. 6.3-6.4 and 6.7-6.11.

3.23   On the basis of the foregoing, the United States has demonstrated that a Section 123 proceeding is an appropriate means to implement the DSB's "as such" recommendations and rulings in this dispute.

3.4.2   Steps in the implementation process

3.24   Turning to the implementation process, the subsections below address the steps required for: (i) implementation of the DSB's "as such" recommendations and rulings through a Section 123 proceeding; (ii) implementation of the DSB's "as applied" recommendations and rulings concerning the *Washers* anti-dumping investigation through a Section 129 anti-dumping proceeding; (iii) the sequencing of the Section 123 and Section 129 proceedings concerning the anti-dumping measures; and (iv) implementation of the DSB's "as applied" recommendations and rulings concerning the *Washers* countervailing duty investigation through a Section 129 proceeding.

3.4.2.1   Implementation of the DSB's "as such" recommendations and rulings

3.25   With regard to implementation of the DSB's "as such" recommendations and rulings concerning the DPM and the W-T methodology, the United States argues that it needs 5 months to conduct internal deliberations prior to the commencement of the Section 123 proceeding, during which: the United States would determine whether a WTO-consistent approach to applying the W-T methodology in anti-dumping proceedings "is possible under existing municipal law"; the United States Trade Representative (USTR) and the USDOC would conduct preliminary consultations; these agencies would conduct "pre-commencement analysis preparation"; and the USDOC would begin devising anti-dumping methodologies in preparation for the commencement of Section 123 and Section 129 proceedings.[43] The United States maintains that, thereafter, it needs "no less than 15 months to complete the entire section 123 process".[44] In considering the period of time required to complete both the initial deliberations and the Section 123 proceeding, the United States emphasizes that implementation requires the United States to redesign, and perhaps replace entirely, its methodology for identifying and addressing potential masked dumping in original and assessment proceedings in a way that, to date, has not been applied by WTO Members.[45] Overall, the United States argues that compliance in this dispute requires a period of 21 months.[46]

---

[43]   United States' submission, para. 55.

[44]   United States' submission, para. 42.

[45]   United States' submission, paras. 15-24.

[46]   In its proposed timetable, the United States indicates that the Section 123 proceeding will conclude in June 2018 (i.e. 21 months following the adoption of the Panel and Appellate Body Reports in September 2016). (United States' submission, para. 55)

3.26   Korea argues that the United States' proposed time period fails to account for available flexibilities and incorporates steps not required under the proposed Section 123 proceeding.[47] Korea also contends that the time periods requested for certain steps are longer than the time periods actually needed to complete those steps. In particular, Korea contests the amount of time required to: (i) conduct initial deliberations and preparatory work; (ii) develop proposed methodologies for determining when to apply the W-T methodology and for calculating the margin of dumping; and (iii) conduct consultations with Congress and the private sector (including time for analysis of public comments on the proposed methodologies).[48] Korea also contests the extent to which the "novelty" of the DSB's "as such" recommendations and rulings and the technical complexities of implementation are relevant factors in determining the reasonable period of time.[49] Furthermore, Korea highlights that in *US – Stainless Steel (Mexico)* the United States requested only 7 months to complete a Section 123 proceeding.[50] Korea submits that in the present dispute the United States requires no more than 8 months to complete the Section 123 proceeding.

3.27   Section 123(g) of the URAA provides, in relevant part:

(g)   Requirements for agency action

(1)   Changes in agency regulations or practice

In any case in which a dispute settlement panel or the Appellate Body finds in its report that a regulation or practice of a department or agency of the United States is inconsistent with any of the Uruguay Round Agreements, that regulation or practice may not be amended, rescinded, or otherwise modified in the implementation of such report unless and until—

(A)   the appropriate congressional committees have been consulted under subsection (f)[51];

(B)   the Trade Representative has sought advice regarding the modification from relevant private

---

[47]   Korea's submission, paras. 42-47.
[48]   Korea's submission, paras. 27 and 42-48.
[49]   Korea's submission, paras. 67-71.
[50]   Korea's submission, para. 48 (referring to Award of the Arbitrator, *US – Stainless Steel (Mexico)* (Article 21.3(c))*, para. 56).
[51]   Subsection (f) of Section 123 refers to "[a]ctions upon circulation of reports" and provides that: Promptly after the circulation of a report of a panel or of the Appellate Body to WTO members …, the Trade Representative shall— (1) notify the appropriate congressional committees of the report; (2) in the case of a report of a panel, consult with the appropriate congressional committees concerning the nature of any appeal that may be taken of the report; and (3) if the report is adverse to the United States, consult with the appropriate congressional committees concerning whether to implement the report's recommendation and, if so, the manner of such implementation and the period of time needed for such implementation.

sector advisory committees established under section 135 of the Trade Act of 1974 …;

(C)   the head of the relevant department or agency has provided an opportunity for public comment by publishing in the Federal Register the proposed modification and the explanation for the modification;

(D)   the Trade Representative has submitted to the appropriate congressional committees a report describing the proposed modification, the reasons for the modification, and a summary of the advice obtained under subparagraph (B) with respect to the modification;

(E)   the Trade Representative and the head of the relevant department or agency have consulted with the appropriate congressional committees on the proposed contents of the final rule or other modification; and

(F)   the final rule or other modification has been published in the Federal Register.

(2)   Effective date of modification

A final rule or other modification to which paragraph (1) applies may not go into effect before the end of the 60-day period beginning on the date on which consultations under paragraph (1)(E) begin, unless the President determines that an earlier effective date is in the national interest.

3.28   The parties agree that subparagraphs (A) through (F) quoted above identify the steps involved in a Section 123 proceeding and that the only prescribed time period is found in Section 123(g)(2), which provides that the final rule or modification may not go into effect until at least 60 days after the USTR and the USDOC have begun consultations with the relevant congressional committees on the proposed modification.[52] From the language of Section 123 and the explanations by the United States it is clear that: (i) the USTR begins consulting with Congress promptly after the circulation of a panel or Appellate Body report to WTO Members[53] and is "constantly consulting from that point onwards"[54]; (ii) time is needed between the beginning of consultations and the time that the proposed modification is published in the Federal Register so as to enable the USDOC to elaborate its proposed modification; (iii) in practice, the USTR consults with relevant private sector advisory committees at the same

---

[52]   Parties' responses to questions at the hearing.
[53]   See Section 123(f) reproduced in fn 51 above.
[54]   United States' response to questions at the hearing.

time that the public is afforded an opportunity to comment on the proposal and both of these steps take place following the publication of the proposed modification in the Federal Register; and (iv) because the USTR's report to Congress must include a summary of the advice obtained from private sector advisory committees and also contains a summary of the comments from the public on the proposed rule, this report can be prepared only after the period for commenting on the proposed modification has elapsed. Consequently, while some steps can be performed at the same time, other steps must, as a matter of law and by necessary implication, occur sequentially. Korea does not disagree with the description and explanations provided by the United States.

3.29   The parties disagree as to the necessity of an initial period of internal deliberations and consultations by the USTR and the USDOC and as to the period of time that is required by the USTR and the USDOC to develop the proposed modification and publish it in the Federal Register.[55] In respect of these deliberative steps, the United States emphasizes the "novelty" of the Appellate Body's findings and highlights that this is the first dispute in which the DSB has made recommendations and rulings regarding the application of the second sentence of Article 2.4.2 of the Anti-Dumping Agreement.[56] The United States further explains that there is significant technical "complexity" in implementing these "as such" recommendations and rulings because it will likely need to: (i) make significant changes to or replace the DPM, including revision of the computer program used to perform a "quantitative" analysis of export prices and the development of a means to perform a "qualitative" analysis[57]; (ii) make substantial revisions to its computer program for determining the margin of dumping under the W-T methodology, including for purposes of administrative reviews[58]; and (iii) revise its approach to explaining why the weighted average-to-weighted average (W-W) and transaction-to-transaction (T-T) methodologies cannot appropriately take into account differences in export prices, including "significant practice development, internal analysis and deliberation, and decision-making" to determine how the USDOC would employ a T-T analysis.[59] The United States indicates that it requires 12 months from adoption of the Panel and Appellate Body Reports until publication of the proposed modification in the Federal Register.[60]

3.30   For its part, Korea asserts that the implementation steps that the United States must carry out are neither novel nor particularly complex and "do not present significant burdens or complications compared to other proceedings".[61] Korea emphasizes that the United States has already undertaken

---

[55]   United States' submission, paras. 12 and 16-24; Korea's submission, paras. 67-71.
[56]   United States' submission, para. 15.
[57]   United States' submission, paras. 18-19.
[58]   United States' submission, paras. 20-21.
[59]   United States' submission, para. 23.
[60]   United States' submission, para. 55.
[61]   Korea's submission, para. 71.

"intense studying" of the issue of how to apply the second sentence of Article 2.4.2 of the Anti-Dumping Agreement over the last ten years and that, just as it was not difficult for the USDOC to modify the Nails II methodology[62] to identify differential pricing under the DPM, it would not be difficult to modify the DPM to implement the relevant recommendations and rulings of the DSB.[63] Korea adds that the United States does not need to conduct lengthy procedures in order to develop a "qualitative test", make technical revisions to its dumping margin calculation computer program, or make significant revisions to the USDOC's policies or regulations. To Korea, the DSB's recommendations and rulings do not require the United States to "redo everything and rethink everything and do every contingency imaginable in every single case".[64] For Korea, it follows that the reasonable period of time should not encompass time for the United States to establish if it might want to use a T-T methodology, what that methodology would be, and how it would apply to all the different industries to which it might be applied. Korea considers that the United States could conduct its internal deliberations and consultations at the same time as it develops its methodology, all of which could have taken place within 90 days of the adoption of the Panel and Appellate Body Reports.[65]

3.31   The first point of disagreement between the United States and Korea relates to the need and the length of time that would be justified for preparatory work. The United States highlights that, following the findings of the Panel and the Appellate Body, "the landscape of how investigating authorities can apply the second sentence of Article 2.4.2 has significantly changed".[66] Korea argues that the United States has already undertaken "intense studying" of the issues involved over the past ten years.[67] Korea also emphasizes that the United States could have and should have begun taking steps towards implementation in this dispute earlier than it has, and that the United States has not demonstrated that it has taken any concrete action in the more than 5 months since adoption of the Panel and Appellate Body Reports.[68]

3.32   Concerning preparatory work, it is important to note that such work, including consultations within government agencies, is a typical and legitimate aspect of "law-making" and is reflected throughout the Section 123 process. Consequently, such consultation and preparatory work should be taken into account in determining a reasonable period of time for implementation. The length of time required for such preparatory work is affected by the number and complexity of the issues and the number of agencies involved. The alleged

---

[62]   For an explanation of the Nails II methodology previously used by the USDOC to determine the existence of "targeted dumping", see Panel Report, fn 54 to para. 7.10.
[63]   Korea's opening statement at the hearing. See also Korea's submission, paras. 65-71.
[64]   Korea's response to questions at the hearing.
[65]   Korea's submission, paras. 44-45 and 49.
[66]   United States' response to questions at the hearing.
[67]   Korea's opening statement at the hearing. See also Korea's submission, para. 65.
[68]   Korea's submission, paras. 24-28; response to questions at the hearing.

novelty and complexity involved in implementation in the current case is addressed below. At this stage, it is sufficient to highlight that an appropriate time for the preparatory steps as identified by the United States (reflection, debate, and the development, testing, and analysis of new approaches) serves the double purpose of ensuring that the resulting methodology is an appropriate means of addressing targeted dumping consistently with the Anti-Dumping Agreement and reducing the time needed to undertake subsequent steps in the implementation process.

3.33   Regarding the alleged "novelty" and "complexity" of the issues involved, it is noted that this is the first dispute in which a panel or the Appellate Body has interpreted the second sentence of Article 2.4.2 of the Anti-Dumping Agreement.[69] Moreover, according to the United States, the interpretation by the Appellate Body requires an approach not yet developed by any WTO Member. In and of itself, the fact that a provision is interpreted for the first time in dispute settlement is not necessarily relevant to the determination of the reasonable period of time to come into conformity with that provision. A "new" interpretation of a provision may be relatively simple to implement depending on the nature of the obligation that it prescribes. Thus, the nature of the specific implementing obligation needs to be considered.

3.34   The current case relates to the second sentence of Article 2.4.2 of the Anti-Dumping Agreement. The right established therein, to use an exceptional methodology to calculate the margin of dumping, is subject to several conditions, each requiring a number of analytical steps to fulfil the parameters of the provision. The scope of the DSB's recommendations and rulings refers to each element of the provision, namely, the manner of establishing the pattern, the explanation as to why the normal methodologies are not appropriate, and the manner of calculating the margin of dumping. Each of these elements has been interpreted for the first time in this dispute. Consequently, the nature of the obligations covered by the required implementation includes a number of interrelated issues with an aspect of novelty. Nevertheless, the novelty and complexity is limited to three elements, and for each the range of options that can be explored is limited by the parameters of what is WTO-compatible as interpreted by the Panel and the Appellate Body.

3.35   Turning to Korea's argument that the United States should have begun taking steps towards implementation earlier than it has, both parties agree that the reasonable period of time for implementation is measured as from the date of adoption of the Panel and Appellate Body Reports.[70] According to the

---

[69]   Although previous panel and Appellate Body reports have referred to Article 2.4.2, second sentence, of the Anti-Dumping Agreement, this is the first dispute in which a panel or the Appellate Body has made a finding of inconsistency in respect of this provision. (See e.g. Appellate Body Reports, *US – Softwood Lumber V (Article 21.5 – Canada)*, paras. 95-100; *US – Zeroing (Japan)*, paras. 130-136; *US – Stainless Steel (Mexico)*, paras. 122-127; and *US – Continued Zeroing*, paras. 296-298)

[70]   United States' submission, para. 9; Korea's submission, para. 13.

United States, implementation steps in the form of internal deliberations and consultations were taken as from that date. However, the United States indicates that it is not in a position to provide evidence of such steps in light of the confidential nature of the internal deliberations and consultations that have occurred.[71] In Korea's view, absent evidence showing that specific actions have been taken, an arbitrator charged with determining the reasonable period of time cannot accept the mere assertion by a Member that it is taking steps towards implementation. Otherwise, explains Korea, "the possibility of abuse is too great" because that Member could make any assertion it wished in order to extend the reasonable period of time determined by an arbitrator.[72]

3.36   By the time of the hearing in this arbitration, over 5 months had elapsed since the DSB's adoption of the Panel and Appellate Body Reports in this dispute. It has been explained that details cannot be provided. Therefore it is not possible to assess how much has been accomplished in this period. Nevertheless, it is important to keep in mind that, in the meantime, measures found to be WTO-inconsistent have remained in place. It is also important to keep in mind that Article 21.1 of the DSU identifies prompt compliance with DSB recommendations and rulings as "essential in order to ensure effective resolution of disputes to the benefit of all Members".

3.37   For the reasons above, and in particular the number and complexity of the issues to be considered, a period of work that enables publication of a proposal only 12 months after adoption of the Panel and Appellate Body Reports is unjustifiably long.

3.38   A second point of disagreement concerns Korea's claim that the timeline proposed by the United States does not make use of possible flexibilities. As noted in paragraph 3.28 above, the United States explained at the hearing that in practice the consultations with the relevant private sector advisory committees foreseen in Section 123(g)(1)(B) take place simultaneously with the public consultation process foreseen in Section 123(g)(1)(C). The United States also explained that, because the report to Congress foreseen in Section 123(g)(1)(D) must include "a summary of the advice obtained" from private sector advisory committees and also contains a summary of the comments from the public on the proposed rule, the report cannot be done in parallel with those steps.

3.39   Lastly, the parties disagree on the length of time that must be afforded to the public to comment on the proposed methodology and the time to be afforded to the USDOC to complete its analysis of those comments. The United States indicates that it requires 2 months from publication in the Federal Register to allow the public to comment, followed by 5 months of analysis of those

---

[71]   United States' response to questions at the hearing.
[72]   Korea's response to questions at the hearing.

comments.[73] Korea submits that the USDOC can complete both of these steps within 60 days.[74]

3.40   In considering this issue, previous arbitrators have noted that "there must be a balance between the transparency and due process rights of interested parties, on the one hand, and the promptness required in implementing recommendations and rulings of the DSB, on the other hand."[75] In the current case, while there is no statutorily prescribed minimum period for public comment, it must be highlighted that a shorter-than-normal period for public comment risks affecting the legitimacy of the modification. Turning to the period for consideration of the comments that may be received, as mentioned in paragraph 3.34 above, the number of issues covered and the options available within the parameters of the legal obligation are relatively limited. Consequently, 5 months from the end of the period for public comment to analyse the responses received seems unjustifiably long.

3.4.2.2   Implementation of the DSB's "as applied" recommendations and rulings concerning the *Washers* anti-dumping investigation

3.41   The United States submits that it requires roughly 9 months to complete the Section 129 anti-dumping proceeding, as from the date of publication of the proposed modification developed in the context of the Section 123 proceeding.[76] The United States explains that the USDOC *may* need to prepare and issue questionnaires to the two respondents in the *Washers* anti-dumping investigation, allow them time to respond, allow interested parties to comment on the responses, issue follow-up questionnaires, and thereafter conduct verifications in respect of the responses.[77] The United States also indicates that it must afford interested parties the opportunity to comment on a preliminary determination in the Section 129 anti-dumping proceeding and potentially hold a hearing with interested parties.[78]

3.42   Korea submits that any additional fact-finding step in the Section 129 anti-dumping proceeding should not be taken into account in determining the reasonable period of time for implementation because the various steps mentioned by the United States are not required by law and are not normally taken in Section 129 proceedings.[79] Korea adds that it is unlikely that implementation of the relevant recommendations and rulings would require the

---

[73]   United States' submission, para. 55.

[74]   Korea's submission, para. 49.

[75]   Award of the Arbitrator, *US – Shrimp II (Viet Nam) (Article 21.3(c))*, para. 3.49 (referring to Award of the Arbitrator, *Japan – DRAMS (Korea) (Article 21.3(c))*, para. 51). See also Award of the Arbitrator, *China – GOES (Article 21.3(c))*, para. 3.46.

[76]   United States' submission, para. 55.

[77]   United States' submission, paras. 27-29.

[78]   United States' submission, paras. 50-52.

[79]   Korea's submission, paras. 54-57.

USDOC to make new factual determinations, and that the USDOC should be able to "narrowly tailor" any information request it may make.[80] Korea also contends that the time periods requested by the United States for certain steps are longer than the time periods normally taken in Section 129 proceedings to complete these steps.[81] Korea submits that the United States requires only 6 months from the date of the adoption of the Panel and Appellate Body Reports to complete the Section 129 anti-dumping proceeding.[82]

3.43   Section 129(b) of the URAA states as follows:

(b)   Action by administering authority

(1)   Consultations   with   administering   authority   and congressional committees

Promptly after a report by a dispute settlement panel or the Appellate Body is issued that contains findings that an action by the administering authority in a proceeding under title VII of the Tariff Act of 1930 … is not in conformity with the obligations of the United States under the Antidumping Agreement or the Agreement on Subsidies and Countervailing Measures, the Trade Representative shall consult with the administering authority and the congressional committees on the matter.

(2)   Determination by administering authority

Notwithstanding any provision of the Tariff Act of 1930 …, the administering authority shall, within 180 days after receipt of a written request from the Trade Representative, issue a determination in connection with the particular proceeding that would render the administering authority's action described in paragraph (1) not inconsistent with the findings of the panel or the Appellate Body.

(3)   Consultations before implementation

Before the administering authority implements any determination under paragraph (2), the Trade Representative shall consult with the administering authority and the congressional committees with respect to such determination.

(4)   Implementation of recommendation

The Trade Representative may, after consulting with the administering authority and the congressional committees under

---

[80]   Korea's submission, para. 55.
[81]   Korea's submission, paras. 56-57 (noting in particular the time taken by the USDOC to perform certain steps in the Section 129 proceeding used to implement the DSB's recommendations and rulings in *US – Countervailing Measures (China)* (DS437)).
[82]   Korea's submission, para. 58.

paragraph (3), direct the administering authority to implement, in whole or in part, the determination made under paragraph (2).

3.44   In addition, Section 129(d) of the URAA provides:

(d) Opportunity for comment by interested parties

Prior to issuing a determination under this section, the administering authority or the Commission, as the case may be, shall provide interested parties with an opportunity to submit written comments and, in appropriate cases, may hold a hearing, with respect to the determination.

3.45   The parties agree that paragraphs (1) through (4) quoted above identify the steps involved in a Section 129 proceeding.[83] The parties' main points of disagreement, however, concern: (i) whether a Section 129 proceeding must be completed within a maximum of 180 days; (ii) whether the time needed for the Section 129 anti-dumping proceeding encompasses time for the USDOC to conduct additional fact-finding; and (iii) the time that the United States requires to address ministerial errors in the final determination. I address these issues below.[84]

3.46   First, the parties disagree on the import of the reference in Section 129(b)(2) to a maximum period of 180 days within which the USDOC is to issue its redetermination. According to Korea, this means that the entire Section 129 process can take no more than 180 days from the date of initiation.[85] The United States, however, stresses that the wording of Section 129(b)(2) explicitly identifies the receipt of a written request from the USTR as the action that triggers the commencement of the 180-day period. The United States explains that this action is decoupled from formal commencement of a Section 129 proceeding by the USDOC.[86] Since this means, according to the United States, that a Section 129 proceeding may be commenced before the letter is sent from the USTR, it follows that the 180-day period is not a maximum period within which to issue a Section 129 redetermination.

3.47   The text of Section 129(b)(2) clearly indicates that the 180-day time period is triggered following the USDOC's receipt of a written request from the USTR. From then on, the USDOC has a maximum of 180 days in which to issue its redetermination. Furthermore, Section 129(b)(1) mandates the USTR to consult with the USDOC and Congress "promptly" after circulation of a panel or Appellate Body report. Likewise, Section 129(b)(3) mandates the USTR to again consult with the USDOC and the congressional committees before the final determination is published in the Federal Register. Thus, the structure of Section 129 includes two consultation phases beyond the 180-day period. Time for each

---

[83]   Parties' responses to questions at the hearing.
[84]   The parties also disagree over the issue of when the Section 129 anti-dumping redetermination can reasonably be expected to begin. This issue is addressed in the next subsection.
[85]   Korea's opening statement at the hearing.
[86]   United States' response to questions at the hearing.

of them must be taken into account. It is clear, therefore, that the 180-day time period does not encompass the entirety of the Section 129 process. This is in line with the findings of previous arbitrators on this issue.[87]

3.48   The second main difference in the positions of the parties concerns whether the reasonable period of time should allow time for the USDOC to conduct additional fact-finding. The United States submits that, because it cannot yet "foreclose that" or "prejudge whether" it will be necessary to solicit additional factual information, conduct verifications, or hold a hearing in this Section 129 proceeding, time must be afforded to conduct such steps.[88] Korea highlights that the United States bears the burden of proving that these steps are necessary and argues that this burden cannot be met simply by making assertions that it "cannot prejudge whether [it] will need" further information, "potentially might need" such information, or, "depending" on the methodology to be developed in the Section 123 proceeding, whether further information may be needed.[89] Korea also points to previous Section 129 proceedings as evidence that the USDOC rarely engages in additional fact-finding or holds hearings during a redetermination proceeding.[90]

3.49   In light of the DSB's recommendations and rulings, the factual information that may be required by the USDOC would be information relevant for: (i) a "qualitative" assessment of export price differences in order to determine the existence of a pattern of significant price differences; and (ii) consideration of "attendant factual circumstances" in explaining why such price differences could not be taken into account through a W-W or T-T comparison.[91] Whether fact-finding and additional steps of verification, a hearing, or even a preliminary determination requires additional time seems an unnecessary question. The text of Section 129 seems to indicate that all steps necessary for a redetermination are to be completed within the 180-day period foreseen in Section 129(b)(2).

3.50   Although the United States draws analogies to the time periods for certain steps to be conducted in *original* anti-dumping investigations, it acknowledges that there is no provision of United States law that mandates that all steps in original investigations must also be taken in Section 129 redeterminations, or that imposes time-limits on the steps taken. Further, the text of Section 129 expressly refers only to an opportunity for comments and, "if appropriate", a hearing. Moreover, as noted in *Japan – DRAMs (Korea) (Article 21.3(c))*, reliance on time periods used in original investigations seems inappropriate,

---

[87]   See Awards of the Arbitrators, *US – Shrimp II (Viet Nam) (Article 21.3(c))*, para. 3.46; and *US – Countervailing Measures (China) (Article 21.3(c))*, para. 3.41.
[88]   United States' response to questions at the hearing.
[89]   Korea's response to questions at the hearing.
[90]   Korea's response to questions at the hearing (referring to "Past USG Implementations of WTO Decisions Addressing AD-CVD Issues" (Exhibit KOR-3).
[91]   United States' submission, paras. 27-28 (referring to Appellate Body Report, para. 5.63; and Panel Report, para. 7.71).

because the implementing Member "is only required to conduct a re-determination to implement a limited number of DSB rulings of inconsistency."[92]

3.51   Concerning the parties' disagreement over the time required to address any ministerial errors before publishing the final determination[93], the United States indicated at the hearing that the process of addressing ministerial errors can be conducted concurrently with the process of consulting with Congress.[94]

3.52   Finally, it is noted that the overall timeframe to complete the Section 129 anti-dumping proceeding is affected by the date of commencement of the 180-day period. The United States has indicated that this cannot be done before publication in the Federal Register of the proposed modification to address the "as such" recommendations and rulings. This sequence is discussed in the subsection below.

3.4.2.3   Sequencing of the Section 123 and Section 129 anti-dumping proceedings

3.53   As described above, the parties disagree over whether the Section 123 and Section 129 proceedings in respect of the anti-dumping measures can take place simultaneously. Specifically, they differ on the extent to which the Section 123 proceeding can or should overlap with the Section 129 anti-dumping proceeding. For Korea, both proceedings should be conducted simultaneously, starting from the date of adoption of the Panel and Appellate Body Reports.[95] The United States, however, maintains that it must develop new methodologies for identifying so-called "targeted" dumping and for calculating the dumping margin using the W-T methodology before it can proceed to apply those methodologies in the *Washers* Section 129 anti-dumping redetermination. For this reason, the United States submits that the Section 129 anti-dumping redetermination could not be initiated immediately upon adoption by the DSB of the Panel and Appellate Body Reports.[96] At the same time, the United States does not contend that initiation of the Section 129 anti-dumping proceeding must await conclusion of the Section 123 anti-dumping proceeding. Rather, the United States submits that the USDOC would be in a position to commence the Section 129 anti-dumping redetermination once it publishes in the Federal Register the proposed modification for implementation of the DSB's "as such" recommendations and rulings.[97]

---

[92]   Award of the Arbitrator, *Japan – DRAMs (Korea) (Article 21.3(c))*, para. 48.
[93]   United States' submission, para. 52; Korea's submission, para. 62.
[94]   See also Award of the Arbitrator, *US – Countervailing Measures (China) (Article 21.3(c))*, para. 3.46.
[95]   Korea's submission, paras. 58 and 85.
[96]   United States' submission, para. 47.
[97]   See United States' submission, para. 55; and response to questions at the hearing.

3.54   Paragraphs 3.21 to 3.23 above explained that the United States has established that a Section 123 proceeding is an appropriate means of implementing the DSB's "as such" recommendations and rulings in this dispute. That proceeding entails publication of a proposed modification after several months of deliberations. The United States has explained that it is on the basis of the proposed modification that the "as applied" recommendations and rulings concerning the anti-dumping investigation will be implemented through the Section 129 proceeding. Effectively, without the proposed modification, the USDOC would not have a methodology for the application of the second sentence of Article 2.4.2 of the Anti-Dumping Agreement different from the ones found to be inconsistent with that provision.

3.55   Consequently, while there is a necessary sequence between the Section 123 and Section 129 anti-dumping proceedings, there is also an overlap. The United States' proposed timetable indicates that the Section 129 anti-dumping proceeding can commence as soon as the proposed methodology is published in the Federal Register. The postponement of the triggering of the 180-day period is explained by the link between the two proceedings described above. At the same time, under the steps of the Section 129 proceeding as described in paragraph 3.43 above, the USTR is obliged to conduct consultations with the USDOC and with congressional committees "promptly" after circulation of a panel or Appellate Body report. While the initiation of the anti-dumping redetermination may need to be on hold until such time as the USDOC has published the proposed new methodology, there does not appear to be any reason why the USTR could not engage in its consultations with the USDOC and with Congress prior to that date.

3.4.2.4   Implementation of the DSB's "as applied" recommendations and rulings concerning the *Washers* countervailing duty investigation

3.56   The United States indicates that the Section 129 countervailing duty proceeding can commence before, or at the same time as, the Section 123 anti-dumping proceeding, following a period of internal consultations and deliberations.[98] The United States indicates that implementation of the DSB's recommendations and rulings in respect of the countervailing measures will take 21 months. The United States explains that this is because of the time requested for implementation in respect of the anti-dumping measures and that, if the United States only needed to implement the recommendations and rulings pertaining to the countervailing duty investigation, it would not request a 21-month implementation period.[99] The United States also notes that implementation of these recommendations and rulings may require the USDOC

---

[98]   United States' submission, paras. 46 and 55.
[99]   United States' response to questions at the hearing.

to solicit additional information from the Government of Korea or from Samsung.[100]

3.57   Korea argues that, in light of the nature of the DSB's recommendations and rulings concerning the *Washers* countervailing duty investigation, the USDOC does not need to collect additional information but simply to reconsider existing evidence.[101] Korea also points out that the United States has not explained why, under its proposed timetable, certain steps in the Section 129 countervailing duty proceeding would take longer than the same steps in the Section 129 anti-dumping proceeding, given that the United States' arguments about "complexity" relate to the anti-dumping measures and not the countervailing measures.[102] Additionally, Korea asserts that, unlike the Section 129 anti-dumping redetermination, in the Section 129 countervailing duty redetermination, the United States does not have to wait for the development of a methodology in a Section 123 proceeding. According to Korea, the United States could and should have already initiated the Section 129 countervailing duty proceeding. Instead, more than 5 months after the adoption of the Panel and Appellate Body Reports, the United States is unable to identify a single concrete step that it has taken, even though in its written submission it stated that it would initiate the Section 129 countervailing duty proceeding by February 2017.[103] Korea submits that the United States requires only 180 days from the adoption of the Panel and Appellate Body Reports to complete the Section 129 countervailing duty proceeding.[104]

3.58   The parties agree that the steps in a Section 129 proceeding, as described in connection with the anti-dumping redetermination in paragraph 3.43 above, are the same as those that would be used by the United States in implementing the DSB's recommendations and rulings pertaining to the *Washers* countervailing duty investigation.[105] They also concur that the Section 129 countervailing duty redetermination will be separate and independent from the proceedings needed to implement the DSB's recommendations and rulings pertaining to the anti-dumping measures. Both parties request determination of a single reasonable period of time for implementation in this dispute.

3.59   As discussed in paragraphs 3.52 to 3.54 above, the period reasonably needed for implementation is affected by a partial sequencing of the proceedings for implementing the DSB's recommendations and rulings concerning the anti-dumping measures. Consequently, the reasonable period of time for implementation in this dispute is necessarily longer than the time required for the Section 129 countervailing duty proceeding. At the same time, no reason has been presented to explain that implementation of the recommendations and

---

[100]   United States' submission, paras. 31-34.
[101]   Korea's submission, paras. 61 and 78-79.
[102]   Korea's response to questions at the hearing.
[103]   Korea's submission, paras. 59-63.
[104]   Korea's response to questions at the hearing.
[105]   Parties' responses to questions at the hearing.

rulings relating to the countervailing measures could not be completed before the expiration of that period. In this context, the principle of prompt compliance contemplated in Article 21.1 of the DSU is important.

3.4.3   Particular circumstances of this dispute

3.60   The United States points to three circumstances that weigh in favour of a longer period of time for implementation in this dispute, namely: (i) the novelty and complexity of the issues involved; (ii) the current workload of the USDOC; and (iii) the change in the United States' administration, including the turnover in and absence of senior officials at the USDOC.[106]

3.61   The novelty and complexity of the anti-dumping issues have been addressed in paragraphs 3.33 and 3.34 above.

3.62   Concerning the remaining two circumstances advanced by the United States, Korea disputes that either of these factors amounts to particular circumstances warranting a longer period of time for implementation.[107]

3.63   Regarding the workload of the USDOC, previous arbitrators have considered that the workload of the implementing authority is not relevant to the reasonable period of time.[108] Further, in light of Article 21.1 of the DSU, it would be inappropriate to prioritize new or ongoing investigations over corrective action vis-à-vis measures already in force and found to be WTO-inconsistent.

3.64   Concerning recent changes in the United States' administration, the United States clarified at the hearing that, although it refers to the change in administration in its submission, this is not a factor built into its proposed timetable.

3.4.4   Conclusion

3.65   In conclusion, for the reasons explained above, the means of implementation proposed, including the flexibilities built into the relevant proceedings under United States law, the complexity and scope of certain issues concerning the anti-dumping measures, and the partial sequencing of the Section 123 and Section 129 anti-dumping proceedings, are the considerations to be given weight in determining the period of time reasonably needed to implement the DSB's recommendations and rulings in this dispute. Having taken account of these factors, 21 months is more than is reasonably needed for implementation. At the same time, 8 months would not be a sufficient period of time for the

---

[106]   United States' submission, paras. 8, 10, 15 and 56-60.
[107]   Korea's submission, paras. 81-84.
[108]   See e.g. Awards of the Arbitrators, *US – Shrimp II (Viet Nam) (Article 21.3(c))*, para. 3.55; *US – Countervailing Measures (China) (Article 21.3(c))*, para. 3.49; and *US – 1916 Act (Article 21.3(c))*, para. 38.

United States to bring itself into compliance with the recommendations and rulings of the DSB in this dispute.

4.   AWARD

4.1   In light of the foregoing considerations, the "reasonable period of time" for the United States to implement the recommendations and rulings of the DSB in this dispute is 15 months from 26 September 2016, that is, from the date on which the DSB adopted the Panel and Appellate Body Reports in this dispute. The reasonable period of time will expire on 26 December 2017.

ANNEX A

EXECUTIVE SUMMARY OF THE
UNITED STATES' SUBMISSION

1.   At its meeting on September 26, 2016, the DSB adopted recommendations and rulings in *United States – Anti-Dumping and Countervailing Measures on Large Residential Washers from Korea* (DS464). Pursuant to Article 21.3 of the DSU, the United States informed the DSB at its meeting on October 26, 2016, that the United States intends to comply with the DSB's recommendations and rulings in a manner that respects its WTO obligations and that it would need a reasonable period of time to do so. The United States engaged in discussions with Korea in an effort to agree on the RPT, but the parties were unable to reach agreement.

2.   The amount of time a Member requires for implementation of DSB recommendations and rulings depends on the particular facts and circumstances of the dispute, including the scope of the recommendations and rulings and the types of procedures required under the Member's laws to make the necessary changes in the measures at issue. Specific circumstances identified in previous awards as relevant to the Arbitrator's determination of the RPT include: (1) the legal form of implementation; (2) the technical complexity of the measure the Member must draft, adopt, and implement; and (3) the period of time in which the implementing Member can achieve that proposed legal form of implementation in accordance with its system of government.

3.   In this dispute, the United States intends to comply with DSB recommendations and rulings with respect to numerous matters. The most practical way under U.S. law to implement these matters is by conducting three proceedings, utilizing both section 123 and section 129 of the Uruguay Round Agreements Act. First, the United States intends to conduct a proceeding pursuant to section 123 to address the Appellate Body's and Panel's "as such" findings under the AD Agreement and the GATT 1994. Second, the United States intends to conduct two separate proceedings pursuant to section 129 to address the Appellate Body's and the Panel's "as applied" findings as they relate to the washers antidumping and countervailing duty investigations. The United States anticipates that it will not be possible to commence the section 129 proceeding relating to the antidumping duty investigation until the section 123 proceeding has been mostly completed. Many of the Panel and Appellate Body findings regarding Korea's "as applied" challenges to the washers antidumping investigation mirror those pertaining to Korea's "as such" challenges. Consequently, the United States expects that, in the section 129 proceeding, the USDOC will apply a number of the revised approaches and methodologies that will be developed in the section 123 determination.

4.　　Both parties, as well as the WTO dispute settlement system as a whole, have a strong interest in setting the RPT at a length that allows for an implementation process that takes account of all available information and uses a well-considered approach to implementing the findings in the Appellate Body and Panel reports. The RPT determined by the Arbitrator in this dispute thus should be of sufficient length to allow the United States to implement the DSB recommendations and rulings in a manner consistent with relevant WTO obligations. Such a result would preserve the rights of the United States to have a reasonable time for compliance and to impose antidumping and countervailing duties where appropriate, while at the same time would preserve Korea's rights to ensure that antidumping and countervailing duties are imposed only in accordance with WTO rules. If the RPT is too short to allow for effective implementation, the likelihood of a "positive solution" to the dispute would be reduced.

5.　　The United States is actively working on administrative actions to bring itself into compliance with the DSB's recommendations and rulings. For the reasons outlined in the U.S. submission, an RPT of at least 21 months is a reasonable period of time for implementation in this dispute.

ANNEX B

EXECUTIVE SUMMARY OF
KOREA'S SUBMISSION

1.   Korea requests that the Arbitrator determine a reasonable period of time of 6 months because implementation can be pursued exclusively through Section 129 proceedings, or 8 months if a Section 123 proceeding were to be considered as part of the implementation steps. This constitutes the shortest period of time possible within the legal system of the United States.

2.   The United States has failed to explain why it requires "at least" 21 months for implementation. The requirements of the U.S. legal system, the complexities alleged by the United States, and the workload of the implementing agency do not justify such an extraordinarily lengthy implementation period.

3.   Almost five months have passed since the Appellate Body and Panel reports were adopted and yet the United States has not taken any significant steps to bring its measures into conformity with the WTO Agreements. The United States should have begun implementation of the Panel's findings on disproportionality as soon as it was aware that these issues would not be appealed, and it should have begun implementation of the other findings immediately after the circulation of the Appellate Body report.

4.   Contrary to the United States' proposal, there is no need to pursue implementation in three phases. The United States can implement the "as such" findings through Section 129 proceedings, and a prior Section 123 proceeding is unnecessary. The DPM is not reflected in the USDOC's regulations nor was it adopted by the USDOC through a formal rule-making process, but was reflected in various memoranda of the USDOC adopted in the context of specific proceedings.[1] Thus, the DPM should be capable of being modified in the context of such kind of proceeding. Similarly, implementation of the Appellate Body's findings with respect to the use of zeroing would require a revision in the USDOC's margin calculation program, which does not require a Section 123 proceeding.

5.   In any case, the 16 months proposed by the United States to conduct a Section 123 proceeding are excessive. The time line proposed by the United States does not make use of the flexibilities inherent in the process, requesting several consecutive months to conduct steps that it could conduct concurrently. Moreover, contrary to the United States' assertions, the "as such" findings do not involve any particular complexities that would warrant additional time.

---

[1]   Panel Report, *US – Washing Machines*, para. 7.100.

6.   The time lines proposed by the United States to conduct two Section 129 proceedings to implement the "as applied" rulings in the anti-dumping and countervailing duty proceedings are also excessive. Section 129 contains no mandatory time lines for each step, and several of these steps can be conducted concurrently. The United States' proposed time line also contains steps that are not required under Section 129, such as collection and verification of additional factual data. Such non-mandatory steps should be given limited, if any, consideration.

7.   Finally, it is well established that the workload of the implementing agency is not a relevant factor in determining a reasonable period of time.[2] Similarly, the "turnover of key decision makers at the USDOC or, in some cases, their absence pending completion of the nomination and confirmation process"[3] are also factors that have been rejected as constituting a "particular circumstance" that warrants additional time.[4]

8.   In conclusion, Korea requests that the Arbitrator award a reasonable period of time of 6 months, ending March 26, 2017. This reasonable period of time reflects the following time line for the two Section 129 proceedings:

Action Under Section 129	Approx. Time Period
USTR consults with administering authority and congressional committees	September 2016
Prior to issuing a determination, the administering authority shall provide interested parties with an opportunity to submit written comments, and in appropriate cases, may hold a hearing.	60 days
Before rendering a determination, USTR shall consult with congressional committees (to continue throughout implementation period)	30 months
Within 180 days of receipt of a written request from the USTR, the administering authority shall issue a determination rendering the action consistent with WTO obligations.	60 days
The administering authority shall publish in the *Federal Register* notice of the implementation	30 days

9.   Finally, if the Arbitrator were to consider a Section 123 proceeding as part of the implementation steps, Korea requests that the Arbitrator award a reasonable period of time of 8 months, ending May 26, 2017.

---

[2]   Award of the Arbitrator, *US – Countervailing Measures (China) (21.3(c))*, para. 3.49.
[3]   U.S. Submission, para. 59.
[4]   Award of the Arbitrator, *US – Stainless Steel (Mexico) (Article 21.3(c))*, para. 62.

Cumulative List of Published Disputes